# COMPUTERS IN SOCIETY

**Fifth Edition**

### Editor

**Kathryn Schellenberg**
**University of Guelph**

Kathryn Schellenberg earned a Ph.D. from the University of Utah and is presently assistant professor of sociology at the University of Guelph in Ontario, Canada. One of her areas of scholarly interest is the social impact of technology, especially computing, and she has taught several sociology courses dealing with this subject. Dr. Schellenberg has also conducted several studies of computer-related topics and her current research centers on the implications of computer-linked technologies on police role relationships.

**Annual Editions**
*A Library of Information from the Public Press*

**The Dushkin Publishing Group, Inc.**
**Sluice Dock, Guilford, Connecticut 06437**

Cover illustration by Mike Eagle

# The Annual Editions Series

Annual Editions is a series of over 60 volumes designed to provide the reader with convenient, low-cost access to a wide range of current, carefully selected articles from some of the most important magazines, newspapers, and journals published today. Annual Editions are updated on an annual basis through a continuous monitoring of over 300 periodical sources. All Annual Editions have a number of features designed to make them particularly useful, including topic guides, annotated tables of contents, unit overviews, and indexes. For the teacher using Annual Editions in the classroom, an Instructor's Resource Guide with test questions is available for each volume.

## VOLUMES AVAILABLE

Africa
Aging
American Foreign Policy
American Government
American History, Pre-Civil War
American History, Post-Civil War
Anthropology
Biology
Business Ethics
Canadian Politics
Child Growth and Development
China
Commonwealth of Independent States
Comparative Politics
Computers in Education
Computers in Business
Computers in Society
Criminal Justice
Drugs, Society, and Behavior
Dying, Death, and Bereavement
Early Childhood Education
Economics
Educating Exceptional Children
Education
Educational Psychology
Environment
Geography
Global Issues
Health
Human Development
Human Resources
Human Sexuality
India and South Asia

International Business
Japan and the Pacific Rim
Latin America
Life Management
Macroeconomics
Management
Marketing
Marriage and Family
Mass Media
Microeconomics
Middle East and the Islamic World
Money and Banking
Multicultural Education
Nutrition
Personal Growth and Behavior
Physical Anthropology
Psychology
Public Administration
Race and Ethnic Relations
Social Problems
Sociology
State and Local Government
Third World
Urban Society
Violence and Terrorism
Western Civilization, Pre-Reformation
Western Civilization, Post-Reformation
Western Europe
World History, Pre-Modern
World History, Modern
World Politics

Library of Congress Cataloging in Publication Data
Main entry under title: Computer Studies: Computers in Society. 5/E.
"An Annual Edition Publication."
    1. Computers and civilization—Periodicals. 2. Computers—Periodicals. I. Schellenberg, Kathryn, comp. II. Title: Computers in society.
ISBN 1–56134–259–9            303.4′834

© 1994 by The Dushkin Publishing Group, Inc., Guilford, CT 06437

Fifth Edition

Manufactured in the United States of America

Printed on Recycled Paper

# To the Reader

In publishing ANNUAL EDITIONS we recognize the enormous role played by the magazines, newspapers, and journals of the *public press* in providing current, first-rate educational information in a broad spectrum of interest areas. Within the articles, the best scientists, practitioners, researchers, and commentators draw issues into new perspective as accepted theories and viewpoints are called into account by new events, recent discoveries change old facts, and fresh debate breaks out over important controversies.

Many of the articles resulting from this enormous editorial effort are appropriate for students, researchers, and professionals seeking accurate, current material to help bridge the gap between principles and theories and the real world. These articles, however, become more useful for study when those of lasting value are carefully *collected, organized, indexed,* and *reproduced* in a *low-cost format,* which provides easy and permanent access when the material is needed. That is the role played by *Annual Editions.* Under the direction of each volume's *Editor,* who is an expert in the subject area, and with the guidance of an *Advisory Board,* we seek each year to provide in each *ANNUAL EDITION* a current, well-balanced, carefully selected collection of the best of the public press for your study and enjoyment. We think you'll find this volume useful, and we hope you'll take a moment to let us know what you think.

We can only guess at how the ever increasing power, diversity, and pervasiveness of computers and other information technologies might affect the patterns of our individual and social lives. However, it is hoped that *Computers in Society* will complement your technical understanding of these emerging technologies by acquainting you with the philosophical, economic, political, and social dimensions of the information society.

Contributors to the fifth edition represent a diverse range of backgrounds. Their collective writings highlight a wide spectrum of issues and views about how the information age will or ought to unfold. For the most part, their writing styles are very understandable and devoid of the kind of unintelligible technical jargon that can be a barrier to becoming informed about technological issues.

Because of its social focus, this book is organized to reflect the major dimensions of society rather than various aspects of computing. The major themes of the book are the economy, community, and conflict. Many of these themes are also examined in an international context. The final section looks at some of the philosophical challenges posed by emerging technologies.

Each article has been selected for its informational value, but "informative" does not necessarily imply correctness or validity. In fact, some of you may find that you strongly disagree with, or are even offended by, a position expressed in one or more articles—I may well agree with you. On the other hand, some may feel simply inspired by arguments that make others irate. *Computers in Society* is meant to generate rather than answer questions on how computers will affect society. Hopefully, such queries will serve to clarify issues, broaden perspectives, provoke curiosity, and stimulate informed discussion of and participation in the computer age.

Readers can have input into the next edition by completing and returning the article rating form in the back of the book.

Kathryn Schellenberg
*Editor*

# Contents

## Introduction: The Computer *Revolution?*

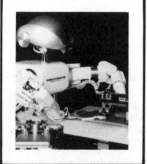

## Unit 1

## The Changing Economy

Nine articles examine some national and global economic implications of emerging technological developments. The building of an "information" infrastructure, manufacturing, speech recognition, fiber optics, nanotechnology, virtual reality, and the electronic movement of funds are highlighted.

To the Reader    iv
Topic Guide    2
Introduction    4

1. **Communications, Computers, and Networks,** Michael L. Dertouzos, *Scientific American,* September 1991.    6
   A renowned scholar argues that developments in computing and communications technologies are spawning a social and economic **revolution.** The new society will be built upon an **information infrastructure.**

Overview    12

2. **The New Democrat From Cyberspace,** Robert Wright, *The New Republic,* May 24, 1993.    14
   Robert Wright discusses the "mission" of Mitch Kapor and the Electronic Frontier Foundation in advancing the development of the **information infrastructure** or "data superhighway." In his discussion, Wright reveals how a complex interplay of social, economic, and political factors might shape technological development.

3. **Who's Winning the Information Revolution?** Myron Magnet, *Fortune,* November 30, 1992.    21
   The merging of computing and telecommunications is "transforming all of business." In this article, Myron Magnet discusses some of the changes taking place in retailing, marketing, insurance, health care, and manufacturing. He argues that, unlike the first industrial revolution that fostered specialization, the new trend is toward global unification.

4. **Tomorrow's Factory,** Jenny C. McCune, *Management Review,* January 1993.    24
   According to Jenny McCune, the factories of the future will be based on **mass customization.** They will also be smaller, more flexible, closer to the customer, more environmentally friendly, and more specialized than today's factories.

5. **The Light Fantastic,** *Business Week,* May 10, 1993.    29
   "**Optoelectronics**" is the current cutting edge of computing. According to this article, this new technological leap "will touch everything from medicine to the waging of war . . . [and foment] a revolution as far-reaching as that wrought by the silicon chip."

6. **How Small Is It, Johnny?** Gino Del Guercio, *World Monitor,* April 1993.    35
   **Nanotechnology** is a new field that is advancing very rapidly with intense global competition. As Gino Del Guercio explains, "whichever country gains control . . . may have an economic advantage [to match that of the Japanese] in the micro-electronics industry."

7. **At Last! Computers You Can Talk To,** Gene Bylinsky, *Fortune,* May 3, 1993.    38
   The decades-old dream of directing computers through spoken commands is fast becoming a reality. As Gene Bylinsky describes it, **speech recognition** will be a great boon to many individuals and businesses. It may also replace some workers.

8. **Virtual Reality,** *Business Week,* October 5, 1992.    41
   This article recounts the current state and future potential of "virtual reality" and suggests how a "computer-generated world could change the real world."

The concepts in bold italics are developed in the article. For further expansion please refer to the Topic Guide, the Index, and the Glossary.

9. **Fast Money,** Peter Passell, *The New York Times Magazine,*    48
October 18, 1992.
Peter Passell describes the staggering sums of money that flow through the Clearing House Interbank Payments Systems (CHIPS) each day. He also identifies some potential vulnerabilities of the system and security measures to protect it from risks of fire, technical failure, theft, and terrorism.

10. **Medical Technology 'Arms Race' Adds Billions to the**    52
**Nation's Bills,** Andrew Pollack, *The New York Times,* April 29, 1991.
Andrew Pollack describes how the cost of new medical technologies can drive up the **cost of health care** and lead to conflict between those who provide medical services and those who pay for them.

**Overview**    56

11. **The Skilling of America,** Jack Gordon, *Training,* March 28,    58
1991.
The popular belief that jobs are becoming more complex and skilled is challenged by Jack Gordon. He claims that in too many cases jobs are actually being **deskilled,** and he offers suggestions on how and why work should be "skilled up."

12. **Telecommuting: A Better Way to Work?** Bob Filipczak,    64
*Training,* May 1992.
Telecommuting is "not idyllic," according to Bob Filipczak, but there are numerous benefits to working away from the office. He offers a number of useful guidelines to successful telecommuting.

13. **Adaptive Technology for the Disabled,** Bob Filipczak,    71
*Training,* March 1993.
In this article, Bob Filipczak discusses social, economic, and political issues, as well as recent technical advances, which make it possible to integrate **disabled employees** into the workplace.

14. **Do It Yourself,** Brian Hayes, *The Sciences,* March/April    79
1991.
Modern society is becoming increasingly **"self-service."** In this article, Brian Hayes speculates on some of the trend's potential effects in the workplace and other areas of society.

**Overview**    82

15. **Challenging the Myth of Disability,** Alan Brightman,    84
*EDUCOM Review,* Winter 1989.
Close to 800 million people in the world are disabled. In this article, Alan Brightman describes their special problems and needs and argues that, "when [the] **disabled are given access to computers,** it becomes clear how these machines can, indeed, change lives."

16. **The Powerful Patient,** Steve Fishman, *Health,* March/April    90
1993.
The author describes a number of organizations, support groups, and computerized **medical databases** that offer information to help patients make better decisions about treatments for diseases and disabilities.

# Unit 2

## Employment and the Workplace

Four articles examine the changing skill requirements of the work force, telecommuting, integrating disabled persons into the workplace, and the "do-it-yourself" trend.

# Unit 3

## Computers, People, and Social Interaction

Seven articles examine present and future implications of computing and other technologies for participation in economic, political, and social life.

17. **The 20 Percent Solution,** Morris H. Shamos, *The Sciences,* March/April 1993.                                    93

Few adults are "sufficiently literate . . . to reach independent, rational judgments on technology-based societal matters." Morris Shamos highlights obstacles to achieving a high level of ***technological literacy*** and offers one approach to bringing technology under society's control.

18. **The Pleasure Machine,** Herb Brody, *Technology Review,* April 1992.                                    95

Herb Brody observes that ***computers are fun*** as well as useful. For some, computers are so much fun that people become obsessed with them. For others, computing is still pretty frustrating. Brody argues that hardware and software manufacturers should put greater emphasis on making computing pleasurable.

19. **Electronic Democracy,** Pamela Varley, *Technology Review,* November/December 1991.                                    100

Citizens of Santa Monica, California, use the Public Electronic Network (PEN) to express their views on a wide range of social and political issues. In this article, Pamela Varley addresses the question, Is the PEN system "a state-of-the-art ***town meeting*** or just a glorified call-in show?"

20. **Superduperitis,** David C. Churbuck, *Forbes,* March 15, 1993.                                    108

In this humorous but revealing article, David Churbuck relates some symptoms of ***computer addiction*** and describes some outstanding examples of victims.

21. **Contracts Without Paper,** Benjamin Wright, *Technology Review,* July 1992.                                    110

It is widely understood that contracts should be "in writing." In this article, an attorney discusses some legal issues surrounding ***"electronic contracts."***

# Unit 4

## Intellectual Property and Individual Privacy

Six articles discuss intellectual property issues— hardware and software patents, copyright, "nonprofit" software, and new technical developments that threaten individual privacy.

**Overview**                                    114

22. **The Great Patent Plague,** Nancy Rutter, *Forbes,* March 29, 1993.                                    116

In this article, Nancy Rutter outlines some of the issues surrounding the patenting of electronic ***hardware innovations.*** She argues that current trends regarding intellectual property claims and litigation will have negative consequences for technical innovation and the company involved.

23. **Why Patents Are Bad for Software,** Simson L. Garfinkel, Richard M. Stallman, and Mitchell Kapor, *Issues in Science and Technology,* Fall 1991.                                    121

The authors of this article strongly criticize the growing number of ***software patents.*** They argue that patents cannot "protect or invigorate the computer software industry; they can only cripple it."

24. **Warning: Here Come the Software Police,** Janet Mason, *Across the Board,* October 1990.                                    127

A good deal of "illegal" ***copying of software*** occurs in the corporate world. As Janet Mason points out, even firms that have policies against piracy can and are being sued if their employees are caught with unauthorized copies of software.

The concepts in bold italics are developed in the article. For further expansion please refer to the Topic Guide, the Index, and the Glossary.

**25. Programs to the People,** Simson L. Garfinkel, *Technology Review,* February/March 1991.

Computer whiz "Richard Stallman believes that companies that sell [computer] programs give their customers the choice of being criminals or bad neighbors," and he is determined to **make software free.** In this article, Simson Garfinkel discusses Stallman's goals and successes thus far.

132

**26. Orwellian Dream Come True: A Badge That Pinpoints You,** Leonard Sloane, *The New York Times,* September 12, 1992.

Researchers in England and California are testing **active badges,** small I.D. card-size badges that allow computers to closely track the movements of persons and things. The badges can be very useful, but they also raise concerns about "Orwellian" electronic monitoring and control.

139

**27. Supermarket Spies,** Erik Larson, *Health,* September 1992.

Most of us shop at the supermarket. But, as Erik Larson relates, the growing sophistication of product coding and **scanning technologies** may soon give marketers "unprecedented power to know us—and therefore to know precisely how and exactly when to make us . . . shop."

141

# Unit 5

# Computer Ethics and Crime

Six articles discuss the unethical use of computer systems, the visual manipulation and potential distortion of information, and computer crime.

**Overview**

146

**28. Dispatches From the Front Line: Computer Ethics War Stories,** Sally Webster, *EDUCOM Review,* July/August 1992.

Sally Webster deals with the use and abuse of computers by students and faculty in the **college and university** setting. She argues that the "entire institution," not just computing services people, need to set policies and "deal firmly" with **computer abuse.**

148

**29. Computer Imaging, A New Branch of Science That Can Turn Truth on Its Head,** Stephen Strauss, *The Globe and Mail (Toronto),* July 4, 1992.

Using the Rodney King videotape and trial as an example of standing "evidence on its head," Stephen Strauss argues that the growing potential to manipulate and distort **visual information** poses serious ethical concerns, especially when visual images are presented as evidence in a court of law.

151

**30. Evidence Set in Motion,** Alexander Jason, *Police Magazine,* June 1992.

Alexander Jason wrote a **computer animation** to represent the sequence of events in a California murder case. The animation was used as prosecution **evidence** in the trial of the accused murderer. In this article, Jason describes and defends computer animation "as an effective new tool in law enforcement."

153

**31. World of Electronic Games: Computer Game Ethics,** Sara Reeder, *Compute,* January 1992.

The author examines concerns about violence, pornography, and other challenges to **cultural values** in popular computer games. Restricting content raises concerns about freedom of expression but "ratings" might be one means of helping consumers avoid games they may find offensive.

156

**32. "The Playground Bullies Are Learning How to Type,"** 160
William G. Flanagan and Brigid McMenamin, *Forbes,*
December 21, 1992.
The authors describe the ethos and activities of a "new genera-
tion of **hacker hoods**" who are at the forefront of a **computer
crime** wave of "epidemic proportions."

**33. Legally Speaking: Can Hackers Be Sued for Damages** 164
**Caused by Computer Viruses?** Pamela Samuelson, and
**Viruses and Criminal Law,** Michael Gemignani, *Communications of the ACM,* June 1989.
Two legal scholars discuss potential benefits and problems in
bringing civil and criminal action against those who plant **viruses
in computer systems.** In both cases the law is highly ambiguous
and has not kept pace with technological developments.

**Overview** 170

**34. The Complexity Problem,** John Sedgwick, *The Atlantic,* 172
March 1993.
John Sedgwick argues that too many technologies are so complex that people cannot use them properly. This can result in
frustration and even danger. Therefore, Sedgwick calls for more
simplicity and a **user-centered approach** to technological design.

**35. Do Cellular Phones Cause Cancer?** David Kirkpatrick, 178
*Fortune,* March 8, 1993.
This article deals with the extremely controversial issue of
whether the **electromagnetic fields** emitted by cellular phones
and other technologies such as computer video display terminals
(VDTs) pose a threat to human health. Research to date has
produced inconclusive evidence, and more thorough studies are
urgently needed.

**36. A System on Overload,** Evelyn Richards, *The Washington* 181
*Post National Weekly Edition,* December 31, 1990–January
6, 1991.
Many sectors of society, such as the economy and the military,
depend on the reliable operation of computer systems. However,
Evelyn Richards describes a number of problems related to
meeting the demand for the **highly complex software** needed to
control vital systems.

**37. Programmed for Disaster,** Jonathan Jacky, *The Sciences,* 186
September/October 1989.
**Software errors** can imperil lives. In this article, Jonathan Jacky
describes some of the more serious programming errors and
offers suggestions on how complex, critical software could be
made more reliable and safe.

**38. Liability for Defective Electronic Information,** Pamela 190
Samuelson, *Communications of the ACM,* January 1993.
Legal scholar Pamela Samuelson draws on the legal protections
and **liabilities** of authors, publishers, and booksellers to outline
some of the legal issues surrounding the production, publication,
and distribution of **defective software** that causes economic or
physical harm.

# Unit 6

# Technological Risks

Five articles examine products that are difficult to use,
electromagnetic fields, society's extreme reliance on
very complex systems, and legal liabilities surrounding
defective electronic information.

The concepts in bold italics are developed in the article. For further expansion please refer to the Topic Guide, the Index, and the Glossary.

# Unit 7

# International Perspectives and Issues

Five articles examine computing-related issues in several countries—Japan, sub-Saharan African nations, Middle Eastern countries, Canada, and Bulgaria.

# Unit 8

# Philosophical Frontiers

Four articles examine the moral and philosophical dilemmas faced by scientists who develop nuclear weapons, the question of artificial "life" and whether computers will ever acquire consciousness, and possible impacts of parallel computing on the way that humans think.

**Overview**      **196**

39. **Why Japan Loves Robots and We Don't,** Andrew Tanzer and Ruth Simon, *Forbes,* April 16, 1990.    **198**
The United States lags behind Japan in the use of ***robots*** to solve practical problems. In this article, the authors discuss economic, cultural, and demographic factors underlying the "robot gap."

40. **Sub-Saharan Africa: A Technological Desert,** Mayuri Odedra, Mike Lawrie, Mark Bennett, and Sy Goodman, *Communications of the ACM,* February 1993.    **202**
Africa is the ***least computerized continent*** in the world. In this article, Sy Goodman brings together three Africans who share their views on the prospects and the complex social, political, and economic problems confronting the effective use of information technologies (IT) in sub-Saharan Africa.

41. **Computing in the Middle East,** S. E. Goodman and J. D. Green, *Communications of the ACM,* August 1992.    **207**
S. Goodman and J. Green relate some of the ***social, political, economic, and religious factors*** affecting the shape and direction of computing and other information technologies in the Middle East.

42. **New Technology Propels Air Travel,** Geoffrey Rowan, *The Globe and Mail (Toronto),* February 1, 1993.    **211**
A proposed alliance between a Canadian and an American airline may lead to a ***computer reservations system*** monopoly in Canada. Geoffrey Rowan explains how the Canadian "Gemini" system and the U.S. "Sabre" system are "slugging it out for control" of Canada's reservations market.

43. **The Bulgarian Connection,** Paul Mungo and Bryan Clough, *Discover,* February 1993.    **213**
Computer ***viruses*** are an international curse. Paul Mungo and Bryan Clough relate the history of some of the more famous and widely traveled viruses and their Bulgarian origins.

**Overview**      **220**

44. **Coming of Age in a Weapons Lab,** Hugh Gusterson, *The Sciences,* May/June 1992.    **222**
An anthropologist discusses the ***ethical and moral challenges*** faced by scientists and engineers whose lifework is designing ***nuclear weapons*** at the Lawrence Livermore National Laboratory in California.

45. **Compelling Signs of Artificial Life,** Mark Nichols, *Maclean's,* June 7, 1993.    **227**
Researchers are creating "digital creatures" that clone themselves and evolve into new forms. Some scientists are claiming that these or future creatures may constitute ***artificial life forms*** and "intelligence is the next frontier."

The concepts in bold italics are developed in the article. For further expansion please refer to the Topic Guide, the Index, and the Glossary.

46. **Is Thinking Computable?** Peter J. Denning, *American Scientist,* March/April 1990.    229

   Peter Denning discusses the debate between John Searle and Paul and Patricia Smith Churchland along with a review of physicist Roger Penrose's book on *artificial intelligence.* Denning concludes that Searle, the Churchlands, and Penrose have, for now at least, "bolstered our confidence in the belief that we [humans] are more than mechanical devices."

47. **New Computers, New Thoughts,** James Bailey, *Harper's,* May 1992.    232

   James Bailey considers whether or not computers will think the way humans think. He relates that throughout history "computing" has always been a *sequential* process. However, new developments in *parallel computing* offer dramatic potential for problem solving and "to *reshape what we think about, and even how we think.*"

**Glossary**    236
**Index**    241
**Article Review Form**    244
**Article Rating Form**    245

The concepts in bold italics are developed in the article. For further expansion please refer to the Topic Guide, the Index, and the Glossary.

# Topic Guide

This topic guide suggests how the selections in this book relate to topics of traditional concern to students and professionals involved with computers in society. It can be very useful in locating articles that relate to each other for reading and research. The guide is arranged alphabetically according to topic. Articles may, of course, treat topics that do not appear in the topic guide. In turn, entries in the topic guide do not necessarily constitute a comprehensive listing of all the contents of each selection.

| TOPIC AREA | TREATED IN: | TOPIC AREA | TREATED IN: |
|---|---|---|---|
| Africa | 40. Sub-Saharan Africa | Economy (cont'd) | 6. How Small Is It, Johnny? |
| | | | 7. At Last! Computers You Can Talk To |
| Artificial Intelligence | 46. Is Thinking Computable? | | 8. Virtual Reality |
| | | | 9. Fast Money |
| Artificial Life | 45. Compelling Signs of Artificial Life | | 10. Medical Technology 'Arms Race' |
| | | | 22. Great Patent Plague |
| Automation | 4. Tomorrow's Factory | Education and Training | 8. Virtual Reality |
| | 14. Do It Yourself | | 11. Skilling of America |
| | 39. Why Japan Loves Robots | | 15. Challenging the Myth of Disability |
| | | | 17. 20 Percent Solution |
| Bulgaria | 43. Bulgarian Connection | | 18. Pleasure Machine |
| Canada | 42. New Technology Propels Air Travel | Electronic Frontier Foundation | 2. New Democrat From Cyberspace |
| Children | 15. Challenging the Myth of Disability | | |
| | 18. Pleasure Machine | Ergonomics | 34. Complexity Problem |
| | 31. World of Electronic Games | Ethics | 24. Warning: Here Come the Software Police |
| Computer Abuse | 28. Dispatches From the Front Line | | 28. Dispatches From the Front Line |
| | | | 31. World of Electronic Games |
| Computer Addiction | 18. Pleasure Machine | | 32. "Playground Bullies" |
| | 20. Superduperitis | | 43. Bulgarian Connection |
| | | | 44. Coming of Age in a Weapons Lab |
| Computer Games | 31. World of Electronic Games | Fiber Optics | 5. Light Fantastic |
| Copyright | 23. Why Patents Are Bad for Software | Freedom of Speech | 31. World of Electronic Games |
| | 24. Warning: Here Come the Software Police | | 38. Liability for Defective Electronic Information |
| | 25. Programs to the People | Germany | 6. How Small Is It, Johnny? |
| Crime | 9. Fast Money | Hacking | 32. "Playground Bullies" |
| | 32. "Playground Bullies" | | |
| Disabled Persons | 7. At Last! Computers You Can Talk To | Health and Medicine | 3. Who's Winning the Information Revolution? |
| | 13. Adaptive Technology for the Disabled | | 5. Light Fantastic |
| | 15. Challenging the Myth of Disability | | 10. Medical Technology 'Arms Race' |
| | | | 16. Powerful Patient |
| | | | 35. Do Cellular Phones Cause Cancer? |
| Economy | 2. New Democrat From Cyberspace | | 37. Programmed for Disaster |
| | 3. Who's Winning the Information Revolution? | Information Infrastructure | 1. Communications, Computers, and Networks |
| | 4. Tomorrow's Factory | | 2. New Democrat From Cyberspace |
| | 5. Light Fantastic | | |

| TOPIC AREA | TREATED IN: | TOPIC AREA | TREATED IN: |
|---|---|---|---|
| Intellectual Property | 22. Great Patent Plague<br>23. Why Patents Are Bad for Software<br>24. Warning: Here Come the Software Police<br>25. Programs to the People | Philosophical Issues | 44. Coming of Age in a Weapons Lab<br>45. Compelling Signs of Artificial Life<br>46. Is Thinking Computable?<br>47. New Computers, New Thoughts |
| International Issues | 39. Why Japan Loves Robots<br>40. Sub-Saharan Africa<br>41. Computing in the Middle East<br>42. New Technology Propels Air Travel<br>43. Bulgarian Connection | Politics and Political Participation | 2. New Democrat From Cyberspace<br>17. 20 Percent Solution<br>19. Electronic Democracy |
| Japan | 6. How Small Is It, Johnny? | Privacy | 26. Orwellian Dream Come True<br>27. Supermarket Spies |
| Legal Issues | 8. Virtual Reality<br>21. Contracts Without Paper<br>29. Computer Imaging, A New Branch of Science<br>30. Evidence Set in Motion<br>33. Legally Speaking<br>38. Liability for Defective Electronic Information | Robotics | 39. Why Japan Loves Robots |
| | | Scientific Literacy | 17. 20 Percent Solution |
| | | Software Reliability | 36. System on Overload<br>37. Programmed for Disaster<br>38. Liability for Defective Electronic Information |
| Manufacturing | 3. Who's Winning the Information Revolution?<br>4. Tomorrow's Factory<br>39. Why Japan Loves Robots | Speech Recognition | 7. At Last! Computers You Can Talk To |
| Middle East | 41. Computing in the Middle East | Telecommunity and Teledemocracy | 18. Pleasure Machine<br>19. Electronic Democracy |
| (The) Military | 5. Light Fantastic<br>36. System on Overload<br>37. Programmed for Disaster<br>44. Coming of Age in a Weapons Lab | Virtual Reality | 8. Virtual Reality |
| | | Viruses | 33. Legally Speaking<br>43. Bulgarian Connection |
| Nano-Technology | 6. How Small Is It, Johnny? | Visualization | 29. Computer Imaging, A New Branch of Science<br>30. Evidence Set in Motion |
| Networks | 1. Communications, Computers, and Networks | Work and Employment | 4. Tomorrow's Factory<br>11. Skilling of America<br>12. Telecommuting<br>13. Adaptive Technology for the Disabled<br>14. Do It Yourself<br>26. Orwellian Dream Come True |
| Nuclear Weapons | 44. Coming of Age in a Weapons Lab | | |
| Optical Computing | 5. Light Fantastic | | |
| Parallel Computing | 47. New Computers, New Thoughts | | |
| Patents | 22. Great Patent Plague<br>23. Why Patents Are Bad for Software | | |

# Introduction:
# The Computer *Revolution?*

Computer "revolution" and information "revolution" are widely used terms these days, and these terms imply that society is undergoing a radical transformation. This was the view of the late British computer expert, Christopher Evans. In his thought-provoking book, *The Micro Millenium*, Evans argued that the societal impacts of computers in general, and personal computers in particular, would rival the effects of the Industrial Revolution that:

> brought about immense shifts in all aspects of society, affecting the individual, his family, his neighbors, his domestic and working environment, his clothes, his food, his leisure time, his political and religious ideals, his education, his social attitudes, his life-span, even the manner of his birth and death. (1979:ix)

Moreover, Evans claimed the future is not one of our choosing. He stated that as we began to apply these powerful new tools to the tasks of bettering our lives, we set in motion a process that took on an independent, unstoppable momentum.

There are those who disagree that a revolution is underway or at least dispute the claim that we have no control over the future. For instance, in his book *The Personal Computer Book,* Peter A. McWilliams argued that computers will have a dramatic impact on our lives and on society, but he also suggested that we are in command of our own fate when he stated:

> For the most part, personal computers will prove their worth to the extent that they fit into your daily life, not to the degree that you adapt your life to be more in step with The Computer Age. (1984:15)

Contradictory predictions about the implications of computing are not surprising since people operate from many different premises about society and human nature. We need to keep this is in mind when we try to make sense of competing claims about the future. This is not easy because we are often unaware of our own assumptions about social life. Mostly, we just tend to take certain things for granted—we believe them so strongly that we simply assume that other reasonable and intelligent people see things the same way.

However, if you think people are fundamentally honest, generous, and altruistic, it is just as clear to someone else

that people are basically greedy, self-interested, and manipulative. If you take it for granted that an orderly, stable society is the result of people cooperating and working toward the common good, there are others who would argue that competition, power, and coercion hold society together. If you are convinced people have agency and free will to create the kind of society they desire, others are more inclined to think the nature of society is determined by forces beyond human will. And, if you believe "idealism" governs society, others are persuaded we live in a "material" world.

The disagreement between Evans and McWilliams basically reflects the difference between how idealists and materialists look at the world. Those who feel that idealism and free will govern societies are uncomfortable with the kinds of claims Evans makes—that cultural, political, and religious ideals can be influenced by technical innovation. They would argue that the ideals come first and are the foundation of society. Technical innovations are accepted or rejected depending on whether or not they harmonize with basic values. This assumption is implied in McWilliams' argument that computers are mere tools that people are free to use or avoid. Materialists, on the other hand, insist that new technologies need not support any basic belief system. They maintain that if a technology can provide real material benefits, such as greater wealth or longer life expectancy to society or to a powerful minority, it will be adopted. If some aspect of the technology clashes with society's values and ideals, then the values, not the technology, will be modified or abandoned. Clearly, Christopher Evans is in the materialist camp.

Social theorists and philosophers have debated for centuries over which of the competing social assumptions are valid. Like the rest of us, they continue to disagree about where the truth lies. The articles in this edition of *Computers in Society* do not put these issues to rest, but they do show us that technology and cultural ideals influence each other in complex, and sometimes strange, ways.

In the lead article of this edition, a leading computer expert argues that a genuine revolution is unfolding. In "Communications, Computers, and Networks," Michael Dertouzos relates that developments in computing and communications will radically affect us as individuals and through our social, economic, and cultural institutions. For

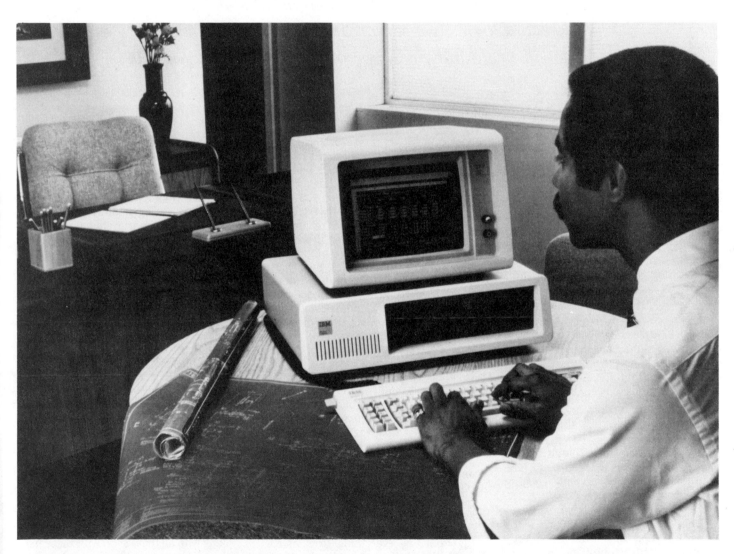

the most part, he is enthusiastically optimistic that the changes will be positive. Dertouzos warns, however, that we cannot take it for granted that everyone will be better off if we do not monitor change and take steps to minimize the negative effects of an otherwise glorious revolution.

## Looking Ahead: Challenge Questions

If society has a choice about which technologies are developed and how they are used, then who should participate in making those choices? Should those with political power, wealth, or technical expertise assume the responsibilities of shaping our society? If everyone should have a say, how should we be given the opportunity to express our views and concerns?

If we discover that we really dislike some of the social changes that result from new technologies, will we be able to discard our inventions and return to the ideals of an earlier age?

# Communications, Computers and Networks

*By fusing computing and communications
technologies, we can create an infrastructure
that will profoundly reshape our economy and society*

Michael L. Dertouzos

MICHAEL L. DERTOUZOS directs the Laboratory for Computer Science at the Massachusetts Institute of Technology, where he is professor of computer science and electrical engineering. He is a member of the National Academy of Arts and Sciences in Greece and a member of the U.S. National Academy of Engineering. He recently chaired the M.I.T. Commission on Industrial Productivity. He received his Ph.D. from M.I.T. in 1964 and joined the faculty at that time. He enjoys playing with computers and sophisticated electronic gadgets, along with dreaming up new interactions between technology and people.

The agricultural age was based on plows and the animals that pulled them; the industrial age, on engines and the fuels that fed them. The information age we are now creating will be based on computers and the networks that interconnect them.

The authors of the 1991 issue of *Scientific American* share a hopeful vision of a future built on an information infrastructure that will enrich our lives by relieving us of mundane tasks, by improving the ways we live, learn and work and by unlocking new personal and social freedoms.

Since the timid debut of the first useful computers almost half a century ago, there has been no shortage of opinion, speculation and prediction about the

magical new world they promise. Why, then, devote this entire special issue to this topic at this time? What is new?

A growing opportunity has attained critical mass as a result of a twofold serendipity: dramatic improvements in the cost-performance ratios of computers and of communications technologies. Independent of each other, computing and communicating tools have been improving at the annual rate of some 25 percent for at least the past two decades. This relentless compounding of capabilities has transformed a faint promise of synergy into an immense and real potential.

Computers have grown so powerful and cost-effective that they can be found nearly everywhere doing nearly everything: Supercomputers, manipulating billions of commands per second, forecast the weather and analyze complex medical images. Sensory computers respond to spoken sentences and visually recognize parts on assembly lines. Robotic computers turn those parts into full products. Like the telescope and microscope, computers are opening up new realms for scientists by simulating everything from astronomical collisions to molecular reactions. Fifty million personal computers along with thousands of varieties of software packages help people at work and at home. And millions of computers disappear every year into the cars, microwave ovens, telephones and television sets that they control.

At the same time, the reach and speed of networks have increased by equally awesome strides: millions of

miles of glass fibers handle most long-haul communications and are capable of relaying data at speeds of up to a billion bits (gigabits) per second. Local-area networks have become indispensable webs, wiring numerous buildings and neighborhoods. Cellular and other wireless networks reach people while they are driving or even walking. And now these two giants, computers and networks, can be fused to form an infrastructure even more promising than the individual technologies.

During the past 10 years, we have, moreover, learned lessons about the many useful possibilities offered by the information infrastructure and the difficulties in building it. For instance, throwing computers and networks together without careful development of common conventions that enable them to communicate easily does not lead far.

As we lay the bricks of the information age, trying to envision the ultimate edifice and its uses is as challenging for us as it would have been for writers in the late 1700s to anticipate the automobile, the helicopter, the jet airplane and the myriad of other modern engines along with all that we do with these machines. So we simply offer readers our best impressionistic glimpses into this future, its underlying technologies and surrounding issues.

In a world in which hundreds of millions of computers, servants to their users, easily plug into a global information infrastructure, business mail would routinely reach its destination in five seconds instead of five days, dramatically altering the substance of business communications. A company's designers and marketers would actively collaborate on a product, even when located a continent apart and unable to meet at the same time. Consumers would broadcast their needs to suppliers, creating a kind of reverse advertising. Many goods would be ordered and paid for electronically. A parent could deliver work to a physically distant employer while taking care of children at home. A retired engineer in Florida could teach algebra to high school students in New York City. And from a comfortable position in your easy chair, you could enjoy a drive through your next vacation spot, a trip through the Louvre or a high-definition movie rented electronically, chosen from the millions available.

Yet the information age has its shadows as well. Will these new technologies widen the gap between rich and poor? I suspect so. Will they cause us to be inundated with "infojunk," mountains of information irrelevant to us? Yes, but we can also use the technologies to shield us from such perils. Will they threaten to dehumanize people? I doubt it. But will these technologies also increase white-collar crimes and violations of privacy? We don't know; we must be vigilant.

And as has been the case for much technological change, the glorious possibilities we describe in this issue stem more from opportunism than they do from pressing human need. Consequently, we, the designers and users of this information infrastructure, bear a serious responsibility: we must understand the value and role of information so that we may better channel our technological miracles into useful rather than frivolous, if not dangerous, directions.

Information touches all human activity. It comes in a multitude of different shapes—speech, pictures, video, office work, software, great art and kitsch, invoices, music, stock prices, tax returns, orders to attack, love letters, novels and the news. We have also created many ways of conveying information, from cheap, large newsprint pages to postal systems to telephone, radio and television networks. Virtually all these schemes require humans at the receiving end to understand and then to act on the incoming information.

Similarly, computers and networks are bound together by information and can fulfill roles roughly analogous to those of people and their communications schemes. Computers accept, store, process and present information; the networks move information among the machines they interconnect. Computers can manipulate information far faster than people ever will. But unlike people, machines almost never understand the messages they are manipulating. To them, information is only a deceptively uniform sequence of numbers—ones and zeros.

One key idea behind the information infrastructure is to relieve people of a good deal of the work of communicating and processing information. To do so, the machines must intelligently handle some of the dazzling diversity of concepts that information represents. They must therefore begin to understand, even at a crude level, what the ones and zeros mean. In contrast, the current state of affairs is tantamount to a community of telephone callers trying to work with one another using only meaningless grunts of different loudnesses to convey messages.

Understanding the value of information, though, is difficult even for people. Although we are continually besieged by information, we have at best only an intuitive grasp of its meaning and almost no sense of how to value it. How valuable is a 300-page report on a company's stock? What makes a 15-page booklet or a well-placed stock tip more valuable?

Until a better explanation is devised, let me suggest that information has economic value to people only if it can lead them to the acquisition of tangible goods. Similarly, information has intangible value if it can enable them to satisfy less tangible human desires. An encyclopedia publisher, for instance, will find a mailing list of prospective buyers useful because it might increase sales. Watching a soap opera has value for those people who want to experience heartrending emotions.

Because information leads to goods only indirectly, it seems reasonable to value it as a fraction of the worth of the tangible goods to which it leads. If information leads to goods through intermediate pieces of information, each one derived from the others through processing, then all the intermediate data and programs should also be somehow valued backward from the end results.

Using these ideas, we can measure the economic value of all that will transpire on tomorrow's sprawling computer-and-network complexes as a fraction of the tangible goods to which

they will lead. Today an industrially advanced and wealthy country such as the U.S. places the value of its computer hardware and software, including the work needed to run computer systems within organizations, at almost a tenth of its gross national product—roughly about $500 billion. Yet because some 60 percent of the work force have jobs that involve information, the value of computerized information handling may well grow to an even larger fraction of the U.S. economy.

Valuing information this way points out some sobering lessons to bear in mind as we embark on the information age. To be valuable to us, tomorrow's computers and networks must help us achieve our tangible goals, even as they shield us from the barrage of infojunk produced by others aiming to achieve their own goals. This objective raises to a still higher premium the need for computers and networks to understand enough content so they can isolate, simplify and present useful information and reject irrelevant data before they clutter users' lives.

Thinking about the value of information brings home another lesson: that information and its processing have less value in poor countries because there are not many tangible goods to which they can lead. Yet there are other ways in which information can play an important role in these countries. It can help teach people to take better care of their health, to fix machinery or to establish better farming practices. Information might also improve the distribution of food and medicine. Countries with well-educated pools of labor, such as India, may even earn foreign exchange by writing software for overseas consumption.

On balance, however, information more naturally boosts the wealth of those who already have material goods—simply because those communities already have so many tangible goods to which information can lead. Unless wealthy countries see it as their duty to help developing nations make good use of the evolving technologies, the information age will likely widen the rift between the haves and have-nots.

Rich nations must also remember that if they become enamoured of and blinded by the glamour of the information era and neglect to produce and improve tangible wealth—such as food, manufactured goods, natural resources and human services—the information colossus will lead to nothing and so will collapse. Information is, after all, secondary to people's principal needs—food, shelter, health and human relationships. In a crisis, even the most dedicated hackers would trade millions of bytes of software for a few bites of bread.

We begin to reap the value of information when we have created an infrastructure that leverages our work. The existing web of computer, telephone, broadcast and other kinds of networks does not constitute the kind of powerful information infrastructure that we envision—no more than the thousands of U.S. dirt roads in the early 1900s made a national highway system. Intrepid travelers could drive from one place to another by navigating over those twisting passages, but such trips were slow and difficult.

Well-established infrastructures, such as the present highway system, the telephone network and the electric power grid, have several simple but powerful properties. They are widely available: accessible to practically every American is a well-paved road, at least one telephone and several electric power outlets. These infrastructures are also easy to use. No more effort is required than pushing a plug into an electric socket or talking into a telephone. And most important, these infrastructures serve as the foundations for countless useful activities. We conduct business deals and family chats over the telephone, ferry people, food and every conceivable good over the highways, and so on.

Using these yardsticks, we can see that no information infrastructure exists anywhere in the world today. Learning how to use a computer still causes headaches. And it is impossible to build even one application that can be used by all the nation's computers.

To escape the present chaos and to fashion our computers and networks into a true information infrastructure, we must endow networks with three key capabilities: flexible information transport capabilities, common services and common communications conventions.

Flexible transport means that the infrastructure can carry information among computers with various degrees of speed, security and reliability. This requirement is vastly different from the capabilities of the telephone infrastructure, which was built to carry digital voice signals at a fixed speed of 64,000 bits per second with uniform degrees of security and reliability.

Humans only talk on telephone networks; computers carry on far more diverse activities. Computers can convey information at a wide range of speeds, from a few thousand bits per second for sending a brief text message to tens of millions of bits (megabits) per second for shipping high-resolution video.

Depending on their tasks, computers also have variable access and security needs: arranging a personal loan electronically demands more security than does chatting openly on an electronic bulletin board about the Boston Celtics. Some messages must also be sent with more precision than others. Conveying software, funds or lifesaving medical data requires perfection. A certain laxness, on the other hand, is tolerated in the transmission of photographs, in which case a few lost bits do not alter the meaning of the message.

If users or their computers can set these "levers," that is, choose the combination of transmission speed, security and reliability appropriate for their task, then they need only pay for the service they want. The alternative—a highly secure and lightning-fast transport service that would satisfy all potential needs—would be so expensive that it would never become widely used.

. . . The U.S. is making gradual progress in building the hardware for a flexible network. . . . Telephone companies and other network builders continue to lay down optical fiber lines that are capable of transmitting thousands of times—or eventually hundreds of thousands of times—more traffic than the traditional copper wire. An emerging standard for future telephone service, called broadband integrated-services digital network, will let users transmit data at speeds of up to 150 megabits per second. By the end of the 1990s, the U.S. may have in place a working gigabit network, capable of conveying video images that will rival prize-winning photographs in their vibrancy and crispness.

Flexible service also means that people can tap into the infrastructure wherever and whenever they want. Wireless networks based on cellular and satellite systems will make this access possible by letting automobiles and people walking on the street be part of the world's information infrastructure.

The second component of a proper information infrastructure is a set of common services that would be available to everyone. At a minimum, there must be a few basic and necessary common resources, such as directories—electronic white and yellow pages—of users and services. But there could be richer, universally shared resources as well: government tax codes and regulations, census data, the paintings in the National Gallery and the 15 million books in the Library of Congress.

To understand the third and most important ingredient of an information infrastructure—common communications conventions—consider again the frustrations of people trying to communicate with grunts over the telephone. Any pair trying to communicate may assign meanings to a few specific grunts so they can understand each other. Crude as it may sound, that method is used today within groups of interconnected computers. A company and its suppliers, or even people within one large firm, draw up agreements to establish specific formats for exchanging information. Although this approach works well for a small number, it becomes absurd for a larger community. It is far more economical for everyone to agree on some conventions—in other words, on a common language.

One way to create such a language for computers involves what I like to call E-forms, or electronic forms. E-forms, the computer equivalent of mail-order forms, would be instantly recognized by any computer on the network that needs to do so. A handful are already in use. Several years ago corporations agreed on a broad format called the electronic data interchange (EDI) for settling business transactions, including sending invoices and ordering parts. Electronic services, such as Prodigy (developed by Sears, Roebuck and Co. and IBM), CompuServe and Dow Jones News/Retrieval, offer E-forms for ordering airplane tickets and some merchandise. Unfortunately, these early E-forms are not universally used by computers but are restricted to those clients who pay for the services.

Eventually E-forms might be filled in by speaking rather than by typing. A few prototypes exist: bond traders at Shearson Lehman Brothers and about 40 other firms use voice-activated assistants to record sales of government securities. The machines have small vocabularies, however, and must be trained to understand a specific broker. A research system at the Massachusetts Institute of Technology, called the Air Travel Information System (ATIS), helps people wishing to book flights. It understands continuous speech by any speaker—including those who have accents—provided the person wants to order a ticket. People normally phrase questions in many different ways. Yet the computer need only fit the question asked into one of a few categories. As a result, voice E-forms are much more feasible than general-purpose systems for understanding speech.

Whether typed or spoken, E-forms can also bridge different languages. For instance, an American ordering a pair of Italian shoes need only fill in an E-form in English; it would then automatically be translated into the corresponding E-form in Italian. Such facile translation may make E-forms a key factor in the European Community's quest for commercial unification, providing the participating countries with an easy means to overcome linguistic barriers in routine business transactions.

An alternative to this E-form Esperanto would be a Knowbot, first developed by Cerf and Robert E. Kahn at the Corporation for National Research Initiatives (CNRI). Knowbots are programs designed by their users to travel through a network, inspecting and understanding similar kinds of information, regardless of the language or form in which they are expressed.

Suppose, for example, that you wanted to create a list of all the available car models that have enough backseat leg room for tall people and cost less than $18,000. If details on various vehicles are available through the information infrastructure but are represented in different formats by the manufacturers, you might unleash a Knowbot to roam the net and scan the various forms. Your Knowbot would understand enough about the different ways the same kind of information may be represented to glean the relevant details from every entry. It would then process and present the information to you in a useful and familiar way. An early prototype Knowbot, designed by the CNRI, combs through data bases developed by the National Library of Medicine for salient facts on people in publicly available data bases.

Because Knowbots can be tailored to meet a person's needs and can tolerate diverse representations of information, they look more desirable than E-forms. But as we ask these programs to act with greater intelligence, they become far more challenging to build.

Beyond creating a proper infrastructure with these three elements, we must also develop computer hardware and software that can more naturally connect people and machines to the information infrastructure and, as a result, to one another. . . . Most important, we must rethink how to link people and machines at the cognitive level so as to communicate understanding

instead of grunts. To this end, . . . the hardware should fade into an inconspicuous feature of the environment, even as it enhances our understanding of the events and people around us.

The most vibrant infrastructure we can build is one that allows free enterprise to flourish. The telephone companies will play a major role in laying down the physical fibers for the network and so bear the responsibility for providing flexible information transport services, some minimal common services and access to major shared resources. But neither the telephone companies nor any other centralized body should decide what common communications conventions should be offered; that should instead be the role of special-interest groups working outside the purview of the carriers. In addition, no central agency should have anything to say about what services will be offered through the information infrastructure. These new products and services should be devised by the millions of people and their computers that will use the infrastructure according to their own plans and for their own purposes.

The information infrastructure will then resemble an old-fashioned village market. A multitude of goods and services will be bought and sold through this new information marketplace, as I like to call it. As in traditional markets, not all transactions will be monetary. Some people will publish free manuscripts, others will engage in debates and still others will collaborate in creative and entrepreneurial ways, all through the network.

We can begin to imagine the information marketplace by thinking about how it will change familiar information-handling services such as today's business mail. There is no reason to treat much of the mail as precious physical goods. The message is usually more important than the paper on which it is printed. This does not mean we are obliged to send a video clip of shimmering red roses to someone we love. But when the content is more important than the medium, it is wasteful to transport the paper conveying the message.

A speedy and flexible nationwide electronic mail service could dramatically enhance the competitiveness of domestic industries. Whether a nation becomes a major producer of manufactured goods and services depends heavily on the quality and cost of the products it generates and the speed

with which the products reach the market. Lowering the cost of production and trimming the time needed to design, produce, sell and service products are all intimately related to the speed and flexibility of communicating and processing business information.

In addition to conventional advertising, manufacturers' computers may respond directly to queries for products with special features and prices broadcast by the computers of potential consumers. Before buying a car, for example, a consumer would interact with the manufacturer's computers: via the infrastructure, she might request certain basic features (namely, four-wheel drive), scrutinize the models that fit, then further tailor the car to her needs and wishes by selecting specific options, fabrics and colors.

Once the sale is made, her order would touch off an explosion of computer network activity. Automatically, her descriptions would expand into a cascade of orders for the necessary systems and subsystems of the car. The order would then generate instructions that would time the arrival of these parts to the production floor and would direct the floor to assemble all these pieces. Such services could lead to the mass production of individualized products. . . . Networks may enable independent contractors to create an organization overnight to fill a customer's specific demand—and then to dissolve it just as quickly. . . .

The information marketplace will also change how we work with geographically distant partners. An increasing number of conferences are already conducted over video links, but these conferences still require all the participants to be in the right place at the right time. New approaches to such collaborations will free people to take part in delayed and distributed meetings. . . .

Other services and opportunities also become possible as the infrastructure dissolves geographic and temporal barriers. Remote medical diagnosis and perhaps, some day, remote manipulation would bring experts close to needy patients who are physically thousands of miles away. The long-promised links between the work-place and the home would finally be forged. Besides offering many people the convenience of working at home, the network would also open up new career opportunities for housebound parents

Because the infrastructure so rapidly handles the transport and processing of information, the services likely to gain the most efficiency from the infrastructure are those that involve only information. Securing advice on a specific legal, financial or medical problem could become a relatively easy and low-cost undertaking. Prospective vacationers could explore a virtual island retreat from their home before booking tickets. Inquiries about government regulations would be answered in minutes rather than in months. Advice on building a house or baking a chocolate soufflé would be at hand at any time.

Computers are already heavily used in military training; specially designed flight simulators for pilots and sophisticated war games for strategists have become standard practice. As networked computers grow cheaper and more powerful, companies, too, will be able to afford such approaches. A firm might train its managers by confronting them with simulated problem scenarios involving employees' complaints, project bottlenecks or one another. Other companies might sell such simulation services through the information marketplace.

Even though much has been said and written about computers and education, we have yet to find the most effective ways of applying computers to help people learn. . . . Computers do not magically improve schools. When used to drill students on rote memorization, the machine add little value. . . . But by enabling students to interact with rich intellectual resources, including distant teachers, libraries and museums, the infrastructure can be a strong ally in general education.

In specific cases, we are discovering approaches that seem effective. At M.I.T., students participating in Project Athena learn French as they engage in a simulation of trying to rent an apartment in Paris. A high-resolution moving image of a French speaker asks questions that students must answer.

Eventually the infrastructure may even couple individualized computer tutors with students. One such tutor might help a student analyze a specific bridge or, at a more ambitious level, design bridges. If we can make research dreams come true, an even more advanced tutor, endowed with the design approach and style of Frank Lloyd Wright, might help a student become a virtual apprentice of the master.

Entertainment and publishing will be greatly enhanced by the information infrastructure. We will have easy access to millions of movies and music performances by renting them from collectors who offer their goods in the information marketplace. Video broadcasters, radio stations and videotape rental stores may lose some of their monopolistic hue as the information marketplace connects every supplier to every consumer throughout the nation and the world.

Printed newspapers are unlikely to disappear because they are so convenient and inexpensive. But the information marketplace will also be an abundant source of timely information—including text, advertisements, music and video—contributed by anyone and perused freely by anyone else. These mountains of information will, in turn, create opportunities for a breed of electronic publishers and entrepreneurs who will sift for diamonds, which they can then edit and publish electronically. Thus, even though publishers may not print their works on paper, the substance of gathering and reporting information will not change. . . .

Not only will the information marketplace enhance specific sectors of the economy, but even greater collective benefits will flow from binding together previously unlinked parts of the economy. Consider, for example, the likely evolution of high-definition television (HDTV). With the information infrastructure in place, all the vexing questions about how HDTV will develop and who will control it will fade. Instead we need only adjust the flexible transport levers to make HDTV a reality, linking every home and office to every broadcaster and video rental service in the information marketplace. Interactive, how-to instructions, virtual museum visits or simulation sessions could exploit the visual power of HDTV, thereby benefiting the suppliers of and the many services that use high-definition video as well as the country that has this infrastructure treasure trove.

Where will this information mania lead us? As we think about how far we might use the technologies to stretch the ways people live, learn and work, we anticipate that a sophisticated information infrastructure should help in three ways. It should relieve many of the repetitive, boring and unpleasant tasks related to processing and communicating information. In this case, the computers' effectiveness will be limited only by the extent to which they have been designed to understand the information that reaches them, regardless of whether the information is supplied by people or by computers.

Second, the information infrastructure should help us improve the ways we do things now, by speeding up existing processes or by improving their quality. Although the flow of information can be greatly accelerated, the ultimate limits to these improvements are governed by the physical work involved, including those tasks that only people can carry out. No matter how fast the information flows, assembling a real car out of real parts still takes real time.

The third major way computers and networks will touch our lives is by unlocking as yet unexplored possibilities. The neighborhoods we play in and the people with whom we do business no longer need be the ones close by but the ones we choose.

There is no question, too, that computers and networks will democratize human communications. Nearly everyone would be able to put his or her ideas, concerns and demands before all others. This freedom will undoubtedly bring sociological consequences, including the formation of electronic tribes that can span physical distance.

The manipulation of video, sound and text by computers will let us explore new vistas. It will also further blur the boundary between virtual and real experiences. Even a plain old movie can deeply color the moods of passive viewers. What might tomorrow's interactive, multisensory movies inspire?

Influential as these tools will be, there are obvious limits to how much they will change our lives: no amount of virtual reality can substitute for people's real needs. Neither can computers and networks augment the human capacity to absorb information or the number of people with whom a person can interact or the quality of human relationships.

The information infrastructure will also introduce new challenges for society. Who should be liable for computer services that misbehave? I believe the people or companies who profit by providing the services should be accountable. How will we ensure personal privacy on the network and yet protect users from computer crimes, worms and viruses? We cannot yet answer questions like these with much certainty, but we should not hesitate to try to anticipate them. . . .

Yet even as some of the promises that we seek will turn out to be mirages, so, too, some of the problems will evaporate like bad dreams. Some people worry that these new technologies will tend to dehumanize us. In the worst technophobic scenario, men and women fixated on computer screens and plugged into networks are rendered spiritless and become trapped in lonely and cruel isolation. I find such concerns implausible. People are neither so naive nor devoid of instincts for self-preservation and control that they will surrender their humanity to their tools.

Information infrastructures will evolve first in those industrialized countries that need and can afford them. Senator Al Gore identifies the role that national governments must take in developing these infrastructures. Like the traditional highway and power systems, these information infrastructures will be woven tightly into the fabric of a nation, hard for others to copy or to emulate. And like these earlier infrastructures, they will give their

builders certain unique economic advantages.

Once several national information infrastructures are in place, countries will tie them together, much as national power grids, airline routes and telephone circuits have been linked in the past. The result will be a global information infrastructure that will help the people of the world buy and sell information and information services and share knowledge and creative energy—we hope to the benefit of all.

The opportunities along with the problems that may well arise on tomorrow's computers and networks will be new, different, unpredictable and worthy of our continual vigilance. Harnessing the electronic agents that will emerge from this infrastructure to support humanity may be our ultimate challenge. And yet the opportunities and shadows we face as we try to achieve our goals in the in-

formation age are consistent with those we have grappled with during the agricultural and industrial eras. The alternative—closing the door to technological discovery so as to avoid societal pitfalls—is unacceptable to the probing nature of the human spirit.

FURTHER READING

THE NATIONAL CHALLENGE IN COMPUTER SCIENCE AND TECHNOLOGY. Washington, D.C., Computer Science and Telecommunications Board, 1988.

SILICON DREAMS: INFORMATION, MAN, AND MACHINE. Robert W. Lucky. St. Martin's Press, 1989.

BUILDING THE INFORMATION MARKETPLACE. Michael L. Dertouzos in *Technology Review*, pages 29–40; January 1991.

M.I.T. PROJECT ATHENA: A MODEL FOR DISTRIBUTED CAMPUS COMPUTING. George A. Champine. Digital Press, 1991.

# The Changing Economy

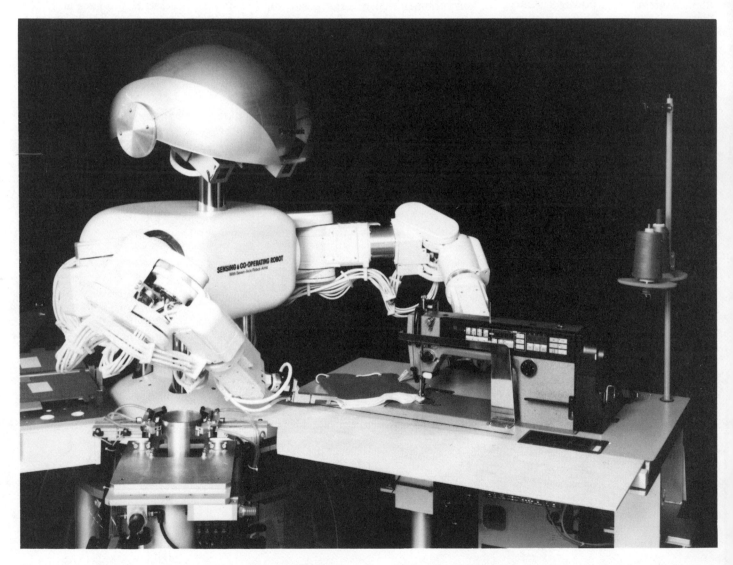

The whole range of inventions we refer to as computers or information technology are having a major impact on the production, distribution, and consumption of goods and services in society. In other words, they are transforming the economy. Because the economy is tied to nearly every facet of social life, this transformation will have some very far-reaching consequences.

To better understand why the economy is so important, consider a few of the social consequences of current economic arrangements in advanced societies. Our system of mass producing goods and services has given us a high standard of living. But it also means that most of us must live in or near a city and work in highly specialized occupations for large organizations over which we have little control. True self-reliance is rare. We depend on countless others to produce the basic goods and services we need to carry out daily life. In addition, our elaborate system of market exchange brings us into numerous brief and close encounters with complete strangers nearly every day. Such factors have helped to make the nuclear family's role in social and emotional fulfillment more important than it was in preindustrial societies.

We tend to take the social dimensions of our economic system for granted, but a significant change in even one part of its underlying structure could lead to unexpected side effects in other areas. For instance, computers and telecommunications now make it technically feasible for workers in many occupations to "telecommute" to work without physically leaving their homes. How might society change if telecommuting becomes widespread? This is not a far-fetched possibility because many current jobs center on various aspects of creating, collecting, analyzing, interpreting, and disseminating information, and they do not require a worker to occupy any particular physical space.

For societies and individuals, accurate, current, information is extremely important to economic well-being. Try to imagine your own day-to-day survival without easy access to such ordinary information as schedules, prices, and telephone numbers. Business and government would screech to a halt without a relatively smooth and continuous flow of masses of reliable information. In "The New Democrat From Cyberspace," Robert Wright discusses the mission of Mitch Kapor, a major proponent of a powerful new "information infrastructure" that will vastly increase the capacity to collect and exchange data. As Wright discusses, the development of the envisioned "data superhighway," as well as its potential effects, depend on a complex interplay of social and political as well as economic factors. In the second article in this section, Myron Magnet looks more specifically at how information is reshaping a number of economic sectors in "Who's Winning the Information Revolution?"

Manufacturing is one sector that has been drastically affected by technological change. The size of the manufacturing work force has been declining over the past few decades, and a significant factor in this trend is that various forms of automation have enabled factories to produce more goods with fewer workers. According to Jenny McCune, this trend will continue. In "Tomorrow's Factory," she relates that factories of the future will be smaller and more specialized than now. They will also be more environmentally friendly and responsive to consumer demands.

The next four articles discuss recent, cutting-edge technological developments—all of which are predicted to have major economic and/or social impacts. The state of "optoelectronic" computing is described in "The Light Fantastic." Gino Del Guercio discusses current research and potential applications of "nanotechnology" in "How Small Is It, Johnny?" Gene Bylinsky describes individual and business uses for computers that can recognize human speech in "At Last! Computers You Can Talk To." The article "Virtual Reality" recounts the current state and future applications of virtual reality.

In "Fast Money," Peter Passell offers us insights into the complexities of the daily transferring of billions of dollars in electronic funds through the Clearing House Interbank Payments System. He also relates that electronic transfer systems require exceptional security measures to protect against the risks of fire, technical malfunction, and unauthorized access.

The cost of new medical technologies frequently drives up the cost of health care. In "Medical Technology 'Arms Race' Adds Billions to the Nation's Bills," Andrew Pollack describes the conflict among those who provide medical services and those who pay for them.

### Looking Ahead: Challenge Questions

Do you think that as the "information age" advances, people will become more dependent on others for their basic needs or more self-reliant?

Is the information explosion helping us become more informed as individuals? Are workers, parents, consumers, voters, more knowledgeable than in the past? Does it matter?

Some historians have observed that every major change in the mechanism of economic exchange has resulted in shifts in the balance of power in society. Do you think the move toward electronic funds transfer will alter the current balance of power? If so, which groups do you think will become more or less powerful?

# THE NEW DEMOCRAT FROM CYBERSPACE

*Robert Wright*

During the mid-1980s, when Mitch Kapor and Bill Gates were America's twin software titans, telling them apart wasn't hard. Before striking it rich, Kapor had spent time as a disc jockey, a stand-up comic, a transcendental meditation instructor and a counselor at a mental hospital (where, he liked to tell journalists, he had performed "the psychic equivalent of emptying bedpans"). Gates had gone straight from college into business, showing the single-minded drive for which he remains famous. Kapor had called his software company "Lotus"—simple, elegant, quietly reflective of his spiritual leanings. Gates, in something shy of a vast creative leap, had named his microcomputer software company "Microsoft." Gates's main product, the operating system DOS, was, like the company's name, serviceable but clunky. Kapor's smash hit, the spreadsheet Lotus 1-2-3, was stylish and user-friendly.

As the decade passed, Gates got richer and richer and Microsoft got bigger and bigger. Kapor got rich and dropped out. He left Lotus, which, he said, had gotten oppressively corporate. He would leave it for Gates to be the "empire-builder, someone who wants to build the Standard Oil of computing."

Kapor, in short, seemed the more authentic embodiment of Silicon Valley's hacker ideals: anti-corporate, nonconformist, vaguely whole-earthish, creative. With time this contrast hardened into hacker iconography. Gates was the anti-Christ, a man whose corporate stranglehold on the software industry had left it awash in ugly products. Kapor was a folk hero.

In 1990 Kapor and Grateful Dead lyricist John Perry Barlow started the Electronic Frontier Foundation, a public interest group devoted to defending the civil liberties of hackers. (Some were getting stifling attention from, for example, federal agents who didn't see the humor in entering government or corporate computers, even if just for kicks.) Kapor's place in Silicon Valley lore seemed secure.

The story has since gotten more complex. The Electronic Frontier Foundation (EFF) has moved its main office from Cambridge to Washington and expanded its domain. In particular, it is paying great attention to Al Gore's pet project, the "data superhighway"—the nationwide fiber-optic grid that, we are told, will revolutionize research, education, entertainment and commerce. Kapor is no longer just a gadfly and defender of the oppressed, but, increasingly, a Washington Player. He is a star witness at congressional hearings and a common quote in stories about the "information infrastructure." He and EFF work closely with the chairman of the House Subcommittee on Telecommunications and Finance, Ed Markey of Massachusetts (Lotus's and Kapor's home state). And they have easy access to the Clinton administration, with which, Kapor says, EFF is "in sync" philosophically.

With power comes suspicion. Kapor says: "You can find people who will go on record as saying 'EFF—that bunch of Washington sellouts.'" Indeed. In expanding from civil liberties to the ideologically complex issues of infrastructure, EFF has alienated some members and some (former) employees who feel it has lost its purity of mission. And the foundation's success in Washington has brought complaints from other groups that occupy roughly the same niche—or would occupy it, at least, if there were room. EFF is "a thousand-pound canary," says Jeff Chester of the Center for Media Education; it is perceived as *the* respectable liberal voice on the information infrastructure. And "because Ed Markey's door is always open, they have incredible influence on Capitol Hill, I think to the exclusion of other groups that are working in the public interest."

Beneath this complaint is a sense that Kapor is drifting from his cultural and ideological moorings, that the Zen-master dropout from corporate America has become a tool of corporations. EFF, originally funded by Kapor and a couple of other computer millionaires, is now underwritten mainly by companies and trade associations from just about every relevant walk of life: IBM, Apple, AT&T, MCI, Bell Atlantic, Adobe, the Newspaper Association of America, the National Cable Television Association. Even the dreaded Microsoft. Jamie Love of the Center for Study of Responsive Law, a Ralph Nader group, says, "You've got the group that's billed as the principal public interest organization in these debates being funded mostly by companies and trade associations."

The question of whose interests are served by EFF is indeed important. Though the data superhighway has been heavily hyped, its significance is, if anything, underappreciated. The visionaries are probably right to say that for decades a growing portion of human interaction will take place electronically—in "cyberspace." And the sizeable cultural and political effects of this fact will depend on the architecture of cyberspace and the laws that govern it, both of which remain up for grabs, and both of which greatly concern companies backing EFF. If Kapor has sold out, he will assuredly not go to hacker heaven.

The data superhighway is much misunderstood. For example: contrary to popular belief, it already exists. AT&T, MCI, Sprint and others have laid gobs of optical fiber from city to city, and these glass lines can handle the commonly cited superhighway services: routine teleconferencing and telecommuting; interactive multimedia education; video on demand; interactive home shopping (eventually featuring 3-D on-line catalogs); remote medical diagnosis; prompt delivery of any book or article in the world, etc. What is lacking are lots and lots of more local fiber links, which will carry signals from superhighway to the home. One reason this distinction gets muddied is that, as one congressional staffer put it, "Saying 'We must build a nationwide superhighway' sounds better than saying, 'We must build nationwide on-and-off-ramps.' "

The "we" part is also misleading. The builder of the data highways and byways won't be the government. The work will be done by cable T.V. companies, regional Bell telephone companies and other private actors. And the Clinton administration won't be footing the bill. It has promised only $1 billion annually for a project that is expected to cost between $200 billion and $400 billion over fifteen to thirty years.

The likely builders of fiber networks are seeking less direct federal support. The regional Bells want to be freed to compete with cable T.V.; then, they say, they'll have an incentive to invest heavily in local fiber networks. They wouldn't mind tax breaks or looser rate controls, either. The cable companies would like to be free of price regulation, which dampens revenues and thus slows their replacement of coaxial cable with fiber. But, having just been re-regulated, they're now talking more about tax breaks.

In Washington the sense of urgency about building a nationwide fiber network has abated a bit since the presidential campaign, when Gore carried the goal to new prominence. One reason is Mitch Kapor. On the day before Clinton's inauguration, in a standing-room-only hearing of Markey's subcommittee, Kapor championed a near-term alternative to a fully fiber network that EFF had been pushing for some time: integrated services digital network, or ISDN. By enabling existing copper phone lines to carry digital signals (on-or-off signals, instead of wavy "analog" signals), ISDN would make the lines much quicker conduits of data. Kapor's testimony inspired the lead paragraph of a story in the next day's *Washington Post*: "Plans advocated by the incoming Clinton administration and others to use fiber-optic cables to create an elaborate new nationwide communications highway may be elbowed out by less costly technologies."

This is a little misleading. Kapor supports a nationwide fiber grid, and sees ISDN as a transitional step, not a substitute. Still, he does oppose big government financing for fiber, and this financing did seem a live prospect in January, after Gore's ambitious campaign rhetoric. Gore now says he was misinterpreted and had never envisioned a big government role. In any event, the interest in ISDN stoked by EFF and Markey helped end discussion of any such role.

Arguments rage over ISDN. Some call it a distraction—a marginal and, anyway, inevitable step that will only sap public support for fiber subsidies. Others call it a waste—sure to be rendered obsolete by fiber fairly soon (though much of the investment in ISDN, such as digital switches, might survive the transition to fiber). Whatever ISDN's technical merits, one thing it definitely succeeds at is illustration. It is a nice example of EFF's ideology—of the shape Kapor thinks the eventual fiber-optic network should assume, and of the political, cultural and economic values embedded in such a network. ISDN helps explain what Kapor means when he calls EFF's worldview "Jeffersonian."

ISDN, which is already available to more than a third of Americans (unbeknownst to most of them), could reach virtually every American home in four or five years. Over existing copper lines, it moves data twenty-seven times faster than a 2400-baud modem. That would mean rapid-fire faxes and database retrievals and the easy transmission of graphics and photographs, both of which are very information-intensive. ISDN wouldn't bring seamless video, but, with the aid of new data-compression tricks, it could bring video worthy of teleconferences.

ISDN could revolutionize, say, house hunting. Sit at your terminal, define the kind of home you're after, and then "tour" each candidate: see color pictures of the house, of every room, of the view from every window. Moving from one room to the next would take a few seconds, versus a couple of minutes at 2400-baud. You wouldn't buy a house without touring the real thing, of course, but you'd remotely reject plenty of houses, saving eons of drive time. The fact that people actually watch those Sunday real estate shows—which offer about four shots of each house and no control over which houses appear—suggests a large potential market for a Home Home Shopping Service.

ISDN would also simplify, for example, expert medical consultation for rural residents. An x-ray or CAT scan comprises vast numbers of bits, and sending one by conventional modem can take ten minutes. Telecommuting, too, would be easier. ISDN would let you remotely control your office computer with little or no bothersome time lag. And because ISDN divides the phone line into three parts, you and a colleague can talk to each other while looking at any text or images you're discussing. Less sexy services—

the electronic magazines, bulletin boards and databases that are already common—would become much cheaper to run and easier to use.

In grasping ISDN's connection to EFF's core doctrines, the most important thing to appreciate is that, even when it is transporting video, ISDN is not like cable T.V. Many politicians talk as if the regional Bells and the cable companies are equally viable builders of fiber networks—whoever can do the job fast and cheap should do it. But a choice between the two could be momentous, assuming they pattern the new fiber systems on their current systems.

Suppose, for example, you want to start the Home Home Shopping Service. Sounds easy: tell people you'll sell their homes for much less than brokers charge; you'll come in, take lots of pictures and file them on a computerized database in your den. But if the pictures have to be accessed via cable-T.V. lines, you'll have a problem. Cable systems aren't generally designed to let you send data; they're designed to let you receive it. And even if the lines are made two-way, you still have to send the data through a central bottleneck to get it to other people; cable systems typically have a "tree and branch" structure, so that getting one branch in touch with another means going through the trunk. To get your Home Home Shopping Service through the trunk, you'd probably have to promise the cable company a piece of the action and do God knows what else to convince it that the operation was viable.

With ISDN, you need nobody's permission. The phone system is designed for decentralized, home-to-home communication; it is a *switched* network—not a tree, but a web in which the shortest distance between two points is a reasonably straight line. What's more, as a matter of law, the regional Bells have to make their system available to everyone at the same rate, since they are "common carriers"; they don't pass judgment on the content of your communication—it's none of their business. So long as you're on the Bell system, you can just set up the Home Home Shopping Service in your den, advertise it and wait for the calls to come in.

In championing ISDN, Kapor has been inspired (seduced, critics say) by his success at Lotus, which hinged on the open architecture of the IBM personal computer. Any software designer could take the computer's publicly available specifications, create compatible software and sell the software without anyone's permission. The result was an explosion of entrepreneurship. ISDN, similarly, would provide an "open platform" for experimentation, a seedbed for enterprise.

The ensuing proliferation of new data services, Kapor thinks, would help solve the chicken-and-egg problem that has slowed the laying of fiber by the private sector. Once the Home Home Shopping Service was a success, a better version—a high-definition T.V. tour through each house—would seem to be a sure bet. So fiber would seem to be a surer bet. Here, again, Kapor speaks from experience. The success of P.C. software—especially Lotus 1-2-3—brought massive invest-

ment in subsequent, more powerful generations of hardware.

The fiber lines that would gradually overshadow ISDN's copper lines should, says Kapor, follow the same basic form: a switched network, open to all, with no discrimination on the basis of content. The coming fiber grid should resemble the phone system, not the average cable T.V. system.

In stressing the superiority of switched, open networks, Kapor seems not especially trammeled by the money EFF gets from the National Cable Television Association. Describing how cable companies have tried to exploit the term "information infrastructure," he says, "They have all these great slides that they make up about it. They say, 'We can deliver information-age benefits, we've got our fiber-optic networks.' And they don't talk about the fact that the networks are closed—you can't put your own content on it. You know, I mean like *fatal* limitations."

To say that the new grids should resemble the phone system isn't to say that phone companies have to build them. Cable companies can build switched fiber networks. In fact, Time-Warner is building a small one in suburban Orlando. And maybe, with a radical attitude adjustment, cable companies could even adopt the mindset of a common carrier. But we certainly can't assume that companies accustomed to the somewhat Stalinist world of cable T.V. will, if left to their own devices, choose to build switched, open networks.

For that matter, we can't assume that the regional Bells, once allowed into the T.V. business, will choose to build switched networks. The Bells' fascination with video programming tends to rest on a kind of cable envy that could foster uncritical emulation.

Whoever the various highway builders are, then, they may need some, well, *guidance*. If the government gives them their cherished incentives to lay fiber, perhaps in return it should get some say over highway architecture and the rules of the road. So far this idea hasn't permeated Capitol Hill. Last year the Bush administration's FCC issued its "video dial tone" ruling, allowing phone companies to carry video programming owned by others. Now a bill sponsored by Democratic Representative Frederick Boucher of Virginia would free the Bells to own some of the programming they carry—a major item on their wish list. Yet the Boucher bill says nothing about network architecture. And it doesn't entirely resolve questions (though it does address them) about whether the Bells' ownership of video content might conflict with the role of common carrier.

Legislation as undemanding as the Boucher bill could mean that in twenty years, after zillions of dollars are spent on fiber optics, some cities will have two centralized, corporatized T.V. systems instead of one. That wouldn't be a total loss. It might keep rates low without regulation. Also, a centralized fiber system would offer much more variety than a centralized coaxial system. Still, it probably wouldn't bring the explosion in consumer choice that Kapor hopes for.

And "consumer choice" isn't the half of it. EFF's argument for a switched, open network is much deeper than the Home Home Shopping Service example suggests. That example covers only the argument's economic dimension. The other dimensions are cultural and political.

One nightmare scenario for a data superhighway, says Kapor, is that it would take the famous Bruce Springsteen lyric and multiply it by ten: 570 channels and nothing on. "I mean, we could have tremendous bandwidth into the home and individuals and groups not have any access to it but continue to be passive recipients for whatever the people who control access to that medium want to do with it." In other words: "just more corporatism."

Surely he exaggerates. Even monopolistic cable companies don't do "whatever they want." They cater to consumer demand in a crude way, since more viewers mean more money. Still, it is true that the vision of 570 channels looks positively retro next to Kapor's vision: a network devoid of centralized control, a network on which everyone can be producer as well as consumer, and no audience is considered too small—a network that supplements popular culture not just with highbrow culture, but with *un*popular culture.

If someone wants to telecast his daughter's cello practice live, to one or ten or fifty people, then let the fun begin. And if the daughter wants to use a camcorder, computerized animation, a desktop editing system, text from the *Bhagavad Gita* and clips from *Birth of a Nation* to produce an interactive multimedia product, fine; let people download it and experience it at their leisure. If she wants to host a teleconference seminar afterward, that's fine, too. Maybe, as her following grows, she'll become a multimedia Truffaut.

And if the content of her product, and of the ensuing tele-discussion, is political (text from the *Federalist Papers* and clips from C-SPAN), *that's* fine. Maybe it will seed a new ideology; maybe she will host ever larger electronic town meetings. In the world of tomorrow, anyone can grow up to be Ross Perot—without becoming a billionaire first.

In this light, the principles EFF wants embedded in the fiber network assume new meaning. Ensuring cheap, easy and equal access becomes more than a lubricant for entrepreneurship; it is a guarantee of free cultural and political expression—the extension of the First Amendment into cyberspace. When Jerry Berman, formerly of the ACLU and now EFF's executive director, is asked what lobbying about the data superhighway has to do with EFF's original mission, he says information infrastructure is "the fundamental civil liberties issue of the twenty-first century."

Berman and Kapor recommend a paradigm shift. The phrase "500 channels," which often crops up in discussions of the superhighway, is best banished from future discourse. The preferred model is internet, the global computer meta-network, which encompasses various institutional archives and millions of personal computers. On internet people can read and post messages on bulletin boards; send e-mail to a friend;

"broadcast" e-mail to lots of friends; search databases and download articles and software; play games by long distance; join in discussions—whether in "real time" or on bulletin boards—that become magazines in progress read by lots of people who don't contribute; and so on. Friendships blossom, clubs form, debates rage. EFF itself arose from internet discussions between Barlow and Kapor, who live half a country apart. And recent debate over EFF's corporate backing and ideological fidelity has been catalyzed by internet.

Internet involves no dominant corporate players, no central source of information, no central source of anything. It is with evident satisfaction that Kapor calls it "one of the world's largest functioning anarchies."

Internet, being hard to access and navigate, is mainly a world of computer jocks. But, says Kapor, "you've got to get past the idea that it's nerds only" and see "the beauty within its soul." Imagine a user-friendly, multimedia internet over a switched fiber-optic network: practically infinite capacity and infinite reach in a world of cheap video equipment, subtly interactive software and so on. Uses of the network would be reminiscent of various mixtures of T.V., radio, telephones, computers, magazines, mass mail, C.B. radios—a new medium of such flexibility and power that there's literally no telling what it will be like. This is the vision of the hackers. They believe that thinking of the new medium as high-octane T.V., as some legislators seem inclined to do, will only lead to bad legislation.

All in all, "Jeffersonian" is probably a defensible description of EFF's vision. And not just because the government's role would be simply to lay the groundwork for the economic, cultural and political manifestation of liberty. Jefferson believed that the basic resource of his day—land—was a "natural right," and that its acquisition by the masses should be promoted, in part to foster self-reliance. These days, land is not such a vital resource. The sine qua non of prosperity, increasingly, is information. "If you give individuals a suitably rich information environment," says Kapor, "whatever their discipline or profession is, you're empowering them economically." Access to data lets people "strike out and have an independent economic existence." And, unlike land, information is potentially infinite. Everyone can cultivate it, and everyone can share in the harvest. But only if the information infrastructure is designed with that in mind.

Putting a gigabyte in every pot sounds like a liberal enough goal. So what *are* the substantive complaints from the left about EFF? They're hard to flesh out. After mentioning shady corporate backing and complaining about EFF's hogging the spotlight, critics tend to lapse into minor or off-the-mark issues (such as "reserving channels for nonprofits," a concern that, though perhaps valid in the short run, EFF hopes to render moot). But there is one genuine and weighty difference between EFF and its liberal critics: how to get the gigabyte in every pot.

# 1. THE CHANGING ECONOMY

Kapor wants to do it by lowering the cost of the gigabytes. As the personal computer industry showed, "Volume goes up, price comes down. The same thing will be the case here." Just structure cyberspace so enterprise can flourish, and access to data will grow cheap, "like televisions and telephones today."

But markets don't do their magic overnight. Highway builders, left to their own devices, will put fiber in affluent neighborhoods first. And even if all homes were suddenly given broad bandwidth, each exotic new service would, for a time, be pricey. Marc Rotenberg of Computer Professionals for Social Responsibility expresses a common fear when he talks about the "network equivalents of Beverly Hills and East L.A." He and some others on the left want to address such disparities by making public schools and libraries information oases in low-income neighborhoods. He wants to "get the network out to K-12," and he worries about EFF's "lack of support for public libraries."

Kapor actually supports subsidies that will get libraries and schools linked to internet, and to the fully fiber network of tomorrow—including subsidies in a second Boucher bill that he finds more meritorious than the first. EFF has managed to avoid an open split with the American Library Association. (Few things are worse for your image than thousands of kindly librarians bad-mouthing you.) Still, tension does exist. Kapor frowns on an idea that some states are considering—building whole fiber-optic networks specially for schools and libraries before the market has lowered the cost (especially of the "boxes" that will connect user to fiber). The best way to help libraries, schools and poor people, he says, "is to get the mass market moving as quickly as possible." The question is: "What are the minimal government interventions required to ensure access? I mean, no doubt there will be some small percentage of people who need to get subsidies, just as there are for telephone service." And "we'd be prepared to hop on it as hard as necessary to ensure equity of access." It's just that "some other issues, like network architecture—like, is it going to be open, and can you put your own content on it?—are much more problematic right now."

Between Rotenberg and Kapor lies an issue that has helped fracture the left over the past twenty years: the relative role of markets and government in realizing liberal goals. The very language they use pinpoints them on the ideological map. Rotenberg, explaining Kapor's attraction to ISDN, says somewhat suspiciously, "Mitch saw very exciting entrepreneurial possibilities." It's "not so much that he was trying to make a buck" as that he naturally identified with business interests. (As if business interests and the public interest necessarily diverge.) Kapor, meanwhile, talks about special interests with the full-throated disdain of a New Democrat (or an old Republican). "They come and they got their hand out," he says. "And it's amazing and disgusting to me to see the parade of people sucking on the government

teat. I mean it's really true. You sit in enough hearings—you know, they're nice people; they're family people; I could have interesting conversations with them. But they're conditioned and adapted to operating in an environment where the way they get resources is by *whining*. And, you know, we can't afford to do that."

Kapor avoids common labels for his outlook. "Neoliberal" is "very déclassé," he says. In fact, any variation on "liberal" (except "postliberal") bothers him, so tainted is the term by its old "programmatic" methods. But he can't dodge "New Democrat"; he's a longtime contributor to Democratic campaigns, and he sure isn't an *old* Democrat.

One possibly apt label for Kapor's ideology is "Silicon Valley"—construed broadly to include the American computer culture anywhere from northern California to Kapor's turf in Massachusetts. Among many hackers, the emphasis on free expression and moral tolerance is unyielding, and is nourished by a deep suspicion of authority. But a thoroughly left-wing aversion to government intrusion, when applied to economic matters, leads to the right end of the political spectrum (or, at least, to the "neo" end of "liberal"). Hence EFF co-founder Barlow's identity, as rendered by Kapor: "an acid-head ex-Republican-county-chairman." (And no, the Republican part didn't precede the acid part.) Though many hackers have at one time or another been on the government dole, typically through the Pentagon's research budget, there is still in Silicon Valley a large suspicion of subsidies, a strong strain of laissez-faire.

All told, Kapor has a plausible line of defense against charges of sellout: coherence. EFF seems driven by a consistent ideology (neoliberal, New Democrat, whatever); and that ideology seems a natural expression of Kapor's worldview, which in turn is rooted in his cultural milieu. His vision of the data superhighway is simply a hacker's vision. It doesn't have that jerry-built quality we expect from an agenda designed to satisfy a dozen different corporations. In fact, simultaneously satisfying the various interests backing EFF would be impossible. There are very few things they all favor.

But by the same token, fear of antagonizing them could induce paralysis. And, though paralysis doesn't yet seem a major problem (witness Kapor's opposition to the large fiber subsidies beloved by cable and the Bells), it is also true that EFF has been slow to take a formal stand on some issues, including the divisive question of the Bells' entry into video programming. This permits Love to observe suspiciously, "A blank slate is a position, when you think about it."

Such suspicions may not be well-founded, but they are not crazy, and they are unlikely to fade completely away. Which is sad. EFF came on the scene as a White Knight, beholden to no one, moved only by a few heartfelt values. This autonomy distinguished it from almost every other interest group, public or otherwise. (Even Love's patron, Nader—who coined the term "public interest group"—gets money from trial lawyers associations, which have quite a stake in the litigiousness he foments.) As long as EFF relies on corporate backing, it can never again claim that special purity. It is true that an earnest neo-Jeffersonianism (that is, Hackerism) seems to be Kapor's driving force. But it is also true that most EFF backers will in the long run profit from a neo-Jeffersonian world, in which data flows fast and free.

Kapor sometimes seems overly optimistic about that world. But here, again, he is being true to hacker culture, which exudes a nearly mystical faith in the benign force of uninhibited information. Barlow often cites Pierre Teilhard de Chardin, the Jesuit priest who envisioned the technological assembly of a planetary "noosphere," a global brain that would seal humanity's spiritual destiny: Point Omega. "Whether or not it represents Teilhard's vision," he has written, "it seems clear we are about some Great Work here—the physical wiring of collective human consciousness. The idea of connecting every mind to every other mind in full-duplex broadband is one which, for a hippie mystic like me, has clear theological implications."

Kapor doesn't put the matter in theological terms. Still, when you ask him about some possibly malign effects of a nationwide fiber grid, he exhibits a trust in cyberspace that verges on faith.

For instance: What about the much-feared cultural fragmentation of America—the death of Cronkite, the Cartwrights and other images that once formed a common American heritage? Remember, Kapor says, people are "quite social and sociable and we depend on shared meanings." So, "I think there will always be some role for vehicles of communication that serve broad markets. They may be less comprehensive and less powerful than they have been, and frankly that would be a goddamn good thing." But "this notion that we all only talk to other people that are just like ourselves is a fear that I actually don't see any rational justification for."

And what about grid-induced gridlock? Surely the new medium will, as internet has already begun to do, spawn groups bound by interests of stunning narrowness. And surely when these interests are political, their weight will be felt in Washington. If Congress is bombarded by letter-writing campaigns now, just wait until minute special interests are coalescing on-line (and often doing their letter-writing on-line). Kapor says: "I think what will happen is that all that stuff will wind up being discounted in the political process. At the point at which anybody can do it, it just won't be taken seriously."

Both of these issues—cultural disintegration and electronic gridlock—deserve deeper analysis, and in neither case would the analysis likely end on as sanguine a note as Kapor's does. These are genuinely scary problems. In fact, they are at some level the same scary problem: the more efficient sorting of people into their designated boxes, whether cultural, political or both. This is one of the darker dimensions of Teilhard de Chardin's superorganism metaphor: the ever sharper division of society into cells of ever more finely specified roles. That such divisive constraint should result from freely flowing information may sound strange, but the early signs are that this perverse correlation holds. Its ultimate test will come with an electronic grid of exactly the sort that EFF recommends.

There's no sense trying to escape the test. The alternatives seem either equally scary or just plain absurd. (A government-mandated return to broadcasting, with only three channels allowed?) America has no real choice but to dance with the guy who brung us: stick with Jeffersonian laws of information flow and address problems as they arise. In the meanwhile, we can have faith in the timelessness of the nation's founding principles. But faith is all it will be.

If there's a silver lining here, it's that national disintegration can have globally integrating effects. Americans of different class, religion, vocation or avocation may indeed have less contact with each other next century than now, but they can have more contact with similarly situated foreigners. Kapor gets gleeful standing at his computer and reading a piece of e-mail from someone in Iran who has just announced the creation of an Iranian "node" on internet. This internationalist impulse, this thrill at crossing deep chasms, is shared by many cybernauts and by genuine liberals in both the nineteenth- and twentieth-century senses of the word. And, obviously, by Teilhard de Chardin, who believed that, as national boundaries weakened under the weight of cross-cutting affinities, war would cease to be practical.

Who governs a global cyberspace? Which nation's constitution defines, or denies, your right to put a radical message on an Iranian bulletin board? "A lot of stuff that we've done has been very United States focused," Kapor says. "And that's a shortcoming, because you have to think globally." EFF has looked into cyberspace questions of an international cast, and "we can see an agenda of issues that we could grow into over the next several years quite comfortably if we had the resources and so on." (Hmmmm. The Standard Oil of public interest groups?)

Kapor is approaching his three-year anniversary as a presence in Washington. And "you know, I don't find it very hard to take, which surprises me." Surprises a lot of people. More than one critic has noted the irony of his having left corporate America with conspicuous disdain for its ethos and then having shifted his focus to Washington. Might as well move from Sodom to Gomorrah.

No, there's a difference, he insists. "The difference is that in business, because you're legally obligated to protect shareholder interests, and because there's a whole culture that virtually demanded disingenuousness and manipulation, it just became increasingly difficult for me, given who I am and what I believe, to feel like I could get up in the morning and do my job without feeling slimy, whereas at least so far, in three years,

## 1. THE CHANGING ECONOMY

I haven't had that problem. I don't mind it being in the environment. I mean environments are environments. I'm a pragmatist. They are the way they are. And sort of holding your nose up in the air and saying, 'This isn't up to my standards' is a pretty foolish posture."

The Electronic Frontier Foundation advised the Clinton transition team, and at one point there was discussion of an administration job for Kapor. The job was "nothing incredibly glamorous." Still, "it got serious enough that I had to think about, well, would I actually want to live in Washington?" Pause. "No way."

Wise move. If there's one thing Washington doesn't need it's another formerly well-meaning apparatchik. And if there's one thing it does need, it's someone who will persist in the nearly impossible task of trying to keep the town focused on the big picture. So far Kapor and EFF have done more than anyone to clarify the deeper data-superhighway issues—more than Al Gore, and more than John Sculley, the administration's high-tech mascot. And in addressing the less deep issues—how do you pay for the thing?—Kapor exhibits a truer sense for the uses of markets than is yet evident within the Clinton administration generally. All in all, he's a model New Democrat. There's always room for a good New Democrat in Washington, but right now there's more room in cyberspace.

# WHO'S WINNING THE
# INFORMATION REVOLUTION

The company of the future is already here, formed by the technological ferment that is transforming all of business. These examples are powerhouses.

*Myron Magnet*

**W**E'VE KNOWN for years that it was happening—the merging of computer and communications power that is the information revolution. But few foresaw how completely human ingenuity and competitive pressure would turn it into a second industrial revolution. As computers routinely talk to one another—about almost every aspect of business—via phone lines, fiber-optic cables, and satellites, companies find their basic metabolisms changing as radically as the ivory statue of Pygmalion's Galatea awakening to life.

The organizing principle of this new industrial revolution is the opposite of the spirit that guided the original revolution two centuries ago. The genius of the first industrial revolution was separation—the breaking up of work into its component parts to allow mass production. Today's principle is unification. Increasingly, thanks to networks of computers, company departments are fusing, and enterprises are growing so closely allied with customers and suppliers that boundaries between them seem to dissolve. Global rather than just local or national, this unification can make a division or a company across the world seem as if it's down the hall, transforming our conception of distance as radically as the supplanting of coaches by railways in the 1840s.

Every revolution is full of opportunity. Here are the new and often surprising ways several outfits, from Texas Instruments to J.C. Penney, have grasped a competitive advantage by advancing to the information revolution's cutting edge.

REPORTER ASSOCIATE *Ricardo Sookdeo*

■ **RETAIL DISTRIBUTION.** McKesson is a good place to start, since the drug distributor helped spearhead—and continues to lead—the reinventing of distribution that has transformed retailing. McKesson, headquartered in San Francisco, pioneered the electronic linking of distributor and retailer in the mid-Seventies to gain the advantages of just-in-time delivery. Today's druggist uses a laser scanner: One swipe over the shelf label, bar-coded with the product's name and usual order quantity, and presto! the order is entered. But that's only a refinement of the original system. Now McKesson has gone a revolutionary step beyond.

It has carried the battle into the warehouses. Though orders come into those depots electronically, with no order taker to introduce mistakes, error can still creep in. The person who fills the order can pick wrong items or wrong quantities, displeasing the customer and costing McKesson a whopping seven times as much as a properly filled order. The solution: a 12-ounce gizmo, worn like a plaster cast on the hand and forearm, that is a computer, laser scanner, and two-way radio in one. Dick Tracy would gape with astonishment.

Designed a year ago in conjunction with Electronic Data Systems, this wonder receives an order by radio from the warehouse's central computer and displays it on a three-square-inch screen strapped to the order filler's arm. It tells him where the items are and plans the most efficient route through the 22,000-item warehouse to get them. As the employee chooses each item, he points a finger, like some lethal space invader, at the bar-coded shelf label

beneath it, shooting a laser beam that scans the label and confirms that he has picked the right product. When the order is complete, his arm-borne computer radios the warehouse's main computer, updating inventory numbers and the bill. The result: a 70% reduction in order errors since April and a hefty rise in the productivity of order fillers.

An important advantage for McKesson—beyond being able to schedule inventory more efficiently and no longer needing banks of telephone order takers—is that the customer becomes dependent on the system. Says ex–Citicorp CEO Walter Wriston, author of a new book on the information revolution: "Once you get the guy on that system, you have a huge competitive advantage. You're very hard to displace."

**N**OW, in act two of the distribution revolution, retailers are returning the fire. To shift the balance of power back in their direction, Dayton Hudson, Kmart, J.C. Penney, Sears, and Wal-Mart, in conjunction with some major suppliers, have opened the system of electronic data interchange by establishing uniform standards for it, so that everyone's system is more or less interchangeable with everyone else's. Says Penney's information systems vice president, David Evans: "We wanted an open system so everyone could participate."

Today all these retailing colossi use the same bar coding on merchandise—Jockey shorts are Jockey shorts in everybody's bar code language—and the same formats for electronic purchase orders, invoices, and advance shipping notices. For big retailers the result is the best of both worlds— unfettered competition among their suppliers and all the advantages of a computer system that manages inventory and links them to manufacturers as if in a single network.

While this open system knocks out the advantages of a supplier's proprietary network, it also gives him valuable information. Penney and other big retailers constantly provide suppliers with updated sales and inventory information electronically so they can plan production. With such data arriving in a standard format from so many customers, a manufacturer like Levi Strauss or Vanity Fair can easily estimate aggregate demand weeks ahead. Penney's system has begun turning out six-month forecasts to help manufacturers plan production even further in advance.

■ **MARKETING.** Using computers to spot buying patterns among customers is old hat; Penney finds that fine-jewelry purchasers also often buy fancy children's pajamas, for instance. Companies then target purchasers of item A with promotions for item B. But the idea has progressed much further: Look at Catalina Marketing, a $50-million-a-year Anaheim, California, outfit that sprang into existence to do a brand-new kind of marketing using point-of-sale scanner information. Catalina's domain is supermarkets, over 5,000 of them serving 70 million shoppers a week. The company operates by connecting a personal computer to a supermarket's scanners and, on the basis of what the scanner shows to be in the customer's shopping cart, issuing coupons on the spot designed to get her to try a related product, to buy more of what she bought next time, or to buy the competitor's product.

Did she buy a bottle of Pepsi? Then the back-room computer sends a message to the printer next to the cash register, which spits out a brightly colored coupon to get a whole case at a discount next time. A Lean Cuisine buyer might get a coupon offering her a sixth frozen dinner free when she buys five. Check out with infant diapers and you might get a coupon for Carnation formula. A more two-fisted kind of coupon, accounting for two-thirds of Catalina's business, tries to get the customer to switch brands—from Crest to Colgate, say.

Along with higher sales, the food companies that sponsor such promotions get key information. If a frozen-dinner maker gives out coupons to buyers of several competitors' dinners, it learns from Catalina how many of each competitor's product triggered the coupons, which give a quick glimpse into the rivals' relative strength. The manufacturer gets a deeper glimpse when it learns that 15% of competitor A's buyers redeemed its coupon vs. only 5% of competitor B's, and further

coupons to loyal B customers can determine just how much the offer must be sweetened to get them even to try its band. Still another round of coupons can show how many of those who tried the new brand liked it enough to buy it again. All this can add up to a new, streamlined way to test-market a product before deciding on full production.

■ **INSURANCE.** The information revolution has made huge inroads throughout the service industries, information-intensive by nature. USAA, the San Antonio financial services outfit specializing in insurance for military officers and their families, decided early that it could deploy information technology as a strategic advantage. Management foresaw at the start of the Eighties that being able to scan documents electronically and store them on optical disks would expedite operations. No longer would a battalion of 200 clerks have to march off to a 39,000-square-foot warehouse in search of files that would take a day to find—or two weeks, if lying on a policy reviewer's desk. No longer would platoons of college kids have to come in nightly from midnight to 6 A.M. to reconnoiter desktops for lost dossiers.

When the necessary technology still wasn't available in 1986, USAA joined with IBM to develop it. Today, with the system operational, employees scan all incoming mail that contains more than a check into USAA's computer network—that's nearly 14 million pieces a year. Now when a customer buys insurance on jewelry, say, which takes effect 24 hours after the postmark on the appraisal mailed to USAA, he can telephone a service rep and get an instant answer to the question, "Did my appraisal come, and can my wife wear her necklace to the theater tonight?" Similarly, a customer who needs to close quickly on a house but hasn't yet received the required confirmation of its insurability can learn if the inspection report has reached USAA and if the policy is being written. Result: markedly better customer service at markedly lower cost. Overall, no competitor is as advanced.

USAA can hardly wait to use the system to process claims. By next year, when a customer calls to say he has had an accident, the system will digitize and store his phone call and scan the photos and the reports from doctors, lawyers, and appraisers that he sends in. Claim dossiers that fill a filing cabinet will be squeezed onto an optical disk or two. Even further out, USAA is working with IBM to develop a multimedia system that in a lawsuit, for example, will allow a USAA employee to hold a conference call with a lawyer in Miami and a doctor in Fort Lauderdale in which all participants can hear the recording of the original telephone accident report and view on their screens documents,

X-rays of injuries, and color videos of damage to the car.

■ **HEALTH CARE.** Sinking under an epidemic of paper, the health care industry needs the benefits of the information revolution more than almost any other. Among the companies applying technology most creatively is a San Francisco startup called InterPractice Systems. Says CEO Dr. Albert Martin: "Health care went from cottage industry to big business, and the systems didn't keep up." Handwritten medical records of idiosyncratic legibility, okay in the days of the solo practitioner, work less well in the HMO era, when patients may see a different doctor at every visit and records have a way of going astray in a multi-clinic organization's myriad file cabinets. According to one dismaying study, doctors in group practices see almost one patient in three without access to his or her record, and at least a quarter of the records available are incomplete or illegible.

InterPractice, in conjunction with its half owner, EDS, has devised a system that goes beyond computerizing records so that they are instantly available to any doctor in the HMO—a boon in itself. The system also automatically sends prescriptions to the pharmacy, relays orders for tests or X-rays to the appropriate department, attaches test results to the patient's electronic record, and triggers the billing system, reducing the need for clerks and cutting over 10% from the cost of each patient visit.

If a doctor finds symptoms that stump him, the computer will help him out. As he ticks off what he sees clinically on a menu on his screen, the computer, programmed with a library of standard treatment guidelines, will tell him what tests to order. InterPractice is testing a home version of this system: A patient can enter symptoms on his terminal, be asked further questions by the computer, and be told whether to use a home remedy or go to the HMO, where his symptoms will have been entered in his electronic record before he arrives. If the situation looks very serious, the computer alerts HMO personnel, who make sure he's on his way. By reducing patient visits, the system further controls costs.

■ **INDUSTRIAL DESIGN.** Like some all-powerful genie out of *The Arabian Nights*, the information revolution has transformed manufacturing companies even more magically than service companies. It has so revolutionized industrial design that at Square D, an electrical component manufacturer in Palatine, Illinois, computer systems now design giant electrical equipment virtually on their own. Since all of the custom switch arrays for power stations and factories that account for 20% of Square D's sales are variations of essentially the same basic elements, a computer, fed by the sales office with the required size, specifications, and features, can lay out the switch and produce a drawing. After a final check by a pair of human eyes, the drawing goes to the factory floor to be turned into actuality.

The information revolution's transformation of design has improved product quality and cut product cycle time. Andersen Consulting partner Leroy Peterson says, "Around 60% to 70% of manufacturing quality problems start with the engineering process." Designs can be just plain flawed; they can invite incorrect assembly; they can be hard to manufacture. To avoid such snafus, the information revolution has sped far past the computer-aided design and manufacturing systems most people have heard of. An example is a dramatic new technique called rapid prototyping, a method of embodying the electronic design information on your workstation in a solid, three-dimensional model of the actual part almost as quickly as waving a wand. You can see and touch just what you've wrought before the plant turns out thousands of them.

The commonest version of rapid prototyping, called stereolithography, builds a three-dimensional representation out of salami-like slices of plastic. The CAD system's digital information guides a laser over a vat of liquid plastic, hardening its surface into a thin slice of the required shape. A little elevator in the vat draws down that slice, exposing enough liquid above it for the laser to harden into the next slice, and so on, until the entire model takes form, made up of the fused slices. Other rapid prototyping systems make models out of powdered plastic or squeeze out plastic models, like icing from a computer-controlled pastry tube.

A one-sixth scale model of United Technology's Comanche helicopter for recent radar testing is a perfect emblem of the information revolution's power: Not only did stereolithography make the model quickly and flawlessly, but computers also acquired and quickly analyzed unprecedentedly huge amounts of data from the tests so that engineers could perfect the design faster and cheaper than ever before. Says UTC science and technology chief Robert Hermann: "It's a true revolution in the way we can do design."

More down to earth is Ford's use of rap-id prototyping to solicit bids for making a new rocker arm for one of its engines. Only three of the four suppliers that received Ford's blueprints submitted bids; the fourth couldn't fully decipher the drawings. Then Ford sent the four prospective suppliers plastic models made by stereolithography. This time the fourth supplier, certain of what was required, submitted a bid 49 cents cheaper than the next lowest. That's a hefty cost savings for Ford, which buys millions of these rocker arms.

■ **NEW-PRODUCT DEVELOPMENT.** Everyone expected the information revolution to make business more global, but few realized just how far and how effectively it would do so. Texas Instruments has long used its resources worldwide to design new products—but how things have changed. Days used to get lost when designers and engineers around the world worked together: Drawings they needed to see before they could talk might take two weeks to arrive. Faxing helped only a little, since blurry faxes of blueprints cut into letter-size pieces and taped back together at the other end were often undecipherable.

Now, with detailed designs sent instantly over the computer network so that TI employees anywhere can work on them simultaneously, development time has dwindled. The time needed to develop a calculator, for instance, shrank 20% as soon as TI began sending drawings electronically in 1989. It has shrunk another 17% since.

Far-flung units of TI routinely work simultaneously—and speedily—on separate parts of a project, keeping everything coordinated over the computer network. Exactly across the globe from Texas, a memory chip design project progresses at TI's engineering facility in Bangalore, India—located there to take advantage of a growing Asian market and a large, lower-cost pool of talented engineers, and connected to the TI system by an earth station that TI had to haul in by oxcart. Engineers in Dallas and in Miho, Japan, provide elements of the design, sent by satellite. When the design is done, Bangalore will forward the complete CAD data to Texas, where the chip will be fabricated before being sent back to India for debugging. Says TI group vice president Wayne Spence: "Problems that used to take three years now take a year."

Time gets compressed another way since departments scattered across the globe can work on a project 24 hours a day. When a U.S. financial exchange asked TI to come up with a quote to make a hand-held electronic bidding device for traders, the company's design department began working on the problem in Dallas, then at quitting time electronically sent what they had done to designers in Tokyo, who when their workday ended passed it on to designers in Nice, France. By the next day in Dallas, TI not only had a pretty accurate quote but could also show the customer a computer-generated photo of what the product would look like.

DISTANCE ALSO disappears. A process engineer in Dallas can look through the network into the process data from TI's assembly and test plant in Kuala Lumpur and spot any disturbing trends that the Malaysian staff must cure. As a result, the Malaysian plant, staffed by relatively low-cost labor, needs few high-priced engineers. Even more global, a TI unit called Tiris (Texas Instruments Registration and Identification System), maker of tiny James Bond–type communications devices used for security and identification purposes, is managed out of England, develops products in the Netherlands and Germany, and manufactures and assembles in those two places plus Japan and Malaysia. All these centers send text, diagrams, and mock-up drawings to each other over the computer network, and they are tied in as well to the nine centers that design the various applications for Tiris's products around the world. The computer network allowed Tiris to create a new business quickly and cheaply out of existing TI facilities. Says Tiris North American general manager David Slinger: "We're probably 18 to 24 months ahead of the competition, partly as a result of this communications expertise."

When the first industrial revolution came to Britain two centuries ago, deep thinkers foresaw a galaxy of dire consequences, from the breaking up of communities to the brutalization of workers. The seers rarely get it right. The real effects of this second revolution are also almost sure to be different from what they predict, not to mention more interesting—and momentously large.

# Tomorrow's Factory

*It's just seven short years away. What will manufacturing facilities look like in the 21st Century?*

## Jenny C. McCune

*Jenny C. McCune is a New York-based business writer.*

A woman peers at the image of a microwave oven on the personal computer in her home office. With the mouse on her PC, she selects from an array of options: size, color, digital display, rotating carousel. As she changes the specifications, the illustration represented on the screen changes. When she's satisfied with the results of her design, she "modems" an order for the microwave to the manufacturer, bypassing the company's order department completely. Presto! Her "personalized" microwave is manufactured that night and shipped the next morning.

Of course, in 1993 a consumer can't order a custom-designed product directly from a factory. Motorola Inc. comes close with electronic ordering for its sales department. A sales rep for its pager products can type up an order on a portable computer and then zap it to the company's factory in Boynton Beach, Fla., where the pager is configured and manufactured.

But the custom-built microwave scenario sketched out above may well become routine by 2000. "You'll be seeing more and more customers self-designing products, which then get manufactured," says William Davidson, associate professor of management and organization at the University of Southern California and co-author of *2020 Vision*, a book on future trends.

What directions are Motorola and other manufacturers taking as we head toward the next century? What will our factories look like in 2000? Who will be at the controls—robots or people? Take a walk into the future with *Man-*

*agement Review* as we explore how manufacturing and the factory will evolve.

In the beginning of the industrial age, factories were huge, smoke-belching entities, the raw materials of an Upton Sinclair novel. While the factories of the future will produce substantially more products than those ancient hulks, they'll be doing so in less space.

Just-in-time manufacturing already has reduced the amount of parts and inventory that must be stored on the premises. In addition, through miniaturization, many industries can make products with less raw material and their products are coming in smaller packages—a plus in the recycling battle.

Manufacturers also are turning to smaller factories for management reasons. Sprawling plants with thousands of employees and hundreds of managers are just too difficult to oversee. Automation has helped cut staffs, of course, but 21st-century factory owners will purposely keep the employee rolls short because small factories are more manageable.

"Large factories are dinosaurs," says Doan T. Modianos, assistant dean of the college of business at Bradley University, Peoria, Ill. "They're too difficult to control."

### HOW SMALL CAN YOU GET?

How small will factories get? Dean Kropp, professor of operations and manufacturing management at the Olin School of Business, Washington University, St. Louis,

---

# BRIEFCASE

The manufacturing goals are the same: more products made in less time with fewer defects and increased customization. But how will factories in the 21st century achieve those aims? Here's how we would describe the factory of the future:

- Smaller, more flexible and able to shift gears quickly.
- Fast, capable of manufacturing at lightning speed.
- Customer-driven.
- Closely integrated with the rest of the corporation, but not necessarily next door.
- Producing highly customized products in smaller lots.

---

estimates that the average factory today employs approximately 1,200 people. That number will decrease to between 400 and 600 people by 2000, he predicts.

Factory facilities will reach new lows as well: Horizontal is in, vertical is out. When Chrysler Corp. rebuilt its Jefferson North Assembly Plant on a 283-acre site on Detroit's East Side, it did away with multiple floors, a fixture of the plant since it was originally built in 1907. The new plant, which started production of Jeep Grand Cherokees one year ago, has just one story compared with the five stories of old, and 1.75 million square feet of floor space, reduced from 3.5 million. "Cars used to go up and down elevators, which slowed down production times," recalls James J. Lyijyen, general manager of Jeep/Truck Platform Assembly. The single-story structure simplifies product flow and helps *increase* the factory's throughput.

Most people assume that the more advanced the manufacturing, the more robots there will be on the factory floor. In fact, some futurists go so far as to predict the "lights out" factory, a facility that is so automated that its owners simply have to program it, turn out the lights on the way out, and the factory will grind out products by night without a single person on hand.

That's the goal we see for ourselves sometime within the next five years," says Leonard de Barros, vice president and director of manufacturing for Motorola's paging and wireless data group. His forecast applies to the company's 500,000-square-foot pager plant in Florida.

Total automation may be theoretically possible, but it may not always be desirable. Many manufacturers who were hell bent on automating during the 1980s have come to realize that automation can't cure all their manufacturing ills.

"We need to automate as much of the process that makes sense," explains Liam Donohoe, external relations manager for Apple Computer Inc.'s factory in Cork, Ireland. "It's not wise to automate everything."

Donohoe points to the short product cycles that are becoming endemic to the computer industry. It's not profitable to invest in automation equipment if the products won't be around long enough for the manufacturer to recoup its capital. So Apple only automates its Ireland facility when the equipment can be used for several different product lines.

Besides, he adds, there are certain jobs that are better left in human hands. People tend to be more flexible than machines. They can adjust their pace or shift to different tasks or assembly lines without much trouble.

Indeed, some vendors have started to "deautomate," according to Kropp. "They are pulling equipment out and replacing it with skilled people just to have the knowledge, flexibility and capability to discriminate and, in the end, get a better job done faster."

Even among those who continue to automate, the need for such flexibility has not gone unanswered. Sophisticated companies are pouring their investment dollars into the software that drives their robotic devices rather than the hardware.

Motorola's pager facility takes that route. It's highly automated, but Motorola keeps it flexible through "soft automation."

Says Motorola's de Barro, "[The software] is pivotal to our flexibility. We can capitalize on our high-technology investment over and over again, even as our product lines change."

Many companies are showing similar flexibility in where they apply automation. These companies are looking beyond the factory floor to processes that lead to and from the factory floor: order taking, design and distribution.

Rytex Co., an Indianapolis manufacturer of stationery, is searching for ways to speed printing, improve product quality and increase customization, but it spends even more time looking for ways to speed its delivery channels.

"You have to look at the entire cycle," says Rytex President Frank A. Diekmann. For Rytex and many older companies, that means investigating electronic data interchange as a way to improve communication between the company, its suppliers and its customers.

Other companies are looking to speed engineering and design. Concurrent engineering—designing and modifying a product in tandem with its manufacture—is already being tested by farsighted manufacturers. That concept will move closer to center stage during the next seven years.

Concurrent engineering will get a big push from leading-edge technologies such as three-dimensional printing. 3-D printing, the logical extension of CAD-CAM, allows a part to go directly from the computerized drawing board into production without building a prototype.

Chrysler used this technique to produce an exhaust manifold for its Viper pace car in last year's Indianapolis 500 because it didn't have time to go through the regular design and manufacture process. Instead, it had engineers come up with a 3-D print of the part, which shaved six weeks off the car's production time.

In fact, by 2000, it's conceivable that factories equipped with 3-D printers could produce hundreds of customized devices each day, without keeping any parts inventory. These factories could simply design and manufacture parts as they go along.

Davidson calls this "real-time design." "It's designing a product in the morning and then having it on my desk the next day," he explains.

Technology may be changing the old adage about location being everything. It certainly isn't everything to American Standard Inc., whose faucet division is based in Piscataway, N.J., with manufacturing plants in Bulgaria, Italy, France, Germany, Egypt, Mexico, Korea and the United States.

It's common for a new American Standard faucet to be jointly developed by engineers based in the United States and Germany. An electronic network links the two facilities so they can exchange CAD-CAM drawings. "For example, Germany may work on the interior valving system and New Jersey would design the cosmetic, exterior part," says Jim Datka, vice president of faucet product marketing.

And once a new model is developed, it can be manufactured in any of those facilities, depending on the new faucet's manufacturing requirements or where it will be sold.

## LOCATION, LOCATION, LOCATION

If factories need to be located close to anyone, it's the customer, says Washington University's Kropp. "Very often we source a product locally because we can have better speed to market and more local knowledge of the market," Datka explains. For example, American Standard's Korean facility usually makes faucets for the company's Asian customers since its management knows the plumbing standards for that part of the world.

Stanley Magic Doors, a manufacturer of custom automatic doors, has brought manufacturing closer to its customers—but not by shifting the location of its factory. Instead, the Farmington, Conn., company brings customers in on a quarterly basis to meet with Stanley Magic Doors' staff, including representatives of the manufacturing department, to provide valuable feedback. The company, a division of the Stanley Works of New Britain, Conn., isn't alone. Corning Inc.'s fiber-optics factory also interviews customers to get feedback on what they want and whether the factory's performance is satisfactory,

says Gerry McQuaid, division vice president of manufacturing and engineering for Corning's telecommunication products.

It's this need to stay close to the customer that has caused some companies to rethink moving their manufacturing facilities overseas in search of cheap labor. Many companies migrated their manufacturing in the '80s, but a few have moved back because of hidden costs or the need for faster order fulfillment. Companies also found that factories were getting too far removed from customers and marketing when they were located halfway around the world.

For example, AT&T moved some of its electronic circuit board manufacturing from Hong Kong to Richmond, Va., several years ago. And American Tourister has brought back much of its manufacturing from Asia to Jacksonville, Fla.

Even if the North American Free Trade Agreement is ratified, experts don't expect a mass migration of manufacturers across U.S. borders. "What looked like cheap labor in the past, may not be," Corning's McQuaid points out. "It's difficult to manufacture overseas and have the degree of customer focus that is necessary."

## KEEP IT GREEN

To comply with government regulations and the wishes of their customers, companies are cleaning up their existing factories and are designing new ones that will be more ecologically responsible.

A glimpse into that green future can be seen today at Chrysler's Jefferson North Assembly Plant, which won an Environmental Protection Agency (EPA) Administrator's Award last April. It was the first car plant to receive that award. The EPA recognized the factory for several innovations, including things as simple as switching from cardboard boxes and wooden palettes to reusable containers. That switch has saved the company an estimated 30,000 tons in annual scrap waste.

The new plant also has attacked the problem of paint sludge, the residue left over from painting its automobiles. Painting cars produces enough paint sludge in a year to fill up three football fields with muck that's four feet deep, says Lyijynen. To recycle that residue, the plant uses machines to remove the water from the sludge and dry it to a powder, which is used to paint the undercarriages of cars.

The factory's paint operations, however, also produce air pollution in the form of paint fumes and particles. Paint-ladened air is funneled into a building where filters remove up to 95 percent of the pollutants before releasing the air back into the atmosphere.

The factory's layout also includes an on-site water treatment plant, which recycles water and then discharges it to municipal sewers.

---

No factory now or in 2000 will be 100 percent environmentally pure. But Chrysler's Jefferson North plant does show how manufacturers are working to reduce waste and make factories more environmentally friendly.

## HOW FACTORIES WILL BE ORGANIZED

Forward-looking companies aren't just updating a factory's layout. They're also analyzing how a factory should be managed, who ought to run it, and how it should fit in with the rest of the corporation.

In 2000, more factories will be "focused." They will concentrate on a particular type of product rather than be a jack of all trades. The concept isn't new. "It's been around for 20 years. But it's only in the past five years or so that American manufacturers have taken the concept to heart and have really paid attention to it," says Bradley University's Modianos.

Companies such as the Maytag Corp., in Newton, Iowa, already are designing factories around this principle. Last May, Maytag opened a $45 million facility called Jackson Appliance Co. in Jackson, Tenn., to produce dishwashers.

That's a different approach for Maytag. Its older factories generally make a variety of products. Before the new factory was built, Maytag's five dishwasher brands were made at several different locations. In fact, Maytag wasn't even making all of its dishwashers; some of them were contracted out to third party manufacturers. (While the factory currently produces only the Maytag brand, the plan is for the Jackson plant to be the hub for all of Maytag's dishwasher manufacturing.)

"Our plant was specifically designed around a product," says William Fowler, director of operations. "In addition, it's organized around functions and is not department-oriented."

For example, while a manufacturing plant would typically have a plastic molding department that would supply different product lines, Jackson Appliances' factory is organized around the various stages of dishwasher construction. Its employees are assigned to cross-functional teams, which may be involved in several different stages of manufacture.

"In older factories, you'd have conflicting priorities as different products compete for the services of a department. We don't have that problem here," Fowler says.

Some manufacturers are moving from specification to differentiation. "We are now building multipurpose chemical plants that can make myriad products," says Peter Neff, president and CEO of chemical company Rhone-Poulenc Inc. "Instead of large plants with long runs and high volumes of one product, we're designing facilities to do a wide variety of things. We can make agriculture surfactants and on the same machines produce shampoo and soaps."

What everyone does agree on is the need for flexible factories and production facilities that can quickly shift gears and adapt, whether it's focusing on one product or several. That also gets back to the idea of mass customization: Factories of the future will be able to churn out differently configured products in very small lots.

## TOTAL INTEGRATION

As we head to 2000, the lines between departments are blurring in nearly every company. "There used to be a wall between each discipline within the corporation," recalls Lyijynen. "The product design people would come engineer a product and then toss it over the wall to the manufacturing guys. Now people are realizing those walls should come down."

The barriers are dropping, not instantly and certainly not with a bang, but factories are getting integrated more closely into the total corporation. By 2000, the separation between manufacturing and the "front office" may not exist. Factory personnel already are getting involved at the earlier stages of product design. They're also more integrated into a company's marketing and sales efforts.

Integrating manufacturing with the rest of the company is also one of the guiding principles behind the Chrysler Technology Center, which opened last June. Chrysler bills the $1 billion facility as "part automobile, part think tank, part factory." The automobile manufacturer says the center will take more than a year out of the time it takes for vehicles to go from concept to production.

## THE FUTURE'S SO BRIGHT

Tomorrow's factories will be more of an extension of what is already going on today rather than a brave new world of manufacturing. Some predict that there will be an expansion of output similar to what has taken place with agriculture. "Today only 1 percent of the population works on farms, yet agricultural output has increased a hundred-fold since the beginning of this century," points out Davidson. "I see the same thing happening with manufacturing."

But the guiding principles of quality, continuous improvement, and just-in-time manufacturing will remain in place. It's just that they'll be further refined and perfected. Sure, there will be more automation, but factories will still need people to run them.

"What will set the factory of the future apart from what is going on today?" asks Etian Zemel, professor of management and co-director of the Masters in Management Program at Northwestern University. "Not a lot really; it's more that what today is frontier and leading edge, tomorrow will become commonplace."

# THE LIGHT FANTASTIC

## *OPTOELECTRONICS MAY REVOLUTIONIZE COMPUTERS—AND A LOT MORE*

Embedded in the new dam spanning Vermont's Winooski River are four miles of glass fibers. Laser light racing through them will warn of strains and stresses long before failures occur. In late April, in fact, the fiber-optic sensors alerted dam operators to a turbine gear that was about to break.

\* \* \*

In a University of Pennsylvania lab, scientists Britton Chance and Arjun Yodh have deciphered the chaotic light patterns created when harmless, low-power laser beams shine through the human body. Their goal: light-based medical imaging that will detect brain tumors and other diseases far more cheaply than today's magnetic-resonance systems.

\* \* \*

Laser beams flash through the AT&T Bell Laboratories room where Alan Huang is designing a computer that moves data via light instead of electrons. His latest optical processor can run a washing machine. "We've come from the crazy to the impossible to the impractical," says Huang. Someday, he believes his technology will spawn astonishingly powerful computers.

\* \* \*

In only a few decades, the enormous power of silicon chips has transported much of the world from the Industrial Revolution to the Information Age. The next great leap, many scientists argue, will come from a technology called optoelectronics—the marriage of light and electricity. Once it's fully harnessed, they say, light will supercharge the speed of communications and computers and bring new ways of probing everything from the atmosphere to the body. The possibilities "are truly amazing," says John Day, president of market researcher Strategies Unlimited. "We are moving from the world of the electron to the world of the photon"—the most basic unit of light.

This light fantastic is already shaping everyday life. Each hour, millions of voices and megareams of data zip through fiber-optic lines on streams of photons. Every time you use a laser printer, buy from a store that has barcode scanners, gaze at a laptop computer, or hear Madonna or Mozart on compact disks, the words, purchases, data, and tunes are communicated by light beams. Sales of optoelectronic devices from At&T, Hewlett-Packard, Sony, NEC, Fujitsu, and countless small innovators have been rising 15% a year and will total $39 billion in 1993, estimates the Optoelectronics Industry Development Assn. (OIDA). "Optoelectronics is becoming the backbone of the Information Age," says Arpad A. Bergh, a top official at Bellcore, the research and development arm of the Baby Bells. "Without it, we could not collect, store, or transmit information."

And yet, the Optoelectronic Age is just dawning. As there was a formative leap in the 1960s from separate transistors wired together to thousands of transistors etched on silicon chips, so optoelectronics is poised to move from individual lasers and devices "toward integrated-circuit technology," says University of Illinois photonics pioneer Nick Holonyak Jr. At Bell Labs, Bellcore, and other facilities, scientists are building prototype chips that contain thousands of microscope lasers. Instead of relying on electrons coursing through tiny wires, these chips will send and receive messages by flashing the lasers on and off millions of times a second.

Foreseeing such advances, the Clinton Administration has made a nationwide fiber-optic "information superhighway" a centerpiece of its technology policy. The Pentagon, meanwhile, is pouring millions into optoelectronics for military gear and civilian spin-offs such as flat-panel displays (page 32).

Both efforts are being spurred by intense rivalry with Japan. The fundamental optoelectronic inventions were U.S.-made. But today, Japan dominates markets for CD players, CD-ROMS, and flat-panel displays. It is investing billions in cutting-edge R&D and plans to link every home and business with fiber optics by 2015. "Japan is betting the country on optoelectronics," says Peter F. Moulton, vice-president of the research unit at Schwartz Optics, a Boston-area laser maker.

# 1. THE CHANGING ECONOMY

**INTERCEPT.** Such a commitment is not surprising, given the potential gains. In telecommunications alone, replacing poky electronics and copper wire with photons can boost capacity of transmission lines 10,000 times. The same approach could make today's computers the equivalent of Model Ts. At IBM, AT&T, Martin Marietta, and Honeywell, engineers are building hybrid systems in which beams of light replace wires that connect chips and computers. Big advances also lie ahead for computer-memory technology, says Scotty R. Neal, president of AT&T CommVault Systems, which makes optical storage devices. "Revolution is an overused word, but it's happening. You'll be able to put more information than all the world's books contain in a box and have it accessible in seconds."

The technology's impact will go well beyond that. The coming decade will bring optosensors that monitor factory processes, spot stresses on buildings and other structures, or detect submarines (page 33). In cars, optical sensors may control engine performance and help avoid crashes. Add it up, and Tokyo's analysts foresee opto-electronics sales in Japan alone of more than $300 billion by 2010. Because of this technology, "the 21st century will be a very different place," muses Phil Anthony, head of optoelectronics research at Bell Labs.

**TOO MUCH HYPE?** How different is still a matter of conjecture. As with any nascent technology, "our predictions will almost certainly be wrong," says Bell Labs physicist David A. B. Miller. When the semiconductor laser—a building block of optoelectronics—was invented in 1962, few expected that its first mass market use would be for listening to music through CD players so complex "we shouldn't let ordinary people buy them," jokes Robert W. Lucky, Bellcore's vice-president for applied research. Still, Lucky and others wonder if visions of optoelectronic miracles are mostly hype. "Photonics is so beautiful, it's got to be good for something else," he says. "But I don't know what."

To the technology's boosters, Lucky's skepticism is reminiscent of the pessimists who called electronic integrated circuits impossible. But it's easy to see where he's coming from. To examine the details of the technology is to enter a world of exotic materials and esoteric devices largely governed by the topsy-turvy rules of quantum mechanics, where light simultaneously acts as particles, or photons, and as waves.

At its simplest, optoelectronics involves transforming electricity to light and back again, largely through the marvel of semiconductor materials. Through intricate engineering of their structure, semiconductors such as gallium arsenide can be made to give off light when a current is passed through them. The simplest of these devices are light-emitting diodes (LEDs), invented in 1961. Today, 20 billion are made a year, for everything from the blinking lights on cellular phones to the high-mounted center brake lights on newer cars.

The next advance came in 1962. The earliest lasers required a ruby or cumbersome tube of gas to generate light. To make smaller devices, researchers at IBM, GE, and other labs put mirrors on each end of tiny, light-producing regions in the semiconductor. When light bounces back and forth between the mirrors, it's amplified until it's bright enough to shine through one mirror—and make a pure beam of a single wavelength, or color, of light. This device, the size of a grain of salt, is a semiconductor laser. Today, these are at the core of CD players and many other products.

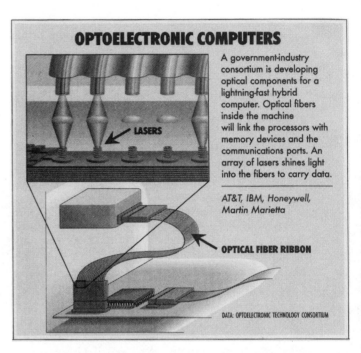

**OPTOELECTRONIC COMPUTERS**

A government-industry consortium is developing optical components for a lightning-fast hybrid computer. Optical fibers inside the machine will link the processors with memory devices and the communications ports. An array of lasers shines light into the fibers to carry data.

AT&T, IBM, Honeywell, Martin Marietta

LASERS

OPTICAL FIBER RIBBON

DATA: OPTOELECTRONIC TECHNOLOGY CONSORTIUM

Semiconductor lasers are also the engines for fiber-optic transmission. Through what Bell Labs' Anthony calls an "accident of nature," some of them produce light at precisely the infrared wave-lengths at which optical fibers are most transparent—the quality that lets them carry data great distances. Until recently, however, there was a bottleneck: Light pulses fade as they travel the fiber. So every 35 miles, they were converted back to electricity, amplified, reconverted to light, and re-sent.

This limitation has disappeared with the invention of the optical amplifier. Emmanuel Desurvire's bosses were skeptical when, as a new Bell Labs researcher in 1986, he attempted to make such a gadget. Desurvire persevered, however. Building on advances in England and Japan, he laced glass fibers with a rare earth element, erbium, and devised a way to pump energy continuously into the fiber from an external laser. This boosts the brightness of light pulses—and ends the need for electronic repeaters. Dramatically faster fiber-optic networks are thus possible—as is light-based computer processing. Desurvire's device "is about to revolutionize the industry," says Tingye Li, who directs light-waves system research at Bell Labs.

**'FLY BY LIGHT.'** Among the most avid followers of all this are defense contractors. In the past decade, Hughes, Boeing, Honeywell, and Lockheed have begun or boosted optoelectonic R&D. The Lockheed-Boeing F-22 fighter and Boeing-Sikorsky Comanche helicopter will use fiber optics to ferry huge amounts of data between their various systems. In addition, the Pentagon's Advanced Research Projects Agency (ARPA) and some companies want to replace electronic controls with a "fly-by-light" system. Both approaches would save weight and keep information free of electromagnetic interference from other equipment, lightning, or nuclear blasts.

Defense companies also are working on sensors and optoelectronic components for radars so sensitive that they'll read license plates from satellites. And they're creating wings that are "smart" enough to telegraph dangerous stresses—for instance, through sensors that analyze how laser light is absorbed or scattered. A Lockheed Corp. system bounces light off of dust particles in the air to spot wind shears, the violent downdrafts that can cause plane crashes.

Essentially the same approach is being applied to such medical jobs as monitoring blood sugar. In fact, when Hewlett-Packard Co.'s Mark Chandler began assessing the biomedical uses of the technology for the OIDA last year, he "was surprised by the size of the market opportunities," he says. The group predicts that the medical market will exceed $10 billion a year by 2013. Lasers are already used to blast plaque from clogged arteries and perform surgery. Now, they're showing promise for imaging. "We could take a big bite out of health-care costs," says Penn's Britton Chance, who thinks optoelectronic detection of brain tumors could cost 99% less than magnetic-resonance imaging.

Perhaps the greatest impact of optoelectronics, however, will be in telecommunications and computing. Even as fiber-optic networks are extended to homes—New Jersey Bell Telephone Co., for example, plans to reach all of its customers by 2010—their capacity will soar. At IBM's Thomas J. Watson Research Center in Yorktown Heights, N.Y., scientists are creating an astonishingly powerful fiber network for rollout by the late 1990s. Their key innovation is boosting the number of wavelengths of light that travel the fiber. Now, optical fibers carry only pulses of light at one wavelength, or color, like a one-lane highway. Using an array of lasers, each producing light with a slightly different wavelength, creates thousands of lanes within the same fiber.

**DIALING FOR DATA.** Each channel is big enough to send the contents of the *Encyclopaedia Britannica* in a second. So the system's overall capacity will be prodigious—large enough to profoundly alter the business of communications. Today, customers typically pay a phone company by the bit to transform information into light pulses and route it through the fiber-optic system. But with what IBM's Paul Green, manager of advanced optical networks, calls a "dumb, dark" network, a company could simply lease unused—or dark—fiber for a flat fee. It would use its own lasers to send data, as though on a private highway.

Optoelectronics will also help solve a resulting problem: where to store such vast amounts of information. Optical CD-ROMs, in which lasers etch information as tiny pits on the disk's surface, offer 100 times the capacity of today's floppy disks. That explains why sales of computer CD-ROM drives have doubled since 1990. And the potential of optical storage has barely been tapped. Scientists at IBM and elsewhere are devising ways to make the pits smaller and closer together—including using lasers that emit short-wavelength blue light—to boost disk storage capacity three- or fourfold.

More exotic solutions lie ahead. Researchers at Microelectronics & Computer Technology Corp. in Austin, Tex., have formed a company called Tamarack Storage Devices Inc. to commercialize a holographic memory system. The gadget shines two laser beams onto a material that changes chemically when struck by light. Much like the wakes of criss-crossing boats, the light waves interfere with each other. The result is a distinctive wave pattern, or hologram, that holds information and can be retrieved with another laser. This technology boosts storage capacity and speeds access times to the data. "It could replace floppy disks, tape drives, CD-Roms, and even some hard disks," says Tamarack President John Stockton, who hopes the first products will reach the market next year.

**NO WIRES.** Optoelectronics also promises the computer power needed to move this mountain of data. In the 1980s, some researchers began laying the groundwork for purely optical computers—entirely light-based machines with no wires inside. In these, data would be moved exclusively by light beams that cross through each other without interference. The dream of an optical computer still lives: Bell Labs' Huang has built an all-optical processor. And in January, University of Colorado researchers showed off a rudimentary optical computer than can do simple mathematics. It's hard to program the machine for more complex tasks, however. So a practical version is still decades away.

In the meantime, most researchers have shifted to an easier goal—a hybrid computer that combines electronics and optics. "What makes sense is optoelectronic computing," says Sadik C. Esener, an engineering professor at the University of California at San Diego. IBM, Martin Marietta, Honeywell, and AT&T have formed the Optoelectronic Technology Consortium, funded with $8 million from ARPA, to develop optical links among a processor, two memory units, and the machine's communications ports. This so-called optical backplane will remove wiring bottlenecks in current machines to let them run faster. "Many people think this will be the next thing in system design, with broad applications for supercomputing and high-speed telecommunications," says David Lewis, head of optoelectronics at Martin Marietta's electronics laboratory in Syracuse, N.Y.

# CAN THE U.S. PUT ITS SCREENS IN THE PICTURE?

Despite Japan's worst recession in decades, Sharp Corp.'s Tenri plant is humming: Its production of 100,000 flat-panel screens a month is expected to double within a year. Hosiden Corp., which makes laptop screens for Apple Computer Inc. and cockpit displays for Boeing Co., is ramping up, too. So are NEC Corp. and Fujitsu Ltd. No wonder. Advanced flat-panel displays—one of today's brightest optoelectronics products—will become even hotter once they're put into HDTVs, cars, and medical gear. That's great news for the Japanese, who have over 95% of a global market that is projected to grow 14% annually, to $9.4 billion by 2000.

The news might be good for America, too. From tiny Kopin Corp. to giant Xerox Corp., U.S. companies are developing new screen technologies. Motorola Inc. and partner In Focus Systems Inc. are building the first major U.S.-owned flat-panel display factory. And the Pentagon's Advanced Research Projects Agency (ARPA) has formed a display consortium that includes American Telephone & Telegraph, Xerox, and eight others. "High-definition displays are the windows into the Information Age," says Lance Glasser, director of ARPA's Electronic Systems Technology Office. "We're determined to get the U.S. back into high-definition displays."

**NIGHTMARE.** America's hopes depend on out-innovating the Japanese. They've invested $3 billion in the leading technology—active-matrix liquid-crystal displays. But making these is fiendishly difficult. Liquid crystal acts as a shutter that blocks or allows light from the back panel to pass through and darken or lighten each dot, or pixel, on the screen. A transistor at each pixel activates the crystal shutter. High-resolution color screens can have a million or more pixels—thus the production nightmare. Only recently have yields of defect-free

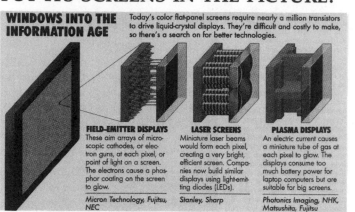

**WINDOWS INTO THE INFORMATION AGE**

Today's color flat-panel screens require nearly a million transistors to drive liquid-crystal displays. They're difficult and costly to make, so there's a search on for better technologies.

**FIELD-EMITTER DISPLAYS**
These aim arrays of microscopic cathodes, or electron guns, at each pixel, or point of light on a screen. The electrons cause a phosphor coating on the screen to glow.
*Micron Technology, Fujitsu, NEC*

**LASER SCREENS**
Miniature laser beams would form each pixel, creating a very bright, efficient screen. Companies now build similar displays using light-emitting diodes (LEDs).
*Stanley, Sharp*

**PLASMA DISPLAYS**
An electric current causes a miniature tube of gas at each pixel to glow. The displays consume too much battery power for laptop computers but are suitable for big screens.
*Photonics Imaging, NHK, Matsushita, Fujitsu*

screens climbed about 60%. Moreover, Japan's display makers haven't fashioned screens larger than 20 inches diagonally or dropped the price much below $1,500.

So the door is ajar for U.S. producers. In Focus has a way to make high-resolution LCDs that don't need a transistor at each pixel—thus slashing manufacturing costs and boosting yields past 90%. The Wilsonville (Ore.) factory should be cranking out six-inch screens for handheld devices by early 1994, says In Focus Chairman Steven R. Hix, "and Motorola is pushing like mad to get up to 12 inches."

Other U.S. innovators are aiming for screens that take over some computer functions—a key to miniaturization. David Sarnoff Research Center in Princeton, N.J., has made four-by-eight-inch prototypes of such a "smart" LCD. And in Taunton, Mass., Kopin mounts high-speed computer-chip circuitry on a display's glass. Kopin's displays will be used in projection-TV systems and tiny screens in military goggles for simulations, guiding weapons, or viewing data.

Very big screens, by contrast, may require abandoning LCDs. Screens in which each pixel produces its own light "are much crisper and more pleasing to the eye than backlit [liquid-crystal] displays," says James A. Ionson, research vice-president for Polaroid Corp. In plasma displays, for instance, a current induces a gas at each pixel to shine. These are easier and cheaper

to make, says Peter S. Friedman, president of screenmaker Photonics Imaging in Northwood, Ohio. "Active-matrix doesn't have a prayer of catching up," he adds.

Chipmaker Micron Technology Inc. in Boise, Idaho, is trying another approach—field-emitter displays that use thousands of arrays of electron beams to light up the phosphor coatings in a screen. One advantage of this technology is that viewers won't discern the failure of a few microscopic field emitters. That's also true for screens using clusters of either light-emitting diodes (LEDs) or miniature lasers to light each pixel. Once researchers can make screens with a palette of colors bright enough for use in daylight, "these displays will take over the flat-panel market," predicts physicist Jan F. Schetzina of North Carolina State University.

The next question is whether U.S. lab breakthroughs can become commercial successes. The Japanese are also working on advanced plasma displays and laser screens. Given Japan's huge investment, manufacturing skills, and enormous lead, says consultant Lawrence E. Tannas Jr., president of Tannas Electronics in Orange, Calif., it will take the U.S. at least a decade to get back in the race. Only then might anyone know who will offer the clearest windows into the Information Age.

*John Carey in Washington, with Neil Gross in Tokyo and Gary McWilliams in Boston*

# DEVELOPING A HIGH-TECH SIXTH SENSE

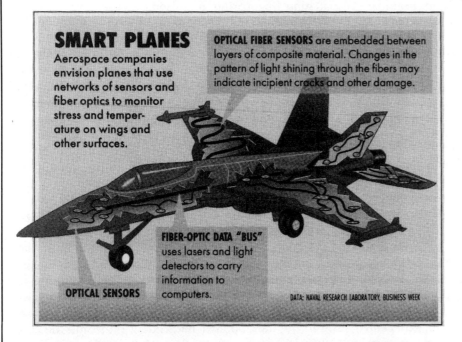

**SMART PLANES**
Aerospace companies envision planes that use networks of sensors and fiber optics to monitor stress and temperature on wings and other surfaces.

**OPTICAL FIBER SENSORS** are embedded between layers of composite material. Changes in the pattern of light shining through the fibers may indicate incipient cracks and other damage.

**FIBER-OPTIC DATA "BUS"** uses lasers and light detectors to carry information to computers.

**OPTICAL SENSORS**

DATA: NAVAL RESEARCH LABORATORY, BUSINESS WEEK

One offspring of the marriage of electricity and light is better technology for probing the world. Researchers are developing optoelectronic sensors that can record stresses in airplane wings or buildings, peer into living cells, or measure levels of air pollution. "No other technology gives the same capabilities," says physicist Alan D. Kersey, a sensor expert at the Naval Research Laboratory in Washington, D.C.

Sensor technology mostly exploits the fact that light travels in waves. Take the fiber-optic gyroscope now used in some planes. Laser light is split into two beams that travel in opposite directions through a coil of fiber. When the plane turns—and the gyroscope with it—light traveling one way around the coil will have to go slightly farther to reach the end of the fiber. The other path will be a bit shorter. So the two streams of light waves will arrive back at the starting point slightly out of sync, allowing a processor to calculate the change in direction. Built by Honeywell Inc. and others, these gyro-scopes are simpler, lighter, and less costly than previous ones.

Light waves can also help peer into solid materials. University of Vermont engineers Peter L. Fuhr and Dryver R. Huston have embedded miles of optical fibers in concrete in a university building and other structures. Light waves shining down the fiber bounce off its internal walls like errant bobsleds, interfering with each other and forming a distinctive light pattern at the end of the fiber. The pattern changes as the fiber is bent or stretched by cracking deep within the concrete—and the change is analyzed by a computer. "This technology shows engineers what is going on inside a structure," says Fuhr. Aerospace companies envision using similar sensors to build "smart" airplane skin, says Kersey, that can "provide real-time analysis of what's going on in the wings."

Other scientists are making sensors by adding impurities to optical fibers that cause the glass to reflect, scatter, or emit light differently when a variable, such as temperature or pressure, changes. A single such fiber can be strung through a factory to monitor the temperature of dozens of machines and furnaces.

**SWEET SPOT.** University of Michigan chemist Raoul Kopelman has built a microscopic fiber-optic sensor that enables biologists to measure the pH level of a single living cell. Similar devices will monitor everything from calcium to sugar levels inside cells—a boon for biomedical research.

Optoelectronic sensors don't always involve optical fibers. Pollution detectors use laser beams that are reflected off tiny particles in the air. And Hewlett-Packard Co. has developed LED sensors capable of detecting even the slightest turn of a car's steering wheel. The information could be used with a microprocessor to adjust an active suspension system so it banks the vehicle into a turn. Mark Chandler, optoelectronics marketing manager at HP, predicts that such sensors will be a $100 million-a-year market by 2005.

So far, much of the cutting-edge work in sensors is being done for defense applications. The Navy is building cheap but sensitive fiber-optic sensors to pick up the faintest ripples created by lurking submarines. And Hughes Aircraft Co. and others are developing phased-array aircraft and satellite radars. Instead of large radar domes, these planes and satellites would use scores of tiny radar-beam emitters mounted on the plane's or satellite's skin. "A fiber-optic connection to each group of emitters makes it possible to steer the resulting radar beam," says Richard Lind, manager of the optical physics lab at Hughes. Such a system, experts say, could see a license plate from orbit. Not much, it seems, will be hidden from optoelectronic sensors.

*John Carey in Washington*

## 1. THE CHANGING ECONOMY

Optoelectronics also offers a radical shift in the way a computer processes information. "The real advantage is that an image [not a bit] is the unit of information," says Purdue University physicist David Nolte. "One image can contain 1 billion bits." To match fingerprints, for example, computers now search for similarities between two pictures by comparing the thousands of individual pixels, or dots, that make up each image. An optical processor, by contrast, can overlay two images and immediately spot similarities. University of Colorado computer scientist Kristina M. Johnson is using this to design an optical chip that can identify cancer cells in Pap smears.

The main hurdles to such bold ideas are complexity and cost. Because current lasers emit light from the side of a chip, each must be cut from the parent gallium arsenide wafer, then aligned by hand with a glass fiber about the width of a human hair—a costly job. A better approach would be to move from single lasers to integrated systems.

That leap will require some wizardry. At startup Photonics Research Inc. in Boulder, Colo., co-founder Jack L. Jewell, in collaboration with researchers at Bellcore, is using techniques adapted from chipmaking to fashion a new breed of microscopic lasers. These emit light upward from the wafer, making it possible to create chips that aim hundreds or thousands of lasers in the same direction, creating a powerful beam. Moreover, the job of aligning this array of lasers with a corresponding array of optical fibers should be much simpler, dramatically reducing manufacturing costs. "There are huge numbers of markets" for the improved devices, says Jewell. These include laser printers, optical memory for computers, and advanced telecommunications networks.

**EAGLE 'EYES.'** Another promising computer technology involves so-called smart pixels—chips with arrays of lasers and transistors—that send and receive information using hundreds or thousands of light beams. These hybrid devices are already capable of such rudimentary processing as routing signals from one path to another in a network. At Bell Labs, Miller's team has built experimental smart pixels that process a hundred million bits per second. Very fast conventional chips can do as well. But the advantage of smart pixels is that they can contain hundreds or thousands of channels operating at that speed. They should thus make it possible to build faster hybrid optoelectronic computers and zippier high-speed switches in communications networks. And smart pixels could be used in computer-vision systems capable of matching fingerprints or serving as the "eyes" for self-guided vehicles.

Smart pixels are a big step toward practical integrated optoelectronic circuits, but they're still tricky to build. The Bell Labs devices, for example, are fashioned from complex wafers that are processed to make both transistors and lasers. Another approach uses less exotic wafers and a technique called selective-area epitaxy. This allows the lasers and transistors to be made separately on the same chip, says Colorado State University electrical engineer Henryk Temkin. He expects the technique to take several years to perfect but predicts it will greatly lower the cost of making many optoelectronic devices.

Some researchers are even trying to coax light from silicon itself. If that becomes possible, manufacturers could build optoelectronic devices without using materials such as gallium arsenide, which is expensive and hard to work with. So far, scientists have gotten a few rays of light by riddling silicon with holes or lacing it with sulfur or germanium, then applying a current. But they're still in the dark about what's going on inside the chips. "We're looking for a breakthrough," says Dennis G. Hall, professor of optics at the University of Rochester, who is working with sulfur in silicon. One lesson from the past, he adds, is that in optoelectronics, it's reasonable to expect new discoveries.

Taken alone, each of these advances represents only a small leap. It may not even be obvious, for example, when optical fibers replace wires in computers—except that the machines will work faster. But the remarkable attribute of optoelectronics is its enormous breadth. It will touch everything from medicine to the waging of war. As the technology creeps into use, the quality of images on videophones will improve dramatically and the amount of information that data bases can hold will rise exponentially. Airplanes made of the smarter materials will be safer, medical devices will be better and cheaper, until one day, optoelectronics will have fomented a revolution as far-reaching as that wrought by the silicon chip.

*By John Carey in Washington, with Neil Gross in Tokyo*

# How Small Is It, Johnny?

**Gino Del Guercio**

*Gino Del Guercio is a regular contributor to WM and a documentary filmmaker specializing in science and technology.*

What we can't show you in this space may change your life. And while you'll never actually see it, it will be all around you. Consider motors so small that *hordes of gnat-sized robots* could clean your house. Electronics so tiny that a $^1/_{200}$th-inch cube could contain *all the world's books*. It's called nanotechnology—as exciting a break-through as the transistor. Germany's racing to beat the leaders, the US and Japan.

It all started 33 years ago, when the Nobel Prize-winning physicist Richard Feynman proposed that if miniaturization were taken to its ultimate limits—fashioning structures atom by atom—absolutely amazing machines could be built. He calculated that all the books in the world combined could be written on "the barest piece of dust that can be made out of the human eye." And he speculated that perfect microscopic machines, which "would have an enormous number of technical applications," could be made to reproduce themselves.

The scientists who heard Feynman's lecture, "There's Plenty of Room at the Bottom," thought he was pulling another of his legendary tricks. After all, no one had even *seen* an atom, let alone manipulated one. But he was serious.

Although Feynman died in 1988, his idea is finally coming to fruition. Scientists and engineers from around the world and from almost every discipline—chemistry, biology, optics, electronics, physics, and many others—are turning to what is called nanotechnology (nano meaning one billionth) to help them explore the world of the ultra-tiny and to build new and useful devices.

The technology has progressed so quickly, in fact, that many people already have at least one nano-device in their home: Most compact disc players use a laser made with nanotechnology. In the future, the number of household nano-devices is likely to increase exponentially. Of course, since they're so small, you'll never see them.

The age of microscopic miniaturiza-

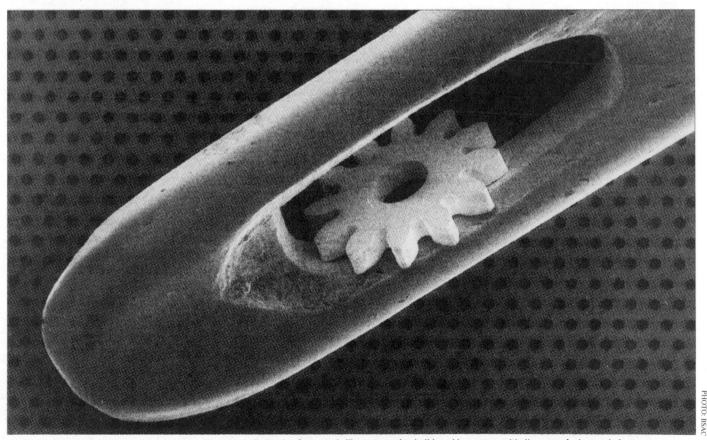

IN THE EYE OF A NEEDLE: Micro-gear from research center in Karlsruhe, Germany, is like ones used to build working motors with diameter of a human hair.

PHOTO: BSAC

tion began in 1947, when scientists at Bell Labs in Murray Hill, New Jersey, invented the transistor, a device that can amplify an electrical signal, serve as an electronic on-off switch, and be made exceedingly small, compared to the thumb-sized or larger vacuum tube that a transistor could replace.

The size kept shrinking. By 1979, 29,000 transistors could fit onto a microchip; by 1989, 1 million. By 2010, if the trend continues, engineers will reach the theoretical limit, squeezing 1 billion transistors onto a chip about the size of your thumbnail.

## Micro-*mechanics*

Miniaturization transformed computers, which 40 years ago were relatively slow and the size of large rooms, into hand-held, lightning-fast calculators. It put personal computers—ones that would have been considered supercomputers just a decade earlier—on the desktop. And it has enabled engineers to build new supercomputers able to perform billions of calculations per second—very useful for predicting large-scale phenomena such as the weather.

Until recently, however, micro-miniaturization was limited to electronic components. Mechanical devices, such as gears and motors, were still made by traditional grinding, molding, and cutting methods. To do work, the miniaturized electronic components had to feed their signals to normal-size motors, sensors, lasers, and other large-scale devices.

However, during the mid-1980s, scientists and engineers realized they could use the existing techniques—those used for packing micro-transistors onto chips—to make micro-mechanical devices. A race began to see who could build the first working micro-motor. The Massachusetts Institute of Technology and the University of California at Berkeley were in a heated competition. And in the summer of 1988, Berkeley won the race, demonstrating a spinning motor about the diameter of a human hair. The images of that first motor, which looked like a tiny pinwheel, were printed in newspapers and magazines around the world.

Finally, mechanical and electronic components could be packed together on the same chip, at least in theory. Such a hybrid device would be able to sense its surroundings, figure out what to do, and then

act upon those calculations, all on the scale of 1/1,000th of an inch. Ultimately, engineers might be able to create robots the size of gnats, or smaller. Hordes of these gnatbots could be produced for pennies, programmed, and then unleashed to perform some useful task—cleaning up all the dust in a room, for example, or building a machine more complex than themselves.

Or a miniaturized personal computer—more powerful than today's laptop—could be strapped on like Dick Tracy's wrist radio.

Or you might have in your pocket a navigational guidance system of the sort reserved for intercontinental ballistic missiles today.

## Germany Advances

At the present rate of development, however, such feats are a long way off. In fact, half a decade after the Berkeley discovery, engineers are still trying to figure out how to attach their micro-motors to gears, so that they

*Back in 1988 Berkeley demonstrated a motor about the diameter of a human hair.*

can do more than just spin their wheels. The trouble is that current micro-manufacturing techniques can make only flat objects. To be useful, mechanical devices generally need to have some bulk.

The solution to this problem may have been found in Germany. A team of engineers at the Karlsruhe Nuclear Research Center has developed a technique capable of making gears and motors 1/1,000th of an inch wide and 6/1,000ths of an inch taller than they are wide. They use high-energy X-rays to cut tiny patterns into a material. This leaves a mold that can be filled with metal to produce a gear such as you might see in an expensive Swiss watch, only 100 times smaller.

The Germans are making up for lost time, having fallen behind the Japanese and the Americans in developing microelectronics. The government is investing more than $70 million in microsystems research, hoping to take the lead in this new field. And it is proposing that the European Community pool its resources

to spend $1 billion on miniaturization technologies. The Germans realize that whichever country gains control of the micro-mechanical industry may have an economic advantage as big as—or bigger than—the Japanese currently have in the micro-electronics industry.

If Richard Feynman were around today he would probably say what he said of miniaturization milestones three decades ago: "That's the most primitive, halting step in the direction. It is a staggeringly small world that is below."

Each tiny part of a micro-mechanical or micro-electronic device contains 25 billion atoms. Feynman proposed that useful devices could be made from just a few dozen atoms, which would be 1,000 times smaller than the smallest micro-part. To do this one must first be able to *see* atoms.

## Writing with Atoms

Most microscopes focus the light that comes bouncing up off an object. This works well for objects down to around 1/10,000th of an inch across, but light cannot resolve anything smaller than its own wavelength. Atoms are 100,000 times smaller. Electron microscopes solve this problem by bombarding the object with a stream of electrons, which are much smaller than an atom. But electrons are hard to focus, and electron microscopes require a vacuum, which destroys fragile materials such as living tissue. For years, scientists struggled without success to improve the electron microscope so they could see atoms.

Fortunately, a very different device has been invented, called the scanning tunneling microscope, or STM. While most microscopes are extensions of the human eye, the STM is more like an extension of our fingers. It uses an extremely fine tip to feel its way across a surface. The tip runs no more than a few atoms' distance above the surface and senses the electrical charge passing between the object and the tip.

In 1981, IBM scientists Gerd Bennig and Heinrich Rohrer used an STM to make pictures of individual gold atoms. Later the pair developed a similar device, which, instead of measuring electric current, measured the attractive force between the atoms in the tip and the atoms on the surface. This they called an atomic-force microscope (AFM). It proved useful for looking at biological materials and other substances that do not normally conduct electricity. In 1986, the pair won the Nobel Prize for their work.

While miraculous in itself, the STM has gone on to do something even more amazing. In 1990, Don Eigler and colleagues in San Jose, California, used an STM to move atoms around one by one. Very slowly, and at a temperature close to absolute zero (minus 459.67 F, the temperature at which atoms stop vibrating), they were able to write their company logo, "IBM," in letters only a dozen atoms

---

*A tiny PC, more powerful than today's laptop, could be strapped on like a Dick Tracy wrist radio.*

---

across. Less than a year later, Shigeyuki Hosoki, an electronics researcher at the Hitachi Central Research Laboratory (HCRL) in Tokyo, took the technique several steps further, writing—more rapidly—"PEACE '91 HCRL" with individual atoms at room temperature.

Suddenly, Feynman's favorite idea of writing all of recorded knowledge on a speck of dust seemed possible.

"Ones" and "zeros" are the two basic components of a digital memory. A structure with a hole created by removing an atom or a small number of atoms could be used to represent a zero. Leave the hole filled and that could represent a one.

Feynman estimated that, even if 100 atoms were used to represent each digital bit, all the books in the world could be written on a cube of material 1/200th of an inch wide. By comparison, the 100-megabyte hard drive on a personal computer—which can hold 200 complete encyclopedia sets—begins to look pretty puny.

## Making It Cheaper

Seeing the potential of such research, the Japanese government has committed $225 million over the next 10 years. When the Japanese and German governments commit resources to pursuing basic research they tend to create central facilities, while research in the United States is usually spread among a large number of universities and corporate research laboratories. However, for the past 14 years the US government has funded a centralized facility for nanotech research at Cornell University—the National Nanofabrication Facility.

The NNF is a low-slung building tucked into the center of Cornell's bucolic campus in upstate New York. Much of the laboratory is operating-room clean. To enter, one must don hat, lab coat, and shoe covers; awkwardly slide over a low counter; and then go through an airlock.

Edward Wolf, emeritus professor of electrical engineering at Cornell and a former director of the facility, gives the tour. Off the main corridor are a variety of sealed rooms with even higher cleanliness standards, requiring full head-to-toe "bunny suits." These rooms are packed with the latest equipment for manufacturing and viewing components no more than a few 10-millionths of an inch across.

The facility is unique in the United States because it actively encourages anyone from the academic or corporate research communities to come use the equipment. It especially likes to see people from unexpected backgrounds, such as biology. The facility's staff of 24 scientists and engineers help guide users in their quest to build a device.

For instance, William Tasker, a senior scientist at Galileo Electro-Optics Corp. in Sturbridge, Massachusetts, is using the facility to develop a new method for making night-vision scopes like those used in Operation Desert Storm. The scopes amplify light by converting photons into electrons and then sending them through a micro-channel electron multiplier. This is a plate made from millions of short, very thin, glass tubes. When a single electron goes in one side of the plate, it spits out scores of electrons from the other. The amplified image can be seen on a small television screen.

The current method Galileo uses to make the micro-channel multiplier takes four to six weeks, and the entire device costs $6,000 to $7,000. Tasker believes he can make a similar device by cutting micro-channels into a material using nanotechnology, which he expects will result in a plate-manufacture time of one week or less and a cost of between $500 and $1,000 per scope.

While much of Galileo's work has been for the military, the company is trying to convert to primarily civilian applications, and this means reducing cost. Tasker believes the result of his research will be night scopes cheap enough for local police departments and individuals who have particular trouble seeing in the dark. This is just one of 467 projects undertaken by the facility so far.

"I think we're at the point where we won't go any smaller in our lifetime," says Robert Buhrman, director of applied and engineering physics at Cornell. "To go any further we'd have to work with individual quarks [subatomic particles], and they're very different. So in that sense we're at the bottom. It's the equivalent of laying the first bricks. Now we can start building things from the bottom up."

# AT LAST! COMPUTERS YOU CAN TALK TO

Sick of dealing with keyboards and mice? The decades-old dream of directing computers by spoken commands is rapidly becoming reality at work and at home.

*Gene Bylinsky*

**W**HEN Jean Kovacs comes into the office each day, she dons a little headset and greets her computer with a brisk "Good morning!" In response, her Sun workstation lights up its screen. "Start mail!" commands Kovacs, executive vice president of Qualix Group, a company in San Mateo, California, that markets SayIt, the $295 speech-recognition software package she uses on her machine. The computer obliges, displaying an E-mail message that has arrived via the office network. Kovacs reads it, directs the machine to forward it to a colleague, then asks for her next message.

Talking her way through the morning's chores, she schedules appointments and scans sales reports without touching her keyboard or mouse. The computer can respond to any of 200 commands but doesn't always understand what Kovacs says. So a little cartoonish character named Simon in the corner of the screen provides instant feedback. Whenever the workstation hears a word it can't make out, Simon scratches his head; Kovacs repeats herself and the computer usually gets the word right on the second try. If the telephone rings, Kovacs says, "Cover your ears!" and Simon covers his ears; she then can converse without worrying about inadvertently triggering the computer into action.

Dr. Paul H. Klainer, director of emergency services at Milford-Whitinsville Regional Hospital near Boston, also talks to his computer. He and the 12 doctors he supervises share a $40,000 system called VoiceEM, developed by Kurzweil Applied Intelligence of Waltham, Massachusetts. To Klainer the machine, which transcribes spoken comments on patients' conditions, is a clerical miracle: He and associates used to write their reports by hand. At hospitals where reports previously had to be dictated into tape recorders and transcribed by overworked typists, VoiceEMs have

REPORTER ASSOCIATE *Alicia Hills Moore*

brought down turnaround time from days to minutes. VoiceEM also has a built-in "knowledge base" of medical data that prompts the doctors to check for symptoms they may have overlooked, thus improving the accuracy of diagnoses and reducing the threat of malpractice suits.

The decades-old dream of directing computers by spoken commands is rapidly becoming reality in workplaces and homes. And not a moment too soon for people who have never mastered a keyboard or mouse, for those who always seem to be doing two things at once, and for those whose physical disabilities make typing difficult—or impossible.

Computer companies—the speech-recognition pioneers like Qualix and Kurzweil as well as the industry giants—are introducing powerful software and add-on equipment that endow ordinary PCs and workstations with the ability to understand their master's voice. Phone companies, eager to streamline service and cut operator time, have begun integrating speech-recognition equipment into their networks so consumers can converse directly with information and call-routing computers. If you've made a collect call from a pay phone recently, you may have had a computerized voice help make the connection.

In the past year IBM has unveiled four speech-recognition products, ranging from a $129 software package for PCs to Speech Server, a $6,995 program for the company's RISC workstation that can transcribe dictation from as many as eight users simultaneously. In September, Microsoft announced Windows Sound, a $289 package that lets users of ordinary PCs do many of the things Jean Kovacs does on her workstation. Later this year Apple Computer is expected to introduce Casper, a voice-command system for the Macintosh.

No wonder analyst John Oberteuffer, president of Voice Information Associates of Lexington, Massachusetts, expects annual sales of speech-recognition equipment, $159 million in 1992, to quadruple by 1996 and to top $1 billion by the year 2000. Says Nathan P. Myhrvold, vice president for advanced technology and business develop-

ment at Microsoft: "Clearly we're reaching a crossover point where speech recognition gets to be mainstream."

**S**PEECH-RECOGNITION technology is finally outgrowing the annoying limitations that have confined it mostly to the lab. Early systems had tiny vocabularies; the latest dictation machines, such as Kurzweil's and IBM's, can recognize up to 50,000 words, or ten times the range needed for routine business correspondence. Where once systems required each user to spend many hours reading test words into a mike to "train" the machine, it took Jean Kovacs only five seconds per command to train her workstation, and some new systems require no training at all.

Most products still suffer the worst bugaboo of speech recognition: an inability to process continuous speech. For example, users of the Speech Server must learn to pause for a fraction of a second after each word they dictate. But even that nuisance will vanish in systems being developed for use in tourist information kiosks and other settings where the vocabulary is predictable and relatively small. Within five years, experts say, the power to recognize continuous speech should extend to large-vocabulary machines.

So rapidly is speech recognition evolving that it has caught up with speech synthesis—the playback of digitally stored sounds that enables computers to speak. Integrate the two technologies, says Arno Penzias, vice president of research at AT&T Bell Labs, and the world will fill with machines that listen and talk to people: "The widespread deployment of computers that can converse now has as much to do with limits on our imaginations as it does with limits on the technology itself." Among the applications he and other technologists see as already here or on the way:

■ **Talking to your phone.** Last summer AT&T began phasing in a nationwide service that automates operator assistance. When a caller dials *O*, he actually gets *C*—a computer that asks whether he means to make a collect, person-to-person, or credit-card call, and carries out the instructions he gives. If difficulties arise—say the machine can't make sense of a person's response—it will signal a human operator to intervene.

Local phone companies, meanwhile, are experimenting with voice-command services. In the New York City suburb of Bay Shore, Long Island, latchkey kids in 400 households can pick up the phone and simply say "Mom" to reach their mothers at work. Their speech is processed by a computer at Nynex's central office. In Boise, Idaho, US West is testing a system it calls Voice Interactive Phone, or VIP. By dialing the octothorpe (#) and 44, then saying "Messages," a subscriber can retrieve voice mail. By saying "Return call," the subscriber can order the system to dial the party who had phoned most recently. Bell Canada wants to make it easy for customers to check their portfolios: It offers a toll-free line on which you name the stock exchange and the company, and a machine responds with its current stock price.

■ **Going beyond keyboards.** As every user knows, modern desk-top computer software typically can perform far more functions than there are keys on the keyboard. Consequence: Giving a single command may require a dozen keystrokes or mouse movements. But if a computer understands spoken commands, the inconvenience vanishes. Users can also perform two tasks at once: A graphics designer drawing an image with a mouse can simultaneously adjust the color of the image by talking to the machine.

■ **Lording it over other gadgets.** How about barking out an order from your couch and having your VCR obey? Voice Powered Technology of Canoga Park, California, offers a $169 voice-activated remote control designed to work with most VCRs and cable TV boxes. It lets you channel-hop and start and stop tapes; you can even skip commercials during playback by simply saying "Zap it." The controller causes the VCR to fast-forward past the next 60 seconds of tape.

As Apple Computer and other manufacturers prepare to market "personal digital assistants," paperback-size computers intended to make address books, calendars, and laptop computers obsolete, some technologists believe the machines will need speech recognition to succeed. Referring wryly to the difficulty of typing on miniature keyboards, Janet Baker, president of Dragon Systems, a Newton, Massachusetts, speech-recognition pioneer, observes, "Nobody wants to enter text by toothpick." She predicts that at least three years will pass before PDAs pack sufficient speech-recognition capability to achieve widespread use.

■ **Dispensing with clerks.** Talking information machines will pop up in all sorts of unexpected places, predicts IBM market strategist Elton B. Scherwin Jr. He says hotel and shopping mall operators have expressed intense interest in systems that can answer customers' routine questions without coming across like automatons. An IBM videotape gives a futuristic look at how one might work on a city street. A tourist couple inquires about the location of the nearest Chinese restaurant. The machine, programmed with the knowledge that one is across the street, wickedly asks, "Have you looked behind you?"

At MIT, researcher Victor Zue has built a demonstration system that can talk about Cambridge, Massachusetts, almost as fluently as a person. Asked "How can I get to Harvard from here?" it responds, "Take the Red Line two stops to Harvard Square." It is also full of tips about restaurants and museums.

Airlines are interested in adapting Zue's and similar systems to stand in for clerks. The machines would be able to answer travelers' questions about flight schedules and issue tickets. Eventually, speech-equipped computers may even replace workers at fast-food chains. In Japan, Toshiba is at work on a machine that in response to a spoken command will produce a hamburger and a soft drink. In an unintentional pun on hamburger flipping, Toshiba has called it the Tosburg.

What makes such intriguing progress possible is the growing availability of cheap computer power and the development of better algorithms, or formulas, for processing speech. Work in the field dates back to the early 1970s, when the Defense Department's Advanced Research Projects Agency, or ARPA (at that time called DARPA), began underwriting speech-recognition programs at Carnegie Mellon and MIT. At first the investigators tried word matching: using computers to compare the energies and frequencies of speech sounds with the stored acoustic profiles of words. But because pronunciation varies wildly from speaker to speaker and also depends on the context in which a word is spoken, the approach proved impractical. "Can you imagine asking for samples of 30,000 words each time a new person wants to use the computer?" asks Dragon Systems' Baker.

Investigators next tried matching spoken sounds with acoustic profiles of "phones," the basic building blocks of speech. The word *cat*, for example, consists of three phones: *k*, *æ*, and *t*. In one sense this made the computers' task more manageable, since a few thousand phones can account for the English language. The hard part lay in sorting out phones' seemingly infinite combinations, a task that could defeat even the fastest computer.

## SOFTWARE TO MAKE YOUR MACHINE LISTEN UP

| PRODUCT<br>Manufacturer | Price | No. of words recognized | What it does |
|---|---|---|---|
| **VoiceType Control for Windows**<br>IBM (Somers, New York) | $129 | 64 | Allows owners of PCs equipped with Microsoft Windows to perform basic chores such as opening and closing files. Comes with a mike that plugs into the PC. |
| **Microsoft Windows Sound Sys.**<br>Microsoft (Redmond, Wash.) | $289 | 3,000 + | Offers same functions as above; also lets users put voice annotations on documents and spreadsheets. Comes with add-on circuitboard, mike, and headphones. |
| **SayIt**<br>Qualix Group (San Mateo, Calif.) | $295 | 1,000 + | Lets users of Sun workstations execute spoken commands. Optional headsets ($100 or $200) improve performance (Sun workstations have rudimentary mikes). |
| **Voice Navigator SW**<br>Articulate Systems (Woburn, Mass.) | $399 | 1,000 + | For most models of the Apple Macintosh. Allows user to execute program commands and dictate some data. Your choice of desktop mike or headset. |
| **DragonDictate-30K**<br>Dragon Systems (Newton, Mass.) | $4,995 | 30,000 + | For PCs. Transcribes sentences spoken with a brief pause after each word. Automatically adapts to user's voice. Comes with add-on circuitboard and mike. |
| **Kurzweil Voice**<br>Kurzweil Applied Intel. (Waltham, Mass.) | $6,000 | 50,000 | Works like DragonDictate. For PCs that incorporate Intel 486 chip. Choice of headset or handheld mike. |

FORTUNE TABLE

## 1. THE CHANGING ECONOMY

**T**HE KEY to that puzzle was uncovered in 1971 when Baker's husband, James Baker, a mathematician, applied the work of a turn-of-the-century Russian mathematician named Andrei A. Markov. He had invented a method for statistically predicting the sequence of letters as they appeared in Pushkin's verse novel, *Eugene Onegin*. Hidden Markov Modeling, as the method was called, worked so well that the U.S. National Security Agency used it to crack codes. Applied to speech recognition, it offered a crucial shortcut: Once a computer identifies the first phone in a sequence, it can narrow its search for the next by statistically calculating which sounds are most likely to follow. Coping with a large range of possible words still requires millions of calculations for each—which is why speech-recognition programs originally required large, fast mainframes. Only recently have desktop computers become powerful enough to handle the job.

ARPA gave the field a second big boost in 1986 when it issued grants to break down the barrier between speech recognition and a branch of linguistics called natural-language studies. Experts from the two disciplines almost never crossed paths: Speech researchers had concentrated on acoustics while natural-language scholars had devoted themselves to the study of syntax and semantics. Their government-prompted collaboration helped establish the U.S. as by far the world leader in speech recognition, a remarkable example of how industrial policy can foster competitiveness. Within a few years the researchers had programmed dictation systems to resolve ambiguity. Confronted with the trick sentence *Our last two presenters were one hour too long,* for example, IBM's Speech Server distinguishes "hour" from "our" and "two" from "too" and delivers an accurate transcription with amazing ease.

But don't toss your keyboard into the trash basket yet. The day is at least decades away when you'll be able to chat with a computer the way astronauts conversed with HAL in the movie *2001: A Space Odyssey*. While today's best speech-recognition systems are fairly dependable—some attain 95% accuracy—they still can make alarming mistakes. For example, when Dr. Klainer of the Milford-Whitinsville hospital recently dictated a report on a patient with angina, his Kurzweil machine typed "cancer" on the screen. But it also typed "angina" as the next best choice; Klainer immediately corrected the misdiagnosis. Another Kurzweil system, when told at a recent demonstration "Make your text bold," typed, "Make your pets old." The young woman operator explained apologetically that she was recovering from a cold and hadn't retrained the machine to take into account her stuffy nose.

Even if they work perfectly, computers that listen won't necessarily be welcome in every workplace. Users tend to speak loudly as they enunciate into the machines, addressing them like not-too-bright menial help. "The prospect of an office full of people all babbling away at their PCs is not something I'd look forward to," a reader recently wrote to the New York *Times*. Michael Pique, a computer specialist at the Research Institute of Scripps Clinic in La Jolla, California, found out the hard way. He installed the SayIt program on his Sun workstation in December, only to find his office neighbors grumbling about noise.

Eventually technology should come to the rescue of Pique and other users: Researchers are working on ultrasensitive directional mikes that can be built into the rim around the screen to pick up the faintest whisper. But for now Pique has found his own way to reconcile civility and progress. He has rearranged his work schedule so that he and his computer do most of their talking at night, after everyone else has gone home.

# VIRTUAL REALITY

## *HOW A COMPUTER-GENERATED WORLD COULD CHANGE THE REAL WORLD*

Psychologists call it "suspending disbelief." Computer jocks call it entering "virtual reality." Whatever the jargon, it doesn't begin to describe what happens in Arlington, Va., at the Institute for Defense Analyses.

You sit in a wood-paneled room as Colonel Jack Thorpe, special assistant for simulation at the Pentagon's Defense Advanced Research Projects Agency, douses the lights, flips on a computer—and sends three five-foot screens in front of you thundering into action. Instantly, you're transported inside a tank rolling across the Iraqi desert. You are performing the same maneuvers as a unit of the 2nd Armored Cavalry during "73 Easting," an actual battle in the Persian Gulf war. The graphics on the screens are only video-game quality. Yet, the illusion works: You duck as shells scream toward you and explode in ear-splitting fury.

It isn't unusual for soldiers participating in this exercise to curse or sweat as the computer-simulated fight unfolds. Something else happens as well: Their scores for battlefield acumen improve dramatically after they practice with these video tank crews. In an era of shrinking defense budgets, such training offers invaluable experience without the cost, damage, and logistical hassle of war games. "We will expect a smaller military to be masters of a wider

ensemble of skills," says Thorpe. "This is an idea whose time is right."

**NEW SENSATIONS.** The cyberspace tank battle is primitive compared with visions of "virtual reality" trumpeted in books, movies, and the TV show *Star Trek: The Next Generation*. There, intergalactic travelers use computers to conjure up Sherlock Holmes's London or a sexy date. But as DARPA's system proves, computer-generated worlds don't have to be super-realistic to evoke real life. That fact is turning virtual reality into a red-hot technology.

---

*Cyberspace simulations may enhance job performance and training, improve product design, assist surgeons, and create interactive forms of entertainment. But it will be years, if ever, before all that is a reality*

---

There's plenty of confusion over what VR is. But to most developers, the core of every system is a data base that contains data from a brain scan, specifications for a car dashboard, the description of a fictional landscape—in short, data that can represent almost anything. A power-

ful computer with sophisticated graphics then renders a "world," often in 3-D, that recreates precisely what the data describe. VR displays vary widely, from images on a computer monitor to theater-style displays such as 73 Easting to projections on stereoscopic lenses mounted inside helmets that VR participants wear.

Whatever the approach, two characteristics distinguish VR worlds from other computer graphics: Increasingly, they convey multiple sensory information—sound or touch—to make environments more realistic. And they are interactive. In some systems, a viewer wearing a sensor-laden glove manipulates objects in the computer as one would naturally. In others, images on the screen or a viewer's perspective are manipulated with a mouse or joystick.

At IBM's Watson Labs in Hawthorne, N.Y., for instance, an engineer seated in front of a projection screen, looking at a sleek, beige dashboard becomes a test driver for a 1997 Chrysler. Wearing 3-D glasses and a glove with sensors, he turns the steering wheel and reaches for buttons as though in a real car. Chrysler Corp. is developing the system with IBM in hopes that the exercise could cut months off the three-year to five-year car-design process by letting engineers spot inconveniently positioned knobs and other problems before they surface in expensive prototypes.

## ANATOMY OF A FASTBALL

Hurling a 100-miles-per-hour fastball down the middle is a special skill worth analyzing. But a big-league pitcher's arm, wrist, and finger movements change so rapidly that they're almost impossible to dissect. This thwarts efforts to learn from good pitchers—or figure out what's wrong when they have injuries or slumps.

Insights into these puzzles of movement could come from a new data-collection tool come from a new data-collection tool that's integral to virtual reality. Greenleaf Medical Systems, a four-year-old startup in Palo Alto, Calif., has licensed the "dataglove" from VPL Research Inc. for medical uses. A black Lycra glove with fiber-optic cables attached relays movement signals to a computer, which quantifies hand motion. In a recent experiment, Greenleaf put datagloves on the hands of four Boston Red Sox pitchers, including team ace Roger Clemens.

Attached to an Apple Macintosh computer, the glove recorded subtle relationships between speed, position, flex, and other variables as the four men threw a variety of pitches. For every three-second pitch, the system compiled 16,000 data points. Red Sox associate team physician William J. Morgan is building graphic images to see what he can learn. By repeating the experiment he hopes to identify movement changes that make a pitcher less effective—and correct them.

Company founder Walter J. Greenleaf sees broader potential in the experiment: He envisions a huge market in analyzing repetitive-stress injuries, an increasingly common malady of office workers, and in diagnosing other orthopedic and neurological ills. He also hopes to make patients who can't speak able to communicate through gestures the computer interprets.

**'PAST THE HYPE.'** Intrigued by this kind of potential, dozens of government, university, and industrial labs, from NASA and the Defense Dept. to the University of Washington (UW), are embracing virtual reality. In the next four years, the military hopes to spend more than $500 million on simulations. This fall, the Army will likely award an additional $350 million, eight-year contract to create an advanced network for battlefield simulations. Industry giants—including Boeing, AT&T, Sharp, and Fujitsu—are investing millions, too. At UW's Human Interface Technology Laboratory, some 19 companies have created the Virtual Worlds Consortium to apply VR to business. "Forget the games and electronic sex," says Bryan Lewis, a researcher at IBM. "We are past the hype and pursuing real applications."

This could be a boon to computer giants such as IBM, DEC, Apple, Sun, and graphics workstation maker Silicon Graphics. VR represents a potentially big market—and a flashy selling point—for their muscle machines. Startups including Exos, Virtual Vision, and Fake Space Labs are building gear to enhance VR worlds—viewing devices, acoustical chips, and sensors. Autodesk, Sense8, VPL Research, and others see their fortunes in systems that business can use.

For good reason. Cyberspace worlds that exist only in the electronic ether can be a powerful tool in the hands of architects, engineers, and scientists. They can also be used to boost productivity, improve product design, and provide more cost-effective training. In medicine, VR tools are being used to create 3-D X-rays to help surgeons plan procedures or assist in surgery miles away. Psychologists want to use the technology to treat patients and to study human behavior. Artists and entertainment moguls are pioneering new attractions—interactive theater, interactive fiction, and even virtual sculpture, cyberspace works that defy the laws of physics.

Whether VR systems will ever match the sophistication they display in fiction is far from certain. The field faces huge technical hurdles: Success will depend on improvements in hardware and software, plus new insights into the human brain and behavior. And as systems become more "real," they will pose thorny ethical questions: Could VR influence people in pernicious ways that conventional media cannot?

Still, VR's social and economic potential seems clear. Democratic Vice Presidential hopeful Al Gore considers VR so crucial to "the way we design new products, teach our children, and spend free time" that last year he chaired hearings on its value to American competitiveness. The conclusion: The U.S. is underinvesting in the technology.

To VR advocates, that's a mistake. Virtual reality represents "the manifest destiny for computers," asserts Eric Gullichsen, founder of VR software producer Sense8. By creating worlds of color, shapes, sounds, and feel, these systems should amplify the powers of the mind to see previously hidden relation-ships in complex sets of data and to absorb, manipulate, and interpret information more quickly and completely. The distinction between immersion in a VR world and analyzing the same information using blueprints, numbers, or text "is the difference between looking at an aquarium and putting on your scuba gear and diving in," says Thomas Furness, director of UW's Human Interface Technology Laboratory.

**BUMP AND GRAB.** Just ask engineers at Northrop Corp., who are using a VR system from Simgraphics Engineering Corp. to help redesign the Air Force's F-18 fighter jet. They model air-intake ducts on computers

# IS VR REAL ENOUGH FOR THE COURTROOM?

On the night of Feb. 27, 1991, San Francisco porn-movie king Jim Mitchell drove to the home of his younger brother and business partner, Artie, in Corte Madera, Calif. Minutes later, Artie was dead, and a dazed Jim was arrested walking away from the scene.

The district attorney didn't buy Jim's story that he shot eight times in self-defense, frightened by a beer bottle an intoxicated Artie wielded in a dim hallway. But there were no eyewitnesses. So, the prosecution persuaded the judge to let the jury watch a video of Artie's death.

This was no candid videotape, however. In the first-ever use of VR in a criminal trial, a ballistics expert recreated the event, complete with bullet trajectories, on a personal computer using computer-aided design software from Autodesk Inc. In the animation, a ghostly figure peeks from behind a door. The figure emerges and walks stiffly down a hallway. A red tube pierces, then exits, the body. The figure continues to walk until another red tube strikes its forehead.

The video, which was created after analyzing evidence found at the scene, had the desired effect. Last Feb. 19, the jury convicted Jim Mitchell of manslaughter and sentenced him to six years in prison. He's appealing, in part because of the videotape, which his attorney, Nanci Clarence, calls "wizardry that has no place in a court of law."

The Mitchell case highlights the ethical dilemmas inherent in VR. Reality is, after all, more than sophisticated software. To the defense's chagrin, for instance, the figure in the tape doesn't wield his beer bottle in a remotely threatening way. In short, VR may raise a thorny question for judges: Even in the best of simulations, can reality be manipulated unfairly?

to make sure they fit through bulkheads, rather than building expensive hard models. An operator wearing wraparound goggles moves parts around with a type of mouse, making sure they fit together in virtual space. The software even simulates resistance, so engineers know when parts "bump" against each other. Project Engineer Robert E. Joy loves the flexibility: "It's like reaching into the workstation and grabbing the part," he says.

VR represents the second major effort in two decades to bring about a dramatic evolution in computers. The aim of the first, artificial intelligence, originally was to build systems that could mimic human reasoning, a goal that has yet to be reached. Virtual reality is the antithesis of what AI tried to do. It aims "to extend the power of the person" says Robert Jacobson, president of WorlDesign, a Seattle VR software startup.

That's what a visualization tool designed by Maxus Systems International does for managers at TIAA-CREF, a New York pension fund with $105 billion in assets. Tracking the performance of a group of stocks against the larger market is a challenge for analysts, who must follow hundreds of ever-changing numbers. Using software from Sense8, the Maxus system converts the numbers to a 3-D schematic of colored squares that move and symbolize individual stocks within grids representing market and industry sectors. It runs on a personal computer and draws on real-time feeds from financial wires.

A specialist in bank stocks may glance at the computer and notice that a box showing banks in the Pacific Rim is active. The squares are red, a signal that the stocks are falling. The analyst uses a mouse to "fly" into the lowest tier of stocks, which have plunged the fastest, and click on the security that has dropped most. Up pops text on that bank. The process takes seconds, so portfolio managers can "identify trends, recognize exceptions, and make decisions more quickly," says Sense8 President Tom Coull. "That can translate into a tremendous amount of money."

**FLYING MICE.** Such a system falls short for VR purists, who argue that only an immersive experience with a helmet holding two stereoscopic screens and headphones will do. That way, you see and hear only what the computer generates, interacting with the environment as in the real world. At NASA Ames Research Center in Mountain View, Calif., this approach lets you look around the surface of Mars, which has been recreated from satellite data. A motion sensor in the helmet lets you look in any direction, and the computer rerenders the scene to reflect your new perspective on the Martian landscape.

Still, theater-style simulations and two-dimensional computer displays can be just as powerful. Using a Silicon Graphics Inc. system, urban planners in Los Angeles are building an 80-block-by-80-block virtual model of renovation plans for riot-damaged areas. The value: It's hard for untrained people to read blueprints, and models are expensive. Yet, community involvement is essential. This way, residents can use a mouse to "fly" through the streets as if they were in a helicopter. And designers can pop in a park bench or delete a 7-Eleven, testing suggestions from those who live in the real Los Angeles.

The idea of using computers to render useful environments dates back to the 1960s. Back then, however, the computing power needed to generate even crude 3-D graphics was so expensive that only government agencies such as Defense or NASA, plus a few university labs, could afford it. Even today, special helmets used for military flight simulators can cost $1 million.

The field began to attract attention when onetime computer hacker Jaron Lanier coined the term virtual reality in the mid-1980s. In 1984, he founded VPL Research Inc. in Foster City, Calif.—the first company dedicated to VR worlds (next page). VPL has developed key VR aids—head-mounted stereo screen displays, or "eyephones," plus the "data-glove" and the "datasuit," which let VR viewers convey information to computers with hand signals. Don a Dataglove, and an image of a hand appears in the virtual world, so you can point to objects, pick them up, or command the computer.

More than anything else, though, the relentless increase in performance—and decrease in price—of semiconductor chips is driving VR by allowing computer makers to build more sophisticated graphics systems. At the high end, Silicon Graphics' new $100,000 "Reality Engine" has a computing speed 1,000 times a fast as most PCs, allowing it to provide quick rendering and real-time motion in VR worlds. On the low end, desktop VR systems based on Intel Corp.'s 486 chip cost as little as $20,000. Richard H. Dym, general manager for multimedia at Autodesk Inc., calls new programming tools and applications for these systems the leading edge of software development.

Entertainment is one of the first beneficiaries. Nintendo Co.'s $99 Powerglove, a simpler version of VPL's $8,800 Dataglove, lets video-game wizards play with hand gestures and has already helped spawn a host of VR-like video games. Virtual World Entertainment LP's VR game site in Chicago, the "Battletech Center," has sold some 300,000 tickets at $7 each since it opened in July to players who sit in an enclosed cockpit to engage in *Star Wars*-like battles. The company has two sites in Japan and plans to open 17 more over the next three years.

**'TELEPRESENCE.'** In business, much VR technology will evolve out of current computer systems. Computer-aided design, or CAD, systems have been around for years. Adding VR's greater resolution and interactivity can enhance their utility, as Chrysler, among others, is discovering.

"Telepresence," a VR tool that refers to the remote manipulation of equipment, shows similar potential. The Japanese construction company Fujita Corp. has hired VPL to help it build a system that lets an operator in Tokyo direct a spray-painting robot anywhere in the world. The operator views the building to be painted on a computer, then works controls that signal the robot to spray. With VR, the image is so painstakingly exact that the human operator makes no mistakes in directing the operation.

In business education and job training, VR's chief benefit would be lower costs. The Electric Power Research Institute has teamed up with MITRE Corp. to determine if an electronic mock-up of a power-plant control room using stereo projection displays can be effective in training plant operators. Today's training rooms for fossil-fuel plants cost up to $1 million. Using VR, the cost might dip under $100,000. And eventually, says Hugh W. Ryan, director of new-age systems for Arthur Andersen Consulting, VR worlds will be used to simulate business interactions—from sales negotiations to general management problems—and will replace some of today's expensive seminars and classes.

VR may also help train workers for flexible manufacturing. Boeing Co.'s project manager for human-computer interactions, Keith Butler, is developing techniques to project job instructions onto see-through goggles worn by assembly workers or onto the work space in front of them. In theory, instructions presented this way could replace hours of training in which workers learn jobs, then must be trained again when the task changes. With such displays, a worker might assemble wing flaps, then switch to nose cones on the same day with little loss of productivity.

In perfecting such systems, developers must solve some novel problems. Why do some people become nauseated when navigating in cyberspace? And if you have to make a trade-off between complex, realistic graphics or live-action motion, which is more important for maintaining the illusion of reality?

The answers to such questions lie in the cognitive and behavioral sciences. Greater knowledge of the structure of the brain, how it processes information, and how people think and perceive is the key. Such research already indicates why VR worlds are so effective in training, says Roger Shank, director of the Institute for the Learning Sciences at Northwestern University. Studies show that in general, people reason or solve problems based on cases, examples, and experience, not by learning rules. "That's why the flight simulator is the best piece of educational software ever made," says Shank.

**GENETIC CUES.** One of the key assumptions of VR work is that the brain can process information better when it is presented through sight, sound, and touch instead of just text or numbers. Scientists also are finding that the responses to certain visual cues—including hand-eye coordination and the ability to detect the edges of objects and to recognize movement across a meadow of grass—are encoded in genes. Our cave-dwelling forebears originally developed these responses in reaction to the world around them, says Ronald M. Pickett, professor of psychology at the University of Massachusetts at Lowell.

Pickett and others are designing software icons that mimic those cues. We want to trick the visual system to evoke quick, natural perceptual processes in the service of analyzing data," he says. To do that, he has created an icon that looks like grass. It changes length, curve, and arc to represent numeric data such as income level, age, and sex. Each icon can convey multiple characteristics

# GOING WHERE NO MINDS HAVE GONE BEFORE

To get a feel for what is different about virtual reality, meet Jaron Lanier, chairman of VPL Research Inc. Dreadlocks crown his ample frame. His Sausalito (Calif.) studio—he's an accomplished musician—is filled with exotic instruments. On the door hangs his image emblazoned on a psychedelic poster. The poster is hot in Europe, where VR is *très trendy* and Lanier is a cult figure, reflecting VPL's preeminent role among the start-ups that are pushing the technology's frontiers.

Lanier, 33, started VPL in his garage eight years ago with money he made from programming an Atari Corp. video game called Moondust. Fiddling with icons and graphics he hoped would make math easier led him to a more sweeping vision. Today, VPL sells hardware devices such as the Dataglove and Datasuit for navigating in virtual space, helmets that surround you with computer-generated worlds, and programming software that even children have used to create virtual environments—kids, and a few other customers, such as Boeing, SRI International, Matsushita, and MCA.

**THE 'BOOM.'** VR's big winners eventually should be heavyweights such as Intel, IBM, Apple, and Silicon Graphics—the makers of graphics chips and computers. Alan Meckler, publisher of the newsletter *The Virtual Reality Report*, sees liftoff toward the end of this decade. But whoever cashes in will owe a debt to VPL and many other innovators. Crystal River Engineering in Groveland, Calif., is selling acoustical circuit boards that let programmers put 3-D sound—say, the sound of a door opening and closing—in a virtual space. Fake Space Labs has invented a stereoscopic viewing device called the "boom"—as in boom microphone—that lets a person move around a virtual space by looking through a viewfinder.

Lanier thinks medicine will be VR's "monster market," partly because of the need for better visualization of diagnostic scans. At a recent San Diego conference, surgeon-inventors mingled with science fiction writers, while Sony Corp. marketers pitched high-definition-television screens. The other products discussed ranged from systems for doing remote surgery to 3-D data bases for analyzing casualty data in a war.

The core of such markets will be software, says Robert Jacobson, founder of WorlDesign in Seattle. StereoCad in Sunnyvale, Calif., and Virtus in Cary, N.C., specialize in architectural and engineering design programs. BioCad in Mountain View, Calif., sells "virtual chemistry" software that lets scientists create 3-D, interactive models of molecules and other chemical structures. Engineering Animation Inc. in Ames, Iowa, makes 3-D graphics and animation programs that recreate accident scenes for use in court. Both Sense8 and VPL sell "tool-kit" programs for VR software programmers. But they may not rule the market for long.

Autodesk Inc. in Sausalito, which has 700,000 customers for its computer-aided-design software, could have an edge when it comes out soon with its own tool-kit program. **BETTER ENTREE.** Such competition has begun to alarm Lanier, a major VPL shareholder. In May, he named a new chief executive: ex-Hewlett-Packard Co. executive Walt Fischer. As white collar as Lanier is not, Fischer may have better entrée to corporate customers. This could be crucial for VPL's plan to become a systems integrator, selling packaged solutions—not just components. "We've sold millions of dollars' worth of hobby stuff," says Lanier. "The transition now is into a real company."

Whether VPL and the other VR upstarts will prosper is impossible to predict. But even if they do not, pioneers such as Lanier are trailblazing a technology that is likely to benefit every industry that relies on computing.

*By Joan O'C. Hamilton in Sausalito, Calif.*

## PIONEERS IN VIRTUAL REALITY
### THESE VR LEADERS ARE ALL PRIVATE COMPANIES

| Company | Location | Employees | Founded |
|---|---|---|---|
| **VPL RESEARCH** Makes hardware and software, including DataGlove and EyePhones | FOSTER CITY, CALIF. | 25 | 1984 |
| **SENSE8** Creates programming packages for virtual worlds | SAUSALITO, CALIF. | 8 | 1990 |
| **FAKE SPACE LABS** Makes stereoscopic viewing device | MENLO PARK, CALIF. | 7 | 1989 |
| **SIMGRAPHICS** Develops engineering visualization programs | SOUTH PASADENA, CALIF. | 15 | 1985 |
| **GREENLEAF MEDICAL SYSTEMS** Adapting the DataGlove for use in medicine | PALO ALTO, CALIF. | 12 | 1988 |
| **EXOS** Sells a device that signals computers through gestures | WOBURN, MASS. | 25 | 1988 |

that can be comprehended at a glance.

Whether people experience virtual worlds as "real" doesn't depend entirely on real-time motion, graphics, or visual cues, however. One of the most difficult challenges is to imbue computer characters with humanlike qualities. As part of that effort, Joseph Bates, a computer scientist at Carnegie Mellon University in Pittsburgh, is trying to create VR drama—interactive programs in which computer characters and people collaborate to create stories or situations. At first, it's hard to understand how an animated landscape with four bouncing blobs could be relevant. The blobs' only activity is jumping up and down, and they are supposed to take turns "leading." But when one ball starts to dominate the activity, the others react. They change color, or slow down. One even turns from red to blue, retreating to a corner, its sides heaving, to . . . well, sulk.

The balls appear to be exhibiting emotion and acting independently because Bates and his colleagues have programmed them based on theories of behavior. These hold that emotion—and the behavior that results from it—arise from goals that are being met, opposed, or otherwise affected. When programmed this way, the blobs begin to act as if they have "personalities," and people can identify with them.

'BARFOGENIC ZONE.' Building on such work, researchers one day hope to populate virtual worlds with creatures—human-looking or not—that people interact with as they would another person. These characters might analyze a problem, monitor an experiment, or play the role of someone in a business simulation—a hot sales prospect, say. They would probably react to voice commands but would also need to convey and understand more subtle human communication such as body language. Sound fantastic? Not to Fujitsu Ltd., which has invested $250,000 in Bates's work. His work reinforces Fujitsu's research in "arti-ficial life," computer algorithms that behave like biological entities and could become the basis of computer-generated characters in VR worlds.

Fine-tuning the sensory and psychological factors that make a VR world "real" is a further technical challenge. Experience shows that VR viewers adjust to low-resolution monitors. The brain also accepts slow, jerky frame speed and much faster live action—30 frames per second. But in between lies what Thomas P. Piantanida, principal scientist of SRI International's Virtual Perception Program, calls the "barfogenic zone" —from 4 to 12 frames per second. At that speed, the confusion between what the brain expects and what it sees can make viewers sick. Until computers can create complex worlds with live motion, Piantanida's work suggests that it's better to run crude displays faster than to run detailed displays in the barfogenic zone.

Putting sound to virtual worlds is one more key to improving people's ability to absorb information. "Our ears point our eyes," says NASA Research Psychologist Elizabeth M. Wenzel, an expert in adding 3-D sound to virtual environments. A military pilot, for instance, often monitors as many as eight conversations from air and ground sources through the same earpiece. Wenzel says that making the sound appear to come from different directions helps pilots key in on high-priority information. A new circuit board developed by NASA and Crystal River Engineering Inc. that produces 3-D sound will make it easier to put sound in virtual worlds. The chips mimic the shape of sound waves as they hit the human ear from different directions, creating the illusion of distance as sounds grow louder and softer.

VR researchers are opening another portal to the brain through so-called force feedback. The idea is to build weight, resistance, or attraction into joy-sticks, so that VR voyagers can "feel" simulated objects. Researchers at Digital Equipment Corp. are working with outside chemists to simulate the forces of molecular attraction and repulsion. Their goal is to develop a system within two years that will help chemists feel these forces as they experiment with 3-D images of molecules to develop drugs and other chemicals. That's important because molecules that appear to be compatible often are not. Knowing this in advance could help scientists avoid blind alleys.

The more sophisticated VR worlds become, the more controversy they may generate. Some psychologists want to use VR in psychotherapy to alter the perspective of patients, or to recreate environments that cause stress or other problems as a way to help treat phobias, depressions, and schizophrenia. British psychologist Peter Ward, who plans to use VR to treat spider phobia, thinks some patients may feel more comfortable with a machine than with a human therapist.

Still, simulations with the power to make soldiers sweat might wreak havoc on fragile psyches. Indeed, widespread use of VR, some worry, could influence people in harmful ways. Could immersion in VR worlds incite violence, become addictive for some people, or lead to computer-generated manipulation of others? It will be years before anyone knows for sure. But, muses Bob Jacobs of Illusion Engineering, which develops military simulations: "We may eventually need a code of ethics for cyberspace."

In fact, a down-to-earth dilemma arose this year when a VR program helped convict a man of manslaughter in California (page 43). And some critics believe that VR training exercises could alter the view of what constitutes valuable work experience. Take two candidates for the job of nuclear-plant manager. Who should get the nod a veteran plant worker with a decade of no mistakes, or a less experienced candidate who scores higher in simulations of disaster? "This scares the hell out of some hierarchical types," says Michael W. McGreevy, principal engineer at

NASA's Aerospace Human Factors Research Div.

**BLURRY VISION.** Formidable hurdles remain before VR systems can reach their full potential. "We need a whole bunch of technologies that are still in their infancy," says VR pioneer Henry Fuchs, professor of computer science at the University of North Carolina. Researchers are only making slow headway toward improving today's often blurry head displays. And a camera that digitizes the image of a room and turns it into a VR environment remains elusive:

So far, computers can't distinguish between edges, lines, and shadows sufficiently to translate a video image into 3-D. It's no easy task to get so many disciplines—programming, behavioral science, and hardware design—to work together to produce those advances.

The task is so arduous that some VR advocates worry about being engulfed by the cycle of hype, then hopelessness, that befell artificial intelligence. Still, VR represents a potent direction in technology. Inevitably, as computers gain more

power, more work will focus on making the interactions between humans and machines more efficient. Watch a roomful of charged-up players in Chicago's Battletech Center go at it—oblivious to the real world—and you can't help thinking that you're seeing the makings of the ultimate tool for the mind.

*By Joan O'C. Hamilton in San Francisco, with Emily T. Smith in New York, Gary McWilliams in Boston, Evan I. Schwartz in New York, John Carey in Washington, and bureau reports*

# FAST MONEY

## Gridlock alert! A trillion a day in electronic money makes the financial world go round. Could it spin out of control?

## Peter Passell

*Peter Passell writes about economics for* The New York Times.

THE OFFICE BUILDING, A dreary block of reinforced concrete and glass on the seedy western fringes of midtown Manhattan, hardly rates a second glance. Nor does a dimly lit extension to the marble and steel lobby tucked beyond the elevator bank and leading to an unmarked beige door, discreetly monitored by a television camera recessed in the ceiling.

If it all seems unremarkable and uninviting, that is by design, something you begin to understand the moment you walk through the door. For you enter a maze of locked anterooms, rigged to trap, or at least slow, a determined intruder. And beyond the maze sits the object of these security measures, the computer system that is the heart of global capitalism. Here, coded requests to make payments of tens or hundreds of millions of dollars on behalf of this emir or that aerospace conglomerate pour in through 134 dedicated telephone lines. Twenty-two electronic black boxes made by the Racal-Guardata Corporation screen the incoming requests for coding flaws that would expose an illicit message before hand-

ing off the orders to a pair of Unisys A-15 J mainframe computers. In less than a second, the funds are on their way to Tokyo or Riyadh, or anywhere else money talks.

While the featureless facades of the refrigerator-size mainframes and the casual slouch of a few technicians in front of their video monitors give little hint of the scope of the operation, the stream of messages is really a torrent of unimaginable scale. Each business day, nearly $1 trillion—more than the entire money supply of the United States—moves through the machines. Were the flow to stop unexpectedly, financial empires would teeter and governments tremble.

The scene could be the prop for a running joke in a Vonnegut novel—the one in which the fate of civilization rests in the hands of a bored switchboard operator. And there are unmistakable overtones of "Star Trek" and "Mission Impossible."

Actually it's not fantasy at all, but Chips, the Clearing House Interbank Payments System owned by 11 big New York banks. And to the thousands of businesses and government agencies that have come to depend on it, there is nothing sinister about a computerized system that reliably zaps multimillion-dollar payments around the globe for less than the price of a first-class postage stamp. Indeed, Chips is widely ad-

mired as a triumphant marriage of information processing technology and free enterprise, the next best thing to a perpetual-motion money-market machine.

But not every economics heavyweight gazes so benignly at Chips—or, more generally, at the uncharted frontiers of finance of which Chips is a part, where money consists of magnetized specks of iron oxide in computer memories and great fortunes move from continent to continent as weightless photons through the electromagnetic ether.

Some worry that electronic money and the speed of its transfer are pushing the control of the world's money beyond the conservative reach of the Federal Reserve and other central government banks. Some focus on the coincidence of electronic transfer and increased volatility in financial markets, which they believe gives lie to the hallowed axiom that markets can never be too cheap or too easy to use. Certainly, the recent currency crisis in Europe did nothing to allay these fears.

The most widespread concern, though—one that could make Europe's currency woes look like the failure of a small-town bank by comparison—is financial gridlock. In the old banking world of paper money and clerks in green eyeshades, the wheels of financial commerce ground slowly, but with

predictable regularity. By contrast, if something were to go seriously awry in the nearly perfect world of electronic money, the whole system could come to a wrenching halt in the twinkling of a gigabyte.

First things first. People make most of their purchases with coins or currency. Indeed, according to a back-of-the-envelope calculation by the Federal Reserve, a shade less than 85 percent of all dollar payments—everything from tipping the bartender to buying the Sunday paper—is made in cash. Checks account for most of the rest, while electronic transfers bring up the rear with a mere 2 percent of total transactions.

**But this order is reversed if the count is made in total dollars in transit, rather than by the number of times money changes hands. Cash covers less than 1 percent of the total value of transactions, while money flashed from computer to computer accounts for five out of every six dollars that move in the economy. And while just one transaction in a thousand is made on the two great "wholesale" electronic transfer systems, Chips along with the network run by the Federal Reserve push around a stunning $1.7 trillion a day — 80 percent of the total payments made worldwide in dollars.**

What's more, the volume

of business on these lightning-fast systems has grown at a rate hardly anyone would have imagined possible a few years ago. In 1980, the daily flow of electronic money was roughly 12 times the balances held in accounts at the Federal Reserve — the money that banks use to settle their debts at the end of each day. By 1991, the daily flow had reached 55 times this base of bank reserves.

Why the explosion of electronic money? Start with the spectacular expansion of Government securities, used to finance the Federal deficit. These securities are, in effect, money that pays interest — the perfect medium for speculating or hedging in dollars. Add the fact that the Government securities market was automated in the 1980's, reducing the mechanical obstacles to transferring ownership by wire: "A Treasury bill," points out James Grant, the editor of Grant's Interest Rate Observer, "no longer exists except as an entry on a computer tape."

Now factor in the growth of the global economy. When securities brokers in Milan or shirt factories in Thailand do international business, they usually conduct it in the only truly international money, the dollar. And when they convert their own money to United States currency (or back again), the dollar "leg" of the transaction usually goes through Chips in New York because the process is swift and cheap. Chips charges the 122 banks now on line to its computers a mere 18 cents per payment order — no matter what the size — and even less if their monthly transactions exceed 80,000.

Cheap and easy is precisely what modern telecommunications and data processing is supposed to be about. And the fact that the world's big economic players want to do most of their playing in American dollars under the rules set by American institutions is surely a tribute to the efficiency and

stability of the American financial system.

So what's the beef? Some analysts worry that the speed, scale and complexity of electronic funds transfer has left the global payments system vulnerable to accident or malice — or worse, a planetwide financial stall caused by a sudden loss of confidence.

JOHN F. LEE, PRESIdent of the New York Clearing House Association, which runs Chips, hastens to point out that Chips has certainly not ignored the risks of fire, mechanical failure or even terrorism. The Manhattan site houses two computers, either of which could handle the business on its own. And the computers themselves are insulated from potential disaster in a variety of ways. The machines run on current from storage batteries fed by the city power grid; that way, the system is protected against surges and outages. A fire in the control room could be snuffed out in seconds by filling the chamber with Halon gas. Moreover, somewhere in New Jersey — Lee is not eager to say just where — Chips has two backup computers linked to an independent communications grid that are ready to process funds transfers at a moment's notice.

The one time backup was needed (Oct. 18, 1991, after a hardware breakdown took out both New York computers), the system worked flawlessly; processing was interrupted for just five minutes. Lee notes that users of the system would never have known about the failure if they hadn't been told.

Chips is well armored against theft. While the speed of transfer and the staggering sums routinely processed make fraud tempting, Lee argues that the problems in penetrating the system and making off with the cash are daunting.

A thief would have to tap into the dedicated phone lines that link member

banks with Chips. Then he would have to crack the electronic authentication barrier — the supersleuth equivalent of a mathematical password — that stands between the central computers and the outside world.

Simply intercepting a message and changing a funds-transfer instruction would get the miscreant nowhere: the code that must be attached to each message is uniquely linked to the content of the message. An order to move, say, $4.2 million requires a different code from one for $42 million. And when a message cannot be authenticated by the black boxes, the dedicated phone line to the transmitting financial institution is automatically severed.

Finally, a thief would have to lay his hands on the fraudulently transmitted funds at the receiving end before the discrepancy was discovered — most likely before the end of the day in which the evil deed was done.

There has, in fact, been a theft using Chips. But that was an inside job, one in which thieves used the system to wire money embezzled from the second-largest bank in Switzerland to the New York branch of an Australian bank. The coded message received by Chips was entirely legitimate.

The story of that robbery, pieced together from Australian news accounts and confirmed by bank representa-

tives, is remarkable for both its simplicity and ingenuity. Vannyasingham Sothirasan, a Malaysian con man, apparently convinced two employees of the Swiss Bank Corporation in Zurich, Basant Singh and Martin Hauseder, to serve as inside men in the plot. They succeeded in forging an order to wire some $20 million to the State Bank of New South Wales on Dec. 7, 1989 — money that had supposedly been deposited in the Swiss Bank Corporation the day before.

But how to claim the money once it arrived and make a clean getaway? Posing as an investment banker, Sothirasan had earlier cut a deal with Malcolm Edwards, an Australian tycoon in desperate need of cash to keep his real-estate empire afloat. The $20 million was to be the first installment of a $500 million loan coming from a fictitious bank, the Beyina Merchant Bank located in the West African nation of Cameroon.

Of the $20 million and change that was transferred to Edwards's account, some $10 million was apparently owed to Sothirasan and his associates by the "borrower" as a fee for arranging the "loan." These funds were quickly wired out of the State Bank of New South Wales by Edwards, broken down into smaller bites and then rewired to other banks.

Edwards used part of the balance to pay off debts and shipped the rest to Edwards-owned companies in Hong Kong and Fiji. Days later, when the Swiss Bank Corporation discovered there had never been a $20 million deposit received on Dec. 6, less than $100,000 was left in the New South Wales bank account.

This crime didn't pay — or, at least, it probably won't. Sothirasan, Singh and Hauseder were tracked down and returned to Switzerland. All three were convicted; if their legal appeals fail, they will serve sentences of two and a half to three and a half years. At last report, though, only $8 million of the $20 million had been recovered. Civil suits against Edwards's companies and the State Bank of New South Wales are pending in Australia.

THE REMOTE THREATS of computer failure or fraud in Chips or one of the other big money networks are enough to keep the techies on their toes. But the scenario that really causes heartburn among the economists who pay attention to electronic transfers is something called systemic credit risk.

If you pay the dry cleaner in currency of the realm, the payment is final — that's why the stuff is called legal tender. If you pay the dry cleaner by check, the settlement is "subject to collection," as they say in the fine print on your bank statement. But even if the check bounces and the dry cleaner takes you to court, the national system of making payments with written orders to transfer money from one bank account to another would hardly be threatened.

Now look again at Chips, where 122 banks are zapping orders to pay to each other at a rate of about $2 billion a minute. These payments aren't final until the end of the day, when all debts are cleared by shuffling dollars among the accounts the banks keep with the Federal Reserve.

Note, too, that the large number of banks and the incredible volume of transactions (typically 150,000 a day and, on occasion, as many as 300,000) make it impractical to make settlements on a bank-to-bank basis. Instead, what everybody owes everybody else is netted: Each institution that is in arrears makes payments into the kitty, much the way the "bank" settles accounts for a half-dozen players at the end of a night of poker.

"Multilateral" clearing of accounts through Chips is thus a daisy chain in which each bank's ability to meet its obligations depends on every other's. And that raises a natural question, one that people have been asking since the early 1980's, when the sums

moving through Chips began to approach gee-whiz magnitudes: What would happen if a bank that owed money to the system failed to come up with the money at settlement time?

Under the rules of last resort adopted by Chips, the deceptively simple answer is that the day's transactions would be "unwound." That means that every transfer involving the defaulting bank would be removed from the day's settlement. But apart from the inconceivable complexity of sorting through the enormous volume of transfers and informing everyone from Exxon to the central bank of Burundi that the money never arrived, an "unwind" could also generate a cascade of failures in other banks that were owed money by the defaulting institution.

That's not just a guess. David B. Humphrey, a former Fed official now teaching at Florida State University, used the actual transactions from a day in 1983 to simulate the consequences of unwinding after the hypothetical failure of just one large bank. Humphrey found that 24 banks ended up owing more money than the capital of the banks' owners.

This does not mean all 24 would have gone belly up. Presumably most of the payment orders flowing through the defaulting bank would have been honored in the end; thus, most promises to pay by the bank would eventually have been collectible. But the likely consequence would still have been days or weeks of financial gridlock, in which tens or even hundreds of billions of dollars would have been frozen and hundreds of corporations would have faced a harrowing struggle to find cash.

And while the experts are reluctant to speculate about it on the record, there is a chance a settlement crisis in Chips could interact with a crisis in the securities markets, turning a merely hairy situation into a catastrophe. Imagine, for example, the

## How do you guard against the Big One, the accident that no one imagines?

fallout if Chips had failed to settle according to Hoyle during that awful day in October 1987, when America's stock markets lost $500 billion in value in a single trading session.

One way around this systemic credit risk, suggests Prof. Elinor Solomon, an economist at George Washington University, would be to work out a way to make every payment final the microsecond it is completed. That, in effect, is just what the Federal Reserve does with the transfers on its own electronic system: If a bank cannot settle at the end of the day, the Fed covers its obligations with a loan. Once, it actually made an overnight advance of $23.6 billion — yes, billion — to the Bank of New York in order to settle the day's accounts on transfers of Government securities that got fouled up in a software snafu.

This story had a happy ending: The Fed got its money back the next day, with interest at a 7.5 percent annual rate. And truth be told, Uncle Sam was never in danger of ending up out of pocket, because the loan was fully collateralized: the Government securities whose sale had caused all the problems never left the Fed's metaphoric vault. But one might ask what would have happened if a similar accident had occurred on Chips, where daylight overdrafts are not backed by the full faith and credit of the United States.

The best answer is that this kind of accident could not have happened. Chips payments must be initiated by the payer, making an involuntary, sorcerer's apprentice-style accumulation of overdrafts impossible. Besides, Chips places a cap on the level of debt that may be incurred by any single bank.

THAT STILL LEAVES THE question of how to guard against the Big One, the accident no one imagines before it happens.

Emergency loans to cope with liquidity problems are available to any solvent bank — that, in fact, is what the Federal Reserve was invented to do. Thus, any American bank that couldn't settle its daily bill with Chips simply because it lacked liquidity would be eligible for a helping hand from Uncle.

Robert E. Hall, an economist at the Hoover Institution in Stanford, Calif., points out that a broader form of Government insurance against default — even default generated by true insolvency — is conceivable. But Hall is hardly enthusiastic about assigning a new insurance function to the good folks who brought us the savings-and-loan crisis.

Chips's own answer to the challenge of systemic risk is a combination of "real time" credit surveillance combined with group self-insurance. Each Chips bank now sets a limit on how much it is willing to be owed by every other Chips bank at any moment in the day. And the total amount any single bank can collectively owe to the others is automatically capped. Chips's computers give all member banks, as well as Chips's own staff, the capacity to monitor the ebb and flow as it is happening.

Moreover, since 1990 all the banks have been required to put up securities as collateral against the risk of failure by any other participating bank — enough, collectively, to cover the risk of three big bank failures. If, say, one member of Chips couldn't come up with $2 billion at settlement time, the others would absorb the losses as a group and then try to get the money back through negotiation or litigation.

E. Gerald Corrigan, the president of the New York Federal Reserve Bank, while not "declaring victory," is confident that Chips could now withstand a very large shock. Michael Urkowitz, an executive vice president of Chase Manhattan Bank who is in charge of Chase's mammoth funds-transfer operations, is more emphatic: "I believe in my heart and soul," he says, "that the gridlock potential is small to nil."

What all the experts fear is what they do not know. Could the technology of funds transfer outrace the mechanisms for control, as it may have done in the early years of Chips? Could Wall Street, in its relentless quest for new products to peddle, invent one that unwittingly destabilizes the payments system? Could a competing payments network offshore, operating under other rules in other time zones, generate some perverse synergy that fatally damages Chips?

Almost anything is possible, suggests James Grant, "in a world in which electronic leverage — the ratio of newfangled photons to old-fashioned banking dollars — is enormous."

# Medical Technology 'Arms Race' Adds Billions to the Nation's Bills

## Concern Over Costs Prompts Limits on Scanners

### Andrew Pollack

*Special to The New York Times*

PALTO ALTO, Calif.—Dr. George M. Segall held up a set of multicolored images of a patient's heart. On one side, the red was not as sharp, indicating that blood flow to that part of the heart was lacking.

The pictures were taken with a machine, one of only 50 in the nation, that has just been installed at the Palo Alto Veterans Administration Hospital, where Dr. Segall is deputy chief of nuclear medicine.

The machine, known as a PET scanner, can peer into the workings of internal organs, providing doctors with previously unobtainable information. It can tell, for instance, whether heart tissue is alive or dead and whether it is worthwhile for a cardiologist to attempt open-heart surgery.

But such information doesn't come cheap. "You're talking about a five-and-a-half-million-dollar investment," said Dr. Segall, who is also an assistant professor at Stanford Medical School, referring to the cost of the scanner and of a cyclotron that makes the radioisotopes administered to the patient for the test. "It's by far one of the most expensive technologies available now."

Once, an advance like the PET, which stands for positron emission tomography, would have been welcomed into the nation's arsenal of medical tools. After all, Americans want, and feel entitled to, the best medical care, regardless of cost, and doctors want to provide it. And with insurance companies or government programs paying the bills, neither patient nor physician has had much reason to weigh the costs and benefits.

But the future of the PET scanner in medical care is far from assured. A move is afoot, driven by strapped Federal health agencies and insurance companies, to rein in what some have called a medical technology arms race. Their hope, a revolutionary one for American medicine, is to limit the uses of costly machines and procedures to instances in which the benefits have been shown to be commensurate with the expense.

Fueling this move is a growing recognition that the uncontrolled use of high-technology medical equipment and procedures, from coronary bypass surgery to new scanning machines to lithotripters that blast kidney stones with shock waves, helps drive the relentless increase in medical costs, which now account for 12 percent of the gross national product.

PET scanning comes on the heels of other major advantages in diagnostic imaging. CAT or CT scanning, which stands for computerized axial tomography, appeared in the 1970's and represented a great advance over conventional X-rays, but at a cost of up to $500 per scan. Magnetic resonance imaging, or M.R.I. scans, appeared in the mid-1980's and offered advantages over CAT scans, but again at a higher cost, up to $1,000 a scan. PET scan fees are higher still, reaching $2,500.

Moreover, there is widespread agreement that many advanced, expensive medical procedures are overused. Coronary bypass surgery, for instance, is performed 300,000 times a year in the United States and accounts for about $1 of every $50 spent on health care. But a study of the Rand Corporation a few years ago found that more than 40 percent of such operations did very little, if anything, for the patients. M.R.I. scans, doctors say, are often done to rule out a minute chance of brain injury, for example, and perhaps most of all to protect the doctor from malpractice suits.

The United States relies far more heavily on technology than other advanced nations. A 1989 study by the American Medical Association found that on a per capita basis the United States had four times as many M.R.I. machines as Germany and eight times as many as Canada. American doctors performed open-heart surgery 2.6 times as often as Canadian doctors and 4.4 times as often as German doctors.

### Driven by Society
### Breakthroughs As Birthright

Technology is only one factor in soaring health care expenses, and diagnostic imaging is only one factor in medical technology. Still, an examination of how such imaging machines are sold, paid for and used reveals much about the medical and business issues feeding the growth in medical technology and how difficult it would be to rein it in.

"The pressure of the introduction of new technologies is inexorable," said Dr. Seymour Perry, director of a program on technology and health care at Georgetown University. "Every day there's a claim of a new breakthrough. Our society wants that. We are different from other societies in the world."

The National Institutes of Health spend billions of dollars each year on medical research. A huge medical technology industry is also in place, spewing out streams of innovations and marketing them heavily, with profit rather than social utility often its prime motivator.

Nor should society try to stifle new technology, experts agree. In addition to providing better health care, technology can lower costs. A new technique for removing gall bladders, known as laparoscopy, can be finished in a day compared with the older approach, which required up to a week in the hospital.

The case of medical imaging is an example of how technology can spread virtually unchecked by considerations of cost. One reason PET machines are undergoing scrutiny is that the last great innovation in diagnostic imaging, the magnetic resonance imager, spread rapidly after it appeared in the middle 1980's. Although offering wonderful benefits, M.R.I. scans are often used to

achieve marginal gains, experts say, and sometimes under conditions that raise at least a suspicion of a conflict of interest.

There are now 2,000 such M.R.I. machines, which cost $1 million to $2 million each, in the United States. Analysts estimate that more than five million M.R.I. scans were performed in the nation last year, at prices of $600 to $1,000 each. That means that magnetic resonance imaging alone is adding about $5 billion to the nation's health bill.

"People want this smart test," said John Caronna, professor of clinical neurology at New York Hospital/ Cornell Medical Center in Manhattan. "There's no way to shut it off. The doctors crave it, it's reassuring, and the patients crave it."

But some critics say the test is overused. "There was never any effort on the part of payers or providers or society in general to develop a rational policy on how to use them," said John L. Cova, director of medical technology assessment for the Health Insurance Association of America, a trade group representing 300 insurance companies. The M.R.I. scans are "used in an inappropriate way in many instances," he said. "It's almost a joke: 'Give him an M.R.I.' "

### Driven by Profits
### Keeping Up With Rivals

A set of forces, indicative of basic traits of the nation's health system that undermine efforts at cost-control, brought about the rapid spread of M.R.I. machines and procedures. Manufacturers constantly pushed new machines on the market. The purchase of a machine by one hospital inspired others to want to keep up. Entrepreneurs, sensing big profits, set up specialized imaging centers, often attracting doctors, who could refer patients to the centers, as co-owners.

Having bought such expensive machines, hospitals and imaging centers had an incentive to push as

many patients through as possible to pay off the machines. Fear of malpractice also contributed to the machines' use. And the tests were largely profitable, in part because of Medicare reimbursement rates that over-compensated radiologists, in the view of many experts, and that failed to come down as the technology became more widespread.

To be sure, M.R.I. machines can have enormous medical value. They use radio waves and powerful magnets to take pictures of the inside of the body and have been particularly useful in finding anomalies like brain tumors and spinal cord injuries. Unlike the earlier CAT scan, M.R.I. does not expose the patient to radiation. Both M.R.I. and CAT scans have largely replaced riskier and more painful procedures, like pneumo-encephalography, in which spinal fluid is removed and air pumped into the brain.

After Medicare greed to reimburse patients for M.R.I. scans in 1985, sales of the machines rose to about $500 million a year in the United States. The leading manufacturer is the General Electric Company, followed by Siemens, Toshiba, Philips N.V. and Picker International.

Hospitals, sometimes under pressure from their own doctors, pushed to buy machines to retain their competitive status as full-service, modern health care centers.

Some states tried to limit the spread of machines under programs that require hospitals to obtain a certificate of need before buying new equipment. But private imaging centers, not subject to those controls, sprang up, including Medical Imaging Centers of America in San Diego and Health Images Inc. in Atlanta.

The New York State Department of Health, for instance, approved the purchase of 43 magnetic resonance imagers in state hospitals. But there are probably an additional 35 private imaging centers in New York City and Long Island alone, said John Milliren, director of appropriateness review for the New York State Department of Health.

## The Imaging Arms Race: Three Scanners

**CAT SCAN**

In computerized axial tomography, also known as computerized tomography (C.T.), X-rays rotate around the body, producing pictures of cross-sectional slices of tissue.

**Common uses:** Diagnosis of brain disorders, sinus problems, complex fractures and abscesses. Evaluation of problems in chest and abdominal organs like liver, spleen and pancreas.

**Cost of Machine:** $400,000 to $1.2 million

**Typical fee:** $300 to $500

**Installed in 1990:** 4,900

**Advantages:** Compared with conventional X-ray, provides far higher resolution and contrast in soft tissues, and useful images of adjacent "slices" of tissue. Taking only minutes, it is often best alternative for evaluating critical injuries.

**Disadvantages:** Less soft-tissue contrast than M.R.I. Exposure to radiation.

**M.R.I. SCAN**

In magnetic resonance imaging devices the body is subjected to radio waves in the presence of a powerful magnetic field. The waves excite atoms in body tissue, which emit detectable energy as they return to an unexcited state. Like CAT scan, produces cross-sectional pictures.

**Common uses:** Detection of brain tumors, disorders of the spinal column, multiple sclerosis. Evaluation of knees and other joints.

**Cost of machine:** $1.2 million to $2.5 million

**Typical fee:** $600 to $1,000

**Installed in 1990:** 1,990

**Advantages:** Compared with CAT, gives more subtle discrimination of soft tissue and is unaffected by bone, which limits CAT in lower head and spine. Can measure blood flow, enables study of cardiovascular structure without injection of agent to provide contrast. No exposure to radiation.

**Disadvantages:** Exam is slow, often lasting one hour; not as good as CAT for images of abdominal area.

**PET SCAN**

In positron emission tomography, radioactive isotopes are injected or inhaled and absorbed by organs. Energy from radioactive decay is detected, providing evidence of where the isotopes are being used.

**Common uses:** Evaluation of the health of heart tissue. Early detection of neurological diseases. Guiding surgery for epilepsy.

**Cost of machine:** $3.6 million to $4.2 million. Includes $1 million cost of cyclotron.

**Typical fee:** $1,500 to $2,000

**Advantages:** Provides valuable data on tissue function, metabolism and other subtle biochemical processes, not just structure as with other imaging devices.

**Disadvantages:** Exams may last more than an hour. Can require presence of cyclotron to generate short-lived isotopes for injection. Exposure to radiation.

*Sources: Drew Consultants, Inc., Concord, Mass.; Institute for Clinical PET*

---

Spurring the formation of these centers was the possibility of big profits. A 1988 letter seeking investors for one such center, East Bay Medical Imaging Services in Castro Valley, Calif., forecast a return to investors "in excess of 25 percent per year and in many cases substantially more." Similarly, Stuart, Coleman & Company of New York solicited investors for several imaging centers with the promise of a cash distribution of 400 percent over 10 years.

The way to realize those profits is to run many tests. A study by the New York State Department of Health estimated that a high volume imaging center could reduce the cost per scan below $250. Despite high volume, prices have not fallen.

To provide themselves with a steady stream of customers, imaging centers often sold part ownership to doctors, who could refer patients for tests. A recent survey for Florida's Health Care Cost Containment Board found that 75 percent of the imaging centers in the state had doctors as part or full owners.

Critics say this practice gives doctors a financial incentive to order tests that might not otherwise be called for.

*'A Black Eye' for Medicine*

"It's going to give all medicine a black eye before it's over," said Daniel P. Chisholm, a radiologist in Little Rock, Ark. "There are too many studies being performed that are not necessary."

A study by Bruce J. Hillman of the University of Arizona published in the New England Journal of Medicine in December found that doctors who owned X-ray or ultrasound machines did 4 to 4.5 times as many tests as doctors who referred patients to radiologists, and also charged more for each test than radiologists did, over $100 more for the ultrasound exams.

Paying doctors a fee for each patient they refer to an imaging center would constitute an illegal kickback scheme, but a mere investment in such a center by a doctor is not illegal.

Starting next January, however, it will become illegal for doctors to refer Medicare patients for blood, urine and other tests to clinical laboratories in which they own an interest. Representative Pete Stark, Democrat of California, who wrote the law, has vowed to try to expand it to cover imaging centers.

### Driven by the System
### Legal Fears and High Fees

Even without the financial incentives, doctors say, there are numerous incentives for ordering diagnostic tests. One is the fear of a malpractice lawsuit if a doctor misses a problem. Malpractice suits are less of a threat in other countries because of different cultural traditions and legal approaches.

Another factor is that there are simply no incentives not to order a scan. The patient has little incentive to refuse a test because insurance usually covers it. And while doctors and patients might think twice if the imaging procedure were painful or risky, that is not the case with M.R.I., although some patients become claustrophobic inside the device during the nearly hourlong test.

"Because it's so good, it's done all the time," said Dr. Caronna, the New York neurologist.

Dr. Caronna said that 90 percent of the time that neurologists order M.R.I. scans no structural damage to the patient's nervous system is detected. Still, he said, ruling out such problems is valuable information in itself.

*Higher Fees for Specialists*

In addition to worrying about overuse of such tests, some say their prices are needlessly high.

In part, this is because the medical system has always paid doctors more for performing sophisticated procedures than for more routine medical care. A study by Victor R. Fuchs and James S. Hahn of Stanford found that doctors in the United States are paid 80 percent more than those in Canada for routine patient evaluation and management, but three times as much for procedures.

Radiologists are the most highly paid specialists, second only to surgeons, according to the American Medical Association. The mean income after expenses for radiologists was $210,500 in 1989, as against an average for all doctors of $155,800.

One reason procedures like M.R.I. tests start out being expensive is that the technology is new. But the price did not fall even as the technology spread.

Blue Shield of California for instance, paid for 1,728 M.R.I. brain scans in 1987 at an average payment of $647. In 1989, it paid for twice as many procedures, 3,578, at an average payment of $708.

"Generally speaking, once a certain level of cost is established, it only goes in one direction from there, and that's up," said Randy Horn, a senior vice president of Mutual of Omaha, an insurance company.

## Stepping on the Brakes
## Forcing Doctors To Consider Cost

Society is now trying to contain its mushrooming health-care costs. Medicare is moving toward a system of payments to doctors based on relative value of the effort involved. The system will generally reduce payments to specialists like radiologists and surgeons.

Already, payments for radiological services are being cut about 20 percent in stages, starting in 1989. This year, Congress voted a special 10 percent cut in the Medicare payments for M.R.I. and CAT scans performed in imaging centers.

Medicare is also changing its rules on how it will reimburse hospitals for capital expenditures. The new rules will make hospitals "think twice" about buying expensive equipment like scanners, said Larry Haimovitch, a medical technology consultant in San Francisco.

In what could be the biggest change, Medicare is also planning to consider cost effectiveness, not just medical effectiveness, in deciding whether to pay for procedures and technology.

*Ethical Questions*

But Medicare officials say they must first develop a methodology for determining cost effectiveness. Medical experts say this could involve some ethically touchy questions, like how valuable is it to keep an elderly person alive for six more months. Or what is the value of a diagnostic imaging procedure that detects a disease for which there is no treatment?

Into this more hostile environment steps the PET scanner, which is even more expensive than the M.R.I. machine and draws fees of $1,500 to $2,500. While CAT and M.R.I. scans show the structure of internal organs, PET scans show the functioning of organs by their uptake of radioactively tagged glucose and other substances.

In heart disease, a PET scan can tell whether heart tissue that appears to be dead is in fact still alive and might be salvaged. PET scans have also proven of great value in guiding surgery to remove part of the brain in people with epilepsy, said John C. Mazziotta, a professor of neurology and radiology at the University of California at Los Angeles. PET scans also show promise for being able to diagnose neurological diseases like Alzheimer's and Huntington's, something that cannot be done with CAT or M.R.I. scans.

*Lobbying for the PET*

But insurance companies are being cautious. So far they will reimburse for PET scans only in selected cases and are carefully weighing whether to extend coverage. The Health Insurance Association of America, for instance, has organized two seminars on PET scans for insurance company executives, the first of a series of seminars the organization plans to hold on new technologies. The Federal Office of Health Technology Assessment, which advises Medicare and other Federal health insurance programs, is also studying PET scans.

Supporters of PET scans, including manufacturers and doctors and hospitals that have used the machines, banded together a year ago to form the Institute for Clinical PET, to win reimbursement for the machines.

The group is financing clinical trials to show how PET scans can improve the outcome for patients. It has also organized conferences and studies on cost and reimbursement issues. Health experts say the fact that such lobbying effort has to be mounted is one of the most visible signs of the changing economics of medical technology.

# Employment and the Workplace

Whether we work and the kind of work we do influence our standard of living, our social status, our self-image and even our sense of spiritual or moral worth. As societies move through various stages of technological change, the nature of work is correspondingly altered. In this process, new jobs are created, while others become obsolete and disappear. During the Industrial Revolution, for example, many people worried that mass unemployment and hardship would result as machines displaced human labor.

While it is true that industrialization made certain types of jobs obsolete, many more different jobs were created. According to U.S. census records, there were only 323 different occupations in 1850. Now there are more than

20,000 job specialties. Furthermore, social reforms eased competition for jobs and gave workers more time for personal and educational pursuits. These include a shortened work week, annual vacation time, paid retirement, and prolonged schooling for the young. Rather than causing impoverishment, these reforms have enabled wages and living standards to rise immeasurably.

The contemporary work scene is not without problems, however. Many of today's jobs require little skill and offer low wages. Some are dangerous. Too many people are unable to find work at all. And as computing technologies enter the workplace at an accelerating pace, many of the same concerns expressed during the Industrial Revolution are again being raised.

One of the most pervasive worries is that new technologies will eliminate many of the jobs that currently exist. Automation and off-shore production have already cost thousands of manufacturing jobs, and the same forces are starting to threaten some clerical jobs as well. There is further fear that the number of new jobs that are created will be less than the number lost. Others claim that existing jobs will be deskilled and the majority of newly created jobs will also be in low-skill, low-pay fields. Optimists, on the other hand, predict that average jobs in the future will be more skilled, more satisfying, and better paying than now.

A Canadian study by Graham S. Lowe (1991) found that white-collar workers tended to report that computers and automation had led to increased job skills and had made their work more challenging and interesting. However, there is no question that computers make a lot of jobs easier (and duller). Supermarket cashiers, for instance, need only a fraction of the skills that were required before bar code scanners became common. As these examples show, deskilling and upgrading are both possible, but they may not be equally probable. In order for jobs and workers to become more skilled (and for displaced workers to move into higher-skilled jobs) there must be a widespread system for retraining those whose skills become obsolete. In "The Skilling of America," Jack Gordon argues that in order for corporations to remain competitive in the new global, high-tech economy, they should be upgrading jobs and training workers to fill them. He claims, however, that most businesses are "looking for ways to cut wages

instead of for ways to skill up jobs." As a result, argues Gordon, the United States could be on the road to resembling a Third World country.

Working at home via computer and telecommunications is an option that is becoming possible for growing numbers of workers, but so far the practice has been controversial and resisted by some managers and unions. In "Telecommuting: A Better Way to Work?" Bob Filipczak identifies several issues related to telework. He argues that although it is not a perfect option for everyone, it does offer several attractive features over more traditional work arrangements. Filipczak also offers some advice on how to make telecommuting successful.

In the next article, the same author discusses some of the legal aspects of the *Americans With Disabilities Act* (ADA) as well as recent technical advances that increase the employment options for disabled workers. As he points out, both employers and workers have a lot to gain by making "reasonable accommodations" to bring disabled employees into the workplace.

In the final article in this section, Brian Hayes takes a philosophical look at the do-it-yourself movement. Technology is making it easier to bypass some of the steps (and jobs) in a complicated sequence of tasks. For instance, with computer-aided design (CAD) engineers can do their own drafting. Current trends, says Hayes, appear to be "bad news" for several occupations. Nevertheless, he notes several reasons to be optimistic about the "do-it-yourself phenomenon."

## Looking Ahead: Challenge Questions

In "The Skilling of America," Jack Gordon describes the training programs of some very large, wealthy corporations. Are the kinds of programs described by Gordon realistic for most organizations (that typically have between a few dozen and a few hundred employees)? What kinds of training strategies could "typical" firms adopt?

Highly trained professionals such as physicians and lawyers sell their scarce, valuable, and expert knowledge. We now see that some of this expert knowledge is being packaged in easy to operate "do-it-yourself" computer programs. What are some of the positive and negative implications of consumers bypassing professionals on legal and medical matters?

# THE SKILLING OF AMERICA

## Do we want to skill up or dumb down jobs? It's time to decide. And blowing smoke at the issue won't help.

**Jack Gordon**

*Jack Gordon is editor of* TRACING.

*Jack Gordon is editor of* TRAINING.

*OUR STORY SO FAR. . . .*

Hunter-gatherers invented agriculture and stopped roaming around all the time. Cities resulted. These were populated in part by tradespeople, artsy-craftsy types who took clay and metal and leather and cotton, turned them into pots and tools and sandals and textiles, and sold them. Then the Industrial Age showed up. People went to work in factories, where big machines made tools and textiles and newfangled gadgets more economically than artsy-craftsy types could.

In America, many of the people available to work in factories were illiterate immigrants. The big machines were alien and baffling to them. Things looked bad. Then Frederick W. Taylor taught factory owners how to design jobs that were extremely easy to learn. The way to do this was to study the production steps the machines could not perform by themselves, and break them down into simple subtasks. Each subtask became a job; each tiny piece of the original production process that an artsy-craftsy type used to perform all by himself—each decontextualized particle of that erstwhile trade—turned into something for a person to do all day, every day. An illiterate immigrant could learn to do such a job very quickly. So could an extremely stupid person. Stupidity was a blessing, in fact, because if you had any brains or imagination at all, one of these jobs would quickly bore you right out of your skull. The only thinking to be done was done by managers, college-degreed professionals and some skilled technicians like machinists and tool-and-die makers. Taylor still catches a lot of guff for this, even though he wasn't really such a bad guy.

Then more and more people started to work in offices instead of factories. Any fool could see that the Information Age would be along shortly, but a lot of office work nevertheless was designed very much like factory work: Each person did one little fragment of some larger task, like "claims processing," then passed the work on to somebody else, who did another fragment, and so on. The difference was that the work being passed around involved pieces of paper instead of hunks of metal.

Then computers and industrial robots arrived. Right behind them came the New Global Economy and lots of shouting about the competitive need for everybody to produce higher-quality goods and services. Some of the college-degreed professionals got very excited. They talked and talked about all the new skills workers would have to learn, and how much smarter workers would have to get in order use the computers and robots, and make better products and perform better services. Most of the time, though, companies went right on designing jobs the same old way: Figure out what stuff the machine needs a human to help it do, break that stuff into parts ("data entry"), and turn the parts into jobs. Plenty of dull jobs in offices and factories got even duller. And the pay got worse. Sometimes the computers and robots just plain took over jobs that people used to do. In came the machines, out went the people.

This didn't occur everywhere. A few companies wanted to see what would happen if they tried to reverse the fragmenting and de-skilling trend that began back in the Industrial Age. They experimented with turning job fragments back into something resembling whole jobs. They started asking workers to think, and sometimes to decide for themselves how to make products and perform services. They did this even though it made the jobs harder to learn, and thus tended to drive up wages. It drove up wages because now the company couldn't just hire any extremely stupid person who happened to walk by, and teach him the job in about an hour, and pay him peanuts. Instead, the company had to do quite a lot of training.

Here's why these few companies were going to all this trouble: They figured that in the long run, they'd make more money and be more likely to survive in the New Global Economy.

The college-degreed professionals proclaimed that these few companies were obviously the leaders, and all the other companies were bound to start following them any minute. And that's more or less where we are today: waiting to see.

For years fashion has dictated that we speak of the average job of tomorrow as demanding a smarter, more highly skilled worker than does the average job today. The notion has become so commonplace that it often is advanced not as a prediction or even as a probability but as a self-evident fact.

The reasoning: Technological gadgets are taking over more and more of the repetitive, the routine and the manual tasks that once constituted a significant amount of human work. That leaves humans with the unusual, the creative and the conceptual. Spurred by the ferocity of global competition, lashed by the universal imperative to improve the quality of goods and services, business is reorganizing itself on a grand scale. And it is doing so in such a way that the work available for people to perform is growing inexorably more complex.

Think of it as an equation: AT = ID.

Advancing technology equates to greater intellectual demands upon the worker. Look at those (formerly) humble factory workers at model companies like Motorola and Corning and Johnsonville Foods. Many of them now tinker with computers and interpret statistical charts. Many of them are organized into teams that perform all sorts of tasks (production scheduling, hiring) once reserved for managers and staff specialists. There's the future of the average worker for you. No doubt about it.

Unfortunately, this is balderdash. True, our future as a prosperous nation may very well depend upon the skilled-up workplace becoming the norm instead of the exception, but there is nothing inevitable about it.

That point was made forcefully last year by the Commission on the Skills of the American Workforce, sponsored by the National Center on Education and the Economy. In a report called *America's Choice: High Skills or Low Wages,* the commission announced its finding that the vast majority of U.S. businesses are not following in the footsteps of the so-called model companies and apparently do not intend to.

Indeed, the commission claimed that the much-ballyhooed "skills gap" in the American work force does not really exist—not in relation to the jobs employers currently want noncollege graduates to perform. Yes, the commission said, most employers do complain about job candidates with low "skills." But when you pin these employers down, in eight out of 10 cases the "skills" they're complaining about have nothing to do with literacy or mathematics or critical-thinking abilities or any sort of technical expertise. Instead, the skills in question boil down to "a good work ethic and appropriate social behavior: 'reliable,' 'a good attitude,' 'a pleasant appearance,' 'a good personality. . . .'"

In other words, what most employers want is workers who will show up on time, smile at the customers, keep the profanity and intramural bickering down to a dull roar, defer to their managers and do what they're told. The complaint about noncollege graduates is that they are uncouth ignoramuses; the desire is for couth ignoramuses instead.

By "noncollege graduates," incidentally, the commission is referring to people it says will perform more than 70 percent of all American jobs in the year 2000.

Furthermore, the commission claims, 95 percent of employers do not expect their skill needs to change significantly in the foreseeable future. They see no reason why the jobs they'll have to offer tomorrow would call for better-educated, more highly skilled workers than the jobs they have to offer today. The exceptional 5 percent are mostly large companies in manufacturing, communications or financial services.

America's choice? The business world is making it right now, the commission says, and the bulk of companies are choosing poorly. They are looking for ways to cut wages instead of for ways to skill up jobs, thus making jobs more productive, thus making the people perform the jobs worth more money.

I must be said that this report seems to have made no significant dent in the national rhetoric, which continues to insist that jobs are growing inexorably more complex and demanding. The 95 percent figure, in particular, draws skepticism from many quarters (see box). But if that figure is even in the right ballpark, it follows that a great deal of the corporate world's howling about the sorry state of the public education system is, to put it mildly, insincere.

Exactly so, concluded professor Robert B. Reich of Harvard's John F. Kennedy School of Government in a *Business Month* article last November: "Forget all the PR about corporate 'partnerships' with local schools. Whatever American corporations are giving through the front door, they're taking away much more through the back." He refers to common corporate practices such as inviting municipalities to engage in bidding wars to attract new plants or to keep old plants from closing. For "bidding wars," read: Which city will offer the biggest tax breaks in order to attract or save some jobs? According to Reich, the corporate share of local property tax revenues, which pay for local schools, dropped from 45 percent nationally in 1957 to 16 percent in 1989.

"The inescapable conclusion," Reich wrote, "is that American Business isn't really worried about the future of the work force. Why? Because American corporations increasingly are finding the workers they need outside the United States, often at a fraction of the price."

This is one form of the "low-wages" option described in *America's Choice.* A key feature of the global economy is that one can now transfer data, information and money all over the planet at lightening speed. This makes it much easier to move jobs to places like Mexico and Thailand, where people will work for less money than Americans can live on.

Another way to make the "low-wages" choice is to use technology to de-skill work even further—to finish the job the Industrial Revolution started. "This plant was so modern, so glorified and so built-up that all they needed were monkeys to push buttons. And that's what we hired," said a supervisor in a high-tech printing plant, quoted last year in *Technical & Skills Training* magazine. If you can hire monkeys to push buttons in high-tech factories or "electronic sweatshops," of course, you get to pay them peanuts.

Economic indicators lend credence to the commission's assertion that the bulk of American companies are choosing the low-wages option. *Business Week* reports that median family income (in inflation-adjusted dollars) has been stagnant since 1973. Worse yet, "real wages" in the United States have dropped by 6 percent since 1980, except in certain industries that export significant amounts of their goods and services. (Among these are aircraft, computers, entertainment, chemicals and, ironically, higher education, which "exports" its product by training foreign students in subjects such as math and engineering, then sending them home.)

The low-wages choice dooms most Americans to a slow but sure trip toward impoverishment, the report concludes. If we keep traveling down this road, we'll eventually start to resemble a Third World country. We will have atomic weapons, of course, but then so does India.

And it's all so hideously pointless, moans the commission. The Japanese aren't beating our pants off in automobiles and electronics and so on by paying their workers lower wages. The way to compete in the global economy is not to design jobs that monkeys can do and pay them peanuts. The way to compete is by creating "high-performance organizations" that operate with well-educated, highly trained and—yes—well-paid workers.

"High-performance organization" is about as good a label for this idea as any other. Reich calls it creating jobs that "add value in the world economy." Tom Peters calls it "train, train, train until you die!" Johnsonville Foods CEO Ralph Stayer calls it "intellectual capitalism." Former Labor Secretary Elizabeth Dole formed task forces and issued calls for national training programs that would provide workers with "portable" skills that would keep them employable if their current jobs vanished. Late last year, that American Society for Training and Development went so far as to hang a price tag on it all, announcing the American employers need to do an additional $15 billion worth of training every year—$15 billion more than they're doing now, that is.

And yet somehow, in the face of all this, the vast majority of companies evi-

# DID *WORKFORCE 2000* GET IT WRONG?

The Commission on the Skills of the American Workforce is not some rag-tag collection of bureaucrats. Its members include two former secretaries of the U.S. Department of Labor; the CEOs of companies including Eastman Kodak, Corning Inc. and Apple Computer; a pair of university presidents; a former governor; union bigwigs including the president of the United Auto Workers; and the head of the National Urban League.

When a group with these credentials issues a report insisting that the conventional wisdom about the job market in this country is dead wrong, one would expect purveyors of that conventional wisdom to sit up and take notice. Last year, in *America's Choice: High Skills or Low Wages,* the commission flatly contradicted the prevailing belief that American jobs, as a whole, are growing increasingly complex, and that it will take workers with more education and higher-level skills to perform them (see main story). Yet to all appearances, the conventional wisdom has emerged virtually unscathed. Why?

One reason may be the widespread credulity attached to the findings of *Workforce 2000,* the 1987 demographic study commissioned by the U.S. Department of Labor and conducted by the Hudson Institute of Indianapolis. According to *Workforce 2000,* tomorrow's average job will demand a more skilled worker than today's, and that's that.

In 1987, William J. Maroni, now a consultant with SJS Inc. of Providence, RI, worked for the Labor Department and was connected to the *Workforce 2000* study. He later served as a field researcher for the Commission on the Skills of the American Workforce.

That field research convinced Maroni that "we oversold those few conclusions in *Workforce 2000* [which said] jobs were being skilled up." He

points out that the Hudson Institute did no "primary research" for that study; it used data from the Bureau of Labor Statistics to make its projections. When the commission's research teams went into actual companies to conduct in-depth interviews and study real jobs, Maroni says, it became clear that BLS skill classifications can be misleading.

"At Ford [Motor Co.], for instance, we talked to a middle-aged guy who was using a computer on the factory floor. He was so proud of being computer literate—never expected to learn about computers at his age, and so on." Maroni's team seemed to be bearing personal witness to a chapter of the inspiring story that has become a classic in the folklore of "model companies": downtrodden factory worker becomes Master of Technology and achieves self-actualization in the Computer Age.

Alas for pleasant illusions, Maroni and his mates made the mistake of hanging around for several hours to watch this man do his job. It became evident that he knew nothing except "which buttons to push" when certain information appeared on his screen. "He had no computer skills that he couldn't have learned in about two days," Maroni says. Yet BLS would classify that as a highly skilled job because a computer is attached to it.

"We promoted *Workforce 2000* so well that now we've got a lot of confusion out there about what a 'skilled up' job is," Maroni concludes.

Another reason why *America's Choice* might fail to shake the prevailing faith in the notion that jobs are being skilled up is that the report lacks a statistical vigor. The commission insists that its field research provided a deep and disturbing understanding of the true direction in which the country is moving, but the companies it studied do not constitute a representative sam-

ple of all U.S. employers. Although the report attaches numbers to some findings (e.g., 95 percent of all American employers do not expect to need more highly skilled workers in the foreseeable future than they do right now), the commission doesn't claim that those numbers are statistically precise.

Finally, the recommendations in *America's Choice* might suggest that the commission itself doesn't really believe its own findings. In one breath, the authors announce their conclusion that only 5 percent of employers give a tinker's damn whether the job candidates they see tomorrow are any better educated than the ones they see today. In the next breath, they propose a sweeping agenda of school reform and government-sponsored vocational training programs intended to ensure that henceforth, every young American who goes looking for a job will be a proud representative of the best-educated and most highly trained work force in the world. The reader is left to wonder why 95 percent of these paragons won't simply be impoverished and numbed by the mindless, low-paying jobs they get.

According to Maroni, the explanation is that the commission expects the tide of history to change the minds of employers who are attempting to compete in the global economy on the basis of low wages rather than high skills. It expects history to get a helping hand in the form of continued proselytizing by model companies, especially winners of the Malcolm Baldrige National Quality Award. A well-educated work force would exert pressure of its own on companies to skill up jobs, Maroni says. And the government, by means of a national training tax and other measures, can nudge the process along as well.      —J.G.

dently are going right on choosing the low-wages option.

Why don't they get the message? It can't be because they haven't heard it; the message has been shouted from every bully pulpit in the country. The problem must be that they don't believe it. Or maybe it all sounds fine as far as it goes, but they don't see how it applies to them. Maybe they don't know what to *do* with it.

And maybe this is because the message so often comes shrouded in large, billowing clouds of mysto smoke.

Mysto . . .as in "high-performance organization" and "value-added work" and "intellectual capitalism" and "portable skills."

Mysto . . .as in prescribing "training" in such relentlessly generic terms and on such a macro-level that it comes to sound like one big homogeneous bucket

of magic dust, or an all-purpose vitamin compound cooked up by Dr. Feelgood at his Knowledge Lab in Learningland. Unfortunately for this line of talk, employers have *seen* "training." Many have paid repeatedly over the years for whoppingly expensive examples of "training" that didn't do much of anything for anybody.

Mysto . . .as in, when somebody does answer the question, "Train them to do *what*?" a great deal of the talk about value-added jobs and intellectual capital turns out to be merely code for the basic-skills issue: Teach them eighth-grade math and reading, if you must, but more importantly, teach them customer service skills (smile), interpersonal communication skills (develop a pleasant personality and keep the profanity down to a dull roar), teamwork (also the intramural bickering), and listening skills (pay attention and do what you're told.)*

Maybe what's needed is a little less macro-level evangelizing from bully pulpits and a little more concrete explaining of how some of this stuff is supposed to work. For example, let's take three aspects of the national discussion about skilling up the work force—creating whole jobs, "train, train, train," and "portable skills"—and see if we can talk about them minus the mysto.

## WHOLE JOBS

"There are three things we know for sure," says consultant Marvin Weisbord of Block, Petrella & Weisbord of Plainfield, NJ. "One, there are no technological exemptions from human decision making yet. That's a fantasy. . . .

"Two, it's a losing proposition, and uneconomic, to try to make people extensions of machines—to have a keyboard operator entering 150 transactions an hour. That's not a fit job for humans." Attempts to use computers this way explain why many a large company has a technological skeleton in its closet—"the $30 million mistake they don't want the stockholders to know about. And it's always because of what these systems left for people to do. . . .

"Three, it's not possible to automate every job, because robots won't buy goods and services from each other. We can't automate everybody out of work and expect to make money. Long term, how can rich people stay rich in a world where nobody can buy anything?"

Companies exporting jobs offshore in search of cheaper workers are making the incorrect assumption that labor costs are the biggest part of their overhead, Weisbord says. "It's not hourly people you need fewer of, it's managers, supervisors and staff people." It is only the fragmentation of work at the bottom of the organization that creates the need for large numbers of managers and staff specialists. "Dumb jobs

lead to huge overhead: You need middle managers and staff specialization to make up for people doing bad work and not caring."

If the key to "skilling up" jobs is to "de-fragment" the work at the bottom of the organization, how does one go about that? Robert Janson, president of Roy Walters & Associates, a Mahwah, NJ, consulting firm, is a specialist in the subject.

You begin with your customers, Janson says. "How do you want customer transactions to work? How do you want to deal with your customers? You design jobs around that."

For instance, many companies find that their customers want "one-stop service." That is, when the customer contacts the company for some reason, she wants to deal with one person who can answer questions, solve problems and get things done. She doesn't want to be bounced around from department to department, from worker to supervisor, etc. (General Electric's GE Answer Center is a prime example of how the skills required to support this strategy can snowball. Customers who call GE's 800 number speak to an employee who now must have a college degree, sales experience and at least six weeks of intensive training on the technical workings of GE products.)

The same principle applies internally, Janson says. For instance, field reps who require information or support from corporate headquarters want to deal with one person or one team that can give them what they need. Technology now allows you to redesign jobs in order to create such people.

To do so, you need to look at the various tasks that make up some process—the fragmented jobs that carry the work from start to finish—and recombine them into whole jobs. In his training materials, Janson uses the reorganization of a major bank's letter-of-credit division as an example.

A letter of credit is "a service provided to finance business transactions between separate concerns working through financial intermediaries." Usually, the separate concerns are in different countries: A construction company in Argentina wants to buy some bulldozers from an American company; an Argentine bank arranges for an American bank to issue a letter of credit, which pays for the deal.

In Janson's example, the paperwork for 450 letters of credit wends its way through this division every day. The division is organized into three clerical departments: issues, amendments and payments. Then there's the accounting department, which records both credits and payments; the customer service

unit, which handles inquiries and complaints; and the main files unit, where records of everything are kept.

It typically takes two weeks for this division to issue a letter of credit. During that time, more than a dozen people do *something* with the batch of forms and papers that each case represents. As customer's application for a letter of credit arrives in the mail room and is sent to a clerk called a pre-processor. The pre-processor sends it to the issues department, where it is received by a log clerk, who assigns it an identification number and then gives it to a typist. The typist fills out an "offering ticket," one copy of which wends its way into a different thicket of the bureaucratic forest for checks and approvals, then straggles back to the main file. By that time, the main file has traveled up to a different floor of the building for verification of the customer's signature, then back down to a preparer, who gives it to a checker, who gives it to a credit typist, who gives it to a fanfold checker. From there the file is passed on to another preparer, a break-out checker, a manager, another checker and a credit-package preparer.

That's just the issues department. In the payment department, five people will handle this wad of paper. And God help the application that a customer wants to alter in some way (as many do), because that means a side trip to the joyless hellhole of the amendment department, where seven different people will fanfold, spindle and mutilate the poor thing.

In short, the letter of credit division is organized into three assembly lines, and everyone who works there performs a single, isolated piece of a production process, over and over again. Our job is to figure out how in the world we might reorganize this place to make it more efficient and competitive in the global economy.

Cutting-edge stuff, eh? Well, yes and no. Janson's 1979 case study is based on a reorganization that took place at Citibank in New York almost 20 years ago. What the bank did was to pare and combine all of those functions into a single job. As of the mid-'70s, the new system worked like this: A letter of credit application arrives and is given to an "account representative" (a former clerk, now retrained) assigned to the appropriate region: Middle East, South America, etc. The account rep sits at a workstation linked to a minicomputer. The computer contains all the necessary information on the customer's credit history and so forth. The account rep handles all the issuing and amending functions, as well as payment processing and accounting. The rep is also

---

*Save the stamp. I know that plenty of the training that goes on under these headings is not just designed to turn uncouth ignoramuses into couth ones. But plenty of it is, too.

the customer service agent for this account.

In case you lost track, that's three assembly lines and two auxiliary functions combined into one job, using the computer technology available in the 1970s. (True, some auditing oversight has been whitewashed out of this picture, Janson says, but the reorganization left behind no such thing as a person who was strictly a "checker.") Five years after the reorganization, revenues had nearly quadrupled while operating expenses had remained flat. The division was running with less than half as many workers; displaced clerks were retrained for other assignments in the bank.

What can we say about all this? Obviously we can agree that these clerks were "skilled up." Their fragment jobs were turned into whole jobs. Efficiency, productivity and competitiveness improved. The clerks undoubtedly care more about their jobs. Their working lives are almost certainly more interesting and enjoyable. We could crank up the mysto machine and rhapsodize about value-added intellectual capital and all, and we'd be perfectly justified. But we could also point out that nobody here had to be magically transformed into a nuclear physicist. What happened was this: The computer allowed a big bank to design a job the way it probably would have done in the first place had it been a small bank that handled only one or two of these types of transactions each day.

## TRAIN, TRAIN, TRAIN

Take two companies, each doing a great deal of training. One is using training, successfully, as a strategic tool to improve its competitive position; it probably will continue to do so. The other is "slopping training on with a bucket," as the old phrase has it; it will probably stop doing so in a recession, or as soon as it becomes clear that business results—quality, service, sales, market share—are not improving.

How would we know which organization was which?

If we're seeking a company with an impressive track record in using training strategically, the exemplar is IBM. "We look at ourselves as a learning organization," says Ken Lay, the corporation's director of education-external programs. New buzzword, old concept: IBM has been a "learning organization" for several decades. When Lay says, "The key to business is education," he's quoting founder Tom Watson, who made that statement in 1933.

Almost nothing you hear anybody say about the "new" need for lifelong, continual learning and education is new to IBM.

IBM currently spends about $1.5 billion a year on training for its 374,000 employees worldwide; that's not counting the salaries paid to people while they're being trained. The company employs 7,000 training specialists. The average employee get 15 days of formal training every year, about 65 percent of it in a classroom and the rest via computer or interactive video. It doesn't seem to occur to the people who run this company that any employee at any level could possibly perform his job competently without being trained.

Yet for all this emphasis on employee education, the notion of training as a homogeneous wonder-substance is utterly alien to IBM. "You can't just have training for training's sake," Lay says. (He doesn't add, "for crying out loud," but it's there in his tone.) "You need the right education for the right person at the right time. You might call it 'just-in-time education.' "

How does the company go about ensuring just-in-time education? Largely by attending to the basics that have been preached for years (by people like Bob Mager, Thomas Gilbert, Joe Harless, Dugan Laird) under the heading, "How to design and conduct effective training in the working world."

Jobs at IBM are classified according to five major functions: marketing, service, information and office systems, technical and finance. Ninety percent of all jobs are further broken down into 85 major "job areas," Lay says. Three years ago the company finished a full-scale needs analysis to determine what people in each of those 85 areas ought to know and be able to do. From the findings came the latest edition of IBM's corporate training curriculum.

According to Lay, all training is designed and conducted using the classic instructional systems design (ISD) approach, about which there is nothing mysto whatsoever. Measurements of a course's effectiveness are built into its design, following Donald Kirkpatrick's familiar four-level evaluation model: Level 1, do the trainees say the course is well-designed and helpful? Level 2, did they master the material they were taught? Level 3, did they apply the skills they learned once they returned to the job? Level 4, has a business goal been met (Are sales increasing? Are customers more satisfied with the service they receive?) as a result of the fact that people *are* applying these new skills on the job?

In some cases, particularly with "soft skills" training, it's unrealistic to try to carry a rigorous evaluation all the way to Level 4, Lay admits. But for the most part, he says, "If we see no business results, we kill the course."

Although the company offers some generic courses that cut across different job functions (time management, effective business writing, many management-training courses), the vast majority of its programs are tied directly to specific jobs. And only a minuscule fraction of all training is remedial. "Through our recruitment and hiring programs, we're able to get highly skilled people," Lay says. "The analogy is, you're starting with someone who has set a record in the 100-yard dash, and you're trying to improve on that."

If IBMers are so wonderful to begin with, why all the training? "In a market-driven company, you're constantly trying to raise your level of performance," Lay says. "You have to be obsessed with customer satisfaction. Our focus is on continual improvement. And that comes from the fact that our jobs change all the time."

Customer satisfaction, continual improvement, the accelerating pace of change—the phrases have become clichés, yet at IBM they are translated into very specific learning challenges. Obviously, many employees are forever having to learn about new products the company introduces—computer technology never sleeps—but it's more than that.

Take marketing, for instance. In days gone by, an IBM sales representative sold products to many different types of companies. Now the marketing function has been reorganized so that salespeople specialize by industry: A rep will sell computer systems only to banks or only to health-care organizations or to universities or to the securities industry. If you're going to do an effective job of selling a computer system to a company, Lay says, "you have to be able to help the customer focus on the processes" that the system will handle. To do that, you have to understand something about the customer's business. Thus, "Introduction to the Securities Industry" becomes a basic training course for an IBM sales rep.

Lay himself began his IBM career as a computer programmer. Then he went into marketing, where he spent his first year shuttling back and forth from training programs to the job. Then he switched to corporate education. That involved traveling to various IBM facilities, learning from specialists in instructional design, computer-based training, classroom instruction, evaluation and so on.

This brings up another heralded but often hazily described benefit of training for which IBM serves as a concrete illustration: the notion that the promise of extensive educational programs will help a company attract and keep good people. When TRAINING asked Lay for examples of in-house educational programs that would provide workers with "transferable" skills that would make them attractive to other employers if they left IBM, he couldn't relate to the question; unless they're accepting early retirement offers, people don't *leave* IBM. The worldwide attrition rate is 3 percent. Leave? Why? Because you're sick of finance and you want to go into sales? Well, hey. . . .

## PORTABLE SKILLS

There is a desperate need, the macro-level talk insists, for a national system of training designed to "reskill" workers. Why? Because we live in a world where jobs are changing, mutating and vanishing faster than you can say, "So long, lithographers," In this utterly unpredictable, rapidly changing world (We're in *permanent white water!* We're in a state of *raging chaos!*), the worker's skills will soon become obsolete, if they aren't already, which is why he needs this retraining. Meanwhile, we'll all pretend not to notice that if things are *that* chaotic, any new skills we teach this guy may just as easily be obsolete by the time he graduates.

Ah, irony.

Yes, but suppose there were a system of training designed to keep workers employable in a fast-changing job market: What might one of those look like?

AT&T's Alliance for Employee Growth and Development Inc. was created in 1986 as part of the company's contract agreements with the Communication Workers of America and the International Brotherhood of Electrical Workers. Its charter is to provide training to AT&T's union workers that will keep them employable, either inside or outside the company. Its services are available to union members currently employed at AT&T and to those who have been laid off. Displaced workers remain eligible for up to two years.

To date, more than 50,000 people, one-third of them layoff victims, have completed at least one course sponsored by the Alliance. As for the other two-thirds, "People at AT&T all consider themselves at risk," says Don Treinen of the communication workers union, who serves as the Alliance's co-executive director. The company's work force has shrunk by 100,000 people since 1984, albeit partly due to the court-ordered breakup of the Bell System.

A worker wishing to use the Alliance's services must first go through 15 to 20 hours of career-planning sessions. These include skill inventories, aptitude tests and discussions with counselors. Through a network of 360 working committees at AT&T sites in 48 states, the Alliance also conducts marketplace surveys and compiles data from the U.S. Bureau of Labor Statistics and other sources, showing what kinds of jobs are available, inside and outside AT&T, and in various regions of the country. The committees also keep tabs on various training resources in their areas—programs available from universities, community colleges, private training vendors, public agencies and so on. Only when the worker settles upon a realistic career plan will the Alliance pay for any training.

"There must be a demand in the marketplace" for the type of job the worker is after, Treinen says, and the worker's aptitude for the job must be supported by the results of the planning sessions. "We won't train you for a job that's not there or for a job you're highly unlikely to get."

Provided the career plan is viable, however, the training options are wide open. The Alliance will pay for training in "anything AT&T doesn't," says Treinen. That is, if the company wants its union workers to learn something, the company does the training. If the worker wants to learn something that will qualify him for a different job at AT&T or elsewhere, the Alliance takes over—and the training occurs on the worker's own time. When some new technology is introduced on the job at AT&T, for instance, "it might mean they'll now need 10 workers instead of 100," Treinen says. "So 10 people will get training from AT&T in the new technology. We'll see the other 90."

The Alliance operates on an annual budget of $15 million, of which $2.5 million is earmarked for college tuition payments. The Alliance picks up the educational expenses for people who want to be teachers, counselors, nurses, software engineers—whatever. It has sent people to vocational-training courses covering everything from secretarial skills to underwater welding (including scuba diving). The Alliance also coordinates and pays for a great deal of computer training, most of which involves basic keyboarding and introductions to various software packages. Once you have "a grounding" in a few different types of computer software, Treinen says, potential employers are much more willing to teach you the specific applications they use.

Even with the emphasis on specific career planning, many Alliance-sponsored courses fall under the generic heading of basic skills. These are defined broadly to include not just academic skills but subjects such as problem solving, time management, teamwork, social skills and leadership (as in, how to take the lead when your work team is involved with some project in which you happen to have the most expertise). Of the 50,000 union members who have completed an Alliance-sponsored course, more than half have taken one or more of these kinds of courses.

When retraining can qualify a displaced worker for a new job within AT&T, the company makes out like a bandit. The Alliance spends an average of $2,000 on training for each displaced worker. The average cost to AT&T to lay off a worker, calculated in 1989, was $24,500: Layoffs are expensive, Treinen says, when you add up things like unemployment compensation, extended medical payments (the company is self-insured) and severance pay, especially since most displaced workers at AT&T have many years of service with the company and their severance packages amount to significant chunks of money. "So every time we place somebody internally at AT&T," he says, "it saves the company about $22,000."

## JUST DO IT

None of these examples are meant to represent the one true path to the enlightened redesign of jobs, the delivery of continuous education to employees or the construction of a mechanism for retraining displaced workers. But they do demonstrate that all of these things can be done—are *being* done—in practical ways by practical people acting for practical business reasons.

It is axiomatic that we quickly forget most things we learn if we have no reason, need or opportunity to practice them. This principle does not vanish because a company decides to call itself a learning organization or a total quality manufacturer, or because its employees are "knowledge workers," or because the "pace of change" is accelerating.

Redesigning jobs, training and retraining may well be the most important economic challenges facing this country for the next decade at least. But they have to be linked. Training has to support jobs that are really changing. Retraining has to prepare people for work that really exists. Otherwise, we're spinning our wheels. And the bulk of employers will listen to the rhetoric, match it against the training they see with their own eyes, and go right on wondering what all the shouting is about.

# TELECOMMUTING
## A BETTER WAY TO WORK?

*The benefits of avoiding the grinding commute to and from work are obvious. It's the hidden advantages, however, that may tip the scales in telecommuting's favor . . . if management finds out about them.*

## Bob Filipczak

*Bob Filipczak is staff editor of* TRAINING *Magazine.*

Here you sit, again, in the line of stop-and-go traffic crawling into the city. Care to glance about at your fellow commuters? Faces full of slow-brewing rage and resigned despair surround you as you swing around the '77 Impala stalled in the center lane. You'll be 20 minutes late for work, again, and you pray the coffee isn't gone when you get there.

Suddenly it occurs to you that you get to do this all over again tonight. You stifle a scream. Your mind thrashes like a wounded badger, trying to recall one of those stress-reduction exercises from the seminar last year.

Finally, breathing deeply, you begin to wax philosophical about your predicament. Is it all worth it? Shouldn't I be spending more time with my family? Isn't there a better way to live?

The best way to forgo the torments of traveling to and from work in most major cities would be, of course, to avoid the commute altogether. That's the idea behind telecommuting. The concept has been around for years but is just now beginning to make significant inroads into the workplace. Telecommuting means, essentially, doing your job at home or at a satellite location (a small branch office near your home, for instance) instead of working at the main office. In most telecommuting arrangements your work remains the same, your benefits stay in place, your salary is unchanged and the hours you work may be identical. The difference is *where* you work—and sometimes that can make all the difference.

Take Robert Duerr of Philadelphia, for example. He's the product manager for Atlantic Bell's speech recognition line, and he telecommutes one or two days a week. His official office hours are 8 a.m. to 5 p.m. On days when he goes to the office, he faces a 40-minute drive—provided he's on the road by 6:30 a.m. to avoid traffic. He stays at the office until 6 p.m., again to avoid traffic, and gets home about 40 minutes later, if he's lucky.

A telecommuting morning, on the other hand, starts for Duerr at 7:45 a.m. He goes downstairs, starts a pot of coffee and turns on his personal computer. By 8 a.m. he's at work. His phone calls can be forwarded from the office to his home, and he has access to his coworkers through voice mail and electronic mail. He works until noon, goes out for some lunch, works the rest of the afternoon and shuts down at 5 p.m.

Nancy Apeles, the telecommuting program manager for Los Angeles County, practices what she preaches by telecommuting two days a week. Her round-trip commute to the county government office where she works is about 80 miles, and she estimates that telecommuting saves her at least 90 minutes in the morning alone. That means she doesn't have to get her son up at 5 a.m. to take him to day care. It also means she has time for exercise; she jogs on the mornings she works at home. Since one of her tasks is legislative analysis, Apeles reads a lot of legislative bills. At home, she says, she gets through about 26 bills in a day. At the office, because of interruptions, she reads about three a day.

### OBSTACLES

It sounds wonderful, but it's not idyllic. Isolation is the most-often cited drawback to telecommuting. Social interaction is an important part of most jobs, so allowing your employees to cloister themselves in their home offices full time probably would be counterproductive. Even the most extreme examples of telecommuting arrangements include at least a half day in the office every week.

And let's face it, most jobs include some duties that demand personal contact. The trick seems to be finding the employees who are interested in telecommuting and figuring out which parts of their jobs can be done at home. That usually results in an arrangement of one or two days of telecommuting supplemented by "regular" days at the office.

---

*'The reality is that the office is a lousy place to work for today's knowledge workers.'*

---

Moreover, telecommuting isn't for everyone. Outgoing, gregarious people who thrive on human contact probably are not good candidates. Others may know themselves well enough to realize that they wouldn't get anything done at home. If you see your home as a refuge from work, telecommuting would certainly violate that sense of safety. The idea behind telecommuting is to remain flexible and do what's best for the employee.

One obstacle, if your workplace is unionized, is that labor unions are officially opposed to telecommuting. Their past battles against sweatshops apparently have been influential in their decision to oppose telecommuting. Unions are generally concerned about issues such as the safety of the work environment when telecommuters are at home and the protection of employees' benefits. For instance, the American Federation of Government Employees (AFGE) is watching a pilot program that is currently under way among a variety of federal agencies, including the Navy and the Department of Agriculture. The union is worried that employees may be submitted to unreasonable monitoring while they are at home. Other than that, AFGE is generally in favor of the federal government's efforts in this area.

Dave Fleming, a partner with Fleming LTD Telecommuting Services in Davis, CA, helped design a telecommuting pilot program for the state of California. He negotiated with some unions during the pilot and believes that, as the rank and file become more interested in this work option, unions will realize that their members' interests will be better served by supporting telecommuting. For the time being, however, if you decide to experiment with telecommuting, you may have to coax unions to cooperate.

Others won't be quite so reluctant, since telecommuting is beginning to sound attractive and feasible to increasing numbers of people. The days of fast-track promotional ladders and large yearly raises for those who spend the most time in the office "looking busy" are all but over in many organizations. In their search for new ways to motivate and retain good employees, companies are looking at flexible work options such as job sharing, compressed workweeks, flextime and telecommuting. When bigger paychecks aren't an option, employees look

for other ways to improve their quality of life. That often means having more time for themselves or their families. Telecommuting can offer that and more.

If telecommuting is so great, exactly how many people are doing it? Link Resources, a New York-based research and consulting firm, conducts a National Work-at-Home Survey every year. According to the 1991 version, about 5.5 million part-time and full-time company employees work at home during normal business hours. That's up 38 percent from 1990.

In another study on flexible work arrangements, The Conference Board, also a New York-based research firm, found that 15 percent to 20 percent of the companies it surveyed offered formal telecommuting arrangements to some of their employees. Closer to 80 percent, however, had informal telecommuting as a work option. Informal telecommuting is usually arranged between a supervisor and an employee without the knowledge of upper management or the HR department. While these arrangements can work out fine, they usually forgo successful elements like a telecommuting agreement, formal training and job analysis.

## WHO BENEFITS?

Most of the benefits to the employee are rather obvious. It's the not-so-obvious benefits to the *employer*, however, that may finally sell organizations on telecommuting in a big way.

Let's look at the easy stuff first. To calculate how much time you spend commuting every year, plug yourself into this equation supplied by Paul and Sarah Edwards' book *Working From Home: Everything You Need to Know About Living and Working Under the Same Roof* (Jeremy P. Tarcher Inc., Los Angeles). Multiply the number of minutes you spend commuting each day by 240, then divide by 60. That tells you roughly how many hours you spend every year traveling to and from work. If you have a one-way commute of 20 minutes, for example, you spend 160 hours a year commuting. That translates to four 40-hour workweeks spent in your car, on the bus or on the train.

Is your commute an aggravating one? By removing the trip, you also reduce stress. Consultant Gil Gordon, president of Gordon & Associates of Monmouth Junction, NJ, and editor of the "Telecommuting Review" newsletter, points out that if you measure work in terms of frustration and stress, many employees have already put in a fun day's work by the time they get to the office. Fighting traffic for 45 minutes can drain you, and your recovery time in the morning or at night might also be counted as time lost.

"The reality is that the office is a lousy place to work for today's knowledge workers," Gordon declares. "The office is really an outgrowth of the factory, in many ways. When we were basically a factory-driven economy, it made sense to have everybody come to the same place and be there at the same time." What once was plain old pragmatism, however, is in some cases merely a habit today.

Another advantage: Telecommuting is flexible and able to accommodate a variety of different work styles. If your body clock tells you that you work best early in the morning or late in the evening, telecommuting can make the best use of your most productive times. Similarly, people who have jobs that involve lots of reading, writing or analysis can benefit from the distraction-free environment that can be set up at home.

Some additional benefits of telecommuting are: less air pollution, less need for office space, money saved on gas, money saved on parking, fewer meetings and less money spent for lunch.

## WORKING SMARTER

This brings us to those less-obvious benefits—the ones likely to appeal to employers. Improved productivity is an enticement often cited by people who sing the praises of telecommuting, especially when they are trying to impress its merits on corporate managers. Advocates boast of productivity gains ranging from 10 percent to 200 percent.

When Gordon is questioned about productivity boosts, he says, "I typically talk in the range of 15 percent to 25 percent, although I have seen gains reported that were so high as to make you wonder what these people were ever doing in the office."

Why would productivity go up if people work at home? Some alleged causes are factors we've already mentioned: less stress, more time, more flexibility and fewer distractions. Strangely enough, reduced absenteeism also has been cited by more than one organization as a reason for increased productivity. At first blush, it seems a non sequitur: less absenteeism because your employees are at home?

Don't laugh, says Paul Rupert, associate director of New Ways to Work, a San Francisco-based nonprofit organization that promotes alternative work schedules. Absenteeism actually can be reduced by telecommuting, he says, because of "sort of" illnesses. He refers to those mornings when an employee wakes up just feeling sort of . . . blaaah. The trip to work and a whole day at the office isn't going to make him feel any better, so he stays home. But at the same time, he's not so sick that he couldn't get a full day's work done—OK, maybe a half day—provided he didn't have to get up early, shower, dress, fight traffic and so on. Telecommuting allows a "sort of" ill employee enough flexibility to get some work done, recover from the illness and save his colleagues from what may be a contagious case of the crud.

By the same token, an employee who is able to stay home with a sick child and still get some work done also has increased her productivity. But there is a major caveat

attached to this idea. As Gordon puts it, nobody should try to use telecommuting as a substitute for day care. In the early 1980s, some enthusiasts began to speak of the "electronic cottage" as a place where a parent could work full time and care for young children as well. That vision was quickly laughed into obscurity by everyone who knew anything about the demands and logistics of child rearing.

## MANAGING FOR RESULTS

The biggest surprise that has popped out of pilot projects at companies like Bell Atlantic and The Travelers, an insurance company in Hartford, CT, relates to a principle that management theorists have been talking about for years. Whether you call it "management by objectives" (MBO) or "management by results," it essentially means that people ought to be managed and rewarded based on what they produce—not on how much time they spend in the office or on the procedures they follow to achieve their results. Telecommuting forces both employees and bosses to ask some serious questions about the real purpose of a job. In organizations that already claim to be managing by results, telecommuting calls supervisors' bluff about the criteria they're using to rate their subordinates' performance.

How's that? Well, one of the first questions that arises when telecommuting is discussed is: How are bosses going to manage employees when they work at home? "The question is always asked, 'How will we know they're working?'" Fleming says. "We said, 'Well, how do you know they're working now?'"

---

*Managers are beginning to embrace MBO simply because they have little choice when they aren't face-to-face with employees.*

---

That response implies a focus on the outputs or "deliverables" of job performance, rather than a concern with "activities." Bev Adante, president of Telecommuting Works, a consulting firm in Morton Grove, IL, says that managers in her client firms are beginning to embrace MBO simply be cause they have little choice when they aren't face-to-face with employees. She claims that many bosses have gotten better at managing telecommuters as well as the subordinates who continue to work in the office.

Rupert is downright adamant about the need for managers to rethink their roles, and he promotes telecommuting as a great way to force the issue. Managers often bring up the issue of "trust," Rupert says, but he discounts trust as the fundamental building block of a good telecommuting arrangement. He quotes the adage former

# TELECOMMUTING FROM THE ELECTRONIC COTTAGE

Futurist Alvin Toffler's discussion of the "electronic cottage" in his 1980 book *The Third Wave* is probably one of the driving forces behind the introduction of telecommuting to business and government. But one question remains: Has the electronic cottage been built yet?

We've seen prototypes, and all the necessary technology is available. Affordability, however, remains the biggest hurdle to the utopian ideal that many envision. Interactive TV that patches into a huge computer network with multimedia and video teleconferencing capability, while possible, still depends on large installed bases of high-tech equipment and the right kind of electronic cables. Since only about 25 percent of all Americans have personal computers in their homes, a fully functional electronic cottage may still be on the distant horizon. Maybe the more important question is: Do we really need all the fancy technology in order to telecommute?

Gil Gordon, editor of the "Telecommuting Review" newsletter, is a proponent of outfitting a home office with precisely what you need to do your work, no more and no less. The minimum equipment for a telecommuter's home office is a telephone, according to Gordon. You could have more, but first be sure you need it.

A personal computer, when combined with a modem, opens up a world of communications and research capabilities. If your office has electronic mail, a PC often can connect you to that system. Many voice mail systems also can be accessed from home. According to Karen Gislason, director of the telecommuting and home-based business markets for Bell Atlantic in Philadelphia: "The use of voice messaging services has proven invaluable. In many respects, people feel they are even more 'available' in a telecommuting situation than in the office."

With the advent of fax/modems, faxing documents with your computer can relieve you of the economic burden of buying a fully functional fax machine.

In short, much of the equipment that might be called the foundation of the electronic cottage is becoming affordable for either companies or individuals—whoever is buying the equipment.

At J.C. Penney, about 200 part-time customer-service employees telecommute. To allow these people to take catalog orders over the phone and register those orders in the computer, the company had to run two business telephone lines into each employee's home. One line is for the phone calls, the other transfers data to the main computer. That's one reason why Carl Kirkpatrick, planning and program manager for J.C. Penney's telemarketing division, isn't planning to expand his telecommuting program. While he is satisfied with the original investment, he can't justify more expenditures until the technology becomes more affordable.

Michael Crampton, a director in the telecommunications division of the information systems department of The Travelers, a Hartford, CT-based insurance company, sees the installation of ISDN (integrated services digital network) lines as a possible solution to Kirkpatrick's current problems. These cables, which are only now becoming available, can transmit video, computer data and telephone calls, all using the same line. If the ideal electronic cottage ever becomes a reality, ISDN lines may be the link between the telecommuter and the rest of the world.

The affordability of personal computers certainly has been a key reason why telecommuting has caught on in the last 10 years, but voice mail and e-mail are the applications telecommuters mention most often as critical to keeping in touch with their peers and supervisors. The most important technology in any telecommuting program, however, is a commodity that's inexpensive but often hard to come by: good communication between managers and employees.—**B.F.**

President Ronald Reagan liked to repeat during disarmament talks with the former Soviet Union: "Trust but verify." Rupert argues that if managers can verify that employees are producing results, there's no need to worry much about "trust."

Says Adante, "What I love about telecommuting is that it [makes managers] take a look at what they really ask of people, their clarity, their expectations, and whether they've actually asked for what they want."

But here Gordon adds a caution to any crusader who sees telecommuting as one more neat opportunity to "force" managers to change their wrongheaded ways: "Managers have had so many bad experiences with having things jammed down their throats—and a lot of the jamming is done by human resources people with good intentions but bad execution. [You should] say to them, 'Hey, this is a tool you can use or not use. If you want to use it, here's the boundary around it.' Then they really get turned on to it."

## PUT IT IN WRITING

According to most experts, serious communication about how the telecommuter ought to be managed doesn't really begin unless employees and managers sit down to draft a telecommuting agreement. This usually is a formal contract that a) states the responsibilities of both parties, and b) lists some of the variables that might alter or cancel the agreement. If that sounds like a document that could easily fall prey to a lot of legal jargon, it is.

The advantage, however, is that on the way to the final written contract, managers and employees have a chance to talk about a multitude of work issues that they may never have addressed before. Gordon, Rupert and Adante all endorse the idea of a formal written contract as a way to eliminate hidden agendas or guessing games.

Many of the objections and concerns about telecommuting can be dealt with during the drafting of a formal agreement. Some problems can come as a surprise to employers. If you're setting up a home office, it's going to cost money. Who is going to pay for it? That debate sometimes causes conflict when an obtuse employer gives the employee a $200 allowance for office equipment. That might just get you a good office chair, but it's not going to put a computer on your desk. Another problem that concerns employees is the "out of sight, out of mind" mentality that might diminish their chances for promotions. If that is a consequence for telecommuters, you should state it clearly up front. Furthermore, if the telecommuter wants to be considered for a promotion, he must be willing to forgo his telecommuting arrangement according to the demands of the job.

Telecommuters themselves face another potential surprise: weight gain. Since telecommuters are only a few steps from the refrigerator, you may want to warn them about eating their way through the hours spent working at home. Some companies even talk about this during telecommuting training.

Gordon has some specific tips about issues that should be covered during the contract discussion:

1. If equipment needs to be purchased—computers, modems, fax machines, and so on—specify who will pay for it, where it will be set up in the employee's home, who can use the equipment and what needs to be returned to the company if the arrangement is terminated. A site visit from the employer may be in order to make sure the employee's home office meets safety standards.

2. Address concerns about workers' compensation insurance. If the employee is injured at home while working for the employer, is she covered by workers' compensation? Do medical benefits change?

3. If equipment is stolen, will the employee's homeowners insurance cover the loss? Also, who will fix or maintain the equipment the telecommuter will be using at home?

4. If either party finds the telecommuting scheme isn't working, there should be an escape clause. If the isolation of working at home is getting to the employee, for instance, he should be able to come back to work at the office. Likewise, if the manager discovers he needs the subordinate at the office more often, the telecommuting arrangement can be scaled back or canceled altogether.

That last point is the most important, according to Gordon. If both employees and managers are reassured that they aren't embarking on a road of no return, there will be less resistance and better communication.

Since the idea behind telecommuting is flexibility, most experts agree that the written agreements should also be flexible and customized to the individual employee. If the right issues are addressed and the communication channels stay open, you can avoid a lot of the potential problems. Even though the agreement will probably go to the lawyers eventually, try to keep the language simple and clear. Says Gordon, "My approach, if I can keep the lawyers out of it, is to write the damn thing in English and not legalese."

---

*Some employees who 'report' to the head office in Hartford live as far away as Iowa.*

---

Formal telecommuter agreements aren't always possible, however, so general guidelines or standards are another option for ensuring that telecommuting runs smoothly. Los Angeles County has the largest telecommuting program in the United States, with 2,000 participants, but the county couldn't sign legal agreements with employees because of union restrictions. Margery Gould, a management analyst and former project manager of the telecommuter program, helped set up standards that took into consideration a lot of the issues a formal agreement would tackle. Still, Gould tried to keep the arrangements as flexible as possible.

At The Travelers there seemed to be no need for formal telecommuter agreements. The corporate culture was already based on management by objectives, open communication and progressive management principles, according to Michael Crampton, a director in the telecommunications division of The Travelers' information systems department.

Crampton says telecommuters are informed that the business needs of the company will dictate whether the arrangement will continue. Apparently things usually go well: The company expanded its program after the 1987 pilot season, and now has hundreds of telecommuters on the payroll. Some employees who "report" to the head office in Hartford live as far away as Iowa. These individuals come to Hartford a few times a year, but are tied into the most extensive voice mail system in the United States, according to Crampton.

### SELECTION AND TRAINING

Almost every organization with a successful telecommuting program is very careful about selecting the right employees and offers some form of training to both managers and telecommuters. "Don't do this on a lark," Crampton warns. "If you do, you have a much higher likelihood of screwing up something with your most valuable resource, which is your people."

So what does a good telecommuting prospect look like? The first criterion, by nearly universal consensus, is that the employee should be a volunteer—preferably an enthusiastic one.

# TELECENTERS: THE MIDDLE ROAD

On the path to developing a telecommuting program, companies can run into obstacles that threaten to kill the process before it starts. Since many managers and employees are not ready for a full plunge into the telecommuting world, some organizations have come up with a compromise. "Telecenters," essentially satellite offices, are yet another piece of the puzzle known as the "flexible workplace." Here's how they work.

A telecenter is basically an office or group of offices to which employees can go every day instead of commuting to the main office. For example, a company with 20 employees living in a suburb 30 miles from headquarters can set up a telecenter in that suburb and shorten a 45-minute commute to five minutes. A telecenter gives these people a structured work environment and can eliminate the sense of isolation that telecommuting from home can cause. On the more practical side, many employees—especially apartment dwellers—don't have space to set up a home office. A satellite office can keep the telecommuting option open for them.

According to Gil Gordon of Monmouth Junction, NJ, editor of the "Telecommuting Review" newsletter, there are a couple of differences between a telecenter and a simple branch office. First, the location of a branch office usually is determined by customers. A realty company, for instance, sets up branches in various parts of the city to be closer to its customers. Second, a branch office tends to be "department specific." For example, everyone in research and development might work in a separate building hallway across the city.

The location of a telecenter, on the other hand, is determined by where employees live. Moreover, a telecenter could have a variety of employees, from the vice president of sales to data entry operators to software engineers. Telecenters may be set up by the company itself or by an independent property management company, which can buy the space, set up the office and rent it to companies. In the latter case, employees from a number of companies might share the same space.

A telecenter can offer some economic advantages over home-based telecommuting arrangements because companies can save on office equipment. Instead of buying a fax machine for each home-based telecommuter, for instance, the company can let people at a telecenter share a fax machine.

According to Gordon, telecenters are becoming especially popular in Japan. The reasons are strictly pragmatic: Japanese cities have serious traffic problems, and Japanese homes tend to be too small to set up home offices.—B.F.

---

Obviously, the volunteer's job must have some tasks that can be accomplished at home. Telecommuting simply is not a viable option for people in many jobs. But as the economy moves further into the Information Age, it generates more and more jobs that *could* be done, at least partially, at home. Crampton sees the people in The Travelers' program, for instance, as perfect examples of modern "knowledge workers." Since the advent of telecommunications, the nature of their jobs no longer demands that they congregate in some particular place.

Many companies also select their best performers from among the employees who volunteer for a telecommuting program. There are two schools of thought on this. Fleming argues that if you're launching a pilot program, you want to design the pilot for success. Therefore it makes sense to load the deck with people who already have proven to be excellent performers. Top performers also are more likely to be trusted by their bosses, so managerial objections may be less extreme. Finally, many employees view telecommuting as a perk, a highly desirable work option that could make their lives a lot easier. Managers may hesitate to bestow this "reward" on average or marginally productive employees.

Rupert disagrees with this assessment. His objection has two parts. First, if you really are managing by objectives, it shouldn't matter what kind of performers you're allowing to telecommute. If you're judging them by their results, why should you care whether they produce these results at the office or at home?

Second, Rupert argues, if top performers can increase their productivity by 15 percent to 25 percent when they telecommute, the potential increases ought to be even greater for average employees. After all, the top performer has a smaller margin for productivity improvement than does the average performer. More over, Rupert continues, telecommuting may be the answer to the very problems that make some of your marginal performers marginal in the first place. If a mother is preoccupied with worries about her children coming home to an empty house every day, or a computer programmer is having trouble with office politics, telecommuting might turn these average performers into excellent ones.

Fleming counters that a pilot program designed for quick success will lead to expansion. Once top management sees that the benefits of telecommuting are substantial and that the obstacles can be overcome, the option is more likely to become available to all employees. He says that's what happened in the telecommuting program he set up for the state of California, which now includes about 200 employees.

Since demand for telecommuting still exceeds supply in most cases, The Travelers is still restricting its telecommuting arrangements to top performers.

Can telecommuting be used as a recruiting tool to attract new employees? This is still more a promise than a reality. Some organizations with telecommuting programs do cite them to prospective employees as a way to demonstrate flexibility and "family friendliness." Most often, however, telecommuting becomes an option only after a person works for the company for awhile and learns the cultural ropes. Fleming supposes that recruiting new employees directly into telecommuting may become more common in the future, but says it's extremely rare today.

Gordon points at the arrival of the Americans with Disabilities Act, however, and suggests that telecommuting may prove a great way to recruit disabled people. When getting to work is half the battle, as it is for many, telecommuting could eliminate a lot of strain. And if it's a good option for disabled people, what about retired people who still want to work but find the commute difficult? Adante is working on a study that will investigate telecommuting as a strategy for recruiting older, retired workers.

So much for recruiting. What about training? Assuming managers are willing to try to manage in a new way, somebody probably will have to teach them how. This suggests training in MBO or whatever strategy people have agreed upon. As for the employees who will be telecommuting, most companies sponsor workshops to help them make the transition. These workshops, usually ranging from half-day to two-day sessions, address some of the concerns people might have: how to keep home life and work life separate, how to manage your work so you don't run out when you're at home, and so on. Also, technical training may be needed on how to use any new equipment involved in the plan—modems, electronic mail systems, and so on.

As you would with any good training program, follow up later to see how trainees are doing. At Bell Atlantic, Duerr heads a support group for telecommuters that's independent of the company. They meet once a month, by conference call, to talk about problems, solutions and general feelings about their new work arrangements.

## THE WRONG WAY

Let's say we all agree by now that the keys to doing this right are good management, open communication, careful selection and appropriate training. What, then, are the traps that can make a telecommuting program go sour for everyone concerned?

Here's a list of "don'ts":

• *Don't make it mandatory.* This is a mistake that really raises Gordon's hackles. Forcing employees to work at home, he insists, is a certain recipe for disaster. Even though many employees are attracted to it, telecommuting isn't for everybody. When J.C. Penney went into its customer service centers to find out who might be interested in telecommuting, the company got about 120 potential candidates out of every group of 500. As Carl Kirkpatrick, planning and program manager for J.C. Penney's telemarketing division in Brookfield, WI, explains, many of his customer service employees took the job to get out of the house. Consequently, telecommuting isn't an attractive option for all of them.

• *Don't cut benefits or compensation.* If you use telecommuting as a way to reduce people's salary, benefits or status, it won't take them long to figure out what your exciting new program is really all about. One of the most notorious examples of a failed telecommuting arrangement was developed by Cal-Western Insurance, an insurance company that formerly resided in Sacramento, CA. Cal-Western decided that a number of its employees should become independent contractors and work at home. All of their benefits were cut, but the strings weren't. The company continued to monitor the workers, manage them and generally treat them as if they were still employees. The newly "independent" workers, who alleged that they were getting none of the benefits and all the hassles of working for Cal-Western, sued the company. The suit eventually was settled out of court. (Shortly after this case, Cal-Western lost its contract with the state of California and was absorbed into its parent company, American General Corp. in Houston.)

•*Don't do it in order to increase productivity.* While productivity gains are often cited as an important benefit of telecommuting, they should not be the primary reason to start a program. Kirkpatrick believes that the quickest way to invoke a "sweatshop mentality" is to start proclaiming to both management and employees how much more work everybody will be doing.

Gordon argues that telecommuting should be presented as a way to retain valuable employees or to make life easier for them. "Do the right things for the right reasons," he says. "Telecommuting should not be used to cover up other problems. For example, if you are experiencing very high turnover or having trouble recruiting people because you're paying 20 percent below the going rate of the market, don't use telecommuting as a way to bribe people to come to work for you."

If a job can be done on a computer,
some remarkable new equipment
will allow most disabled people to do it.
But the question remains,
what's a 'reasonable accommodation'?

# ADAPTIVE TECHNOLOGY FOR THE DISABLED

## BOB FILIPCZAK

**Bob Filipczak** *is staff editor of TRAINING Magazine.*

### PART ONE: ADAPTATION

It was an eerie feeling, sitting in front of a computer that did everything but read my mind. At the 10th annual Closing the Gap conference in Minneapolis, a show dedicated to adaptive technology for people with disabilities, a woman sat me down in front of a modified computer monitor to show me what her system did. What it did was just a little less amazing than what I did *not* have to do in order to use it.

A small device beneath the monitor fired an infrared beam that bounced off my cornea and onto the computer screen. Consequently, a red dot appeared on the monitor representing where my eye was looking. With this red dot I could call up a menu of items that included environmental control, speech output and a keyboard. With the keyboard represented on the screen, I could eye-type my name—albeit slowly—or ask for a beer or express my chagrin over the federal deficit. If an audience couldn't read my words from the screen, a voice synthesizer would speak them aloud. With other menus I could turn off a light, turn on a TV or turn up the heat.

What I didn't have to do was move. Except for the flickering of my eyes, I was completely still. Even wearing my eyeglasses didn't interfere with the system. No equipment was strapped to my head. The calibration the technician did to get the system used to me took only about a minute.

I began to get an inkling of what Richard Ring, an editor of a computer magazine for the blind, would later confirm. Ring, who is blind, says of adaptive technology, "[Using a computer] means more to us than it ever did to you."

The advent last year of the Americans with Disabilities Act (ADA) has made it illegal to discriminate against a disabled job applicant who is capable of doing the job. At the same time, adaptive technologies are rewriting the book on what disabled people are, in fact, able to do. The system I used, called Eyegaze, is manufactured by LC Technologies of Fairfax, VA. It makes computers accessible to people so severely paralyzed that they can move nothing but their eyes. That kind of disability used to render a person hopelessly unemployable. No more.

Unless you've seen a presentation by Steven Hawking, the world-renowned physicist and author of the best-selling *A Brief History of Time,* chances are you don't begin to suspect the kind of technology that is now available. Here's an introduction.

## COMPUTERS THAT TALK

The range of human disabilities generally can be grouped into four areas: visual, auditory, mobility and cognitive. Of those four, the most

**The Eyegaze system from LC Technologies is one of the more advanced examples of adaptive technology.**

dramatic technological developments are for impairments of vision or mobility.

For visually impaired people, the simplest accommodation for using computers is a software program that will expand the size of the letters on the screen or reverse them to black letters on a white background. This is the computer equivalent of large-print books and is a built-in feature of most new Macintosh computers. Special software is also available for IBM-compatibles.

For blind people (that is, people who can't see at all), large print is not an option. The next step on the technology ladder is a screen reader, which consists of special software that interacts with a voice synthesizer that reads aloud whatever is on the computer screen. With this system, any document that can be put on a screen becomes accessible to people who are blind. That includes electronic mail, documents developed on word processors or news services that can be accessed via modem.

Add a scanner to this screen-reader system and a blind person can access almost any written document, including newspapers, books and memos. A scanner is essentially a mainstream computer device that takes a picture of a document—not unlike the one a fax or copy machine takes—and turns the print on the paper into print on a computer screen. Then a screen reader can read it to you.

If you put a scanner, a computer, appropriate software and a voice synthesizer into one integrated system, you've got a reading machine. It can take any paper document and read it to a person who can't see. The two best-known systems are from Arkenstone, a nonprofit developer in Sunnyvale, CA, and the Kurzweil reader from Xerox. (Ray Kurzweil, a pioneer in optical character recognition technology, developed the first reading machine for the blind in 1975. He later sold the technology to Xerox and

went on to develop a system of voice recognition for computers, his current project.) The advantage of the Kurzweil reader in its latest configuration is portability.

A reading machine scans a page of print and reads it aloud. While that may sound simple, the doors it opens for blind people are almost unlimited. This is the sort of thing that helps level the playing field by giving blind people information parity. As Ring puts it, "If I have access to any information you do, and I can use it in the same way that you do, then I can do the job that you do."

Computers are also creating a kind of renaissance for braille. Before personal computers, braille books were expensive, bulky and very hard to find. Now braille printers make most written materials accessible to anyone who can read braille. The next generation of technology in this area is the braille monitor or refreshable braille system. This device allows a braille reader to use a keyboard modification to read a line-by-line braille representation of whatever appears on the computer screen.

One of the most popular pieces of technology among braille users is the Braille 'n Speak from Blazie Engineering in Forest Hill, MD. This little device, about the size of a brick, is outfitted with a braille keyboard (which consists of eight keys), a voice synthesizer, 640K of memory and a port that allows you to download your notes to a computer. It's often used for taking notes during meetings and seminars.

Glenn Kroll, technical director of information systems at Travelers Insurance Co. in Hartford, CT, admits that he has never been very good at reading braille. He can, however, write braille pretty well, so he takes notes with his Braille 'n Speak and lets the voice synthesizer read the notes to him later. He can also hook up the device to any computer and use the voice synthesizer as a kind of portable screen reader.

## KEYBOARD ALTERNATIVES

On the mobility-impairment front, a number of access solutions are available because so many are needed. Whether the cause is a spinal-cord injury or multiple sclerosis or cerebral palsy, people with mobility impairments often need specially customized access to whatever job they are hired to do. For the severely disabled, something as advanced as the Eyegaze system may be necessary, but extreme efforts to accommodate the mobility-impaired are rare.

Many people with mobility impairments need special technology only to get them to work and get them home. Motorized wheelchairs and accessible transportation may be all they require to be fully functional members of the work force. If the impairment is more severe, special access to keyboards and computers can still be a simple and cheap solution.

"Keyboard solutions" are simple software programs that alter the way the keyboard interacts with the computer. Apple has keyboard solutions built right into its new computers and IBM has a DOS (disk operating system) program called AccessDOS

# SOMETHING FOR EVERYONE?

Clearly, there have been some miraculous advances in technology—especially in computer technology—during the past two decades. And some of these developments, like screen readers and voice-recognition systems, hold promises for everyone, not just disabled people. Just like curb cuts in sidewalks that serve bicycles as well as wheelchairs, many of the solutions that make the world more accessible to people with disabilities can also make life easier for the rest of us.

For example, John Roberts, product manager for IBM's Special Needs Systems in Boca Raton, FL, says that screen readers can help employees do inventory. The computer reads what's supposed to be on the shelves so the user can concentrate on what's actually on the shelves, making the inventory process more efficient.

Voice-recognition systems have obvious applications for people who need to do things with their hands and take notes at the same time. Jerry Thompson, president of Business Machines Sales and Services in Minneapolis, sells Dragon Dictate, a voice-recognition system for personal computers. Some buyers, he says, are able-bodied people who have found a use for the device on the job.

For instance, the quality control inspectors for a ceramics manufacturer discovered the advantages of a computer they could talk to. The line inspector used to pick up a piece of ceramic and write notes about its color, pattern and any flaws he could spot. The information on each slip of paper was later entered into the computer. With a voice-recognition system, the inspector wears a headset and simply describes each piece to the computer. This system not only sped up the inspection process, it also got rid of all the paperwork and data entry that the old system demanded because the information goes directly into the computer.

As voice recognition becomes faster and more accurate, it should be able to enter words into the computer at conversational speed (80 to 120 words per minute). When that happens, a lot of us may be exchanging our keyboards for microphones.—**B.F.**

---

that's free to anyone who wants it. (Call 1-(800)-426-7282. In Canada, 1-(800)-465-1234.)

Stickykeys, a program available to both Macintosh and IBM users, allows a person with a mobility impairment to type combinations of keys using only one finger. To type a capital "T," for instance, it isn't necessary to press the shift key and the "T" key at the same time. Hit the shift button, and the computer remembers you did it. Then hit the "T," and the letter is capitalized.

Other keyboard solutions include taking the repeat function off the keyboard so a person who has limited control of his hands won't type three rows of "E's" before he can lift his finger off the key. For others who tend to hit more than one key with whatever appendage they use, a keyboard solution can be set up so that the "F" key will signal the computer to type an "F" only when it is held down for more than a second. Finally, a keyboard overlay can be installed so fingers can rest on the keyboard without pushing the keys down and inadvertently typing nonsense. This overlay is simply a plastic panel with a hole in it for every key.

If these simple keyboard solutions aren't enough to make a computer fully functional for a given individual, the technology can lead in two directions: Make the keystrokes more efficient or leave the keyboard behind completely. "Word-predictive software" increases efficiency by reducing the number of keys you have to type to get the word you want. For people who can type only a few words a minute, word-predictive software can speed up a laborious process by providing a list of words every time a key is entered. Type the letter "T" and the software will give you a menu of common words that start with "T": the, this, that, then, etc. If the word you want doesn't come up on the menu, type the next letter and a new menu appears until you've either typed the whole word or found the one you want.

Word-predictive software also learns from its user. If you use a word often in your writing, it will begin to appear on the menu more often as you type the first letters of the word. Rick Creech is an augmentative communication specialist for the Pennsylvania Assistive Technology Center in Harrisburg. Because he uses the words "augmentative communication" a lot, his software has learned to spit out that phrase after only a few keystrokes.

Creech's mobility impairment, caused by cerebral palsy, also keeps him from using his voice. His computer is outfitted with a voice-output device called the DECtalk, from Digital Equipment Corp. in Maynard, MA. When he types a word, the computer speaks it aloud. This is very similar to the system Steven Hawking uses, and it allows Creech to communicate in ways that were impossible just five years ago. His job includes giving presentations about augmentative systems like the one he uses. He can type these presentations ahead of time, store them on computer and deliver them with a speech-output device that is surprisingly clear and easy to understand.

While conversations with someone using an augmentative communication system tend to be considerably slower than normal, they are still genuine conversations. Here's part of a telephone interview with Creech.

**TRAINING:** I saw a presentation by someone using a similar system…. He did a half-hour demon-

**The technology can lead in two directions: Make the keystrokes more efficient or leave the keyboard behind completely.**

**Xerox's Reading Edge is the sixth generation of a reading machine for the visually impaired.**

stration, maybe 45 minutes. It was very clear; it made a lot of sense, but I wondered...I understand that you do presentations as well?

**Creech:** Yes.

**TRAINING:** I'm just wondering how long it takes to prepare a demonstration of 15 minutes or a half hour or something along those lines.

**Creech:** If I know what I want to say, it doesn't take all that long. You're hearing the speed at which I am communicating now, and that's my average speed.

**TRAINING:** Do people talk to you slower or louder because they figure you can only hear as fast as you can talk?

**Creech:** Yes, and sometimes that drives me up a wall.

That exchange took a little less than two-and-a-half minutes. The voice-output device says each word as it is typed and then repeats the whole phrase when the person has completed the sentence.

Assuming she can speak, a person with a mobility impairment can gain access to computer technology by using voice-recognition systems. These consist of software and hardware that allow the user to speak into a microphone and put her words on the screen. You can speak at about 40 words per minute with 90 percent accuracy provided you pause one second between each word. These voice-recognition systems have varying degrees of power and sophistication based on the speed of the computer and the size of the internal dictionary. A 30,000-word dictionary, for example, uses up to 8MB of RAM because all those words have to be instantly available to the computer as you speak. This software, like word-predictive software, also learns your speech patterns and adjusts itself accordingly. It can even accommodate regional accents. (See Tech Trends, TRAINING, June 1992.)

One surprising form of communication is making a comeback among mobility-impaired people who want access to computers: Morse code. For those who can't use a keyboard but have some motion left in a finger or toe, using Morse code to enter text and

send commands is often a viable option. A little software manipulation reinterprets the dots and dashes as letters and the disabled person can then have full use of the computer.

## TELEPHONE ALTERNATIVES

People with hearing impairments generally don't need any special equipment to use computers, but other office equipment presents problems.

The telephone is perhaps the least user-friendly device a hearing-impaired person encounters in the business world. Two products are currently available to overcome this hurdle. One is the Telecommunications Device for the Deaf (TDD). This is a keyboard and small screen that displays one or two lines of text. It can be plugged directly into the phone line or hooked up to a regular phone.

The drawback to this technology is that you must have a TDD in order to call someone else who has a TDD; it's a closed system. If your company has customers with hearing impairments, you may want to look into getting a TDD. In fact, depending on how things shake out in the expected blizzard of lawsuits and court rulings involving the Americans with Disabilities Act, your company may have no choice in the matter.

The other adaptive technology for people with hearing impairments is a product from IBM called PhoneCommunicator. It connects the phone to a computer so that the screen blinks when the user gets a call. When the hearing-impaired person answers the phone, he can type a message on the computer and a voice synthesizer will read it to the caller. The caller can likewise type messages across the phone lines using the letters associated with the numbers on the keypad of a touch-tone phone. The hitch is, of course, that each number on a telephone might stand for three different letters. The software on the computer end of the line makes educated guesses, with pretty good accuracy, about the words being typed and displays the message to the person with the hearing impairment.

Producers of commercial training videos have recognized the limitations of their medium for people who can't hear, and many suppliers have followed the lead of television producers by providing closed-captioned videos. Surprisingly, some trainers have found that the captions also help participants who can hear because they find it easier to take notes when the subtitles appear on the screen.

## COGNITIVE IMPAIRMENTS

As far as technological help is concerned, cognitive impairments are probably the trickiest kinds of disabilities. It's difficult to imagine someone with a severe brain injury or Alzheimer's being able to accomplish meaningful work on a computer. Under the broad umbrella of cognitive impairment, however, are people who have learning disabilities such as dyslexia or attention deficit disorder.

According to Peter Moulton, manager of disability resources at Apple Computer's Worldwide Disability Solutions Group in Cupertino, CA, people with learning disabilities make up the largest segment of the disabled community. Some of the built-

# DOES HIGH TECH MEAN HIGH PRICE?

**M**ost forms of adaptive technology are designed to make a computer accessible to a person with a disability, so let's assume you've already got a computer in the office where the newly hired employee is going to work. Here are some ballpark prices on the kinds of equipment discussed in the accompanying article.

**Under $500:** keyboard overlays, software that alters keyboard functions, print enlargers for computer monitors, some low-end screen-reading software, some voice synthesizers, Telecommunications Devices for the Deaf (TDDs).

**$500 to $1,000:** word-predictive software, midrange voice synthesizers, most screen-reading software.

**$1,000 to $5,000:** reading machines, voice-recognition systems, top-of-the-line voice synthe-

sizers, some braille printers, Braille 'n Speak.

**$5,000 to $10,000:** braille printers, braille monitors, completely portable communication systems (like the one used by physicist Steven Hawking).

**$10,000 to $20,000:** completely compatible braille laptop computers, Eyegaze System (as described in attached article).

For more information on adaptive equipment and the companies that make it, contact Closing the Gap (P.O. Box 68, Henderson, MN 56044, (612) 248-3294) and ask for its annual resource directory. For literature on adaptive technology, contact the Trace Center (S-151 Waisman Center, 1500 Highland Ave., Madison, WI 53705, (608) 262-6966) and ask for its publications and media catalog.—**B.F.**

---

in features of the Macintosh, like the graphical user interface and mouse, are particularly useful for the learning disabled, says Moulton. (Adding Microsoft Windows and a mouse to an IBM-compatible computer achieves much the same effect.)

Other kinds of technology already mentioned can help, too. With a screen reader, for example, a dyslexic individual can get through a production report in half the time it would take him to read it himself. Often reading is easier if the entire screen isn't filled with text, so programs that expand the size of the type on the screen, and thus reduce the total amount of information assaulting the individual, also can help.

Word-predictive software can assist people who have trouble spelling words correctly when they write. If they know what they want to say, learning-impaired people can choose the words from a menu of correctly spelled words instead of trying to extract it from memory.

# PART TWO: REASONABLE ACCOMMODATION

**A**s we've seen, computers can help people with almost every type of disability adapt to the workplace. Consequently, a tremendous variety of office jobs could be handled by disabled people. But handled how well, how quickly and at what expense to the employer? If access is one side of the coin, competitiveness with nondisabled workers is the other.

This is where the concept of reasonable accommodation, a phrase written into the ADA legislation that enters into almost every discussion of the law, needs some interpretation. The courts are wrestling

with it, the disabled community is wrestling with it, and before long your company probably will have to wrestle with it, too. The fact is, all of this adaptive technology costs money—and seeking the least-expensive solution may not be a solution at all.

What it boils down to is choosing the technology that will make an employee with a disability as productive as his able-bodied peers. For example, a visually impaired worker may be able to *get along* using a screen expander that makes the computer text large enough to see. If, however, the person can read only 20 or 30 words a minute using this system, or if it tires his eyes quickly, a more expensive screen-reading system might make sense. This way, the disabled worker might be able to perform at the same level as everyone else. But at what initial cost?

Cathlene Schroeder is a systems analyst for the New Mexico Department of Labor in Albuquerque. She is blind. When choosing the adaptive technology she needs to do her job, the acid test she uses is competitiveness. She uses a screen reader and voice synthesizer. Like many people, Schroeder isn't crazy about the quality of the voice—its tone, pronunciation and clarity. But she opted against the clearer digitized voice of a system like DECtalk, because she needs a faster system. "The problem with the DEC[talk] is that it's clearer speech, but I'm in a competitive situation," says Schroeder, "I need response instantaneously." In other words, her job programming computers and making sure out-of-work New Mexicans get their unemployment checks demands speed and accuracy. We'll talk more about speed in a moment.

Darren Gabbert, coordinator for the Adaptive Computing Technology Center at the University of Missouri-Columbia, agrees that competitiveness— not just accessibility—is the key issue. Gabbert and his colleagues have developed an expert system

**What it boils down to is choosing the technology that will make an employee with a disability as productive as his able-bodied peers.**

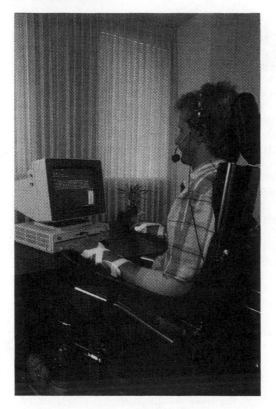

VoiceType from IBM allows access to computers through voice-recognition technology.

In some cases, disabled people using adaptive technology can be *more* productive than their coworkers. We noted earlier that Cathlene Schroeder listens to her screen reader at an accelerated pace. The fact is, many blind and visually impaired people can listen to speech output at about 300 words a minute. When I heard it at this speed, it sounded like gibberish to my untrained ear.

I timed myself and found that I can read, silently, at about 120 words per minute. Greg Guidice, the director of marketing for Xerox Imaging Systems in Hayward, CA, says some visually impaired people are able to use his company's reading machine, The Reading Edge, at its top speed of 500 words a minute.

## DON'T TRY THIS AT HOME

How do you determine what kind of adaptive technology a given individual needs to do a given job? Gabbert's expert system, still under development, is refining a list of generic questions designed to zero in on the right choices, but most experts suggest that the best way to get started is to ask the individual in question. As often as not, says John Roberts, product manager for IBM's Special Needs Systems in Boca Raton, FL, the disabled person will have a good idea of what she needs—especially if she has been employed before—and may know of some cheap, simple solutions.

A qualified professional, such as an occupational therapist, can also help. You can contact these people at local hospitals, state vocational rehabilitation departments and through national organizations like the National Easter Seal Society. Also, ADA centers located around the country can help you make intelligent decisions about hiring people with disabilities and making your business accessible.

One such ADA facility is the Trace Center at the University of Wisconsin in Madison. Communications director Peter Borden suggests that if you're looking for expert advice about adaptive technology, be sure to find someone who is up-to-date. Your state vocational and rehabilitation department is an obvious place to turn; it's in the business of placing disabled people in jobs. But, warns Borden, understaffed and underfunded departments may not have the latest information about adaptive technology. If you can find the right expert, however, "You could have one conversation with a person who knows what they're doing and you'd be on the right track," he says.

Berlis is particularly sensitive to people making decisions about equipment without enough information. "The greatest danger," she says, "and the thing that's going to cause the greatest output of money is *assuming* what someone needs and buying it for them."

But the responsibility for deciding what technology to buy does not necessarily rest solely with the employer. Pledger insists that disabled employees bear some of the burden. While the employer may be responsible for hiring the person and buying the equipment, the employee should be responsible for doing the research on the technology and finding out what works best. "In order for ADA to really take

called AC/ES that helps determine the appropriate technology for disabled people based on the limits imposed by their disabilities.

If you tell the AC/ES system that you are blind, you read braille, you'll be using a computer to do accounting work and you need a portable system for on-site accounting for customers, the software spits out a list of equipment that fits your needs. Some of this equipment likely will be pretty high-tech and costly. But, as Gabbert asserts, "there are a lot of cheaper, very clever little devices that will give you computer access, but that's not always the same as being competitive with your nondisabled peers."

Jeff Pledger, a data-base administrator in the Federal Systems Division of Bell Atlantic in Silver Spring, MD, insists that disabled employees ought to have to prove themselves just like other employees. Pledger, who has been blind for eight years, recommends that a worker with a disability begin by asking for the least-expensive or least-intrusive adaptive solution. Once she's shown the employer that she can do the job and do it well, she can start asking for more sophisticated equipment that will make her more productive and make the equipment more cost-effective.

Jane Berlis is access products director for Berkeley Systems in Berkeley, CA, a software developer that makes a screen reader and screen enlarger for Macintosh computers. She agrees that adaptive solutions should be, above all, cost-effective. When asked for her definition of reasonable accommodation, she asserts that a $1,000 speech output system looks pretty reasonable if the employee is generating $20,000 in profits.

off, to really be effective and to be worth something more than writing on a piece of paper," he says, "it has to be a shared responsibility."

## FUNDING HELP

When the smoke clears, the employer is left with one question: How much is this accommodation going to cost me?

The air is full of statistics about how reasonably priced reasonable accommodation is. Conventional wisdom states that half of all accommodations for disabled employees or customers cost less than $100 and another 30 percent cost less than $1,000. That leaves 20 percent in the $1,000-and-up range.

As with computer technology in general, however, prices are dropping fast. The Kurzweil reader cost $50,000 when it was introduced in 1975. The current, sixth-generation model costs about $5,000. Dragon Dictate, the voice-recognition system, has decreased in price while increasing in power and accuracy over the last three years. That pattern presumably will continue. (For more on prices, see box page 75.)

Nevertheless, the ADA affects almost all employers, including small businesses with very little extra money lying around. If a company wants to hire people with disabilities, can it get some financial help? The answer is a qualified yes.

Lewis Golinker is the funding coordinator for Project Mentor in Ithaca, NY, a program sponsored by the United Cerebral Palsy Association. He is a firm believer in the idea that employers should push for as much help as possible, both advice and funding, from their state vocational and rehabilitation (VR) departments.

Golinker points out that while a VR agency can't give funds to a company, it can buy adaptive equipment for a disabled person who is either already at work or about to be hired. Employers who seek this kind of help from VR departments may have to get pushy, he says, because initial resistance is almost guaranteed. His advice: Go ahead and push.

That means arguing that your company can't afford, say, a $10,000 braille monitor that falls outside *your* definition of a "reasonable accommodation." Your state VR agency will make the same argument: It doesn't have the money. It's up to you to point out that your company is in business to make bicycles or sell insurance while the VR agency is in business to place people with disabilities in jobs. You may even have to threaten a court action to get some movement.

As Golinker sees it, people with disabilities "get caught in the door because the VR agency refuses to pay, saying it's the obligation of the employer, and the employer doesn't do anything, and the placement gets lost....To me, without any question, it's the VR agency's responsibility."

Ring suggests taking this tack when approaching a VR agency: Tell the person in charge of saying no, "I'm going to take one of your clients and set him free. I'm going to give him a life here, give him the ability to make his own decisions." And if you want to get really cold about it, "I'm going to take him off your [pay]roll."

If, however, you work for a large corporation that is turning a good profit, you're unlikely to win many arguments with the state VR agency. (Also, the agency may be telling the truth when it says it hasn't got the money to buy the adaptive equipment your prospective employee needs.) Furthermore, Golinker says, a court will interpret what's "reasonable" based on your company's size and bank balance.

Madalaine Pugliese, a partner in the Boston consulting firm Pugliese, Davey and Associates, travels the country delivering seminars on adaptive technology. Finding alternative funding sources is a topic that comes up often in her discussions with school administrators, occupational therapists and employers. She acknowledges the limited funds of VR agencies and helps her clients seek other funding solutions. For example, if you can get a doctor to write a prescription for one of these devices, Medicaid will pay for it. You may have to educate the doctor about adaptive technology, however, to get him to write such a prescription.

Pugliese also recommends a packet of forms, letters and advice about finding funding that is distributed by Prentke Romich, a Wooster, OH, company that designs systems for people whose mobility impairments have robbed them of speech. Prentke Romich set up the system that allows Rick Creech to be gainfully employed, write books and converse with people. Its forms are the kind that use Medicaid jargon and governmentspeak to cut a swathe through roadblocks in the bureaucratic jungle.

And don't forget about corporate and private philanthropy, adds Pugliese. There's a lot of funding out there for people with disabilities if you know where to look. One New York-based philanthropic organization, called simply The Foundation, has branches in almost every state. These branches maintain libraries of vast collections of information about potential sources of funding. Pugliese suggests picking the brains of the librarians in charge of these collections; they are often funding experts in their own right.

Some money is also available from a coalition of foundations led by the Dole Foundation in Washington, DC, and the J.M. Foundation in New York City. This coalition offers funds to community projects promoting cooperation between business and the disabled community. Some of these funds can be used to buy adaptive equipment.

Finally, Borden suggests the book *Financing Adaptive Technology: A Guide to Sources and Strategies for Blind and Visually Impaired Users* by Steven Mendelsohn (Smiling Interface Publishers, New York).

## HOW REASONABLE ARE YOU?

As technology removes the physical barriers to employment for disabled people, the social and attitudinal barriers become that much more frustrating. Apple's Moulton laments that ignorance is often the most formidable obstacle a disabled worker faces. Of all the disheartening stories he hears, perhaps the worst is the recurring one about the person "who could be employed doing the job that he or she was trained to do—before they had an accident that

> **'In large measure, the unemployment and under-employment of people with disabilities is a national disgrace.'**

resulted in a disability—but has been at home doing nothing for five or six years. And we *know* the technology was available to put that person back to work as soon as he was done with his rehabilitation program."

According to Moulton, there are 43 million Americans with disabilities. According to IBM's Roberts, between 70 percent and 80 percent of them are unemployed.

That means there is a gold mine of untapped potential out there. Golinker states the case bluntly: "In large measure, the unemployment and underemployment of people with disabilities is a national disgrace."

Those statistics create a catch-22 for Jim Fructerman, president of Arkenstone. Because so few blind and visually impaired people are employed, there's not enough of a market for his company to build Arkenstone Readers at a profit. The price of his reading machines can't come down until demand goes up. And there won't be more demand if the high rate of unemployment for disabled people persists. The same is true of high-priced equipment like braille monitors and braille printers.

Adaptive technology is making "reasonable accommodation" cheaper, faster, better and more portable. If we take into account the studies indicating high degrees of loyalty and productivity from people with disabilities, as well as low absentee rates, it makes more sense than ever to bring these people into the work force. Never mind the mandates of the ADA. With the help of adaptive technology, disabled employees can do the job—if we let them.

**Editor's note:** *This article is available for visually impaired individuals on computer disks (Macintosh- or IBM-compatible) or on audiocassette.*

# Do It Yourself

*Brian Hayes*

*BRIAN HAYES is the editor of* AMERICAN SCIENTIST.

They say we live in a service economy, that today the main business of business is not making things but tending to people's needs. We do for one another—you flip my hamburgers and I baby-sit your kids—and by some magic, wealth is created out of the transaction. Three-fourths of all jobs in the United States are service-sector jobs. And yet, to a remarkable degree we inhabit a self-service world.

Within living memory, people who were no more than respectably rich needed servants to help them dress in the morning and bathe in the evening. Now most families wash their own clothes, cook their own meals, clean their own house, drive their own car, mow their own lawn, shine their own shoes. The self-service elevator is all but universal. The telephone company has persuaded us to dial our own calls and now expects us to install our own telephones. In the past decade we have learned to pump our own gas. When we move the household, some of us rent a truck and haul our own furniture. We go to an automatic teller machine to do our own banking. There is even do-it-yourself surgery: after a minor operation not long ago, I was sent home with instructions on how to remove my own sutures.

The new emphasis on doing it yourself has brought with it tremendous social and technological change. Consider the supermarket, an institution founded on the idea of self-service shopping. The supermarket was made possible by changes in the packaging of goods, and it has given rise to further changes in both packaging and marketing, not to mention eating habits. Do-it-yourself laundry has a similar history. It was not enough to develop the automatic washing machine. A precondition for the success of that device was a detergent that would clean with a mere swishing in water rather than heavy-duty rubbing. And the advantages of the washing machine were not fully realized until the textiles industry developed fabrics that respond well to such treatment, thereby eliminating the need for the ironing board as well as the washboard.

The automobile provides another example. Do-it-yourself transportation is favored so strongly in most American cities that alternative means of getting around can barely survive. The result of the attachment to the automobile has been a thoroughgoing transformation of the landscape, the atmosphere, the world economy and the urban way of life. Nations are ready to go to war for the right to sit in a rush-hour traffic jam.

Not all the changes brought on by the do-it-yourself movement are entirely for the best. Supermarket packaging is overflowing our garbage dumps; phosphate-rich detergents are suffocating our lakes; the automobile is suffocating *us*. Nevertheless, the social effects of the do-it-yourself movement seem primarily beneficial. They reinforce the more democratic and egalitarian tendencies in American society. In my own life, at least, the new order is welcome. I believe self-reliance is a virtue. I am made uncomfortable by the close attention of personal servants. I will drive an extra mile to find a gas station with a self-service pump. I certainly want no one else to draw my bath for me in the evening.

I would also like to believe that the self-service economy would be welcomed as an emancipation by those who toiled at pumping gas, shining shoes or pressing linen at steam-driven mangles. But of course the change in their lives has been a change for the better only if they have been put to better work; too often they have merely been put out of work.

The most dramatic social changes—but also the most ambiguous—are the ones that affect the roles of women. When the middle-class family gave up household servants in the 1930s, 1940s and 1950s, the work of those servants was taken on by the wife, who became cook, butler, valet, chauffeur. Indeed, wives are the heroes and pioneers of the do-it-yourself revolution. For some years—for a generation or two—a life of doing it yourself at home was the only choice available to many women. Lately that way of life has changed, as women have been welcomed back into the work force or have been compelled by economic necessity to rejoin it. One might therefore suppose that even men would now be learning to do for themselves. Perhaps some of us are.

Most of the developments mentioned above focus on the home and private life. There is a similar movement toward self-reliance under way in the workplace. In decades past the middle-class man of affairs—the one whose household included a cook, a gardener and a charwoman—was surrounded at the office by an equally elaborate support staff. In Dickens and Melville we read of copyists and clerks and office boys—all male. With the invention of the typewriter and carbon paper, copyists were eliminated, and subsequently women were admitted to office work as typists, stenographers and secretaries. Then came the photocopying machine and another shuffling of personnel; the typing pool was abolished. Now further changes are in progress or in prospect, driven this time by the availability of cheap computing power.

One case in which the issues are particularly clear is electronic mail (known to

This article is reprinted by permission of *The Sciences* and is from the March/April 1991 issue, pp. 13-15. Individual subscriptions are $18.00 per year. Write to The Sciences, 2 East 63rd Street, New York, NY 10021 or call 1-800-THE-NYAS.

those who use it as e-mail). In my work I carry on a fair amount of correspondence, most of it on paper but a growing proportion flowing over the electronic networks. Most people who write to me on paper employ secretarial help to produce their letters. Electronic mail, in contrast, is strictly a do-it-yourself operation. As far as I know, I have never received an e-mail message that did not come directly from the hand of the sender. My own habits reflect the same pattern: when letters must be sent on paper, I often dictate them, but e-mail messages I always write and dispatch on my own.

An important reason for the difference is the greater convenience of electronic mail, even when each kind of missive is prepared with the aid of a computer and word-processing software. With e-mail there is no need to feed letterhead stock through the printer and follow it with an envelope; once you have written the message, a single keystroke sends it on its way. Furthermore, standards of formality are more relaxed on the electronic network; no one bothers about typographical errors, and there is no such thing as a second draft. The tone is conversational, which is to be expected in a medium in which messages are delivered in seconds or minutes rather than in days. Perhaps most important, the sociology of network communications is quite different from that of the U.S. mail. The idea of e-mail was born on the ARPANET, the national computer network set up by the Department of Defense twenty years ago. The early users of that system belonged to the research community, and most of them were computer enthusiasts. They would no more ask a secretary to sit at their terminal and read their e-mail than a sports car enthusiast would hire a chauffeur to drive her Ferrari. (Of course some people in the academic world do not have a secretary—or a Ferrari.)

Another area in which the do-it-yourself movement has had a remarkable influence is engineering. A few years ago a mechanical engineer required the support of a cadre of subordinate designers, draftsmen and detailers, who spent most of their time preparing drawings. Today an engineer working alone can readily produce finished drawings and specifications entirely without (human) assistance. This feat is made practical by computer-aided design, or CAD, in which three-dimensional shapes are sketched and refined on a computer screen, while a corresponding data base records the evolving properties and relations among the represented objects. In some cases the output of the CAD program can directly control a computer-driven machine tool, so that the engineer not only designs the object but even manufactures it single-handedly.

In electronic engineering, computer assistance is all but mandatory. The designer of an integrated circuit works with a CAD program to define the structures that will be built up in various layers of metal, semiconductor and insulator on the surface of a silicon chip. Another program verifies that the design obeys all the geometric rules established for a given semiconductor technology, and still another program simulates the operation of the circuit. When the design is complete, the data files can be transmitted (over the same networks that carry e-mail) to a "silicon foundry," where the chip is fabricated. Again a single individual has been given control of an entire manufacturing process.

What prompts these reflections on doing it yourself is a recent personal experience that has given me a sense of liberation similar to what I imagine an engineer might feel on turning an idea directly into hardware. Part of my work is to devise illustrations—drawings, diagrams, graphs and the like—for magazine publication. For many years I have done this by collaborating with an artist, who would attempt to draw what I dreamed up. The process would start with my sketch, however crude, which would serve as an aid in communicating with the artist. Then the artist would show me a more refined sketch, which I would revise; after two or three iterations of this process we would converge on a finished illustration. The multiple cycles of revision were needed not because the artist failed to follow my instructions but because I never seemed to know what I wanted to see until I had seen it.

Now I have discovered, to my surprise, that with the help of certain computer software I can prepare many routine illustrations on my own. The computer has not made an artist of me, but it offers so much assistance with the elementary, mechanical aspects of drawing—making round circles, ruling straight lines—that someone without much aptitude or training can fake it quite successfully. As a drawing tool the computer is not so much a better pencil as a better eraser. It allows you to see immediately where you have gone wrong and to revise endlessly without rubbing a hole through the paper. It also solves the "Plan Ahea" problem: if an illustration drawn on paper does not fit its allotted space, the artist may well have to start all over; working on a computer, however, one merely tugs at a corner of the drawing to rescale it.

Computer programs for drawing and illustration make up part of the technology called desktop publishing. Getting a bit of prose printed was once a collaborative effort of at least eight people. A writer wrote it; an editor edited it; a compositor set it in type; a proofreader checked the compositor's work; a designer laid out the pages; a printer or a paste-up artist put the type into the pages; a lithographer or a stereotyper created printing plates; a pressman (or a press crew) ran off the copies. Most of this work can now be done by one person, sitting at one machine. Writing, editing, setting type, proofreading, designing and putting type into pages all are tasks for the solitary desktop publisher; only platemaking and printing still require investments of craft and capital that are beyond the means of the individual.

In music too, as in the graphic arts, there is the promise of a new autonomy. The computer will not turn you into a musician or a composer, but it will remove some of the emphasis on performance skills. With a computer program called a sequencer you can piece together a melodic invention note by note, as slowly as you please, and the machine will then play the composition at its proper tempo. You can keep trying different notes until you finally stumble on the right one. Moreover, you become conductor as well as composer, and you can hear your work in its fully orchestrated form without hiring Carnegie Hall. A one-man band indeed.

Even in areas as cool and forbidding as statistics and mathematics the computer has introduced a new spirit of self-sufficiency. There was a time when a biologist with experimental results to analyze might have asked the advice of a statistician and would surely have enlisted the help of a graduate student to perform the numerical work. Computer programs have now taken the drudgery out of the more routine mathematical tasks—fitting a curve to data, say, or estimating statistical significance. What is more remarkable is that there is mechanized help available even for higher mathematics: with a program for symbolic manipulation I can solve equations beyond my capacity with paper and pencil. I feel sheepish in saying it, but I can come up with answers to problems I do not understand.

What about do-it-yourself computing? A long-standing dream of computer science is to dispense with the profession of programming and enable those who use computers to create their own software. A lot of that is going on: much excellent software is being written by people whose training is not in computing. So far, however, people have been adapting to the needs of the machine, not the other way around. Physicists learn to speak FORTRAN; astronomers control their telescopes with programs they write in

FORTH; businesspeople master the intricacies of linear programming and other algorithms for optimization. The software that will make computing easy for everyone does not yet exist, but it may not be an altogether vain notion.

I have said that I welcome the social effects of self-reliance in personal life, but what about the consequences of such changes in the workplace? The various trends described above would appear to be bad news for secretaries, draftsmen, illustrators and proofreaders, among others. The compositors who once operated stately Linotype machines have already been displaced. The jobs of programmers may one day be in jeopardy, and for that matter editors are not totally secure.

On the other hand, one ought to keep in mind that telling a machine what to do will always be more difficult than telling a person what to do. It seems unlikely, therefore, that captains of industry will ever give up their trains of aides and assistants. As a matter of fact, the social milieu of most large corporations seems set up to reward dependency and to discourage self-reliance. After all, it is a milieu dominated by people whose very function is not to do it themselves but to tell someone else to do it. The way to get ahead in that world is to manage people, not to operate machines. As long as the boss claims she cannot type, the secretary will not disappear; but with any luck, he might get to do more interesting work.

There are other reasons for having misgivings about the do-it-yourself movement. In the arts and the sciences the changes under discussion here amount to a triumph of amateurism. Computer-based tools may compensate to some extent for the amateur's lack of skill, but they cannot make up for a failure of taste or judgment. Professional artists and designers cringe at some of the products of desktop publishing, which tend to show the exuberant recklessness of a child's first adventure with a can of spray paint. Even when the worst offenses are avoided, it often seems that something is missing. A living and breathing artist will listen to your plans and then respond, "I have a better idea." Computer programs do not volunteer.

In the end the main effect of the computer on aesthetic sensibilities may be to increase our appreciation of those arts and crafts that continue to resist mechanization. I have learned to produce meticulous diagrams of carefully plotted geometry, but what I admire most is the sure brush stroke of the watercolorist, who works in a medium that supplies no erasers, in which it has to be done right the first time.

Finally, I must admit to a doubt about the healthfulness of all this autonomy and self-sufficiency. Doing it yourself offers important psychological rewards and gratifications, but as a way of life it can surely be taken too far. Ultimately we are left with a vision out of science fiction: the isolated mastermind, seated at a vast control panel full of dials and knobs, pushing a button to synthesize a string quartet or publish a book or start up an assembly line. It is a vision of power and control, but rather lacking in human warmth.

# Computers, People, and Social Interaction

The economic system provides members of a society with the means of acquiring goods and services. As important as these functions are, a thriving society also needs a sense of community or identity among its members. This point was stressed by the French social scientist Emile Durkheim (1858–1917). He criticized those who thought that economic factors alone could tie society together, and he argued that unless people had common beliefs, values, and expectations, an economy based on exchange would be difficult to maintain. Economic interests alone, argued Durkheim, make people friends one day and enemies the next. In order for economic exchange to work, parties must agree in advance on the terms of trade. Each must trust the other's integrity to fulfill his or her

obligations—perform the labor, deliver the goods, pay the agreed price.

In traditional societies, strong kinship ties and a shared religion provide a basis for group identity and common values. People have common life experiences. They work at the same occupations (farming, hunting, fishing) and face the same challenges of existence. Social norms and expectations are dictated by tradition. Because of strong group ties and shared beliefs, members have a "collective conscience."

In modern societies, however, social cohesion is harder to achieve. Though mass production results in an outward appearance of a homogeneous culture, other forces foster differences between people. Rather than a single unifying set of sacred values and beliefs, there are countless competing moral and philosophical perspectives. Families have weaker ties with extended kinship groups. Individuals work in very diverse occupations. Differences in work and social position can make it difficult for people to identify with each other's needs and interests. People are often anonymous to each other as they go about their daily affairs, and they can feel insignificant, powerless, and alienated.

Under these conditions, social cohesion can easily be splintered by factionalism. Group solidarity can be eroded by self-interested individualism. In his day, Durkheim felt that social problems such as crime, divorce, and suicide were symptoms of isolation and social disintegration. He was concerned with finding ways to reduce the alienation of modern life and reunite society with itself. He hoped that ultimately, a new form of social stability would emerge, one based on the rule of law and contracts. However, the continuing debates and clashes over such issues as abortion, sex education, surrogate parenting, women's rights, and gun control underscore the difficulty in formulating laws and contracts that all the people will uphold.

The first two articles in this section examine how computers can reduce the sense of alienation or powerlessness felt by many people who are ill or disabled. In "The Powerful Patient," Steve Fishman discusses some new services, including computerized data bases, designed to help people make more informed decisions about their own health care. By giving people more knowledge about medical conditions and treatment options, these services are also changing the relationships between patients and their doctors. In "Challenging the Myth of Disability," Alan Brightman describes the experience of disability and how one computer company is striving to change the "quality of life of the disabled person and how disability is perceived by the rest of society." Brightman also encourages the rest of us to get involved in building "a bridge to a new community."

Articles 17 and 19 focus on citizen participation in the political process. A dilemma of modern democratic participation is that for most of us it is hard to make informed choices about complex scientific and technological issues. The important topic of scientific and technical illiteracy is discussed by Morris Shamos in "The 20 Percent Solution." In "Electronic Democracy," Pamela Varley describes an experimental program designed to increase opportunities for residents of Santa Monica, California, to share ideas on community issues. As Varley reports, some observers praise the PEN (Public Electronic Network) for giving everyone a voice, while others argue that some groups are still being excluded.

The unit continues with articles that deal with computing on a more personal scale. Herb Brody describes how some people experience intense personal satisfaction or distress from using computers in "The Pleasure Machine." David Churbuck describes those whose attraction to computing extends to extreme levels in the article "Superduperitis."

As noted earlier, Emile Durkheim predicted that social relations would become increasingly characterized by legally binding contracts. In "Contracts Without Paper," Benjamin Wright looks at whether contracts "signed" electronically carry the same legal weight as contracts sealed with pen and ink.

### Looking Ahead: Challenge Questions

Can you identify some "marginal" groups or people who might achieve greater social acceptance and participation through computer networking? Which groups might be hurt even further?

How do feel about your own level of scientific/technological "literacy?" Which technological issues do you feel really knowledgeable about?

# CHALLENGING THE MYTH OF DISABILITY

*WHEN DISABLED CHILDREN AND ADULTS ARE GIVEN ACCESS TO COMPUTERS, IT BECOMES CLEAR HOW THESE MACHINES CAN, INDEED, CHANGE LIVES*

## Alan Brightman

*Manager of Special Education and Rehabilitation at Apple Computer, Inc., Alan J. Brightman received his PhD in education from Harvard University. His newest book is,* Independence Day: Designing Computer Solutions for Individuals with Disability, *1991.*

*A computer can change your life.* When I first came to Apple more than five years ago, that was one of the phrases I heard most often. The advertising and, particularly, the marketing staff repeated this slogan frequently. I can remember, however, that no matter how much I heard it and no matter how often I saw it on bumper stickers and buttons, it rang a little false to me. It seemed that if it were true a plastic box could change your life, then that was *more of a comment on your life than on the plastic box.* What kind of a life must you have if it could be changed so easily?

Five years later, I still hear the same words. Frankly, they still sound somewhat overstated, but, in one area at least, I've become a total and passionate believer. Every day across the country, when disabled children and adults are given access to computers, it becomes clear how these machines can, indeed, change certain lives. Often the changes can be at the most fundamental level imaginable.

### THE RHETORIC OF DISABILITY

Anyone who has been involved with disabled people for any length of time *must* be extremely observant of (if not actually petty about) the apparently casual use of some common words and slogans. The difference that rhetoric has made in the field of special education and rehabilitation—and in the lives of disabled individuals—has been so insistent, so dramatic, and so consequential, that as professionals in this field we would be blatantly irresponsible if we were not vigilant about the words we use.

Almost 20 years ago, I spent some months in Denmark and Sweden trying to discover, firsthand, why the Scandinavian special education and rehabilitation system was regarded as the most humane and progressive in the world. I returned from that visit (and from subsequent visits) with a refreshing new respect for common sense and, in particular, for the ability to

---

*It is not too ambitious to set as our goal fundamentally changing the experience of being disabled.*

---

match reality with rhetoric. I was walking in the halls of a school building in Sweden at about 10 or 11 o'clock in the morning. In the corridor there were five or six doorways leading to various classrooms. I remember entering a speech class. It seemed fairly typical. Then I went into a reading class. It looked like a reading class. And then I opened a door to a resource room for retarded students. It was lit only by red bulbs. A juke box was playing. Several pairs of students were on a dance floor. They were dancing. Other students stood or sat at a bar drinking and chatting. A silver ball rotated in the ceiling.

*This was a disco.* It was literally a classroom in "disconess" held at 10 o'clock in the morning in a resource room of a public school. It all seemed a little strange to me at first. But in the context of both the Scandinavian value system and pervasive Scandinavian rhetoric, I was soon discover that this classroom wasn't strange at all. It made perfect common sense.

The Swedish people believe that school is a place that should help people—all people—fit into society and, as much as possible, to become full participants in it. A discotheque is one of the places in our society where a retarded person might, through some inap-

*EDUCOM Review,* Winter 1989, pp. 17-23. Copyright © 1989 by EDUCOM. For information about this article or *EDUCOM Review,* contact: EDUCOM, 1112 16th Street, NW, Suite 600, Washington, DC 20036, (202) 872-4200.

propriate behavior, signal that he or she does not fit in. Therefore, why shouldn't school be the place to learn how to behave in a disco? One needs to know how to ask someone to dance and then to be able to dance, how to order a drink and then to pay (and tip) for it, and how to initiate a casual conversation and then to continue it.

I recall this scene in order to consider the critical implications of rhetoric in the fields of special education and rehabilitation. In Sweden, very clearly, the rhetoric is essentially about *mainstreaming*. When you listen to the Scandinavians speak about mainstreaming (and about normalization), you hear very pretty, very proud words. But their sparkling rhetoric would have remained just that if classrooms such as the one I've described had not sprung forth from those words. From a special education and rehabilitation perspective, it is, therefore, not trivial to ask: What is our rhetoric? Furthermore, what might *our* discos be?

If we examine the development of special education and rehabilitation in this country, we will find that what has largely driven its twists and turns is the engine of rhetoric. Two kinds of rhetoric have historically influenced, if not dominated, the design of our discos in special education and rehabilitation. Yet there is a third kind of rhetoric, a new way of thinking and talking about disability, that I am confident will be more forceful, more dramatic, and simply and finally more correct in bringing us to the future. It should become clear in the midst of this discussion why we, at Apple, believe that it is not too ambitious to set as our goal nothing less than *fundamentally changing the experience of being disabled*, in terms of both the quality of life of the disabled person and how the disability is perceived by the rest of society.

The first, and by far the most prevalent rhetoric, is the rhetoric of platitudes. Disability makes most nondisabled adults somewhat awkward. We feel as if we're not quite ourselves in the presence of others who seem so different, others with whom we have so little practice at interpersonal relations. If we could hear the things we say when we're feeling awkward, we'd probably choose to be silent, but we don't. So we issue forth with the kind of safe platitudes that we might seriously question, if we had more insight. Only children, especially those under the age of 12, tend to be free of our platitudes; they make clear and true attempts at understanding. Here, for example, are the kinds of questions children ask when confronted with disability.

- If that girl's blind, why does she keep her eyes open?
- If I yell into that deaf child's ear, will he hear me better?
- Why does that retarded boy do those stupid things?
- How does a person in a wheelchair go to the bathroom?

These are terrific questions. They are real, visceral, curious, and challenging. More often than not, though, if a child directs any one of them to a teacher in a public school, for example, the teacher's answer is something like: "Don't you think it's time we finished our spelling now?"

It seems that we're simply more comfortable pretending not to notice, or else we're driven by a tremendous need to disavow the *fact of difference* in our society. These kinds of disavowals are by no means limited to verbal platitudes. In the name of providing care to disabled individuals, for example, we have built enormous institutional settings as far away from populated areas as possible. We have also put disabled children either in separate schools altogether or in segregated classrooms, typically in the basement, next to the boiler room. These might be called physical platitudes: way out of sight, comfortably out of mind. These physical platitudes turn out to be a breeding ground for one very curious phenomenon, which can only be described as the active and consistent disregard for common sense. In fact, nowhere, in my experience, has common sense proven to be less common than in institutional settings or organizations designed for disabled people.

Many years ago I worked at a large eastern state school for retarded persons. Some of the severely retarded young adults in one of the wards were apparently chewing on the rugs and causing a significant amount of damage. The institution did not bother to notice either that these day rooms, occupied for endless hours by their students, were devoid of books, games, and other diversions or that there was absolutely nothing else to do there. Instead, each individual was brought to the institutional dentist to have all of his or her teeth removed. Thus, the problem was solved.

In a similar institution, the problem was an increase in the number of pregnancies among mildly retarded women who, as a reward for appropriate behavior, were allowed off the grounds on day passes. It seems that some of the local men were taking easy advantage of these vulnerable women. Unbelievably, the institutional response was to implement a new policy whereby the women could no longer go into town on their own. Instead, they had to be paired with a buddy, another woman who had also earned the right to leave the grounds for a day. Within four months, of course, the pregnancy rate was found to have doubled.

It is significant that this common *nonsense* phenomenon isn't limited to places designed to serve only disabled individuals. Sometimes it can occur spontaneously when a disabled person simply enters a place designed for the mainstream population. In the late 1960s, a good friend of mine lost a leg in a freak boating accident. About a year and a half later, he was called to report to the draft board, and, good citizen that he was, he responded. He presented himself to the orientation interviewer—with his right pant leg pinned up—and sat while she noted his name, address, and other pertinent information. One interview question, though, made him get up and leave: Looking first at his pant leg and then straight into his eyes, the draft board interviewer asked, "Will this disability be of lasting duration?" Common sense seems to take flight in the presence of disability. Our comfortable reliance on the rhetoric of platitudes cannot hide our preference for not noticing.

On the other hand, the second category of rhetoric, which I call high drama, is the rhetoric of noticing too much. We have always cast disabled individuals as special, as exceptional, and we believe that nothing less than the grace of God has prevented us from becoming like them. Their lives are the stuff of grand themes: Frankenstein, Quasimodo, Captain Hook, Dr. Strangelove, Mr. Magoo, and all of the seven dwarfs (not just the one named Dopey). Their lives are the stuff of pity and heroism, which is to say, the stuff of telethons. Theirs are the lives of intense drama, in which countless obstacles are forever having to be overcome.

Yet none of this high drama is real, at least in the experience of the disabled person. In fact, the hardest thing about being disabled really is not the pain, or the dependence, or the expense, or even the inaccessible bathroom. The hardest thing about being disabled is that you're never perceived as just plain ordinary. The world always sees you as someone peculiar, as someone uncommon, as someone who doesn't quite fit in. When you're disabled, we, the nondisabled, regard you as nonordinary, as extraordinary.

## THE REALITY OF DISABILITY

The truth is, however, that being disabled has nothing to do with exaggerated melodramatic themes. It has everything to do, instead, with basic, gritty, mundane details: getting through a day and getting through a life, a real life, and being somebody. Several years ago, I edited a book called *Ordinary Moments*, which was an effort to capture the experience of disability from the disabled person's point of view, from the locker room, as it were, rather than from the poet's desk. A chapter written by a friend of mine in Boston begins by offering some definitions for the word "handicapped."

- Being handicapped is when you're the guest of honor at the "Handicapped Person of the Year" award luncheon and the rest room doors are too narrow for the wheelchair so you have to urinate in a broom closet.
- Or when someone actually says to you: "Oh, you have muscular dystrophy? If that happened to me, I'd kill myself."
- Not being able to turn the radio on. Or the television off.

- Accomplishing microscopic tasks well.
- Going to the museum and getting in free.
- Seeing everything from always only four feet off the ground.
- Hating having to ask. All the time ask.
- Having the ability to sit in one place for nine hours without going mad from restlessness. And after nine hours of not moving, coming home to sit in a different chair for seven hours more.
- Being handicapped is worrying about being handicapped too much.
- But damn it, this room is a mess, and I can't clean it.
- I'm hungry and I can't cook. The window is open and it's freezing outside; I can't shut it. The record player's skipping but the bike's in the way of the player. I hate that scratching noise.
- I can't find a pipe that's not clogged, so I can't even get high. And I don't feel like masturbating.
- The incredible pettiness gets wearying at times. I'm always worrying about getting to bed, getting up, getting into a chair, getting out of a chair.
- Being handicapped creates a pettiness syndrome. All you think about is simple stuff.[1]

So much, then, for the rhetoric of high drama, the rhetoric that has historically justified our treating disabled individuals as little more than objects of charity.

There is a new kind of rhetoric that needs to saturate our thinking and our actions in special education and rehabilitation. While doing so, it must also reflect the true reality of disabled children and adults. Simply stated, it is the rhetoric of expectation. A wonderful poster was put out several years ago by the Spastics Society of Great Britain. In it, a fourth- or fifth-grade child is sitting at a computer that he's operating with a head wand. He looks proud and serious. The monitor screen is covered with lines of text. Across the top of the poster, a bold caption reads: "Just because I couldn't speak, they thought I had nothing to say."

I know a lot of nonvocal people who also have much to say and who, with access to a computer, are, for the first time, finally being heard: across a room, over a phone, even on public assembly stages. I know people who will never be capable of actually seeing a printed page but who are now, with combination braille-text printers, able to share written assignments with sighted classmates. I know some profoundly retarded individuals, as well as mildly learning disabled ones, who are finally discovering that education doesn't need to be a perpetual experience in failure.

Disabled people form a significant part of our world. Close to 40 million children and adults with disability live, work, and play in the United States alone. Close to a million and a half of them are attending colleges and universities today. An additional 750 million disabled people live in other parts of the world. And their number, both in this country and abroad, keeps growing every day. In this country, the growing number of disabled people is largely due to advances in medical technology. In other countries, the increase is caused by such factors as war, malnutrition, and insidious disease. Furthermore, out of every seven disabled people alive today, six were not born that way. Eighty-five percent of people who have a disability today acquired it *after birth*, which is why disabled activists frequently refer to you and me as TABs—Temporarily Able Bodied individuals.

## THE CHALLENGE OF DESIGNING FOR DISABLED INDIVIDUALS

For the vast majority of disabled individuals, the microcomputer doesn't simply represent the ability to accomplish tasks a little faster or a little better. It represents the ability to do things previously considered unthinkable. In other words, the computer *can* indeed change lives. It can give new, varied, and multifaceted expression to personal identity and, not incidentally, increase and improve self-confidence and self-esteem.

Consider a 15-year-old child in a wheelchair, who is paralyzed from the neck down and without speech. How is that child typically regarded by his peers? Perhaps even by his teachers? What's truly expected of him? And given how he's probably seen by others, how is he conditioned to see himself? Now we say to that child, "You can raise your eyebrows up and down. You have a movement you can control that enables you to pass instructions along to a computer, so you can do word processing, use a modem, and draw pictures. You can even acquire a voice. For the first time in your life, you can say 'here' when attendance is taken. You can demonstrate what a whiz you are at baseball statistics. You can display your artistic talents. You can become known, in other words, for *who you know you are* rather than for what others have interpreted you to be."

Once we say all this to the child, two things will happen. We will make him aware of astounding new, but very real, possibilities. And we will probably cause this young individual to ask a few questions, such as "How can I make those possibilities real for me?" As a matter of fact, these two things have been the primary concerns of our Office of Special Education and Rehabilitation since we created it four years ago.

- First, we try to generate awareness of how the personal computer can provide new options and opportunities for disabled children and adults.
- Second, we try to fashion a comprehensive response capacity to deal with the inevitable questions about actualizing these options and opportunities.

This twofold agenda of ours is written in the rhetoric of expectations, that is to say, where other people may look at a disabled individual and see only diagnosis, we see promise, usually a great deal of promise. We have chosen to regard the disabled person as someone who can rather than as someone who *probably* can't. Together with his or her family members, friends, teachers, and coworkers, we approach the disabled person eagerly and hopefully, and we always offer answers.

Over the past four years, Apple has developed a response capacity that we believe is second to none in the industry. Our response capacity is rooted both in a comprehensive and carefully maintained database of adaptive technology and in a growing network of close to 40 community-based resource centers that we have established around the country.

## PRODUCT DEVELOPMENT

While the history of Apple's response capacity is instructive, it is more useful here to consider the technology involved in product development.

To understand how we approached the area of product development, you have to understand only one basic premise: *This is not a world that was designed or built with disabled people in mind*. The natural world is difficult enough and there are so many man-made obstacles: curbs, steps, doors that are too narrow, and public phones that are too high. To make matters worse, a premium is put on physical beauty, making it an ideal that everyone should strive for. And if you don't have it, you belong to someone else's world, perhaps with people who can't see enough or know enough to tell that you, too, are imperfect. All of which leads, of course, to those favorite worldwide pastimes: the stigmatization and segregation of others and the creation of deviance yardsticks by which some people can assure themselves they are normal. Nevertheless, particularly over the last 15 years or so, largely because disabled activists have grown tired of being told to "just be patient" and have demonstrated that they can conduct sit-ins and chain themselves to fences just as effectively as nondisabled protesters, the physical world has changed significantly. It's a much easier terrain to navigate today than it was not so very long ago.

When the personal computer entered that terrain, it promised disabled people access to all kinds of new

---

*Close to 40 million children and adults with disability live, work, and play in the United States.*

---

power and capabilities, provided that they could get access to the machine in the first place. And that's the rub. Even the Macintosh, the computer "for the rest of us," was effectively sealed off, shutting out the disabled. To them, *ease of use* was pretty much a hypocritical concept. It is true that by the time the Macintosh arrived, the Apple II product line had become enormously accessible, mostly because of the hundreds of small third-party manufacturers who developed switches, keyboards, keyguards, printers, and specialized software that enabled people with all kinds of disabilities to use the computer, even though they had to operate it in very different ways. But that wasn't the case with the Macintosh, which in the beginning had many barriers for disabled users.

At first glance, none of these obstacles might seem to be too imposing. Yet a 2-inch curb is enough to prevent a motorized wheelchair from getting up on the sidewalk. For that reason, we set ourselves the task of trying to identify where we needed to build, in effect, *electronic curbcuts* into the computer. Suppose, for ex-

---

*For the vast majority of disabled individuals, the microcomputer represents the ability to do things previously considered unthinkable.*

---

ample, that you're working with your Macintosh and you make a mistake. Your machine will beep at you, which is a terrific warning signal; however, if you're deaf, the signal is irrelevant. Or consider the repeat key. Most good typists report that it's a wonderful feature. Most good typists, however, don't have poor gross or fine motor skills. If they did, they'd discover the frustration that's caused by not being able to remove their fingers from the keys quickly enough and, as a result, ending up with rows of repeating characters filling up the screen. There are also other obstacles, generally born of an attempt to improve hardware or software technology. For example, most software programs now and again require you to press down two or three keys simultaneously. This is impossible if you happen to be able to type only by using a head wand or a mouth stick, or if you are able to use only one finger. Finally, the mouse is obviously another major problem for the disabled user.

Our challenge, then, was to educate our own designers and engineers about the needs of those users typically ignored in the generic design process. Incidentally, the reason our designers and engineers don't ordinarily think about these users is not because they're instinctively insensitive, but, like most people, they need to be reminded now and then that disabled people make up a significant fraction of the population. Several years ago, we brought together about 20 people from different parts of Jean-Louis Gassee's organization and sat them down in front of an Apple IIe. "You know this thing inside and out," we reminded them. "You made it." Then we put an Apple-works disk in front of them and said, "You all know how to use this." Finally, we asked them to put their hands in their pockets, put a pencil in their mouth, and type a memo. As soon as they decided to take the challenge seriously, the protests began. "How about if

I just turn the machine on first?" one of the participants asked. "It's going to be a little hard to do with this pencil." "Let me just put the disk in the drive first, okay?" asked another.

In a short while, virtually on their own, the group identified a list of more than 60 design features that might prove to be an obstacle for one type of disability or another. Most of these barriers have, by now, been addressed. We've either fixed them or we've found simple ways around them. For instance, on those machines where the power switch is not on the front, a power strip affords the user the same function quite handily. It is probably well-known that the beep and the repeat key are both adaptable from the control panel. By sliding the volume control bar down to zero, a video analog of the beep appears in the form of a menu–bar flash. The repeat key feature, of course, can simply be shut off entirely. Simultaneous pressing of more than one key and full use of the mouse are both possible through the two utilities that are included in *Easy Access:* sticky keys and mouse keys. There is also *Close View,* a system utility that enables you to enlarge screen contents up to 16 times, which is helpful not only for the visually impaired person but also for someone who is necessarily sitting farther than usual from the screen, in a bed or a wheelchair, for example. It is also possible to invert the contents of the screen with this program. Of course, the documentation for *Close View* is presented in large print in the system manual.

There are also a number of much less obvious curbcuts built into the Macintosh. We have no latches on our disk drives, for example, and the drives themselves require that very little pressure be exerted on the disk before they accept it. Also, they push the disk out when it's ejected, giving fingers or mouth tongs something to grasp. In fact, the 3.5-inch disk medium itself proves to be an interesting example of a disability-appropriate device. Its increased storage capacity, for one, means that a user will have to do much less disk swapping. It is encased in hard plastic and can, therefore, withstand the often tortuous slamming to which some users (particularly those with poor gross motor skills) subject it before they insert it into the drive.

In this area, our ultimate goal is to *establish, within the product development group, a permanent filter* that enables our designers and engineers both to recognize that there are many users in the world who are quite different from them and, therefore, to make our *generic* machine as accessible as possible. Apple is concerned with these product design issues for many reasons. In the first place, our engineers consider them important. They understand that the products they build are intended for individuals. That is, after all, Apple's design focus. Disabled users merely happened to strengthen the focus on individuals. So when our product designers realized that they had been ignoring this particular group of individuals, they were almost embarrassed. It was obvious, as well, that they were intrigued by the challenge of inclusion. More pragmatically, perhaps, they began to realize that conveniences that are initially invented and implemented for disabled people very soon become conveniences for nondisabled people as well. For example, many users who work in desktop publishing or graphic design have commented to us on how much easier it is for them to use mouse keys, rather than the mouse itself, to move objects on the screen with precision. The fact that conveniences for one turn out to be conveniences for all shouldn't be that surprising. Consider the simple curbcut on the sidewalk. It was put there specifically for disabled people and now nine out of ten people who use it are, of course, nondisabled.

We'll never be completely finished with this design task. In fact, there can never be a generic disability machine, one that meets the needs of all disabled users. Sometimes features that are useful for one set of

---

*The challenge grows ever more urgent as the world of computers moves closer to standardization.*

---

needs conflict with another set of needs. Consider the curbcut again. Everyone praised it when it began to become popular and legally required, that is, everyone except certain blind people whose guide dogs had been carefully trained to stop at curbs and were now leading them out into busy streets. Nor is the problem for blind people limited just to real-world curbcuts. From an access point of view, this population represents our biggest product design challenge by far. That challenge grows ever more urgent as the world of computers moves ever closer to standardization on graphical interfaces and multiple windows, things that must be seen in order to be used. At this point, we are

actively engaged in pursuing several possible avenues of response.

## CONCLUSION

Although I have been thinking about it for 20 years, I still find it difficult to say what our special education and rehabilitation programs might look like if they were to truly fulfill the promise of the rhetoric of expectation.

Perhaps the answer can best be found by understanding and appreciating for *yourself* how your knowledge of computer technology could have a tremendous influence on the lives of disabled individuals. *Spend a few hours at the center for disabled student services on your campus.* Find out why that center exists and what needs are being fulfilled there. Forget for a moment about things like *computer literacy* and come to know at least a few people who are involved in the business of *life literacy*. Find out how the technology you know so well, the technology of diversity, might be creatively applied to very real and very pressing human needs.

You needn't be an expert in special education or rehabilitation to learn quickly how you might forge a mutually satisfying association. All that is necessary is an interest in "hanging around until you've caught on," as Robert Frost defined education. Or, to paraphrase Yogi Berra, "You'll be able to observe a lot just by watching." Then you can build a bridge to a new community, which will prove to be a fertile turf for new ideas. Let it be a two-way bridge and encourage a lot of active traffic on it. It might lead, perhaps, to a brand-new disco.

## REFERENCE

1. *Ordinary Moments: The Disabled Experience*, ed. Alan Brightman (Syracuse, N.Y.: Human Policy Press, 1985), p. 81.

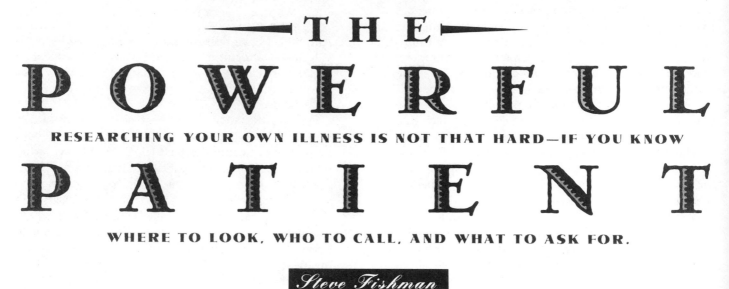

# —THE—
# POWERFUL

### RESEARCHING YOUR OWN ILLNESS IS NOT THAT HARD—IF YOU KNOW

# PATIENT

### WHERE TO LOOK, WHO TO CALL, AND WHAT TO ASK FOR.

*Steve Fishman*

*Steve Fishman is a contributing editor based in New York.*

**MARK ROMAN** WAS TAKING A KARATE CLASS THREE TIMES A WEEK AND FEELING EXCEEDINGLY FIT. "I CAN PUT MY FIST THROUGH THREE INCHES OF WOOD," HE'D SAY, HOLDING OUT HIS RIGHT HAND TO SHOW OFF BIG CAULIFLOWER CALLUSES ON HIS KNUCKLES. ROMAN, 31 YEARS OLD, LIVING IN NEW YORK CITY, WAS INVESTING HIMSELF

with strength. "I feel invincible," he'd say.

Then one day as he undresses for bed he notices a hard lump, about the diameter of a dime, on his right testicle. Roman calls his HMO, explains what he's found, and is scheduled for an immediate doctor's appointment—the first thing that frightened him, he recalls.

The next day, Roman is given an examination, an ultrasound, and a blood test. In his blood the levels of hormone-like chemicals—telltale signs of testicular cancer—are elevated. The doctor recommends surgery to remove the testicle.

So much for popping his fist through floorboards, Roman says. In a 45-minute operation with a local anesthetic, the cancerous testicle is removed. A silicone prosthesis takes its place. Roman's family waits in

his hospital room, and when he returns, he thinks, It's over.

But ten days afterward, his urologist, cheery, white-haired, conscientious, says, "It's not over yet." Roman's cancer, he says, is what they call stage one, the most contained and thus the least dangerous. Still, there's a chance—the doctor doesn't say how much—that it has spread to the lymph system.

The urologist says the standard follow-up is lymph node dissection—surgery that can last as long as 12 hours, during which the abdomen is sliced open so that the doctors can remove the lymph nodes and examine them for cancer.

"This is surgery that's been around for a long time, and a lot of urologists would recommend it," says the doctor. Roman isn't impressed by the procedure's pedigree. "What are the side

effects?" he wants to know. In addition to the ordeal of the surgery itself, and the weeks of recovery, there's a chance that the operation could sever the nerve that permits ejaculation, the doctor says.

Sterility, Roman thinks. He is stunned. The idea of fatherhood is important to him. Between breaking two-by-fours, he's fallen in love with a fellow karate student. He'd like children someday; she's said she would, too.

The obliging urologist says the decision is up to Roman. Now the usually in-control karate student is running through emotions as though they were a deck of cards. He's never had to make a decision like this before. "The doctor is pushing a serious operation to possibly save my life, but what about the quality of life after survival? If I have the

surgery, I could end up unable to ejaculate. And if I don't have the operation, there's the chance that cancer cells may remain hidden in my body, and I'll die before I have a chance to *be* a father."

The doctor's words echo in Roman's ears: "It's up to you."

It's true that patients can do whatever they want. They can refuse any procedure, out of whimsy or orneriness. Or, more rationally perhaps, they can learn enough to take an active part in the decisions.

Roman, feeling scared and confused, decides to bone up fast. "I felt victimized, but what made me feel out of control," he says later, "was my lack of knowledge."

Not knowing where to start, he calls the National Cancer Institute in Bethesda, Maryland, and requests the names of the country's biggest cancer treatment centers. He calls up the closest one, Memorial–Sloan Kettering Cancer Center, asks for the urology department, and eventually gets a doctor on the line. He wants to learn everything he can, please, on lymph node dissections. The doctor offers to lend him a special report, the jauntily titled "Testicular Cancer: A Multidisciplinary Approach."

Next, Roman heads for the library, where he thumbs through back issues of the medical journal *Urology*. He finds that Indiana University Medical School in Indianapolis is doing major work, and he calls them up. He's referred to more studies to read. "It's my life," he reasons. "It's worth some time."

After a few days' reading, Roman learns that the lymph node surgery in this country has high cure rates—especially when combined with chemotherapy. And, he reads, physicians in Denmark, which has the highest testicular cancer rate in the world, have achieved high cure rates by using chemotherapy alone—rarely the lymph node dissection surgery.

Roman, taking a plodding tone, more Columbo than Perry Mason, bounces what he's learned off his urologist. Roman doesn't have the answers, but he works up to some specific questions: Is there any way to avoid the surgery, for instance? How do doctors know it's the surgery, and not the chemotherapy, that kills the cancer? What about chemotherapy alone? What about holding off on either surgery or chemotherapy?

In the end, Roman and his doctor agree on a wait-and-see approach—no lymph node dissection—since the tumor that was removed had been so contained, and since the cancer had been caught at such an early stage. They also decide to postpone the chemotherapy for the time being. Roman wants to avoid the side effects.

The risk he runs in saying no to the surgery is a 20 to 30 percent chance that the cancer will recur, but he'll be monitored with sensitive monthly blood tests and quarterly CT scans—high-definition X rays of the lymph system—which will pick up any cancer early. And if there is a recurrence, he now knows, the same treatments will still be available, with an overall cure rate still above 90 percent. Roman has learned enough to know his risks, and he's content with his decision.

While some doctors are put off by give-and-take sessions with patients, Roman's experience has been positive. "Doctors like it," he says. "They rarely have patients who take such an active interest."

Three years later, his cancer hasn't recurred, nor has his fertility been hampered—an enormous relief, since he bought his girlfriend, the one he met at karate class, an engagement ring for Christmas.

"You really owe it to yourself to do what I did," he says.

. . . . . . . .

"BECOME AN EXPERT," says Arthur Levin, director of the Center for Medical Consumers. "It's the only way to make rational judgments about quality, to assess diagnosis and treatment options—in short, to make up your own mind."

In some cases, it can even save lives. The film *Lorenzo's Oil*, for example, tells the real-life story of Augusto and Michaela Odone, who, through persistence and seat-of-the-pants research, succeeded in finding a substance to save their young son's life after they'd been told there was no cure.

As soon as you start digging, you'll find there's more help out there than you might think. Government departments, hospitals, and private companies have introduced simple, affordable systems to make information available to the public.

Roman made a lot of headway using just a phone, a library, and a little time and luck; not everyone who calls a medical school gets a doctor on the line. But there are easier ways to go about it—taking advantage of a computerized search firm, for instance. Some modern gadgetry will help you—a computer, a modem, a fax. But you can choose your own level of investigative comfort, from reading medical journals at the library to hooking into a computerized network.

As you set out to become your own expert—on your illness or that of someone close to you—here are some suggestions and phone numbers to get you started.

### HELPFUL ORGANIZATIONS

DISEASES AND DISABILITIES that afflict enough people have their own organizations—the American Lung Association, the American Cancer Society, the American Heart Association, just for starters. There are more than 200 of these, all user-friendly repositories of general information. Most of the organizations will send free booklets about their diseases.

Some national organizations are listed in the local yellow pages, or you can order a printed listing of private and public sources for $17.25 postpaid by writing to Resource Information Guide, P.O. Box 990297, Redding, CA 96099.

The National Health Information Center can also refer you to the appropriate organizations. Call ☎ 800/336-4797. Don't be shy—the center gets calls for every disease imaginable, and its staff is armed with 1,100 phone numbers.

For less well-known illnesses, try the National Organization for Rare Disorders. It was created by Abbey Meyers, after she discovered how hard it was to get information on Tourette's syndrome, which her three children have. Now her organization supplies the public with the kind of information

she wishes she'd had easier access to—reports on any of 950 diseases, covering symptoms, therapies, as well as current research. The first request is free; subsequent reports cost $3.25 each. Call ☎ 203/746-6518.

For women's illnesses, the National Women's Health Network provides information and referrals on 75 topics. Call ☎ 202/347-1140.

### THE HOT LINE CONNECTION

YOU CAN LEARN a lot these days just by picking up your phone. Hot lines are usually staffed by trained volunteers. A prostate hot line, for instance, offers advice on treatments (☎ 800/543-9632). The Y-ME National Organization for Breast Cancer Information and Support is at ☎ 800/221-2141 or ☎ 708/799-8228. The Centers for Disease Control and Prevention operates an AIDS hot line (☎ 800/342-AIDS).

For a list of some 100 hot lines, dial the number of the National Health Information Center at ☎ 800/336-4797. For $1, they'll send a roster of toll-free health information numbers. Some operate from nine to five, others are on call 24 hours.

### SUPPORT GROUPS

PEOPLE SUFFERING from everything from dwarfism to electrical shock injuries have formed their own local and national groups. While most people think of such groups merely as sources of emotional support, they also serve the powerful function of information exchanges.

When Marie Grimes developed a rare disease that caused such frequent urination that she couldn't leave the house, her doctors said they knew of no treatment. Then she heard about a self-help group for people who shared her illness, the San Diego branch of the Interstitial Cystitis Association. From the group, she learned about a drug that offered relief, not yet approved in the United States, but which some members were getting from Europe and Mexico. Armed with this information, Grimes returned to her doctor, who obtained the drug for her through an experimental program. For the first time in years, she can go out to dinner.

The American Self-Help Clearinghouse at St. Clares–Riverside Medical Center in Denville, New Jersey, tracks more than 700 groups and publishes the *Self-Help Sourcebook*. It's available for $10; call ☎ 201/625-7101. They'll also provide numbers for clearinghouses in 19 states (Calif., Conn., Ill., Iowa, Kan., Mass., Mich., Mo., Neb., N.J., N.Y., N.C., Ohio, Ore., Penn., S.C., Tenn., Texas, and the District of Columbia), which can direct you to specific local support groups. The National Self-Help Clearinghouse will also send a list of support group information. Send an SASE to 25 West 43rd St., New York, NY 10036.

### THE COMPUTER SEARCH

MORE THAN any other tool, the computer has diminished the gap between what doctors and patients know. Plug in. There are as many as 245 data bases—computerized indexes of information.

The most important index, and the one on which most searches are based, is Medline, a data base of 3,600 medical journals. With a personal computer, a modem, and a $30 software package (one is known as Grateful Med), you can conduct your own search for in-depth articles on any medical subject.

For the Grateful Med software, call ☎ 800/638-8480;

for a free demo disk and brochure, call ☎ 301/496-6308.

A guide to other data bases, *Directory of Online Healthcare Databases,* is available for $38; call ☎ 503/471-1627. This is a far-reaching directory—with a data base on acupuncture alone, for instance, and 12 on AIDS. Some major libraries also subscribe to Medline, and a reference librarian can walk you through the steps.

Some larger libraries, hospitals, and HMOs have desktop terminals—it's the new wave in library furniture—for the nonscientific public.

Health Reference Center is a commercial data base of 4,000 consumer and medical publications. For the center nearest to you, call ☎ 800/227-8431; ask for marketing.

MDX Health Digest contains 200 health-oriented publications. Call Medical Data Exchange, a private company, to learn which libraries have it; ☎ 503/471-1627. Both services rely mainly on secondary sources, such as newspapers. Both are usually free.

### COMPUTER BULLETIN BOARDS

IF YOU'RE already into computer technology—or eager to learn—you can scan all kinds of exchanges between people delving into various medical subjects, via some 300 electronic "bulletin boards." You can also send out a message and await the serendipity of a reply.

For a list of health-oriented computer bulletin boards, send $5 and an SASE to Black Bag BBS, 1 Ball Farm Way, Wilmington, DE 19808. With a modem, dial ☎ 302/994-3772.

An extension of the computer bulletin board is the on-line conference, a sort of electronic self-help group accessible from your own living room. The American Self-Help Clearinghouse organized the first on-line conference for agoraphobics—people who are afraid of open or public places. They linked up without

having to leave the house, chatting via keyboards. It's also a boon for people in rural areas.

CompuServe, an on-line information service, hosts several groups (for a membership fee of around $40, plus a small monthly charge). There is, for instance, a diabetes forum. Call ☎ 800/848-8199 for general information.

For cancer patients, there are numerous data bases. Designed for both doctors and the public, they're among the most complete and easy to use. Medline, for instance, offers a separate cancer data base called CANCERLIT.

A list of treatment centers, plus some 1,500 experimental treatment programs—is available through the National Cancer Institute's data base called Physician Data Query. PDQ also has a directory of physicians and organizations that provide cancer care. It's designed for doctors, but you're invited to tap into PDQ by using the Grateful Med software. Or else call ☎ 800/4-CANCER and request a free PDQ search. They'll mail it along.

If you have a fax, try Cancer-Fax at ☎ 301/402-5874, and an automated voice will tell you how to obtain detailed prognosis and treatment summaries on 80 kinds of cancers. The information is updated every month, and you can request a version intended for either doctors or for the public.

### DATA BROKERS

TO MEET the needs of doctors, lawyers—and most recently, patients—a growing number of these have sprung up. The four listed below rely heavily on Medline, tend to be consumer-oriented, and are staffed by professionals.

"I would have loved to have had these at the beginning of my illness," says Jane Perlmutter, a director with the organization for people who suffer from chronic fatigue syndrome,

CFIDS Activation Network (☎ 212/627-5631). These services run from around $25 to as much as $175 for a single search, but you'll be assured of some expertise.

The Health Resource Inc., a commercial enterprise, will provide Medline searches, article summaries, book excerpts, medical journal articles, as well as lists of self-help groups. They cover alternative and holistic, along with the more mainstream, sources of help. A report of 50 to 150 pages costs from $175 up; a mini-report (20 to 25 pages) runs $85. There's a 30-day money-back guarantee if you're not satisfied. Call ☎ 501/329-5272.

The nonprofit Planetree Health Resource Center provides an in-depth packet on a particular illness for $100. They'll do a PDQ search for $25 per topic or a Medline search for $35 per topic.

Medline searches are included in the comprehensive package, as are book excerpts and magazine articles. They'll also help you get in touch with other people who have the same condition. Contact them at ☎ 415/923-3680.

The Medical Information Service of the Palo Alto Medical Foundation was founded as a nonprofit service for doctors. More recently, most of its clients come from the general public. A standard search, including Medline, costs $89. Call ☎ 800/999-1999.

The Medical Data Exchange offers a search on its own consumer health data base, MDX Health Digest, at a cost of $25. A Medline search is $48.

If you're in need of a more exhaustive, customized search, it's $60 an hour. This company also began as a data source for health professionals, but recently has launched into searches for lay people. Call ☎ 503/471-1627.

"If I had known about these kinds of services," says Mark Roman, "my job would have been a lot easier."

# The 20 Percent Solution

## Morris H. Shamos

*MORRIS H. SHAMOS is professor emeritus of physics at New York University. He is a past president of both the National Science Teachers Association and the New York Academy of Sciences. He is at work on a book about scientific literacy.*

Until quite recently most educators and policy makers regularly cited two reasons for their support of the massive reform movement now under way to improve scientific literacy in the United States. The first was a concern that the nation faced a serious shortfall of scientists, engineers and science teachers, which could be offset only by improving the science education of all students. The alarm was first sounded urgently in October 1982 by a select commission of the National Science Board, and it pretty much propped up the science-education community for a decade. I argued in these pages some time ago [see "The Lesson Every Child Need Not Learn," July/August 1988] that such a fear failed a simple test of logic. Since then Congress too has joined in the critical attack on the studies of the scientist "pipeline" done by the National Science Foundation, from which the shortfall is inferred. In particular, Congress has criticized the studies for poor design, and they are now widely recognized as having been faulty.

The second rationale for seeking widespread literacy in science is a social and democratic one. Many controversial societal issues have a scientific (usually meaning technological) base. Hence—or so the argument goes—the public must be made more literate in science to deal rationally with such matters.

How many Americans could now be considered scientifically literate, in a sense relevant to that social concern? The estimates range from roughly 3 percent to 6 percent of the adult population. Thus, to sketch in the main contours of the issue, roughly one in twenty American adults may be sufficiently literate in science and social mores to reach independent, rational judgments on technology-

based societal matters. That criterion, incidentally, may be the only practical definition of the elusive concept of scientific literacy. How one measures it and how one achieves it in an appreciable number of students and adults both remain a mystery.

No one seriously believes that any amount of tinkering with science education will ever elevate all or even most Americans to such a state of scientific literacy. But given the general goal of technologically informed judgment on societal issues, and given the current dismal level of success in meeting that goal, it becomes possible to set some bounds to the problem. Consider how issues are dealt with by groups of varying size: a family gathering, a jury, a tenants' meeting in a city apartment building, a city council, a New England town meeting. One would naturally like such groups to reach reasoned conclusions and take informed actions on issues involving science or technology. Wouldn't such an outcome be much more likely if one or more individuals, who happen to be scientifically literate according to the practical criterion given above, are members of the group?

A "what if" exercise suggests itself here. Given that a certain fraction of the overall population satisfies the literacy criterion, what is the probability that in a group of a given size at least one member will be literate in science? What would happen to the probabilities if the overall literacy rate were raised? And what literacy rate would ensure a reasonably high probability that deliberative groups would reach scientifically and technologically informed decisions? Perhaps even a modest improvement in the scientific-literacy rate could have a marked influence on public attitudes in society and on the outcome of public debates.

Assume, then, that the scientific-literacy rate is 5 percent. Standard probability analysis shows that for groups numbering fewer than about fifty people the probability that at least one group member is scientifically literate is not very high. For example:

In a group of  6 the probability is 0.26.
In a group of 12 the probability is 0.46.
In a group of 25 the probability is 0.72.
In a group of 50 the probability is 0.92.

Thus for the first of those groups, which might be typical of a small family gathering or a civil trial jury, the chances are less than three in ten that at least one group member is scientifically literate. For the twelve-member group, as in a full trial jury, the chances that one or more members are literate in science are still less than fifty-fifty. (Thus, the conventional wisdom that committees ought to be small to be manageable may actually work to society's disadvantage when the committee's charge involves technical matters and no attempt has been made to select members for pertinent technical expertise.) Even in the fifty-member group, as in, say, the urban tenants' meeting or the New England town meeting, though there is a fairly high probability, there is still no certainty of finding someone scientifically literate in the group.

Doubling the literacy rate to 10 percent of the population markedly improves the odds, of course, but not enough to provide real comfort about the presence of a scientifically literate person in the smaller groups.

In a group of  6 the probability is 0.47.
In a group of 12 the probability is 0.72.
In a group of 25 the probability is 0.93.
In a group of 50 the probability is 0.995.

Doubling the literacy rate again—to 20 percent of the general population—makes it likely that even smaller groups, such as congressional committees, will include at least one member who is scientifically literate.

In a group of  6 the probability is 0.74.
In a group of 12 the probability is 0.93.
In a group of 25 the probability is 0.996.
In a group of 50 the probability is 0.9999.

Given a 20 percent literacy rate it is almost certain, with a probability of 99 percent, that there will be at least one scientifically literate person in groups as small as twenty. Incidentally, for a 99 percent probability in groups as small as twelve, the overall literacy rate of the population would have to be about 32 percent; for groups as small as six, 54 percent. Anyone with a calculator that computes exponents can explore the further ramifications of probabilities and literacy rates by evaluating the formula $P=1-(1-f)^N$. Here $P$ is the probability of finding at least one scientifically literate person in a group of $N$ people, and $f$ is the fraction of such people in the general population.

But including only one scientifically literate person in a group may not suffice. One participant in a large group, who may be literate in science generally, may not be a recognized expert on the issue being considered. That person probably would not satisfy any members of the group who have fixed contrary opinions based on rumor or belief. But two scientifically literate people in the group would be more convincing—provided, of course, they agreed with each other. If they did not agree, one would like to include a third such person.

Consider again the fifty-member group. For the current literacy rate of 5 percent it turns out that the probability of finding two or more scientifically literate people in such a group is only 72 percent; and the probability of finding three or more is 46 percent. If, however, the overall literacy rate could be increased to 20 percent, each of those probabilities would increase to a virtual certainty. In smaller groups the probability of finding three or more scientifically literate people decreases fairly rapidly. In a group of thirty members the probability is still about 96 percent, but for twenty it decreases to 80 percent, and for twelve it is only 44 percent. Similarly, the probability of finding two or more scientifically literate people in a group of twelve is 73 percent.

There are some obvious caveats to the foregoing analysis. One is that it assumes group members are randomly selected from the adult population—an idealization that rarely occurs in practice. Furthermore, the makeup of citizens' groups or committees often must satisfy some political, racial, ethnic or economic considerations; hence they cannot be purely random. And even in trial juries, for which the initial selection process is often as random as one could hope for, trial lawyers usually exclude those jurors they believe may have independent knowledge of a subject.

Once those points are understood, there is both good news and bad. The good news is that "only" a 20 percent national scientific-literacy rate would profoundly alter the way society deals with technical matters. Indeed, if all college graduates were literate in science, a 20 percent solution would be achieved, and the problem would be solved. The bad news is that society has no better prospect of obtaining a 20 percent literacy rate than it does of achieving 100 percent literacy, which everyone agrees is impossible. In spite of all the efforts of the past half-century or so, the U.S. population has not budged beyond a literacy rate of about 5 percent. A 20 percent solution, enticing as it may seem, is only an illusion.

Illusion notwithstanding, there is enlightenment to be gained from my thought experiment. It puts into sharper focus the problem that greater scientific literacy is supposed to solve: How can reliable information be made available on the purely technical aspects of certain public issues? The only feasible solution to that problem lies in the sensible use of scientific experts. Such experts should act not as surrogates for the public in determining the desirable course of action on an issue but only as the ultimate sources of information for the public debate. But how can society extract credible, reliable information from experts who disagree?

The concept of a science court, proposed by the physicist Arthur Kantrowitz of Dartmouth University a quarter-century ago, offers a novel and imaginative means of resolving the dilemma. Kantrowitz envisioned a formal, courtroom-like adversarial procedure in which panels of technically competent judges would establish the factual components of an issue. As a means of separating fact from fiction, rumor, speculation or emotion, the proposal seemed to many observers at the time an ideal start on a perplexing problem, and it even prompted a few serious experiments. Regrettably, however, the concept soon floundered and died for lack of strong support outside the scientific community. The legal profession opposed it for obvious reasons. But so did many sociologists and most citizens groups; they objected that such a reductionist approach tended to emphasize facts over social values, thereby violating their belief that even scientific "facts" could be value-laden and should therefore not be considered unquestionable.

Yet if the American public really wants to have a say in societal issues with a scientific or technological component, some mechanism must be developed to seek out and act on credible expert advice. After all, society has learned how to rely on experts for advice in other areas of personal need: in law, medicine, finance, politics. All those specialties frequently involve issues of value as well as fact. Why should specialized knowledge in science and technology be so different? One can wish that reason may yet prevail and that public-policy debates will move toward a system incorporating some form of science court or a similar device. The alternative is to give up all hope of society's control of technology and become resigned to a future whose technology is determined solely by a technological elite.

# The Pleasure Machine

◆

*Why do people get such a thrill from using computers?*
*How can this "ecstasy" help guide the industry?*

◆

## Herb Brody

*Herb Brody is a senior editor of*
Technology Review.

My sons have progressed though many of the usual childhood obsessions— Matchbox cars, Legos, trains, bicycling, marbles, baseball. They, like millions of other children, have taken to these low-tech activities with energetic glee. In fact, I thought for a while that our family was going to maneuver through the child-raising years largely unaffected by the technological revolution swirling around us.

Fat chance. By the time my oldest son was 5, he had discovered my old IBM PC. Now 8, he steals up to my attic office at every opportunity, boots up, and goes to work. He writes. He plays games. He creates bar charts. He squeals with delight when a new program enters the house, and he even creates little programs of his own to do common word-processing tasks with a keystroke or two. He proudly shows off his mastery of the machine to peers and adults, and passes on his knowledge to his younger brother, who now exhibits similar (though admittedly less intense) enthusiasm. In fact, when sitting at the keyboard, my son experiences a high-energy eu-

phoria that I can only describe as a state of ecstasy.

What's going on here? My family isn't an aberration. Teachers report that children who can't sit still through a 10-minute lecture on fractions remain transfixed by a computer game for hours. In the grown-up world, people who started using computers to speed up routine tasks find themselves smitten with the machine's power, spending an ever larger fraction of their day—and their budget—on software. Novice programmers sit down at the screen after dinner and become so engrossed constructing a program that they don't look away until midnight.

Most discussions of computers focus on their utility. Do they increase productivity? Are tasks done better, or quicker, or both, with a computer than without one? What's less often noted is that many people see computers not just as a practical tool but as a source of pleasure.

In the popular mind, the phenomenon of computer-driven ecstasy means intense, greasy-haired characters who spend their waking hours at a terminal, seemingly nourished only by soft drinks, junk food, and the ethereal glow of the screen. In this milieu, they are in general retreat from life into a synthetic world of acronyms and unintelligible syntax.

But the phenomenon with greater ramifications captures people who are not typical computerphiles: doctors, professors, musicians, writers, children. They do not set out to become computer experts, or even hobbyists. Typically they begin using a computer—almost always a personal computer, such as a Macintosh or an IBM-compatible—to accomplish some task. Then the computer takes hold of them in a way that other machines do not.

Computers are undeniably liberating. Children can escape adult-structured chores by burrowing into a computer game that leaves their parents hopelessly baffled. A writer is freed from the finger-numbing tedium of typing draft after draft, instead able to massage sentences and words to refine the piece. Engineers can build and tear down structures repeatedly in an attempt to get something that looks and works right—without waiting for the machine shop to build a prototype.

Computerphiles thus use words like control, mastery, and magic. And they often express joy at their independence from other people's skills. This is what the revolution in so-called desktop publishing is all about: anyone with a computer and a laser printer can churn out pamphlets, newsletters, and other small publishing jobs without turning to professional typesetters and print shops. The result may be an overall lowering of aesthetic standards as millions of typographical novices grapple with fonts, leading, and kerning. But the practitioners of desktop publishing tend to feel the same glee as a 3-year-old walking up the stairs without holding an adult's hand—the "I can do it myself" epiphany is powerful indeed.

Computer users also describe their machines in more rapturous ways, suggesting reveries on sensual experiences such as sex and chemical intoxication. Howard Liptzin, a San Francisco-based graphic designer, says that using graphics software on his computer gives him a "weightless feeling, like my mind has been freed of the constraints of gravity." Tom Valovic, senior editor of *Telecommunications* magazine, talks of the "pure, fuguestate, mind play involved in connecting with the PC." Lily Pond, who uses a Macintosh to produce a San Francisco-based literary quarterly called *Yellow Silk*, says that the thrill is "almost, but not quite, sexual—it's more like growing a foot taller in just a second or two."

## A Magnificent Obsession

A few years ago, when I joined the staff of a new computer magazine, I was astounded by how passionately readers cared about their computers. Each issue of the magazine drew scores of letters to the editor—intensely written little essays arguing the relative merits of various pieces of PC hardware and software. The stack of letters from that magazine's premier issue was about six inches high. I spent a few lunch hours reading through them. The writers referred lyrically to their favorite word processors and spreadsheets, and likewise lashed out bitterly at products that did not square with their standards. These readers exhibited about their computers the kind of emotional, possessive pride usually associated with one's children or alma mater's sports team.

Thus the implications of computing pleasure go beyond mere hedonistic interest. If computing is a pleasurable experience, people will—for better or for worse—spend more of their lives at computers. Staying afloat in the rapidly rising information-rich ocean requires a certain degree of comfort in using information technologies—a comfort that can best be achieved if computing is a pleasurable experience.

But just as parents find their children alternately delightful and infuriating, so do computer users experience much that is far from euphoric with their machines. Indeed, the very notion of computer ecstasy puzzles people who have never felt it. For them, working with a computer raises no more emotion than using a toaster. They don't join user groups, sign on to bulletin boards, or lust after the latest products. They are not seduced by what Provincetown, Mass., poet Sarah Randolph calls the "new porn—thick glossy computer magazines and instant-gratification phone-order catalogs."

This indifference arises in part from the correct observation that the influence of the computer has not quite fulfilled its promise. If computers are such wonderful information-management machines, then "why do I see so many computers with Post-It notes stuck all over them?" wonders S. Joy Mountford, manager of advanced technology in Apple Computer's human interface group. Beyond this inadequacy, computers still hold the terrifying power to lose or destroy information. "A computer lets you make more mistakes faster than any other invention in human history, with the possible exceptions of handguns and tequila," says Mitch Ratcliffe, a staff writer for the Macintosh publication *MacWeek*.

And of course, the power that the computer confers to endlessly revise, to tinker, to edit, is not necessarily all

*Even in serious software, there is a game-like feel: good programs invite users to explore— in effect, to play.*

to the good. Corporate managers complain about the new breed of business school graduates who are adept at spreadsheet manipulation but who confuse the ability to produce an attractive chart with sound business analysis.

In fact, computers seem to encourage people to obsess over what are, ultimately, secondary concerns. Office workers don't just dash off handwritten memos anymore, complains Mountford. Instead, she observes, "they spend hours getting the layout just right." As a result, she says, work progresses not much faster than it ever did.

I have been a writer and editor since the late 1970s. Wild editors-in-chief could not drag me away from my Macintosh and plunk me in front of a typewriter, scissors, and tape. But I cannot honestly claim that the ability to massage paragraphs endlessly before ink ever touches paper has made me a better or more productive writer. (Truth be told, I almost missed my deadline on this article—I became absorbed in learning the features of a new version of my word processor.)

## Going with the Flow

The essence of computer-using pleasure appears to be the machine's responsiveness. Computers give instant, unambiguous feedback that is inherently satisfying—and that is lacking in most human encounters. Indeed, the "computer is a little Skinner box, dishing out rewards at regular intervals," says Robert LaRose, professor of telecommunications at the University of Michigan. Put the program through the right gyrations and you get a beautiful on-screen graphic. Use different keystrokes or movements of the mouse, and a document is perfectly formatted. This constant cycle of positive reinforcement is well known to psychologists as an effective way to condition behavior, LaRose points out.

And, he says, once a person comes to expect satisfaction from a computer, a Pavlovian anticipation can develop. If computer use is, overall, a satisfying experience, then the user will experience little bursts of pleasure from the machine's many sensual cues—its beeps, the whirr of its disk drives, the sound of the keystrokes.

"My computer has become my metronome," explains Arthur Kleiner, a writer based in Oxford, Ohio. "I construct my pauses, my breaks of attention, to match the rhythm with which the computer brings up programs, saves files, dials a network, or stalls while processing a heavy data base."

At its best, computing's rapid and rhythmic give-and-take resembles the "high" people experience from any activity in which their skills are well matched to the challenge of the task at hand. If the challenge exceeds the skill, the person feels anxiety; if the reverse is true, boredom ensues. The optimal match, posits University of Chicago psychologist Mihali Csikszentmihalyi, produces a euphoric involvement that he dubs "flow."

Computer games, in particular, are highly challenging, require skill, and offer rapid feedback. The level of difficulty ratchets upward incrementally, ensuring that the player is always challenged but never overwhelmed. "There can be little doubt," says Csikszentmihalyi, "that the flow experiences they engender explain much of the popularity" of computer games. Even in more serious software, there is a game-like feel: good programs invite users to explore, to test new commands and menus—in effect, to play.

A common theme that runs through these and other odes to computers is a keen appreciation of the machine's power. To enthusiastic computer users, power is not just a set of numbers signifying microprocessor speed and memory size. Power means leveraging one's mental resources, accomplishing tasks dramatically quicker than without a computer.

The computer's blend of flow, play, and power is especially apparent in children. "We often see kids in school who have never been turned on by anything, and who are not doing well, and then we introduce the computer," says Seymour Papert of MIT's Media Laboratory. "They get very excited, and begin to do work that astounds their teachers—and themselves. The kids are thrilled that they can do something that seems so complicated."

In the most dramatic instances, Papert says that several schoolchildren who have been classified as learning-disabled have surpassed their supposedly "normal" classmates in their ability to construct programs. Often, says Papert, kids who gain confidence through their computer abilities then improve their performance generally.

A fundamental verity of education is that motivation is everything. Children (or adults, for that matter) will learn when it turns them on. For many kids, computers are a turn-on—and they will learn very rapidly and effectively using the computer as a teaching tool. Using a single program called *PC Globe*, my son has taught himself more about world geography, and about how to

*The companies that make software dare not take for granted the geyser of enthusiasm they have tapped.*

read graphs, maps, and charts, than I learned from years of conventional instruction. The secret is that he is willing to try again and again, to plumb the depths of the information contained in this piece of software. He could have used encyclopedias and other traditional materials, but they aren't anywhere near as much fun. "The phrase we hear a lot from the kids we work with," says Mitchell Resnick, a researcher at the MIT Media Lab, "is that computer work is 'hard fun.' "

Computers at their best give kids the opportunity to work in their own style. Even video games offer this versatility, which appeals to children's desire for self-expression and individuality. "Look at a game like *Super Mario Brothers*," says Resnick. "Some kids explore the world the game has created. Others try to pile up points. Others try to last a long time. That's the secret—lots of different kids like it because they can play it in different ways to suit their individual styles."

Good software is riveting because it can continue to offer new challenges just a notch above the ones just surmounted. This is, after all, what keeps people (young and old) plunking quarters into video games. The game greets success by immediately posing a new

97

challenge, just harder enough to keep the game interesting without becoming unplayable. If only human educators were as consistent in their ability to incrementally ratchet difficulty when teaching kids new skills and ideas.

More generally, says Papert, computers provide constant "challenges to perfection." A word-processed document stands ready to be instantly edited, a spreadsheet tinkered with, a game played one more time for a higher score. Other activities also can be refined—playing a musical instrument, for instance, or athletic performance—but they require a much larger investment of effort. "It's the low cost of the 'one more go' that makes computers unique," says Papert.

All this helps account for computers' holding power—but what of the intensity of the computing experience? Why do people get so immersed in their interactions with these machines?

"A computer is as close as you can get in this world to magic," says Nathan Myhrvold, vice president for advanced technology and business development at Microsoft. Computers, he says, "let you manipulate things without physical constraints." Working with a computer, there's little barrier between thought and deed. Software, after all, is essentially crystallized and codified thought. In a program, says Myhrvold, "you just describe something, and it comes true. That doesn't happen with anything but computers. The only limit is the cleverness of the programmer, and cleverness is a virtually boundless resource."

That sense of magic keeps coming up in conversations with computer enthusiasts, especially programmers. "To me, writing a computer program is like playing with electronic Legos," says Chris Peters, general manager of the Microsoft business unit that produces *Word*, a popular word processor. Writing a program, he says, is like "building a piece of incredibly compli-

# Computer-Based Communities

THE era of the island-computer is coming rapidly to a close. Many computer users now have modems for connecting their machines to the telephone network, which promises to amplify computing pleasure greatly. Networking is extending the typical session at a computer beyond the traditional activities of massaging information into useful and attractive forms.

"A computer without a modem is a pretty sorry excuse for a computer," says Reva Basch, a professional database searcher. "I love tracking down arcane facts in on-line indexes, or amassing, in minutes, piles of useful information that would take days to track down in a library, assuming you could find it at all. When a difficult search works out perfectly, I feel like I've pulled a rabbit out of a hat."

Few people have the opportunity to regularly experience the thrill of tapping enormous information banks; the costs of these on-line services are too high to allow for casual use. To a far larger population, the joy of computer outreach comes from the ability to electronically chat with other people. And that's as it should be, because communication resonates deeply in the human spirit. Thus, computing is coming more and more to mean communication.

Electronic mail is bringing back the lost art of letter writing, but with an important twist: e-mail messages often generate an immediate response from the recipient, and the ensuing exchange is more like a transcribed telephone call than a written correspondence. It is just this immediacy that many computer users find stimulating; e-mail exchanges provide the informality of telephoning without the hassle of linking up at a particular time.

E-mail is just one part of the broader phenomenon of electronic communities: people can use their computers and modems to connect to any of thousands of local bulletin boards or nation-wide conferencing systems. "There's a random quality to inhabiting that information space that's quite appealing—like going to a coffee house and not knowing who you'll happen to run into," says energy economist David Kline of the National Renewable Energy Laboratory in Golden, Colo.

"Armed with nothing more than a laptop computer with a built-in modem, I can, from anywhere there's a telephone, pursue conversations that help me think about a problem more clearly, watch debates forging new ideas, or drum up additional consulting business," says Tom Portante, an anthropologist and management consultant in Belmont, Mass. By connecting to what he calls this "ethereal intellectual bazaar," Portante gets "a feeling — not infrequently an Olympian one — of being on the moving edge of something, of somehow finding one's place on a rough-and-tumble frontier." It is this thrill of adventure more than any abstract desire to form new kinds of societal relationships that is driving the emergence of computer-based communities.

—*Herb Brody*

cated machinery, totally unconstrained by physical reality. You don't have to worry about getting the gears to mesh."

The programming community's almost child-like enthusiasm can infect software users. "Software is at its best when it is at it's most human, when you can feel the designer trying to imagine you, the user," says poet Sarah Randolph. Macintosh software in particular, she says, is "often full of small presents from the programmers. It's a kind of seduction, or romance."

## Beyond User Friendliness

While some computer companies make a point of producing easy-to-use systems, they are not, by and large, consciously pursuing the "joy angle." Makers of hardware and software still stress productivity. Even Apple—arguably the computer company most tuned in to computers' emotional appeal—has concluded that advertisements for its products work best when they address the practical aspects.

Computers have not yet progressed to the commodity status of automobiles, where the public is already sold on the notion that a car is useful. Would-be computer buyers still need to be convinced that the machine will save them time, make them money, or make their lives easier. They'll accept fun as a fringe benefit.

Still, some major computer companies are striving to make their products more enjoyable. Microsoft, the largest producer of personal computer software, has established a "usability lab." Software developers give test users new programs and assign them a task. The developers then watch through one-way mirrors. The goal, says Peters, is to produce a program that can be manipulated largely without manuals.

It is through such testing that Microsoft—and other software companies—have discovered some basic principles of user-friendliness. For example, says Peters, "it is very important that the screen always show something happening. If there has to be a 30-second delay for the computer to recalculate a modified spreadsheet, there ought to be some visual indication—such as the spinning watch hand familiar to Macintosh users—that work is in process and that the computer has not frozen up."

Apple has taken this idea even further by observing workers not just when they are at their computers. Mountford's group takes a video camera "on the road," where it can watch people do their job all day long. And she has found, for example, that "a lot of people spend 80 percent of their time just looking for things." To reduce frustration, then, computers should make it easy for people to know where things are. In a good user interface, Mountford says, it's always obvious where users are in the program, where they can get to next, and where they have come from.

There are other ways that software can cultivate what makes computer use enjoyable. One way is for a program to sense what the user is doing and then suggest a shortcut—an "over-the-shoulder interface."

But even those who get great satisfaction from working with computers can see that the technology has a long way to go. In a sense, today's most advanced computers are only whetting our appetites for what might follow—machines that reliably respond to human speech, for example, and software that is far more tolerant of human variability. Even the supposedly "intuitive" Macintosh computers really aren't—"double-clicking" a mouse button has no real equivalent outside the computing domain.

There is a burden, then, on the computer industry. If computers remain merely useful appliances, their potential impact on society will barely be realized—even though the machines will continue to infiltrate the workplace and, to a lesser extent, the home. An essentially captive audience will put up with arbitrary commands, irrational procedures, and ugly screens just to get its work done.

But the companies that make software, in particular, dare not take for granted the geyser of enthusiasm they have tapped. Already, a rift is growing between the computer cognoscenti and those who muddle through, relying, like Blanche DuBois in *A Streetcar Named Desire*, on the kindness of strangers. Computer developers should target the silent majority. They should be paying close attention to what annoys people about today's computers and taking appropriate action.

It is an axiom of the computer business that raw hardware power—memory size, processor speed—doubles roughly every two and a half years. It is largely up to the software developers to exploit this appreciating asset. They can continue to complicate their products—adding feature after feature that intensify their appeal to the dedicated few—the equivalent of car manufacturers upping engine horsepower every year while ignoring refinements in the dashboard. Or they can apply this escalating computational power to improving the computer's own "dashboard"—the user interface. That means making computers not just easy to use but a *pleasure* to use.

And that's a much bigger challenge than mere user friendliness. Ecstasy, after all, is a short-lived phenomenon: excitement abates, the novel becomes mundane. But with computing, more so than with any other technology, we are building mirrors of the human brain. The potential for computer ecstasy—like the potential for human creativity—is essentially unbounded.

Which ought to please my sons.

# Electronic Democracy

*The citizens of Santa Monica use computers to talk with City Hall and each other.
Is the system a state-of-the-art town meeting, or just a glorified call-in show?*

PAMELA VARLEY

PAMELA VARLEY is a Boston-based journalist and case writer at Harvard University's Kennedy School of Government. She has written a case study of PEN for the Kennedy School's program on innovation in state and local government.

With its enticing beaches, gourmet eateries zany public artworks, and radical-chic sensibility, Santa Monica has long been known as a playground for celebrities and affluent tourists. But the residents of this gleaming seaside town in Southern California are lately putting their community on the map for yet another reason: a curious social and political experiment. The idea is to create a new kind of public meeting ground—different from City Hall, different from a city park or plaza—where citizens can talk to public officials and city servants on equal footing, where people can get to know one another in safe environs and chat about local political issues or anything else on their minds.

This egalitarian meeting ground—where all voices are equal, anyone can speak at any time, and no one can be silenced—is not a physical place at all. It is a computer system, called the Public Electronic Network (PEN), that residents may hook into, free of charge. PEN provides electronic access to city council agendas, staff reports, public safety tips, and the public library's on-line catalog. It also allows residents to enter into electronic conferences on topics ranging from the political (discussions about rent control or human rights) to the utterly apolitical (such as TV's *Simpsons* or household pets). Santa Monicans can tap into PEN from a home or office computer or use one of the public terminals in libraries, community centers, and elderly housing complexes.

Each time a PEN user enters a comment, it immediately appears on the screen of other PEN users logged on to the same discussion item. As many as 64 people can use the system at once, so the comments can come thick and fast, just as if people were sitting around a room chatting. Sometimes the conversations are elongated—with a comment made one day and responses coming several days later. Discussions on a single topic may last for months. In addition to having access to these public conferences, each PEN user gets a private electronic mailbox for exchanging messages with city bureaucrats, politicians, and fellow citizens.

In a sense, Santa Monica is appropriating for public purposes technologies that had previously been mostly the province of businesses and individual computer devotees. Corporations use electronic mail to communicate with their customers and with one another. Private computer networks, such as CompuServe, allowing subscribers with common interests to meet without the traditional constraints of time and space. Using such a network, for example, a chess aficionado in Nebraska might strike up a friendship with a like-minded soul in London.

Applying these innovations to a public-sector network, a couple of visionary Santa Monicans thought, would give residents more direct access to their local government. The system could offer citizens a new way to be heard politically, free from the conventional gatekeepers in City Hall and the press. More broadly, it might prove a powerful antidote to the isolation and anomie of modern urban life by offering a new way for Santa Monicans to interact and forge alliances. This, in turn, might eventually involve more residents in civic affairs. "Engagement is what democracy is all about," says municipal court judge David Finkel, a member of the Santa Monica City Council in the late 1980s and an early fan of PEN. "The more people communicating on PEN, the more potential political activists there are to jump in and stir up the pot."

In its two and a half years of operation, PEN has had a tangible impact on Santa Monica. For instance, through PEN, a group of residents—including three or four homeless men—formed an on-line political organization that lobbied successfully for new city services for the homeless (*see "Helping the Homeless"*). But PEN also has its detractors. Some dismiss the system as a high-tech toy kept alive by a few computer enthusiasts with nothing better to do. And in fact, a relatively small group of Santa Monicans dominates the conferences, which often degenerate into mean-spirited verbal duels. The system also suffers from the lack of participation by most local officials. Nevertheless, PEN is a brave experiment. After all, not many municipal governments would play a wild card that could shift the balance of local political power.

## Pioneering PEN

A city of 96,000 tucked between Los Angeles and the Pacific Ocean, Santa Monica has a reputation for leftish politics. Heavily populated with "frumpies"—formerly radical upwardly mobile professionals—the city has elected '60s rebel leader Tom Hayden to the California State Assembly since 1982. The city has responded with unusual tolerance to its burgeoning population of homeless people; police refrain from rousting them from city parks, and every weekday afternoon a community group provides a free hot meal on the lawn in front of City Hall.

The city does have a contingent of moderates and conservatives, but nearly all of political Santa Monica embraces certain basic principles. Mark E. Kann, author of *Middle Class Radicalism in Santa Monica,* defines this ideology as a belief in "human-scale community, participatory democracy, and one-class society." Thus the city is well suited to pioneer a system like PEN.

The system's chief architect and champion is Ken Phillips, director of the Information Systems Department in Santa Monica City Hall. Phillips had already presided over the introduction of an electronic mail system at City Hall in 1984, allowing 600 of the city's 1,500 employees to communicate via computer. The seven city council members received laptop computers with which to send messages to city bureaucrats and to each other.

The idea of expanding the system beyond City Hall came in 1986, when council member Herb Katz mentioned to Phillips that a constituent was trying to get hold of some city documents and wondered whether he might be able to hook his computer up to the city's system. Phillips was not, at first, enthusiastic. The city computers are filled with sensitive information, and the idea of opening them to the public sounded like a security nightmare. Phillips did not reject the idea outright, however. As a subscriber to private computer networks, he began to see the potential for applying the same technology to a public system. He figured out a way around the security problems: set up a separate city computer that would contain public information and that would allow citizens access to City Hall via e-mail.

In October 1987, Phillips conducted a survey of local residents. To his surprise, it revealed enormous interest in a public computer network. The survey also showed that a third of the respondents already owned personal computers and that almost three-quarters of this group owned modems as well. Despite these numbers, the Santa Monica city manager was reluctant to ask the council for the hundreds of thousands of dollars in equipment necessary to launch an elaborate public computer network. Undaunted, Phillips persuaded Hewlett-Packard (maker of the city's existing computer system) to donate $350,000 worth of equipment to the venture and Metasystems Design Group to contribute $20,000 worth of software. On February 21, 1989, the system opened for public use. In the next few weeks, 500 curious Santa Monicans signed up for PEN. To ensure equitable access to the system, the city provided the service free of charge.

One of Phillips's early concerns in designing PEN had been the prospect of on-line obscenity or slander. Would the city be liable for comments that appeared on the system, the way a television station is for material it broadcasts? Or would the city be no more responsible for such communications than the telephone company? There was no suitable legal precedents. After some discussions, the city decided not to play the role of censor at all, unless a court declared a particular comment only a slanderous or obscene.

A related question was whether residents should be required to log on under their own names. One worry was that by using real names, PENners might feel exposed and therefore less inclined to enter debates. The city opted for real names, however, in part to deter irresponsible or obscence comments.

## The Lure of Conferences

City planners had expected the heaviest use of PEN to come from residents seeking information from one of the city's databases. They were wrong. From the beginning, the public conferences were by far the most popular attraction, accounting for more than half the calls. Electronic mail was the second most popular feature, followed by access to city databases. One of the clearest lessons of PEN, according to William Dutton, a professor at the University of Southern California's Annenberg School for Communications, is that people do not crave new sources of information so much as new venues for talking to one another.

In fact, many PEN users report that when they first began logging onto the PEN conferences, they went through a period of addiction (PENaholism, some call it) and found themselves mesmerized for hours in front of the screen, night after night. Most addicts settled down after a few weeks or months, although a few continued to log on every day for several hours.

What makes PEN so seductive? "You start playing with electronic mail and then you start looking forward to logging on in the morning to see if you got any mail in return," explains Phillips. "And then you post a comment in a conference, and the the next time you log on, 15 people have said something about what you've said. That's a heady brew."

Kevin McKeown, chair of the PEN Users Group, compares the system to a traditional New England town meeting—except that PEN is every day. "It's not like writing a letter to the editor of the local newspaper, where you have a chance in a thousand that it will be published, and no one ever responds to you even if it is," he says. "You put something provocative on PEN, and you get responses. And then other people chime in and pretty soon you've got a good debate going."

PEN also is casual and chatty, so a user does not need to measure every word. PEN offers housebound people a way to socialize. And it is always available: "PEN is the only place in town where I can have a decent conversation about a meaningful subject at a moment's notice," says one user.

Another draw for many users is the leveling effect of the PEN conferences. Judged solely on what they say on-line, people can easily cross social barriers. Homeless people talk to the well-to-do, teenagers talk to adults, political neophytes talk to City Hall's old hands. Even gender lines blur if a resident registers using only initials or an androgynous first name. "It's been a great equalizer," says Don Paschal, who was homeless until November 1990 and began using PEN while living on the street.

The leveling effect of PEN means that when PEN users do finally meet face to face, there can be surprises. McKeown remembers his shock at finding that some of the most thoughtful comments on PEN were written by a precocious teenager. City council member Ken Genser remembers meeting a PEN user he had assumed to be an elderly curmudgeon only to find that he was 25, with a pony tail.

## Trouble in Paradise

PEN's egalitarianism also makes the system vulnerable to abuse. PENners quickly discover that they must contend with people who feel entitled to hector mercilessly those with whom they disagree. It is, Phillips says, a little like trying to hold a meeting while "allowing somebody to stand in a corner and shout."

"Part of what makes PEN so volatile," says McKeown, "is that you're not face to face. There's not a chance you're going to get popped in the chops for what you say, so you feel like you can get away with more. In a way, that's liberating. But then you have the occasional 'flamer,' as they're called in on-line circles, who doesn't care if he or she hurts people."

As active PEN user Robert Segelbaum puts it, com-

# EAVESDROPPING ON PEN

Topics of PEN conferences range from the frivolous to the weighty; the level of discourse is sometimes tawdry and sometimes almost poetic. Following is a sampling of what Santa Monicans are saying to each other over the network:

### ABORTION

**RICHARD GROSSMAN 04-JUL-91, 9:24**
There are a lot of different ways women have attempted to induce abortions, most of them ineffective, and some very dangerous. That's why passing laws making abortion [illegal] will be such a disaster. It's not even a freedom of choice issue. The fact is, women who need abortions will go to any length to get them. Without proper medical care, the body count from abortions will rise to a level that is truly criminal. So-called "right to lifers" will end up being the cause of tens of thousands of needless deaths. I actually spoke to one of these fanatics about this, and her response was that it was the choice of the women to attempt an illegal abortion, and if they died from it, tough luck. Right to life indeed.
· · · · · · · ·

**JACK KOLB 04-JUL-91 10:24**
Right to life should be forced to staff hospital wards.
· · · · · · · ·

**THOMAS LEAVITT 04-JUL-91 10:41**
Feminists are setting up (I suspect even more determined and avidly) underground networks to ensure "safe" abortions for women who desire them. As well, they are working on developing self-induced abortion techniques, etc. They are also developing contacts with sympathetic doctors willing to perform them despite sanctions.
· · · · · · · ·

**ROBERT SEGELBAUM 04-JUL-91 16:42**
There's not going to be any need for an "underground." Abortion will always be legal in enough states, with wide enough geographical distribution, such that all any woman will have to do will be to get to a neighboring state.

puter conferencing turns writing into "a performing art." Michele Wittig, a psychology professor at California State University at Northridge and an active PENner, contends that "public postings take on the character of ripostes because, like fencing, PENning often occurs between two or three people interacting before an audience."

When the system started up, women—greatly outnumbered by men—had problems with harassment. "Several men would badger us a lot when we came onto the system," Wittig says. "We'd started on line discussions about sexism and equality of women in the workplace. They made disparaging remarks and innuendos." Even worse, she says, "several of the 17- and 18-year-olds started to post their very violent fantasies. They would use initials of women on PEN and say that they would dismember us and rape us." By the summer of 1989, the few women on line were fed up and ready to drop out.

Another kind of problem comes up when one or two PENners "go off thread," straying from the conference topic into a personal reverie or chitchat that all participants must wade through. PEN etiquette allows everyone to discuss any topic and express any opinion, no matter how arcane. But instead of interrupting discussion, a PENner who wants to change the subject is expected to open a new conference item. Some PEN users, for instance, enjoy chatting on-line about their stuffed animals. That's fine, McKeown says, provided they confine their ruminations to a special "stuffed animals" conference item.

PEN occasionally suffers as well from the tyranny of those with too much time on their hands. In a few cases, PENners have been known to comment not only on every topic but on virtually every *comment* made on every topic. Since thousands of comments are entered in PEN, this metacommentary can be oppressive, especially if the PENner is ill-mannered and given to name-calling. "There are people who have dominated on-line discussions for months now," says McKeown. "And there's no way to shut them up." Most PEN devotees cringe at the antics of the system's resident bullies because—aside from the immediate unpleasantness they produce—these troublemakers tend to reduce the

---

**JOANNE LEAVITT 04-JUL-91 18:19**
Robert is talking about a privileged class. . . those who can afford a trip to another state and a few nights hotel accommodations. How about a single mother with a couple of little ones at home? How about a teenage girl who is afraid to tell her family? How about. . . .
. . . . . . . . .

**CLAUDIA KRIEGER 04-JUL-91 18:23**
Glad you brought up those examples, Joanne. There are so many.
. . . . . . . . .

**RICK SAVAGE 04-JUL-91 18:24**
My guess is that this issue will get even more polarized after the fall of Roe vs Wade and that states that vote to keep abortion legal will also vote to make it affordable/free. Travelling to another state is relatively easy and cheap. In most parts of the country it only takes 1-2 tanks of gas.
. . . . . . . . .

**CLAUDIA KRIEGER 04-JUL-91 18:27**
Babysitting costs, loss of the

day(s) wages, overnight(s) stay, etc. . . .
. . . . . . . .

**JERRY NEWPORT 06-JUL-91 15:34**
Stay tuned for the grand opening, on the Arizona-CA border, or maybe Nevada-CA: Gloria's Baby Motel (shaped like a big roach motel); "Fetuses check in, but they don't check out."
. . . . . . . .

**JOANNE LEAVITT 08-JUL-91 17:57**
The Greater Los Angeles Coalition for Reproductive Freedom is holding a rally, Sunday, July 14th, 10:00 a.m. at the Westwood Federal Building. If you would like further information, need a ride or whatever, send me an e-mail for the appropriate phone numbers. Also needed are letters to both the President and our local papers regarding the Gag Rule (Rust v. Sullivan).
. . . . . . . .

**CLAUDIA KRIEGER 08-JUL-91 18:40**
Will do, Joanne. . . Stormin' the Bastille!

**RESPONSE TO A TRAGEDY**

**SUSAN DAVIDSON 01-SEP-91 8:17**
James Burgess died Saturday after trying to flag down an RTD bus in West Hollywood. He accidentally lost his balance and fell under the wheels of the bus. If you have any information about his relatives, please call the sheriff's station at 855-8850. They do know that he was from Washington and living at a homeless shelter in S.M.
. . . . . . . . .

**RICHARD GROSS 01-SEP-91 8:42**
That is really sad and upsetting news. James had just started living in an apartment in the valley, and was in the process of finding a job.
. . . . . . . .

**ROBERT SEGELBAUM 01-SEP-91 12:30**
Someone should sue RTD on his behalf. RTD drivers are, in general, utterly callous about passengers trying to board their buses once they decide to pull

out. They seem to take some sort of sadistic pride in making people wait for the next bus when it would cost them no more than 5 seconds of their time to pause and open the door. I am quite certain that this horrible incident came as a DIRECT RESULT of such callousness.
. . . . . . . .

**MARGARET WILLIAMS 01-SEP-91 15:54**
There should be an inquiry. I've seen RTD drivers close doors in people's faces after they've sat and watched them run to try to catch them in time. James was deaf. It is appalling to think of him (or anyone) dying this way.
. . . . . . . .

**FRANCEYE SMITH 01-SEP-91 16:01**
A few years ago when my boss went to China, he showed us pictures of the tour bus they took. This bus had a closed-circuit TV camera at the back with the screen in front so the driver would see anyone in the road behind him. Our buses need something like this—or better rear-view mirrors. No one

forum's apparent importance in the eyes of the general public. "Sometimes it degenerates into nothing better than one of those $5-a-minute telephone lines," says one regular user.

Of course, just about any public forum has a similar problem. At every Santa Monica City Council meeting, for instance, one woman gets up to speak on each item on the agenda—prolonging meetings by as much as an hour. "Any system can be abused," McKeown says. "What you have to look at is the balance—how many people are you enabling and empowering and how many people are going to abuse that kind of power?"

PENners have come up with a number of ways to cope with on-line bullying. In response to harassment, for example, the women on PEN banded together in July 1989 to form a support group called PEN Femmes. The group makes a point of welcoming women when they begin to participate in PEN conferences. Harassment has subsided as more women have become active. The city has also made available private conferences, so that groups of like-minded people can work on a project in peace—an idea Phillips likens to allowing a community group to meet in a private room at City Hall.

E-mail, too, has proved useful against PEN abuse. For one thing, if two PEN users get off track in a conference—suddenly realizing that they want to chat about football, say, instead of property assessments—they can do so privately. E-mail is also a good way to let someone know he or she is breaching PEN's etiquette without dressing the person down in public. "One of the worst things you can do," McKeown says. "is respond to a blowhard on-line, because he'll blow hard right back at you, in an endless cycle." Sometimes, when approached by e-mail, a PENner can be persuaded to delete an offending comment from a conference, or at least to temper his or her future comments. Says Phillips, "The ability to operate behind the scenes with e-mail is the glue that keeps the conferences running."

## Coping with a Hard Core

PEN's biggest disappointment has been the domination of its conference discussions by a small number of users.

---

should ever die under the wheels of a bus!
. . . . . . . .

**RICHARD GROSSMAN 02-SEP-91 21:46**
Has anyone found out anything about James's family?
. . . . . . . .

**DONALD PASCHAL 03-SEP-91 12:32**
re the Late Mr. Burgess: He was deaf, gay, and a human being, in reverse order. He simple asked people to get to know him. I wish I did. Rest in peace, Mr. Burgess.

### THE HOMELESS

**BILL MYERS 21-AUG-91 10:07**
Is there a reason for our city not to allow the homeless shelter at night when public facilities are locked until morning? City Hall itself could be open to the public at night for such a service, no? Naturally, there would be "problems" to iron out, but this shouldn't be too difficult with a few good minds at work. Other cities could follow our lead, too,

which might force public officials to take a more serious look at homelessness. And this might prove to speed up this slow process of actually ending homelessness.
. . . . . . . .

**DONALD PASCHAL 21-AUG-91 10:13**
Where EXACTLY in City Hall. . . .I'm sitting in the place right now, and I can't see, based on the layout of the place, how that can be feasible. You have to have some sort of security, a way to control bathroom flow, and how are you going to accommodate 1000 people inside city hall? Good suggestion, wrong building.
. . . . . . . .

**SUSAN DAVIDSON 21-AUG-91 10:22**
How about the Auditorium?
. . . . . . . .

**DONALD PASCHAL 21-AUG-91 10:26**
Again, where. . . on stage. . . and how do you accommodate for events. . . .let's say Guns'n'Roses were playing at the Auditorium. . . can you imagine telling Axl Rose he has to cut his set short

because a bunch of homeless people were waiting to sleep on the stage?
. . . . . . . .

**SUSAN DAVIDSON 21-AUG-91 10:28**
How often is that white elephant used, anyway?
. . . . . . . .

**DONALD PASCHAL 21-AUG-91 10:29**
Enough to know that (a) it would not be practical and (b) anyone suggesting that would be laughed out of council chambers.
. . . . . . . .

**SUSAN DAVIDSON 21-AUG-91 10:33**
Well then it's worth a try!

### THE SOVIET BREAKUP

**DONALD PASCHAL 25-AUG-91 16:18**
Remember. . . Communism itself is not dead. . . only the party in the USSR. What form Communism takes is what the administration is watching.
. . . . . . . .

**BRIAN HUTCHINGS 25-AUG-91 16:21**
I mean, both Bush & Gorbachev

have ties to the bad-assed sides of their respective intelligence agencies (Gorby having been hand-picked by mister Andropov.)
. . . . . . . .

**DONALD PASCHAL 25-AUG-91 16:39**
A good point, but what of Yeltsin. He seems to be going headstrong in trying to eliminate Communism altogether. . . and he is very popular. Plus remember, both are politicians in the new (TV-oriented) school, something only one other Soviet leader seemed to be. . . .Nikita Kruschev.
. . . . . . . .

**SUSAN DAVIDSON 25-AUG-91 19:05**
Nick was a tad heavy handed, tho.
. . . . . . . .

**CURTIS SHENTON 25-AUG-91 20:36**
Anyone watch *60 Minutes* tonight? It had an interesting piece by a Soviet reporter that brought to light the fact that the majority of Soviets didn't oppose the coup. Not that they supported it, but many, if not most, of the Soviet peoples feel that

More than 3,000 people are signed up for PEN, but only 500 to 600 log on each month and most never add any comments to the conference discussions. PENners talk about the "50 hard-core" users whose names appear again and again. While the average PEN user logs on to the system about 12 times a month, some PENners do so 8 or 10 times a day.

Most of the hard-core PENners tend to be pro–rent control, antidevelopment, and sympathetic to the plight of the homeless. But according to city council member Genser, the core users differ from other community activists in town. The PEN group is "less of an insider crowd," he says. They tend to approach government with a "wide-eyed innocence."

Those active in the conference discussions tend to be articulate; they also tend to be thick-skinned and to enjoy verbal skirmishes. Says active PENner Bill Myers, "The attacks have been quite vicious at times, creating a kind of survivalist attitude among PENners. It is like an electronic pack of wolves who gather together for strength and companionship."

Santa Monica's political movers and shakers have, for the most part, stayed clear of PEN's crucible. If the active PENners are, as Myers suggests, an electronic wolf pack, then a politician on PEN becomes a computerized rawhide bone. PENners tend to pounce on any officeholder bold enough to enter the on-line fray, making accusations and demanding a response. Politicians are accustomed to guarding their public comments closely, working out their positions ahead of time with core constituents and then "going into meetings with relatively fixed positions," says judge and former council member Finkel. But politicians who "think out loud" on PEN and respond conversationally to questions subject themselves to intense scrutiny.

Most PEN users, says Katz, are "fringe" types, like the people who call in to radio talk shows. "They're both liberal and conservative, but way over, one way or another, on an issue," he says. Chris Reed, a council member who has participated in the conferences, agrees. She characterizes PEN's hard core as "mean-spirited people who pound out their anger on the keyboard. They've poisoned the system and driven off the reasonable people." Reed quit PEN in August 1990, an-

---

democracy and perestroika have ruined the country.
· · · · · · · ·

**THOMAS LEAVITT 25-AUG-91 21:55**
Hmm. . . Ukraine declared itself independent, Russia is going around recognizing the Baltic states as independent, various and sundry republics and autonomous regions are squawking. . . question will eventually be faced. . . why the defense establishment? Is that the reason Bushie baby is busy trying to support Gorby to the max?
· · · · · · · ·

**DANIEL BRIN 25-AUG-91 23:57**
Am I the only person who is appalled that Yeltsin unilaterally shut down the Communist Party's newspapers? Is this the action of a democrat?
· · · · · · · ·

**PHILLIP CARTER 26-AUG-91 9:39**
Actually, the Communist newspapers, i.e. Pravda, Red Star, were state run, censored, and full of false news and propaganda. They were not newspapers in any true sense of the word, so I don't see why we should be appalled at all.
· · · · · · · ·

**DAVID MORGAN 26-AUG-91 15:43**
The *60 Minutes* show was quite interesting. Yeltsin is not popular among the workers, and the Moscow reporter thinks they have a year, at most, to make democracy work. Most of the people interviewed thought things were much better under communism. I guess because there was food in the stores, and they had jobs.

---
**WHERE ARE THE POLITICIANS?**

**WILLIAM NOBLE 12-JUL-90 23:34**
How come [Tom] Hayden isn't on PEN anyway. Let's all write him nasty letters saying that we won't vote for someone who can't take the time to listen to us directly (through staff even)
· · · · · · · ·

**JOANNE LEAVITT 13-JUL-90 0:42**
Seems to be a problem with the way the equipment is set up. The ones tied into Sacramento are on dedicated lines. Can't use them for both. Still don't understand, but something like this is the problem.
· · · · · · · ·

**ROBERT SEGELBAUM 13-JUL-90 10:11**
Joanne, there is absolutely NO technical problem with someone signing on from Sacramento or anywhere else on earth.
· · · · · · · ·

**JON STEVENS 13-JUL-90 12:03**
What I don't understand is why we don't have more political participation on PEN from public officials? Our city seems to be behind pen but for some reason we can't even get local media to open up a conference to hear from their audience. As for getting Tom Hayden online, William, some of us feel he would be the perfect politician to use this system to promote grass roots participation in the electoral process. I have been accused of driving people off PEN because of some of my confrontive and adversarial responses online. I have told the misguided souls in no uncertain terms that they need to have a good bowel movement and to do to themselves what only certain species of worms and slugs have the anatomical capacity to accomplish. I cannot take credit for driving people off PEN and in fact have been trying very hard for over a year to do just the opposite. Forgive me for being persistent and impatient.

---
**WHAT SANTA MONICA NEEDS**

**PHILLIP CARTER 05-MAR-91 21:30**
I think that the city needs to promote bicycling more by establishing more safe routes and paths along Santa Monica streets. Our city is a very environmentally conscious city, and cycling to work or school is one way to cut down on pollution. I'm not sure how many people on PEN use bicycles as transportation. I do because I don't drive yet.
· · · · · · · ·

**WILLIAM NOBLE 05-MAR-91 22:21**

nouncing that she was fed up with being attacked. "If people had been the least bit polite, or respectful of the need for people in a democracy to differ," she says, "I would have stuck it out."

Reed was not the only local politician to give up on PEN in exasperation. When city council member Judy Abdo, who had been active on PEN during its first year, diverged from her liberal council colleagues by supporting a local beachfront hotel development, she too incurred the wrath of PEN regulars. After battling it out on-line for a while, she stopped participating.

Another reason that politicians shun PEN is their perception that the network is a time sink. A few months after the system started, Santa Monica's congressman, Mel Levine, agreed to sponsor several on-line discussions about national and international policy. Levine's district office staff monitored the conferences and, when questions arose, either answered them or (more often) sent them to Washington for research and reply.

Yet this arrangement has not satisfied anyone. PEN users resent that it takes several weeks to get their questions answered and that Levine does not enter the debates personally. Levine's staff, meanwhile, is frustrated at having to do a great deal of work to respond to the demands of a small number of constituents—and then being lambasted for failing to do more. "We take a beating on a system we volunteered to participate in," says Blaise Antin, staff assistant and PEN coordinator in the congressman's district office. Even Santa Monica's guru of participatory democracy, State Assemblyman Tom Hayden, insists that he and his staff don't have time for PEN.

Phillips believes that much of the problem could have been averted if PEN had started up a little differently: "I recommend to people that if they're going to do a system like this, they start with a group of community leaders, and let them set the tone of the system."

### Breaking New Ground

Some PENners argue that it's too early to conclude much of anything about the experiment, which, they point out, is still in its infancy. "It's going through growing pains," says Finkel, and despite its shortcomings, he still believes it to be a "wonderful new First Amendment tool."

---

specific building codes designed for gray water irrigation.
. . . . . . . .

**BILL MYERS 06-MAR-91 0:15**
I think our city would make a move in the right direction by creating another task force regarding methods of conservation and ideas promoting our more informed and new age society.
. . . . . . . .

**ROBERT SEGELBAUM 06-MAR-91 9:29**
One thing this city desperately needs is housing for low- and middle-income people and one thing it absolutely does NOT need is more office space.
. . . . . . . .

**JERRY NEWPORT 06-MAR-91 15:28**
The best way to provide affordable housing here is to allow rental of rooms in single homes, and allow landlords to charge higher rents to those who can afford them, with a controlled pass-through of a fair portion of that profit to subsidize affordable units.
. . . . . . . .

**WILLIAM HANDELSMAN 06-MAR-91 15:35**
As an aside, the Coroner-select for LA recently turned down the job because even with a loan for 30% from the County a comparable house of 5000 sq.ft. like he has in Pittsburgh would cost at least $1,000,000 in LA.
. . . . . . . .

**PHILLIP CARTER 18 MAR 91 18:51**
Our city needs to revitalize its streets to hold water. Up in Seattle, where it rains a lot, their streets can handle the water. Here, when it rains, the next day the roads really suck. On a bike you notice this. Also, our roads aren't designed to absorb the runoff of oils, paints, and other chemicals onto the street which in turn make it slippery. As well, the sewer system that collects street water is not adequate. Though we are at a budget premium, how much extra would it take the next time S.M. redoes its roads to make them watersafe.
. . . . . . . .

**GERALDINE MOYLE 18-MAR-91 18:53**
Phillip: there is no sewer system to collect waste from the streets. Water, and everything else spilled on the streets, flows down into storm drains, which, although they have catchment basins for solid trash, essentially carry rainwater etc. into the ocean.
. . . . . . . .

**JACK KOLB 18-MAR-91 19:01**
An ocean which has been smelling unctuous all day.

# Helping the Homeless

DESPITE the lack of participation by Santa Monica's political leaders, PEN has been instrumental in forming one civic project: an effort to provide better services for the homeless. The initiative began with on-line discussions of homelessness in the winter and spring of 1989, a time when surveys showed that this issue was the number-one local concern of Santa Monica residents. Several homeless men took part in the discussion using public terminals at a city library. As participants read their stories and comments, says Kevin McKeown, who chairs the PEN Users Group, they began to realize that not all the homeless were mentally ill or drug-addicted. "There's a significant percentage who are involuntarily homeless because of something that happened. How many people, if they missed two or three pay checks, couldn't make the rent?"

In July 1989, as a result of a proposal by Michele Wittig, a psychology professor [at California State University at Northridge] and PEN enthusiast, PEN users formed a group to work on community projects and made homelessness its first agenda item. One PENner proposed that what homeless people really needed to seek employment was early morning showers, a place to wash their clothes, and a locker in which to store their belongings. That was the beginning of a project dubbed "SHWASHLOCK" (for SHowers, WASHers, and LOCKers).

The PEN Action Group, about 20 people in all, took stock of the community's existing resources and came up with a proposal for a facility near the beach with showers and lockers. There were some stumbling blocks along the way—neighborhood resistance to one proposed site for the facility, for instance. But the action group persevered and in May 1990 brought its proposal to the City Council, which has since approved it. The PEN Action Group has worked with social service groups to provide homeless people with vouchers so they can use the showers and lockers for free, as well as use washing machines at a nearby laundromat. Through a fund-raising clothes sale and donations, the group raised more than $4,000 for this effort.

Acting on the suggestions of Don Paschal (a homeless man who participates in PEN ), the group has begun work on another way to help the homeless: an on-line job bank that will be run as a cooperative venture with local social service and business groups.—*Pamela Varley*

---

McKeown agrees. "I see PEN as a way to change the whole political process, the whole exchange of information with voters, the whole way that we interact with our city government," he says. "Five or ten years down the road, we're going to have candidates for City Council and other positions that will run only because they got involved through PEN."

Gary Orren, a professor of public policy at Harvard University and co-author of *The Electronic Commonwealth,* is less sanguine about the prospects. New communication technologies tend to acquire a following of true believers who have utopian notions of what they will accomplish, he says. Orren believes there will never be more than "a very small subgroup of unusual people" who take part in computer conferencing that requires typing on a keyboard and reading from a screen. An audiovisual communication medium will be more likely to attract users, he believes. But even a more sophisticated interface may ultimately prove futile. The sad truth, he says, is that "people have a limited and declining taste and hunger for politics."

And in fact, other U.S. communities have yet to copy PEN. More than 100 other municipalities are experimenting with public computer networks. But in most cases, that simply means that a resident can approach a multimedia kiosk—say, in a shopping mall—and, after viewing a videotaped message from the mayor, dial up the city computer for land-use records. Most local governments, gasping and struggling financially, are not inclined to risk a sizable chunk of their budget on something that may be branded a frill. No one else has created a system as interactive as PEN or as socially ambitious.

Nevertheless, PEN has broken important new ground, and it may yet inspire future efforts. What is unusual and exciting about PEN, says Jerry Mechling, director of strategic computing and telecommunications at Harvard's Kennedy School of Government, is that a public-sector entity is doing something that is normally done only by the private sector—namely, using technology not merely to automate an existing method of doing business but to "rethink the basic way things are done." With PEN, he says, Santa Monica is "using technology to explore different ways of reaching the public. If we encourage many such experiments, I'm optimistic that we'll find better ways of doing things."

# Superduperitis

There are ordinary personal computer users, there are serious users
and then there are users who go off the deep end.
Are you a computer widow or widower?

**David C. Churbuck**

TRIPP LILLEY, a sophomore at Virginia Tech, doesn't just have an Aberdeen 486 computer in his off-campus apartment, he has a computer network. The network connects Lilley's machine with a Mylex 486 belonging to his roommate and with a used TRS-80 Model 100 he has installed in the kitchen "for reading E-mail and newsfeeds over orange juice in the morning."

The system is not quite powerful enough, Lilley has decided. He says he needs another 112 megabytes of chip memory and an upgrade to a hard disk with space for a gigabyte of files. Lilley is also saving money from a part-time job in order to buy a $300 bar-code reader, so he can scan food packages as he puts them in the freezer. Then he can dial his apartment computer from the campus computer center before deciding whether to hit the nearby Pizza Hut or walk home for lunch.

Lilley rationalizes all this equipment as being a useful background for an engineering major who will probably use computers in his career. Maybe so, but what we see here looks an awful lot like an incipient case of Geek Syndrome. Victims of this affliction start out with a basic computer purchase, then feel they have to trade up to something faster, and then have to buy again and again each time a new generation of microprocessor or hard disk comes out.

James Gordon Upton, 69, a former Manhattan advertising and marketing executive now retired to a farm in Bedford, N.H., bought his first computer four years ago. Today he has a custom-built 486SX computer that clocks at 25 megahertz and has a Zoom Telephonics interval modem running at 9,600 bits per second. Upton spends up to two hours a day in front of the box. His passion is playing Links 386 Pro computer golf against prerecorded players contained in the software. You don't need a lot of iron to run that software, but just in case, Upton has two printers, a scanner (a Logitech, costing around $200) and, for playing digitized sound, a $180 Sound Blaster sound board.

Still not enough. Upton is now thinking of moving into multimedia, which would, of course, mean buying at least one compact disk reader at $400 and adding on a 24-bit color video capture board ($600) so he can edit his home videos and capture still images from the tube.

"These are very seductive tools, like sports cars," says Russell Walter, 45, author of *The Secret Guide to Computers* and a computer consultant in Somerville, Mass., who has witnessed PC addictions firsthand. "Most people can get what they need from a computer for $1,000. But if you spend just a little bit more you get so much more power, and a little more leads to a little more power. . . ."

Walter has 45 computers in his home, most of them stacked in 6-foot-high piles on the living room floor. But the bedroom, he says, is where he puts his "emotional" equipment, by which he means hardware that makes sounds. That's where his five music synthesizers are, including his Roland Jupiter-6, which he plans to hook up to a Synergy 386 computer and a sound card.

Walter explains the addiction: "It's like drugs. To support your habit you deal to others, and get into the industry yourself. You write programs and give them away, a pusher encouraging others to become users."

That's how retired adman Upton got hooked. His supplier is a self-employed cabinetmaker who developed an expensive taste for electronics and set up shop as a computer consultant in order to pay for it.

Penn Jillette, 38, the loquacious half of the demented comic magic act Penn & Teller, has been a PC fanatic since 1985, when he talked a young hacker into showing him the ropes in exchange for free tickets and lunch. Now the compulsive carrier of a 486SX Toshiba T4400C notebook with color screen and 20 megabytes of RAM and 120-meg hard drive ($7,000), Jillette says he gets the same charge from computers that his artist friends get from their paints. "The glow of the screen makes me happy," says Jillette, who advocates painting hot-rod flames on the side of fast computers.

Do you have a problem with home computers? Are they taking over your life? You know you are in trouble if you buy a $200 sound board just so you can get your computer to say the time rather than display it, or if you buy a $600 video board so you can watch television on your monitor.

Another danger sign is practicing what the geeks call homebrewing—manufacturing your own personal computers for the thrill of it. Paul Matthews, 37, a Boston-area computer consultant, is a brewer. He combed flea markets and computer magazine ads for the parts to build a custom 486 PC on his kitchen table. But Matthews' obsession is virtual reality. The ultimate in computer interfaces, these three-dimensional immersion systems cost lots of money when bought off-the-shelf. So Matthews is making do. He is rewiring and programming a Mattel Power Glove, a kids' videogame accessory, to substitute for an $8,800 VPL Research Dataglove, the Spandex and fiber-optic glove used in commercial virtual reality systems.

On-line benders are something to watch for, especially if you are using a service like CompuServe's message board that bills for every minute of connect time. "On-line services can be a serious problem to some people. They should be controlled substances," says Thomas Mandel, a futurist at SRI International in Menlo Park, Calif. and a recovered on-liner.

Kamal Singh, 28, a systems analyst at Lehman Brothers in New York City, has three computers in his apartment, including a Sun Sparcstation workstation running Unix ($11,000 with 32 megabytes of memory and a 400-meg hard drive). Between them and his workstation at work, he spends 16 hours a day, six days a week in front of a screen. "My wife says it is my first wife," he says. She might have left him by now, he jokes, except that he was once able to pull up a key research paper on podiatry for her from Medline, the on-line database available from Dialog Information Services (60 cents per minute).

How bad can it get? A 1987 medical journal article relates the case of an 18-year-old Dane who spent 12 to 16 hours a day at the keyboard. Doctors at Copenhagen's Nordvang Hospital said the young man took on the persona of his computer, saying things like: "Line 10, Go to the bathroom; Line 11, Next."

If you get to this state, get help. Get an Internet account, preferably with a high-speed modem connection, and tap into the Usenet system. A Usenet newsgroup addressable as alt.irc.recovery is a digital encounter session for people addicted to real-time computer conferencing.

# Contracts Without Paper

◆

*Conventional legal wisdom requires ink on paper to make a contract enforceable. Businesses need to get past this anachronistic attitude as computer transactions become more common.*

◆

BENJAMIN WRIGHT

*BENJAMIN WRIGHT, a Dallas-based attorney, is the author of* The Law of Electronic Commerce: EDI, Fax and E-mail *(Little, Brown, 1991).*

"*Get it in writing.*"

So warns a long-distance phone company in its advertisements warning consumers to distrust its competitors' promises. The meaning is unmistakable: a promise is valid only if it is printed on paper.

This long-standing creed is being challenged as businesses and governments replace paper with electronic documents, which are more economical to create, transmit, and store. But despite the technology's advantages, conventional business wisdom questions the validity of using purely electronic messages to form contracts. This doubt springs from the belief that computer messages inherently provide less reliable evidence than paper messages: they can be easily altered without leaving a telltale "scratch-out" mark that would betray a tampered-with paper document. Embodying the conventional wisdom, Hans B. Thomsen, writing in an influential business-law text, advises businesses to confirm electronic contracts with paper—even while acknowledging how cumbersome this procedure could be.

Relying on such cautious legal counsel, many organizations remain hesitant about forming contracts without paper. As recently as 1990, for example, a lawyer for Exxon stated publicly at an oil industry conference that his company would not form contracts solely via computer-generated documents. The oil giant, he said, insisted on paper to seal every deal. Exxon's lawyers knew of no legal precedent that established the validity of computer-generated contracts; their conservative instincts said their client should avoid them.

This slavish adherence to ink on paper is evident in government as well as industry. The Bureau of Land Management—a federal agency that leases government property to the private sector—requires that all submitted requests for leases be "manually signed." In 1987, the bureau rejected a lease offer submitted by fax machine because it did not fulfill this requirement. The applicant—Reed Gilmore—appealed the decision to the Ninth Circuit U.S. Court of Appeals. Although the court ruled last November that Gilmore's application did not comply with the letter of the regulation and therefore that the rejection was proper, the judge chided the bureau for its enforcement of a meaningless and hypertechnical signature requirement. Despite the scolding, the bureau has yet to amend its regulation—a clear-cut case of a large institution maintaining an outmoded legal policy that ignores the last decade's technological advances.

Reluctance to rely on electronic contracts is understandable—old habits die hard—but it is also uneducated and counterproductive. If appropriate data-processing controls are in place, computer messages can be just as reliably authentic as paper documents. And since computer messaging can reduce the seemingly endless paper shuffling that marks today's commerce, it is more economically efficient.

With businesses today staking sizable sums on electronic messages, legal controversy has begun to mount. Recently, for example, two companies fought the first reported lawsuit over whether an exchange of computer messages constitutes a binding contract. (*See "Suing over an Electronic Contract."*)

There are few limits on the types of transactions organizations now convey electronically. The Securities and Exchange Commission, for example, accepts corporate regulatory filings electronically. The SEC's program that

From *Technology Review*, July 1992, pp. 57-62. Copyright © 1992 by Benjamin Wright. Reprinted by permission.

makes this possible, the Electronic Data Gathering, Analysis and Retrieval (EDGAR) system, has been operating in pilot mode since the mid-1980s. Ultimately, the SEC will require virtually all filers to use EDGAR. And cotton farmers and buyers around the world are forming paperless contracts of sale with a PC-based system called Telcot.

But the messaging format that promises the most for automating commerce is electronic data interchange, or EDI. Here, humans step back and let the computers control the whole process, automatically generating and reading such business documents as purchase orders, checks, and official regulatory filings. Some 20,000 organizations worldwide (most of them in North America) now use EDI, and the number is growing at 45 percent a year.

An EDI transaction might happen like this: A computer program for a retail chain monitors the sales of 10-gallon hats in the retailer's stores. When the level of hat sales exceeds a predefined threshold, the program composes an EDI purchase order and transmits it to the hat-maker's computer, which then automatically commences action to acknowledge and fill the order. Legally, the retailer's purchase order is an offer, and the manufacturer's acknowledgment an acceptance. The parties form a contract without paper and without human involvement.

### What Is a 'Signed Writing'?

A 300-year-old law called the statute of frauds, aimed at ensuring that no contract is disputed in court unless the parties possess substantial evidence that the contract exists, is at the heart of the misunderstanding about the legality of computer messages. This statute—embodied in Section 2–201 of the Uniform Commercial Code, which virtually every state incorpo-

*Despite strong intuitive reservations from lawyers, recent cases suggest that courts are likely to accept any computer message as "writing."*

rates into its laws—says that many types of contracts are unenforceable without a "signed writing," which conventional wisdom defines as a paper document ending with an autograph.

According to standard legal thinking, the physical properties of paper and ink—such as the difficulty of changing ink marks, the unique features of handwritten pen strokes, and the chemical consistency of different grades and brands of ink and paper—enable a forensics expert to determine a paper document's authenticity. A corollary is that a simple computer message, which has no properties to prevent it from being fabricated or altered inconspicuously, cannot provide similar forensic evidence and thus should not be relied on as a legal document.

This thinking has a ring of logic, but it is based on an archaic view of the law. In fact, through the centuries, courts have invented many exceptions to the statute of frauds and have, in effect, read the statute off the books. The law now holds, for example, that

a contract is enforceable as long as both parties admit its existence—even if no signed writing exists. A deal, after all, is a deal.

Moreover, it is not fundamentally very difficult to insure the authenticity of a business document, even if it is transmitted electronically. In fact, the prevention of forgery rarely even requires sophisticated technological safeguards. Business messages are often very specific—an order to buy 5,014 jars of picante sauce, for example, would specify date, time, quantity, flavor, price, place of delivery, and so on. To create a message that is not obviously fake, a forger must know a great deal about the parties. Anyone with that much knowledge would, of course, be an early suspect if anyone were to uncover the wrongdoing.

### Adequate Safeguards

Password schemes provide further protection. Two users can agree to use a password in their messages to establish authorship. Banks, for example, have long relied on a special kind of password to authenticate the telex messages used to transfer funds. The sender appends to its message a "test key"—a number that represents the product of a previously agreed-upon mathematical formula based on a regularly changing set of numbers from a code book and a portion of the contents of the telex message, such as the dollar amount of the funds involved. The recipient verifies the message by recomputing the test key and comparing its version with transmitted the test key. Any alteration of the telex contents during transmission would be apparent because the original test key and the recomputed test key would not match.

Callback routines can provide another form of security. The message-sending computer calls the computer of the intended recipient. Then the second computer calls the first computer back at its secret telephone number. This procedure makes it difficult for an electronic intruder to masquerade as a legitimate user. (When the second computer calls back, it can, if sophisticated enough, detect that call-forwarding is being used—and if so discontinue the call because it is not going to the intended telephone number.)

Encryption can offer still greater security. One of the most promising technologies is public-key cryptography, whereby the transmitted data are scrambled with one key and unscrambled with another key. Each key is a number that, when incorporated into a specified algorithm together with numbers representing the content of the message, permits the message to be coded or decoded.

Under a public-key system, a neutral party assigns the message sender both a scrambling key (which is kept secret) and an unscrambling key (which is made public). Senders use their private keys to scramble their outgoing messages. The receiver tries to unscramble the message using the sender's public key—an endeavor that can succeed only if the message came from the expected sender and if the message has not changed since the sender released it. (Although the two keys are mathematically related, it is virtually impossible to derive the private key from the public one.) Thus no one can forge a message and claim it came from the sender. Although highly effective, public key cryptography is not widely used in commercial electronic messaging because it requires considerable advance coordination among the parties.

Computer-message users can employ passwords, callback routines, and cryptography, together with other authentication methods, in different degrees and combinations. Determining which blend of safeguards is best boils down to a decision balancing the risks of fraud against the expense and inconvenience of using one combination or another.

This judgment call is a familiar one. In conventional communications, we choose from a variety of devices to authenticate paper—single signatures, dual signatures, witnessed signatures, safety paper, notary stamps, bank signature guarantees, and so on. The combination we choose for any particular document depends upon a similar balance of risk versus expense and inconvenience.

The most popular paper authentication device—a single handwritten signature—is itself rather weak. Signatures can be forged, and message recipients rarely check them against specimen signatures. The truth is that signatures secure paper documents from forgery far less than do the circumstances surrounding the documents: the time of creation, the contents, the special knowledge of the parties. This experience with paper suggests that for many routine legal transactions, electronic messages need not require extremely robust authentication. Cryptography, for example, is seldom necessary.

## Evidence in Court

Even if messages can be authenticated, conventional legal wisdom still protests that since computer records can be changed after their creation, they do not suffice as legal evidence.

But this argument misunderstands the role of courtroom evidence. Little of that evidence provides *absolute* proof of anything. Any document can be forged or altered. Any witness can lie, forget, or embellish. A judge generally requires only that a piece of evidence be "reliable," meaning that an observer has good reason to believe it, even though it may be false.

U.S. courts have decided that at least some computer records pass this reliability test and have accepted them as evidence. In a landmark case in 1965—*Transport Indemnity Co. v. Seib*—the Supreme Court of Nebraska

*Many courts have ruled that telegrams, mailgrams, and telexes qualify as "signed writing."*

allowed an insurance company to present in court computerized accounting records of payments the company had made over a period of years. The court considered the records reliable largely because they had been kept in the ordinary course of the company's business. The court did not require that the company show beyond all doubt that the records were trustworthy.

Where a court is particularly concerned about the reliability of a computer record, it can examine the data-processing controls in the computer system. A judge can ask, for example, whether the hardware and software, as a result of testing or broad public use, are known to be reliable in receiving, processing, and storing computer messages. Most off-the-shelf computers and programs meet this test. In addition, most computers can automatically create a log of who opens files and what modifications they have made. Alternatively, the system can write the record of each message onto an unalterable medium, such as an optical disc. A permanent serial number on such a disc could prevent a forger from replacing the original with a bogus copy.

Controls involve more than just the computer system. Data reliability also depends on organizational procedures. Magnetic tapes containing the digital records of messages, for example, can be locked in a secure room, with the key held by a neutral person.

It is also important that the people who create the data are not the same as those who operate the computer system. If the purchasing department is issuing EDI purchase orders, then an internal audit department could serve as the company's custodian of all electronic records. To insure its neutrality—and diminish any incentive to permit the fabrication of EDI records—the audit department could report directly to a special committee composed of only members of the board of directors who are not company officers. Such segregation of corporate duties is a routine form of control in government and business.

Despite lawyers' reservations, then, courts have become more tolerant of electronic documents as evidence. Indeed, in a very high-stakes case—the Iran-Contra prosecution of Adm. John Poindexter—the court allowed as evidence an e-mail message from Poindexter to Oliver North after the e-mail system operator explained the system's functions and the routine data-processing controls it incorporated.

Moreover, courts have been liberal in defining what qualifies as a signed writing under the statute of frauds. Many, for example, have ruled that telegrams, mailgrams, and telexes—telecommunicated messages that end as words typed on paper—so qualify, even though they do not fit the conventional image of signed writings. The senders never see, approve, or autograph the final paper, and forgery is easy. Nevertheless, courts have considered them signed writings; judges have held that the simple typewritten names on such messages constitute the "signatures" because the senders intended them as such. Thus despite strong intuitive reservations from lawyers, legal issues pose no fundamental barrier to electronic contracting; courts are likely to accept as "writing" any computer message. In one 1989 case—*Hessenthaler v. Farzin*, which ruled that a mailgram was a signed writing even though the signature on it was just a machine-printed name—the Pennsylvania Superior Court explicitly suggested that the same conclusion should apply to an e-mail message.

Technologies and procedures are readily available to insure that computer-generated messages are at least as secure as paper ones—and the benefits are clear in faster turnaround times and reduced administrative paperwork. But unlike new generations of technologies, which typically arrive on the scene every few years, the law changes at a glacial pace. The precedents set in cases such as *Hessenthaler* are likely to remain part of the legal scaffolding for decades to come. And though Exxon will probably rescind its policy against electronic contracts, according to a company lawyer, business too is shedding its reluctance very slowly.

But legislatures and government agencies can help accelerate this acceptance. Many statutes and regulations that require transactions to be "signed writings"—such as the statute of frauds—are now outdated. Although courts can read around many signed-writing requirements to permit the enforcement of electronic transactions, it only confuses matters to keep such restrictions on the books. In many cases, signed writing requirements have little meaning and should be repealed. In other cases, the requirements should be revised to permit electronic practices explicitly. They should be changed to be brought in line with modern commercial practice.

Once such antiquated laws are swept away—and once the legal community breaks free from its paper-centered mentality—then business and government organizations can enter the bright new dawn of electronic commerce.

---

# Suing over an Electronic Contract

IN the first lawsuit over a disputed electronic contract, the court in effect acknowledged the validity of computer-generated contracts.

The 1989 suit revolved around a dispute between Lederle Laboratories, a pharmaceutical company, and Corinthian Pharmaceutical, a customer. Lederle had installed an order-taking computer system, called Telgo. A customer could place an order—without speaking to anyone and without paper—by dialing into Telgo with a touch-tone telephone.

The conflict arose over an order that Corinthian placed, via Telgo, for 950 vials of Lederle's DTP vaccine. Telgo responded by electronically issuing Corinthian an order-tracking number. The next day, Lederle raised the price of the vaccine from $51 per vial to $171—and rejected Corinthian's order, which was placed at the lower price. Corinthian believed that the Telgo response had confirmed its contract to buy the vaccine at $51 and that it was being overcharged by $114,000—so it sued Lederle.

Although the federal district court in Indiana ruled in favor of Lederle, its decision indirectly affirmed the validity of electronic transactions. The court held that Corinthian's message to Telgo was a legal offer but that the order-tracking number from Telgo was only an administrative number—and not a true acceptance. The court treated the electronic nature of the transaction as irrelevant, implying that if the tracking number *had* constituted an acceptance, the contract would have been binding.

—*Benjamin Wright*

# Intellectual Property and Individual Privacy

Given the diversity and complexity of a modern society, it is inevitable that groups and individuals will clash over social, political, and economic interests. Most social conflict is of the kind found in the debate of the political forum, the competition of the marketplace, and the labor/management negotiation table. These types of conflict are socially approved and desirable because they provide appropriate opportunities for the expression of dissent and the exercise of choice—vital elements of the democratic process.

Unfortunately, conflict does not always lead to a beneficial resolution. Often, one party's gain is another's loss. In this unit, we examine issues related to economic conflict surrounding intellectual property and threats to individual privacy in the information age. In unit 5 we will look at computer ethics and crime.

Our "information" society has spawned some unanticipated problems over intellectual property rights. Traditionally, information has been treated as a public good rather than a private resource—except under circumstances where individuals may copyright written works or patent inventions. The first two articles in this unit condemn the use of patents to protect hardware and software innovations. In "The Great Patent Plague" and "Why Patents Are Bad for Software," the authors outline a number of problems with the current system of issuing patents. They claim, among other things, that patents impair creativity and will stunt development of the computer industry because small firms are usually the most innovative, but they lack the resources to compete against large powerful patent holders.

Today, most commercial software is copyrighted, which means it is illegal to make copies without the permission of the copyright holder. However, unauthorized copying of software is common. And as Janet Mason explains in "Warning: Here Come the Software Police," firms that allow their employees to pirate software can face stiff penalties.

A movement against intellectual property rights is being spearheaded by Richard Stallman, who insists that all software should be free. Some of his initiatives toward this end include the Free Software Foundation, the GNU project, and the Copyleft software licensing agreement. Details about Stallman's efforts and successes are provided by Simson Garfinkel in "Programs to the People."

While the first four articles in this unit focus mainly on relationships among organizations, the last two articles center on the relationships between powerful organizations and individual people. Governments, employers, commercial businesses, and even charities are amassing ever greater quantities of data about individual people and their habits, whereabouts, and attitudes. Moreover, such data can and has been used to manipulate and shape people's behavior. This trend has raised concern about threats to individual freedom and privacy in an information society.

The greatest concerns over freedom and privacy usually center on potential government abuse and a great deal of material has been written about the Orwellian threat of "Big Brother." An example of such abuse was provided in the spring of 1989 when the People's Republic of China used information technology to identify dissidents who participated in prodemocracy demonstrations. News reports of foreign journalists, as well as telephone and facsimile messages to and from China, were intercepted and studied by the government in its search for "counterrevolutionaries." On the other hand, information technology in the hands of the governed is a powerful tool against oppression. More than one observer has noted that a good "democracy barometer" is the number of telephones relative to the size of the population: the higher the telephone to people ratio, the more democratic the society because it is simply too hard for a government to keep track of who is calling whom or what they are talking about. (There are still very few telephones in China.) The technological empowerment argument has, of course, been extended to computing. When ordinary people have access to computing, information can be generated and spread very quickly. As encouraging as this is, the proliferation of information in electronic data bases is still cause for concern.

Some of the threats to privacy are quite unintended and derive from legitimate and socially desirable uses of information technology. In "Orwellian Dream Come True: A Badge That Pinpoints You," Leonard Sloane describes "smart badges" that allow computers to keep track of exactly where people are at all times. For many people, such as those who work in dangerous situations or who

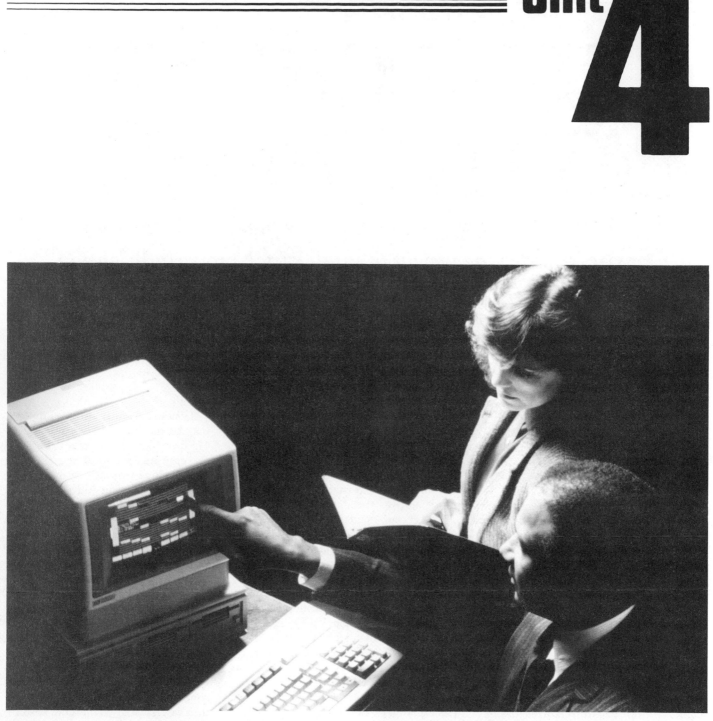

need to keep in close communication with others, this is a promising technology indeed. However, others fear the technology will be used in ways that are too intrusive for most people. Sloane's discussion focuses on the workplace but there are many other potential applications for this technology. The article "Supermarket Spies" highlights the ordinary, everyday habit of buying groceries. As Erik Larson explains, the scanning technologies will soon reveal a great deal about us to those who want our business.

**Looking Ahead: Challenge Questions**

Should all software be free? Why or why not?

Have you ever "pirated" software? Do you feel guilty? Why or why not?

How many potential uses can you think of for "smart badges?" How many of the uses you can identify enhance personal freedom and choice? Under which circumstances would you want and not want to wear one?

A few years ago Yoneji Masuda of Japan argued that the right to privacy is an outmoded social value and proposed that the "human right to protect secrets . . . change into a human duty or ethic to share information." What are the pros and cons of Masuda's proposal? Must we give up our right to personal privacy for the sake of the "Information Society"?

# THE GREAT PATENT PLAGUE

*More and more of technology's big players are crushing
progress under the weight of intellectual property litigation.
And the courts are playing the villain's role.*

NANCY RUTTER

*Nancy Rutter is an Atherton, Calif.-
based freelance writer.*

George Hwang's second American dream is entangled in a web of high-tech litigation, and chances are slim it will ever get free.

This would have been unthinkable to the Chinese-born, Taiwanese-bred Hwang a few years ago. Smitten by U.S. free-market capitalism, the skinny, intense engineer emigrated here in 1967 to pursue the American dream. He found it in high technology. His first company, memory chipmaker Integrated Device Technology Inc. of San Jose, Calif., went public in 1984 after just four years in business. By age 43, Hwang had become another unlikely Silicon Valley millionaire.

Yet it was Hwang's second stab at entrepreneurship, ULSI Systems Inc., that seemed destined to become really big. ULSI planned to produce a line of low-cost, hugely profitable coprocessor chips in 1987, a time when giant Intel Corp. was generating hundreds of millions of dollars and dominating the market with its coprocessor chip. "We saw that it took about $10 to make these

chips and that they sold for $800 to $900 a pop. What margins!" recalls the 51-year-old Hwang in his still-thick accent. "We figured we could do [the product] better, give the customers an alternative. We figured this was the American way."

But Hwang figured wrong. He and six-year-old ULSI have been battling Intel since 1989, not in the marketplace but in the courtroom, fighting patent infringement and, more foreboding, criminal and civil trade-secret theft charges. The criminal allegation is an unusual one for Silicon Valley. Those involved with high-tech litigation in Santa Clara County remember only about half a dozen cases deemed serious enough to try in criminal court in the past 30 years. A guilty charge for entrepreneur Hwang will mean a jail term.

Tiny ULSI has not had a smooth ride through the court system. It was wiped out in round one of the infringement case, enjoined in the process from using the Hewlett Packard Co. foundry in Oregon that was making its chips. The injunction was suspended in the appeals process, however. Hwang's criminal proceedings were scheduled to start in late February, which would keep him away from ULSI for three to four months, since defendants in criminal cases must appear in court every day.

Lost management time, however, may be the least of Hwang's worries. The deputy district attorney in charge of the case has accumulated allegedly incriminating evidence against Hwang and fellow defendant Alfred Chan, who was on the team that designed Intel's 387 math coprocessor, the product ULSI is accused of copying.

Chan left Intel to join ULSI in 1987, and, according to Hwang's lawyer, Thomas J. Nolan, some Intel documents "ended up" at Hwang's company. Although the papers were subsequently returned, those materials, plus four other boxes of Intel documents found in Chan's garage, form the basis of the criminal case. When his lengthy criminal trial is over, Hwang will face yet another lawsuit, the civil trade-secret theft case. He may do this from prison.

ULSI, meanwhile, has survived only by virtue of Hwang's own estimated $3 million investment, half of which he's shelled out for legal bills. Housed in a stucco low-rise in a low-rent district of San Jose, ULSI employs 40 rather than the hundreds Hwang once envisioned. And the company remains a bit player in the coprocessor chip market it set out to attack, having lost out to newcomers such as Cyrix Corp., Richardson, Tex., which sneaked into the market while ULSI was tied up in court and quickly gained some 20 percent of the market.

Cyrix, however, was also sued for patent infringement as soon as it entered the business by—you guessed it—Intel.

On the face of it, Intel's continuing squabbles with ULSI and Cyrix appear to be about infringement of the company's intellectual property. Some within the industry believe these battles have as much to do with Intel's desire to slow down and stomp out competitors as anything else.

Faced with increasing competition, eroding margins, escalating R&D costs and shrinking market share, some high-tech companies are using the legal process to achieve business goals that should rightfully be determined by the rigors of the marketplace. Structural changes in the courts coupled with other legal developments have made it possible for companies to use intellectual property lawsuits as intimidating and often deadly competitive weapons—companies that can afford protracted, big-ticket litigation, that is. This usually means big companies, like Intel.

But hold on. Wasn't the technology business built by small companies that freely traded ideas and talent, unimpeded by lawsuits? This bit of history seems to have been forgotten by many of today's high-tech plaintiffs. Says the always-glib T. J. Rodgers, CEO of San Jose-based Cypress Semiconductor Corp., "Some of the biggest proponents of intellectual property litigation today were some of the best rip-off artists of the past."

The industry's entrepreneurial ardor could be dampened if it decides to forsake its free-spirited heritage in favor of burdensome litigation. George Hwang, for one, is embittered, and his company is all but destroyed, thanks to Intel's legal tactics. In a less litigious scenario, Hwang—even if he had been found guilty of filching trade secrets—might have been allowed the chance to compete after misappropriated documents had been returned. ULSI might have been a major employer in San Jose; its engineers might have produced innovative products. That's the way Silicon Valley worked 10 years ago.

Litigation may also prove repellent to technology investors, who can find better things to do with their capital than use it to fill lawyers' pockets. There are some indications that this is already happening. "We steer very wide of any project that has the threat of litigation," says C. Richard Kramlich, managing partner of the $700 million venture investment firm New Enterprise Associates, San Francisco. Adds New York City venture investor Fred F. Nazem, "The litigation surrounding new companies is a darned ugly area. It's scaring investors away from innovators."

Worse yet, the distraction of intellectual property litigation could impair the industry's ability to bring fast-paced innovations to market, a knack that's made the U.S. electronics industry second to none. Already lawyers and legal issues have become ubiquitous in some areas of high technology, restricting this country's ability to compete globally as European and Asian companies steer clear of unproductive legal battles.

Although protecting U.S. inventions is important, one can go too far in employing lawsuits and courts to do so. Fifteen-year veteran Silicon Valley lawyer Michael Ladra warns, "We could go too far with intellectual property litigation.... The industry could choke itself on it."

## Founding Fathers' Special Favor to Technology

Patents have always been troublesome in our free-market economy. When this country's Founding Fathers set out in 1789 to "promote the progress of science and the useful arts," they did so by granting patents, which gave an inventor exclusive rights to his or her creation for a period of 17 years. This was a tough measure for them to adopt. "You have to remember that these people were not fans of big government," notes Boston University School of Law patent professor Robert P. Merges. "They really didn't like the idea of monopolies."

But they coveted the promise of innovation. "The men who wrote the Constitution thought that by offering a monopoly on an invention, by granting the right to exclude, people would be induced to...invent. Innovation was that important to them," says Donald S. Chisum, an intellectual property law professor at the University of Washington, Seattle, and author of *Chisum Patents*, the eight-volume bible of the patent law industry. Adds Merges, "Our patent policy was our original industrial policy, even though broad-based. The Founding Fathers wanted to do a special favor for new technology."

Clearly, the system worked, propelling the United States to the forefront of technology, from early farming inventions such as the cotton gin to high-tech innovations like the personal computer. But the system is now 200 years old, notes Chisum, and "something of that vintage often gets to be a problem. The statutory language is vague and ancient. And there have been too many court cases trying to interpret that. This leads to litigation and to expense."

Apparently, this has been the case for some time. Chisum notes that in 1836, Congress complained that patent statutes were causing too much litigation. The Patent Office (now the Patent and Trademark Office) was created in response to this perceived problem so that patents, which had previously been issued on a casual basis, could be formally granted, thereby limiting legal disputes.

The methods used to curb litigation in the 1840s, though, actually contribute to it in the 1990s. The PTO, as it is called by members of the patent bar, is today a government agency burdened with poor guidelines and overwhelmed by too much work. "Ballpark, there are 1,400 patent examiners who must look at more than 150,000 patent applications a year," observes Washington, D.C., lawyer Gary M. Hoffman, who put in a five-year stint as a patent examiner. "Some do have technical backgrounds [in the areas they review], but they have quotas to meet, which limits their ability to be thorough. And their files are not always complete. They do not always have access to all the prior art."

Chisum believes that high turnover and poor morale among examiners compromise some patents. In addition, he complains that some rules are just plain silly. For example, in Europe patents are published 18 months after they are filed so that prior art—current technological inventions—is revealed, which keeps inventors apprised of developments in specific industries. In the United States, inventions remain secret until they are patented, which sometimes takes years. This means many patents are issued without full knowledge of existing technology. Says San Francisco lawyer Harold McElhinny, "What we are getting as a result [of the agency's problems] are very broad patents that can cause a lot of mischief." Adds Chisum, "The PTO has a quality-control problem."

From the looks of $6 billion chipmaker Intel, few would guess that the U.S. patent system has run amuck. However, Intel is a company that has employed aggressive patent policing practices to gain marketing edge, and its new gray and blue Santa Clara, Calif., headquarters serves as testament to this fact. The building's cavernous lobby functions as a museum, showcasing Intel's scientific accomplishments and honoring its heroes. The company's patented achievements, some of the country's technical crown jewels, are enshrined in Plexiglas cases for visitors to admire.

Etched on the wall among the other displays at the museum is a statement made in 1970 by Robert N. Noyce, an Intel founder and semiconductor pioneer. It reads, "Don't be encumbered by history—go off and do something wonderful."

Noyce did just this when he and seven other engineers defected from Shockley Semiconductor Labs in 1957 to form Fairchild Semiconductor in Mountain View, Calif. Their work at Fairchild revolutionized the electronics industry, but Noyce was not content to stop there. He did "something wonderful" again in 1968, this time leaving Fairchild to create Intel.

Joining Noyce in the new venture were Fairchild defectors Gordon E. Moore, who would become Intel's chairman, and Andrew S. Grove, now Intel's CEO. Dozens of others followed them. Altogether, recalls a former Fairchild assistant patent attorney, some 70 to 80 people were gleaned from Fairchild's ranks to fatten those of Intel. Adds the lawyer, "And a lot of their ideas went with them too."

But Fairchild didn't sue Noyce, Moore or Grove. That wasn't considered the sporting thing to do. Nor is it likely that Fairchild would have been able to enforce its patent case anyway. Cases at the time were litigated in various federal district courts spread throughout the country; some were far more likely to uphold a patent's validity than others. Their standards varied wildly.

This wasn't necessarily bad for some U.S. industries, the semiconductor industry among them. "A weak patent policy did not slow things down in the development of the integrated circuit and microprocessor," Merges observes.

"In fact, it sped things up. The legal environment of the 1970s allowed Fairchild, Intel and others to get their start, carrying the lesson that strong patents for every industry are not always good."

These new technology companies further thrived in the 1970s by embracing a policy of broad, long-term technology cross-licensing, an industry custom that prevailed for more than 20 years. Cross-licensing allowed companies not only to share their technical innovations but to use each other's technologies. It was a good deal. It kept everyone out of court and gave everyone access to technological advances. It also provided innovators with returns for their efforts through a reasonable royalty, typically one percent of the market value of the products made from the patent. A Palo Alto, Calif., patent lawyer, William L. Anthony, Jr., sums up the period this way: "Companies wanted to battle in the markets, not the courts."

But that mindset vanished in the mid-1980s as a number of external developments collided to make high-tech litigation more attractive. For starters, the Reagan administration's laissez-faire antitrust attitude took hold, making it more acceptable to adopt strong-arm litigation tactics to enforce patents. Legislation was also passed that signaled increased interest in protecting intellectual property: The Computer Software Protection Act of 1980 defined software under the Copyright Act, and the Semiconductor Chip Protection Act of 1984 protected some patented chip designs, such as DRAMs (dynamic random access memory), that had been ripped off by Asian competitors.

Still, the high-tech run on the courthouse would not have occurred if the U.S. Court of Appeals for the Federal Circuit hadn't been established in 1982 to handle patent appeals. The court streamlined the appeals process by establishing a unified standard that had been lacking. Curiously, the electronics industry's outcry over the need to protect intellectual property seems to have had little, if anything, to do with the creation of the circuit court. Rather, it was a pet project of Carter administration Attorney General Griffin Bell that was later shepherded through Congress by Senator Edward M. Kennedy (D-Mass.).

The circuit court's stated intent was

to create a uniform, streamlined venue for patent challenges. The Carter administration was also worried that the U.S. was lagging behind other industrial nations because innovators, disillusioned by weak patent protection, had stopped creating things. Thus, the court's "not so hidden agenda" was to be pro-patent, says Boston University professor Merges. "The original judges who sat on the federal circuit court had a political mission," adds lawyer McElhinny. "They were picked for their pro-patent views, and they ruled on them with a vengeance."

The new court quickly showed its stripes. In 1985, it ruled in favor of Polaroid in *Polaroid* v. *Kodak*, eventually awarding the company almost $1 billion in damages and interest. The decision also tossed Kodak, the infringer, out of the instant photo business.

## Out With Cross-Licensing, In With Litigation

This didn't go unnoticed in the legal department of Dallas-based Texas Instruments Inc.

TI had been a bright light in the electronics industry for dozens of years. It created and patented the integrated circuit, the first handheld calculator, the first commercially produced transistor radio and even the first single-chip microprocessor, an innovation wrongly associated with Intel. But by the early 1980s, TI was in terrible shape. It was reeling from increased domestic competition and laboring under poor marketing decisions. It had also been crippled by Asian manufacturers' dumping of cheap, cloned DRAMs on world markets.

But lawyers and the courts provided a cure for TI's ills. "Texas Instruments was the first to notice the changed environment, in terms of the value of patents, that was brought about by the federal circuit court," says Merges. Melvin Sharp, former chief patent counsel for TI and principal architect of the company's patent strategy, remembers, "For years we had a legal environment that was so weak that we couldn't enforce patents. That had materially changed by 1985."

In 1986, TI embarked on a campaign to capitalize on this new environment, demanding high royalties on its patented products. The new premiums were, in some cases, 10 times the old royalty rate of one percent of the market value of the products made with the patents.

The campaign marked a risky break with industry tradition, but TI was betting that, thanks to the new court of appeals, more money could be made by suing than cross-licensing. "The value of patents was clearly going up in the courts, making the incentive to cross-license go down," Merges explains. "That would mean leaving too much on the table."

Richard L. Donaldson, current chief patent counsel for TI, puts it this way: "We had companies coming into the industry who were not innovating. They were not investing in R&D. They were just copying technology. They could not return the same value on a cross-license as companies that contributed to innovation, so we had to come up with another way."

TI flexed its litigation muscle in 1986, suing nine Asian companies in U.S. federal court and before the International Trade Commission for infringing on some of its DRAM patents. The nine—Hitachi Ltd., Oki Electric Industry Co. Ltd., Fujitsu Ltd., Samsung Co. Ltd., Toshiba Corp., Matsushita Electric Industrial Co. Ltd., NEC Corp., Mitsubishi Electric Corp. and Sharp Corp.—were targeted to pay the high royalties because they could afford to. When they refused, TI sued.

And TI won. The nine defendants eventually gave in and paid up, though it took more than three years, 29 law firms, nearly 350 lawyers and an estimated $10 million (TI isn't saying) to get the desired result. Was it worth it? You bet. The company's aggressive royalty program has put more than $1 billion into its coffers since 1986 (almost $260 million in 1991 alone), and has sopped up the red ink on its balance sheet for the last seven years.

Consequently, there's no end in sight. In 1990, TI sued five domestic chipmakers—Analog Devices Inc., Cypress Semiconductor, Integrated Device Technology Inc., LSI Logic Corp., and VLSI Technology Inc.—when they refused to pay increased royalties. At issue are fees paid on a patent covering the dollop of plastic in which some chips are packaged, an intellectual property TI contends is so dear that it felt compelled to go to court. Others see it differently. Roger B. McNamee, a Silicon Valley investor and high-tech stock

analyst, calls TI's legal claim "complete horse pucky."

TI is also trying to force its PC clone manufacturing customers to pay, for the first time, royalties on some of its patented computer "system" chips that enable the machines to interact with printers and keyboards and to perform other functions. The tariff could be up to three percent of the cost of the computers containing the patented systems—up to $30 per machine. At least one of TI's PC customers, Tandy Corp., didn't take kindly to the gesture. After a series of legal wranglings that included faulty license agreements, infringement charges and countersuits, the case was settled.

"We realize some companies feel our fees are too high," says Donaldson. "But that's because they've never had to pay for using our technology before. We have spent millions—billions—on R&D, and we need to protect that investment to get a fair return on our intellectual property for our shareholders."

Hogwash, cries Cypress Semiconductor's Rodgers. "It's hard to listen to such high-blown intellectual property rhetoric when a company is putting a billion dollars in the bank."

## Intel Doesn't Always Win— Does It Matter?

F. Thomas Dunlap, Jr., Intel's general counsel, isn't well liked in the chip business as a result of the company's lawsuits, but he doesn't much care. A smallish, balding, brilliant lawyer, Dunlap is the perfect front man for CEO Andrew Grove's front office, shrugging off criticism and chalking it up to business sour grapes. "If Intel wasn't doing so well, no one would care about its lawsuits," he says.

Dunlap says Intel sues only companies that steal or infringe on its intellectual property, companies Intel calls "copycats." Strictly speaking, infringement is defined as copying a patented invention outright—not too difficult to accomplish since the patent office publishes the invention. At issue in many infringement cases is whether inventions are duplicated or achieve the same functionality through a different design.

"We won't cross-license copycat companies like Cyrix that make an imitation of our product, who don't spend anything on R&D," says Dunlap. "This kind of company comes into the market saying, 'The closer I get to Intel, the less

business risk I have. I have no R&D costs, so I can lower my price and win.' But what we've said is, 'If a company does business this way, it will have an increased legal risk.'

"We do not sue companies that contribute to the industry through R&D," he adds. "If we both innovate, then we both add value. But R&D is a bigger investment risk than ever. Our first fab [fabrication facility] cost $1 million. Now a fab costs $1 billion, so we can't give our innovations away. We have to protect our shareholders' investment, which is allowed by the U.S. Constitution."

Semiconductor analyst Thomas A. Thornhill III, like many on Wall Street, applauds Intel for its trusteeship of the industry's inventions. "It is absolutely critical to U.S. competitiveness to protect our intellectual property," says Thornhill, of Montgomery Securities, San Francisco. "It is important to protect the value of R&D funded by shareholders."

Still, Thornhill suspects Intel isn't always doing just that—Cyrix being a case in point. "I don't believe Cyrix is copying Intel's chip," he says. Cyrix board member and former TI lawyer Melvin Sharp adds, "We were careful to avoid Intel's patents. Cyrix is not a copycat." The company says its product is an original design that achieves the same functionality as Intel chips.

Nevertheless, Cyrix has been fighting Intel on that point for two years. A sizzling startup in the coprocessor market—it captured 20 percent of the market in its first year and generated $25 million in revenues—Cyrix made one critical error: It claimed its chips were "100-percent compatible" with those from Intel. This fueled Intel's fury. "We knew we were in the wrong, and we said we would stop [using compatibility] slogans," says CEO and president Jerry Rogers. "But they also asked us to get out of the [coprocessor] business. We couldn't do that because at the time, that was our entire business." Intel subsequently played hardball with the startup, threatening to sue its Taiwanese supplier if it sold product to Cyrix, among other tactics. So Cyrix hired a team of lawyers. "We knew that Intel would use the legal system, so we felt we should get there first," Rogers explains. Cyrix filed an antitrust claim against Intel in December 1990; Intel sued for patent infringement just 15 days later.

The legal rigmarole has cost Cyrix, a profitable but still private company, several million dollars, plus "every day we have given it," says Dennis J. Gorman, a partner in Sevin Rosen Funds, a venture capital fund that backs Cyrix. So consuming was the litigation that Gorman left Dallas-based Sevin Rosen for 18 months to manage the lawsuits for Cyrix. "Litigation is very devastating for a small company from a time-and-energy point of view," he says. Adds CEO Rogers, "Intel has kept us in court and in depositions. I've been in two depositions in the last 90 days. Our vice-president for engineering has been up [to court] four times."

Yet it's effective, even when Intel doesn't win. "Intel has a pretty miserable record in court," observes patent litigator Anthony. "But as a business policy, its legal strategy has been a big winner. It has managed to keep competitors tied up in court and entrepreneurs away from the field. That's why we do not have a third, fourth or fifth generation of chip companies in this country. Intel has scared entrepreneurs to death."

Adds a San Jose lawyer who has fought Intel and won but nevertheless declines to be named, "A competitor can win a case against Intel, but it doesn't matter because it took five years to litigate the claim. By then, the market has moved on and the competitor has lost out."

Competitors also cried foul last fall when Intel began threatening to impose a royalty on computer manufacturers who use "system" chips patented by Intel. The program is similar to the controversial one underway at Texas Instruments, with one exception: TI is demanding royalties from all of its targets, while Intel plans to command a steep royalty—as much as $25 to $30 per computer—only from computer-makers that use competitors' chips. Manufacturers that use Intel's chips get what Dunlap calls "an automatic license," meaning that no royalty is required. Says Dunlap, "This is not about antitrust; this is about making no-name clonemakers, who have no intellectual property, pay."

Nevertheless, Advanced Micro Devices promptly sued Intel for

## The American Way—As It Used to Be

| Name | Left | To Start |
|---|---|---|
| Gordon Moore<br>Andrew Grove<br>Robert Noyce | Fairchild Semiconductor | Intel |
| Jerry Sanders | Fairchild Semiconductor | Advanced Micro Devices |
| T. J. Rodgers | Advanced Micro Devices | Cypress Semiconductor |
| Rodney Canion | Texas Instruments | Compaq Computer |
| John Warnock<br>Charles Geschke | Xerox PARC | Adobe Systems |
| Finis F. Conner | Seagate Technology | Conner Peripherals |

antitrust violations, and Cyrix, in a motion filed in its pending suit with Intel, appealed to the court to bar the giant chipmaker from collecting fees from Cyrix customers. "We think this is a direct violation of the antitrust laws," says Thomas B. Brightman, co-founder of Cyrix and its vice-president of business and technology. "This is just another way for Intel to intimidate us and our customers."

Intel is undaunted by such accusations and even its losses to courtroom competitors. Dunlap compares Intel's legal record to that of the Denver Broncos in that ball club's bid for the Super Bowl: You can't win 'em all. But the Broncos would never have gotten to the Super Bowl if they lost as many critical games as Dunlap has. Intel was defeated in the first round of its patent lawsuit with Cyrix, for example, and it has an uneven track record against rival AMD, suffering a key loss two years ago in a case over its numerical denotation for chips, which has allowed AMD and other competitors to use Intel's 386 and 486 terminology. (Intel dubbed its latest chip Pentium rather than 586 so that its trademarked name could not be used by anyone else.) To be fair, Intel has licked AMD too. The latest victory came last December, when a judge expanded a ruling barring AMD from using one par-

ticular Intel chip microcode to include use of any of Intel's microcode.

With each round of litigation, the war heats up, ensuring that the feud will continue.

There isn't any way to quantify the degree to which litigation influences entrepreneurship or hampers technical innovation. "There are no numbers on those who didn't invent," observes Boston University's Merges. "There is no record of the venture capitalists who haven't funded innovative companies. Those of us who study the area have a suspicion that the intellectual property litigation boom may have had some negative impact."

Cyrix CEO Jerry Rogers is not merely suspicious of this; he's certain of it. "This litigation is the biggest detriment to innovation to come along in 20 years," he says. "Companies like Intel gave us so much innovation, and now they want to choke it off.... There is no longer an opportunity for a company like Intel to be created."

By the letter of our intellectual property laws, Intel makes a plausible case against that statement. But the intent of those laws may be perverted in the process. Says patent lawyer Anthony, "The patent as hammer, while permitted, was not intended to keep competition from doing its thing—that is, to improve a breed of technology."

# Why Patents Are Bad for Software

*Patents can't protect
or invigorate the
computer software
industry; they can
only cripple it.*

## Simson L. Garfinkel, Richard M. Stallman, and Mitchell Kapor

Simson Garfinkel is a senior editor at *NeXTWORLD* magazine (San Francisco) and the coauthor of the book *Practical UNIX Security*. Richard M. Stallman is one of the founders of the League for Programming Freedom (Cambridge, Massachusetts) and the recipient of the Association for Computing Machinery's Grace Hopper Award. Mitchell Kapor, a founder of the Lotus Development Corporation, is president of the Electronic Frontier Foundation (Cambridge, Massachusetts).

In September 1990, users of the popular XyWrite word processing program got a disturbing letter in the mail from XyQuest, Inc., the program's publisher:

"In June of 1987, we introduced an automatic correction and abbreviation expansion feature in XyWrite III Plus. Unbeknownst to us, a patent application for a related capability had been filed in 1984 and was subsequently granted in 1988. The company holding the patent contacted us in late 1989 and apprised us of the existence of their patent.

We have decided to modify XyWrite III Plus so that it cannot be construed as infringing. The newest version of XyWrite III Plus (3.56) incorporates two significant changes that address this issue: You will no longer be able to automatically correct common spelling errors by pressing the space bar after the misspelled word. In addition, to expand abbreviations stored in your personal dictionary, you will have to press control-R or another designated hot key."

XyQuest had been bitten by a software patent—one of the more than two thousand patents on computer algorithms and software techniques that have been granted by the U.S. Patent and Trademark Office since the mid-1980s. The owner of the patent, Productivity Software, had given XyQuest a choice: license the patent or take a popular feature out of XyWrite, XyQuest's flagship product. If XyQuest refused, a costly patent-infringement lawsuit was sure to follow.

Some choice.

XyQuest tried to license the patent, says Jim Adelson, vice president for marketing, but Productivity Software kept changing its terms. First Productivity said that XyQuest could keep the feature in some versions of XyWrite, but not in others. Then the company said that XyQuest could use one part of the "invention," but not other parts. And Productivity Software kept increasing the amount of money it wanted. XyQuest finally gave up and took the feature out.

XyQuest was lucky it had that option. Other firms—including some of the nation's largest and most profitable software publishers—have been served with notice of patents that strike to the heart of their corporate vitality. In one of the most publicized cases, a company called Refac International—whose sole business is acquiring and litigating patents—sued Lotus, Microsoft, Ashton-Tate, and three other spreadsheet publishers, claiming they had all infringed on patent number 4,398,249, which spells out the order in which to recalculate the values in a complicated model when one parameter in the model changes. (Refac has since dropped its claims against all the companies except Lotus, but only because company lawyers anticipated a better chance of success if they faced just one opponent.)

Patent 4,398,249 does not have anything to do with spreadsheets in particular; the technique also appears in some graphics drawing and artificial intelligence programs. And the idea that values in a spreadsheet should be recalculated in the order specified by the patent is so obvious that it has probably occurred to nearly everyone who has written a spreadsheet program. But the Patent Office's standard for obviousness is extremely low; patents have been granted for ideas so elementary that they could have been answers to problems in a first-year programming course.

Practically once a month, the nation's computer networks are abuzz with news of another patent issued on a fundamental concept that is widely used. Although the Patent Office isn't supposed to grant patents on ideas, that's essentially what it's doing with software patents, carving up the intellectual domain of computer science and handing little pieces to virtually any company that files an application. And the practice is devastating America's software industry.

If Congress does not act quickly to redefine the applicability of patent law to computer programs, the legal minefield confronting the introduction of new computer programs will be so intimidating—and potentially so costly—that small companies will effectively be barred from the marketplace, while large, established firms will become embroiled in litigation that will have a stultifying effect on the entire industry.

## What's being patented?

Software patents do not cover entire programs; instead, they cover algorithms and techniques—the instructions that tell a computer how to carry out a specific task in a program. Thousands of instructions make up any one computer program. But whereas the unique combination of algorithms and techniques in a program is considered an "expression" (like a book or a song) and is covered by copyright law, the algorithms and techniques themselves are treated as procedures eligible for patenting.

The judicial basis for this eligibility is tenuous at best. U.S. law does not allow inventors, no matter how

*The Patent Office is carving up the intellectual domain of computer science and handing little pieces to any company that files an application.*

brilliant they are, to patent the laws of nature, and in two Supreme Court cases (*Gottschalk v. Benson*, 1972, and *Parker v. Flook*, 1978) the Court extended this principle to computer algorithms and software techniques. But in the 1981 case *Diamond v. Diehr*, the Court said that a patent could be granted for an industrial process that was controlled by certain computer algorithms, and the Patent Office seems to have taken that decision as a green light on the patentability of algorithms and techniques in general.

Software patents are now being granted at an alarming rate—by some counts, more than a thousand are issued each year. Unfortunately, most of the patents have about as much cleverness and originality as a recipe for boiled rice—simple in itself but a vital part of many sophisticated dishes. Many cover very small and specific algorithms or techniques that are used in a wide variety of programs. Frequently the "inventions" mentioned in a patent application have been independently formulated and are already in use by other programmers when the application is filed.

When the Patent Office grants a patent on an algorithm or technique, it is telling programmers that they may not use a particular method for solving a problem without the permission of the idea's "owner." To them, patenting an algorithm or technique is like patenting a series of musical notes or a chord progression, then forcing composers to purchase a "musical sequence license."

## Systems at odds

The traditional rationale for patents is that protection of inventions will spur innovation and aid in the dissemination of information about technical advances. By prohibiting others from copying an invention, patents allow inventors to recoup their investment in development while at the same time revealing the workings of the new invention to the public.

But there's evidence that the patent system is backfiring in the computer industry; indeed, the system itself seems unsuited to the nature of software development. Today's computer programs are so complex that they contain literally thousands of algorithms and techniques, each considered patentable by the Patent Office's standards. Is it reasonable to expect a software company to license each of those patents, or even to bring such a legally risky product into the marketplace? To make things even more complicated, the Patent Office has also granted patents on combinations of algorithms and techniques that produce a particular feature. For example, Apple was sued because its Hypercard program allegedly violates patent number 4,736,308, which covers a specific technique that, in simplified terms, entails scrolling through a database displaying selected parts of each line of text. Separately, the scrolling and display functions are ubiquitous fixtures of computer programming, but combining them without a license from the holder of patent 4,736,308 is now apparently illegal.

Another problem with patenting software is the amount of time it takes to do so. The two to five years required to file for and obtain a patent are acceptable if a company is patenting, say, the formula for Valium, which hasn't changed in more than 20 years. But in the software industry, companies that don't continually bring out new versions of their programs go out of business. Success for them depends on spotting needs and developing solutions as quickly as possible.

Unfortunately, conducting a patent search is a slow, deliberative process that, when harnessed to software development, could stop innovation in its tracks. And because patent applications are confidential, there is simply no way for computer programmers to ensure that what they write will not violate some patent that is yet to be issued. Thus XyQuest "reinvented" its automatic spelling-error correction system and brought the product to market between the time that Productivity Software had filed for its application and been awarded the patent.

Such examples are becoming increasingly common. In another case, the journal of *IEEE Computer* in June 1984 published a highly efficient algorithm for performing data compression; unbeknownst to the journal's editors or readers, the authors of the article had simultaneously applied for a patent on their invention. In the following year, numerous programs were written and widely distributed for performing the so-called "LZW data compression." The compression system was even adopted as a national standard and proposed as an international one. Then, in 1985, the Patent Office awarded patent number 4,558,302 to one of the authors of the article. Now Unisys, the holder of the patent, is demanding royalties for the use of the algorithm. Although programs incorporating the algorithm are still in the public domain, using these programs means risking a lawsuit.

Not only is the patent approval process slow, but the search for "prior art"—the criterion the Patent Office uses to determine whether an invention already exists at the time of a patent application—is all but impossible to conduct in the realm of computer software. After more than 25 years, the Patent Office has not developed a system for classifying patents on algorithms and techniques, and no such system may be workable. Just as mathematicians are sometimes unaware that essentially identical mental processes are being used in separate areas of mathematics under different terminology, different parts of computer science frequently reinvent the same algorithm to serve different purposes. It is unreasonable to expect that a patent examiner, pressed for time, would recognize all such duplication. For example, IBM was issued a patent on the same data-compression algorithm that Unisys supposedly owns. The Patent Office was probably not aware of granting two patents for the same algorithm because the descriptions in the patents themselves are quite different even though the formulas are mathematically equivalent.

The search for prior art is complicated by the fact that the literature of computer science is unbelievably large. It contains not only academic journals, but also users' manuals, published source code, and popular accounts in magazines for computer enthusiasts. Whereas a team of chemists working at a major university might produce 20 or 30 pages of published material per year, a single programmer might easily produce a hundred times that much. The situation becomes even more complex in the case of patented combinations of algorithms and techniques. Programmers often publish new algorithms and techniques, but they almost never publish new ways of combining old ones. Although individual algorithms and techniques have been combined in many different ways in the past, there's no good way to establish that history.

The inability to search the literature thoroughly for prior art is crucial, because unless an examiner can find prior art, he or she is all but obligated to issue the patent. As a result, many patents have been granted— and successfully defended in court—that are not "original," even by the Patent Office's definition. It was simply the case that neither the patent examiner

*The most effective
course of action
is to encourage
Congress to amend
patent law
to disallow
software patents.*

nor the defendants in the lawsuit knew of the prior art's existence.

Some members of the commercial software community are now proposing the creation of a "Software Patent Institute" to identify software's prior art that existed before 1980. But even if such an institute could catalogue every discovery made by every programmer in the United States, it makes no sense to arbitrarily declare that only pre-1980 work is in the public domain. Besides, what would be the purpose? To allow the patenting of nature's mathematical laws?

## Bad for business

Even when patents *are* known in advance, software publishers have generally not licensed the algorithms or techniques; instead, they try to rewrite their programs to avoid using the particular procedure that the patent describes. Sometimes this isn't possible, in which case companies have often chosen to avoid implementing new features altogether. It seems clear from the evidence of the last few years that software patents are actually *preventing* the adoption of new technology, rather than encouraging it.

And they don't seem to be encouraging innovation, either. Software patents pose a special danger to small companies, which often form the vanguard of software development but can't afford the cost of patent searches or litigation. The programming of a new product can cost a few hundred thousand dollars; the cost of a patent search for each technique and combination of techniques that the new program uses could easily equal or even exceed that. And the cost of a single patent suit can be more than a million dollars.

"I'm not familiar with any type of ligation that is any more costly than patent litigation," says R. Duff Thompson, vice president and general counsel of the WordPerfect Corporation. But Thompson's greatest fear is that software patents will wipe out young, independent programmers, who until now have been the software industry's source of inspiration. Imagine what happens, says Thompson, when "some 23-year-old kid who has a terrific idea in a piece of software is hammered by a demand letter from someone holding a patent."

As for aiding the exchange of information, the expansion of software patents could mean instead the end of software developed at universities and distributed without charge—software that has been a mainstay of computer users in universities, corporations, and government for years. Many such programs—the X Window system, the EMACS text editor, the "compress" file-compression utility, and others—appear to be in violation of existing patents. Patents could also mean an end to public-domain software, which has played an important part in making computers affordable to public schools. There is obviously no way that an author who distributes a program for free could arrange to pay for royalties if one of the hundreds of techniques that were combined to create the program happens to be patented.

Few programmers and entrepreneurs believe that patents are necessary for their profession. Instead, the impetus for patents on algorithms and techniques comes from two outside sources: managers of large companies, who see patents as a means for triumphing over their competitors without having to develop superior products, and patent attorneys, who see the potential for greatly expanding their business.

Today, most patenting by companies is done to have something to trade or as a defense against other patent-infringement suits. Attorneys advise that patenting software may strengthen competitive position. Although this approach will work for large companies such as Microsoft, Apple, and IBM, small and even mid-sized companies can't play in their league. A future startup will be forced to pay whatever price the giants choose to impose.

## Copyright and trade secrecy

The best argument against the wisdom of software patents may be history itself. Lotus, Microsoft, WordPerfect, and Novell all became world leaders in the software publishing industry on the strength of their products. None of these companies needed patents to secure funding or maintain their market position. Indeed, all made their fortunes before the current explosion of software patents began. Clearly patents are not necessary to ensure the development of computer programs. And for those who want more control over what they see as their property, the computer industry has already adopted two other systems: copyright and trade secrecy.

Today, nearly all programs are copyrighted. Copyright prohibits the users of a software program from making copies of it (for example, to give to their friends) without the permission of the individual or company that licenses the program. It prevents one company from appropriating another company's work and selling it as its own. But the existence of a copyright doesn't prevent other programmers from using algorithms or techniques contained in the program in their own work. A single software technique can be implemented in different ways to do totally different jobs; copyright only prohibits appropriating the actual code that a particular programmer wrote.

In general, copyrighting and patenting are thought to apply to very different kinds of material: the former to the expression of ideas, and the latter to a process that achieves a certain result. Until just a few years ago, computer algorithms and techniques were widely seen as unpatentable. And as Harvard University policy analyst Brian Kahin notes, this is the first time in history that an industry in which copyright was widely established was suddenly subjected to patenting.

Indeed, without conscious action by Congress or the Supreme Court, the most fundamental rule of software publishing—if you write a program, you own it—will change. The new rule will be that you might own what you write—if it is so revolutionary that it owes nothing to any previous work. No author in areas other than software is held to such an unrealistically high standard.

The U.S. patent system was created because the framers of the Constitution hoped that patents would discourage trade secrecy. When techniques are kept secret for commercial advantage, they may never become available for others to use and may even be lost. But although trade secrecy is a problem for software, as it is for other fields, it is not a problem that patents help to correct.

Many of the useful developments in the field of software consist of new features such as the automatic correction and abbreviation expansion feature in Xy-Write III Plus. Since it is impossible to keep a program's features secret from the users of the program, there is no possibility of trade secrecy and thus no need for measures to discourage it. Techniques used internally in a software system can be kept secret; but in the past, the important ones rarely were. It was normal for computer scientists in the commercial as well as the academic world to publish their discoveries. Once again, since secrecy about techniques was not a significant problem, there is little to be gained by adopting the patent system to discourage it.

The place where trade secrecy *is* used extensively in software is in the "source code" for programs. In computer programming, trade secrets are kept by distributing programs in "machine code," the virtually indecipherable translation of programming languages that computers read. It is extremely difficult for another programmer to glean from a machine-code program the original steps written by the program's author. But software patents haven't done anything to limit this form of trade secrecy. By withholding the source code, companies keep secret not a particular technique, but the way that they have combined dozens of techniques to produce a design for a complete system. Patenting the whole design is impractical and ineffective. Even companies that have software patents still distribute programs in machine code only. Thus, in no area do software patents significantly reduce trade secrecy.

## Reversing direction

Many policymakers assume that any increase in intellectual property protection must be good for whoever works in the field. As we've tried to show, this is assuredly not the case in the field of computer programming. Nearly all programmers view patents as an unwelcome intrusion, limiting both their ability to do their work and their freedom of expression.

At this point, so many patents have been issued by the Patent and Trademark Office that the prospect of overturning them by finding prior art, one at a time, is almost unthinkable. Even if the Patent Office learns to understand software better in the future, the mistakes that are being made now will follow the industry into the next century unless there is a dramatic turnaround in policy.

The U.S. Patent and Trademark Office recently established an Advisory Commission on Patent Law Reform that is charged with examining a number of issues, including software patents—or what it prefers to call patents on "computer-program-related inventions." Unfortunately, the commission's subcommittee on software does not include any prominent software industry representatives who have expressed doubts about software patents. But the subcommittee is required to consider public comment. The commission's final report is not due until August 1992, so there is still time to make one's voice heard.

Although influencing the Patent Office might produce some benefits, the really necessary reforms are likely to come only through intervention by the Supreme Court or Congress. Waiting for Court action is not the answer: No one can force the Supreme Court to rule on a relevant case, and there is no guarantee that the Court would decide to change Patent Office practice or to do anything about existing patents. The most effective course of action, therefore, is to encourage Congress to amend the patent law to disallow software patents and, if possible, invalidate those that have already been awarded. The House Subcommittee on Intellectual Property and the Administration of Justice, chaired by Representative William J. Hughes (D-N.J.), should take the lead by scheduling hearings on the subject and calling for a congressionally sponsored economic analysis of the effect of software patents on the industry.

The computer industry grew to be vibrant and healthy without patents. Unless those who want software patents can demonstrate that they are necessary to the health of the industry, Congress should feel justified in eliminating this barrier to innovation.

*Recommended reading*

Brian Kahin, "The Software Patent Crisis," *Technology Review* (April 1990): 53–58.

Mitchell Kapor, Testimony at Hearings before U.S. House of Representatives, Subcommittee on Courts, Intellectual Property and the Administration of Justice, of the Committee on the Judiciary (March 5, 1990).

Pamela Samuelson, "Benson Revisited: Should Patent Protection Be Available for Algorithms and Other Computer Program-Related Inventions?" *Emory Law Journal* (Fall 1990): 1025–1154.

Pamela Samuelson, "Should Program Algorithms Be Patented?" *Communications of the ACM* (August 1990): 23–27.

# WARNING: HERE COME THE SOFTWARE POLICE

Are you sure your firm's
employees haven't made illegal copies
of computer software?
*Really* sure?

## Janet Mason

Janet Mason is a freelance writer in Philadelphia who writes frequently on business and computer topics.

Todd Weiss (not his real name), a chief executive officer of a *Fortune*-500 financial institution, recently received a $35,000 lesson in the perils of computer software piracy. Like many CEOs, he had believed that the anti-piracy statement his employees signed annually would thwart illegal copying at his company. He also had thought that the signed statements would protect him from software-vendor lawsuits. On both accounts he was wrong.

In the corporate world, commercial software is no longer locked securely away in the information systems department. Thanks to the rise of the personal computer, commercial software is found throughout the far reaches of corporate offices. Today any employee with access to a PC—from managers and executives to clerks and warehouse employees—can make an illegal duplicate of commercial software in less than two minutes. Ron Palenski, general counsel of the software industry group, Adapso, estimates that one out of every two copies of software used by corporations is illegal. In the United States alone, says the U.S. Trade Representative's Office, the software industry is suffering $40 million annual losses because of software piracy.

Recently, the software industry has decided that it will no longer turn the other cheek to this drain on its profits. The result:

Companies across the nation must now beware of the software police. Since September 1989, the Software Publishers Association (SPA), a Washington, D.C.-based organization representing 565 software vendors, has filed 36 lawsuits and conducted 40 audits against corporations, computer dealers, electronic bulletin boards, and individuals who allegedly have illegal copies of software. Several software companies are also taking independent legal action against companies misusing their products.

The software vendors' ammunition is the United States Code Section 17 Copyright Law—commonly known as the shrink-wrap license—which says that once the purchaser breaks the seal of the software package he can make copies of the software only for backup or archival purposes. It is illegal for the software copies to be used by various people simultaneously, without a separate license. Companies and individuals who break this agreement can be liable for as much as $50,000 for each illegal copy of the software.

The SPA enforces the copyright protection law by way of the corporate audit, such as the one conducted against Weiss's company, and through fines averaging between $20,000 and $50,000. The SPA targets a company based on tips from callers to its piracy hotline and the extent of the alleged violations. The hotline is advertised in trade publications, at trade shows, and in SPA literature. Although no reward is offered for tips, the hotline receives approximately 20 calls a day.

Once a firm is targeted, the SPA contacts it to warn it of the upcoming audit. Audits are voluntary, but less than 4 percent of companies refuse to cooperate: If they do, the SPA will take them to court.

The audit itself is frequently inconvenient and protracted. A company must escort SPA inspectors throughout the premises to check floppy disks and the hard disk drives in employees' PCs for unauthorized software. Then investigators begin reconciling the companies' purchase records with those of the vendor—a procedure that can take from six days to six months. It's a process that can be eye-opening for the executives involved.

When Todd Weiss's company underwent an SPA audit, he greeted Mary Jane Saunders, SPA's general counsel, at the door by saying: "We can afford to buy our software and we do." Sitting down at the first computer with the audit team, the CEO found that the hard disk, which stores information, including software, contained eight illegal commercial packages. By the time the third computer was audited, revealing electronic games as well as illegal software, says Saunders, "Weiss realized that he didn't know what his employees were doing with their PCs."

With the increase in lawsuits and audits, the responsibility of preventing software piracy falls to the senior managers of a company. Many of these executives believe—as Weiss did—that their companies are protected from lawsuits by the written policies against software piracy that are included in company code of ethics statements or information systems department documents. Although these documents are usually signed by all employees when first hired or on a

---

## Facts on File's anti-piracy policy did nothing to protect the company in court from a multimillion-dollar lawsuit.

---

yearly basis, they are useless as protection unless accompanied by stringent enforcement policies. Facts On File Inc., a New York-based publishing firm, found this out firsthand last year when they were slapped with a multimillion-dollar lawsuit; the company's anti-piracy policy, which was unenforced, did nothing to protect it in court.

Management neglect of software piracy implicitly condones the practice, says Saunders. Oftentimes, unbeknownst to senior executives, employees bring in a favorite software package that is not provided by the

company and copy it for co-workers. This "backdoor" type of piracy is more prevalent than management-condoned piracy, Saunders says, but that doesn't let management off the hook. "The only employees more suspect than others," she says, "are employees who aren't educated in copyright law—and it's up to management to educate them."

Top management sometimes unwittingly encourages software piracy by cutting corners on their budgets. "An executive might say that there is no reason for the accounting department to have word processing software," Saunders says. "But the fact is that sooner or later every employee has to write a letter." Illegal copies may also circulate if employees prefer to use software other than the company standard for a specific task.

In some instances, the SPA has found that top management does sanction software piracy. "In one case," recalls Saunders, "an employee called and told us that the information systems director at his company was making illegal copies." When the concerned employee complained to top management, he was told: "Don't worry, the software police won't get us." Managers may also condone the practice in a less blatant way—by ignoring the fact that it's occurring. "Software piracy is like personal telephone calls," says a high-level information systems executive with a leading retail institution, "people aren't supposed to do it but some do." This executive, who wishes to remain anonymous, says he views spot checks of employees' hard disks as "draconian."

Invasive as the checks may be, the alternative of multimillion-dollar lawsuits and the attendant publicity is even less appealing. As the senior management of Facts on File learned, lawsuits are expensive and embarrassing. From the software companies' point of view, they are also necessary. Saunders says that although each illegal copy does not constitute a lost sale for the software industry, the piracy rate is high enough to damage the industry by limiting research and development funds and driving up retail prices. To mitigate the damage, companies are beginning to litigate aggressively.

"Often a company will buy one copy of our software and make illegal copies from it," says Curt Blake, general counsel of Aldus Corporation. "They are our customers so we don't want to alienate them, but we also don't want our property stolen." Aldus, a Seattle-based software developer of Page-

Maker, a popular desktop publishing package, is a member of the SPA and also conducts litigation on its own.

One of the SPA's largest piracy suits was filed this May against the National Business Academy. Working in conjunction with Federal impoundment marshals, the SPA raided three California locations—Glendale, Vanuys, and Englewood—of the nationwide computer training company and seized 600 pirated disks. The illegal software represented a quarter of a million dollars in unauthorized programs from Lotus Development Corporation, Microsoft Corporation, and WordPerfect Corporation.

At the time of the raid, the SPA had affidavits of piracy activity from a former administrator, student, and teacher. "Since 1986 the company has trained 4,000 students," says Saunders. "We think they gave copies of illegal software to every one of those students. Even though software vendors all give reduced rates to training companies, the company chose to teach students on unauthorized software. In doing so, it also communicated to students that it's okay to pirate software."

In addition to the 600 disks that it found, the SPA alleges that the school gave away 3,400 pirated programs to former students. The SPA estimates damages at $250 for each pirated copy of Lotus and WordPerfect and $100 for each copy of Microsoft's disk operating system, all of which adds up to a $2.5 million lawsuit.

To educate corporate consumers on the hazards of pirating, Adapso, the software industry group, sends interested companies its "Thou Shall Not Dupe" brochure, which explains copyright law. The SPA distributes a similar brochure, which several software companies send out with new releases of their product. The SPA also provides self-auditing kits for companies that want to take matters into their own hands.

A number of companies have already developed effective anti-piracy programs out of a sense of ethics and good management. They realize that unlike those who have legally purchased software, users of pirated software do not receive technical support, instruction manuals, or software updates from the vendors. Many of these companies keep an inventory of their software and, for the purpose of comparison, conduct periodic audits of their employees' hard disks. Audits are often overseen by individual department managers.

At EDS, the Dallas-based provider of information technology services, each local manager maintains the inventory of software for his division. The actual auditing of the employees' hard disks is done quarterly by a corporate-level auditing team. At Chemical Banking Corporation, each business unit has one or more data security managers responsible for preventing software piracy. An official auditing department conducts random spot-checks of employees' hard disks in each department. Like EDS,

## Some companies conduct random spot-checks of employees' hard disks in an effort to stop piracy.

Chemical Banking Corporation includes an anti-piracy stipulation in its company code of ethics.

"Our company treats software just like any other company property," says Jim Mayer, senior vice president and processing services director of Chemical Bank. "When we sign a license with a commercial software vendor, that package becomes a company asset that needs to be protected," he says. "An employee pirating software is equivalent to an employee walking out of the building with a typewriter."

In general, companies are vigilant about insuring that employees sign the anti-piracy statements, but are lax when it comes to enforcing stipulations. Saunders of SPA says that although 90 percent of *Fortune*-500 corporations have anti-piracy contracts, fewer than 40 percent enforce the regulations through inventory controls and spot-checks of hard disks.

The software vendors' crackdown on corporate offenders has caused an old question to resurface: If companies don't want their software pirated, why don't they put in some type of technical barrier? Up until the mid-1980s, vendors did routinely include copy-protection devices in their software. These devices were simply a computer code written in the software that prevented users from making more than one or two backup copies.

The problem with the technology was that much of the copy-protected software required users to insert the original disk into the computer each time they used the program—even if they had a hard disk drive. This cumbersome procedure made copy-protected software unpopular with consumers. A further problem was that not all of the software packages were compatible with the various computer models. As a result, some copy-protected software would not run on certain IBM-compatible personal computers.

# The EC's Crackdown On Software Piracy

As corporate audits and court action prove increasingly effective in protecting software copyrights at a national level, the U.S. software industry is now turning its concern toward proposed changes in copy-protection law in the European Economic Community. The EEC's proposed copyright-protection law claims to be compliant with U.S. law but is not, says Michael Brown, president of Central Point Software Inc. According to Brown, under the proposed directive, European consumers will not have the right to break technical copy protection on commercial software, even to make backups of software.

In the United States it is legal to make an unlimited number of archival or backup copies as long as they are used only by the licensed user. Consumers have plenty of legitimate reasons to make extra copies, says Brown. Software programs can be easily erased by reformatting, placing the disk near a magnetic field, or spilling coffee on it. Brown himself has somewhat more at stake than the consumer: The proposed EEC legislation would make one of Central Point Software's products, Copy II PC, which unlocks copy protection on commercial software, illegal.

Mary Jane Saunders, general counsel of the Software Publishers Association (SPA), says, however, that a clause has been added to the directive that would protect software packages such as Copy II PC. The proposal's language, she says, was changed in recognition of the need for consumers to make legitimate backup copies.

Although the backup debate looks like it may be resolved, another sticky area remains—reverse engineering. Reverse engineering, which involves breaking down a software program to its machine code to discover how it has been made, is often done by computer programmers who hope to improve on the program to create new software products. The EEC copyright proposal would make reverse engineering illegal in Europe.

Michael Brown argues that reverse engineering, which is done routinely in the United States, is inevitable. "This is how good software is built," Brown says. "People build on other products. It's like taking a toaster apart and building a better one."

Saunders of SPA disagrees. "When people read the machine code, they know everything about the product they need to know to create cheap imitations of it," she says. "This isn't fair to software vendors who put in the time, creativity, and money to develop the program."

Although the copyright section of the EEC document will not be decided until March of next year, Saunders is confident that the prohibition on reverse engineering will pass. "It's backed by key figures in the U.S. House and Senate as well as by business leaders," she says.

—J.M.

---

The software industry responded to customer complaints by abandoning copy-protection devices for all their products except those sold overseas or occupying certain niche markets. Computerease Soft Inc., for instance, protects its niche-market applications for the typesetting industry with a software copy-protection device but leaves its word-processing software package unprotected.

To some extent, software companies have resigned themselves to software piracy; the alternative often is going out of business. "There are companies starting up all the time," says Donn B. Parker, a senior management consultant at SRI International, "and they are ready to jump in when established companies do something unfriendly, such as putting copy restrictions on software."

Vendors are also skeptical about safeguarding their software with copy-protection technology because computer hackers often find it easy to break. Michael Brown, in fact, launched a successful software business in 1982 with Copy II PC, a copy-protection-breaking software package. In its first year his company, Central Point Software Inc., sold several hundred thousand copies of Copy II PC, which was promoted as a legitimate backup device rather than as a pirating tool. "In the early days of copy protection, you had to go back and get the original disk whenever you wanted to use the software program," says Brown, "and users wanted to make backup copies on their hard disks." Because few software vendors use copy-protection technology today, Copy II PC has become an almost nonexistent part of Brown's business, purchased primarily by consumers with games and home-computer programs, which are still commonly copy protected.

Paradoxically, copy-protection technology has markedly improved since software vendors discontinued using it. "Although there's always a modicum of inconvenience with copy protection," says David Mosby, president of Softguard Systems Inc., "current technology allows copy-protection software to run smoothly on a variety of IBM-compatibles. Also, newer devices do not require that the user insert the original disk each

---

**Piracy lawsuits and audits are causing companies to be more concerned about copy protection than vendors are.**

---

time." Software packages that use Softguard's copy-protection product take the average consumer about two extra minutes to install. Softguard is also working on making its security product more effective. Within the next year it plans to introduce a program that can be customized by each software vendor, making it more difficult for hackers to break. Currently, each vendor uses the same program, which is periodically updated by the company.

Although few are predicting a widespread return to copy protection, vendors may be

forced to provide such security for their corporate clients. Piracy lawsuits and audits, says Charles Adler, a spokesman for Software Security Inc., "are causing corporations to be more concerned about copy protection than vendors are." To address their anti-piracy needs, Software Security is planning to introduce a combination software and hardware device that will attach to each personal computer in a company and will sell for about $30.

Software vendors are also attacking piracy on the PC networking front. Both Softguard Systems and Lotus Development Corporation sell products that include a security device that prohibits a company from adding new people to its personal computer network unless it purchases a networking license upgrade. David Schnepper, a software architect with Ashton Tate Corporation, which uses Softguard Systems' product, LANmark, says LANmark "does not prevent the user from copying the software, but it does prevent users from adding unlicensed users onto the existing PC network."

Given the corporate trend toward PC networking, anti-networking products are likely to have more of a future in the battle against software piracy than copy-protection devices. For corporations, however, the best protection against the software police rests not in any security device, but in rigorous enforcement of their anti-piracy statements.

*Computer whiz Richard Stallman
is determined to make software free—even
if he has to transform the industry
single-handedly.*

# Programs to the People

## Simson L. Garfinkel

*Simson L. Garfinkel is a free-lance science writer and a doctoral candidate in the MIT Media Laboratory. He is writing a book about Richard Stallman and Project GNU.*

ACCORDING to the Software Publisher's Association (SPA), more than half of all programs currently in use are illegal copies. SPA estimates that unauthorized copying costs the software industry nearly $2 billion a year in lost revenue. The crooks aren't just pimply-faced pirates or vendors in Southeast Asia copying programs and shipping them back to the United States. Rather, all of us are to blame—small offices buying one copy of a word processor and using it on two computers, or people copying a program from work for use at home. After all, a copy of a program works as well as the original, so why pay?

Richard M. Stallman, president of the Cambridge-based Free Software Foundation (FSF), believes companies that sell programs give their customers the choice of being criminals or bad neighbors. People can break the law by copying programs for friends, or they can force friends to go and buy their own. "Imagine if somebody was going around your neighborhood saying 'I will give you all of these wonderful things if you promise not to let your neighbors have them,' " says Stallman. "To many people, that person would be the Devil." Six years ago, when he started the work his foundation supports, his motivation was to be part of a software-sharing community in which people can freely give copies of programs to their friends: "I decided that I was going to do it even if I had to write all the software myself."

What might have been an impossible task for anyone else was just a matter of punching in coding for Stallman, who many consider to be one of the world's greatest and most prolific programmers. Already he has helped create dozens of programming tools, many of them vastly superior to their commercially available counterparts, and broad acceptance by users has convinced several companies, such as Hewlett-Packard and Digital, to include his programs with their computer systems. At the forefront of his achievements is EMACS, a powerful program used by hundreds of thousands of people throughout the world. EMACS lets programmers perform an extensive range of tasks—from editing files to playing games—and they can alter it to their own liking and add their own features.

Moreover, the free-software movement Stallman has spearheaded is taking off. He has convinced hundreds of programmers to contribute their time and efforts. Most of the programs these people have produced are small improvements to other free programs that are already available, but others have been substantial projects, conceived, developed, and distributed as free software. Also, FSF has attracted more than $600,000 worth of gifts in cash and computer equipment. And last summer, Stallman was awarded a "genius grant" from the MacArthur Foundation in recognition of his work.

Stallman wants to create a family of free software so good that companies who do not use it could be driven out of business. In the process, he hopes to free computer users and return youthful hacker idealism to the computer world.

He may just do it.

## Back to the Source

Programs, which allow computers to be word processors today and electronic spreadsheets or payroll-printers tomorrow, are something like a cross between a cookbook recipe and a mathematical proof. Each line of a program contains a set of instructions for the computer to execute at a certain time; around the instructions are comments that explain how the program works. Programmers call the collection of instructions and comments the "source code," and in the early days of computing, companies almost always provided it with the programs they sold. Programmers read the code to learn how programs worked and modified it to fix problems and add features. They even built new programs by taking parts from old ones and reassembling them.

But as the business of computing exploded in the 1970s and 1980s, companies began restricting access to source code so that competitors couldn't see how a program worked and write their own versions. Richard Stallman thinks that was a big mistake. Making source code available again is key to his free-software movement. He likes to explain why it's so important by telling the story of the first two laser printers at the MIT Artificial Intelligence Laboratory, where he was a researcher from 1971 until 1983.

The laser printers of the mid-1970s were the size of today's compact cars. When Xerox gave the AI lab a Xerox Graphics Printer, the only place for it was in the lab's ninth-floor machine room. Researchers connected the printer to the local area network that the lab was developing, and soon anybody in the building could print a 100-page document by typing in a few commands.

That worked fine, except that sometimes the printer would run out of paper or jam, and dozens of other jobs would pile up. Other times there would simply be a lot of people wanting to print long documents, and the person who needed to print a single page would have to run up and down the stairs or babysit the printer until that page appeared. But since the programmers at the lab had the source code to the program that ran the printer, they could add features that solved these problems. Soon the printer was helping the lab run smoothly. "It would send you a message when your document had actually been printed," recalls Stallman. "It would send you a message if you had anything queued and there was a paper jam."

All this changed in 1978, when Xerox replaced the machine with a new laser printer called a Dover but wouldn't share the printer's source code with the lab. "We wanted to put those features into the Dover program, but we couldn't," Stallman says. Xerox wouldn't put the features into the program either. "So we had to suffer with paper jams that nobody knew about."

Keeping source code proprietary hurts users in a wide variety of other ways as well. Say a real estate company with an accounting-system program that allows for 10 checking accounts suddenly finds itself in charge of 13 properties. The program may not be able to handle the additional accounts, and if the company doesn't have the source code, it will either have to change accounting practices or find a new program. If the real estate firm lacks the source code, it may not even be able to hire an outside programming firm to make the necessary changes. "It is a monopoly because only one company can provide you with fixes or updates or changes to that program," says Robert J. Chassell, FSF's treasurer. "It's like you bought a car but there was only one mechanic who was permitted to work on it, and he lived in another city. Americans and American law have been against monopolies for years and for good reason—it is bad for both industry and the public."

Although consumers theoretically have the choice of being able to buy a different program, that choice is often illusory. "People have spent money on a specific program, but more significantly, they have become habituated to it," explains Chassell, who was trained as an economist at Cambridge University in England. "The expense of changing to a new program is not buying it: the expense is unlearning one program and relearning a second one."

To add to the cost, most programs store their data files in a format that is not compatible with competing programs. Most people, says Chassell, will put up with two or three major problems with a program rather than make a change.

## The Rise of UNIX

Until recently, people had the same problems switching between computers made by different companies that they have today switching between different application programs. The problem had to do with the operating system, the master control program that orchestrates the functions a computer performs: every computer had a different one, and all of them were incompatible. Computers made by IBM used an operating system called VM, while those made by Prime used PRIMOS. Digital Equipment Corp. had a variety of different operating systems—sometimes more than one for each computer that it sold.

For the hardware manufacturers, this was good business, because even if a company lost its competitive edge, it would still have a captive base of users who would have to keep buying its computers to run their old programs. And these users could be counted on to pay just about anything the company asked. From the users' point of view, this state of affairs was simply a fact of life. It added to costs, and there was nothing they could do about it. But for computer researchers, such "closed systems" were a nightmare.

If someone developed a program on one computer, those who had other kinds of machines had no access to any of the research that person had done.

Today, "open systems," which let users mix hardware and software components built by different vendors, are changing the computer industry. Compatibility makes more services and products available, while competition cuts prices. Open systems are, in fact, central to Stallman's mission to liberate software, though he can hardly be credited with originating the idea. At its core is a special operating system called UNIX and a programming language called C, both developed at Bell Labs in the 1970s.

UNIX, a pet project of AT&T researchers Ken Thompson and Dennis Ritchie, evolved into a programmer's dream. The system was composed of compact programs called tools, each of which performed a single function. By putting tools together, programmers could do complicated things. The operating system mimicked the way that programmers think. C, the programming language UNIX programs were written in, was created by Ritchie expressly to make them "portable"—that is, able to run on different computers. And unlike other portability schemes under development at the time, C was designed to be sleek, simple, and fast.

Nevertheless, problems remained. UNIX, which the AT&T researchers had developed on DEC computers, handled data a little differently than the operating system on IBM computers—which meant that UNIX programs, even if they were scrupulously written in C, didn't always work on an IBM. The Honeywell operating system was a little different still, creating a whole new set of obstacles. Programs that worked on one machine would mysteriously fail on others.

Then somewhere around 1976 Thompson and Ritchie made a breakthrough. They decided that although writing their programs in C was certainly a good idea, it wasn't enough. What they really needed to do, they reflected, was to move UNIX itself—after all, an operating system is just another program, and users could simply run UNIX instead of the system the computer manufacturer had supplied. It was a radical idea in an age when every computer and its particular operating system seemed to be inextricably linked.

By this time, UNIX had become more than just a research curiosity. As early as 1973, some 25 Bell Labs computers were running it, and the operating system soon spread outside of the telephone company. By 1977, more than 500 sites were using it, 125 of them at universities, among them the University of California at Berkeley.

UNIX took a new turn at Berkeley that shows just how much can be done when a source code remains available to users. Like other schools, Berkeley had paid $400 for a tape that included the complete source code to the operating system. But instead of merely running

UNIX, two bright graduate students, Bill Joy and Chuck Haley, started making changes. In 1977, Joy sent out 30 free copies of the Berkeley Software Distribution (BSD) UNIX, a collection of programs and modifications to the UNIX system.

Over the next six years, the BSD UNIX grew into an operating system of its own that had significant advantages over AT&T's. For example, a programmer using the BSD UNIX could switch between multiple programs running at the same time. AT&T's UNIX allowed the names on files to be no more than 14 letters long, but on Berkeley's they could stretch out to 255 letters. Berkeley also developed software to connect many UNIX computers together using high-speed networks. If there had been a popularity contest between the two systems, the BSD UNIX would have won hands down. And Berkeley never charged more than a modest duplication fee for its software.

Yet Berkeley didn't make a dent in AT&T's sales: since the university's system was based on UNIX, anybody who wanted to run it first had to purchase a source-code license for UNIX from AT&T. What's more, the company was beginning to realize the true value of the operating system it had spawned. In 1977, a commercial source-code license for UNIX cost $17,000, but by 1981, that price had jumped to $43,000.

Educational source-code licenses for UNIX were still under $1,000, so many universities bought the AT&T license, put the system that went along with it on the shelf, and ordered the BSD UNIX from Berkeley. But the businesses that were turning to UNIX couldn't justify spending tens of thousands of dollars just for a source code. Instead, they spent the few hundred dollars AT&T charged for versions of UNIX that didn't include the code. These firms couldn't make changes or see how programs were written, but they could still write their own applications.

### Software War

Back at MIT, Richard Stallman and the AI lab had had their own brush with commercializing software—with very different results. In the late 1970s, the lab was peopled with students, professors, and staff that had drifted in during their high school or college days and never left. This tightly knit community of hackers seemed to live for programming alone. In many ways, what united them was that the lab had built its own computer, the Lisp Machine, and a whole new operating system designed for AI applications.

Progress in developing software for the Lisp Machine was swift: whenever somebody discovered a bug, it was fixed. If people wanted to add a feature to a program—make it do something useful that it hadn't done before—they went right ahead.

Encouraged by the academic success of their

machine, a group of hackers left the lab in 1980 to set up a company to commercialize the computer. They called it Lisp Machine Inc. (LMI). Soon a second group left and set up a company called Symbolics. Both companies licensed the Lisp Machine operating system from MIT, and a clause in their contracts specified that any improvements they made had to be returned to the Institute. So although competition between the two companies was fierce, they shared everything they learned. Any time anyone made an advance, everyone in the embryonic industry benefited. The hackers at the AI lab saw the cooperation between Symbolics, LMI, and MIT as a model for software development.

Then in 1982, Symbolics' lawyers reread their licensing agreement with MIT and discovered that while they had to give any new software they created back to the Institute, they didn't have to grant MIT the right to redistribute those ideas. Programmers at Symbolics developed a new feature for the operating system and refused to let MIT share it with LMI. Although the feature wasn't in itself a major advance, Symbolics' new policy was the death knell to software sharing.

"Stallman and I went into a crash mode," recalls Richard Greenblatt, the Lisp Machine's inventor. They refused to accept Symbolics' terms, and decided to reinvent the company's new feature for themselves. "We hacked around the clock for two solid weeks and finally put a comparable feature into the MIT sources."

For the following two years, Stallman took every improvement that Symbolics' programmers made and rewrote it for the operating system used by MIT and LMI. Programs that took Symbolics months to write he would rewrite in a matter of days. The only reason he did it, he says, was to punish Symbolics for breaking its promise to share software. He called it "the war."

But while he fought the war, Stallman's beloved AI lab fell apart. All the old hackers slowly left, siphoned off by LMI and Symbolics. "Machines would break and there was no one to fix them anymore—they had to be turned off and abandoned," he remembers. "It was a society that could no longer keep itself going. I was the last one who could keep it going, but I couldn't, because one person wasn't enough."

He also came to realize that his fight had little significance. The evolution of computer systems had bypassed the Lisp Machine, which was too specialized and expensive to produce. Stallman saw that the real enemy was not Symbolics but the entire software industry that was restricting access to source code.

In 1984, he decided that it was time to start a counterattack: "Instead of continuing to punish those who had destroyed the old software-sharing community, I wanted to start a new one." He quit his job at MIT. More than anything else, he didn't want a repeat of the Lisp Machine debacle—spending years on a project just to have it pulled out from under him and licensed to a company on MIT's terms. Then he sat down and started the task of building a new operating system.

## What's GNU?

He called his brainchild GNU, a recursive acronym meaning GNU's Not UNIX.

As early as 1984, UNIX appeared to be on its way to becoming the operating system of the future. It was taking over the computer research world and making strong inroads in commercial computer systems. Versions of it were already available for most computers—from microcomputers to supercomputers—and engineers were rapidly adapting it to others. UNIX could even run on the lowly IBM PC. Stallman reasoned that a free version of the operating system, written completely from scratch, would have a large user base eager to accept it.

★ ★ ★ ★ ★ ★

*Richard Stallman's mission to liberate all software begin at MIT's Artificial Intelligence Laboratory back in 1982, when fellow hackers reneged on their tacit promise to share their ideas. Today, the movement he has spearheaded has taken off.*

★ ★ ★ ★ ★ ★

But GNU would *not* be UNIX, even though all GNU software would also run on UNIX. Most significantly, the source code for any GNU program would be available to anyone who wanted it, and people would be able to freely redistribute their own copies of the software—both identical copies for friends and enhanced copies, like Berkeley's version of the original UNIX.

Stallman's main worry was that some company would take the operating system he wrote, make some changes, and then say that their "improved" programs were separate inventions and proprietary. To prevent that, he invented a new kind of licensing agreement, the "Copyleft," which lets people do anything they want with the software except restrict others' right to copy it. As Stallman says, "Forbidding is forbidden." The Copyleft furthermore requires that anybody who distributes a GNU program make its source code available for a nominal fee. And if any piece of a Copylefted program is included into another program, the entire resulting program is Copylefted.

Although Stallman expected that other programmers would eventually help him out with his project, at first he was on his own. When he discovered that nobody else had been assigned to his old office at the AI lab, he started sneaking back at night: he needed a computer to write GNU, and the machines at the lab were available. Soon he was working there days as well. Patrick H. Winston, the AI lab's director, knew about it, but he didn't say anything, since he saw Stallman's resignation as largely symbolic. If Stallman was going to continue writing good programs that other people in the lab could use, Winston wasn't about to tell the 13-year veteran to leave.

Within a year, Stallman's first program was out: GNU EMACS, which edits programs and does a much better job of it than the standard editor that comes with UNIX. EMACS is so powerful that people can use it to write programs, try them out, read electronic mail, browse through online documentation, find programming mistakes with the help of a debugger (also written by Stallman), and even play games. Programmers immediately saw the caliber of the promised GNU software and shared the program with their friends.

And then, just as Stallman had hoped, they started fixing his bugs and adding new features. The hard thing about writing a major program like EMACS, he explains, is starting it. Once the first version is available, people play with it and easily make substantial contributions. By producing just one crop of free software, Stallman bootstrapped a movement that has grown in momentum as the software has improved. Today hundreds of significant subsystems for EMACS have been contributed from around the world, and programmers have adapted it to more than 50 different kinds of computers. It runs on everything from desktop microcomputers to Cray supercomputers.

The success of EMACS led Stallman to found the Free Software Foundation, which gives a tax deduction to companies and individuals who want to contribute to Project GNU. Stallman describes it as "a charity for writing computer programs," and from that perspective, it has been highly successful, receiving $267,782 in donations in 1989 alone. The foundation also earned $330,377 from the sale of manuals and computer tapes containing GNU programs. Moreover, Stallman and the other FSF programmers no longer sneak around to use the AI lab's computers, since they have a fleet of high-performance workstations donated by Hewlett Packard, Thinking Machines, Sony, and even Bell Laboratories. Companies have donated cash as well, and paid for technical staff to spend a year in Cambridge working with Stallman.

The foundation uses the money it garners to pay its staff of fourteen, which includes nine programmers and three technical writers. Even though Stallman works for free, he doesn't expect everybody else to do the same. Nevertheless, FSF programmers earn only $25,000 a year, which is one-half to one-third the salary they would command on the open market. Paying low wages lets FSF take on more staff members, and it guarantees that they're all committed to the cause.

## A Programming Coup

In the workstation and minicomputer market, GNU has already caught on strong. Many computer companies that sell UNIX-based systems—including Convex Computer Corp., which makes mini-supercomputers, and DEC—already include GNU software as part of their standard operating-system distribution. Data General and NeXT, Inc., the billion-dollar startup of Apple Computer's founder Steve Jobs, use GNU as the basis of their workstation line. About the only territory that remains untouched by GNU—and by UNIX as well—is the personal-computer market: the UNIX that runs on the IBM PC often costs more than $1,000 for a usable configuration. But the situation is due to change. As soon as the core of GNU is operational, something that Stallman expects before the end of 1991, GNU software will run on any personal computer based on the Intel 386 microprocessor—what is quickly becoming the standard machine—for free.

If EMACS made the computer world suspect that Project GNU was a force to be reckoned with, what clinched the matter was Stallman's second GNU program, something called the GNU C Compiler (GCC). Compilers are those critical programs that translate source code into "machine code," or language that a machine can use. But not all compilers are equal. Given the same source code, different compilers will produce different machine code. A certain compiler may generate machine code that is more efficient than another's, or it may make mistakes, so that its machine code doesn't work properly.

Stallman knew that he had to write a good C compiler; otherwise people wouldn't want to use it. But he didn't intend to write one of the best. Because it is free software, GCC simply *became* one of the best. Stallman implemented ideas that had been in textbooks for years, and then, since the compiler was distributed with the source code, programmers all around the world helped make it better.

Today the machine code GCC generates is more reliable than that from other commercially available compilers. The reason, say its users, is that people who discover bugs can figure out the fixes themselves by looking through the source code. All the bug reports—and the fixes—end up back on Stallman's workstation. New releases of the compiler come out nearly every month instead of every year, as is the case with most commercial software.

GCC can also generate code for more than 11 different kinds of microprocessors, while most commercial compilers are tailored to a specific microprocessor. Before Stallman wrote GCC, nobody believed a compiler that generated code for more than one kind of machine could be efficient, but Stallman's compiler is efficient indeed: it consistently produces machine code that runs 20 to 30 percent faster than the code from other commercially available compilers.

"The only way for other commercial compilers to continue to exist in the face of GCC is to offer features that GCC does not," says Don Seeley, a senior systems programmer at the University of Utah. "The many vendors whose compilers are not even current with old technology will lose. New compilers must be at least as good as GCC, or the market won't accept them."

It was rave reviews like Seeley's that convinced Ralph W. Hyver, who now manages Hewlett-Packard's Information Architecture Group, to give FSF a $100,000 cash grant and another $350,000 in equipment. Helping Stallman made sense, says Hyver, because many of the research groups that Hewlett-Packard was supporting were using GNU software. The company was also using GNU programs internally.

Another convert is NeXT. All of the software that it delivers with its computers is compiled with GCC. "The issue for us had nothing to do with proprietary versus non-proprietary," says Bud Tribble, NeXT's vice-president of software engineering. "We benchmarked many compilers, and found the GCC code produced to be excellent. The internal structure of GCC was also very clean and allowed us to extend it in several ways. If there had been another 'non-free' compiler that was better, we probably would have used it instead."

## Conflicting Definitions of Freedom

Nevertheless, other companies have been reluctant to use GNU software. Some have spent millions of dollars developing their own C compilers and may feel threatened by a compiler Stallman developed essentially by himself. Engineers at Sun Microsystems, for example, refuse to even talk about GCC anymore. "They have all spoken with people about GCC in the past and believe that comparing our compilers with GCC quickly becomes a fairly unproductive philosophical discussion," says Erica Vener, a spokesperson for the company. "Bottom line, Sun is in the business of selling the products it develops."

But ironically, it is probably the Copyleft, more than anything else, that is preventing more widespread adoption of GCC and other GNU programs. Most companies aren't comfortable with the idea of selling a program only to have the customer turn around and make a copy for a friend. And they don't like the requirement that the source code be made available to anybody who asks for it.

At Berkeley, UNIX developer Mike Karels says that the software he writes is actually more free than Stallman's. Since the mid-1980s, Karels and the other researchers at Berkeley's Computer Systems Research Group (CSRG) have been working to isolate their pro-

grams from AT&T's. And it has paid off. By now, a "significant fraction" of their code has been "written from scratch," Karels notes. Berkeley gives those programs away to companies that do not have AT&T source-code licenses and imposes essentially no restrictions. The companies, in other words, may modify and resell the software without providing the source code to their customers.

Throughout the 1980s, CSRG developed a set of programs for networking computers. Firms bought the software, sometimes altered the source code and added features as they saw fit, and marketed the finished product. Today nearly every UNIX manufacturer sells a version of the Berkeley networking software, and some companies have even placed the programs into integrated circuits that are used inside IBM personal computers. Karels says none of that would have happened if Berkeley had required that the networking source code be made available to customers: companies would have been frightened away by the idea that they would somehow lose their competitive edge. And he adds that many users aren't interested in seeing the source code anyway.

Unfortunately, Berkeley's terms also mean that customers who buy Karels's programs from vendors have to rely on the vendors for bug fixes. This matters the most with security problems. In 1988, for instance, the infamous computer worm written by Robert T. Morris got through a hole in Berkeley's network mail program and shut down thousands of computers across the country. The fix, like many security-related fixes, required changing a single line of the mail program, and it was distributed over the network within a few hours after the worm had been stopped. But it was useful only to those schools and businesses that had the source code. Others had to get new versions of the mail program from their vendors, some of whom took more than a month to distribute them.

"We have been pushing for vendors to ship source code for security-critical functions," Karels says. But vendors haven't complied.

## The Question of Support

Advocates of FSF believe it is precisely because of the Copyleft that GNU software will eventually dominate the computer industry. And, they say, by voting with their checkbooks, people are already forcing manufacturers to abandon their proprietary operating systems. Given the opportunity to use free software, many computer users might soon refuse to purchase anything else.

The pressure will become even more intense once FSF follows through on its plan to produce a spreadsheet program for workstations and advanced PCs that competes with Lotus's best-selling 1-2-3. Although at first the GNU spreadsheet will lack many of the features of

1-2-3, they will surely be added over time. Soon the only competitive advantage of 1-2-3 will be its name.

But who would pay for programmers to eat if all software were free? The same people that are now, says Stallman. Most programs are written for internal use, not for resale, and that will continue, he argues. A company that pays a programmer to write a word processor for drawing up reports and other such applications shouldn't care if that program is shared with another company—especially if the second company gives bug fixes and improvements back. GNU software will make programmers more productive, since they won't have to write each new application from scratch, Stallman points out. He's looking toward a future in which companies that sell computer programs earn their money not by using the copyright law to prevent people from making copies, but by offering services like support and training. If you had a personal computer, for example, you would pay company programmers to add extra features or help you use the ones already provided.

Naturally, not everyone is enthusiastic about the idea. "It is nice to say that we should just sell support and give away the software, but why?" asks Tom Lemberg, vice-president of Cambridge-based Lotus Development Corp. "The way our economic system works is that people who create value are able to get value by selling it."

Other critics note that in fact product support for GNU software has been lacking so far—and that this could prevent businesses from wholeheartedly adopting the programs. "Digital supports people in mass quantities," says Jon Hall, one of Digital's product managers for ULTRIX Workstation Software. "Thousands of customers at one time. Some of the customers are not even computer literate, much less UNIX literate." He contends that Digital can provide that level of support only by charging for its software and using the copyright system to prevent people from making their own copies.

But companies that exclusively supported free software would have lower costs. Michael Tiemann, who wrote a compiler for the G++ programming language, is banking on that idea: last January he founded Cygnus Support, a firm that writes, sells, and supports Copylefted software. Tiemann believes that wholesale adoption of GNU programs will be inevitable once there's a company willing to sign its name on the dotted line, charge an annual fee, and guarantee to fix any bugs and answer any questions a customer might have. Cygnus is that company.

In its first year of operation, Cygnus signed over a million dollars in support contracts. One of the clients is Intel, which needed a C compiler for a new microprocessor that it has developed. "They want to ship GCC as their standard compiler, but companies that they sell to are concerned that it is not a supported product. So they contracted with us to do the support for it," says David Wallace, another Cygnus founder. "We are also starting to get calls from people whose potential clients are telling them 'if it doesn't run the GNU software, we are not going to buy your hardware,'" he adds.

Wallace acknowledges that it will take years to wean the computer industry away from proprietary software. Yet he maintains that Stallman isn't just a fluke programmer, and that GCC is not just a lucky success. "The free-software part isn't a gimmick," he points out. "It is the very thing that makes the software so good."

# Orwellian Dream Come True: A Badge That Pinpoints You

## Leonard Sloane

Is Big Brother your boss?

Another tool that lets "them" check up on "us"—where we are and with whom we are—is on the way. It is the active badge, a small clip-on microcomputer, about the size of an employee I.D. card, that transmits signals to a central system. As long as you wear the badge, the system can track your movements around an office building or even a larger area.

"When different people need to be found, I can ring directly to where they are," said Roy Want, who invented the active badge while at the Olivetti Research Laboratory in Cambridge, England, and who is now a member of the research staff at the Xerox Research Center in Palo Alto, Calif. "It's in your interest as a professional to stay in touch with your colleagues."

Andy Harter, a research engineer at the Olivetti lab, added: "I get my communications so much faster when I carry the badge. And it's all completely hands-free."

For many people, however, privacy issues overwhelm any technological virtues of active badges. They see the badges as an intrusion into the lives of employees, eroding workplace privacy. And they compare the badges with the already widely used electronic monitoring devices that can quantify the number of keystrokes on a terminal, peek at voice and computer mail messages or listen to employees transact business on the phone.

"George Orwell would have been pleased," said Donald A. Norman, chairman of the cognitive science department at the University of California at San Diego. "This technology makes snooping easy. Especially intrusive technology should be under the control of the person using it, not of management."

---

## Visions of an electronic sweatshop.

---

Evan Hendricks, editor of the Privacy Times newsletter, said: "There's a lot of surveillance in the workplace these days. They could say you were in the men's room or the cafeteria too long or that you were sitting in so-and-so's office too long. It has the potential of changing the modern office into an electronic sweatshop."

Mr. Harter of Olivetti said that although active badges were still being tested, there were plans to make them available commercially starting next year.

The target market includes not only office workers who are away from their desks, but also doctors and patients in hospitals or nursing homes, lawyers and laboratory scientists.

In addition to being worn by people, badges can be attached to objects, like luggage in airports or raw materials in factories, to track their progress.

Olivetti officials say active badges were initially developed about four years ago as a means of making telephone communication more effective. Scientists at the laboratory found that with a badge emitting an identification code every 15 seconds—in the form of an infrared beam—to a network of wall-mounted sensors around a building, information about the location of the person wearing it could be constantly updated. The badge functions the same way that a remote control device does in transmitting a code to a television set.

The second generation of active badges is now being tested, with researchers in England and the United States wearing them for the purpose. This version, called the authenticated badge, is designed to assure that the signal is authentic, to prevent tampering with the system.

Currently, the information provided by active badges worn at a particular site is shown on a central computer screen in the form of five columns in a table: the badge wearer's name, the telephone extension nearest the present position, the room where the person is, the number of other badge-wearing people in the room and the approximate length of time the badge wearer has been at that location.

The data from the badges can also be displayed on a screen showing a model of an entire office floor, thus visually indicating where each badge-wearer is in relation to everyone else. Anyone with access to the computer screen can then quickly get in touch with the badge wearer by telephone or electronically.

"In the environment in which we work, people are not always in their offices," said Veronica G. Falcao, who helped to develop active badge software while employed by Olivetti in the United States. "Active badges are the most useful thing to round people up for a meeting, to go out to lunch or celebrate someone's birthday."

Murray Mazer, a member of the research staff at the Digital Equip- ment Corporation, which helps to finance the Olivetti laboratory in England, said: "I view this technology as interesting in itself. It allows the acquisition of dynamic location information."

Other computer experts see active badges in a far different light, however. "We're saying that they are a form of computer monitoring," said Gary Chapman, director of the Cambridge, Mass., office of the Computer Professionals for Social Responsibility, an organization that has studied electronic monitoring. "They can keep a diary of how long you've been talking to Joe Blow."

And legislation pending in both houses of Congress would require that employees be given notice of the forms and frequency of monitoring being used by an employer. "There's such a strong potential for abuse because employers are allowed to spy at will on their employees," said one Congressional staff member who requested anonymity.

Professor Norman, who is writing a book called "Things That Make Us Smart," summed up that view succinctly: "Active badges are a really excellent example of the horrible trade-off technology gives us. This technology makes snooping easy, and what technology makes easy, we tend to do."

# Supermarket Spies

## They tail us through the aisles, watch from hidden cameras as we study the labels, and eavesdrop as we do battle with our kids over Frosted Flakes, Cheetos, and Coke.

### Erik Larson

*Erik Larson is a staff writer with the* Wall Street Journal.

When I met up with Paco Underhill, he was sitting on a bench in front of a store in a treeless shopping complex called The Crossings in Tannersville, Pennsylvania. Underhill was clearly in his element, doing what he does best and, incidentally, what he does for a living. Watching. Observing. Mentally cataloging and sorting.

Spying.

In the 1970s, when he was a student of urban geography at Columbia University, Underhill became fascinated with the techniques of urban analysis pioneered by William "Holly" Whyte, the noted critic of cityscapes who used cameras to analyze how well public spaces served the public. Underhill adapted Whyte's techniques to the commercial landscape and founded Envirosell Inc., a Manhattan company that specializes in the surreptitious filming and tracking of consumers in retail stores and malls throughout the world. His company's client list includes a number of corporate giants, among them Quaker Oats, Burger King, and Noxell Corporation, a cosmetics unit of Procter & Gamble.

Underhill's special brand of store surveillance helps retailers learn how to get people to buy more items per visit, or not lose patience with long lines at the checkout counter. If you've shopped in a store when Underhill and his team have been at work, you've likely been captured on

One researcher hid a camera in a box of Cheer detergent, then stuck stickers on the box that read *Now Sweetened With Nutrasweet.* "No one looked," he said. "No one even noticed."

film. Moreover, one of Underhill's agents probably followed your every step through the store, noting on a layout map the exact moment at which you entered, the direction you traveled, where you paused, what items you touched, what you bought, and the precise moment of your departure.

At no time, however, would you have known you were under surveillance.

IT ISN'T ENOUGH anymore for companies to know precisely what we buy; they want to know *how* we consume: How do we comport ourselves in the aisles of our grocery stores? How do we

do our wash, *really?* The pressures of today's marketplace drive retailers to pursue the most subtle nuances of buyer behavior. But time and again, they run into that most daunting of obstacles: the consumer.

We consumers simply cannot tell the whole truth, it seems. We dodge, duck, and mislead even when we don't intend to. When grabbed in a supermarket by someone with a questionnaire, we don't disclose the real truth, but respond instead with answers meant to please the interviewer, to conform to some cultural standard of correct behavior, or to fit some wishful dream of our own.

The dialogue goes something like this:

SURVEYOR: "Hello, Ma'am. I see you have your son with you. Could you list for me exactly what you served him for lunch yesterday?"

CONSUMER: "Why, yes. Let's see. A banana. And some homemade chicken soup. No salt, of course. Then I made him a tuna salad sandwich. For a dash of color, I sliced him a tomato from my own garden." (She pats child on head.)

THE INNER CONSUMER: "What did I serve? What did I *serve?* I'll tell you what I served. I opened a can of Chef Boy-ardee Ravioli. I poured the ravioli into a bowl and stuck the bowl in the microwave. Then I popped open one of those little boxes of Ninja Turtle juice. I took the bowl of ravioli out of the microwave, but it was too hot so I stuck it in the freezer. I had to rearrange the fish sticks, microwave pizzas, and Eskimo Pies. The little angel threw a tantrum, so while I waited for the ravioli to cool I gave him a couple of Oreo cookies. Okay? *Okay?*"

To counter this natural tendency to present ourselves favorably, the marketers deploy anthropologists, sociologists, and psychologists to observe us in the very act of consumption. Their intimate surveillance, their loitering in stores and hanging out behind one-way mirrors, goes by many labels, among them such neutered terms as "observational research," "unobtrusive research," and even "account planning."

Plain old spying.

PACO UNDERHILL let me follow him into a store he was surveying in the Tannersville complex. Eight cameras stared down from the tops of display partitions, like shiny black crows eyeing rodents on the forest floor. The cameras recorded the travels of shoppers continuously on videotape or jaggedly at two-second intervals on Super 8 film. Three "fieldwork specialists," Craig, Tony, and Carole, tracked the progress of target shoppers on maps attached to clipboards. Each female shopper was an O, each male an X. Typically the agents marked one map for each customer, charting each path with a colored pen. Arrows noted the direction of travel. An O marked on the path itself indicated where the shopper had paused, an X where he or she had touched something.

Underhill's agents moved stealthily. They masked their true interest by pretending to take inventory of store merchandise. Heads bowed, eyes sliding ever so discreetly, they tracked their targets no matter how long they stayed, no matter how many times they returned to the same displays.

In this and other studies, Underhill has captured on film shopping phenomena no one had previously noticed, or at least been able to quantify. It has long been an axiom of retailing, for example, that shoppers approach stores from the right and tend to turn right once they enter. Underhill's films have documented this right-leaning tendency in irrefutable detail.

Underhill also knows that long lines at a cashier counter—known in the retail game as the "cash-wrap"—will discourage shoppers from coming into a store; yet a certain level of crowding, which Underhill has dubbed "laudable crowding," can actually attract shoppers.

"We know that kids are powerful motivators," Underhill said. They grab things from promotional displays, bring them to

**K**ids stymie the researchers. "Don't think of children as small adults," says an observer. "Think of them as big Martians." If you bring them to the store, you will spend a lot more money than if you go alone.

their parents, and, as Underhill puts it, "introduce" the adults to the product. "We've captured kids climbing into the racks to pull things off—literally climbing up the shelving!" Retailers can harness this power, he said.

Underhill has proposed, for example, a way that a grocery store could improve its chances of selling a kids' cereal emblazoned with a cartoon celebrity. Place the box or promotional display so the child can see it from far enough away to build up a powerful demand whine. Put it in the middle of the aisle, he said, not the end. Have it jut a bit into the child's range of vision. "Now you get 'Daddy, Daddy, Daddy, Daddy, Daddy, Daddy, Daddy, Daddy!!'" Underhill whined, mimicking exactly my eldest daughter. "If you put it closer to the head of the aisle, you might get only three 'Daddies.'"

Langbourne Rust, founder of Langbourne Rust Research in Briarcliff, New York, has spent more than 20 years observing kids, often from behind one-way glass, for such prestigious clients as Children's Television Workshop (creators of "Sesame Street"), Quaker Oats, General Foods, Lipton, and McDonald's.

Rust attributes his interest in observation to having been raised a country boy who spent a lot of time "sitting on a stump" watching wildlife pass by. "I've always been a critter watcher," he said. "Now I just watch different critters."

And kids are critters unto themselves. They don't function like adults, said Rust. Kids stymie researchers who approach them with traditional adult tactics.

"Don't think of children as small adults," one researcher advised at a Miami Beach marketers' conference. "Think of them as big Martians." Kids have minimal powers of discrimination. They like virtually everything they see. They lack the ability to report on their own behavior. They try desperately to please their elders, especially strange elders with clipboards. And they have a disturbing knack for giving detailed reactions to products they've never even tried.

Once, for example, Rust asked a group of second-graders what they thought of Big Bird toothpaste. They liked it. They liked the way it looked. It tasted good.

There was one problem: The product did not exist.

Recently Rust spent a lot of time standing discreetly in toy stores and candy and cereal aisles studying the ways kids and parents interact when they shop together. The project, commissioned by the Advertising Research Foundation, captured some behaviors that marketers would be foolish not to pounce upon:

• Girls get more involved in grocery shopping and choosing which brands to buy than do boys, and thus, Rust concluded, "may perhaps be a more productive target for advertising."

• Parents, it appears, control the intensity of their kids' product demands through deft navigation of store aisles, "thereby avoiding the dangers lurking around certain retail corners."

• The youngest children do most of the asking for products when they shop with parents, but older kids are more cunning, "more skilled negotiators."

It is here that Rust and his colleagues exposed a great and important secret that I, as a father who takes my kids shopping, would have preferred the marketers never discover—something that every mother has always known, and every father with an ounce of integrity will concede to be true. The Advertising Research Foundation report trod this ground gingerly: "Fathers are often less skilled at negotiation than their usually more seasoned female counterparts."

In short, dads are suckers.

Imagine the marketing potential! Father-and-son days at the local Piggly Wiggly. Candy racks in hardware stores. Discount motor oil at Toys R Us. Action figures on sale at the beer display!

There is reason, nonetheless, to take heart. The process of getting suckered is less painful than is suggested by the common wisdom, with its lurid tales of tantrums among the Goobers and episodes of rapid oxygen depletion. "In general," Rust told me, "the parent-child interactions in grocery stores are a very positive, upbeat social time between parent and child that both seem to enjoy a lot."

Look closely enough at adult shoppers alone, the spies say, and you'll still find creatures of strange habits. Lee Weinblatt, president of the Pretesting Company, an innovative New Jersey market research business, has secured cameras to shelves to take a close look at how grownups react to individual products.

In a study of frozen food displays, Weinblatt discovered an intriguing behavioral quirk: People spend one-third less time examining frozen foods displayed in new vertical freezer cases (the kind with the glass doors) than when the foods are set out in the old open horizontal cases. The old cases, nicknamed "coffins," encouraged browsing and increased the odds that shoppers would notice new products. Now, however, shoppers march directly to the door they want, open it, reach in with icy precision, then close it fast.

The reason? "We were all taught well by our mothers to close the refrigerator door," Weinblatt said. "I can't remember though—was it to keep the cold air in, or the warm air out?"

During another of Weinblatt's shelf studies, a hapless shopper picked up a cereal box containing a hidden camera and, oblivious both to its unusual weight and to the video cable that ran from its rear, pulled it toward his cart. The cable stretched. Boxes erupted along 40 feet of shelf and tumbled to the floor. The man looked to see if anyone had noticed, replaced the box, and walked briskly away.

Another study demonstrated beyond a doubt just how oblivious we consumers can be to product choices. Weinblatt hid a camera in a box of Cheer detergent, then stuck stickers on the box and its neighbors that read NEW AND IMPROVED, this to test whether anyone paid attention to those weary but ubiquitous adjectives.

"No one looked," he said. "No one even saw it."

He got bolder. This time he pasted a three-inch disk on each box that said NOW SWEETENED WITH NUTRASWEET!

Again, none of the shoppers under surveillance blinked an eye. "Not even people who picked the boxes of detergent up and put them in their shopping carts! We had an interviewer meet them at the end and ask, 'Did you notice anything new about this?' They said no."

L
ook into the glass supermarket scanner and you'll see the red-rimmed gaze of Sara Lee and the Pillsbury Doughboy watching your every purchase. You may as well dance on the scanner naked, for your secrets are known.

Okay. So maybe some people didn't know what NutraSweet was. Maybe they didn't know it had no business being in a laundry soap.

Weinblatt took off the gloves. This time he placed labels that exclaimed NEW IMPROVED TASTE!

"Finally people noticed," he told me later. "When we asked them what it meant, they said, 'I don't know. Maybe it works better?'"

SUPERMARKET SCANNERS and the shimmery red filament they cast over our soups, toothpastes, and cereals have by now become a familiar part of our grocery-shopping experience. Some of us watch the light, even peer down deep inside the glass to observe its glowing helium-neon source, but most of us long ago tucked the scanner into that cupboard of commonplace technologies we don't understand and have no desire to understand, like fiber optics. To the marketers of America, however, that plate of glass embedded at the end of the cashier's conveyor belt has become a window into our consuming souls.

Look back into that scanner and what you really see is the red-rimmed gaze of Betty Crocker, Aunt Jemima, Mrs. Paul, Mrs. Smith, Sara Lee, and the Pillsbury Doughboy watching your every purchase. You may as well get up on the glass and dance there stark naked, for your secrets are known. You have a cold sore, arthritis, and suffer a nasty case of hay fever every spring. Your 12-year-old son just bought a package of condoms. You suspect you are pregnant.

The marketers have discovered things about consumers they never could have known before scanners came along. Scanner data has, for instance, allowed researchers to quantify a truth we parents have known since the invention of the fold-down seat in a shopping cart: If you bring the kids with you to the grocery store, you will spend a lot more money than if you go alone. To be precise, if you are a woman you will spend 29 percent more, if a man 66 percent.

Such discoveries are just icing on the store-bought cake, however. Knowledge mined from scanners has given marketers new powers of manipulation. I don't mean the vague and indirect power conferred through the deft kneading of image and sexual desire. That's old stuff. No time for that now, with markets imploding like newly snuffed stars.

I mean directly.

Pull the lever, the dog bites.

Some 4,000 stores in 53 major grocery chains, including Giant, Safeway, Foodtown, Alpha Beta, Dominick's, Schnuck's, and Tom Thumb, have installed a system called Checkout Coupon, built by Catalina Marketing of Anaheim, California. You may have seen it—it's that insolent little cream-colored box that spits out coupons geared to lure you into future purchases, prompted by the items you've just bought. The Catalina system, first tested in 1984 (of course), seeks to modify your shopping behavior. It watches the codes that flow through the store's checkout computer as the cashier scans each product from your cart. When the system spots a given code, the so-called "trigger" product, it prints a coupon as if by autonomic reflex. When you buy hot dogs, for example, you get a coupon for mustard.

Catalina's clients spent $32 million on the service in 1991, mostly for the purposes of ambushing their competitors. When they spot a shopper who has bought something from the competition, they leap from the machine brandishing a coupon for *their* products.

On one trip to my own local supermarket, the Giant on York Road in northern Baltimore, I bought a package of Sun Chips, a new snack chip made by Frito-Lay. It triggered a coupon for Nabisco's Harvest Crisps.

I bought Gorton's fish sticks for my kids; an incensed Mrs. Paul snapped off a coupon for *her* fish.

I bought Cascade dishwashing detergent; Palmolive offered to take a buck off the price of its liquid gel soap.

I bought Stouffer's microwave French-bread pizzas; the Pillsbury Doughboy shot me a 75-cent chit for Oven Lovins, his microwave pizzas.

Catalina has surprised, possibly even dismayed, some shoppers with its offerings. For a time, women who were breast-feeding and who bought breast pads received coupons urging them to try a brand of prepared baby formula. A condom maker offered coupons to anyone who picked up a tube of Ortho-Gynol spermicide. The same company also issued condom coupons to shoppers who bought baby diapers, as if in a mechanized rebuke for some previous moment of passion and abandon.

"It ran for one day," chuckled Daniel D. Granger, Catalina's senior vice-president for marketing. "If we have something in like that we get an *immediate* reaction. You have to be careful."

COLUMNS OF NUMBERS jolted slowly down the screen of a computer monitor in Bannockburn, Illinois, as Connie Latson demonstrated A.C. Nielsen's intelligence-gathering prowess. The numbers, generated through a service Nielsen calls ScanQuick, constituted the ultimate proof of the power of supermarket scanner technology to speed the collection of consumer sales information.

Five hundred miles away at a grocery store in Kansas City, shoppers were moving through the checkout line. I watched their every purchase the instant it was registered in the store's computer. I felt I'd been let in on a monumental secret.

The left-hand column contained the numbers that identified each checkout line. Next across were the 12-digit price code numbers of each item being purchased, and just beyond this, an abbreviated description of the product. The prices came next, then the quantity, and then the exact time of the purchase, in hours, minutes, and seconds.

In aisle nine, at exactly 11:41:40 A.M., someone bought Sanka coffee packaged as single, one-cup servings. Did the shopper have a sleeping problem? High blood pressure? Was the buyer single, as the packaging might indicate?

The same shopper also became the owner of Royal gelatin (11:41:47), chicken breasts (11:41:48), fresh liver (11:41:49), a greeting card (11:42:28), plums (11:42:33), hot dog buns (11:42:37), and—oh, how

The spies are zeroing in on the intimate details of our daily lives: Well, well, Mr. Grumbach! Suddenly you go from butter and bacon once a week to margarine once a month. Do we detect a brush with mortality, Mr. Grumbach?

predictable—Ballpark franks (11:42:49).

What possible benefit could this real-time data provide? Edward Tunstall, director of the Nielsen Advanced Information Technology Center, had some ideas. Data showing exactly what products people bought on a given trip could provide a clearer glimpse at the demographics of each store's territory. "You can start to infer behavior from what's in the market basket," Tunstall said. "If it's around Passover and you're in Chicago and someone goes in and buys matzoh balls and Pampers, you've probably got yourself a young Jewish family."

Such finely grained data could be used to prospect for patterns among demographic groups—what other items do young couples who buy kosher food also tend to buy? The spies could shake out correlations among various product purchases. How often do Coke buyers also buy Doritos? Do Pepsi buyers, possibly, tend to purchase potato chips instead?

Tunstall let his imagination run free. He envisioned a time when real-time scanner data might lead companies to change their prices to reflect changes in shopping patterns over the course of a day. The prices could be adjusted instantly at any shelf through the use of electronic price labels, which by 1991 had begun to appear in some advanced supermarkets. The labels show each price in a tiny liquid crystal display monitor mounted on the shelf.

"Here's a sexist example," Tunstall said. "It's ten o'clock in the morning and Mrs. Housewife goes in to do her shop-

ping of the day. The reason she chose ten o'clock is the babies are up from their morning naps and they haven't gone down for their afternoon naps. So the price of Pampers is a dollar lower.

"At five o'clock in the afternoon, Dad's on his way home. His wife called him and said bring home some Pampers. The price of Pampers is up," said Tunstall, "but the price of a six-pack of beer is down. So he's going to buy the Pampers *and* a six-pack of beer and head home.

"The use of the information inherent in the data collected by scanning devices has not been scratched," Tunstall said. "It just hasn't been touched."

IN JANUARY 1991, Gerald Saltzgaber, then head of Citicorp's scanner intelligence unit, told a meeting of the Advertising Research Foundation that it was his goal to build a "census" database containing the names and purchase histories of 40 million households. With a smile, he glibly dismissed privacy as a worthy issue: "We just don't think consumers are all that concerned about their groceries."

The audience laughed in agreement.

Saltzgaber was right, of course. We don't worry about our groceries. We don't even think about our groceries, beyond their ability to satisfy a current nutritional need. But scanner technology—its power to collect so much minute detail about each of us and over long periods of time—has imbued our lowly purchases with descriptive powers no one ever intended them to have.

At the same time, our grocery stores have swollen in size to accommodate this crush of precisely targeted products, to the point where they provide a little of everything. In 1985 the average supermarket stocked 11,036 distinct products. By 1990, the number had increased almost 50 percent to 16,486. In 1991 manufacturers tried force-fitting another 12,000 *new* products, or roughly 33 a day, into the mix. The 1992 shopper faces at least 20,000 products on each trip to the supermarket. The narrower the market niche a product fits, the more intimately it describes the buyer. Increasingly, products function like shards of mirrored glass, each capturing a glint of identity.

One summer afternoon I took a walk through my local Giant supermarket with the express purpose of looking for products that might betray some *concrete* clue about the people who buy them. I observed my fellow shoppers, imagining myself in Paco Underhill's unobtrusive moccasins. I tried seeing the shelves through the eyes of the next generation of scanning system, programmed to track individuals through their lives.

Produce came first. Clearly most of the products here had no inherent descriptive power. Grapes? Tomatoes? Iceberg lettuce? Potatoes? What could a sack of Idahos possibly say about you?

Ah. But suppose you just bought fresh ginger, fresh basil, a handful of deadly hot serrano peppers, a little radicchio, arugula, jicama, some ugli fruit—now we're starting to get a hint of personality. You're an adventurer. You like to cook. You've got bucks—who else pays that kind of money for basil? Maybe we'll just pass your name to Williams-Sonoma. Or ship you a brochure on cookbooks. Or offer you a gastronomic tour of Europe.

I moved on to the dairy and meat department, imagining a shopper observed: Well, well, Mr. Grumbach! Suddenly you go from buying butter and bacon once a week to buying margarine once a month? You buy chicken without the skin, you buy fish, and unsalted peanuts, when before you got yourself a nice juicy porterhouse, a bag of potato chips, and a container of sour cream at least once a week? Do we detect a brush with mortality, Mr. Grumbach? High cholesterol? Heart attack? The death of a friend?

Saltzgaber has noted how Citicorp's scanner data could identify which households were health conscious, and could be used to track a family's progress from one life phase to the next, from formula to cereal to teen magazines. Indeed, in 1991 Citicorp became the first company to begin peddling mailing lists derived from a frequent-shopper program. Among the selections: a list of 511,227 "weight-conscious" consumers.

The intelligence technologies are merging. The real-world observations rounded up by Paco Underhill, Langbourne Rust, and their fellow spies, combined with the mass intelligence gathered by direct-marketers and scanner-research companies, now provide retailers with hitherto unavailable details about how the rest of us shop—not only how we move through the store and what we touch, but just how much money we spend, when we spend it, and just what we buy.

Marketers now routinely send us mail timed to arrive on our birthdays and in the wake of such major changes in our lives as marriage, birth, and the purchase of a new home. But the marketers want to get even closer, and the coalescence of mass-surveillance technologies may soon enable them to target us by our most immediate daily needs. A man buys Preparation H, probably he is not happy; the retailers think of products to cheer him up. Someone buys roses and condoms; perhaps coupons for aftershave lotion and chocolates are in order.

One day soon a shopper who rushes out at midnight for an emergency pack of disposable diapers may receive a letter from the local cloth-diaper service explaining how front-door delivery can prevent such unplanned sorties. We buy a pregnancy test; we hear from the big obstetrics practice up the street. We pick up a package of spermicide; we soon receive an angry letter from the Vatican.

The marketers say the rush to know us is powered only by their desire to satisfy our needs. Their increasingly sophisticated methods and undivided attention indeed promise to erase the last barriers between consumer and marketer. But it may create in its place a seamless Pavlovian realm in which companies possess unprecedented power to know us—and therefore to know precisely how and exactly when to make us rise from our chairs, go forth, and shop.

# Computer Ethics and Crime

In unit 4 we saw some examples of how the ability of computers to store and manipulate data has posed (some unintended) threats to individual freedom and privacy. In this section, the articles focus on issues related to unethical and/or criminal uses of technology.

In some cases, negative outcomes of computer use have resulted from conflicting social and cultural values. As discussed in the article "World of Electronic Games: Computer Game Ethics," many of the best-selling computer games, including children's games, have violent themes. Other popular programs are pornographic or contain other content that offends many people. The article suggests that one possible means of warning consumers about potentially objectionable software may be to "rate" games the way movies are rated.

Opposing views are offered in the articles "Computer Imaging, A New Branch of Science That Can Turn Truth on Its Head" and "Evidence Set in Motion." Stephen Strauss observes that computer imaging makes it possible to manipulate and distort visual information. He further argues that it is inappropriate to use computer images in a court of law because it would be difficult for jurors and judges to assess the validity of what they see. Alexander Jason, on the other hand, describes the use of a computer simulation he wrote to show the participants in a murder trial how the events of the crime unfolded. In "Evidence Set in Motion," Jason defends electronic imaging as a useful new tool in law enforcement.

The university campus cases presented by Sally Webster, in "Dispatches From the Front Line: Computer Ethics War Stories," offer examples of unethical computer conduct with the intent to commit harm. Webster argues that all members of the university community need to take greater responsibility to define and enforce ethical computer conduct.

In "Playground Bullies Are Learning How to Type," William Flanagan and Brigid McMenamin move the discussion from questionable ethics to criminal behavior. They claim that outright computer crime has reached epidemic proportions. They reject the popular image of computer crimes as mere mischief that sometimes results in inadvertent damage to computer systems or persons. Instead, they argue that many of today's computer criminals are a "new generation of hacker hoods."

Typical examples of computer crime include the electronic theft of funds or the fraudulent manipulation of computerized information. In some cases, the target of criminal activity is the computer system itself. During a four year period in the late 1970s and early 1980s, more than two dozen computer installations in Europe were attacked by terrorists. But one does not need to resort to terrorism to cripple a computer system. As hundreds of articles in the mass media have made clear, computers can be programmed to sabotage themselves with "viruses." A rash of publicity surrounding computer viruses was spurred by the "Internet" virus planted by a Cornell graduate student in November 1988. Though the damage was unintentional in this case, the virus disrupted the operations of several thousand computers on the Internet Network. In response, several prominent computing organizations issued statements on computer ethics and condemned the placing of unauthorized code in computers. This topic is explored in depth by two legal scholars who discuss issues related to obtaining civil and criminal redress for damages caused by viruses. The civil issues are presented by Pamela Samuelson in "Can Hackers Be Sued for Damages Caused by Computer Viruses?" and the criminal issues are covered by Michael Gemignani in "Viruses and Criminal Law."

## Looking Ahead: Challenge Questions

It is difficult to detect, investigate, and prosecute computer-related crime without some technical knowledge of computing. According to Bryan Kocher, a former president of the Association for Computing Machinery, some computer expertise is necessary to make good computer laws in the first place. He observes that legislatures tend to have "many lawyers, morticians, and tavern keepers, but few computer professionals." This lack of computer experts could lead to some very bad laws, argues Kocher. Do you agree? Why or why not?

# Dispatches From the Front Line:
## Computer Ethics War Stories

## Sally Webster

*Sally Webster worked for eleven years in Academic Computing Services at Syracuse University. For several of those years, she served as the assistant director for the user services group and was responsible for talking to faculty and students who didn't abide by the University's computing policies. She became active in the EDUCOM Software Initiative (now EUIT) in 1986 and has worked on EUIT projects concerning social and ethical computing and network issues since 1988. She is coleader of the Ethics Kit project and leader of the Ethics War Stories project. In 1990, she joined the State University of New York's College of Environmental Science and Forestry as professor of computer applications.*

### THE CASE OF THE HATEFUL HARASSER

You are in charge of the user services group in the academic computing organization on campus. One of your staff tells you that a young male student, X, has been receiving harassing mail messages from another user threatening to expose that he's gay, that his e-mail account has been broken into, and that sexual solicitations have been sent to others. The victim is pretty sure who broke into his account. He claims he is being slandered and mumbles something about suing the university for allowing slanderous attacks to take place with university computing resources. He wants the computer center to find and punish his tormentor. You see copies of the offensive messages, and they are subtly, not overtly, harassing.

Your systems people quickly locate from whose mail account the threatening messages have been coming. The owner of the account is a computer science major who, when in high school, was arrested and convicted for breaking into his local telephone company's computer records. When confronted, he denies sending the messages, claiming someone else must have been using his account. But he also says that "everybody knows that X is gay." X belongs to LISTSERVs of gay people and sometimes wears makeup in the dorm, so how could a message that says X is gay be considered slander? Your experience tells you that this obnoxious student probably did send the offensive messages and that he has the skills and mind-set to have broken into X's account. However, you cannot prove anything, yet.

### THE CASE OF THE IRASCIBLE RESEARCHER

As the person in charge of campus computing, you get an irate telephone call from a professor well-known both for his research reputation and for his miserable treatment of graduate students, particularly women graduate students. He's complaining that a graduate student doing research for him has left the university without giving him the data she had been working on for a joint project, soon to be published. The professor has been told by the systems people that only an account holder can have access to an account. The professor is unmoved; he wants access to the student's account *now*. After all, the research is his, the data are his, and the graduate student is his, too.

These scenarios, amalgams of ones submitted to the War Stories Project of EDUCOM or recounted in many conversations over the past several years, illustrate conflicts among competing values, such as the right to privacy, freedom of speech, the right to be free of abusive or offensive speech, the right to ownership of information or data for which one has paid, and so on.

In each case, the institutional responses were different, sometimes very different. In the case of the hateful harasser, one college's response was to investigate with almost FBI-like intensity, until it had evidence against the harasser, and then to cut him off from any access to computing resources for the rest of his college career; another's was to take the case to the judicial board, which recommended counseling for both students and a stint of community service for the harasser. In the case of the irascible researcher, one institution's response was to

From *EDUCOM Review*, Vol. 27, No. 4, July/August 1992, pp. 18-21. For information about this article or *EDUCOM Review*, contact: EDUCOM, 1112 16th Street, NW, Suite 600, Washington, DC 20036, (202) 872-4200.

transfer all data files to the professor, on the theory that he actually did own them; another's was to refuse access to the data until *they* obtained permission from the graduate student.

Each of these and similar scenarios have been enacted in many academic institutions over the past decade. Although the issues that crop up are virtually the same at each institution, the responses vary widely. It might be expected that after all this time we would be closer to consensus on how to handle them. One of the aims of the War Stories Project is to get a better idea about why the same event evokes such wildly divergent reactions.

Preliminary project results suggest a number of possible explanations for the varying responses.

• Campus culture (a glib phrase that occasionally means something tangible) dictates the tone of official reactions to incidents. For instance, a service academy's reaction to the irascible professor's request for "his" data might be closer to "the person in authority must be right" end of the spectrum than that of a liberal, four-year private institution.

• The presence or absence of a code of conduct explicitly about or including "computer abuses" will affect the process by which they are resolved. Campuses whose codes of conduct do not include acceptable "computer behavior" have a hard time justifying disciplinary or punitive actions they take in response to violations. Students will claim that they didn't understand, didn't know, didn't think about it because it wasn't mentioned. Some will say that if it wasn't forbidden, it must be allowed. Their litigious parents and the parents' lawyers will try to drive through the loophole. Some administrators fear being sued if they take a stand against behavior that isn't explicitly mentioned in an official publication. It's harder to use these excuses if the campus has a code of conduct that does explicitly mention these issues or if students sign a contract before they use campus computing resources.

• When different official bodies are responsible for treating "computer abuses," they respond differently. Their charges are different, their resources are different, the personalities of their staffs are different, and their "bags of responses" are different. Technical people tend to respond with technical solutions, judicial people with legalistic ones, campus policemen with policelike ones, and so on.

• Campuses that are part of a state system respond differently from their private counterparts because they have the additional burden of being bound by state laws and scrutinized by state legislators. Students at state universities have more claim to First Amendment rights than do students at private universities. Administrators at state universities have to explain and defend campus policies all the time—particularly at budget time—in ways private university officials do not.

• On an individual level, the personalities of the people in charge of responding to "computer abuses" may affect the philosophy of the response, specifically in situations when only one person handles these issues. One vice provost of information technology said he does whatever he is told by any official higher in the chain of command than he is, no matter what he privately thinks about it, because his definition of loyalty includes following orders.

Another person given the same order successfully changed her president's mind by appealing to his belief in the benefits of having the students discuss the issues. Her definition of loyalty included educating her president about the conflicting values.

• Possibly the most significant reason why "computer abuses" are handled so disparately is that for too long they have been handled by too few people, whose major responsibilities have not prepared them for the job: the computing services people. We owe the computer services people a great debt for taking on the responsibility when nobody else would and for educating the rest of the campus. But by continuing to accept the idea that because "they brought the technology onto the campus in the first place, letting loose all these disasters, they'd jolly well better take care of the problems," they help perpetuate the fallacy that they are dealing with something new and founded totally in the technology itself.

A bank clerk who steals money using the banking network is not considered "a network problem," but a thief. Likewise, harassing people over the network is not a network problem. Copying software and breaking into computer accounts are not computer problems. They are human problems which use a computer or network as a tool. The technology contributes to the way the crimes are committed, but it is not the cause of the crime, so technologically bound solutions will be unsatisfactory. We don't close down hardware stores because criminals use hammers to break into houses, and we don't ask the store manager to solve the problem. We don't stop building and driving cars because thugs use them for getaways, and we don't ask the dealers to take care of the problem.

But too many of us still think the computer center is solely responsible for preventing people from using their wares in antisocial ways. And too many computer services people accept that responsibility.

Computing services people should use their knowledge and tools to create an environment for research, teaching, and learning, in which people can be trained to use the information technology tools that will be necessary to life in the twenty-first century. This means installing reasonable safeguards, such as passwords, tracking software, and software protections, so that people can and will use computers and computer networks comfortably, humanely, safely, and effectively; so that users understand their citizenship obligations to one another and to the institution; and so that the institution acts as a responsible member of any consortia to which it belongs and as a responsible party to contracts.

However, computer people are not the only ones responsible for creating the right climate. People whose responsibility it is to educate students about and handle violations of acceptable behavior are ultimately responsible for responding to unacceptable computer behavior. The entire institution must deal with "computer abuses" the same way it deals with any kind of abuse: fairly, firmly, consistently, and in keeping with the mission of the institution to educate.

How do institutions begin to create this environment? After listening to people in colleges and universities who have dealt with such issues, several lessons are apparent. First, a clear policy or set of policies that cover such incidents must be developed and become a part of regular institutional policies.

In many cases, the computer center has been the first and only organization to write a policy or invent a contract for users. If the only policy that deals with "computer abuses" is one written by the computer center, it's time to bring in the groups that handle other misbehavior on campus, such as the judicial boards, the academic councils, the campus police, and the student affairs offices, and to acknowledge that they already have responsibility for handling "computer abuses" and in fact can handle them in the usual ways. The "computer" policy can then be subsumed in student and faculty handbooks or codes of conduct, at which point computer center people can act as technical advisers, sources of information, and consultants.

If a college or university does not have language in its codes of conduct to cover computer-mediated misbehavior and wants to understand the issues, computer center staff can advise and can get from file servers examples of institutional computer policies. Even though thoughtful people still disagree on the form of such policies, human misbehaviors that are carried out through computers or over computer networks should be understood as examples of what is generally not acceptable.

Because most computer abuses are committed by people who simply haven't thought the issues through, everybody needs to think through and talk through the underlying unethical or antisocial acts that often get obscured by our fascination with or horror at the ways in which the acts were committed. Reaching through a computer network and taking someone's work is the high-tech equivalent of inappropriately photocopying or photographing the work. The same amount of damage is done with the new method as with the old. The understandings, social contracts, and rules and laws that apply to one apply to the other as well—or they should.

And that is another lesson: The time has come to demystify "computer abuses," to strip away from the act the tool with which it is committed, and to concentrate on the abusers and what they have done to each other. "Computer abuses" should carry the same sanctions and consequences as the same misbehaviors committed with more ordinary tools. The consequences for harassing someone over a computer network should be consistent with those for harassing over the telephone or postal networks.

If we're serious about expecting computer users, most of them students, to adhere to social norms, then we have to talk to them about acts and their consequences, about social norms and the reasons we have them, in a much more serious and committed way than we have been doing. And we have to clean up our own acts, otherwise we have, and deserve to have, no credibility with our

## Too many of us still think the computer center is solely responsible for preventing people from using their wares in antisocial ways

students. A common, sad finding to emerge from the War Stories Project is that often the worst offenders on a college campus are faculty members. It is odd that people whose reputation often depends on the fruits of intellectual labors can so cavalierly steal copyrighted software, not recognizing what they are doing, or, worse, excuse in themselves behavior they condemn in others.

"Computer abuses"—those flashy, high-tech, sometimes clever, newsworthy events—give us a perfect opportunity to educate people. How can we, as educators, pass up those chances?

We don't have to be professionals to talk about ethical and social norms. It's enough merely to be human beings who have thought about and struggled with ethical dilemmas and, most important, made mistakes from which we have learned.

Nor should we shrink from discussing behaviors and their consequences because some people believe or fear that discussing them is the same as prescribing the answers. The important thing is to ask people to think about their actions and who is affected by them and to try to figure out the likely consequences for everybody. It is the habit of thinking about such things that has value, not necessarily the conclusions that are reached while the student is at college.

Nor is it useful to succumb to ethical exhaustion and conclude that the problems are so widespread, so apparently sanctioned, so easy to do and hard to stop that it is useless to make the effort. To say nothing in the face of misdeeds is to shirk responsibility and become a party to the misdeed.

Let us use the educational opportunities presented by computer and network misdeeds to teach students (and faculty) to think about ethical and social norms and the reasons human societies all have them. Let us use them to teach students to arrive at community standards and experience all the issues that arise when a community tries to agree on standards. Let us use them as another legitimate way for students to participate in university decisions that will affect their lives while they are with us, and later. Let us use them to make ourselves—faculty and staff—into the kind of role models we can be proud of.

# Computer Imaging: A New Branch of Science that Can Turn Truth on Its Head

## Stephen Strauss

Let's call it *Rodney King's* contribution to your science awareness.

Most of us have tried to imagine how the *Rodney King* jury was able to take what looked like a gang of Los Angeles policemen bashing a prostrate motorist and stand the videotape evidence on its head.

Running the tape frame by frame, defence lawyers were somehow able to convince 12 jurors that what they were seeing was a pod of beleaguered policemen delicately defending themselves against a monster crazy.

And what clearer and more graphic way is there to show the perils for science of visual data. If seeing is believing, then simple seeing is anathema to science. Science doesn't want to believe; it wants to know.

To avoid being too sight-conscious, fastidious scientists have always tried to express as much of their observations as possible into numbers. To quote Lord Kelvin: "If you can measure that of which you speak, and can express it by a number, you know something of your subject; but if you cannot measure it, your knowledge is meagre and unsatisfactory."

Then came Mr. Magic Number Cruncher—the computer. Suddenly researchers were able to generate thousands and millions and billions of data points, with no end in sight. Indeed, the U.S. National Aeronautics and Space Administration is building a series of Earth-observing satellites that it believes will generate data amounting to 1,000 times the amount of text currently stored in the U.S. Library of Congress. Every day two trillion bits of information about vegetative cover, atmospheric moisture, temperature, etc., will hail down on Earth's scientific community.

How is anyone ever going to understand this information glut? The answer has increasingly been: Make a moving picture out of it. Simulations of the evolution of the universe, chemical interactions on a molecular scale, the opening and closing of ozone holes have all used images to express a mathematics too complicated for the human mind to grasp. In less than a decade, scientific visualization has moved from what some saw as a kind of Hollywoodian trickery to what now is being termed the third branch of science. That is, it joins experimental data and mathematical formulae as elements of scientific proof.

However, the spectre of the *Rodney King* reverse-image jurors has begun to enter into the expanding universe of visualization. Increasingly, researchers are presenting moving pictures—often with sound or three-dimension cues built in—as their entire data. Arresting stuff, but how scientifically true are the pretty pictures?

Sometimes it looks as if the answer is: Not very. Recently, NASA has been chastised for committing cosmic cos-metological crimes. Apparently some of those wonderful images of Earth's sister worlds and brother moons were doctored. Low-lying, almost invisible Venusian volcanoes were made 22.5 times taller than they really are.

So egregious was the alteration that one puckish investigator called for the formation of a Flat Venus Society, "to promote the fact that our sister planet is mostly flat rolling hills."

And another roaring debate emerged after NASA released images of the asteroid Gaspara that showed it to be butterscotch yellow. Members of the imaging team demanded a true colour image of the pocked-face rock, a transformation that would make Gaspara grey. NASA critics have intimated that the agency has a built-in bias toward producing dramatic, colourful pictures that, on some not-too subliminal level, graphically communicate to the public that tax dollars have been well-spent.

For most people, this may seem rather too in-group and ingrown. However, be apprised that all the truth-in-advertising issues underlying scientific simulations are coming your way.

A full-bodied forensic-simulation industry has already begun to gather steam. SEA Inc. of Columbus, Ohio, tells potential lawyer clients, "We have always believed that the most effective way to prove our point to juries is to create an image in their collective minds that pleads our case and is so vivid that it cannot be forgotten."

From *The Globe & Mail*, July 4, 1992, p. D8. Reprinted by permission.

## 5. COMPUTER ETHICS AND CRIME

Based on evidence gathered at an accident scene, companies have produced simulations that seem to show crashes from above, from inside the vehicles in question, from the point of view of bystanders and in ways that simulate nighttime visibility.

Fascinating, but is it real? Is there something of what Waterloo University visualization critic William Cowan calls "invisible smoothing" that has made the images a better television but a distorted reality? And what has been left out? And how will a graphically illiterate juror know something has been dropped? Can there be standards that simulations must adhere to—some judicial definition of when a simulation crosses the border into reality?

And what will happen when rival lawyers hire simulation firms that come up with two highly convincing but contradictory scenarios, complete with virtual-reality graphics, that seem to put the jurors right inside the car as the train smashes into it?

Something tells me we may yet fondly recall the simple days when our biggest problem with video realities was figuring out how 12 apparently sane Californians could turn a brutal beating inside out.

# EVIDENCE SET IN MOTION

## *Computer Animation in the Courtroom: The Mitchell Brothers Murder Trial*

## Alexander Jason

*Alexander Jason is a ballistics consultant and investigative technologist with the ANITE Group in Pinole, Calif. He is the creator of several videos on firearm and ballistic subjects and he is also VP of the International Wound Ballistics Association and Editor of its Journal,* The Wound Ballistics Review.

Jim Mitchell drove to his brother Artie's house in Corte Madera, Calif., on February 27, 1991. It was about 10 p.m. He parked two blocks away and walked with a fully loaded .22 caliber, lever-action, rifle and a loaded five-shot .38 caliber revolver in a shoulder holster. Once he arrived in front of the house, he took out a knife and slashed two tires on his brother's car parked in the driveway. He then waited a few minutes. Inside, Artie and his girlfriend, erotic dancer Julie Bajo, were naked in bed discussing plans for a vacation in Mexico. Their conversation stopped suddenly when they heard noises from the front of the house. Julie later described them as sounding like doors slamming.

Artie shouted out, asking who was out there. There was no answer, just more loud noises. He got out of bed and asked Julie for something to wear. She handed him some pants and, as he slipped them on, he asked her to give him a "bat." She quickly looked for one in the closet, but Artie told her to forget it, that he'd got something. He opened the bedroom door carrying only a half-filled Heineken beer bottle.

Julie had taken the phone and gone into the bedroom closet. She dialed 911 and as soon as the dispatcher said, "911 emergency," Julie said softly, "23 Mohawk" (the address) and told the dispatcher that they'd heard shots. As she talked, two more shots could be heard and Julie began to scream out to Artie, telling him to not go "out there." Artie's voice could be heard asking loudly, "What's going on?" There were more shots. Fifty-six seconds after the call began Artie lay dead in the bathroom down the hall shot through his right eye. The .22 caliber bullet penetrated through his brain and exited out his skull behind his left ear. Julie would not learn of Artie's death until much later.

The Twin Cities police response to Julie's call was quick. One unit was only a few blocks away. Ofc. Ken Haas quickly terminated his traffic stop and responded to the call of "shots fired" with his lights and siren off. He knew the address and planned to pull up a few houses before number 23 and approach carefully. As he stopped, he noticed a man walking away from him down the sidewalk. His head was almost hidden inside an opened umbrella and he was limping.

Haas didn't know who he was or where he came from but he knew the guy was hinky. He asked him to stop. The man kept walking, not even looking toward him. Haas shouted, "Stop, police!" There was no response. When he shouted his order a third time, the man moved quickly, jumping behind a parked car and ducking down. Haas moved in, his pistol out and with a finger on the trigger. He could see the crouched man desperately trying to pull something from his pants. He recognized the rifle butt and his finger tightened on the trigger as the rifle was pulled all the way out. Suddenly another officer came up behind the man with pistol drawn and told him to put his hands up or get his head blown off. The man slowly complied.

The man was Jim Mitchell; one half of the notorious San Francisco-based Mitchell Brothers' porno movie and "sexual fantasy" theater business. He was arrested and charged with the murder of his brother Artie. He made no statements.

From a forensic aspect, it was an unusual case and one which serves as an excellent example of the need to carefully preserve and collect physical evidence—even when the case appears "solved" at the start. The police had a suspect who had been arrested carrying the murder weapon (the rifle) down his pant leg. The victim was dead and the only other potential witness to the incident had been hiding in the back bedroom's closet. She never actually saw the suspect or the shooting. Jim Mitchell refused to state what had happened. The case could only be built on the dead body, the gun, and other items of physical evidence which included a taped recording of the 911 call.

What had been regarded as a simple, "open and shut" case began to get more complicated when the suspect's attorneys started leaking their strategy to the press.

Jim Mitchell would not deny he shot his brother, but claimed he only fired in panic when Artie advanced toward him in a threatening manner: essentially a self-defense strategy. Because the suspect was the only living person who could testify as to what actually happened, the prosecution realized their sole source of objective information would be the physical evidence.

## 5. COMPUTER ETHICS AND CRIME

Every bit of evidence was now very important to determine if the suspect's claim was valid or false.

---

*After the judge ordered some alterations the computer animation was admitted as evidence. I was later told it was the first use of 3-D computer animation in a criminal trial.*

---

The Marin County District Attorney's office realized the need to have a ballistic reconstruction performed to learn if the five shots on the tape and the three made before the 911 call could be sequenced and matched to the various bullet holes and impact marks on the walls, the bedroom door, and the three wounds in the victim's body. They called in Luke Haag, of Forensic Science Services in Phoenix, Ariz. Haag is one of the most respected ballistic reconstructionists in the world. He asked me to assist him on the case and he also called in acoustics expert, Harry Hollien, a professor of linguistics and criminal justice at the University of Florida, to analyze the 911 audio tape.

After a computer analysis, Hollien was able to locate five gunshot impulses on the audio tape. After further tests, he was able to identify them as having the acoustical signature of a .22 rifle. What was most revealing was the timing of the shots. There were some very long pauses between shots (4.8, 15.5, and 28.3 seconds) which contradict any claim of "panic" shooting.

As we went over the evidence, examined the crime scene, and began the reconstruction, it became obvious the events in this case would be difficult for the jury to understand when presented verbally. We realized that some form of visual aid would be very helpful. Haag, knowing my experience with computers, asked if I could create some sort of computer animation to show the events. I spent several weeks researching animation software and finally bought "Autodesk 3D Studio" ($3,000) made by the Autodesk Corporation of San Rafael, Calif.

I began working on the project as a test case not knowing if I could produce anything practical or useful. After two weeks of intensive work surrounded by crime scene photos, evidence reports, and transcripts, I created an animation showing the victim's house, bullets being fired, the door opening, and the victim moving down the hallway and hiding in the bathroom after being shot twice. I then showed the victim taking the fatal shot into his head and slumping to the floor where he ended up in the same position as shown in the crime scene photos. Each shot was labeled to show the sequence and timing. I also created an additional animation segment showing the same events but from a top "bird's eye" view to provide the jury with a good perspective of the crime scene.

The District Attorney John Posey found the animation effective and after several days of revisions, he moved to have it admitted as evidence. The defense strongly objected and tried all sorts of tactics to prevent its being admitted. (One of the defense attorneys privately described the animation as potentially "devastating" to their side). After the judge ordered some alterations the computer animation was admitted as evidence. I was later told it was the first use of 3-D computer animation in a criminal trial.

The benefits of using a computer animation are many, but primary is the animation's ability to communicate; to help the jury understand the events. One reporter who had sat through virtually all the month-long trial testimony saw the animation and said, "Oh, *now* I understand what happened." Her reaction was typical of many others who saw the animation and it underscored the difficulty in trying to understand the prosecution's view of the events from the trial's verbal testimony.

Much of the testimony from Haag and other forensic experts was very difficult to follow. For example, a typical description would be: "The victim then walked approximately eight feet west from the east bedroom. He was near the doorway of the bathroom located north of the east to west hallway. The shot was fired from approximately 26 feet east and a few degrees north and perforated his torso before exiting in yaw in striking the south end of the west bedroom doorway 45.3 inches above floor level and then deflecting into the south bedroom where it struck the south wall at 62.5 inches above floor level and was found on a table at the north end of the bedroom." Such testimony is difficult to comprehend under the best of circumstances and particularly difficult when it is constantly interrupted by objections.

The jury found Jim Mitchell guilty of voluntary manslaughter. The prosecution had sought a first-degree murder conviction, but the verdict revealed the jury did not accept the defendant's self-defense claim, nor the various assertions that he had "accidentally" shot his brother.

There was, of course, more to the trial than computer animation. To put it in perspective, the computer animation file was labeled "Exhibit 95b": One bit of evidence in a long trial with many other items. Some question whether computer animation is "unfair" because it is so visually powerful that it could overwhelm the jurors. I say that no computer animation will ever come close to the power of a persuasive attorney.

---

*Forensic animation is not simply a representation of what either side "thinks" happened. The animation must be based on physical evidence and/or the testimony of witnesses.*

---

There are two important points to be understood about computer animation: First, the animation is *not* created by the computer or the animation program. The computer and the software program "know" nothing about ballistics or forensics. They only allow a trained operator to create a scene and then move (animate) human figures, doors, cars, bullets, or anything else. Computer animation may be new in the criminal courtroom but it is *not* new technology requiring legal validation (like DNA "printing"). The computer is really nothing more than a high-tech slide projector that displays images very fast providing the illusion of motion. If you would be allowed to show a series of drawings in court, then it would not matter whether the drawings were created by hand or by a computer. Nor would it matter whether the artist drew each drawing by hand in front of the jury or if they were simply displayed on a computer monitor.

Second, forensic animation (or any other court exhibit or evidenceiem) is not simply a representation of what either side "thinks" happened. The animation must be based on physical evidence and/or the testimony of witnesses.

I was very careful to "build" the walls of the house with the exact dimensions, the human figures to the right height and width, the angles of the bullet trajectories, the exact placement of bullet impact points, and the location of the victim each time he was shot. I also omitted emotional elements like blood splattering or pained facial reactions. I tried to keep the animation as close to "just the facts" as possible, and I only

started the computer animation *after* Luke Haag's ballistic reconstruction was completed. This involved an examination of all the physical evidence (bullets and bullet fragments, cartridge casings, the firearm used, the crime lab evidence reports, photos, autopsy data, and an actual examination of the crime scene that included shining lasers through bullet holes to determine actual angles, trajectories, and positions.

Although I have recently been creating forensic animations on other (non-ballistic) homicides, automobile accidents, medical, and other subjects, I only do so with the approval of a technical expert. Animation can only be used in a courtroom if there is an acknowledged expert to support all the details shown. With a proper legal foundation, computer animation can be an effective new tool in law enforcement.

*Editor's Note:*

Police readers can obtain a VHS video tape of the animation along with some background media coverage and legal commentary. Send $12 to: ANITE Group, PO Box 375, Pinole, CA 94564.

# WORLD OF ELECTRONIC GAMES: COMPUTER GAME ETHICS

## *WHAT CULTURAL VALUES DO COMPUTER GAMES COMMUNICATE TO THEIR USERS?*

## Sara Reeder

Consider these notes from the computer-gaming press:

In 1983, Atari seeks to halt the distribution of *Custer's Revenge,* an independently produced game in which the player's objective is to rape an Indian woman bound to a post.

In 1987, one of the most popular Macintosh programs on the market is *MacPlaymate,* an adult-oriented game in which the player undresses an animated woman and stimulates her with a wide variety of sex toys.

In the summer of 1990, California Assemblywoman Sally Tanner introduces a bill to prohibit the depiction of alcohol and cigarettes in computer games distributed in the state. The bill is defeated in committee.

In 1991, an underground game creates a small flurry in the American computer press. The game, which is circulated on BBSs in Europe, puts players in charge of a Nazi concentration camp and rewards them for the quantity and brutality of their executions.

For game designers, software publishers, and parents who are already uneasy about their children's all-encompassing Nintendo obsessions, news items like these strike an ominous chord. As the novelty of personal computers wears off and electronic games find their way into the mainstream of American culture, thoughtful developers and con-

sumers are starting to face the tough ethical questions. What effect do these games have on kids? Why are they so violent? And, perhaps most centrally, what cultural values do computer games communicate to their users?

The questions aren't new, but they're becoming more pressing as the market grows. The time is fast approaching when game designers and publishers must reckon with the moral questions that have dogged their colleagues in other media for decades.

### Is the Medium the Message?

"Computer games are definitely not value-free," asserts Chris Crawford, a veteran designer noted for the strong ethical content of his games. "We can't argue that they're mindless entertainment with zero moral value, because it's obvious that there is some form of cultural communication going on whenever someone sits down to play a game. And I think it's very appropriate for people to be concerned about what messages are being communicated."

Roberta Williams, head of development for Sierra On-Line and designer of dozens of games for both children and adults, agrees. "Computer games communicate values the same way any other medium you watch or participate in—movies, books, TV, or magazines. And I'm

not convinced that we should hold games to any different moral standards than we hold the movie or TV industries to."

According to Crawford, computer games do get extra scrutiny, mainly because they're perceived as children's entertainment. "Freedom of speech is paramount when you're creating entertainment for adults, who are better able to accept or reject the values presented to them. But we've also established the legal principle that freedom is appropriately restrained when you're addressing children. Right now, computer games are closely associated with children, and I think that the public debate about their moral content comes largely out of that association. Our image as a 'kiddie medium' gives us increased exposure to censorship."

### Death, War, and Gore

As any parent can tell you, most of the ethical concerns about computer games centers around their notoriously high levels of violence. "It's the one issue that cuts directly to the heart of the industry," says Crawford. Computer game violence comes in a variety of flavors, including the following.

Repetitive death games in which the player's character dies over and over. After each "death," you typically insert another quarter or reload the saved game and start over. (Nervous adults have expressed concern that kids who spend too much time with driving simulations might actually think you can drive that way.)

Military games that simulate (and some say glorify) war. "A goodly portion of Americans find the rather strident militarism of these games objectionable," says Crawford, who has designed several war simulations. "They often present war as an exciting adventure, a noble quest by brave men and women. In short, they tell the player that war is fun."

In his games, Crawford attempts to redirect this message by working some humanity into the manual or right into the game itself. Take, for example, his upcoming game, *Patton Strikes Back.*

"After each major battle, there are these interruptions that stop the game to tell you personal stories about Patton and other people in the war—how this battle affected them personally. Some of them are quite graphic. People will still be entertained, but I hope they also walk away with a deeper sense of how horrific a real battle is."

Sid Meier of MicroProse, a company known for its war simulations, takes a different attitude. "You can make a case that war is full of terrible consequences—but I don't think that's news to anyone. There are a lot of movies and books about war, with a lot of different points of view. And I think that's because 'war is terrible' is not the only lesson to be learned; there's also the decision making and leadership and personal growth that occur because people have been through that situation. In our simulations, we want you to come to understand the decision process, the tradeoffs that are involved, the kinds of things people in battle are faced with.

Shoot-'em-up games in which the object is to blow away everything that moves. "It's instructive that all the early computer games were shoot-'em-ups," notes Meier. "In the beginning, it was just technically easier to do those kinds of games. And people didn't know what computer games were all about, so you had to make it clear who the good guys and the bad guys were. It's easy to do that in a battle context." These days, notes Meier, the last bastion of the shoot'em-up is "your classic Nintendo game, where violence is the focal point of everything that happens."

"This sort of generalized blood-thirstiness, which a lot of games have, makes people very uncomfortable, and I think rightly so," muses Crawford. "This sort of rampant, dehumanized killing generates an aura of tawdriness that does our industry no favors."

---

## IF OUR IDEAS OF CONFLICT ARE LIMITED TO VIOLENCE, WE'VE GOT A LOT TO LEARN ABOUT GAME DESIGN

---

**Blood and gore.** Designers are widely divided about the morality of showing up-close-and-personal scenes of blood and death. "Of the games I've done, I've stayed away from gore; I don't think it adds anything to the game to show blood and arms and legs flying around," says Meier.

Tom Loughry, who designed the close-range combat simulation *Gunboat* for Accolade, wrestled long and hard before coming to the opposite conclusion. "The fact is, when you shoot people, they bleed and die. You're not telling them the truth about war if you sanitize the death scenes."

Why are computer games so violent? According to most of the designers interviewed, they don't need to be. "Violence is a symptom of lazy design," asserts Crawford. "All games must have conflict of some kind, and violence is the most direct and intense form of conflict there is. As the industry matures, we should move away from it, but for that to happen, people have to make the effort to design games that take other approaches."

Several thoughtful designers and publishers are already making the effort. "We've all but banned death from our games," boasts Brian Moriarty, a senior game designer at Lucasfilm Games. "The possibility of death is a convenient and easy way to create game conflict, which is why you see so much of it. But I don't buy the notion that you need it to create dramatic tension. There's almost always a more elegant way to move the plot along if the designer is willing to think a little more creatively. Our perception is that people equate death with failure. And failure is not fun."

Among Moriarty's more recent games is *Loom*, "which took this idea even further—not only can't you die, you can't fail. The fun of the game is in making choices for your character. Like all good stories, it also has a strong moral.

"After all, computer games do teach people things about the world," he concludes. "If our ideas of conflict are limited to violence, we've got a lot to learn about art, storytelling, and game design."

Moriarty, Crawford, and Williams project that shoot-'em-ups, war games, and other types of violent games will soon be only small niches in a much broader market. In fact, the game shelf at your local Egghead might ultimately be as diverse as your local video rental store with a full spectrum of comedy, drama, mystery, adventure, and children's software. And the analogy may extend one step further to include X-rated adult games behind a curtain in the back of the store.

### For Adults Only

Games with strong sexual content have been around almost as long as personal computers. Along with the infamous *Custer's Revenge*, the more notable efforts include *Interlude*, a 1982 text adventure that contained several X-rated scenarios; *Leather*

*Goddesses of Phobos,* a 1986 game that was actually a lot tamer than its hype led one to think; and Sierra's Leisure Suit Larry series, a tacky spoof on the hot-tubs-and-gold-chains singles lifestyle.

Perhaps the most famous of all, however, are *MacPlaymate* (1986) and its second incarnation, *Virtual Valerie* (1989). "They're probably the most pirated games in the history of Macintosh," sighs creator Mike Saenz, who cobbled *MacPlaymate* together in just three days. "I don't even think the games were very erotic. I did them for a laugh because I think the idea of interactive sexual computer entertainment is patently absurd. *MacPlaymate* was a spoof of all the fetishistic trappings of the average male's preferred sexual imagery.

Saenz says there's no question that his two products objectify women as sexual playthings. "It's like having your own 'Stepford date-on-a-disk'; you don't even have to send her roses," he muses. "But I was hoping that the absurdity of it would sink in, that by putting it into such bold, simplified relief, men would realize how unreal it is to expect women to behave that way sexually. I was hoping to make some of this outrageousness clear. But I overestimated my audience; it ended up in the hands of a bunch of nerdy guys who'd never talked to a woman besides their mother.

---

## WE DECIDED AT THE TIME WE DID LARRY THAT THAT WAS OUR ABSOLUTE LIMIT

---

Although it seems that there are always one or two popular adult-oriented games on the market at any given time, most mainstream publishers regard X-rated games as a very small niche. "Every company has its moral or ethical limits," says Williams. "There might be some company that decides it wants to make money doing *Playboy*-type

games. But that's not what Sierra is about. We decided at the time we did Larry that that was our absolute limit, as far as the R-rated stuff is concerned."

Williams adds that some of her designers approached her about doing a more explicit game, but she refused. "It's not just that I don't like the way women are portrayed in these games. It's also that we'd be shooting ourselves in the foot if we sold them. We might sell quite a few to the men who buy that kind of thing, but over the long run, we'd lose the respect of our market. Even those same men would hesitate to buy our kids' games for their families—and women wouldn't go near us. It would be a long-term loss for us. If some other company decided that that's who they were, fine, but we're in the business to make software for everybody."

Saenz admits to feeling a similar backlash. He recently published a mainstream fantasy game called *Spaceship Warlock*—"an old-fashioned space opera that's nostalgic in a Flash Gordon/Buck Rogers sort of way, complete with sophomorically bombastic dialogue. Unfortunately, if you really try to capture that 'golden age of science fiction' feel, it will inevitably be somewhat chauvinistic, although it looks very liberated compared to, say, the first Star Trek series. Still, because of *MacPlaymate* and *Valerie,* people are looking for me to have this attitude. It turns out that there are a whole bunch of people who love what I do—a lot of closet Mike Saenz fans out there and a lot of other people who think, 'That guy's sick.' I've been typecast as a terrible misogynist."

### Of Demons, Drugs, and Censorship

Sex and violence may be the big ethical issues, but they're not the only ones. Over the years, the television, film, recording, and publishing industries have felt pressure to watch their language (as in the recording

industry's well-publicized debate over parental warning stickers), Just Say No (as part of the federal government's much-ballyhooed War on Drugs), and beware of demons (at the behest of the fundamentalist Christian movement). Through it all, though, computer game developers have managed to stay well out of the range of fire.

You would think that Mike Saenz, for example, would be an obvious target. "But none of the pressure groups seem to have found me yet," he marvels. "I haven't heard from Tipper Gore or Women Against Pornography. I think the hardliners and fascists must be very small groups that exert a lot of focused pressure—and right now they're going after the record companies."

"Sure, we've all gotten letters from parents who scream that hack-and-slash fantasy games are inspired by the devil," concurs Crawford, "but the numbers are so small that we tend to think of it as a marginal concern."

As computer games go mainstream, though, they're starting to attract at least some attention. And, surprisingly, one of the early battlegrounds wasn't violence or sex, but drug abuse. "Drugs and tobacco just aren't usually a part of the context of most games," says Moriarty. Crawford echoed this, adding that "sometimes players will come across a vial that says, 'Drink me,' like in *Alice in Wonderland,* and you float over the river or something as a result of taking it. But nobody's ever suggested that this promotes drug abuse."

Because designers and publishers regard drugs as such a nonissue, the introduction of California Assembly Bill 3280 in June 1990 took them completely by surprise.

The bill, introduced by Assemblywoman Sally Tanner (D-El Monte), would have prohibited designers from placing any alcohol or tobacco company logos in games or showing characters holding or using alcohol or tobacco products. Even though it was drafted with the loftiest of intentions, the computer game industry was quick to perceive a threat and moved quickly to block the bill. "We ship a children's product called *Mixed-Up Mother Goose*, which has been widely used in classrooms for years, says Williams. "In the game, King Cole loses his pipe, and the child helps him find it. It didn't make sense. Under this bill, reading a book of nursery rhymes would be perfectly legal, but I could go to jail for animating the same nursery rhyme. I don't like my kids seeing people smoke or drink, either, but to be restricted where other media aren't isn't fair."

### A Kinder, Gentler Future?

All the designers and publishers interviewed for this article were optimistic that the ethical nature of computer games will continue to improve as the audience broadens in numbers and sophistication.

"Right now, we're locked into a traditional, hobbyist market that has a specific set of expectations about the kinds of games they want," Moriarty observes. "A lot of us want to move beyond those expectations but feel held back. Still, I'm convinced that there are a lot more computer owners out there who are interested in using their machines for entertain-

ment but aren't attracted to the traditional offerings."

He's pleased that *Loom* has been very popular with first-time gamers and women—two groups outside the core market—but complains that publishers are often reluctant to support games that fall outside of standard genres, even if they might open up the world of computer gaming to a broader market.

---

## A RATINGS SYSTEM WOULD BE USEFUL BECAUSE YOU'D KNOW WHERE BOUNDARIES EXIST

---

As game developers look toward the big time, they're taking their cues from the film and recording industries. Many publishers have long adhered to their own internal standards. At Sierra, for example, games are categorized as either adult games, like *Leisure Suit Larry* and *Space Quest*; family games, like *King's Quest*, that children and parents will likely play together; or children's games, in which blood, death, and violence are entirely banned. "Our goal is to make software for everyone," says Williams.

There's also widespread talk of an industrywide rating system, based on the system the MPAA uses to rate movies. "We're kind of in this window where we don't have a ratings system yet because we're still a new industry and not all the pieces are together," Saenz says. "But I think a ratings system would be useful because you'd know where boundaries exist and it would help both the developers and the audience clear up a lot of the confusion in the marketplace. I don't want to limit freedom of expression, and a rating system might be one way to protect it."

Crawford points out that, as with books and movies, the truly outrageous games appeal only to very small and specialized niche markets. (The numbers bear this out. *MacPlaymate*, despite its tremendous popularity, was only available through mail order. The concentration-camp game is only distributed via BBS, and no American game designer interviewed had actually seen it.) "Mass marketing will be the key to improving the ethical climate in computer games," Crawford predicts. "You can only push people so fast, but the messages we communicate will certainly improve as we slowly learn how to design games for a larger audience."

# "The playground bullies are learning how to type"

*Computer crimes committed by a new generation of hacker hoods might cost anywhere from $500 million to $5 billion a year. Whatever the number, it's clear that a computer crime wave is reaching epidemic proportions.*

## William G. Flanagan and Brigid McMenamin

Leonard Rose, a 33-year-old computer consultant and father of two, is also a felon. He recently completed 8½ months in a federal prison camp in North Carolina, plus 2 months in a halfway house. His crime? Passing along by computer some software code filched from Bell Labs by an AT&T employee. Rose, who now lives in California, says he is still dazed by the harsh punishment he received. "The Secret Service," he says, "made an example of me."

Maybe so. But if so, why are the cops suddenly cracking down on the hackers? Answer: because serious computer crime is beginning to reach epidemic proportions. The authorities are struggling to contain the crimes, or at least slow their rapid growth.

Rose agrees the hacker world is rapidly changing for the worse. "You're getting a different sort of person now," he says of the hacker community. "You're seeing more and more criminals using computers."

One well-known veteran hacker, who goes by the name Cheshire Catalyst, puts it more bluntly: "The playground bullies are coming indoors and learning how to type."

Rose and the Cheshire Catalyst are talking about a new breed of computer hackers. These aren't just thrill-seeking, boastful kids, but serious (if boastful) cybercrooks. They use computers and telecommunications links partly for stunt hacking—itself a potentially dangerous and costly game—but also to steal valuable information, software, phone service, credit card numbers and cash. And they pass along and even sell their services and techniques to others—including organized crime.

Hacker hoods often exaggerate their escapades, but there is no doubt that their crimes are extensive and becoming more so at an alarming rate. Says Bruce Sterling, a noted cyberpunk novelist and author of the nonfiction *The Hacker Crackdown* (Bantam Books, 1992, $23): "Computer intrusion, as a nonprofit act of intellectual exploration and mastery, is in slow decline, at least in the United States; but electronic fraud, especially telecommunications crime, is growing by leaps and bounds."

Who are these hacker hoods and what do they do for a living? Take the 19-year-old kid who calls himself Kimble—he is a very real person, but for reasons that will become clear, he asks us to mask his identity.

Based in Germany, Kimble is the leader of an international hacker group called Dope. He is also one of the most celebrated hackers in his country. He has appeared on German TV (in disguise) and is featured in the December issue of the German magazine *Capital*.

From his computer terminal, Kimble spends part of each day cracking PBX systems in the U.S., a lucrative form of computer crime. PBXs are the phone systems businesses own or lease. Hackers break into them to steal access numbers, which they then resell to other hackers and, increasingly, to criminals who use the numbers to transact their business. These are hardly victimless crimes; businesses that rightfully own the numbers are expected to pay the billions of dollars of bogus phone bills charged on their stolen numbers each year (FORBES, *Aug. 3*).

Kimble, using a special program he has written, claims he can swipe six access codes a day. He says he escapes prosecution in Germany because the antihacking laws there are more lax than in the U.S. "Every PBX is an open door for me," he brags, claiming he now has a total of 500 valid PBX codes. At Kimble's going price of $200 a number, that's quite an inventory, especially since numbers can be sold to more than one customer.

Kimble works the legal side of the street, too. For example, he sometimes works for German banks, helping them secure their systems against invasions. This might not be such a hot idea for the banks. "Would you hire a former burglar to install your burglar alarm?" asks Robert Kane, president of Intrusion Detection, a New York-based computer security consulting firm.

Kimble has also devised an encrypted telephone that he says cannot be tapped. In just three months he says he has sold 100.

Other hacker hoods FORBES spoke to in Europe say they steal access numbers and resell them for up to $500 to the Turkish mafia. A solid market. Like all organized crime groups, they need a constant supply of fresh, untraceable and untappable telephone numbers to conduct drug and other illicit businesses.

Some crooked hackers will do a lot worse for hire. For example, one is reported to have stolen an East German Stasi secret bomb recipe in 1989 and sold it to the Turkish mafia. Another boasted to FORBES that he broke into a London police computer and, for $50,000 in deutsche marks, delivered its access codes to a young English criminal.

According to one knowledgeable source, another hacker brags that he recently found a way to get into Citibank's computers. For three months he says he quietly skimmed off a penny or so from each account. Once he had $200,000, he quit. Citibank says it has no evidence of this incident and we cannot confirm the hacker's story. But, says computer crime expert Donn Parker of consultants SRI International: "Such a 'salami attack' is definitely possible, especially for an insider."

The tales get wilder. According to another hacker hood who insists on anonymity, during the Gulf war an oil company hired one of his friends to invade a Pentagon computer and retrieve information from a spy satellite. How much was he paid? "Millions," he says.

Is the story true? The scary thing is, it might well be.

No one knows for sure just how much computer crime costs individuals, corporations and the government. When burned, most victims, especially businesses, stay mum for fear of looking stupid or inviting copycats. According to *Law and Order* magazine, only an estimated 11% of all computer crimes are reported.

Still, the FBI estimates annual losses from computer-related crime range from $500 million to $5 billion.

The FBI is getting more and more evidence that the computer crime wave is building every day. Computer network intrusions—one way of measuring attempted criminal cracking of computer systems—have risen rapidly. According to USA Research, which specializes in analyzing technology companies, hacker attacks on U.S. workplace computers increased from 339,000 in 1989 to 684,000 in 1991. It's estimated that by 1993, 60% of the personal computers in the U.S. will be networked, and therefore vulnerable to intrusion.

While companies dislike talking about being ripped off by hackers, details sometimes leak out. In 1988, for instance, seven men were indicted in U.S. federal court in Chicago for using phony computer-generated transactions to steal $70 million from the accounts of Merrill Lynch, United Airlines and Brown-Forman at First National Bank of Chicago. Two pled guilty; the other five were tried and convicted on all counts.

According to generally reliable press reports, here are some other ways computer criminals ply their trade:

• In 1987 Volkswagen said it had been hit with computer-based foreign-exchange fraud that could cost nearly $260 million.

• A scheme to electronically transfer $54 million in Swiss francs out of the London branch of the Union Bank of Switzerland without authorization was reported in 1988. It was foiled when a chance system failure prompted a manual check of payment instructions.

• Also in 1988, over a three-day period, nearly $350,000 was stolen from customer accounts at Security Pacific National Bank, possibly by automated teller machine thieves armed with a pass key card.

• In 1989 IRS agents arrested a Boston bookkeeper for electronically filing $325,000 worth of phony claims for tax refunds.

• In 1990 it was reported that a Malaysian bank executive cracked his employer's security system and allegedly looted customer accounts of $1.5 million.

• Last year members of a ring of travel agents in California got two to four years in prison for using a computer reservation terminal to cheat American Airlines of $1.3 million worth of frequent flier tickets.

U.S. prosecutors say that members of a New York hacker group called MOD, sometimes known as Masters of Deception, took money for showing 21-year-old Morton Rosenfeld how to get into the computers of TRW Information Services and Trans Union Corp. Caught with 176 credit reports, Rosenfeld admitted selling them to private investigators and others. In October he was sentenced to eight months in prison.

The newest form of cybercrime is extortion by computer—give me money or I'll crash your system. "There's no doubt in my mind that things like that are happening," says Chuck Owens, chief of the FBI's economic crime unit. But Owens won't talk about ongoing cases.

Many hackers are young, white, male computer jocks. They include genuinely curious kids who resent being denied access to the knowledge-rich computer networks that ring the globe, just because they can't afford the telephone access charges. (To satisfy their needs in a legitimate way, two smart New York young hackers, Bruce Fancher and Patrick Kroupa, this year started a widely praised new bulletin board called MindVox—modem: 212-988-5030. It's cheap and allows computer users to chat, as well as gain access to several international computer networks, among other things.)

Then there are the stunt hackers. Basically these are small-time hoods who crash and occasionally trash supposedly secure computer networks for the sheer fun of it. They swap and sell stolen software over pirate bulletin boards. One of these hackers sent FORBES an unsolicited copy of MS-DOS 6.0—Microsoft Corp.'s new operating system, which isn't even scheduled to be on the market until next year. It worked fine. (We first had it tested for viruses with Cyberlock Data Intelligence, Inc. in Philadelphia, an electronic data security firm with a sophisticated new hardware-based system that's used to detect viruses.)

The more malicious stunt hackers like to invade company voice mail systems and fool around with so-called Trojan horses, which can steal passwords and cause other mischief, as well as viruses and other computer-generated smoke bombs, just to raise hell.

This kind of hacking around can wreak tremendous damage. Remember Robert Tappan Morris. In 1988 Morris, then a 22-year-old Cornell University grad student, designed a worm computer program that could travel all over computer networks and reproduce itself indefinitely. Morris says he meant no harm. But in November 1988 Morris released the worm on the giant Internet computer network and jammed an estimated 6,000 computers tied into Internet, including those of several universities, NASA and the Air Force, before it was stopped. Damages were estimated as high as $185 million.

That event was something of a watershed for the law enforcement people. In 1990 Morris was one of the first hackers to be convicted of violating the Computer Fraud and Abuse Act of 1986. He could have been sentenced to five years in prison and a $250,000 fine. Instead, Morris got just three years' probation, a $10,000 fine, 400 hours of community service and had to pay his probation costs. Today he'd probably be thrown in the slammer.

After the curious kids and the stunt hackers, a third element in the hacker underworld is made up of members of organized crime, hard-core cybercrooks, extortionists, shady private investigators, credit card cheats, disgruntled ex-employees of banks, telephone and other companies, and various computer-savvy miscreants. These are computer thugs who hack for serious dollars, or who buy other crooked hackers' services and wares.

One of the peculiarities of hackers is that many cannot keep their mouths shut about their illegal exploits. They boast on their underground bulletin boards and in their publications about all the nasty things they can, and occasionally do, pull off. They brag to the press and even to the authorities. Witness Germany's Kimble and the many other hacker hoods who talked to FORBES for this article.

Over their own underground bulletin boards, hackers have brazenly broadcast all kinds of gossip, software and trophy files brought back like scalps from intrusions into other people's computers. The most infamous example is the 911 file purloined from BellSouth, which prosecutors said had key information about the vital 911 emergency telephone network. The file turned out to be far less valuable than alleged. Nonetheless, its theft and, later, its mere possession got a whole raft of hackers—including a group called the Legion of Doom—in big trouble. Over the past three years, several of them have been busted

and their computer equipment seized. A few drew stiff jail terms.

The hackers even have their own above-ground magazines. One, 2600, the Hacker Quarterly, is sold on newsstands. In the current issue, there is an article on how to crack COCOTs, customer-owned, coin-operated telephones, and get free long distance service. While the publisher of 2600 advises readers not to try such schemes, the easy-to-follow instructions are right there, in black and white.

The publisher of 2600, Eric Corley (alias Emmanuel Goldstein), claims that he is protected by the First Amendment. But readers who follow some of the instructions printed in 2600 magazine may find themselves in deep trouble with law enforcement. Notes senior investigator Donald Delaney, a well-known hacker tracker with the New York State Police: "He [Corley] hands copies out free of charge to kids. Then they get arrested."

An even bolder magazine, Hack-Tic, is published by Rop Gonggrijp in Amsterdam, a hacking hotbed thanks in part to liberal Dutch laws. Hack-Tic is something like 2600, but with even more do-it-yourself hacking information.

The hacker hoods stage their own well-publicized meetings and conventions, which are closely watched by the authorities. On the first Friday of every month, for example, at six cities in the U.S., 2600 magazine convenes meetings where hackers can, in the words of the magazine itself, "Come by, drop off articles, ask questions, find the undercover agents."

FORBES dropped by 2600's Nov. 6 meeting in New York. it was held in the lobby of the Citicorp Center on Lexington Avenue, a sort of mini urban mall, with lots of pay phones—phones are to hackers what blood vessels are to Dracula.

On this particular Friday the two or three dozen attendees consist mainly of teenage boys and young men wearing jeans and T shirts and zip-up jackets. Most are white, though there are some blacks and Asians. Most of these young people pretty much resemble the kids next door—or the kids under your own roof. A few look furtive, almost desperate.

Moving easily among the kids are a few veteran hackers—and, watching them, some well-known hacker trackers, sometimes even New York State Police's Don Delaney. He might lurk on one of the upper levels of the Citicorp Center or stroll past the pay phones looking for a suspect wanted in New York. Don't the suspects stay away? Not necessarily. At one meeting Delaney walked right past three young men he had arrested, and not one of them even noticed him. "They're in their own world," he explains.

On the edge of the crowd stands a slight, intense young man wearing an earring and a neatly folded blue bandana around his head. Twenty-year-old Phiber Optik, as he calls himself, is currently under federal indictment in New York, charged with sundry computer crimes. According to federal authorities, he and other members of the hacker group called MOD sold access to credit reporting services and destroyed via computer a television station's educational service, among other things. Phiber Optik claims that he's innocent.

As the group grows, *2600* publisher Corley makes a dramatic entrance. He looks as if he's in his mid-30s and wears 1960s-style long black hair. A baby-faced assistant stands at his side, selling T shirts and back issues of *2600* magazine.

Now and then Corley darts to the pay phones to take phone calls from other hacker meetings around the world. After taking one call he turns around with a worried look. He has just heard that the *2600* meeting at a mall in Arlington, Va. was busted by mall security and the Secret Service. Authorities there demanded the names of the two dozen or so attendees, confiscated their bags containing printouts and computer books, and booted them out of the mall.

The group in Arlington was lucky compared with what happened to some hackers attending "PumpCon," a hacker convention held at the Courtyard by Marriott in Greenburgh, N.Y., over the recent Halloween weekend. Responding to a noise complaint, the police arrived, then got a search warrant and raided the hackers' rooms. The cops confiscated computer equipment and arrested four conventioneers for computer crimes. Three were held in lieu of $1,000 bail. No bail was set for the fourth, a 22-year-old wanted for computer fraud and probation violation in Arizona.

Around the country, computer users of every stripe are growing concerned that law enforcement officials, in their zeal to nail bigtime cybercrooks and computer terrorists, may be abusing the rights of other computer users. In some cases, users have been raided, had their equipment confiscated, yet years later still have not been charged with any wrongdoing—nor had their equipment returned.

In 1990 Lotus Development founder Mitchell Kapor and Grateful Dead lyricist John Perry Barlow, with help from Apple Computer cofounder Stephen Wozniak and John Gilmore, formerly of Sun Microsystems, started a non-profit group called the Electronic Frontier Foundation (EFF). Its aim is to defend the constitutional rights of all computer users.

But if you know someone who likes to hack around, pass along this advice to her or him: While it is a common myth among hackers that the authorities will let them go if they reveal how they accomplished their mischief, the days of such benign treatment have disappeared as the computer crime wave has built.

"If it's a crime, it's a crime," warns the New York State Police's Don Delaney. "The laws are there for a good reason. For the most part, law enforcement is just reacting to complaints from victims."

## Why cybercrooks love cellular

Cellular phones provide cybercrooks with golden opportunities for telephone toll fraud, as many shocked cellular customers are discovering. For example, one U.S. West Cellular customer in Albuquerque recently received a hefty phone bill. Total: $20,000.

Customers are not held responsible when their phone numbers are ripped off and misused. But you may be forced to have your cellular phone number changed. The cellular carriers are the big losers—to the tune of an estimated $300 million per year in unauthorized calls.

How do the crooks get the numbers? There are two common methods: cloning and tumbling.

Each cellular phone has two numbers—a mobile identification number (MIN) and an electronic serial number (ESN). Every time you make a call, the chip transmits both numbers to the local switching office for verification and billing.

Cloning involves altering the microchip in another cellular phone so that both the MIN and ESN numbers match those stolen from a bona fide customer. The altering can be done with a personal computer. The MIN and ESN numbers are either purchased from insiders or plucked from the airwaves with a legal device, about the size of a textbook, that can be plugged into a vehicle's cigarette lighter receptacle.

Cellular companies are starting to watch for suspicious calling patterns. But the cloning may not be detected until the customer gets his bill.

The second method—tumbling—also involves using a personal computer to alter a microchip in a cellular phone so that its numbers change after every phone call. Tumbling doesn't require any signal plucking. It takes advantage of the fact that cellular companies allow "roaming"—letting you make calls away from your home area.

When you use a cellular phone far from your home base, it may take too long for the local switching office to verify your MIN and ESN numbers. So the first call usually goes through while the verification goes on. If the numbers are invalid, no more calls will be permitted by that office on that phone.

In 1987 a California hacker figured out how to use his personal computer to reprogram the chip in a cellular phone. Authorities say one of his pals started selling altered chips and chipped-up phones. Other hackers figured out how to make the chips generate new, fake ESN numbers every time the cellular phone was used, thereby short-circuiting the verification process. By 1991 chipped-up, tumbling ESN phones were in use all over the U.S.

The cellular carriers hope to scotch the problem of tumbling with instant verification. But that won't stop the clones.

How do crooks cash in? Drug dealers buy (for up to $3,200) or lease (about $750 per day) cellular phones with altered chips. So do the "call-sell" crooks, who retail long distance calls to immigrants often for less than phone companies charge. That's why a victim will get bills for calls all over the world, but especially to Colombia, Bolivia and other drug-exporting countries.

—W.G.F. and B.McM.

# legally speaking

## Can Hackers Be Sued for Damages Caused by Computer Viruses?

The law can be a rather blunt instrument with which to attack a hacker whose virus has caused damage in a computer system. Among the kinds of damage that can be caused by computer viruses are the following: destroyed programs or data, lost computing time, the cost of system cleanup, and the cost of installing new security measures to guard against a recurrence of the virus, just to name a few. The more extensive and expensive the damage is, the more appealing (at least initially) will be the prospect of a lawsuit to seek compensation for the losses incurred. But even when the damage done is considerable, sometimes it may not be worthwhile to bring a lawsuit against the hacker whose virus has damaged the system. Careful thought should be given to making a realistic appraisal of the chances for a meaningful, beneficial outcome to the case before a lawsuit is filed.

This appraisal must take into account the significant legal-theory and practical difficulties with bring-

ing a lawsuit as a way of dealing with the harm caused by a hacker's virus. This column will discuss both kinds of difficulties. A brief synopsis of each type of problem may be helpful before going into detail about each. The legal theory problem is essentially this: There may not yet be a law on the books or clearly applicable legal precedents that can readily be used to establish a right to legal relief in computer virus situations. The law has lots of experience with lawsuits claiming a right to compensation for damage to persons or to tangible property. But questions may arise if someone seeks to adapt or extend legal rules to the more intangible nature of electronically stored information. The practical difficulties with using the law to get some remedy for harm caused by a hacker's virus can be even more daunting than the legal theory problems. Chief among the practical difficulties is the fact that the lawsuit alone can cost more than can ever be recovered from the hacker-defendant.

To understand the nature of the legal theory problems with suing a hacker for damage caused by his or her virus, it may help to understand a few basic things about how the law works. One is that the law has often evolved to deal with new situations, and evolution of this sort is more likely when fairness seems to require it. Another is that the law generally recognizes only already established categories of legal claims, and each of the categories of legal claims has its own particular pattern to it, which must be matched in order to win a lawsuit based on it. While judges are sometimes willing to stretch the legal category a little to reach a fair result, they are rarely willing to create entirely new categories of law or stretch an existing category to the breaking point. Because of this, much of what lawyers do is pattern-matching and arguing by analogy: taking a given set of facts relevant to a client's circumstances, sorting through various possible categories of legal claims to determine which of them might apply to the facts at hand, and then developing arguments to show that this case matches the pattern of this legal category or is analogous to it.

Whenever there is no specific law passed by the legislature to deal with a specific issue, such as damages caused by computer viruses, lawyers look to more general categories of legal claims to try to find one that matches a particular client's situation. "Tort" is the name used by lawyers to refer to a category of lawsuits that aim to get money damages to compensate an injured party for harm caused by another person's wrongful conduct. Some torts are intentional (libel, for example, or fraud). Some are unintentional. (Negligence is a good example of this type of lawsuit.) The harm caused by the wrongful conduct may be to the victim's person (as where someone's negligence causes the victim to break a leg) or property (as where a negligent driver smashes into another car, causing it to be "totaled"), or may be more purely economic losses (as where the victim has to incur the expense of renting another car after his or her car has been destroyed by a negligent driver). In general, tort law permits a victim to recover money damages for all three types of injuries so long as they are reasonably foreseeable by the person who causes them. (Some economic losses, however, are too remote to be recoverable.)

Among the categories of traditional torts that might be worth considering as the basis of a lawsuit seeking compensation for losses caused by a computer virus is the law of trespass. Though we ordinarily think of trespass in connection with unlawful entry onto another's land, the tort of trespass applies to more situations than this. Intentional interference with someone's use of his or her property can be a trespass as well. A potential problem with the use of trespass for computer virus situations, however, might be in persuading a judge to conceive of a virus as a physical invasion of a computer system. A defendant might argue that he or she was in another state and never came anywhere near the plaintiff's computer system to show that the tres-

pass pattern had not been established. The plaintiff would have to counter by arguing that the virus physically invaded the system, and was an extension of the defendant who was responsible for planting it.

Another tort to consider would be the law of conversion. Someone who unlawfully "converts" someone else's property to his or her own use in a manner that interferes with the ability of the rightful owner to make use of it can be sued for damages by the rightful owner. (Conversion is the tort pattern that can be used to recover damages for theft; *theft* itself is more of a criminal law term.) As with trespass, the law of conversion is more used to dealing with interferences with use of tangible items of property, such as a car. But there would seem to be a good argument

---

*The law of negligence allows victims of accidental injury to sue to obtain compensation for losses caused by another's negligence.*

---

that when a virus ties up the computing resources of a firm or university, it is even more a conversion of the computing facility than if some component of the system (such as a terminal) was physically removed from the premises.

Even if a claim, such as conversion, could be established to get damages for lost computer time, that wouldn't necessarily cover all of the kinds of losses that might have been caused by the virus. Suppose, for example, that a virus invaded individual accounts in a computer system and sent out libelous messages masquerading as messages from the account's owner or exposed on a computer bulletin board all of the account owner's computer mail messages. Libel would be a separate tort for a separate kind of injury. Similarly, a claim might be made for invasion of privacy and intentional misrepresentation to get damages for injuries resulting from these aspects of the virus as well.

So far we have been talking mostly about intentional torts. A hacker might think that he or she could not be found liable for an intentional tort because he or she did not intend to cause the specific harm that resulted from the virus,

but that is not how tort law works. All that is generally necessary to establish an intentional tort is that the person intended to do the conduct that caused the harm, and that the harm was of a sort that the person knew or should have known would be reasonably certain to happen as a consequence of his or her actions. Still, some hackers might think that if the harm from their viruses was accidental, as when an "experiment" goes awry, they might not be legally responsible for the harm. That is not so. The law of negligence allows victims of accidental injury to sue to obtain compensation for losses caused by another's negligence.

Negligence might be a more difficult legal claim to win in a computer virus case because it may be unclear exactly who had what responsibilities toward whom under the circumstances. In general, someone can be sued for damages resulting from negligence when he or she has a duty to act in accordance with a standard of care appropriate to the circumstances, and fails to act in accordance with that standard of care in a particular situation. Standards of care are often not codified anywhere, but depend on an assessment of what a reasonable person would do in the same set of circumstances. A programmer, for example, would seem to have a duty to act with reasonable care in writing programs to run on a computing system and a duty not to impose unreasonable risks of harm on others by his or her programming. But the owner of the computing system would also have a duty of care to create reasonable safeguards against unauthorized access to the computing system or to some parts of the computer system because the penchant of hackers to seek unauthorized entry is well-known in the computing community. The focus in a negligence lawsuit, then, might not be just on what the hacker did, but on what the injured party did to guard against injury of this sort.

# 5. COMPUTER ETHICS AND CRIME

Sometimes legislatures pass special laws to deal with new situations such as computer viruses. If a legislature was to consider passing a law to provide remedies for damages caused by computer viruses, there would be a number of different kinds of approaches it could take to formulate such a law. It is a tricker task than one might initially suppose to draft a law with a fine enough mesh to catch the fish one is seeking to catch without creating a mesh so fine that one catches too many other fish, including many that one doesn't want to catch.

Different legislative approaches have different pros and cons. Probably the best of these approaches, from a plaintiff's standpoint, would be that which focuses on unauthorized entry or abuse of access privileges because it limits the issue of wrongful conduct by the defendant to access privileges, something that may be relatively easy to prove. Intentional disruption of normal functioning would be a somewhat more demanding standard, but would still reach a wide array of virus-related conduct. A law requiring proof of damage to data or programs would, again from a plaintiff's standpoint, be less desirable because it would have stiffer proof requirements and would not reach viruses that merely disrupted functioning without destroying data or programs. The problem of crafting the right law to cover the right problem (and only the right problem) is yet another aspect of the legal theory problems posed by computer viruses.

Apart from the difficulties with fitting computer virus situations in existing legal categories or devising new legal categories to reach computer viruses, there are a set of practical difficulties that should be considered before undertaking legal pursuit of hackers whose viruses cause damage to computer systems.

Perhaps the most important set of practical difficulties with suing a hacker for virus damages is that which concerns the legal remedy one can realistically get if one wins. That is, even if a lawyer is able to identify an appropriate legal claim that can be effectively maintained against a hacker, and even assuming the lawyer can surmount the considerable evidentiary problems that

might be associated with winning such a lawsuit, the critically important question which must be answered before any lawsuit is begun is what will one realistically be able to recover if one wins.

There are three sets of issues of concern here. One set relates to the costs of bringing and prosecuting the lawsuit. Lawsuits don't come cheap (and not all of the expenses are due to high attorney fees). Another relates to the amount of damages or other cost recoveries that can be obtained if one wins the lawsuit. It's fairly rare to be able to get an award of attorney's fees or punitive damages, for example, but a lawsuit becomes more attractive as an option if these remedies are available. Also, where the virus has spread to a number of different computer systems on a network, for example, the collective damage done by the hacker may be substantial, but the damage to any one entity within the network system may be sufficiently small that, again, it may not be economically feasible to maintain individual lawsuits and the collectivity may not have sufficiently uniform interests to support a single lawsuit on behalf of all network members.

But the third and most significant concern will most often be the ability of the defendant to write a good check to pay the damages that might be awarded in a judgment. Having a judgment for one million dollars won't do you any good if it cost you $10,000 to get it and the defendant's only asset is a used computer with a market value of $500. In such an instance, you might as well have cut your losses and not brought the lawsuit in the first place. Lawyers refer to defendants of this sort as "judgment-proof."

While these comments might suggest that no lawsuit should ever be brought against a young hacker unless he or she has recently come into a major inheritance, it is worth pointing out the law does allow someone who has obtained a judgment against another person to renew the judgment periodically to await "executing" on it until the hacker has gotten a well-paying job or some other major asset which can be seized to satisfy the judgment. If one has enough patience and enough confidence in the hacker's

future (or a strong enough desire for revenge against the hacker), there may be a way to get some compensation eventually from the defendant.

Proof problems may also plague any effort to bring a successful lawsuit for damages against a computer hacker. Few lawsuits are easy to prove, but those that involve live witnesses and paper records are likely to be easier than those involving a shadowy trail of electronic signals through a computer system, especially when an effort is made to disguise the identity of the person responsible for the virus and the guilty person has not confessed his or her responsibility. Log files, for example, are constantly truncated or overwritten, so that whatever evidence might once have existed with which to track down who was logged onto a system when the virus was planted may have ceased to exist.

Causation issues too can become very murky when part of the damage is due to an unexpected way in which the virus program interacted with some other parts of the system. And even proving the extent of damages can be difficult. If the system crashes as a result of the virus, it may be possible to estimate the value of the lost computing time. If specific programs with an established market value are destroyed, the value of the program may be easy to prove. But much of the damage caused by a virus may be more elusive to establish. Can one, for example, recover damages for economic losses attributable to delayed processing, for lost accounts receivable when computerized data files are erased and no backup paper record was kept of the transactions? Or can one recover for the cost of designing new security procedures so that the system is better protected against viruses of this sort? All in all, proof issues can be especially vexing in a computer virus case.

In thinking about the role of the law in dealing with computer virus situations, it is worth considering whether hackers are the sorts of people likely to be deterred from computer virus activities by fear of lawsuits for money damages. Criminal prosecution is likely to be a more powerful legal deterrent to a hacker than a civil suit is. But even criminal liability may be sufficiently remote a prospect that a hacker would be unlikely to forego an experiment involving a virus because of it. In some cases, the prospect of criminal liability may even add zest to the risk-taking that is involved in putting a virus in a system.

Probably more important than new laws or criminal prosecutions in deterring hackers from virus-related conduct would be a stronger and more effective ethical code among computer professional and better internal policies at private firms, universities, and governmental institutions to regulate usage of computing resources. If hackers cannot win the admiration of their colleagues when they succeed at their clever stunts, they may be less likely to do them in the first place. And if owners of computer facilities make clear (and vigorously enforce) rules about what is acceptable and unacceptable conduct when using the system, this too may cut down on the incidence of virus experiments.

Still, if these measures do not succeed in stopping all computer viruses, there is probably a way to use the law to seek some remedy for damages caused by a hacker's virus. The law may not be the most precisely sharpened instrument with which to strike back at a hacker for damages caused by computer viruses, but sometimes blunt instruments do an adequate job, and sometimes lawsuits for damages from viruses will be worth the effort of bringing them.

*Pamela Samuelson*
*Visiting Professor*
*Emory Law School*
*Atlanta, Ga.*

---

# Viruses and Criminal Law

Harry the Hacker broke into the telephone company computer and planted a virus that he expected would paralyze all telephone communications in the United States. Harry's efforts, however, came to naught. Not only did he make a programming error that made the virus dormant until 2089 instead of 1989, but he was also unaware that the telephone company's computer was driven by a set of preprogrammed instructions that were isolated from the effects of the virus. An alert computer security officer, aided by automated audits and alarm systems, detected and defused Harry's logic bomb.

A hypothetical situation, yes, but not one outside the realm of possibility. Let us suppose that Harry bragged about his feat to some friends in a bar, and a phone company employee who overheard the conversation reported the incident to the police and gave them Harry's name and address. Would Harry be guilty of a crime? Even if Harry had committed a crime, what is the likelihood that he could be convicted.

Before attempting to answer these questions, we must first know what a crime is. A crime is an act that society, through its laws, has declared to be so serious a threat to the public order and welfare that it will punish anyone who commits the act. An act is made criminal by being declared to be a crime in a duly enacted statute. The statute must be clear enough to give reasonable notice as to what is prohibited and must also prescribe a punishment for taking the action.

The elements of the crime must be spelled out in the statute. In successful prosecution, the accused must have performed acts that demonstrate the simultaneous presence of all of the elements of the crime. Thus, if the statute specifies that one must destroy data to have committed an alleged crime, but the act destroyed no data, then one cannot be convicted of that crime. If the act destroyed only student records of a university, but the statute defines the crime only for a financial institution, then one cannot be convicted under the statute.

All states now have criminal statutes that specifically address certain forms of computer abuse. Many misdeeds in which the computer is either the instrument or object of the illicit act can be prosecuted as more traditional forms of crime, such as stealing or malicious mischief. Because we cannot consider all possible state and federal statutes under which Harry might be prosecuted, we will examine Harry's action only in terms of the federal computer crime statute.

The United States Criminal Code, title 18, section 1030(a)(3), defines as criminal the intentional, unauthorized access to a computer used exclusively by the federal government, or any other computer used by the government when such conduct affects the government's use. The same statute, in section 1030(a)(5)(A), also defines as criminal the intentional and unauthorized access to two or more computers in different states, and conduct that alters or destroys information and causes loss to one or more parties of a value of at least $1000.

If the phone company computer that Harry illicitly entered was not used by the federal government, Harry cannot be charged with a criminal act under section 1030(a)(3). If Harry accesses two computers in different states, and his action alters information, and it causes loss to someone of a value of at least $1000, then he can be charged under section 1030(a)(5)(A). However, whether these conditions have been satisfied may be open to question.

Suppose, for example, that Harry plants his logic bomb on a single machine, and that after Harry has disconnected, the program that he loaded transfers a virus to other computers in other states. Has Harry accessed those computers? The law is not clear. Suppose Harry's act does not directly alter information, but merely replicates itself to other computers on the network, eventually overwhelming their processing capabilities as in the case of the Internet virus on November 2, 1988. Information may be lost, but can that loss be directly attributed to Harry's action in a way that satisfies the statute? Once again, the answer is not clear-cut.

And what of the $1000 required by the statute as an element of the crime? How is the loss measured? Is it the cost of reconstructing any files that were destroyed? Is it the market value of files that were destroyed? How do we determine these values, and what if there were adequate backups so that the files could be restored at minimal expense and with no loss of data? Should the criminal benefit from good operating procedures on an attacked computer? Should the salaries of computer personnel, who would have been paid anyway, be included for the time they spend to bring the system up again? If one thousand users each suffer a loss of one dollar, can one aggregate these small losses to a loss sufficiently large to be able to invoke the statute? The statute itself gives us noguidance so the courts will have to decide these questions.

No doubt many readers consider questions such as these to be nit-picky. Many citizens already are certain that guilty parties often use subtle legal distinctions and deft procedural maneuvers to avoid the penalities for their offenses. "If someone does something wrong, he or she should be punished and not be permitted to hide behind legal technicalities," so say many. But the law must be the shield of the innocent as well as a weapon against the malefactor. If police were free to invent crimes at will, or a judge could interpret the criminal statutes to punish anyone who displeased him or her, then we would face a greater danger to our rights and freedoms than computer viruses. We cannot defend our social order by undermining the very foundations on which it is built.

The difficulties in convicting Harry of a crime, however, go beyond the questions of whether he

has simultaneously satisfied each condition of some crime with which he can be charged. There remain the issues of prosecutorial discretion and the rules of evidence.

Prosecutors have almost absolute discretion concerning what criminal actions they will prosecute. That a prosecutor can refuse to charge someone with a crime, even someone against whom an airtight case exists, comes as a shock to many citizens who assume that once the evidence exists that someone has committed a crime, that person will be arrested and tried.

There are many reasons why a prosecutor may pass up the chance to nail a felon. One is that the caseload of the prosecutor's office is tremendous, and the prosecutor must choose the criminals who pose the greatest danger to society. Because

computer crimes are often directed against businesses rather than persons and usually carry no threat of bodily injury, they are often seen as low priority cases by prosecutors. Even computer professionals themselves do not seem to think that computer crime is very serious. In a 1984 survey by the American Bar Association, respondents rated computer crime as the third least significant category of illicit activity, with only shoplifting and illegal immigration being lower. With such attitudes among those responsible for computer security, who can blame prosecutors for turning their attention to crimes the public considers to be more worthy of law enforcement's limited resources?

Underlying the assessment of priority is a general lack of understanding about computers among prosecutors. Thus, a prosecutor would have to spend an unusual amount of time to prepare a computer crime case as opposed to a case that dealt with a more traditional, and hence better understood, mode of crime. Moreover, even if the prosecutor is quite knowledge-

able about computers, few judges and even fewer jurors are. The presentation of the case, therefore, will be more difficult and time consuming, and the outcome less predictable. I am familiar with a case that took hundreds of hours to prepare and resulted in a conviction, but the judge sentenced the convicted criminal to pay only a small fine and serve two years probation. With such a result, one cannot be surprised that prosecutors ignore computer criminals when there are so many felons that courts obviously consider more worthwhile.

Suppose, for the sake of argument, that we have a prosecutor who is willing to seek an indictment against Harry and bring him to trial. Even then, computer-related crimes can pose special evidentiary problems. Remember that to convict Harry,

---

*Even if the prosecutor is quite knowledgeable about computers, few judges and even fewer jurors are. The presentation of the case, therefore, will be more difficult and time consuming, and the outcome less predictable.*

---

the prosecutor must convince a jury beyond a reasonable doubt that Harry committed an act in which all of the elements of the crime were found simultaneously. The elements of the crime cannot be found to exist in the abstract; they must be found to apply specifically to Harry.

Apart from having to prove that the act caused the requisite amount of damage and that the computers used were those specified by the statute, the prosecutor would have to show that Harry committed the act and that he did so intentionally and without authorization. Because Harry was using someone else's account number and password, tying Harry to the crime might be difficult unless unusual surveillance was in place. A gunman and his weapon must be physically present at the teller's window to rob the bank, but a computer criminal may be thousands of miles away from the computer that is attacked. A burglar must physically enter a house to carry off the loot and may, therefore, be observed by a witness; moreover, it is generally assumed that someone carrying a television set out of a darkened house in the middle of the night is up to no good. By contrast, a computer criminal can work in isolation and secrecy, and few, if any, of those who happen to observe are likely to know what he is doing.

The evidence that ties the computer criminal to the crime, therefore, is often largely circumstantial; what is placed before the jury is not eyewitness testimony, but evidence from which the facts can only be reasonably inferred. Although convictions on the basis of circumstantial evidence alone are possible, they are often harder to obtain.

Adding to the prosecutor's difficulties in getting convincing evidence about Harry's acts are the unsettled constitutional issues associated with gathering that evidence. Does Harry have a reasonable expectation that his computer files are private? If so, then a search warrant must be obtained before they can be searched and seized. If Harry's files are enciphered, then must Harry furnish the key to decryption, or would he be protected from having to do so by his Fifth Amendment right against self-incrimination? The evidence that would convict Harry won't do the prosecutor much good if it is thrown out as having been obtained by impermissible means.

In the face of these difficulties, some have introduced bills into Congress and into some state legislatures that prohibit planting a virus in a computer system. But drafting a responsible computer crime bill is no easy task for legislators. The first effort at federal computer crime has proscribed, and even imposed heavy penalties for, standard computing practices. It did not clearly define what acts were forbidden. It was so broad that one could have been convicted of a computer crime for stealing a digital watch, and it did not cover nonelectronic computers. The bill was never enacted.

If we want a statute that targets persons who disrupt computer systems by planting viruses, then what do we look for in judging the value of proposed legislation?

Is the proposed statute broad enough to cover activity that should be prohibited but narrow enough not to unduly interfere with legitimate computer activity? Would an expert be able to circumvent the statute by designing a harmful program that would not be covered by the statute? Does the proposed statute clearly define the act that will be punished so as to give clear notice to a reasonable person? Does the act distinguish between intentional acts and innocent programming errors? Does the statute unreasonably interfere with the free flow of information? Does it raise a First Amendment free speech problem? These and other questions must be considered in developing any new computer crime legislation.

Where do I personally stand with regard to legislation against viruses, logic bombs, and other forms of computer abuse? It is not enough to say I am against conduct that destroys valuable property and interferes with the legitimate flow of information. The resolution of legal issues invariably involves the weighing of competing interests, e.g., permitting the free flow of information v. safe-guarding a system against attack. Even now, existing criminal statues and civil remedies are powerful weapons to deter and punish persons who tamper with computer systems. I believe that new legislation should be drawn with great care and adopted only after an open discussion of its merits by informed computer professionals and users.

The odds are that Harry the Hacker will never be charged with a crime, or, if charged, will get off with a light sentence. And that is the way it will remain unless and until society judges computer crimes, be they planting viruses or stealing money, to be a sufficiently serious threat to the public welfare to warrant more stringent and careful treatment. If such a time comes, one can only hope that computing professionals and societies such as the ACM will actively assist legislatures and law enforcement officials in dealing with the problem in an intelligent and technologically competent manner.

*Michael Gemignani*
*Senior Vice President and Provost*
*University of Houston at Clear Lake*
*Houston, TX 77059*

# Technological Risks

The introduction of any new and powerful technology poses unforeseen hazards. In conducting research for a popular magazine article on the history of American technological achievements, engineer/writer Samuel Florman found that nearly every new technological triumph was initially accompanied by disastrous side effects. He learned, for example, that during the early days of steamboat transport, 42 explosions killed 270 persons between 1825 and 1830. These events, and public outrage, led to government-funded research that ultimately resulted in legislation on safety standards. Florman tells a similar story of the early days of railroading, and, in particular, railroad bridges:

In the late 1860s more than 25 American bridges were collapsing each year, with appalling loss of life. In 1873 the American Society of Civil Engineers set up a special commission to address the problem, and eventually the safety of our bridges came to be taken for granted.

As these examples illustrate, the solution to these terrible problems was not to abandon but to improve technology. Florman summarizes the pattern of technological advance as "progress/setback/renewed-creative-effort."

Computers have been relatively common for a few decades now. Compared with the steamboat and railroad examples above, computers have caused very few se-

rious injuries to humans. Yet, as the articles in this section show, several aspects of computing (and other new technologies) are sources of frustration and even danger.

The lead article focuses on the complexity of many technologies. In "The Complexity Problem," John Sedgwick argues that too many technical systems are confusing and difficult to understand. He offers examples ranging from digital watches to the control systems of nuclear reactors. Obviously, the implications of a confused reactor operator are far more serious than the irritations of not knowing how to set a watch, but Sedgwick calls for more simplicity in all types of technological designs.

Many believe that the electromagnetic fields emitted by cellular phones and other technologies such as computer video display terminals pose a threat to human health. This controversial issue is addressed in the article "Do Cellular Phones Cause Cancer?" Research to date has proved inconclusive, and more thorough studies are urgently needed.

Another and potentially greater source of danger stems from the software that controls complex computerized operations. At the individual, organizational, and societal levels, we are dependent on computer systems, some of which are so crucial to the preservation of life and/or societal functioning that they must be 100 percent reliable. However, as technical systems become ever more complex, the goal of reliability is increasingly difficult to achieve.

Sociologist Charles Perrow has argued that danger is increased when highly complex technical systems arise from and operate within equally complex social systems. Disaster can occur if either system breaks down. An example is provided by the Challenger space shuttle that exploded because rocket seals failed to function properly in cold weather. The engineers who had worked on the rocket system knew of these defects, and when they learned the temperature at the launch site was significantly below normal, they tried to have the launch delayed. They were unable, however, to get their warnings

past "organizational" barriers to those in command. Thus the tragedy that ensued was a consequence of organizational as well as technical failure.

The next two articles in this section provide examples of malfunction in complex computer systems. Both articles discuss relevant organizational, political, and labor issues as well as technical problems in producing software that may contain up to several million lines of code. Evelyn Richards' article, "A System on Overload," focuses on the complexity of commercial and military software. In "Programmed for Disaster," Jonathan Jacky focuses on medical computing and discusses how computer safety can be improved through the use of software engineering, formal methods of software analysis, and possible government regulation.

The final article examines issues related to legal accountability for defective software that causes economic or physical harm. In "Liability for Defective Electronic Information," Pamela Samuelson argues that issues surrounding electronic information liability are unclear because software is more like a book than a machine. Traditionally, courts have been "reluctant to impose liability on authors, publishers, and booksellers for defective information" because of constitutional protection of the free exchange of ideas and information. However, Samuelson concludes that providers of electronic information should think not only about their rights but about their responsibilities as well and start addressing liability problems.

### Looking Ahead: Challenge Questions

Should the principle of *caveat emptor* (let the buyer beware) apply to software?

As complex computer systems become more widespread, do you think they will become more reliable and thus safer, as happened with steamboats and railroads, or will safety risks increase? What political, social, economic, and technical factors should be taken into account when assessing computer risks?

*A pragmatic school of
industrial designers aims to make the
controls of a machine—be it a VCR,
a telephone, or a nuclear reactor—reflect the
people who will use the machine
rather than the engineers who want to
show off new technology*

# THE COMPLEXITY PROBLEM

## JOHN SEDGWICK

*John Sedgwick is* Self *magazine's national correspondent. His most recent book,* The Peaceable Kingdom: A Year in the Life of America's Oldest Zoo, *was published in 1988.*

IT IS BECOMING INCREASINGLY CLEAR THAT THE comfort of a good fit between man and machine is largely absent from the technology of the information age. Consider the humble wristwatch, which has been transformed into a kind of wrist-mounted personal computer, with a digital display and a calculator pad whose buttons are too small to be pressed by a human fingertip. In fact, the very usefulness of the digitization of time is open to question. People generally care less about knowing the time to the nanosecond than about seeing how long they've got until lunch. With digital watches that requires a little figuring (the purpose of the calculator pad, perhaps), whereas with the old analog watches, the ones with hands, it's clear at a glance. Worse, by replacing the watch's conventional stem-winding mechanism with a mystifying arrangement of tiny buttons, the manufacturers created a watch that was very hard to reset. One leading manufacturer was distressed to discover that a line of its particularly advanced

digitals was being returned as defective by the thousands, even though the watches actually worked perfectly well. Further investigation revealed that they were coming back soon after purchase and thereafter in two large batches—in the spring and the fall, when the time changed.

Charles Mauro, a consultant in New York City, is a prominent member of a branch of engineering generally known as ergonomics, or human-factors—the only field specifically addressing the question of product usability. Mauro, who has won many awards for industrial design and human-factors research, was brought in to provide some help to the watch manufacturer, which was experiencing what Mauro calls "the complexity problem." With "complexity" defined as "a fundamental mismatch between the demands of a technology and the capabilities of its user," the term nicely captures the essence of our current technological predicament. That mismatch might be measured by the increasing length of the instruction manuals required to work so many of the new gizmos. About the digital-watch manufacturer Mauro asks, "Can you believe that the company actually expected you to carry around a thirty-page manual in your wallet?"

According to Mauro and other experts in the field, the solution to many such problems lies in a new approach to technological development called user-centered design. As the name suggests, this strategy takes the ultimate user into account from the very beginning of a product's development. Elementary as it sounds, this user-centered approach could drastically revamp American business.

## Domestic Confusion

THE COMPLEXITY PROBLEM IS EVERYWHERE, but it is most apparent around the house. Americans' deficiencies in programming the VCR are so well known that they have become a staple of comedy. According to one consumer survey, a third of all VCR owners have given up trying to program their machines for time-delayed viewing. It is a measure of Americans' desperation that a multi-million-dollar industry has sprung up to sell other technology, involving reference numbers, to provide assistance. And our troubles are not confined to the VCR. According to a survey by the marketing specialist Laurence Feldman, 50 percent of Americans can't work other programmable equipment either, and, thanks to the ubiquitous computer chip, that now includes almost everything: telephones, fax machines, thermostats, even coffee makers. Soon we may add the house itself to the list, as plans proceed to link up these various unworkable components into a single unworkable whole, the "smart house," in which occupants will run everything—security system, coffee pot, kitchen stove—from a single remote-control unit at their fingertips.

When confronted by some mystifying piece of high-tech gadgetry, consumers naturally feel that there is something wrong with them if they can't figure it out. In truth it is usually not their fault. Mauro attributes the confusion to the fact that most products are "technology-driven," their nature determined not by consumers and their needs and desires but by engineers who are too often entranced by the myriad capabilities of the microprocessors that lie at the devices' hearts. "They have this idea that if they *can* do something, they *should*," he says. The main effect of the extra capabilities is in a great many cases to badly muddle the essential functions. Mauro was once hired by a sewing-machine manufacturer disturbed to learn that customers buying its latest high-tech sewing machines were abandoning them after a brief trial period and returning to their previous, supposedly outmoded models. Mauro quickly figured out why: "The new machines required as much mechanical training and information processing as it took to fly a light plane on instruments."

Donald Norman, a cognitive scientist now at Apple Computer, has written about such design screw-ups in *The Design of Everyday Things*. Besides the malady he terms "feature-itis" he describes a number of common design bloopers that boost technological complexity. There is "bad mapping," in which, for example, the burners of a stove are arranged in a square but the con-trols are in a row, necessitating labels like "RF" and "LR" to designate which knob governs which burner; a lack of "forced constraints" to ensure that a user will perform each programming step correctly before going on to the next one; and the absence of feedback, such as the beep emitted by a pressed telephone key, to reassure the user that a system is working. But beneath it all, Norman believes, the fundamental confusion is due to the essentially inscrutable nature of the technology itself. "In the mechanical systems of the old days you could wiggle a knob or a lever and see something happen," he says. "Today's technology concerns information that is invisible and abstract, so the designers have to give a sense of control by different means."

All too often those means are dense instruction manuals, which Mauro regards as the clearest sign of design failure. The best-designed products require no instructions at all: their appearance tells you what to do as surely as a coffee mug's handle says "Hold here." This notion is reinforced by product-liability laws, which first consider the product's physical design, then its labeling, and finally its instructions. In the minds of most engineers that list is inverted.

According to Alan Frank, a consumer-products specialist at the telecommunications firm BNR Ltd., the "manufacturer's showroom mentality" also adds complexity. The extra features are merely an eye-catching consumer come-on, not unlike the chrome on a 1952 DeSoto; they are never intended to serve any real purpose. In their eagerness to outdo their rivals, many manufacturers engage in a kind of features warfare. If one company offers twelve buttons, another must offer fifteen. Manufacturers themselves are under few illusions that the added features do anyone any good. Amar Bose, the founder and chairman of Bose Corporation, has worked for years to simplify the controls on his company's stereo equipment. He is always shocked by the graphic equalizers he encounters in rental cars. "It makes the music sound *absolutely terrible*," he says, putting his hands to his ears.

The need for product differentiation produces another misery for consumers, which is that no two products in any category ever work the same way. In the human-factors world this is known as the negative-transfer problem, and it has added a good deal to consumers' cognitive overload. To take one small but revealing example, the telephone industry is engaged in a heated dispute over the question of where to add the letters Q and Z, now missing from conventional keypads, to complete the alphabet for the newly automated caller-interactive switchboards. Some companies put the Q and Z on the 1 key, which otherwise has no letters. Others, led by AT&T, have put them in alphabetical order on the 7 and 9 keys, even though that has meant adding a fourth letter to each. "You wouldn't believe how many studies have been done on this," says Miriam Kotsonis, a technical manager at AT&T's Bell Laboratories. "We concluded, You don't mess with the alphabet."

## 6. TECHNOLOGICAL RISKS

### Matching Machines to Men

FROM ROBOTS TO LASERS, INDUSTRIAL TECHNOLOGY is infinitely more high-powered and challenging than the household variety. Companies can pay their employees to devote their working lives to learning how to operate a single piece of equipment, and they take full advantage of this fact, ratcheting up the cognitive demands to the point where they pose a real strain and in some cases a positive hazard. These machines are VCRs from hell.

Stuart Card, a cognitive psychologist and computer scientist at Xerox Palo Alto Research Center (PARC), holds up a paperback-sized Hewlitt Packard calculator. It performs 2,100 functions, all of them explained in a 700-page manual. Card marvels, "You can even set it to perform certain functions at certain times—say, to do a symbolic evaluation of an integral at 12:04 P.M. on January 12th in the year 2014." Not that he knows why anyone would want to. "They brook no compromise at Hewlett- Packard. Their idea is that if you can't work this thing, *you're not good enough.*"

Some users, not surprisingly, have come to resent the computers that have transformed their work lives so drastically. Mauro was once called in to a newly automated paper mill where workmen were sabotaging the system by deliberately entering incorrect information into the computers and, if all else failed, hosing the computers down until they shorted out. One might dismiss them as Luddites, but Mauro came to a different conclusion. "The workmen were frustrated that the company demanded greater productivity from them while depriving them of the control over the machinery to deliver it," he says. "They were caught in a terrible bind."

Enticed by the potential cost savings of eliminating jobs, companies have added technology at an impressive clip, including desktop publishing equipment, laser-scanning cash registers, and factory robots. "The standard approach in the United States is to add technology and then figure out what problems you've got," says William Rouse, the CEO of Search Technology, a software products and engineering services firm. Oftentimes, as when unworkable VCRs spawned reference-number inputs, the solution to the problems is still more technology. With each round of technological intervention the human role grows more tightly circumscribed. This is the flip side of the complexity problem: just as people can be overtaxed by technology, they can be undertaxed as well.

In the early stages of the computer revolution it was tempting to view the emerging man-machine mismatch as an issue best addressed by ergonomics. The field has roots in Frederick Winslow Taylor's time-and-motion studies at the turn of the century, but it first flowered during the Second World War, when the fate of the Allies hinged on soldiers' ability to work complicated machinery. For example, Alphonse Chapanis, one of the fathers of the modern human-factors movement, examined the

MANY MANUFACTURERS ENGAGE IN A KIND OF FEATURES WARFARE. IF ONE COMPANY OFFERS TWELVE BUTTONS, ANOTHER MUST OFFER FIFTEEN. THE NEED FOR PRODUCT DIFFERENTIATION PRODUCES ANOTHER MISERY FOR CONSUMERS, WHICH IS THAT NO TWO PRODUCTS IN ANY CATEGORY EVER WORK THE SAME WAY.

mysterious runway crashes of B-17s which composed one of the largest categories of noncombat accidents in the war. Chapanis discovered that the plane's cockpit had two identical toggle switches side by side, one to raise the flaps, the other to raise the landing gear. Exhausted at the end of a long flight, the pilots inadvertently pulled up the landing gear rather than the flaps. Their planes plunged down onto the tarmac and sometimes burst into flames. The Allies' human-factors work may have proved decisive in the air war, because it allowed pilots to fly fighter planes with less training than they might otherwise have needed.

After the war human-factors specialists worked to fit machines to men. They tended to focus on physical interaction, making endless anthropometric measurements to determine the range of human foot size, fingertip width, peripheral vision, hearing perception, color sensitivity, and the like. Such issues should certainly not be overlooked: the first wave of Japanese cars into the United States, for example, failed to catch on largely because their makers had underestimated the length of the average American's legs, and produced cars that felt cramped to U.S. buyers.

But there are other issues to be addressed. It is perhaps an index of the very complexity of the complexity problem that no one field can fully address it, and human factors is no exception. One reason that complexity has gotten so far out of hand is that it has come to reflect the divergent interests of the forces that shape the technology in the first place. "There are basically two camps," Charles Mauro says. "You've got the engineers and designers on the one side, and you've got the psychologists and the applied psychologists on the other. The two groups are constitutionally unable to talk to each other. Basically, the psychologists define problems and the engineers propose solutions. The human-factors people get on a track where they think they're both designers and engineers, when in fact they're neither. But you get in real trouble when designers start thinking they're psychologists."

Most human-factors specialists are too physically oriented to address successfully the heavily cognitive issues imposed by today's technology. But then, few engineers are likely to give them a chance to, since engineers believe they can speak for the user perfectly well themselves. "Engineers have this idea that since I'm human and I'm an engineer, I'm a human engineer," Mauro says, referring to another term for a human-factors specialist. Such attitudes may explain why some human-factors professionals often do more work presenting expert testimony in product-liability cases than they do helping to design workable products in the first place.

Mauro has devised something he calls the User Merit Index, largely in order to present the usability issue in numerical terms that engineers can appreciate. His index plots the difficulty of various aspects of operating a technological device, from turning it on to programming it. He has been amazed by how avidly engineers will attack a problem once it has a number.

## What Comes Naturally

THE ENGINEERS' BLINDNESS TO CONSUMERS' needs may be at the root of a deeper problem —how so much baffling technology enters the market. Donald Norman blames it on the "waterfall method": new technological equipment tumbles out of a corporation, never encountering a typical user until it is bought.

A growing number of technologists think that the development process should be reversed, and they speak of user-centered design as a means of scrupulously maintaining the user's perspective from start to finish, adding technology only where necessary to accomplish a particular task. Far from being a simple idea, user-centered design has a host of implications for technology around the house, at work, and in the military. The key principle is not to assume that more technology is always better. The design of AT&T's new videophone, for example, shows the advantages of the user-centered approach—and illustrates the battle a company often faces in trying to keep things simple. "To tell you the truth," says AT&T's Miriam Kotsonis, "when the company first thought about the product, the techies started to go wild, dreaming about a camcorder that lets you make phone calls, with a zoom lens and pans and tilts, and all that. But we said, 'Let's not make this so hard for our customers. Let's make this as natural as holding a telephone.'" In the debate between those who cared primarily about technology and those who cared primarily about users, the defining moment during the planning came over the question of how to handle "self-view" mode, which allows users to check their appearance before each transmission. The technologists were inclined to present the image as the camera sees it, with the left side of one's face on the right side of the screen. But the user-centered designers knew that people expected a mirror image, with the left side of the face on the left side of the screen, and in the end that is what they got. The technology was strained so that the user would not be. At its best, user-centered design can seem almost poetic in its grasp of human nature.

Much of the work is a matter of finding the "mental

models"—like the mirror mode—by which users instinctively interpret a technology. Especially when the workings of a device are invisible, these models may very well be erroneous. For instance, many people set an electric burner on high thinking that it will heat up faster that way: they have the mental model of a gas stove, whose knobs actually do increase the heat's intensity. On an electric stove, however, the knob is merely a switch that turns on the burner and then turns it off when a certain temperature is reached. A cause of fatal mining accidents was once the peculiar configuration of the controls on the trams shuttling along mineshafts. Each tram had a steering wheel that rose straight up from the floor, with a brake pedal on one side and an accelerator pedal on the other. There was no room to turn the tram around, so to reverse direction the driver simply took a seat on the other side of the steering wheel, whereupon what had been the brake became the accelerator, and vice versa. While this may sound ingenious, it proved disastrous. Some designers are trying to restore the logic to otherwise arbitrary controls through what they term "product semantics," which evokes a natural-seeming vocabulary for things like control knobs. A good example is the "up" and "down" designations for the power-window control introduced on the Ford Taurus. The "up" side is marked by a convex surface, the "down" side by a concave one.

No single approach will eliminate all the complexity problems posed by current technology. But user-centered design can certainly help solve these problems, if only by encouraging manufacturers to consider the needs and abilities of the average user early on in the product-development process. With VCRs a truly user-centered manufacturer would have recognized that programming them might prove extremely difficult for the average person and would have taken steps to simplify the process. It would have helped, for instance, to have the VCR's controls all visible, the way a typewriter's are, rather than having them be accessed by a series of complicated commands, like a personal computer's. By the same token, a user-centered digital-watch maker would not have tried to introduce a whole new, mind-bending system of resetting the time by pressing tiny buttons but would instead have relied on the well-established model of the stem-winding mechanism.

User-centered design would probably also encourage businesses simply to forget about certain ill-conceived products like the "smart house." "That's an engineer's idea of user-centered design," Mauro says. "Nobody went out and asked anyone if it would make his life at home better. Some engineer thought, 'Gee, we have all this great technology to control electrical systems and information systems. Let's try to do something with it.'" Mauro would even jettison the so-called user-agent, a piece of computer programming that is being advocated in some circles as a way of assisting us in certain routine aspects of our lives. In one configuration a user-agent could produce a customized newspaper from a computer

# 6. TECHNOLOGICAL RISKS

**A** GROWING NUMBER OF TECHNOLOGISTS THINK THAT THE DEVELOPMENT PROCESS SHOULD BE REVERSED, AND THEY SPEAK OF USER-CENTERED DESIGN AS A MEANS OF SCRUPULOUSLY MAINTAINING THE USER'S PERSPECTIVE FROM START TO FINISH. THE KEY PRINCIPLE IS NOT TO ASSUME THAT MORE TECHNOLOGY IS ALWAYS BETTER.

network by pulling out articles on topics—the Texas Rangers, the stock price of Pfizer—that are known to be of interest to the individual reader. Mauro believes that such a strategy fails the essential test for user-centeredness because it overlooks one reason that most people read newspapers—for those odd bits of information that are interesting precisely because they are outside one's experience.

A piece of true user-centered design is currently in development to increase the "situation awareness" that is so critical for operators of highly automated systems. Called the Pilot's Associate, it is being created by the Air Force to assist the fighter pilot in managing all the information available in the cockpit. "It tells him what he needs to know when he needs to know it," says Richard Pew, of the consulting firm Bolt Beranek and Newman. The Pilot's Associate eschews simple just-leave-it-to-the-computer automation and instead works from the pilot's perspective to expand his capabilities. The same approach would help on commercial aircraft and in other risky enterprises, because it keeps the operator involved at all times.

User-centered computerization can also enhance a worker's feeling of control instead of depriving him of it. Mauro has helped redesign automated systems for paper manufacturers to boost the operators' awareness of the process. "The workers used to hit the paper with an oak stick to get a feel for the variation in water content," he says. "No computer can do that any better. But it can do a lot of other things to help workers stay on top of their job. Instead of using the computer to cut the workers out of the loop through automation, we used it to plug them in."

User-centered design might even be able to forestall accidents, by dictating that mock-ups of a product be tested with users before it goes into full production. Too often manufacturers don't realize the hazards their products present until the liability lawsuits start coming in, which may explain why product-liability law is such a lucrative segment of the legal profession. Bolt Beranek and Newman has developed a piece of software dubbed the "mythical man" to test the cognitive workloads required by certain military flight-control equipment—while it is still in development. The company has also come up with

something called simulator networking, or SIMNET, an extraordinarily realistic audio-video simulation of operating an M-1 tank, among other vehicles. SIMNET was designed to allow soldiers to train on a battalion of M-1s under battle conditions without actually being shot at. Because it is an easily alterable software package, SIMNET has proved helpful in testing the usability of new tank designs as well.

User-centered design applies no less to a large technology such as nuclear power. Mauro served on a nuclear-power task force in the aftermath of the near-meltdown at Three Mile Island. In his opinion, safety issues have been badly neglected by most nuclear designers. "Most nuclear power stations were designed primarily to accommodate the latest engineering theories and other political and technological issues," he says. "Only after they were built did anyone ask if human decision-making was properly factored into the system to make it safe." One way to build safety in from the start would be to require that all control rooms be highly standardized, as they are in France, to allow standardized training and also to facilitate outside intervention in an emergency. As it is, most individual nuclear plants in the United States have gone to considerable expense to produce exact reproductions of their control rooms for training purposes—yet most important skills are not directly transferable to any other plant. Similarly, user-centered design in the military could reduce the hazards of friendly fire for ground vehicles by having them emit the electronic signals indicating "ally" that have long been standard on military airplanes. Only after the calamities of the Persian Gulf War did military designers recognize this problem.

## New Genres

USER-CENTERED DESIGN IS NOT EASY TO IMPLEMENT, first because it means revamping the way that technology reaches the marketplace, and second because it calls on a broad range of expertise—in marketing, human factors, psychology, sociology—that is rarely found in one place. "You can't just hire a user-centered-design person," Mauro says.

For these reasons very few companies in the country are doing much user-centered design. One of the few is Xerox, whose Palo Alto Research Center is using these principles to redesign the personal computer. "We want to use the incredible technological power inside the box to create simplicity outside," says John Seely Brown, a chief scientist at Xerox and the director of PARC. Rather than blindly creating more features, PARC is harnessing the power of the computer to make it easier to use.

Apple's Macintosh computer, using innovations developed at PARC, has set the standard for user-friendliness with its representational icons, such as a trash can (to get rid of a document) and a manila folder (to collect a group of files). But such symbols have served mainly to lessen resistance to computers; they do little to enhance the operator's power over the machine once he or she has gotten going. Some even argue that user-friendliness actually reduces control for the experienced user, just as automatic transmission takes something away from drivers accustomed to standard transmission.

Xerox PARC has responded to this argument by trying to break the computer out of its box entirely, scrapping the conventional configuration of keyboard, central processing unit, and screen. In order to bring more power to a business meeting, one group has computerized a white board, adding such basic computer functions as saving and editing to a large computer screen on which users draw by hand.

Another PARC group, led by Stuart Card, has added depth to the flat world of conventional personal-computer screens through the use of 3D, virtual reality, and Disneyesque animation. This is perhaps the ultimate in user-centeredness: it allows the operator to all but enter into the data. The three-dimensionality means that there is a place to stash a lot of background data while the user focuses on the foreground. The resulting information is wonderfully concentrated. The system can present the top 600 senior managers of Xerox on a single screen by arranging the hierarchy in the shape of a twelve-inch-high 3D Christmas tree (this has the added benefit of showing the relationships among the various jobholders). Without depth such a list would shoot up to twelve feet high.

Depth also makes possible a more natural arrangement for clusters of information. Instead of the "windows" on the current generation of personal computers, Card's team developed the concept of 3D "rooms," one for each project, connected by "doors." With 3D the system can rely on the user's natural intuitions, developed in the real world, and arrange the various entries like sections of a private library. It also allows the user to visualize a long list of files by viewing them as if on three sides of a folding screen, which angles out from and back into deep space as the files scroll by. More startling still, the system allows the mapping of information into lifelike 3D space through computer graphics. In one configuration, Card took me on a tour of the lab itself, occasionally veering off to land on a ceiling or settle on a wall. The world of the computer had become the world of the world.

User-centered design can go only so far to make a new technological system seem natural, though. Some operations simply have to be learned. For instance, does a computer's UP arrow mean that the text goes up (and the screen down) or the screen goes up (and the text down)? Neither mental model is more intuitive than the other; the correct answer has to be memorized.

Over time such things become natural, just as driving a car does—both for individuals and for society. But it does take time. John Seely Brown explains the process for society as a whole as a matter of developing the appropriate technological "genres." Just as popular culture has genres (the romance novel, the slasher flick) to help people interpret a new experience, so technology has genres (the motorcycle, the calculator) to help people come to terms with a new product. In Brown's view, the problem is that technology is coming out faster than the "social mind" can establish genres for it. "In the old days there was real stability," Brown says. "A piece of technology stayed on so long that we had a wonderful, socially constructed genre that helped us read the technology and inform our views. Now the technology is changing so fast that the genre doesn't have time to get enacted or constructed."

Brown believes that there are ways to stimulate the social mind to create new genres, the most valuable of which is to encourage the development of informal technological networks, where he believes the real learning takes place—coffee klatches, user groups, electronic mail. Unfortunately, these networks' free-form conversations are too often stifled by corporations as unproductive.

Brown took me down a hall to look at a high-powered Xerox 5100 copier, which, he told me, embodies many of the principles he had just been discussing. The machine itself does the bulk of the work, of course, but it allows the operator to direct and oversee the process via an icon-laden touch-sensitive computer on top of the machine, which presents a visual display of the internal operation. The whole business seems somehow comfortable, human. The housing is clean and spare, the image of order. Should you need to investigate the cabinet underneath, the color scheme tells you most of what you need to know: red says don't touch, green says grasp here. Brown shut the cabinet door and ran a hand lovingly along the smooth exterior. "This is very nicely designed," he said with a smile. "The scary part is all inside."

# DO CELLULAR PHONES CAUSE CANCER?

One researcher for Motorola wouldn't use them more than 30 minutes a day. But there's an appalling lack of convincing research on risks from electromagnetic fields.

*David Kirkpatrick*

THE BOTTOM LINE of all the hullabaloo over whether cellular phones cause brain cancer: Nobody knows. Why not? Because—as with electromagnetic radiation from other sources like video display terminals (VDTs) and power lines—industry and the U.S. government haven't done enough research. Despite a correlation between proximity to power lines and some forms of cancer, and worrisome experimental results involving cellular phones and VDTs, follow-up remains minimal—largely for lack of money.

In 1971 an advisory council of radiation experts originally appointed under President Johnson warned of "a distressing lack of data on the possible . . . subtle, long-term, and cumulative effects" of low-level electromagnetic radiation, the type that's produced by cellular phones, power lines, hair dryers, baby monitors, pencil sharpeners, electric shavers, some desk lamps, and dozens of other devices people use every day. After more than 20 years of desultory funding and piecemeal research, the council's scary conclusion remains all too accurate.

The world is at the brink of what many giddily call "the wireless revolution." Computers and telephones are shedding their tethering wires and roaming freely with their ever more mobile owners. Companies are peddling wireless cash registers, highway toll collectors, vehicle guidance systems—even wireless mice for use with PCs. All these require transmitters that send out electromagnetic radiation. "We are bathing ourselves in this stuff," says Paul Saffo, a researcher at the Institute for the Future in Menlo Park, California, and a leading U.S. expert on information technology.

So the need to identify and evaluate potential risks—or else dismiss them conclusively—grows increasingly urgent. Ten million Americans already use cellular phones, and their number is rising fast. Says Louis Slesin, publisher of *Microwave News*, an activist who cautions regularly against this sort of risk: "If we're going to have 50 million Americans holding these devices to their heads, don't you think we ought to find out if they're safe?"

What scant evidence of possible hazards there is applies mostly to the extremely low frequency, or ELF, electromagnetic fields created by transmitting electricity. (Cellu-

lar phones transmit higher-frequency radio waves, not electricity, and radiate a completely different field.) The ELF research is more and more worrisome. Most disturbing so far: two long-term epidemiological studies in Sweden that showed clear associations between exposure to ELF fields and various forms of cancer. The results were announced last September. One study found increased brain cancer and leukemia in men exposed to ELF fields in a variety of work situations. The other found three times the normal rate of leukemia in children who live near high-tension lines.

These were among the largest and most careful studies of possible hazards from ELF fields ever conducted. Both suggested that a danger to health appears at very low exposure levels—only a couple of times greater than what hundreds of millions of people experience every day from appliances and wiring in their homes and offices. Says Granger Morgan, who heads the engineering and public policy department at Carnegie Mellon University: "The likelihood that there is a problem has moved up closer to even odds now. There's clearly cause for concern."

In Sweden, those two studies moved the government to action. The day the results were announced, the National Board for Industrial and Technical Development, a regulatory body, declared that it will proceed "on the assumption that there is a connection between exposure to lower frequency magnetic fields and cancer, in particular childhood cancer."

As a result, in January Sweden's Radiation Protection Institute recommended taking steps to reduce the fields "where such countermeasures can be made at reasonable cost." A homely example: moving a bed away from the corner of the room where electrical lines enter a house. Sweden stands alone in taking the issue so seriously, but its actions are slowly gaining attention elsewhere. (For more information on the Swedish response, see box on page 180.)

Scientists are by no means unanimous. The most outspoken skeptic is certainly Robert Adair, a professor of physics at Yale, who asserts flatly: "Worries about cellular phone and power line frequencies range from inane nonsense to foolish inane nonsense. Nothing happens, and there are no experiments that show that anything has happened." Policymakers in the Reagan and Bush Administrations tended to down-

play the issue, and so far the U.S. government has only yawned at the Swedish data.

But the American public seems increasingly fearful. Last year *USA Weekend* magazine, distributed to 33.5 million Sunday newspaper buyers nationwide, asked its readers to name the health issues they worried about most. Topping the list: electromagnetic fields. In January, when CNN's *Larry King Live* publicized a single lawsuit in which a Florida man alleged that a cellular phone caused his wife's fatal brain cancer, the reaction was explosive. Some cellular industry stocks dropped 20%. (They later rebounded.)

How do power lines relate to cellular phones? Both emit low-level electromagnetic radiation, but at very different frequencies. ELF fields from power lines are a byproduct of the flow of electricity through the wires. Similar fields are also produced by such devices as appliance motors or the transformers in VDT or TV picture tubes. Cellular phones, on the other hand, use transmitters to send much higher radio frequency (RF) signals to nearby relay stations. The latest cordless telephones use frequencies near those of cellular phones.

Both ELF and RF fields carry very little energy. That's why scientists find it so hard to imagine how either type could affect living cells. The RF emitted by cellular phones *can* cause heating in tissue at higher power levels than the phones are allowed to produce. After all, microwave ovens operate not awfully far in the spectrum from cellular phones, and they do a fine job of warming things up. The much less energetic ELF fields from power lines cannot by themselves induce any heating. Even now there are no widely accepted theories about how exposure to a so-called nonthermal electromagnetic field—one that can't heat anything—could affect living cells, much less threaten health.

DESPITE THE LACK of a scientific explanation, several developments raise the possibility that nonthermal fields do affect people. The first is the growing body of epidemiology suggesting a connection between exposure to power-line ELF and various cancers, mostly leukemia and brain tumors. The Swedish studies are the most notable, though several U.S. researchers have also shown similar correlations, especially in children. Louis Slesin of *Microwave News* calls the Swedish results a "smoking gun."

REPORTER ASSOCIATE *Ricardo Sookdeo*

He adds, "A few years ago it was considered impossible for either ELF or RF to have health effects. But if you show that one may be risky, you've got to open the book on the other. It's just common sense."

One provocative fact: The incidence of diseases that epidemiologists suggest may be related to electromagnetic fields has increased significantly over the past 20 years. For example, among children under 15 in the U.S., brain and nervous system cancer rose 28.6% from 1973 to 1989, and one of the most common forms of leukemia increased 23.7%.

In addition to the epidemiology associating electromagnetic fields with cancer, an important study in Finland completed last year found a correlation between ELF and miscarriages in women who use VDTs at work. The study was the first anywhere to compare actual magnetic field measurements with the health of VDT users. Magnetic field intensity is measured in gauss. The background level in a typical house or office is about 1 milligauss (mG). The Finnish researchers found that women exposed to over 3 mG from a VDT had more than three times as many miscarriages as those exposed to less than 1 mG. Many VDTs emit 3 mG or more, though shielded models are now widely available.

Epidemiology alone proves nothing about what *causes* a disease. All it does is demonstrate a statistical correlation. It's possible, for example, that children living near power lines are more exposed than others to carcinogenic defoliants sprayed beneath the wires to retard plant growth. Indeed, many who are convinced that electromagnetic fields contribute to cancer believe that the fields act more to promote the disease once it has struck than to cause it in the first place.

As epidemiologists have been mustering their evidence, biophysicists conducting experiments on living cells in test tubes and petri dishes, and in a few cases on animals, claim to have identified a variety of biological effects from exposure to nonthermal levels of both ELF and RF fields. Their work is critical. Finding a biological effect in a cell is by no means the same thing as demonstrating an effect on human health, but it does increase the likelihood that the epidemiology is correctly connecting electromagnetic fields with cancer.

The data are sketchiest for RF fields, the kind associated with cellular phones. Though many investigations have failed to identify any adverse effects, several recent efforts cry out for further exploration. Two studies published in 1990 by Stephen Cleary, a biophysicist at the Medical College of Virginia, showed that both normal human blood cells and one type of cancer cell grew abnormally after two-hour exposures to either the frequency at which microwave ovens operate or a lower frequency emitted by industrial equipment that uses high-intensity RF to fuse plastics. (In that case he was exploring possible dangers to the operators.) Cleary, who testified before a House subcommittee in February, says he would not use a cellular phone until the uncertainties are resolved.

N THE much lower ELF range, at least 11 studies have found effects of nonthermal fields on immune-system cells exposed to frequencies little higher than those of power transmission fields. While none involved intensities anywhere near as low as those the Swedish studies associated with cancer, they nonetheless buttress the notion that something does go on. Several have shown that ELF exposure modifies the concentrations of calcium inside a cell. That may be significant, since calcium levels are closely related to many fundamental cell functions, including the ability to divide and make proteins.

Critic Adair of Yale says that until demonstrable effects of radiation are readily and independently replicated, nothing meaningful has been shown. But others counter, for example, that one paper published in December verified earlier results showing effects on cellular calcium from rock-bottom ELF fields. Many scientists accept Adair's criticism that they need to reproduce more results, though they say the reason they haven't is largely lack of funds. And there are still no studies that show anything happening to cells or tissue at the exact intensity and frequency of cellular phones.

A key observer disagrees, perhaps surprisingly, with Adair's blanket dismissal of the results: Stanley Sussman, who manages electromagnetic field research at the Electric Power Research Institute in Palo Alto, California, which is funded by the electric utility industry. Says Sussman: "Knowing some of the researchers involved and their labs and the way they do experiments, I think it's likely that some of them are showing true results."

One reason it's so hard to know what to make of all the lab research is the sheer dumbfounding complexity of factors that can come into play. Among the variables:

## SOME TIPS ON PLAYING IT SAFE

While it's far from proven that electromagnetic fields are harmful, a little caution can't hurt.

In addition to power lines and wiring, many devices around your home or office produce fields when they are turned on, including video display terminals (VDTs) and almost anything with an electric motor—air conditioners, coffee grinders, computer printers, copiers, clocks, dishwashers, electric razors, and hair dryers. Evidence for possible harmful effects is stronger for children than for adults, probably because growing tissue is more vulnerable.

The strength—and presumably the danger—of a field diminishes dramatically with distance: Four feet from the source, it's only one-sixteenth as powerful as it is one foot away. Even a small space between your body and an emitting device greatly reduces your exposure. Granger Morgan of Carnegie Mellon University, who developed the concept of "prudent avoidance," suggests you analyze where you spend most of your time. Try to stay several feet from any source of a field.

For maximum prudence, you can measure the fields around wiring or appliances with a gaussmeter. These generally cost more than $100 and can be hard to find. (For a list of manufacturers, send a self-addressed stamped envelope and $1 to *Microwave News*, P.O. Box 1799, Grand Central Station, New York, New York 10163.)

A few ways that a growing number of experts say you can limit exposure:

■ Opt if you can for a cellular phone that has the transmitter separate from the handset, as car phones do.

■ Don't work with your head close to a fluorescent or halogen desk lamp.

■ Don't work closer than arm's length from your VDT, or use laptop computers instead—their liquid crystal display (LCD) screens emit negligible radiation. Don't lean back in your desk chair and put your head near the VDT screen behind you. Avoid the backs of VDTs, where fields are more intense.

■ If you use a wireless baby monitor, don't put the transmitter within five feet of the child.

■ Keep children five feet from TV screens.

■ Don't stand next to the dishwasher or microwave oven when it's running.

■ Check around your bed and make sure devices like clocks and air conditioners are at least three feet from your sleeping position.

■ Avoid electric razors—and hand-held hair dryers too, or else buy the kind with the fan far from your head.

■ If you use an electric blanket, pick one of the newer low-intensity-field designs.

wavelength, intensity, duration of exposure, time of day, interaction with the earth's magnetic field (which some experiments show could alter the impact of radiating fields), and other fields that might be affecting an experiment, such as those emanating from lighting or power supplies in the laboratory. Many experiments haven't been repeated partly because it's so difficult to precisely duplicate this long list of experimental parameters.

Dr. Ross Adey, a neurologist at the Veterans Administration Medical Center in Loma Linda, California, and perhaps the most eminent U.S. researcher in this area, believes scientists may eventually discover that what most affects human health is the aggregate effect of exposure to many different frequencies. He points out that when you switch on an electric motor, the initial surge of power creates a range of harmonic frequencies much higher than the basic household current frequency. Says Adey: "I wouldn't focus on cellular phones when other things we have around our heads, like electric hair dryers and shavers, may be much more biologically active."

Adey is conducting research under contract for Motorola, the No. 1 cellular phone maker. The company has cited his work as evidence that the phones are safe, but Adey doesn't put it so simply. He says he would still use one—but for no more than 30 minutes a day. He also worries about the next generation of phones, which will employ digital compression to allow more phones to operate on the same channel. Instead of emitting a continuous signal, each phone will spritz out RF in quick pulses, perhaps as brief as one-fiftieth of a second. "That opens up a Pandora's box of knowns and unknowns," says Adey. "One thing we do know is that when a continuous radio signal is interrupted at that kind of low frequency rate, it interacts with tissue more powerfully than does an uninterrupted signal. I can't say if we should be worried, but I certainly think we should look into it."

THE CELLULAR PHONE industry has yet to address public fears convincingly. In a January statement, Thomas Wheeler, president of the Cellular Telecommunications Industry Association, insisted cheerily, "I'm comfortable using my portable phone, and I'm comfortable telling others to continue using their portable phones." But he conceded the need for more reassurance and announced that the industry would spend over $1 million on research—but only "to revalidate the findings of the existing studies, which have found that the radio waves from cellular phones are safe."

That won't do. Says Samuel Koslov, a physicist at Johns Hopkins and, along with Adey, a member of that presidential panel back in 1971: "It's something of a national scandal that government and industry are so unwilling to fund research to get an adequate understanding of what's going on." No studies of the health of cellular phone users exist. Slesin of *Microwave News* rejects statements by the industry association and Motorola that 10,000 studies prove cellular phones safe. Says he: "Almost none of the studies address cancer or any other long-term effects. Are you telling me that an industry that's invested $10 billion in capital projects can't afford it?"

At the Electric Power Research Institute, spending on electromagnetic field health studies this year will total about $15 million, more than double what it was two years ago. Granger Morgan of Carnegie Mellon terms the dearth of ELF research dollars "a disgrace." He adds, "We've done enough research to suggest there may be a problem, but not enough to resolve it. If we don't crank up and get some answers we're going to have a long, expensive period of chaos." He thinks total federal support for ELF research, now about $7 million a year, ought to top $20 million.

While the measurable danger from electromagnetic radiation so far seems much less than the risk you run if you don't fasten your seat belt, the public won't be reassured by anything less than thorough, conclusive studies.

## MAYBE THE SWEDES ARE RIGHT

Anders Ahlbom is hardly a revolutionary. Sitting in his tidy, light-filled office at Stockholm's Karolinska Institute medical school, the researcher whose results are frightening a lot of people seems not the least anxious himself. His 1992 study found a significant correlation between exposure to electromagnetic fields around power lines and the incidence of leukemia in children. But he won't take a position on what ought to be done, warning that "the worst mistake we can make is to overinterpret the data." He cautions that the mechanism that caused the cancers remains unknown.

On a recent visit to Sweden, FORTUNE interviewed many students of electromagnetic radiation, including epidemiologists like Ahlbom, biophysicists, doctors, and experts from government agencies, unions, and power companies. A number of them pointed out that Ahlbom's study could have been done nowhere else. He had access not only to a comprehensive historical registry of all cancer cases ever reported, but also to detailed logs of electrical loads carried by specific power lines at any given time. Only Sweden keeps such careful records.

The Swedish government is already responding. Olov Östberg, an official at the Agency for Administrative Development, has started to provide "electrical and magnetic sanitation" in government offices, removing unnecessary electrical equipment and designing work areas to minimize exposure. By this summer, Swedish regulators expect to propose a ban on construction of houses within about 330 feet of high-tension lines.

Electromagnetic fields are the talk of Sweden. But a visitor who expected to hear everyone discussing the risk of cancer found greater concern about a phenomenon called "electrical allergy"—hypersensitivity to electricity.

The malady appears to be common nowhere else, but nearly every high-tech workplace in Sweden has people who suffer from it. They generally attribute the onset of symptoms to unremitting work at a video terminal. Eventually, sufferers report a range of allergic reactions, from burning sensations on the skin and headaches to memory loss, nausea, and even complete disorientation. Some can talk for only a few minutes on an ordinary telephone, which uses a minuscule one watt of electrical power.

At Ellemtel, a research partnership between Ericsson and Swedish Telecom that likes to consider itself the Bell Labs of Sweden, as many as 30 out of 750 were afflicted in 1990, including a top software engineer. Ellemtel eventually got them all back to work, in part by reducing fields with rewiring and shielding.

Many doctors in Sweden believe it's all in the mind—but not Gunnar Hovsenius, chief environmental researcher for the nation's power companies. Says he: "I definitely don't believe these problems are psychosomatic in most cases. I have met people willing to do anything to come back to society, but they have no chance." In the U.S. the condition is virtually unheard of, but experiments by Charles Graham of the Midwest Research Institute in Kansas City do show clear variations in how people react to electromagnetic exposure.

Under pressure from its powerful unions, Sweden began moving toward requiring lower VDT emissions in the mid-1980s—well before there was any solid evidence for doing so. Now the national VDT standards, called Swedac, are generally accepted worldwide as the ultimate in user safety. (IBM and Apple have adopted them for reduced-emission monitors.) It's too soon to know whether Swedish officials are once again ahead of the curve in limiting exposure to radiation and taking these allergies seriously.

# A System on Overload

## Our unlimited appetite for software strains our ability to produce it

**Evelyn Richards**
*Washington Post Staff Writer*

It was exactly 2:25 p.m. last Jan. 15 when, out of the corner of his eye, Jim Nelson spotted an alarming sea of red spreading across the screens of 75 video monitors in the control center of AT&T's vast long-distance network.

The screens normally are filled with bland charts and maps of the United States. For Nelson, the manager of the Bedminster, N.J., center, the red warning signals were an unmistakable sign of crisis.

"We have the big one," an assistant exclaimed.

The nation's largest telephone network had virtually collapsed, frustrating millions of Americans who were blocked from making long-distance calls for nine hours and sending a team of more than 100 phone company technicians on a frantic search for the cause.

They found it in the software that controls the system's computers and electronic switches—a small, undetected error in the web of written instructions that tell the equipment what to do. An unexpectedly heavy flow of calls had overwhelmed a weak point in the system, and American Telephone & Telegraph Co. computers, lacking instructions on how to deal with the unforeseen overload, simply shut down.

The calamity that struck AT&T that Monday afternoon is just the kind that many experts have increasingly come to fear as software reaches deeper into everyday life. In a generation's time, software has emerged as the ubiquitous control system of an automated society, a $125 billion-a-year industry that is an essential underpinning of America's economic and political standing in the world.

Software controls banking and airline reservations networks and is critical to U.S. defense systems. It decides when to buy and sell huge blocks of stock. It is buried inside video-cassette recorders and the dashboards and fuel systems of automobiles. It picks lottery winners and flushes toilets in the new Boeing 747-400. It helps physicians select and administer treatments. And, by crunching billions of instructions each second, it can simulate nature to help researchers unravel man's genetic makeup or predict hurricanes.

A miracle of human ingenuity, software instructions translate the tasks requested by humans into electronic commands that computers can follow. Software converted this reporter's keystrokes into letters on a computer screen; other software converted those letters into type for this newspaper page. The computers involved in those operations are lifeless combinations of silicon chips and electronic parts that only software can activate.

Most software routinely performs as expected, but as society demands more and more from software and the computers it controls, errors and failures like AT&T's could easily become more common. According to scores of computer scientists and other specialists, the nation's ability to produce software on time and with high reliability is in jeopardy.

Software problems already affect many sectors of society. One of the most important is the Pentagon, whose increasingly high-tech weapons systems depend—with uneven success—on some of the world's most elaborate computer programs. Another is human health, which can be threatened by faulty software. And at giant corporations, huge investments can be undermined by delayed and over-budget software projects, which are now routine.

The Bank of New York once had to borrow $24 billion overnight from the Federal Reserve, incurring $5 million in instant interest costs, because a software glitch left it without enough funds to balance its account with the Fed. Inadequate software used to process student loans may cost a group of international lenders up to $650 million. Fargo Bank in California vastly overstated the income of 22,000 employees in reports to the Internal Revenue Service because a programming error moved the decimal point two places to the right.

Last year, a mysterious defect paralyzed the American Airlines reservations system for nine hours. Though the carrier located the general problem area, it still isn't certain exactly why the software ran amok.

Perhaps one-quarter of all software projects are so troubled that they are simply canceled in midstream, according to Software Productivity Research, a Cambridge, Mass., consulting firm. The state of Washington, for example, last year pulled the plug on a seven-year, federally backed $20 million automation effort designed to give social service caseworkers more time to spend with their clients. One complaint: The program kept caseworkers waiting 20 minutes for computerized files.

While such problems are multiplying, the supply of new programmers and software designers is declining. After a sharp rise in the late 1970s and early 1980s, interest in computing jobs has plummeted among college freshmen, the fastest collapse ever recorded for a career preference in the 23 years that the University of California at Los Angeles has conducted such surveys. The reason most commonly given: Computer jobs are no longer considered glamorous.

But demand for software is expanding relentlessly, driven by society's insatiable appetite for new uses and the ability of computers to perform calculations at ever greater speeds. Each year, computers have been providing 25 percent more power per dollar, while the productivity of people who produce software has been rising at less than half that rate.

"The amount and quality of software we need is increasing constantly, and our ability to produce it is essentially stagnant. Those two things are on a collision course," warns William Wulf, former head of the National Science Foundation's office of computer and information science. It is "absolutely a problem of much larger dimension than most people realize," says Wulf. The consequence, he fears, will be a slowing of technological progress and in turn a decline in the country's economic competitiveness.

"Software can well become the limiting factor in what we can do in building systems in the future," says Norman Augustine, chairman of Martin Marietta Corp. in Bethesda, Md. The bottleneck could affect "space systems, telephone systems, automobile systems or any other complex technological device," he says.

Other experts warn that, as computers increasingly take over decisions formerly made by human beings, software producers and the public may be placing too much confidence in a technology that defies perfection.

"I'm worried that people are putting too much reliance on computers without enough understanding of the potential risk that they may be adding," says Nancy Leveson, a professor specializing in software reliability at the University of California at Irvine.

Problems with software have claimed a handful of lives, and the potential for software-triggered breakdowns to affect public health and safety "will be much worse in the future than it has been in the past," says John Guttag, an industry consultant and Massachusetts Institute of Technology computer science professor.

Large software systems, in the words of John Shore, a Washington author and software engineer, are "by far the most complex artifact" built by man. It is impossible for designers to predict how complex software will function in every circumstance, and when failures do occur they may never be fully comprehended even by those who crafted the code.

"The programs we construct are effectively too large for humans to understand," says Wulf. "Yet every characteristic of them depends upon the human's ability to understand them, to cope with them."

The challenges confronting the software industry center on the tension between the rigid, precise demands of electronic technology and the spontaneous creativity of programmers and software designers—with their capacity for human error.

Hidden and intangible when in operation, software takes form as the excruciatingly detailed instructions known as computer "code." Generally written by professional programmers, the code is gibberish to the uninitiated. But it actually is a logical structure of step-by-step commands and decisions, bearing some resemblance to English in its use of letters, numbers and symbols. A line of code is akin to a sentence of instruction.

The instructions are either stored electronically in computer chips, like those inside video games, calculators and automobile emission-control systems, or recorded on magnetic disks and tapes linked to computers.

In recent years, software programs have swelled from something easily handled by a lone "hacker"—as computer enthusiasts are known—to systems too large to be grasped by a single mind.

One popular software program for personal computers known as "dBase," designed to manage large amounts of data, was written a decade ago by two programmers and required fewer than 50,000 lines of code. It took a team of more than 100 people three years to write a new, more sophisticated version of the program, and even then the 400,000 lines of code they delivered—six months late—were so laden with defects that publisher Ashton-Tate Corp. of Torrance, Calif., provided buyers a "bug list" of flaws during the 21 months it spent making further corrections.

Still, a program like dBase is a small job compared with the software produced by the aerospace and defense industries. Those projects often run more than 1 million lines—roughly equivalent to the listings in the Manhattan phone book.

As a product of human minds—with their wide variances in skill and judgment—software is not a task easily reduced to tools, mass production or standard parts. Nor is there enough effort to transfer know-how from project to project, causing wasteful duplication.

"The problem is that software has the highest manual labor content of almost any manufactured item in the second half of the 20th century. It's like building pyramids or handcrafting Rolls-Royces," says Capers Jones, chairman of Software Productivity Research.

"We're still building software in many ways the same way we were 30 or 40 years ago," says Max D. Hopper, senior vice president for information systems at American Airlines in Dallas.

Indeed, software development frequently is treated more like an art than a science, with design and testing often dictated more by personal choice than by regimen. Software developers, a fragmented community of independent-minded souls, lack the widely accepted safety standards and engineering discipline applied to the manufacture of mechanical and electrical equipment. Programmers need no license, no particular academic degree and no other official credential to build a software structure, though their creation may be as critical as any bridge or skyscraper.

Software problems begin long before the first line of code is written. In trying to take on tasks or decisions formerly handled by people, or new challenges never before conceived, software must translate all the ambiguity of human thought into rigid commands that a computer can follow.

This means that even before writing code, software developers must try to imagine all the different circumstances to which the computer or electronic equipment ultimately may need to respond, a virtually impossible task. And often the people writing the software have little understanding of the industry that is going to be using it.

"Imagine building a skyscraper and then realizing you forgot to leave space for a water system," says William Scherlis, software technology program manager at the Pentagon's Defense Advanced Research Projects Agency. "That's what happens in software all the time."

There is also the endless temptation to keep tinkering with and adjusting what has largely been completed, a practice that can cause other parts of a program to unravel.

Poor management, as much as anything, is to blame for poor software, experts say. Top corporate managers, many lacking an understanding of software, often don't know how to plan for something they can't see or touch. With little in the way of a standard blueprint to help visualize the outcome of a software effort, many companies and government agencies fail to gauge the challenge or create a structure necessary to see large projects through to completion.

Those in charge of software projects routinely miscalculate the magnitude of their project, a mistake Allstate Insurance Co. officials, for instance, readily acknowledge making.

Allstate, based in Northbrook, Ill., hoped a new computer program would cut as much as 75 percent of the time it takes to devise new life-insurance policies. In 1988, just before the system was supposed to be completed, the company realized the project was badly off track, and it started over. Now it predicts that the work will not be completed until 1992—and at three times the original cost.

"I don't believe we had recognized the level of planning that was needed," says project chief Ben Currier. "I don't think we had the proper management procedures in place."

American Airlines paid a steep price when it tried to add international fares to existing software before managers had the right information at hand. Too late, they discovered the fare-calculation formulas were incorrect and insufficient, causing development time and costs to double and leaving agents unable to function as planned. "We totally screwed up," senior vice president Hopper concedes.

Many companies that develop software for their own payroll, inventory tracking and other essentials of business estimate that they are so backed up in their software development that if they stopped getting new assignments today, programmers would spend the next three years completing their backlog of requests.

major software failure like the one last January at AT&T can be traced to any combination of human error, design flaws and project mismanagement.

The problem with AT&T's software turned out to be a mistake made in just one line of a 2 million-line program used to route calls. Software is structured much like a road map, with many of the lines directing the software where to go next. The flawed line, or software "bug," in the AT&T program sent the call-processing mechanism to an incorrect place in the code, where the next instruction it encountered made no sense, thus disabling the equipment.

As is often the case, the fatal bug had been injected into the system when AT&T altered the software a month earlier to fix an unrelated flaw. The ability to alter software with relative ease causes many of its problems, since small changes can cause larger disruptions elsewhere.

The glitch surfaced only when telephone traffic was so heavy that two calls happened to arrive at a troubled switch within one-hundredth of a second of each other. Despite months of testing, AT&T had failed to prepare for this exact sequence and pace of events.

The AT&T breakdown underscored the trade-off between achieving greater performance and taking greater risk. Software has evolved as the technological backbone of modern society because, in most cases, it is much quicker and more reliable than humans. Many of today's conveniences are possible only because software has taken over where humans or machines left off, carrying on tasks with amazing speed and without wearing out or tiring. And like humans, software has a seemingly endless capacity to adapt to change.

But ultimately, software's performance depends on humans—on people's ability to turn imprecise human preferences into a master plan that can operate flawlessly, without the benefit of common sense to guide it through unexpected situations. These days, as the people who write software race on an accelerating treadmill to keep up with demand, concerns are rising that they are being pushed too far, too fast.

As the Bell Laboratories vice president who presided over the AT&T software-repair mission, Karl Martersteck knows that dilemma well. "With complexity," he says, "you increase the number of things that can go wrong."

# For the Military, Getting
# With the Program Is Half the Battle

When the contract was first awarded in 1984, the U.S. Army hoped to develop a largely automated battlefield.

Computers would determine what gun to fire at what target, and precisely when. They would select routes for artillery and trucks to travel. They would track troops as they moved across the terrain. Commanders would manage the battle from computer consoles.

After six painful years, the Advanced Field Artillery Tac-

tical Data System (AFATDS) is a monument to the perils of reliance on sophisticated computer software to fulfill complex military assignments. The skeleton of a system that can automate bits and pieces of the battlefield has been created. But synchronizing the whole operation, the Army now acknowledges, is still years—and many millions of dollars—away. Nearly $80 million has produced nothing that is yet usable on a battlefield.

AFATDS (pronounced a-FA-tids), far from the Pentagon's largest software project, captures in miniature a software logjam that has affected the entire defense establishment.

The Pentagon is the biggest software customer in the world. Its spending on software projects is estimated to be about $30 billion a year, or 10 percent of its budget, an amount that has tripled in the past five years.

But the Defense Department is also a huge bureaucracy with old habits that aren't well-suited to the computer age.

Numerous Pentagon officials concede that the department has failed to master the administration of complex software projects. "We don't know how to manage it," says Virginia Castor, a Pentagon official who is helping to develop a Defense Department policy for improving software production.

Software problems have caused major delays of weapons systems, created malfunctioning aircraft and cost the Defense Department billions of dollars in unanticipated costs. Officials acknowledge that virtually every troubled weapons system, from the electronics in the B-1B bomber to satellite tracking systems, has been afflicted with software problems. Even straightforward record-keeping systems can get bogged down; last year, the Navy canceled a software accounting project nine years in the making after its costs quadrupled to $230 million.

The software problem steadily compounds itself because of the rapid expansion of the Pentagon's dependence upon software. The F-4 fighter-bombers that saw combat in Vietnam had no software at all. Today's fighters have more than 1 million lines of computer "code"—each line a written instruction to a computer—while the Navy's latest submarine combat system has roughly 3 million lines. The Strategic Defense Initiative, the high-tech U.S. anti-missile program, would require an estimated 30 million lines. With each additional line, the danger of error multiplies.

Never has the military's software dependence been more evident than in the current Persian Gulf crisis. From the F-16 fighters and seaborne Aegis air-defense system to the ordering of spare tires and food, software serves as the central nervous system of the U.S. build-up. "There isn't anything over there except the foot soldiers that doesn't have software," says Lloyd Mosemann II, deputy assistant secretary of the Air Force for communications, computers and logistics.

Ultimately, a failure to perfect military software problems can endanger American fighting men and women and the effectiveness of the U.S. military. One example is the huge C-17A transport plane being developed by McDonnell Douglas Corp. at about $150 million each. Three years into its development, engineers discovered that a faulty software design created an unacceptable risk that the plane could crash when landing. The design was scrapped and developers had to begin anew—increasing the cost of the plane and adding to delays.

Such delays are typical. A review of 82 large military procurement programs conducted by Air Force Col. Joseph Greene Jr. found that those relying heavily on software generally ran 20 months behind schedule, three times longer than projects less dependent on computer programming.

Greene, who retired this year as head of a Pentagon software research effort, calculated that such delays cost the Defense Department one-tenth of its $100 billion annual research and procurement budget.

A separate study showed that Pentagon contractors deserve some of the blame: Three-fourths of 55 aerospace and defense projects were found to be run in an "ad hoc" and even "chaotic" manner.

"The department is paying a huge penalty for not dealing with its software problems," Greene says. "The penalty is not just late software—it is degraded war-fighting capability."

In the case of AFATDS, the Army hoped for a computer system that would be able to set priorities in the heat of battle, decide what firepower should be used against which targets, distribute critical information to units in the field and at headquarters, manage ammunition, assess road conditions and advise commanders where to place artillery.

The contract to develop this capability was awarded in May 1984 to Magnavox Electronic Systems Co., based in Fort Wayne, Ind. The project posed big technical challenges for Magnavox, which had never before won such a large government software contract. But from the beginning, the dream was frustrated by a persistent problem of a different sort, one not uncommon to large projects: The Army couldn't communicate what it wanted the computer software to do.

"The contract was signed for a total system when the government and contractor didn't have a good understanding of what it is that we wanted," says Robert Giordano, now the Army's deputy program executive officer of command and control systems.

Such confusion continuously dogged Magnavox, where software chief Harold "Skip" Carstensen and a staff of 100 others often spent weekends cloistered in conference rooms, reading through line by line what ultimately became the official AFATDS program requirements—nine blue binders totaling about 2,000 pages.

They frequently encountered new snags. Some were caused by Ada, the "universal" computer language adopted by the Pentagon in 1983. So new was Ada that Magnavox had to train nearly 300 people in the language—only to have many hired away by other defense contractors hungry for Ada talent.

Magnavox made its share of outright mistakes, contributing to repeated schedule delays beyond the original 33-month plan. The company had to alter the AFATDS software, for example, because it displayed the same information about the status of troops and ammunition to all levels of personnel. The Army pointed out that generals and privates hardly needed the same information. "I as an artillery officer should have realized that," says Carstensen, an Army officer before joining Magnavox. "You can't think of everything."

He calculated that readjusting the software would take six "man-months"—say, six people working one month. Instead, the job took two man-years, and instead of affecting 6,000 lines of code, it involved 12,000, Carstensen says.

Army gaffes caused setbacks, too. One requirement of AFATDS, for example, was that its users be able to exchange information with the older computer-based battle-management system used by the Army. But the Army failed to supply Magnavox with up-to-date technical details to make the links possible, causing several man-months of extra effort.

Invariably, delays resulted from the Army and Magnavox not seeing eye to eye on what AFATDS was supposed to do. Many misunderstandings stemmed from both parties' use of imprecise English.

One requirement, for example, reads: "The operator will receive notice of this new position when the movement requirement is delivered." To the Army, that meant that when artillery changed locations, the person manning the computer would be notified by an alarm or message on the screen. Magnavox insisted, however, that the requirement meant that the news could simply be delivered by one person handing another person a piece of paper.

Such misunderstandings led to endless paperwork. One report by a Magnavox employee outlined this conversation with an Army official: "The paragraphs in the item were 3.2.3.2.8.d and 3.2.3.2.8.d.1 on page 124. There are no such paragraphs on that page." The matter subsequently was resolved when the parties agreed that a "2" had been dropped from the designations.

Snags like these, though troubling, were overshadowed by managerial shortcomings and political pressures that distracted attention from productive work. As the Army and Magnavox bickered, the project fell behind schedule, prompting the Pentagon to freeze payments and ultimately cap the cost of the program at $46 million, up from the original $34 million.

Like most procurement programs, software acquisition is subject to congressional pressure and interference. In the case of AFATDS, the House defense appropriations subcommittee repeatedly challenged the Army and Magnavox about the cost and feasibility of the ambitious project. The subcommittee ordered at least five General Accounting Office reports on AFATDS and related programs and at one point warned that it was growing "increasingly concerned with the Army's repeated . . . disregard of congressional direction."

Under this scrutiny, the Army increased its pressure on Magnavox, whose officials became overwhelmed by visiting investigators. Some of those visitors were, they themselves acknowledge, ill-prepared to pass judgment. Richard Stanley, then an Army official, was on military business in Texas in early 1987 when he was hastily called to Indiana to investigate Magnavox's progress. "Half the people [on the review team] couldn't spell software if their life depended on it," he says. "Most of us there had very little firsthand knowledge of AFATDS."

At one point, Carstensen says, an Army official requested a photo of a "compiler" that was causing problems. Magnavox people just shook their heads. A compiler is a batch of software code, not a piece of hardware, as the Army official had presumed.

Finally, in the spring of 1989 the software emerged from field testing with remarkably few flaws. Magnavox was two years late and had spent $30 million of its own funds on AFATDS, but in the end it joined the Army in rejoicing that the complex software actually worked.

But for all the agony, Magnavox had been asked to complete merely what is known as a "concept evaluation"— enough software to confirm that computers can support a broad range of troops and weapons, yet far short of what actually would be needed to automate the battlefield. That dream, once expected to become reality starting in 1990, has been broken apart into smaller, incremental steps, and it will be at least three more years before any troops will be even partially equipped with AFATDS gear.

Now, officials say, AFATDS software development is moving forward on schedule, thanks to improved cooperation among everyone involved, with a new $60 million Magnavox contract. Still, so much has changed since the Army first sketched out AFATDS that Magnavox has concluded that half of the software written in the first phase is unusable.

Maj. Gen. Peter Kind, who for a time oversaw AFATDS, says the experience taught an important lesson about software: "With large programs, it's a very difficult thing to get it all working and out there in one fell swoop. It just doesn't work that way."

# PROGRAMMED FOR DISASTER

## Software Errors That Imperil Lives

JONATHAN JACKY

*Jonathan Jacky, a research assistant professor in the radiation oncology department at the University of Washington School of Medicine, in Seattle, is designing software for a computer-controlled radiation-therapy machine.*

On MARCH 21, 1986, oilfield worker Ray Cox visited a clinic in Tyler, Texas, to receive radiation on his back, from which a cancerous tumor had been removed. On the basis of previous visits, he knew the procedure should be painless, but that day he felt a jolt of searing heat. Outside the shielded treatment room, the technician was puzzled by his complaint: the computer terminal used to operate the radiation machine bore only the cryptic message "Malfunction 54," indicating either an overdose or an underdose. Clinic staff were unable to find anything wrong with the machine, so they sent Cox home and continued treating other patients. But Cox's condition worsened. Spitting blood, he checked in to a hospital emergency room, where doctors suspected he had received an electric shock; in fact, he had received a lethal overdose.

Less than a month later, Malfunction 54 occurred again at the Tyler clinic, this time striking Verdon Kidd, a sixty-six-year-old bus driver. Kidd died in May of 1986, reportedly the first fatality ever caused by an overdose during radiation treatment. Meanwhile, Cox became paralyzed and lapsed into a coma, and four months later he, too, died of the injury.

As news of the Tyler incidents spread, similar mishaps in other clinics came to light: one patient in Canada and another in Georgia had received mutilating injuries in 1985; an overdose occurred in Washington State in January of 1987. In each case, the radiation had come from the Therac-25, a computer-controlled machine manufactured by Atomic Energy of Canada. After the fifth such accident was reported, the U.S. Food and Drug Administration advised—but did not order—clinics to discontinue routine use of the Therac-25 until safety features could be installed in the equipment.

Ironically, by the time the accidents occurred, radiation therapy had become a routine, safe, and frequently effective procedure, used on nearly four hundred and fifty thousand new patients a year in more than eleven hundred U.S. clinics. Much of that success was due to linear accelerators, which began to replace cobalt treatment units in the 1960s. (Linear accelerators are electric machines, capable of producing radiation beams whose energy can be adjusted. The earlier equipment used a lump of cobalt-60 as the radiation source; the units could not be adjusted, and the intensity of the radioactivity diminished over time.)

The million-dollar Therac-25, introduced in 1983, was among the first of a generation of computer-controlled linear accelerators. With the earlier accelerators, electricity and mechanical forces were used to transmit the operator's directions directly to the wheels, levers, and cables controlling the radiation beam. But with computers, it was necessary to transmit only information, not force, so the operator's commands could be processed by software —lists of coded instructions that tell the computer what to do. Thus, complex electromechanical control systems were replaced by minicomputers, and the traditional operator's control panels, festooned with switches, buttons, and lamps, were exchanged for computer terminals. With these changes, manufacturers hoped to capitalize on the speed and versatility of computers to make radiation machines faster and more convenient.

The proper operation of an electromechanical radiation machine largely depended on the soundness of the control mechanism. When it malfunctioned, the problem could be traced to relay switches that had failed, tubes that had burned out, hydraulic fluid that had leaked away. These failures were caused by manufacturing defects or wear and could be prevented by inspecting the product and replacing faulty parts.

Computers also can wear out, but most of their problems are not so easy to understand; they are design weaknesses, caused by flaws in the logic, not the mechanics, of the control mechanisms, so there are no material defects to track down. True, faults may exist in the hardware—the chips themselves—but, more frequently, they crop up in the software.

It was a software error, involving the operation of a switch, that killed Cox and Kidd. Linear accelerators can produce two kinds of radiation: electrons, which are used to treat superficial tumors, such as skin cancers, and X rays, which are more effective against such deeply embedded tumors as those of the cervix and the prostate. An electron beam can be produced by the accelerator directly, or an X-ray beam can be created by placing a tungsten target in the path of the electron beam, so that, as the target absorbs electrons, X rays emerge from the other side. Because this process of producing X rays is inefficient, the intensity of the electron beam must be increased tremendously when the target is in place.

To guard against the grave danger that the electron beam might attain its higher intensity without the target in place, and be driven directly into a patient, accelerators were equipped with protective circuits, called interlocks. In the Therac-25, however, both target position and beam intensity were computer-controlled. When the operator switched the machine from X ray to electron mode, the computer was counted upon to set the beam to low intensity before the target was withdrawn.

Usually, it worked that way. (At Tyler, more than five hundred patients had been treated without mishap in the two years preceding the accidents.) But if, because of a software error, the operator first selected X rays and then switched to electrons, by hitting the up-arrow key and typing over the previous instruction, the target was withdrawn while the full-intensity beam remained on. In the cases of Cox and Kidd, the Therac-25 delivered about twenty-five thousand rads of electrons, more than a hundred times the prescribed dose.

The problem in the software itself was compounded by a weakness in the user interface (the system the computer employs to inform the operator of what it is doing), which encouraged operators to run the machine in a hazardous fashion. According to a therapist at the site of the Georgia accident, the Therac-25 typically issued as many as forty error messages a day, most of which indicated that beam intensity was slightly less than it should be. Such messages could be canceled by pressing the terminal's *P* key, and operators quickly learned to respond this way to virtually all error messages—each one difficult to interpret, because the problem was referred to by number instead of being described in words. At Tyler, the only indication of trouble the operator saw was the code "Malfunction 54." She repeatedly pushed *P*, turning on the beam again and again. Ray Cox was burned twice before he managed to move out of the way.

The fault cannot be placed simply on the programmers who wrote software for the Therac-25; even the best programmers make lots of mistakes, because software writing is a painstaking task. The underlying problem was

that Atomic Energy of Canada failed as an organization to guard against such errors. One of the earlier models, the Therac-20, contained electric circuits that prevented the beam from being turned on in such instances of malfunction. This mechanism was omitted from the Therac-25, and it is evident that no sufficient review of the safety implications of this omission ever was made.

Fortunately, only eleven Therac-25s were in use when the hazards became known. But the incidents raised concerns about therapy machines soon to be introduced by other manufacturers, and about other kinds of computer-operated medical equipment, as well. The FDA anticipates that by 1990, virtually all devices produced by the eleven-billion-dollar-a-year medical-electronics industry will contain computers. And the Therac accidents were just the worst examples of a trend the agency has been tracking for several years: computer-related problems in medical devices are on the increase.

Twice as many manufacturer recalls of computer-controlled medical equipment occurred in 1984 as in 1982 or any year before, and most were due to software errors. One blood analyzer displayed incorrect values because addition, rather than subtraction, had been programmed into a calibration formula. A system for monitoring the blood pressure, heart rate, and other vital signs of several patients at once mixed up its data, so the name of one patient was attached to the readings for another. And in one ventilator, a software error allowed concentrations of oxygen and other vital gases to drop without warning. In many of these applications, failure of the computer-controlled system could be deadly.

Such problems are not restricted to medicine. Because of their low cost and versatility, computers are replacing mechanical operations in all kinds of products. The Airbus Industries A320 airliner attracted great press attention when it was introduced last year, because it was the most extensively "fly-by-wire" commercial airliner ever built. (Computers, rather than cables and hydraulics, connect the pilot's controls to the airplane's engines, rudder, and ailerons.) In new cars, computers manage fuel injection and spark timing, and, in some cases, the suspension and antilock braking mechanisms, as well. (General Motors is experimenting with a "drive-by-wire" automobile, in which there is no physical connection, except the computer, between the steering wheel and the tires.) On railroads, computers operate the track switches that are supposed to prevent trains from colliding. Computers are used widely to direct assembly line equipment in factories and generators in power plants; even some emergency shutdown systems in nuclear reactors are computer-controlled. And in weapons systems, computers warn of imminent attack, identify and track targets, aim guns and steer missiles, arm and detonate explosives.

A file of problem reports maintained by Peter Neumann, at SRI International (a computer-industry think tank, in Menlo Park, California), under cosponsorship of the Association for Computing Machinery, lists more than four hundred incidents in a range of industries in which software problems caused or threatened serious injury or significant financial loss. Unless steps are taken to ensure that computer-operated machinery is every bit as safe as the mechanical equipment of old, such alarming software failures are bound to multiply.

WHEN MANUFACTURERS began installing computers in medical equipment and other machinery, they introduced a problem never encountered in strictly mechanical devices: programming errors, popularly known as bugs, which are the natural result of the way software is produced. The process begins when the designers draw up specifications for the software, which requires that they anticipate every task the computer is supposed to be able to direct its machine to perform, as well as every response it should make to situations it might encounter. (For a radiation machine, say, designers would specify that the computer be able to turn on the machine, adjust the beam to various intensities, and keep X ray–strength radiation from operating in the absence of the shield.) Then the design is divided into modules, which are work assignments for individual programmers.

Each programmer, acting independently, creates the software for his module, by entering into a video terminal a list of statements, in programming language, instructing the computer to behave as the specifications direct. Because computer programming is a highly creative endeavor—no less creative than composing a novel, for example—there is no single correct approach. Just as the novelist relies on inventiveness to get a story convincingly across to the reader, the programmer must rely on ingenuity to impart complete and unambiguous instructions to the computer. That is why no two programmers will write the same program in exactly the same way, and why there is so much room for introducing errors or for coming up with instructions not comprehensive enough to work properly.

During the final stage of software production, the individual modules are woven into the finished program. Regrettably, it is not always possible to predict how modules will interact. As Marvin Minsky, dean of American artificial intelligence researchers, put it:

When a program grows in power by an evolution of partially understood patches and fixes, the programmer begins to lose track of internal details, loses his ability to predict what will happen, begins to hope instead of know, and watches the results as though the program were an individual whose range of behavior is uncertain.

Consequently, producing quality software is as much a function of how well the entire program is designed, and how well the steps are coordinated, as of how well the individual lines of code are written.

The only way to tell whether a program has been properly designed is to test it. But even the most rigorous of trials can overlook flaws, because the number of situations a program must contend with is limitless. To check whether a computerized calculator adds numbers correctly, for instance, one could add hundreds of random numbers and see whether the program consistently produces the correct result, but since the supply of numbers is virtually infinite, it is hopeless to try testing every possible sum, and the few that might trigger an error, owing to some software flaw, are likely to be missed. So errors routinely remain in software when it reaches the market, to be discovered and corrected over time.

Programmers accept that they are likely to introduce, inadvertently, about fifty errors in every thousand lines of code. Most of these are weeded out during testing; market versions typically contain only two to three errors in a thousand lines. But this means that even a good program—with, say, fifty thousand lines of code—may contain more than a hundred errors. Usually, the damage can be repaired, though at some cost in time and annoyance. The state sends you a twenty-million-dollar tax bill? Clear it up with a telephone call—or several calls. The telephone switching computer cuts off your connection? Hang up and dial again. A word processor deletes your letter? Type it over, and this time make a backup copy. Experienced computer users develop a defensive style, a whole repertoire of tactics to keep software errors from getting the better of them. Only human adaptability and ingenuity make it possible to base a computerized society on imperfect products.

But some products require better defenses against errors; when a computer controls a linear accelerator or a jetliner, the results of an error cannot always be overcome or ignored. If the patient dies or the plane crashes, the computation cannot be redone.

IT IS POSSIBLE to improve computer products for which safe operation is critical, by adapting, for software development, the principles of safety engineering now used to minimize hazards in non-computer-operated assembly line equipment, medical devices, and the like. The first step is to recognize that safety must be designed into a product, not added on as an afterthought. That requirement alone might lead to a design quite different from one that would be used if cost and performance were the only considerations.

One way of keeping hazards to a minimum is through a process known as software engineering, by which each stage in the programming of a computer is described in writing, and the descriptions are reviewed by outside programmers. Typically, the documents produced include such things as a specification, describing in exhaustive detail what the product is supposed to do; a design guide, telling how the program is organized; a test plan, spelling out a series of trials that are supposed to show that the program works as promised; and a test report, presenting results and explaining how any problems were resolved. Requiring programmers to obtain approval of each document before proceeding to the next step enforces an orderly development process, and, ultimately, helps ensure quality. It is analogous to a standard practice of civil engineering whereby detailed designs are subjected to thorough analysis and review before anyone starts pouring concrete.

Such a system runs counter to the stereotype of the eccentric genius programmer. It requires that programmers spend half their time on planning and design, much of the rest of it on testing, and only fifteen to twenty percent actually writing code. Software engineering is also time-consuming, and therefore costly, though studies have shown that fixing an error after a product has reached the customer may cost as much as a hundred times more than catching it early in development.

Software engineering is practiced on a large scale by the

U.S. Defense Department and its contractors, who must produce sixteen documents for each computer program. Even that system is not foolproof. Some software developed to the department's standards still reaches the field with serious errors: One computer-controlled wing-mounted launcher improperly retained its grip after its missile was ignited, creating what was described as the world's largest pinwheel, when the aircraft went violently out of control. And a jet crashed when its flight-control program was confronted with an unanticipated mechanical problem. But despite its imperfections, the military's documentation process has been mainly beneficial. Something as complex as a fly-by-wire aircraft, for example, could never be relied upon to operate safely if it were produced by traditional techniques, and, for the most part, the military's planes have flown safely.

Unfortunately, the Defense Department's approach is elaborate and expensive, and thus it is practical only for huge projects costing no less than tens of millions of dollars, employing scores of programmers, and generating hundreds of thousands of lines of code. It is not economical for smaller-scale programming projects (those required to produce automated switches for railroad tracks, say, or computer-controlled medical equipment). The Institute of Electrical and Electronics Engineers recommends the production of only six documents, and FDA officials are considering a similar approach for medical-equipment software. But some medical-equipment vendors oppose the additional documentation effort, calling it ineffective, costly, and time-consuming. Apparently, the cost of correcting hazardous errors has not yet caught up with them.

Another way of improving safety in programming involves the application of "formal methods," or techniques of mathematical logic, to software analysis. Designers create models of computer programs in specialized notations resembling equations. A model's behavior can then be analyzed before the product is actually constructed—in much the way the carrying capacity of a bridge can be calculated from an engineer's blueprints—and attempts can be made to prove that a program is error-free, employing the kind of mathematical logic used to prove the validity of theorems in geometry. The aim is to supplement trial-and-error testing, after the product is completed, with logical analysis beforehand.

Although computer scientists have been developing formal methods for more than twenty years, this approach is hardly ever put into practice. Some scientists believe the techniques are too difficult and cumbersome to be useful in evaluating any but the simplest programs (those that are only a few hundred lines long). Others caution that they promise too much, since formal proof does not guarantee that a program is perfect.

Yet formal methods need not ensure perfection to be useful, for they can uncover errors sometimes overlooked by trial-and-error testing and documentation review. Recently, the British Royal Signals and Radar Establishment, the electronics research laboratory of Britain's Ministry of Defense, applied formal methods to program fragments drawn from NATO's military software inventory. One in ten fragments was found to contain errors, many serious enough to result in the loss of the vehicle or machine controlled by the program. The British are betting heavily on formal methods to ensure software safety; new defense ministry regulations will require their use for some safety-critical products, and a government-sponsored report strongly encourages their use in civil products, as well. Nothing similar to this is planned in the United States.

IF MANUFACTURERS of computer-controlled medical devices, production-line equipment, and other potentially hazardous machinery continue to resist using safety engineering and formal methods, it may become necessary for government agencies to force their hands. We regulate all kinds of other things that pose risks to human life—buildings, bridges, airplanes, and drugs are just a few. We also require that the people who provide safety-critical services satisfy certain education requirements and pass examinations: physicians, pharmacists, lawyers, and even automobile drivers all must be government-certified.

Still, software remains largely unregulated. Aviation, nuclear power, and weapons systems purchased by the Defense Department are the few cases in which software is subject to government approval. There is no education standard required of programmers, and many computer-science curricula fail even to mention safety. Studies have found that the best programmers can be more than twenty-five times as competent as the worst and that many software-design supervisors are unable to evaluate or even understand their programmers' work. Of course, efforts to regulate software or certify programmers are likely to meet resistance. "I'll fight them to the death," says Robert Ulrickson, president of Logical Services, a Santa Clara, California, company that designs computerized instruments. "I don't want to be part of an economy that's run by the government."

But, for the most part, the mere appearance of government interest in software safety has had a positive effect. In September of 1987, in the wake of the Therac-25 tragedies, the FDA announced its intent to regulate some computer software in medical devices and began to work out guidelines. At about the same time, a staff member of the U.S. House of Representatives Committee on Science, Space, and Technology began investigating software quality–assurance practices on behalf of Congress. Seeing the writing on the wall, manufacturing and professional associations are instructing their members in software-quality assurance and acceptance testing. Employees are being sent to courses on computer-system safety, and unusually thorough attention is being devoted to checking for hazards in new machines. Some manufacturers have even contracted with outside firms to perform independent tests and evaluations. Given the low priority traditionally assigned to software safety, such efforts promise considerable improvement.

# Liability for Defective Electronic Information

## Pamela Samuelson

*Pamela Samuelson is a professor of law at the University of Pittsburgh School of Law.*

"Sticks and stones may break my bones, but words can never hurt me." This children's refrain may never have been completely true, but it has been definitively disproven now that computer program instructions control the operation of so many machines and devices in our society. Those who develop computer programs know programs often contain defects or bugs, some of which can cause economic or physical harms. Many people in the computing field are rightly concerned about what liability they or their firms might incur if a defect in software they developed injures a user.

The general public seems largely unaware of the risks of defective software. Even the popular press generally subscribes to the myth that if something is computerized, it must be better. Only certain freak software accidents ("Robot Kills Assembly Line Worker") seem to capture the mass media's attention. Within the computing field, Peter Neumann deserves much credit for heightening the field's awareness of the risks of computing through publication of the "RISKS Forum Digest." But even this focuses more on technical risks than legal risks.

It is fair to say that there have been far more injuries from defective software than litigations about defective software. Some lawsuits have been brought, of course, but they have largely been settled out of court, often on condition that the injured person keep silent about the accident, the lawsuit, and the settlement. No software developer seems to want to be the first to set the precedent by which liability rules will definitively be established for the industry.

The topic of what liability may exist when software is defective is too large to be given a full treatment in one column. But I can summarize in a sentence what the law's likely response would be to a lawsuit involving defective software embedded in machines such as airplanes, X-ray equipment, and the like: The developer is likely to be held liable if defects in the software have caused injury to a consumer's person or property; under some circumstances, the developer may also be held liable for economic losses (such as lost profits). That is, when an electronic information product behaves like a machine,

the law will treat it with the same strict rules it has adopted for dealing with defective machines.

Less clear, however, is what rules will apply when software behaves more like a book than a machine. Courts have treated books differently for liability purposes than they have treated machines. They have been reluctant to impose liability on authors, publishers, and booksellers for defective information in books out of concern about the effect such liability would have on the free exchange of ideas and information. Only if erroneous statements defraud or defame a person or are negligently made by someone who claims to have superior knowledge (such as a professional) has the law imposed liability on authors, publishers, or booksellers. Whether the "no liability" rule applicable to print information providers will be extended to electronic information providers remains to be seen. There are some differences between the print world and the electronic world that may put electronic information providers at a greater risk of liability than print information providers.

### AN EXAMPLE OF SOFTWARE BEHAVING LIKE A BOOK

To explore the liability questions that may arise when software behaves like a book, I want you to imagine that a fellow named Harry wrote a computer program which he calls "Harry's Medical Home Companion." Harry works as a computer programmer for a manufacturer of medical equipment, but his avocation and deepest interest has been for many years the study of medical treatments for human diseases. He has read all the major medical textbooks used by practitioners today, as well as many books about herbal and other organic treatments used in traditional societies before the modern era.

Harry's goal is to sell his program to ordinary folk so they can readily compare what today's medical professionals and traditional societies would recommend for treatment of specific diseases. Harry believes people should be empowered to engage in more self-treatment for illnesses and that his program will aid this process by giving ordinary people knowledge about this subject. To make the program more user friendly and interesting, Harry has added some multimedia features to it, such as sound effects and computer animations to illustrate the effects of certain treatments on the human body.

Harry cannot, of course, practice medicine because he does not have a license to be a medical doctor. But that does not mean he cannot write a book or a computer program discussing treatments for various diseases, for in our society no one needs a license to be a writer or a programmer. Harry arranges for the program to be published by Lightweight Software. Lightweight intends to focus its distribution of this product initially to health food stores throughout the country.

If there is a defect in the information contained in "Harry's Medical Home Companion" on which a user relies to his or her detriment, what responsibility will Harry, Lightweight Software, or the health food store at which the user bought the program have if the injured consumer sues? (It is easy for computing professionals to imagine what kinds of errors might creep into an electronic text like Harry's program. A "0.1" might have been accidentally transposed as a "1.0" or a fleck of dust on a printed page might, when processed by an optical character recognition program, cause a "1" to be recognized as a "7" which would cause the quantity of a herb or drug for use to treat a specific disease to be incorrect. Or Harry may have included some illustrations in the program, one of which turned out to be a deadly poisonous mushroom which his artist friend didn't know because she was not a trained botanist.) Interestingly, under the present state of the law, neither Harry nor the publisher nor the health food store may have much to worry about from a liability standpoint.

## NO IMPLIED WARRANTY FOR INFORMATION IN BOOKS: *CARDOZO VS. TRUE*

Injured consumers have been largely unsuccessful when they have sued publishers or booksellers for breach of warranty involving defective information contained in books. Even though judges have regarded books as "goods to which implied warranties of merchantability apply (see "Liability Categories"), they have not treated the information contained in the book as covered by these warranties. Information has instead been treated as an unwarranted part of the goods. The intangible information is treated as though it was a "service" embodied in the goods. The strong warranty rules that apply to goods do not apply to services which, of course, often include the delivery of information to the customer. (See box for a discussion on breach of warranty claims and the "goods" vs. "services" distinction.) Typical of the case law rejecting warranty liability for defective information is the *Cardozo vs. True* case decided in Florida in 1977.

Cardozo got violently ill after she ate a piece of rare plant while preparing to cook it in accordance with a recipe in a cookbook written by True. To recover the cost of her medical expenses, she sued True and the bookstore where she bought the book. Against the bookstore, Cardozo claimed the bookseller had breached an implied warranty of merchantability (that the product was fit for the ordinary purpose for which it might be used) by failing to warn her the plant was poisonous if eaten raw.

Although finding the bookseller was a "merchant" whose books were "goods" subject to the Uniform Commercial Code's (UCC) implied warranty of merchantability rules, the court decided the implied warranty for the book only applied to its physical characteristics, such as the quality of the binding. The court regarded it as "unthinkable that standards imposed on the quality of goods sold by a merchant would require that merchant, who is a bookseller, to evaluate the thought processes of the many authors and publishers of the hundreds and often thousands of books which the merchant offers for sale." Consequently, the court affirmed dismissal of Cardozo's complaint against the bookseller.

(The issue before the court was only whether the bookseller could be liable for breach of warranty, not whether the author could be. But here is the problem with suing authors for breach of warranty when information in books is defective: The UCC only imposes implied warranty responsibilities on "merchants" of "goods" of the sort the case involves. Publishers and booksellers are "merchants" of books, and books are "goods" within the meaning of the UCC. Authors, however, are not merchants of "goods." They are at most sellers of intangible information that may later be embodied in goods when printed and bound by publishers.)

The *Cardozo* opinion is one of many in which judges have stated that publishers and booksellers cannot reasonably investigate all the information in the books they sell and should therefore not be subject to warranty liability when information in the work is defective. Judges worry that imposing a responsibility on publishers and bookstores to verify the accuracy of all information contained in the products they sell would unduly restrict the free flow of information and chill expression of ideas. It would thus be unwise as a matter of public policy. In addition, courts have feared a torrent of socially unproductive litigation if readers were able to sue publishers and bookstores whenever their expectations were disappointed after acting on information contained in books.

If the same rule is applied to "Harry's Medical Home Companion" as has been applied to purveyors of printed information, neither Harry, nor Lightweight Software, nor the health food stores that sell the program would have to worry about a lawsuit by a user of the program to recover damages for injuries resulting from defective information in the program on a breach of warranty theory.

## NO STRICT LIABILITY IN TORT FOR BOOKS: *WINTER VS. PUTNAM*

There have been a number of cases in which injured consumers have asserted that publishers of books containing defective information should be held strictly liable in tort for having sold a defective product (see box on strict liability in tort). In general, these cases have not been successful.

Typical of the case law in which courts have rejected strict liability in tort claims made against publishers is *Winter vs. G. P. Putnam's Sons* decided by a federal appellate court in California in 1991. Winter sued Putnam to recover the cost of the liver transplant he had after

# LIABILITY CATEGORIES

There are three distinct categories the law employs when dealing with claims that defective products have caused physical or economic injury to someone other than their producer: breach of contractual warranties, negligence, and strict liability in tort.

## Warranty

A warranty is a promise made by a manufacturer or seller of goods which is considered to be a part of the contract under which the product is sold. Warranties are of two sorts: express and implied.

Express warranties are created by a seller's statements about the product, its characteristics, or its performance which affect the consumer's decision to buy the product. Express warranties may arise from statements made in advertising, on the package in which the product is shipped, or by the salesperson who persuaded the consumer to buy it. Merely recommending purchase of the product or making statements about it that a reasonable consumer would understand to be mere "sales talk" or puffery will not create an express warranty. However, a seller need not intend to expressly warrant a product to do so.

When the seller is a merchant, the law will regard the act of selling the product in the marketplace as giving rise to an implied representation the product is of fair and average quality for goods of that kind and fit for ordinary consumer purposes. This is known as the implied warranty of merchantability. It attaches automatically by law to all sales transactions in jurisdictions that have adopted Article 2 of the Uniform Commercial Code (UCC). (In the U.S., this includes every state but Louisiana.) Implied warranties of fitness for a particular purpose will also automatically arise when a seller knows the purpose for which a customer is acquiring the goods and the customer relies on the seller's judgment that a particular product will fulfill that purpose.

Implied warranties can be disclaimed by a seller. However, the disclaimer must be explicit, unambiguous, conspicuous, and often must be in writing before the disclaimer will be effective (as are the bright orange stickers saying "as is" or "with all faults" appearing on the windows of automobiles in used car lots).

These warranty rules do not apply to all sales transactions, but only to sales of "goods." Sales of "services" are not subject to these rules. The law for services contracts more closely resembles the 19th century when "caveat emptor" (let the buyer beware) was the rule across the board.

The question of whether computer software should be treated as "goods" or "services" has been much discussed in the legal literature and in some case law. Insofar as software is an embedded component of a hardware device, such as an X-ray machine, it will almost certainly be treated as "goods" within the meaning of the UCC. It is somewhat less clear how software will be treated when it merely automates an information process previously done manually (which would then have been described as a "service"). The more customized the software or the more it resembles a book or a pure information service, the less likely it is to be treated as "goods" under the UCC. Even when an electronic information product is treated as "goods" under the UCC, there is some case law suggesting that warranties will not attach to the information in the work if it behaves like a book. (See article's discussion of the *Cardozo vs. True* case.)

## Negligence

When a person (or a firm) acts in a manner a reasonable person in the same circumstances would have recognized does not live up to a duty of care owed towards others and thereby causes harm to another, that person can be found liable for negligence. Negligence is generally harder to prove than breach of warranty because negligence requires a showing of fault on the part of the person being sued, whereas warranty liability can exist when a product simply fails to perform as stated or expected. There are also some occasions in which negligence claims fall because the law has not imposed a duty of care on the person being sued.

There is a long history of successful negligence lawsuits against manufacturers of defective products. Sometimes manufacturers have been found to have failed in the duty of care owed to consumers in not having taken sufficient care in the design of the product. Sometimes they have been found not to have provided adequate information about how the product should be used or what dangers might exist if the product is used in a particular way.

There have been far fewer successful lawsuits when claims of negligence are made after someone has provided inadequate or inaccurate information to a customer. It is fairly rare for the law to impose a stringent duty of care on information providers unless the information provider holds himself or herself out in the marketplace as having substantially superior knowledge, skill, or expertise. Professional information providers, such as doctors or lawyers, can be held liable for malpractice, for example, when they have conveyed inaccurate information (or otherwise provided a negligent service) and a less knowledgeable consumer relied on it to his or her detriment. It is generally quite

*(box continued on next page)*

*(box continued from previous page)*
difficult to win a malpractice action against a professional for delivering defective information, for one will need to show the provider was acting incompetently in delivering the defective information. There is often a difference of opinion among professionals in a field about what is or is not appropriate information to convey in particular circumstances. In addition, professionals generally do not like to call someone in their field an incompetent practitioner in a public forum such as a court and usually one will need an expert in the field to testify to a professional's incompetence.

I am aware that many people who develop software have ambivalent attitudes about whether they should be considered "professionals" in the sense in which this term is used in other fields. While I will not reignite the tired debate over whether software developers should be "licensed," as most other professionals are, it is an issue which may need to be revisited as greater responsibilities (i.e., duties of care) are imposed by law on publishers of electronic information.

## Strict Liability in Tort

Manufacturers and sellers of defective products are held strictly liable, (that is, liable without fault) in tort (that is, independent of duties imposed by contract) for physical harms to person or property caused by the defect. This liability arises notwithstanding that "the seller has exercised all possible care in the preparation and sale of the product." These strict liability rules do not apply to all commercial transactions. Along similar lines to UCC warranty law, strict liability in tort exists only for "products" and not for "services."

When computer programs are embedded components of airplanes, X-ray equipment, and the like, they will almost certainly be treated as "products" for strict liability purposes. (The *Winter* case discussed in this article is such an example.) While some tricky causation questions may arise in product liability cases involving software, strict liability will be imposed on a software developer if there is a defect resulting in an injury to the consumer (and a defect will generally be easy to show if a consumer or user has been injured), almost as surely as night follows day.

But there are some computer programs which may not be treated as "products" for strict liability purposes. When programs behave more like a book then a machine or when they otherwise resemble an information service, strict liability rules may not be imposed on them. As this article explains, courts have decided that books should not be treated as "products" for strict liability purposes and that publishers of books should not be held strictly liable in tort when their products contain defective information.

## Remedies

When a seller has breached implied or express warranties in connection with the sale of goods, the buyer can sue the seller to recover money damages for certain kinds of injuries arising from the breach. If, for example, a consumer is physically injured by a defective lawnmower and has to pay $10,000 in medical expenses, that $10,000 may be recovered from the manufacturer or the firm from which the consumer bought the lawnmower. If the lawnmower must be repaired or replaced, the consumer can generally recover in contract for these damages as well.

Contract damages, however, tend to be more limited than tort damages. Monetary damages to compensate an injured person for pain and suffering, for example, are recoverable in tort actions (such as negligence and strict liability) but may not be in contract actions. Some economic losses are also not recoverable in contract cases. Unless, for example, the manufacturer (or other seller) of a lawnmower had reason to know at the time of the sale that a particular buyer of the lawnmower needed it to operate a lawn-mowing service, the buyer would not be able to recover lost profits on his lawn-mowing business during the time the business was out of operation after the defect in it evidenced itself.

In negligence actions, successful plaintiffs can generally recover damages for a broad range of injuries flowing from the negligent act, including pain and suffering and some economic losses. In strict liability actions, only damages arising from physical harms to persons or property are generally recoverable.

One other respect in which tort and contract actions tend to differ is in the kinds of persons who can bring claims for what kinds of damages. Contract law tends (except where physical injury to persons or property is involved) to limit the class of possible plaintiffs to those who bought the goods and are thus beneficiaries of the warranty promises that are part of the contract. Tort law is more generous about who can bring a lawsuit (e.g., if the buyer of the product gives it to another person as a gift and that person is harmed, he or she can sue in tort whereas that person might not be able to sue in contract).

Multiple volumes of thick treatises have been written to explain all the nuances of contract and tort liability arising from defective products. This brief synopsis is necessarily incomplete but will, I hope, give those in the computing field some grounding in the basics of these legal categories.

eating a mushroom erroneously depicted as safe for human ingestion in the Encyclopedia of Mushrooms published by Putnam. He claimed the publisher should be held strictly liable in tort or should be found negligent for publishing a book in which a poisonous mushroom was depicted as safe. The court upheld dismissal of both claims.

On the negligence claim, the court ruled the publisher had no duty to investigate the accuracy of information it published. Without a duty of care owed by the publisher to readers of the books it published, no negligence could be found (see box). Even though authors of books may be more vulnerable to negligence claims than publishers, authors may successfully defend against such a lawsuit by showing they exercised reasonable care (e.g., hiring someone to check all the data for correctness) under the circumstances. Also, unless an author claims to be an expert on the subject, the law may not impose a higher duty on the author than it would impose on the reader (who, after all, must use his or her own judgment before taking an author's advice).

The judges in the *Winter* case decided that the strict liability in tort doctrine should only apply to the manufacture of tangible "products," such as tires and insecticides, for which the doctrine had been created. Expansion of the doctrine to make publishers strictly liable for intangible information contained in books would unduly interfere with the free exchange of ideas and information:

*We place a high priority on the unfettered exchange of ideas. We accept the risk that words and ideas have wings that we cannot clip and which carry them we know not where. The threat of liability without fault (financial responsibility for our words and ideas in the absence of fault or special undertaking of responsibility) could seriously inhibit those who wish to share thoughts and theories.*

It was not that the judges thought no one should ever be held liable for delivering erroneous information injuring consumers. Professionals, for example, should be held responsible for injuries caused by their delivery of defective information, but not even they should be held strictly liable in tort:

*Professional services do not ordinarily lend themselves to "strict liability" because they lack the elements which gave rise to the doctrine. There is no mass production of goods or a large body of distant consumers whom it would be unfair to require to trace the article they used along the channels of trade to the original manufacturer and there to pinpoint an act of negligence remote from their knowledge. . . . Those who hire "professionals" are not justified in expecting infallibility, but can expect only reasonable care and competence.*

If the same rule was applied to "Harry's Medical Home Companion" as was applied in *Winter*, Lightweight Software and the health food store would have nothing to worry about from a liability suit against them by an injured consumer. Under the *Winter* ruling, Harry would not have to worry about a strict liability suit. And he would have a reasonable chance of defending against a negligence lawsuit by showing he had exercised reasonable care in preparing the program. He might also point out that he was not holding himself out as a professional in the medical field so he should not be held to the same standard of care as would be imposed on a licensed doctor.

## STRICT LIABILITY IN TORT FOR AERONAUTICAL CHARTS: *AETNA VS. JEPPSEN*

There is, however, at least one circumstance in which an information product has been held to be a "product" for strict liability purposes. Ten years before the *Winter vs. Putnam* decision, the same court ruled that aeronautical charts were "products" for strict liability purposes. The case was *Aetna Casualty & Surety Co. vs. Jeppsen & Co.* Aetna persuaded the trial judge that a defect in the design of an aeronautical chart manufactured by Jeppsen had caused an airplane insured by Aetna to crash at the Las Vegas airport. Interestingly, Aetna's claim was not that the chart contained inaccurate information, but that it failed in its design goal of graphically representing this information in a readily understandable way.

Jeppsen's principal argument on appeal was that the chart was not the sort of "product" to which strict liability rules should be applied. In explaining why it disagreed with Jeppsen on this point, the appellate court emphasized the chart was mass-produced for commercial purposes and those who used the chart relied on Jeppsen's expertise as much as consumers might rely on any other manufacturers' expertise. Aeronautical charts were, said the court, "highly technical tools" resembling compasses which would be treated as products for strict liability purposes. The court contrasted the charts with "how to do X" books which were "pure thought and expression."

If the same rule was applied to "Harry's Medical Home Companion" as was applied in *Jeppsen*, Lightweight Software and the health food store might well be held strictly liable in tort for physical injuries to a user resulting from a defect in the program. Because Harry does not himself sell the program to the public, he might not be held strictly liable in tort even if the publisher and health food store were . The strict liability in tort rules only apply to "sellers" of "products" of the kind that injured the consumer.

## MORE LIABILITY RISKS FOR ELECTRONIC INFORMATION

The law proceeds by analogy. Judges faced with deciding a case brought by an injured consumer against a seller of a multimedia program containing defective information on medical treatments will decide what liability rule to apply by asking him- or herself whether to treat the case like *Winter* or like *Jeppsen*. I can think of a number of reasons why electronic information providers may be more at risk from liability suits than print information providers.

For one thing, electronic information products have a more technological character than books. Even when these products behave mainly like books, they also behave like machines. And there may be no simple way to separate their book-like and machine-like characteristics. In addition, electronic information products are often "engineered" similar to other manufactured products. They are certainly more engineered than books.

Given the emphasis the field places on the technological character of electronic information products, the field should not be surprised if the law takes it seriously by treating its products the way it treats other technological products. One of these days, for example, an electronic information provider's assertion that its product is "user friendly" may be treated not as mere marketing puffery, but as creating an express warranty, leading reasonable consumers to expect that "usability engineering" or "hypertext engineering" techniques or user interface standards or guidelines were used to develop it.

As the electronic information industry moves from handcrafted demonstration projects to mass-marketed products distributed to distant and anonymous customers, the argument for extending liability when defects in these information products cause injury to consumers grows stronger. Consumers of electronic information products and services provided by a distant vendor will probably rely heavily on the expertise of the electronic information provider. The more naive among these customers may well think (however erroneously) that because the information has been computerized, it is more trustworthy than if delivered orally or found in print. In addition, electronic information providers are likely to be in a better position than consumers to control the quality of the information delivered and to insure against liability. This is especially true when firms (and not just individual programmers like Harry) begin to develop electronic information products for the mass market.

Another reason providers of electronic information may in time have greater responsibilities than book publishers is that electronic information products are less readily inspectable by ordinary consumers than books. With books, a consumer can go to a bookstore and browse through the whole thing before buying it. The consumer can, not only examine the binding, but also skim the contents to see if it meets his or her needs. With electronic information products, nothing about the product (except advertising hype) can generally be seen before the purchasing decision is made. One cannot even examine the disk to see if it is scratched or warped. Once out of the box, the disk, of course, reveals nothing about its contents which can only be comprehended through extensive use of the software. With on-line services for which the consumer is charged by connect-time, the contents are similarly invisible until a charge is incurred for usage.

When so little of value in an electronic information product lies in its physical characteristics (such as the disk on which software may be borne), it is difficult to believe courts will not in time extend liability to the contents of such products.

In addition, it is worth noting books merely instruct a reader how to perform a task whereas software does the task. By making the reader an intermediary between the instructions and their execution, a book keeps the reader in the judgment loop which means he or she bears some responsibility for how well or poorly the task is done. The reader also has to exercise judgment about whether it is really a good idea to follow a particular author's advice. By contrast, electronic information products only leave the user in the judgment loop when they have been explicitly designed to do so. Thus, more of the control over and responsibility for proper execution of the task will lie with the electronic publisher. This too may contribute to an extension of liability to providers of electronic information. Moreover, some have argued the liability rules for print publishers should be changed [1], and if they are, electronic publishers would be affected as well.

One unexplored bulwark against liability for electronic information providers is the First Amendment. What has protected print publishers from liability for dissemination of defective information has largely been concerns about the effect liability rules would have on the free exchange of ideas and information. At the moment, many commercial electronic information providers may think the work of groups like the Electronic Frontier Foundation which seek to define civil rights in Cyberspace are somewhat remote from their core concerns. But when they realize First Amendment concerns may provide the best chance electronic information providers have to protect against liability for defective information, they may find more reason to support the work of such organizations.

Electronic information providers should, of course, be thinking not only about what kinds of First Amendment rights they may have, but also about what kinds of First Amendment responsibilities they may have. In law, rights and responsibilities tend to be intertwined. One generally does not get rights without some responsibilities as well. As broadcasters and cable TV firms have discovered to their dismay, print publishers often have greater First Amendment rights than other media types do, in part because of the greater historical role of print publishers in promoting free speech interests. Electronic information providers may want to begin thinking more about First Amendment issues and where they stand (or want to stand) in relation to print publishers and other media types.

Another set of questions people in the computing field should ask themselves is what liability standards they think ought to apply to their field. Should injured consumers be able to recover damages for defective delivery of electronic information or not, and why or why not? In addition, the field should be asking what steps can be taken to self-regulate to promote development of high-quality software production to forestall or at least limit the degree to which regulation will come about through lawsuits about defective electronic information products. Liability will be with the field for a long time. It is time to stop worrying about the problem and start addressing it.

## REFERENCES

1. Arnold, R. The persistence of caveat emptor: Publisher immunity from liability for inaccurate factual information. *U. Pitt. Law Rev.* 53 (Spring 1992), 777.

# International Perspectives and Issues

The implications of computerization for economic production, value systems, and conflict are global in scope. Every society on Earth will be touched to a greater or lesser extent by the spread of information technology. In addition to the direct effects of these technologies, nations will be indirectly affected through their participation in the intricate global network of economic, cultural, and political alliances. Because all nations are ultimately linked to all other nations through this complex exchange system, a major change in even one part of the system implies some degree of change in all other parts. The economic and geopolitical implications of microelectronics and other cutting edge technologies are thought to be so great that advanced nations are engaged in a superstruggle to achieve or maintain global technological leadership.

The lead article in this collection highlights the point that the extent to which a society is able to develop or implement new technologies reflect cultural as well as economic and technical factors. Both North American and Japanese manufacturers have been moving toward factory automation, but as Andrew Tanzer and Ruth Simon explain in "Why Japan Loves Robots and We Don't," the process has been faster and smoother in Japan where robots enjoy a positive cultural image.

Less developed nations (LDCs) are also striving to establish viable high-tech ventures. Although there are huge incentives for all nations to develop domestic high-tech industries, it is a very difficult challenge for the world's poorest countries. In order to close the technological gap, poor nations must be able to stay abreast of global developments in science and technology. According to Rohan Samarajiva (1989), in one LDC, Sri Lanka, a new Ph.D. earned about $1,300 a year in 1989. In contrast, the journal *Chemical Abstracts* costs more than $10,000 a year, and so it is not surprising there is only one subscription to the complete journal in the entire country. Moreover, it costs a Sri Lankan scientist about $10 to get the full copy of a 20-page article that is published in a foreign country (if the regular mail system is used). If the scientist had access to a personal computer, a telephone, and a modem (all luxuries) and an article is available in elec-

tronic form, it could cost even more to receive an article on-line.

As discussed in "Sub-Saharan Africa: A Technological Desert," the poor nations of Africa face similar obstacles to computerization. In this article, three Africans and a North American recount the continent's need for information technology and the economic, cultural, political, and geographic challenges to bringing more than 500 million people into the "global information society."

In "Computing in the Middle East," S. E. Goodman and J. D. Green observe that the role of information technologies in this "important, unstable, and rapidly changing part of the world" has been largely overlooked by most of the world. Even though some of these nations are "oil rich," there are numerous noneconomic (social, cultural, religious, political, linguistic) factors that make the overall acceptability and value of information technologies ambiguous.

The following article, "New Technology Propels Air Travel," focuses on Canada's air travel and travel reservations industries. Here Geoffrey Rowan describes concerns that can arise when technical systems encompass more than one nation. As this edition of *Computers in Society* goes to print, it is still unclear whether the U.S. Sabre system or the Canadian Gemini system will dominate Canada's air travel reservations market.

The last article in this section addresses a very different kind of international computing problem. As Paul Mungo and Bryan Clough relate in "The Bulgarian Connection," computer viruses are easily spread from country to country, and some of the most notorious originated in Bulgaria.

## Looking Ahead: Challenge Questions

How could information technology be used to reduce hostilities between nations and foster international understanding and cooperation?

What are the implications for national sovereignty when computer systems cross national borders or, as is the case for most African nations, most of the electronic data about a country are held in foreign databases?

# Unit 7

# Why Japan loves robots and we don't

Always looking to the future, Japanese businesses are pinning
many of their industrial hopes on increasing use of factory robots.
So what if robots don't pay back their investment right away?
They are a great bet for improving manufacturing
quality and countering rising labor costs.

## Andrew Tanzer and Ruth Simon

IN A FACTORY where Matsushita Electric makes Panasonic VCRs, a robot winds wire a little thinner than a human hair 16 times through a pinhole in the video head, and then solders it. There are 530 of these robots in the factory and they wind, and then wind some more, 24 hours a day. They do it five times faster and much more reliably than the 3,000 housewives who, until recently, did the same job with microscopes on a subcontract basis in Japan's countryside. The robots even inspect their own work.

A U.S. company can't get this technology—even if there were an American consumer electronics industry to take advantage of it. Matsushita invented and custom-made all 530 wire-winders to gain a competitive edge.

Robots were invented here, and the U.S. still leads in advanced research, from robotic brain surgeons to classified undersea naval search-and-destroy robots. But when it comes to using robots to solve practical problems—on the factory floor and in everyday life—Japan has no equal.

What may sound like science fiction to most Americans is taken for granted by ordinary folk in Japan. The Japanese are now accustomed to having robots do everything from make sushi to perform Chopin. Ichiro Kato, a roboticist at Waseda University, designed Wabot, a famous piano-playing, music-reading robot. Says Kato: "There will be one or more robots in every house in the 21st century."

Wabot's creator expects to see robots in people's homes doing dishes and washing floors. He envisions a humanoid robot with movable arms and a synthesized voice that will provide mobility and companionship to lonely old people. Kato, 64, says: "I'd like to live to see that day." Advances in artificial intelligence will put all this in the realm of the probable.

You probably haven't heard much about robots lately in the U.S., and for good reason. Robots have been an embarrassing disappointment for many American manufacturers. But in Japan companies of all sizes have embraced

robots. The robots make it easier to quickly alter a production line to make several different product models. Japanese suppliers are in the forefront of these "flexible manufacturing systems," in which robots play a crucial role.

Now the technology is moving beyond the factory into hospitals, concert halls and restaurants.

In 1988 Japan employed two-thirds of all robots in use in the world, and last year it installed about $2.5 billion worth of new ones. Compare this with the U.S., which added only about $400 million worth of robots last year. "The total population of robots in the U.S. is around 37,000," says John O'Hara, president of the Robotic Industries Association. "The Japanese add that many robots in one year." To be sure, Japan has enough antiquated and small factories to leave its overall manufacturing productivity below that of the U.S. But robots will help narrow the lead. For example, U.S. carmakers are heavily robotized. However, the Japanese are installing new robots not simply to automate but also to make production lines more flexible. For example, Nissan's newer auto plants can produce hundreds of different variations on a given car model simply by reprogramming robots that paint auto bodies and install car seats, engines, batteries, windshields, tires and doors. In Japan, even small companies use robots in simple applications such as welding.

It is one more example of Japan's skill at grasping a new technology and putting it to work while others dither. It happened in consumer electronics, memory chip production and machine tools. Now it's happening in robotics.

As Japan's robot population grows explosively, the U.S. market for metal employees is inching up after falling sharply in the mid-1980s. In February Deere & Co. decided to can the robots it uses to paint tractor chassis and hire humans. The robots take too long to program for endless permutations of paint orders. Whirlpool's Clyde, Ohio washing machine plant has used articulated arms that resembled the human wrist, elbow and shoulder to remove washtubs from injection molding equipment. But the complex robots aren't up to running around-the-clock production. Whirlpool gave up on the idea of using robots for this job, opting for fixed automation—a technology the U.S. excels in.

"Robots give you a lot of flexibility, but there's also a lot of complication," says James Spicer, a director of engineering operations at Whirlpool. "To lift one cylinder at a time you don't have to duplicate the motion of a human arm."

So many other manufacturers have sent robots to the junkyard or slowed plans to add new ones that the U.S. robot industry is in shambles. Early robot producers like Westinghouse and General Electric abandoned robotics in the late Eighties because of disappointing sales. And one-time highfliers such as Unimation and GCA Industrial Systems have disappeared into bigger companies, while Prab and Automatix founder under heavy losses.

One of the few profitable U.S. robot companies is GMFanuc, a 50/50 joint venture between the carmaker and Fanuc, a leading Japanese robotmaker. The venture last year earned a few million dollars on sales of $165 million. Japanese producers aren't making any real money in robots, either. But many Japanese firms design and make robots for their own use to boost competitiveness and quality, so profits are not the issue. They don't buy robots based on a spreadsheet showing payback periods.

Now U.S. companies, having invented industrial robots and licensed the technology to Japan back in the 1960s, are in the awkward position of licensing back new Japanese technology. Cincinnati Milacron, number three in the U.S. robot business, aided Matsushita Electric's push into robotics by licensing it technology. Last year Milacron became a U.S. distributor for small welding robots produced by none other than Matsushita.

Why is Japan so robot-happy? It has to do with a lot more than economics. Japanese managers and government officials consider robots a key tool in combating a severe labor shortage at home. The alternatives would be moving the labor-intensive operations abroad or letting immigrants into Japan. The first alternative would deprive Japan of its manufacturing skills. "If you can fully automate manufacturing, there's no reason you have to go to Southeast Asia," argues Tadaaki Chigusa, a director of McKinsey & Co., Inc. (Japan). The second alternative, immigration, is unacceptable in the homogeneous, somewhat racist Japanese society.

While Chinese, Filipino or Korean laborers would not be very welcome in Japan, no such prejudice exists against robots. The Japanese seem to have been primed for robots with positive images in their popular culture as far back as the 1950s—much earlier than in the U.S. Japanese toymakers have churned out millions of toy robots, and the country's cartoons and comic books are filled with robot heroes. The prototype is Astro Boy, developed in Japan in 1953 and later exported to the U.S.

"Astro Boy is as well known in Japan as Mickey Mouse and Donald Duck are here," says Frederik Schodt, author of *Inside the Robot Kingdom* (Kodansha International, 1988), which argues the Japanese have been conditioned to feel comfortable with robots from a young age. "He's a very cute, friendly robot who's always fighting for peace."

Mostly, robots are portrayed favorably in Western popular culture nowadays, from *Star Wars'* R2-D2 to the futuristic Jetsons cartoon family. However, in Western tradition, robots have frequently been stereotyped as soulless humanoid machines or evil characters in works such as Fritz Lang's 1920s silent film *Metropolis* and the 1920 Czech play *R.U.R.* by Karel Capek, in which the word "robot" was coined to describe man-created monsters that turned on their masters, killing them

In Japan, friendly, peace-loving robots are seen as solving a growing blue-collar labor shortage. The number of Japanese high school graduates is stagnant, and fewer graduates are willing to get their hands dirty. "Young people would rather work at the Hotel Okura or McDonald's than in the factory," says Naohide Kumagai, associate director of Kawasaki Heavy Industry's robot division. Shirking factory work doesn't carry a heavy penalty: Last year's typical high school graduate had 2.5 job offers to choose from.

Robots are more than a mere substitute for human labor. They can do some things better than humans. "Robots are becoming indispensable because they provide a precision, quality and cleanliness man can't," says Toshitsugu Inoue, senior engineer in Matsushita's robot development department. Because robots work at a precise speed and don't make mistakes, inventories are easier to control.

As electronic components are miniaturized, robots are becoming essential for quality and high yields in the production of everything from very large scale integration chips (some of Japan's "clean rooms" are already unmanned) to watches and VCRs. The inverse is also true: Because Japanese manufacturers have robots, they can further miniaturize the product. The process is redefining the product. Many consumer electronic products are designed from scratch to be efficiently assembled by robots.

The Victor Co. of Japan (JVC) Ltd.'s Yokohama camcorder factory is bathed in an eerie silence. Automated guided vehicles quietly deliver pallets of components to 64 robots, which perform 150 assembly and inspection tasks. Two workers operate the robots, which assemble eight models on the same production line. Before the robots were installed in 1987, JVC needed 150 workers to do the same job. Just as important, JVC has redesigned the camcorder and its components, some almost microscopic, to be more efficiently assembled by robots. The robots also provide flexibility: They'll work around the clock—no overtime, sick leave or bonuses.

Japanese government industrial planners have since the 1970s provided a raft of incentives for robot research, development and use. The government allows accelerated depreciation for purchase of sophisticated robots and established its own leasing company to provide low-cost robots to the private sector. Japan's Ministry of International Trade & Industry provides small and medium-size companies with interest-free loans to buy robots. MITI is also pouring $150 million into developing hazardous-duty robots for use in nuclear power plants or fighting fires at oil refineries. This would be unthinkable in the U.S., because it smacks of industrial policy.

Politics and national differences aside, why has the U.S. lagged so far behind Japan in applying robots to manufacturing? "The companies selling robots plain lied about the capabilities of their equipment and the circumstances under which they could perform," says Roger Nagel, manager of automation technology for International Harvester (now Navistar Corp.) in the early 1980s and now a professor at Lehigh University. After struggling for two years to debug a robot brought in to load and unload stamped parts from a press, Nagel finally junked the robot. A Japanese customer would probably have worked more closely developing the robot with the supplier, incorporating ideas from the engineers and even from assembly workers on the customer's own factory floor.

One reason for the overblown expectations is that U.S. robot engineers often came from the field of artificial intelligence and had little if any experience on the factory floor. They were enamored of the idea of a mechanical human, an idea readily embraced by corporate executives who hoped to replace workers in "lights out" factories.

---

## "I'm a guru when I get to Japan"

**W**hen American industrialist Joseph Engelberger arrived at Tokyo's Narita Airport in the spring of 1987, he was met by a limousine and whisked to the television studios of NHK, Japan's national broadcast network. There Engelberger, who built the first industrial robot in 1961, was interviewed on a popular national news program. The conversation followed what had become to Engelberger a familiar pattern. "Didn't the U.S. found the robot industry?" the interviewer asked. "Doesn't Japan dominate it today?"

"We all have a good laugh about it," says Engelberger, 64, who founded Unimation, the first robot-maker, and in 1968 licensed its technology to Japan's Kawasaki Heavy Industries. "I'm a guru when I get to Japan. I'm [considered] the founder of Japanese robotics."

He's no guru at home. Here, few people not related to Engelberger recall his last big network TV appearance, when he instructed his robot to open a can of Budweiser and pour it for Johnny Carson on the *Tonight Show* in 1966. "I had a hard time getting people in the U.S. to take me seriously," he says.

Engelberger's exploits may have been good for a few laughs at home, but they caught the Japanese government's attention. In 1967 it invited him to address 600 Japanese scientists and business executives. The session lasted five hours and led to an agreement with Kawasaki to license Unimation's technology.

Kawasaki remains a powerhouse in robotics, but Engelberger's Unimation has all but disappeared in the U.S. Its problems started almost immediately after its 1983 purchase by Westinghouse, which paid $107 million for Unimation with the hope of turning the $70 million company into a $1 billion business.

Unimation sold its first robot to General Motors in 1961 but was battered by GM's 1982 decision to start its own robot company in partnership with Japan's Fanuc. With Westinghouse putting little money into research and development, Unimation's sales and market share withered. The hydraulic robots it pioneered were soon supplanted by newer and more versatile electric robots. Unimation's West Coast researchers left en masse and formed Adept Technology, now a hot little maker of light assembly robots.

After years of heavy losses, Westinghouse sold Unimation's two main operations—the robotics unit to Staubli International A.G., a private Swiss outfit, and its factory automation unit to AEG, a unit of Daimler-Benz.

Engelberger left Unimation in 1984 but remains a robot evangelist. His new venture, Transitions Research Corp., is developing robots for the service industry in a low-slung building in Danbury, Conn., down the road from Unimation's former offices.

Engelberger isn't hurting personally. He received around $5 million when Westinghouse bought Unimation, enough to buy a 62-foot sailboat with some money left over to continue researching robotics on his own. But he wishes his countrymen would pay him at least a fraction of the attention the Japanese pay him.—R.S.

---

The result was overengineered robots that were costly and didn't work well on the shop floor.

"U.S. companies made robot hands that were so ungodly complex that in many cases they had no chance of standing up in a real industrial environment," says Dennis Wisnosky, former vice president of GCA Industrial Systems Group, once the number two U.S. robotmaker. The Japanese, by contrast, started with simpler robots such as spotwelders in car plants and then used their experience to build more complicated machines, such as robots that inspect the paint finish on car bodies with visual sensors.

In the U.S., robots have been slow to spread beyond automakers and their first-tier suppliers. A survey last year by Deloitte & Touche found less than 30% of U.S. manufacturers believed they had received significant benefits from new technology, down from more than 60% two years earlier.

It is a situation that should trouble those who recall the sad story of the U.S. numerically controlled machine tool industry. The technology was developed at the Massachusetts Institute of Technology in the 1950s and then exploited by the Japanese. "U.S. manufacturers didn't push the machine tool industry hard enough from a technology point of view," says George Chryssolouris, a professor of mechanical engineering at MIT. Japanese companies demanded more sophisticated machine tools so they could better compete in export markets. The result? When U.S. companies finally awakened to the need for sophisticated, high-quality tools, they were forced to turn to Japan.

One reason U.S. manufacturers aren't pushing robotmakers as hard as their Japanese counterparts is that companies here tend to be run by salesmen or accountants.

Here, manufacturing engineers get scant respect; in Japan they frequently run companies. The best known include Honda's Soichiro Honda and Sony's Akio Morita. By contrast, it's hard to name an American manufacturer who has made it to the top since the days of Henry Ford and Charles Kettering. While the Japanese revere manufacturers, Americans lionize entrepreneurs and inventors. That helps explain why a U.S. manufacturing engineer with a couple years' experience makes only $37,000 a year, compared with $44,000 for a software applications engineer. Why should a smart American kid tinker with robots and assembly lines when he or she can strike it rich writing a new personal computer software program or designing a hedging strategy for an investment firm?

The Japanese have been able to accept a slower payout. If they used the U.S. standard formula of about 30% return on capital investment—instead of the 20% return common in Japan—robot investments would be cut by half, says Edwin Mansfield, director of the University of Pennsylvania's Center for Economics & Technology. The Japanese prefer a simpler comparison. The average cost of an industrial robot is $40,000—about the same as the annual income, with bonus, of a skilled worker in a Nissan factory. But the cost of robots is dropping, while labor costs are rising. Investing now could save money ten years from now.

Will robots make a comeback in the U.S.? Yes, eventually. Companies that sacked robots for complex jobs are rehiring them for simpler tasks. Deere, for example, decided to kick robots off its spray-paint line, but now uses them to torque a series of about 20 identical cap screws on tractor transmissions, a boring, repetitive job with a high degree of human error. Instead of using robots as a quick

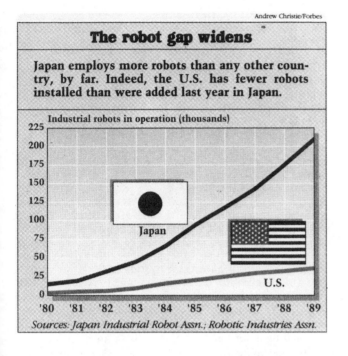

Andrew Christie/Forbes

## The robot gap widens

Japan employs more robots than any other country, by far. Indeed, the U.S. has fewer robots installed than were added last year in Japan.

Industrial robots in operation (thousands)

Japan

U.S.

Sources: Japan Industrial Robot Assn.; Robotic Industries Assn.

fix, some companies are including them as part of a broad revamping of their entire manufacturing process. Electrolux Corp. designed a new upright vacuum cleaner to be more easily assembled by robots and employees in its new $40 million automated plant in Bristol, Va.

But it will be a long and slow road. The latest hot robot application in Japan is in construction. Komatsu Ltd. has developed a robot that installs panels of up to 1,100 pounds in the exterior walls of buildings, boosting labor productivity sixfold. Shimizu Corp. produces its own robots to spray fireproofing materials on steel structures, to position ceiling panels in buildings, to plaster floors and to lay concrete segments in tunnels.

Is the U.S. construction industry interested? Not a chance. "There's basically nothing going on," complains David Panos, assistant director of Carnegie Mellon University's Field Robotics Center, which is trying to ignite interest. "It's the same old story. They're focused on the short term. [The Japanese are focused on] the long term." Not to mention the outcry from powerful construction unions if jobs were threatened by robots.

Pioneered in the U.S., exploited in Japan. It's getting to be a too familiar story.

# Sub-Saharan Africa: A Technological Desert

## M. Odedra, M. Lawrie, M. Bennett and S. Goodman

Africa seems to be the "lost continent" of the information technologies (IT). The second largest continent is the least computerized,[1] and its more than twoscore countries have an average telephone density that is an order of magnitude smaller than that of the European Community. A recent graphic on world computer densities used the map of Africa simply as a place to display the overflow data for Europe [7].

It may be argued that deficiencies in the use of IT are the least of the problems of a continent plagued by a history of exploitation, postcolonial political difficulties, bloody civil conflicts, and extensive health, educational, demographic and economic problems. Nevertheless, attention should be given to the fact that more than 500 million people have largely been left out of the "global information society."

"International Perspectives" brings three Africans together—notably through the use of the electronic networks—to discuss a few of the issues and problems confronting the effective us of IT in sub-Saharan Africa (see [2] for some discussion of Arab North Africa). We start with Mayuri Odedra's provocative perspective. A Kenyan who has written extensively on IT in Africa, Odedra helped launch and edit the journal *PC World Africa* before her recent move to the National University in Singapore. Her statement is followed by responses from Mike Lawrie, director of computing at Rhodes University in Grahamstown, on the southern coast of South Africa, and Mark Bennett, director of computing at the University of Zambia in Lusaka.

Intra-African communications still leave much to be desired. Electronic and transportation connections between sub-Saharan

countries and their former European colonial metropolises are often better and more frequent than direct connections across the continent. Not surprisingly then, former French, British, Belgian, and Portuguese colonies have relatively little communication across ex-colonial lines. All three of our African writers are from former British colonies; this choice being influenced by my email and travel opportunities. Furthermore, space limitations prevent us from doing justice to an entire continent—even a "lost continent"—in a single essay. Consequently, our coverage of sub-Saharan Africa outside of the former British empire has necessarily suffered, and reader input is welcomed with the hope of collecting enough suitable material for another article.

## MAYURI ODEDRA: TOO MUCH FOREIGN DEPENDENCE, INADEQUATE INFRASTRUCTURE AND EDUCATION

Information technology is widely preached as having the power to narrow the gap between the advanced industrial and the less developed countries (LDCs), as having the capabilities which will allow the LDCs to leapfrog development, and as having the potential to help tackle many social and economic problems. Yet few LDCs, especially those in sub-Saharan Africa, have succeeded in exploiting this potential.

Although the number of computers has increased rapidly in some places (e.g., Zimbabwe's computer population has grown from a handful of mainframes and minis in the 1970s to around 1,000 such machines and 10,000 micros in 1990), the process of computerization has not been as successful as it should be in a majority of these countries. The technology has penetrated many sectors, including banking, agriculture, mining, transportation, research, defense, medical services, accounting and communications, but the levels of software applications, business practices, and IT-related government policies and regulations vary greatly from country to country. Several, including Kenya, Nigeria, Ivory Coast and Zimbabwe, are making some

---

[1] Antarctica has no indigenous human population, but its transplanted, transient population (mostly in scientific stations of many nations) must have a higher per capita use of IT than Africa.

progress, but others such as Uganda and Tanzania have lagged far behind.

Africa is plagued by extensive underutilization of equipment and by the failure of major computer-based projects [3, 4, 5, 6]. Examples abound of systems that are simply not used because of the lack of secondary equipment, suitable electric power, or training. Hard selling from manufacturers and vendors, the urge to keep up with the latest technology, donations from international assistance organizations (half of the computers in Africa acquired in the early 1980s were "aid-donated"), self-interest, and pressure from computer professionals have all done more to spread computing in Africa than successful use in solving real problems.

In many sub-Saharan African countries, there exists a blind notion that if the more developed countries use the technology and tell us to do so as well, then we should. But no IT policies or strategic buying plans exist which clearly identify the needs that are likely to bring overall benefit to a nation, or which determine what may be achieved with the available resources. Some regulatory policies covering procedures for the acquisition of hardware and software do exist in a few places. These regulations typically mandate centralized acquisition for the public sector and tax private companies and nongovernment organizations in order to discourage imports or to raise convertible currency for the state. Such taxes range from 0% in Mauritius to over 100% in Kenya. However, a number of countries such as Botswana, Zimbabwe, Nigeria and Mauritius have recently taken initiatives to formulate more comprehensive IT policies.

Although IT has been a mixed blessing in different sub-Saharan countries, overall there have been many negative consequences. Scarce foreign currency has been spent on equipment which is not used. The dependency on multinational corporations and expatriate personnel has increased, and sociocultural conflicts introduced. Moreover, what Africa has experienced for the most part so far is not IT transfer but transplantation, the dumping of boxes without the necessary know-how (donor agencies have a reputation for doing this).

Certain prerequisites, such as reliable power supply to operate the computers, a well-functioning telephone network to transmit data, foreign currency to import the technology, and computer literate personnel, are necessary for successful use of IT. Such infrastructural elements remain inadequate in many sub-Saharan countries. For instance, with the number of telephones per 1,000 people ranging between 12 and 50 depending on the country, Africa's telecommunications infrastructure is woefully inadequate. Many of the lines that do exist are out of order much of the time (e.g., sometimes large pieces of telephone cable are cut out by thieves and the metals resold).

Sub-Saharan Africa lacks computer skills in all areas, including systems analysis, programming, maintenance and consulting, and at all operational levels from basic use to management. Most countries lack the educational and training facilities needed to help people acquire the proper skills. The few training centers that do exist have not been able to keep up with demand. Only a handful of countries such as Nigeria, Malawi and Zimbabwe have universities that offer computer science de-

grees. The programs available in the other countries are mainly diplomas and certificates. As a result of unskilled and untrained personnel, user organizations are forced to hire expatriate staff, who in turn lack knowledge about local organizational cultures and thus design poor systems. Many African governments and organizations are waking up to this situation, but few serious measures have been taken. For instance, the University of Nairobi has developed a Bachelor of Science major on paper, but it is yet to be implemented because of the bureaucracy. Moreover, it will not be enough to merely institute courses; books, teachers and equipment are also required but unfortunately have been overlooked.

Unless computer literacy is among managers, poor strategic decisions will continue to be made. The application of computers in sub-Saharan Africa have so far been mainly the result of isolated initiatives without preconceived strategies or plans. The lack of long-term business plans at many organizations results in systems being purchased but not used properly. Managers need to understand that planning is essential before, not after, hardware and software is bought. At present, the most pressing need in sub-Saharan Africa is not new systems, but rather the know-how to effectively use what is already there.

IT can be of great value in various economic sectors if used for decision-making. But computers are still largely used for routine data processing in sub-Saharan Africa with very little computer-aided decision-making. There is still minimal recognition that information is one of the major determinants of economic and social development. One of the reasons for Africa's underdevelopment is bad or ineffective public sector management because of the lack of or inadequate use of data. Computers are often introduced to overcome some of these problems but few realize that blind computerization does not correct ineffective manual systems.

The sub-Saharan countries, largely because of the influence of foreign suppliers, consultants, and organizations, have come to believe and accept that computers systems can help organizations make more effective use of financial, managerial and socioeconomic resources. Furthermore, with the cost of IT falling dramatically, and with systems becoming much easier to use and maintain, some of the prohibitive cost and infrastructural problems are being lessened. So an increasingly affordable and broadly applicable technology is available to play an essential part in the process of development. How should this be done?

Instead of trying to "catch up" with the industrialized world, sub-Saharan LDCs should instead use IT for selected and discriminated applications to bring substantial benefits to their economies and people. The choice of applications must match the priorities set by government and have a high developmental impact. The automation of the telecommunications system in The Gambia, the Expenditure Monitoring System in Ghana, and the Road Safety and Planning System in Nigeria are a few examples of applications which should be encouraged.

What Africa needs most is the ability to exploit existing products effectively, and this can only be achieved through education. Development is all about people, their needs and their potential, and not about the sophistication of technology.

# 7. INTERNATIONAL PERSPECTIVES AND ISSUES

## MIKE LAWRIE: THE RICH NATIONS CAN AFFORD THE INEFFICIENCIES, THE POOR CANNOT

There is a general theme of frustration in Odedra's essay, and this must be shared by many IT people who are trying to assist LDCs in Africa. Some of the issues that have been raised apply to so-called developed countries as well, but they can afford the inefficiencies whereas the poorer nations cannot.

---

*It is painful to see an underutilized machine in a less developed country because somewhere in that country is someone with a great need who is crying out for a computer.*

---

It is painful to see an underutilized machine in an LDC because somewhere in that country is someone with a great need who is crying out for a computer. The underutilized resource is in the wrong place and nothing can be done about it. Likewise, seeing a broken fileserver (and the unusable workstations) in an LDC is somehow very different from seeing this in the so-called first world because it should take but a little labor and a few parts to fix, but this is unlikely to happen because the skills are not available and there are no parts in the local electronics store. Indeed, there is probably no local electronics store.

The shortage of training is certainly a serious problem, as is lack of experience. The costs of training are horrendously high in hard cash, and the cost of obtaining experience can be crippling. If in the process of obtaining experience, a piece of equipment is broken or a bit of software is erased, it may not be possible to replace—donated equipment might be too old to have spares readily available, and export laws of the U.S. can make it extremely difficult to obtain a software release.

There is the frustration experienced by people who have too much well-meant but misguided "help." There is at least one individual in an African developing country who has been forbidden from making telephones calls to send/receive email—this on the justifiable grounds of expense. Yet within the last 12 months he has been sponsored to attend at least four international meetings dealing with email—three in the first world—with all the costs these trips entail. Were these travel funds directed instead toward a telephone bill, email would have been given a big boost in Africa.

African social practices may be difficult for a Westerner to understand. As a member of an extended family you must always give assistance to someone who is even remotely related to you, no matter what the cost. This can be viewed as nepotism when it comes to giving "jobs for pals," but in a rural society there is no need for orphanages and the aged are looked after— not as a burden but as a normal way of life. This is far removed from what happens in most societies that use IT extensively and successfully, so the experts from those societies do not even appreciate, for example, that staff selection in an organization does not necessarily work best by choosing the most technically qualified persons for the job. You might end up with a well-qualified staff, but not necessarily with a working team.

Hard-selling by IT vendors does take place. There is the story about the vendor who took his African client to the U.S. to demonstrate his product, yet did not let the client find out about the multivendor trade show held a few miles away. That this action is accepted as "fair trading" in the Western world is one thing, but it smacks of very poor taste in an LDC.

Dependency on expatriates does occur. There are differing views about this, however. Good African staff leave for the wide world (and maybe some political freedom) and will not go home anyway, so how is the IT function to be staffed? Expatriates in African countries could be making a sacrifice by living under what to them must be very trying conditions, and certainly some of them do this out of a kindly feeling towards their fellow human beings. Integrating IT into the fabric of an LDC does not happen overnight, and certainly some "expats" are doing a great job of overseeing this process.

There is no one correct way to introduce IT. Governmental planning in itself is not the solution, nor is allowing individuals to develop whatever entrepreneurial skills they have without there being some overall strategy. It is difficult to define the line between on the one hand simply throwing technology at a problem and on the other simply waiting for someone to call for technology to help with a problem. This may well be the essence of the frustration over IT in sub-Saharan Africa. Whatever is done is criticized.

Odedra has made a very relevant point that "development is all about people, their needs and their potential, and not about the sophistication of technology." It will be better for the developed world to adapt to this approach to African IT than to have Africa adapt instantly to the developed world. Africans are going to have to live with the warts of Western IT, but it will be easier all around if the IT vendors and aid agencies in turn take note of her comments.

## MARK BENNETT: FOR GROWTH, IT IS AS VITAL TO AFRICA AS IT IS TO AMERICA OR EUROPE

A problem with writing about IT in Africa is that Africa itself is a very diverse entity. The differences among countries in their economies, levels of education, languages, underlying cultures, and historic associations all have considerable effects on the likely success in the uptake of a new technology such as computing. It is thus with great care that one undertakes analysis of this immensely complex scene and can only do so from a perspective of limited experience and inevitable subjectivity.

Odedra's comments are perceptive, despite this necessity to speak to the whole of the African IT condition. And yet there is room for additional perspectives.

She begins by suggesting that IT may have turned from a potential tool for development into something of an obstacle to it. Many of the problems she cites with the introduction of IT would be echoed by others who have worked in the African environment. These include complex purchasing procedures, vendor control of technical direction, dependency on outsiders, poor maintenance procedures, poor training and underutilization of machines and human potential.

But such criticisms could be equally leveled at other imported technologies such as the motor car: equally liable to break down, creating equal dependence, and even more consumptive of valuable foreign exchange. Furthermore, in some countries up to 80% of vehicles lie idle in garages, gardens and scrapyards for want of spare parts or trained engineers to maintain them. Yet few suggest that such transport technologies are not appropriate; they are essential to the economy despite their many difficulties. IT too should be considered to be going through "growing pains" in the development process. It needs to be carefully analyzed and considered, but as a tool for growth it is as vital to Africa as it is to America or Europe.

IT is not, and never will be, a way to leapfrog development, an immensely complex process having its roots in educational and infrastructural building which cannot be by-passed.

Some people have therefore questioned whether Africa needs IT in the management of its operations, bearing in mind its rural nature and shortage of capital and foreign exchange. However, every society needs to be an "information society" to a greater or lesser degree. The question remains, therefore, whether the current manual systems with their plenteous supplies of manpower are managing to generate that information?

The answer appears to be "no." Most LDCs are beset with numerous manpower-related difficulties that may not be fully understood elsewhere. Many stem from lack of education and experience or from environments with no formal systems of control. But difficulties also include poor infrastructure and services (telephones, post, transport, etc.) and lack of a consistently available work force (for reasons which result from low standards of living). In particular, it is common to have a whole skilled middle layer of management missing (e.g., trained accountants and competent administrators).

In the West, primary reasons for the use of IT include the ability to gain access to fast and accurate information, to provide better customer service, and to save costs, which often means reducing manpower. In the South, with its plenteous supply of cheap manpower (a microcomputer in the West may cost one month's wage for a programmer; the same machine in Zambia would cost 6 years wages), justification for reduction of manpower might seem to be almost altogether removed, especially since unemployment is morally undesirable in economies with no social security provisions.

But computers do not always replace manpower per se. Manual systems may not improve however many people are applied to them. Computers instead are being used to transform inefficient systems into efficient ones. This accords with UN thinking that "the analysis and systematization that occurs when computerization takes place can be recognized in itself as a most significant contribution to improving management decision-making and resource allocation" [1].

So the computer may substitute for semiskilled and middle-management staff who are simply not available, or may be part of a stable and reliable system with no clerical counterpart. It reduces the constraints on expansion which may not have resulted from lack of manpower alone, but absence of supervision and control, slowness and lack of firm policies. By this token IT is worth introducing in its own right and may well overcome some of the constraints to accelerated development.

But increasingly today IT in Africa is being used as it should be for the importation and production of vitally needed information. Information represents power in both the economic and political spheres. Yet it has been estimated that at least 90% of data on Africa may reside on databases in the West [8]. If African economies are to improve, they need to have access to the same markets and the same information within the same time frame as more developed countries. Such access is only achievable through IT.

In education this need is perhaps even more manifest. Many universities in Africa suffer from lack of access to the latest books or journals. Academics may be unable to publish internationally accepted papers as a consequence. Travel opportunities become fewer and a sense of isolation easily sets in. (A 20 minute phone call from Zambia to the U.S. can cost a month's wages.)

One important contribution IT can make under these circumstances is the introduction of electronic mail services. The degree to which African telecommunications can support such services varies greatly, but recent signs are encouraging, and this would appear to be one area (with considerable encouragement from "outside") where a leapfrog approach could be viable.

Computing in Africa may appear presumptive: in areas of drought or malnutrition it is hard to persuade some people that IT is something on which money should be spent. But IT is about information, and information is needed to help cure illness and bring food, bolster production or foster education. Information is needed to allow Africa to find its own ways forward.

## FOLLOW-UPS AND POINTERS

Correspondence with the African guest coauthors of this column is possible via electronic mail: Mayuri Odedra, odedra@iscs.nus.sg; Mike Lawrie, ccml@hippo.ru.ac.za; Mark Bennett, mark.bennett@fl.n761.z5.fidonet.org.

Mike Lawrie has been providing an invaluable fidonet hub for several countries through the computer center at Rhodes. His "record distance" is to Ethiopia, with regular links to Botswana, Mauritius and Zambia (the only affordable outlet for Bennett). He also has regular uucp links with Zimbabwe and Namibia, and hopes to have another with Mozambique soon. More generally, he points out that IT development in South Africa is extensive, and there is much willingness to cooperate with other sub-Saharan countries.

Most of Africa still has a greet need for PCs and ancillary equipment which may be considered outdated elsewhere, e.g.,

286s, XTs, or even VT100s. Such equipment is now "junked" in many countries while universities and other institutions in Africa would make grateful use of it. Transport arrangements would be covered by the recipient. Please contact Mark Bennett if you have equipment to pass along.

Readers are encouraged to send comments, suggestions, anecdotes, insightful speculation, raw data, and submissions for guest columns on subjects relating to international aspects of IT. Correspondence should be addressed to:

**Sy Goodman**
MIS/BPA
University of Arizona
Tucson, AZ 85721 **or**
goodman@bpa.arizona.edu **or**
fax: (602) 621-2433

## REFERENCES

1. Bogod, J. *The Role of Computing in Developing Countries,* British Computer Society, London, 1979.
2. Goodman, S. E., Green, J. D. Computing in the Middle East, *Comm, ACM 35,* 8 (Aug. 1992), 21–25.
3. Janczewski, L. J. Factors of information technology implementation in underdeveloped countries: Example of the West African nations. In *The Global Issues of Information Technology Management,* S. Palvia, P. Palvia and R. M. Zigli, Eds., Idea Group, (1992), 187–212.
4. Odedra, M. Information technology transfer to developing countries: Cases from Kenya, Zambia and Zimbabwe. Ph. D. thesis, London School of Economics, Sept. 1990.
5. Odedra, M. Much more than human resource development for Africa. In *Information Technology Manpower: Key Issues for Developing Countries,* S. C. Bhatnagar, Ed., Tata McGraw-Hill, 1992, 189–200.
6. Odedra, M. Enforcement of foreign technology on Africa: Its effect on society, culture, and utilization of information technology. In *Social Citizenship in the Information Age,* C. Beardon and D. Whitehouse, Eds., 1992, 143–154.
7. Who's got the computers? *World Mon.* (Oct. 1992), 9.
8. Zwangobani, E. Communications for development: A developing country perspective. In *Conference Proceedings of Africom '87,* Computer Society of Zimbabwe, Harare, 1987.

# Computing in the Middle East

## S. E. Goodman and J. D. Green

*Seymour E. Goodman, a professor of management information systems and policy at the University of Arizona, studies international developments in computing. Jerrold Green is Director of the Center for Middle Eastern Studies at the University of Arizona.*

The role, status and future of the information technologies (IT) in the Middle East, with the partial exceptions of Israel and Turkey, have been largely ignored or misunderstood by most of the world. The economic, political and strategic significance of this region make technological lacuna about it inexcusable. Oil, a strategic locale, a complex range of economic and social problems, and conflict on many levels (e.g., Arabs/Israel, Iran/Iraq, Iraq/UN, Lebanon, Somalia) combine to make this an important, unstable, and rapidly changing part of the world.

Largely uninformed external coverage of the Middle East tends to project the image of peoples intent upon the eradication of modernization, the abolition of technologies synonymous with the West, and a generalized desire to revert to some earlier epoch in history. In our view, this impression of regional technophobia is oversimplified and exaggerated. As the following examples illustrate, there have been important applications of IT in the region, including some with unique indigenous characteristics. Yet, as we describe in this column, economic, political and cultural circumstances are such that the overall acceptability and value of these technologies remains ambiguous.

## Snapshots

### Egypt

Egypt is the most populous country (about 55 million) in the region as well as one of the most cosmopolitan. It has the largest, most capable, and most internationally oriented computing community in the Arab world, and trained people are among its most important high-tech exports. Mohtassem Billah Kaddah exemplifies this sophistication as head of the Debt Management Project of the Information and Decision Support Center (IDSC), the lead IT-related organization under the Egyptian Cabinet. Because Egypt has one of the world's largest foreign debts, Kaddah and his staff have had to develop an information system for modeling different debt rescheduling schemes. The system is heavily used by senior officials, and is credited with playing a key role in producing a model that resulted in the negotiation of very favorable terms from foreign creditors. As a result, other developing countries with severe debt problems look to Egypt for technical assistance with debt rescheduling.

In a different realm, Fathy Saleh and his team at the Regional Information Technology and Software Engineering Center (RITSEC) in Cairo are working on cultural multimedia projects. Their goal is to capture some of the most valuable artistic and library treasures in computerized forms accessible to large numbers of people. A prototype system exists for storing and displaying ancient manuscripts in the National Library on CD-ROM, including one of the oldest known copies of the complete Koran. Saleh, Robert Cribbs, and Mahmoud Effat did a Fourier analysis of the digitized sound recordings of two original and five exact replicas of ancient Egyptian flutes dating from the 18th Pharaonic Dynasty (around 1500 B.C.). They concluded that the Western musical scale was probably invented by the ancient Egyptians and not by Pythagoras as has been believed for centuries. A similar analysis suggests that the Arabian musical scale, credited to the Persians, may also have been invented by the ancient Egyptians [9].

### Iran

An interesting irony may be seen in the fact that a powerful synthesis of modern technologies and traditional ideas were instrumental in the overthrow of the Shah and the victory of Iran's Islamic Revolution of 1978–79. Without IT, this upheaval may not have occurred [8]. The Shah had invested heavily in these technologies as a means to secure his own position. Particular attention was paid to the development of a state-of-the-art TV and radio infrastructure which was used to further centralize his authority and cement his control. SAVAK, the Shah's secret police, was equipped with computers to keep track of Iran's large and growing community of political dissidents. Copy machines, shortwave radio, and an improved telephone system all became key elements in state-building. Yet just as the Shah had hoped to use these tools to support his control, his opponents turned them against him. Copy machines churned out antigovernment material, while cassette recorders were used to play tape-recorded exhortations by Ayatollah Khomeini from his places of exile in Iraq and France. People listened to the BBC and the Voice of America, which broadcast the exiled Ayatollah's instructions to his followers in Iran. In less than a year, the region's strongest leader with its best-equipped military and secret police was chased out of the country by a movement headed by an elderly cleric who never had a bank account nor driven an automobile.

## Jordan

The Middle East is home to an unparalleled concentration of great archaeological sites. There is a growing threat of damage to many of these sites due to the rapid growth of population and the attendant need for housing, utilities, roads, telephone lines, and agricultural land. In recent years, government and international agencies concerned with the preservation of antiquities have started programs for establishing and maintaining computerized inventories of their archaeological heritages. One of these is the Jordan Antiquities Database and Information System (JADIS) project headed by Gaetano Palumbo. The goals of JADIS include providing detailed information to government and private organizations undertaking construction near antiquity sites and helping archaeologists to more effectively plan their excavations and surveys. The hardware used for antiquities projects covers the full range of computer systems from mainframes to PCs. Many, including JADIS, are trying to combine databases and Geographical Information Systems (GIS) to provide a wide spectrum of useful outputs. Palumbo estimates that over 20,000 sites in Jordan will be recorded in JADIS and that there are hundreds of potential users [6].

## Syria

The most striking feature in Syria is the omnipresence of pictures of President Hafez al-Assad. Every building has at least one, and many government buildings have at least one on every piece of glass and wall. Even taxis (often pre-1970 American-made cars) have two or three photos. The ruling Baath Party and government generate new Assad posters frequently, and no one dares to remove old ones. Only 360 people from an electorate of 6.5 million voted against Assad in last December's one-candidate election [4]. This ostentatious display of control is backed up by over a dozen enforcement and intelligence agencies.

Assad's control is different in some ways from that of other "socialist" leader-worshipping states like Iraq or Romania [1]. The merchant class—including smugglers and entrepreneurs—is largely left alone in return for various forms of support. Food is good and reasonably plentiful, and Damascus is a lively city, as the capitals of police states go. There is little control of domestic use of technology, and PCs, photocopy machines, and telephones are in common use, subject more to cost constraints than to the heavy government control that existed in places like pre-1986 Romania, East Germany, and the USSR. PCs must be registered with an office that is connected with the military, but no one seems to consider this threatening, and reregistration is not necessary if the ownership of the machine changes.

Electronic communications with the outside world are a different matter. The government is acutely aware of the potential power of IT. Syria has no international email links and limited international phone service. The importation of telefax machines is illegal. Some people do have fax machines—often smuggled in from nearby Beirut—but these are usually kept out of sight in desk drawers.

Foreign contact of another sort has given Syrian merchants a problem they deal with using an electro-optical technology not seen much elsewhere. They have electronic scanning devices for checking the authenticity of American currency. Apparently the former Soviet Union used to pay some of its local clients in counterfeit $100 bills supposedly printed under the auspices of the KGB.

## Building Software Capabilities

There is no computer hardware manufacturing industry of great consequence in the Middle East. However, many of the countries in the region have good universities and send large numbers of people abroad for technical and business training. Many Middle Easterners live in or have good contacts within the industrialized countries. Taken together with existing or prospective domestic and regional markets for IT applications, these factors have stimulated several countries to try to build indigenous software engineering and marketing capabilities to serve a variety of national needs and to provide export opportunities. Software industries are being nurtured in Egypt, Jordan, Libya, Morocco, Saudi Arabia, Sudan, Syria, and Tunisia, among others. So far, Egypt seems to have the most extensive and successful record, one which we hope to cover in more detail in a future column.

Tunisia's efforts are illustrative of activities in several countries. The Tunisian government has officially made informatics a "privileged sector." The National Informatics Plan is formulated by the Council for Computing and Telecommunications, which is chaired by the Prime Minister and whose membership consists of a small number of cabinet ministers and other "key players." The National Informatics Center in Tunis has been Tunisia's lead IT organization since 1975. Its 250-member staff tries to do everything from overseeing the implementation of the Plan to playing a major role in the design and construction of a national data transmission network. The government recently cut tariffs on computer imports from 50% to 10%. These efforts are contributing to increases in the use of IT: computers are heavily used in banks and public utilities, and during 1987–91 Tunisia had a 31.5% average annual rate of increase in the value of its computer equipment stock, to a current value of over 200 million dinars (1 dinar = U.S. $1.12 on Jan. 13, 1992) [5].

Even the Sudan, one of the poorest countries in the region (and still suffering from a prolonged civil war), is trying to develop a software industry. The Sudan was an early serious user of computing, with two mainframes in 1965, one for data processing and one for scientific computation at the University of Khartoum. But this start was not sustained, and computing in the Sudan has suffered from the migration of some of its best technical people to oil-rich neighboring countries. There has also been a lack of government priority since return on resources spent on computing was less tangible than in other areas [7]. Nevertheless, the computing community is growing and doing what it can to improve its software capabilities, including the 1929 introduction of a graduate program in software engineering at the Sudan University of Science and Technology.

A common concern, and the focus of much effort from Morocco to Saudi Arabia, has naturally been the Arabization of software. The large regional population, and the localized utility of Arabic, guarantee a substantial amount of work and market for Arabized software products. An Arabic computer standardized code (ASMO-449) was established in 1985 under the Arab Standards and Metrology Organization (ASMO) and the Arabization Coordination Bureau, specialized organizations under the Arab League. However, both groups died of political and budgetary problems and the codes have not been updated, resulting in a proliferation of many new codes and additions [2]. (Arabic letters take different written forms depending on their position in a word. So Arabic word processors have to be a little smarter than those for European languages because a previously typed character may have to change shape, depending on what is typed after it.) One of the serious barriers to building national and regional software industries is the widespread software piracy that exists in most of the Middle East. Frank and open discussions of this sensitive subject were recently held at a major regional software engineering conference hosted by RITSEC/IDSC, under the direction of Hisham El-Sherif, in Cairo in January, 1992. Although extreme positions were stated (ranging from "let's take what we can and let Bush worry about the New World Order" to "pirating countries should be ostracized from the world community"), most of the discussions centered on the need to respect intellectual property and to become legitimate members of the international software community. There was general agreement that piracy has done much to increase computer literacy in developing countries. But so has the availability of inexpensive microcomputers, and users in pirating countries always seem to find enough money to buy PCs from Taiwan or Korea, although they claim they are too poor to buy software. It is simply much easier to steal software than hardware, and little respect for intellectual property has evolved in most developing countries, at least partially because so little software is created there (see also the December 1991 "International Perspectives" column). A concern of the Middle Eastern software engineering communities is that little commercial software will ever be created where piracy is so prevalent since the practice undermines their incentives. Compromises in pricing strategies were advocated as ways to balance the needs of foreign and domestic software producers and users in developing countries, e.g., poor country discounts similar to educational discounts used by book producers, or special site licenses.

## Information Technologies and Social-Political Control

In a part of the world where monarchies, dictatorships, and theocracies are dominant, and where traditional values are still important, the acceptability of IT is mixed. Controls and technological inhibitions remain prominent and widespread.

During this time of incredible global proliferation of computer networks, the Middle East is noteworthy for the near absence of this technology. Although plans for national or regional data networks have been raised in several countries, we know of no extensive implemented network in any of these countries. According to Larry Landweber's international connectivity table [3], there are no Bitnet, Internet, UUCP or Fidonet sites in Algeria, Bahrain, Iraq, Jordan, Kuwait, Lebanon, Libya, Morocco, Oman, Qatar, Somalia, Sudan, Syria, UAE, or Yemen. Egypt and Saudi Arabia have small numbers of domestic sites. Tunisia is the Arab country that is most extensively connected, with at least five Internet sites and fewer Bitnet and Fidonet sites. Of the three prominent non-Arab countries in the region, Iran is unconnected, but Israel and Turkey are.

Why is there so little network activity? We have no simple, credible explanation. Money is often cited as a reason, but unconvincingly. The cost of the technology is decreasing rapidly, there are inexpensive linkages available in significantly poorer parts of the world, and many Mideastern countries that can easily afford sites are among the most conspicuous nonusers. Cultural factors may provide a partial explanation. In a part of the world in which distrust for government is high, Middle Easterners may be unwilling to send communications which can be easily collected and read. Islamic religious constraints have been cited by some as inhibiting the introduction of new technologies, but we have not found any generally accepted tenets to this effect. Indeed, some Muslims with whom we spoke believe that Islam encourages the progressive use of new techniques. A better explanation may be found in cultures where personal contact is preferred to colder and more abstract long-distance ties. Middle Easterners rely heavily on face-to-face communications; a handshake is often as good as a written contract. There is still a strong human element to a telephone conversation, but people may think computer networks deprive individuals of any personalized contact.

A significant part of the explanation is political. Regional politics have always been difficult and contentious, and are likely to have impeded the regionalization of IT. At least some frustrated Jordanian computer scientists think so: "Plans to create a national network in Jordan . . . operating within a Central Arab Network and linking it to other Arab national networks through Gulfnet and Maghrebnet, under the umbrella of Aris-Net, are still a glimmer in the eyes of infocrats because of regional political reason" [2].

As the example of faxes in Syria illustrates, there are higher-level political controls in some places. One senior computer scientist blamed the region's IT troubles on the kinds of governments most of the countries have, where people with power think and have the authority to act as if power is in controlling and containing information (especially information that crosses borders) rather than in distributing it. But a few controls are loosening. During the Gulf War hundreds of Saudis purchased previously restricted satellite dishes to watch news of the conflict. After the war ended, certain government officials felt that the dishes should be registered, monitored, or dismantled. They were reportedly overruled by the King himself who recognized how disruptive such a policy might prove. Once people are exposed to a useful new technology, they cannot be forced to forget it.

Not all of the political controls on IT are of local origin. Some come from outside, e.g., the unilateral U.S. export controls on such items as personal computers. Imposed on Syria for its purported support for terrorist activities, controls on these particular products do little more than punish affiliates of American companies like

IBM and NCR (the latter has been operating in Syria since 1952). Microcomputers based on Intel Corporation's 80286, 80386, and 80486 microprocessors are imported from the Far East and Europe without impediments and in whatever numbers the market will bear.

## Conclusions

We have tried to make the case that the heterogeneity and complexity of IT use in the Middle East is far greater than many Western observers may realize. What is particularly noteworthy is the openness of the computing professionals whom we encountered during our visit to the region in January 1992, when we gathered much of the information presented here. Although it might be trite to emphasize the degree to which commitment to technological development seems to transcend individual nationalisms, we were both struck by the degree to which our colleagues in the Middle East were eager to discuss with us the role of IT in their individual countries. It is this kind of openness that may ultimately undermine the opposition to further pursuit of the types of studies advocated in this column. We would be interested in hearing from colleagues sharing an interest both in IT and its applications throughout a highly variegated Middle East.

## References

1. Goodman, S. E. Computing and the resuscitation of Romania. *Commun. ACM 34*, 9 (Sept. 1991). 19–22.
2. Kanaan, T., Alul S., Abdullah, G. Jordan: Country briefing note. Regional Seminar on Establishing Regional Software Centers. Cairo, Jan. 14–16, 1992.
3. Landweber, L. *International connectivity, Version 5.* Apr. 10, 1992.
4. Miller, J. Syria's game: Put on a Western face. The *New York Times Magazine* (Jan. 26, 1992), 12–21.
5. National Center for Informatics. Informatics in Tunisia. Regional Seminary on Establishing Regional Software Centers. Cairo. Jan. 14–16, 1992; and Center brochure, undated.
6. Palumbo, G. Jordan antiquities database and information system. Unpublished project description. Amman, Jordan, Jan. 15, 1992.
7. Status of software engineering and information technology in the Sudan. Regional Seminar on Establishing Regional Software Centers. Cairo, Jan. 14–16, 1992.
8. Tehranian, M. Iran: Communication, alienation, revolution. *Intermedia* (Mar. 1979), 6–12.
9. Wafai, C. Music's new Rosetta Stone. *Alam El-Computer* (Dec. 1991), 49–51.

## Follow-ups and Pointers

**Jerrold Green** is Director of the Center for Middle Eastern Studies at the University of Arizona. He regularly visits the region and has lived for extended periods in Egypt, Israel, and Iran.

As discussed in the April 1992 "International Perspectives," the economic crisis currently devastating Brazil has been particularly hard on the university computing communities there. Samuel Oliveira and others have organized an effort to send used hardware and software to Brazilian universities. Oliveira may be contacted at: Samuel R. Oliveira, Department of Physics—RLM 9.216, University of Texas at Austin, Austin, TX 78712-1081 or (512) 471-4700 or 322-0369 or sam@einstein.ph.utexas .edu; BRAS-NET@CS.UCLA.EDU—(Brazilian email list) soc.culture.brazil—(newsgroup on Brazil)

Readers are encouraged to send comments, suggestions, anecdotes, insightful speculation (especially on the issue of social-political controls or inhibitions on IT in the Middle East), raw data, and submissions for guest columns on subjects relating to international aspects of IT. All correspondence should be addressed to:

**Sy Goodman**
*MIS/BPA*
*University of Arizona*
*Tucson, AZ 85721 or*
*goodman@mis.arizona.edu or*
*fax: (602) 621-2433*

# NEW TECHNOLOGY PROPELS AIR TRAVEL

*Lucrative Reservation Systems Shaping Debate on Industry's Future*

## Geoffrey Rowan

*The Globe and Mail*
*Toronto*

Over the past 60 years, the technology used to book a seat on an airplane has changed more dramatically than the airplanes themselves, evolving from pencil on paper or chalk on slate to big-money international computer networks.

In the process, the computer reservation systems (CRSs) that started out as a creation of the airlines to help them manage their seat inventories have, in some cases, replaced the airplane as their main source of profit.

Besides airline tickets, travel agents use these computerized marvels to book hotel rooms, rental cars, theatre tickets, bon voyage gifts, flowers, limousines, yacht vacations, tour packages and other products—and every transaction generates a fee for the airline-owned system.

That's why it's no coincidence that this travel agents' lifeline has become the focus of PWA Corp.'s life-and-death struggle, and has helped shape the debate about the future of Canada's embattled airline industry.

The federal Competition Tribunal is scheduled to begin three to four weeks of hearings in Ottawa today. At issue is whether an airline—Calgary-based PWA's Canadian Airlines International Ltd.—should be allowed to survive at the possible expense of a monopoly in the CRS business, or whether a CRS should survive at the possible expense of an airline monopoly.

When the hearings are wrapped up, the tribunal will decide whether the Gemini Group CRS—co-owned by Air Canada, PWA and United Airlines Inc.'s Covia Group—should be drastically altered.

PWA wants desperately to be released from its commitments to the Gemini partnership so that it can pursue a relationship with AMR Corp., the parent of American Airlines Inc., which has its own CRS, the highly profitable Sabre Travel Information Network.

Some fear that if PWA severs its ties, it could weaken Gemini, paving the way for Sabre to dominate the CRS market in Canada. Conversely, if PWA's bid to ally itself with American is stymied, that could set the stage for Canadian Airlines' demise, making Air Canada the country's only national airline.

The CRS has utterly transformed the way travel agents do their jobs. Agents who once needed only to know how to find their way around the world to be considered expert at their profession must now be able to find their way around a computer keyboard.

When Larry Finn, the president of Toronto-based TTI Travel (Canada) Inc., went to work as a travel agent 14 years ago, he would jot down on a piece of paper information from a customer needing a flight, hotel and rental car.

Then he would start making phone calls. First, he'd phone an airline, where he might be put on hold for 10 minutes or more waiting for a reservation agent. If no seat was available, he'd try another airline. Next, he'd call hotels until he found one with an available room and he would repeat the process with the car rental companies.

With any luck, he could get back to the customer the same day. If any of the bookings were unsatisfactory, Mr. Finn would have to start over.

Now, he has desktop access to American Airlines' high-powered Sabre system, which enables him to handle 80 percent of all reservations on the first client call. Flights, hotel, car and any number of other services can be booked and confirmed in minutes, while the client is still on the line.

The Toronto-based Gemini CRS gives its customers the same type of fingertip power.

Gemini and Sabre are slugging it out for control of the $120-million a year CRS market in Canada, with Gemini hanging on to a 65-percent share—for now.

But control of the CRS market in Canada has come to mean much more than control of that market by itself.

PWA is trying to close a deal with AMR that would see the Fort Worth, Tex., company invest $246-million in Canadian Airlines.

But AMR has said it will go ahead with the deal only if Canadian is able to break its ties with Gemini and move its business to Sabre.

That conflict has spawned several billion-dollar lawsuits and created an air of uncertainty for travel agents, who would be unable to function without the sophisticated CRSs, and would have to invest time and money to switch to another system.

As is often the case when an airline finds a profitable new route or type of service, once the value of CRSs was fully realized everyone got into the game. As a result, the products offered by the different systems are remarkably similar.

"I think you can say that, today, the two main CRSs in Canada are comparable," said Reet Muur, managing director of Sabre's Canadian operations. "That wasn't the case a few years ago."

What's critical now to win market share is the ability to find out what travel agents need most and to figure out a technology that will give it to them.

Both Sabre and Gemini provide back-office accounting programs, word-processing programs and a variety of software bells and whistles designed to improve productivity.

"In 1979, the average productivity of a consultant (travel agent) might have been $500,000 to $600,000 a year," Mr. Finn said. "Today it is more like $1.5-million to $2-million a year."

In a business where profit margins are low and competition fierce—there are 850 agencies in Toronto alone—productivity is often what separates the survivors from the failures.

"If a customer calls, they don't want to wait until tomorrow to see if you can get a hotel for them," Ms.

Muur said. "They want to know now. The agency that can be more responsive to their customers' needs is the one that is going to get that customer's business."

If the competing CRSs are basically the same, how do travel agents choose? For some it's a matter of going with what they know.

"I wanted to go with Sabre, but my partner said we should do the made-in-Canada solution," said Kit Manley of Intra-Travel Corp.'s Scarborough office. "We decided to stick with Gemini."

Also affecting their decision were reports they were hearing about difficulties some agents were having with biases built into Sabre's system. The system presented information in ways that helped its owner, American Airlines, or hurt its competitors.

"American now says there is no bias," Ms. Manley said.

But just as the Sabre system had its shortcomings years ago, Gemini had its own problems. It is the product of a merger in 1989 of Air Canada's Reservac system and Canadian Airlines' Pegasus, both of which were based on technology that is now obsolete.

Until last summer, when a conversion to modern technology was completed, Gemini lagged behind Sabre. As a result, the U.S. system managed to pick up 35 percent of the Canadian market.

Now that Gemini is on equal technological footing, it has stopped the erosion of its market share. But with all the controversy surrounding it these days, Gemini sales representatives are fighting an uphill battle to regain lost customers.

"If I give them the benefit of the doubt, there is parity in the product," Mr. Finn said. "There would have to be a further inducement for me to go through the conversion process, to turn off 45 computers on a Friday night and look at restarting something different on a Monday.

"If there is parity, what would induce me to make that change? Right now, with what's happening between Canadian Airlines, Air Canada and Gemini, we feel most comfortable being a Sabre user."

# The Bulgarian Connection

*Many of the Smartest Viruses Poised to Destroy U.S. Computers Can Be Traced to a Single Bored Eastern European Hacker.*

## Paul Mungo and Bryan Clough

The first call came in to the Help Desk of a California magazine publisher just after 5 P.M. on Thursday, June 27, 1991. The company has 1,500 interlinked computers spread around three buildings. The Help Desk, part of the technical-support department, works as a sort of troubleshooter for the entire networked system, dealing with routine problems and helping the less computer-literate staff with their hassles.

"My computer has started making a noise," said the caller. In the normal run of events, noises, apart from the standard beep when starting up or the low-pitched whir of the machine's cooling system, are not part of a computer's repertoire. A noise usually suggests a problem.

Seconds later the Help Desk received a call from another user with the same problem. Then the switchboard lit up. There were callers from all over the company, all with the same complaint: their computers were making odd noises. It might be a tune, one of the callers added helpfully, coming from the computer's small internal speaker. The sixth caller recognized the melody. The computers were all playing tinny renditions of "Yankee Doodle."

To the specialists in the technical-support department, the tune was confirmation that the company had been hit by a virus, and a well-known one at that. The Yankee Doodle virus had first been seen in 1989. There are a number of variants of the bug, and this particular variant, known as Version 44, played the tune at 5 P.M. every eight days.

The company arranged for antiviral software to be shipped overnight by Federal Express. The publishers of the software assured the Help Desk that they would simply need to run the program on the computers to locate the infected files and kill the virus; the files wouldn't be damaged and no data would be lost.

On Friday morning the technical-support staff began the time-consuming task of checking every computer in the company. They discovered that 18 of their machines had been hit by the virus but that the killer function of the software they had just bought wouldn't work on their particular variant of Yankee Doodle. To clean the bug out they would need to delete all infected files and replace them.

The virus they were fighting is generally transferred by diskette. It attaches itself to an executable file—a word-processing program or a game, for instance. Once loaded on to a computer, it searches out other programs to infect. It is generally harmless, in that it never attacks data files—the ones users actually work on—so it can't cause serious damage. Its nuisance value lies in the time it takes to eradicate it.

To stop the virus from spreading, the company decided to shut down its entire network. The technical-support specialists had estimated that killing the bug and replacing the programs would take them two or three hours at most. But by midafternoon they realized that they had underestimated the size of the job. In the end, the technical staff worked for four days, Friday through Monday, before they were satisfied that all the machines were free of the virus. During that time computers and staff were idle.

The computers worked well for the next three days. Then, at 10 A.M. on Thursday, July 4, in a routine scan of one of the computers with the new anti-viral software, a member of a small crew working over the holiday received a big shock: Yankee Doodle was back. The technical specialists, called in to the offices from their homes, discovered to their horror that this time 320 machines had been infected. When they asked the software maker for an explanation, they were simply told, "You missed a spot."

THE COMPANY WAS FORCED TO SHUT DOWN ITS COM-PUTERS, AND AGAIN STAFF AND MACHINERY SAT IDLE WHILE THE SUPPORT STAFF searched through every program on all 1,500 machines. There was no damage: the bug was eradicated and the pro-grams were reinstalled without even a byte of data lost. But the lack of dam-age disguised the virus's real cost. By the time Yankee Doodle had been com-pletely eradicated, the company had suffered one week of lost production, one week of irrecoverable business. The company never quantified its loss, but it is estimated to run into the hundreds of thousands of dollars—all from what was purported to be a harmless virus.

Since 1990 virus researchers have pieced together a history of Yankee Doo-dle. It was first spotted in 1989 in the United Nations offices in Vienna on a computer game called Outrun. The game is proprietary, though unautho-rized pirate copies are often passed around on diskette. Someone, some-where, is thought to have infected a copy of the game, accidentally or deliberately, and the virus began its travels, first to Vi-enna, then around the world, courtesy of the United Nations. Although there are 51 known versions of the virus, they are all based on one original prototype. And that program, despite the virus's all-American name, was written in Bulgaria.

In the same month that the California publishing company was trying to eradi-cate Yankee Doodle, a major financial-ser-vices house on the other side of the coun-try was hit by another bug. This one wasn't a joke; it was deliberately ma-licious.

The first symptoms appeared when one of the secretaries was unable to print out a letter she had just entered into her computer. When the specialist arrived, he began running tests on the affected machine. First he created a new docu-ment and tried printing it out, but that didn't work. He then guessed that the word-processing program itself was de-fective. He went to another computer and copied out the list of program files used by the company, which showed the names of the programs and their size, in bytes (or characters). He then compared

---

*Most virus-detection programs look for known characteristics of familiar viruses and are unable to detect new or modified viruses.*

---

the files on the problem machine with the list. Everything matched, except that eight of the files on the affected com-puter were slightly larger than on the other. He checked the differences, and in each case the files on the problem ma-chine were exactly 1,800 bytes larger.

With that information, the specialist knew immediately that the company had been hit by a virus; he also knew it was 1,800 bytes long and attached itself to program files. He called his supervisor, who hurried over with a virus-detection diskette. They inserted it in the infected computer. After five minutes a message appeared on the screen: 83 files had been checked and no virus had been found. In exasperation the supervisor called the vendor of the virus-detection program.

"It does sound like you've got a virus," the vendor agreed. "But if it's not getting picked up by our software, then it must be a new virus. Or a new strain of an old one."

Most virus-detection programs look for known characteristics of familiar viruses—in other words, for a string of text or a jumble of characters that is known to be contained within the pro-gram of a previously discovered bug. Such virus-detection kits are, of course, unable to detect new or modified viruses.

At the suggestion of the vendor, the technical-support staff began a search of one of the infected files, looking for text or messages. Specialized software is needed to inspect the inside of a program file; during the inspection the screen dis-plays a jumble of computer code. But

within the code the staff saw two strings of text: EDDIE LIVES . . . SOMEWHERE IN TIME! said the first. The second an-nounced: THIS PROGRAM WAS WRIT-TEN IN THE CITY OF SOFIA 1988–1989 © DARK AVENGER.

The supervisor phoned the vendor again: "Who the hell is the Dark Avenger?"

The short answer, the vendor ex-plained patiently, is that no one knows. The Dark Avenger is an enigma. Most virus writers remain anonymous, their viruses appearing, seemingly, out of the ether, without provenance or claimed authorship, but the Dark Avenger is dif-ferent: not only does he put his name to his viruses, he also signals where they were written—Sofia, the capital of Bul-garia. The Dark Avenger's viruses be-gan seeping into the West in 1989. They are all highly contagious and ma-liciously destructive.

"The virus you've been hit with is called Eddie, or sometimes the Dark Avenger," the vendor told the increasingly worried technical-support supervisor. "It must be a new strain or something. That's why it wasn't picked up. Is there any other text message, a girl's name?"

The supervisor took a closer look at the virus. "I missed it before. There's an-other word here. 'DIANA P.' What does this thing do?"

"Well, as it's a new version, the answer is I don't know. Until we've seen a copy, it's anybody's guess."

To discover what a virus actually does, it has to be disassembled, its operating in-structions—the program—taken apart line by line. This is a difficult and time-con-suming process and can be carried out only by specialists. In the meantime the technical-support staff could only wait and watch as the virus spread slowly through the company, bouncing from machine to machine via the network cables that in-tertwined the company's computers.

Viruses like Eddie work by attach-ing a copy of themselves to an exe-cutable file; whenever an infected pro-gram is used, the virus springs into action. It usually has two tasks: first, to find more files to infect; then, after it has had enough time to spread its in-fection, to release its payload. It was obvious that Eddie was spreading, so it was already performing its infection task. What was worrisome was what its payload would prove to be.

To arrest the spread of the bug, the company decided to turn off all its com-puters and wait until the virus could be cleaned out. It was a difficult decision— it would mean downtime and lost business—but it was a sensible precaution. It was later discovered that the payload in the Eddie variant is particularly malicious. When unleashed, it takes occasional potshots at the hard disk, zapping any data or programs it hits.

In this instance some data were irrecoverably destroyed, even though only 60 machines were found to be infected. But in a sense the company had been lucky: because Eddie had taken a potshot at a secretary's word-processing program and knocked out its print capability, it was discovered fairly early. Had it lurked undetected for longer, it could have destroyed even more data.

The process of checking all 2,200 computers took four and a half days, with a team of 12 people working 12 hours a day. Every executable file on every hard disk on every machine had to be checked. The team had special programs to help with the task, but viruses can easily get wrapped up inside "archived" files—files that are compressed to save computer space—where they can escape detection. All archived files had to be expanded back to their full size, checked, and then packed away again. That took time. Also, all diskettes had to be checked, a nearly impossible task given the difficulty in finding them: diskettes have a habit of disappearing into black holes in desk drawers, in briefcases, in storage cupboards.

After 700 hours of intensive effort, the technical-support staff felt confident they had eliminated all traces of Eddie. Their confidence was short-lived. Within a week Eddie was back. This time they lost a further one and a half days' work.

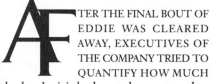FTER THE FINAL BOUT OF EDDIE WAS CLEARED AWAY, EXECUTIVES OF THE COMPANY TRIED TO QUANTIFY HOW MUCH the bug's visit had cost them—not that any of it would be recoverable from insurance. "We lost $500,000 of business— really lost business—not orders deferred until we could catch up but business that had to be done there and then or it went to a competitor," said the company's chief financial officer. "We also lost data. That cost us $20,000. But what really hurt was the lost business. If we force a customer into the hands of a competitor, he might go there again. I guess that could cost us another $500,000."

The company tried to find out how the virus had got into its machines in the first place. Sometimes disenchanted employees (or ex-employees) have been known to cause havoc deliberately on computer systems, but it seemed unlikely in this case. The company concluded that the infection was almost certainly accidental, probably introduced on a diskette brought in from outside. All it knew for certain was that some Bulgarian who called himself the Dark Avenger had cost it $1 million.

By 1990 everyone involved in computer security had become aware that something odd was going on in that obscure Eastern European country. Increasingly sophisticated and damaging viruses that affected IBM-type PCs were moving into the West, carried on diskette or transferred by electronic bulletin boards, and all had one thing in common: they had been written in Bulgaria.

Though only a few of the viruses had actually been seen "in the wild"—that is, infecting computers—reports from Bulgaria suggested that two new viruses were being discovered in that country every week. By mid-1990 there were so many reported Bulgarian viruses that one researcher was moved to refer to the existence of a "Bulgarian virus factory." The phrase stuck.

The origins of that factory go back to the last decade. In the early 1980s the then-president of Bulgaria, Todor Zhivkov, decided that his country was to become a high-tech power, with computers managing the economy while industry concentrated on manufacturing hardware to match that of the West. Bulgaria, he decided, would function as the hardware-manufacturing center for Eastern Europe, trading its computers for cheap raw materials. Bulgaria had the potential, in that it had many well-educated young electronics engineers; what it didn't have, with its archaic infrastructure and ill-managed economy, was any particularly useful application for its own hardware.

With the resources of the state behind Bulgaria's computerization, the country began manufacturing copies of IBM and Apple models. The machines were slow— very slow by today's standards—and were already obsolete even when they first started crawling off the production line. They had been "designed" at the Bulgarian Academy of Sciences, but without the help or blessing of either IBM or Apple. The Bulgarian machines were poorly manufactured clones that used the same operating systems and computer language as the real IBMs and Apples.

In the latter half of the 1980s shiny new computers started to appear in state organizations, schools, colleges, and computer clubs. Many were destined to sit on the boss's desk, largely unused, symbols of a high-tech society that never really

---

*Bulgarians began copying Western programs, cracking any copy-protection schemes that stood in their way, and became skilled at hacking.*

---

existed. Few businesses had any real need for computers; some used them simply to store personnel records. It was a gloss of technology laid over a system that, at its core, wasn't functioning.

In addition, Bulgaria didn't have any software. While the factories continued to manufacture PCs, the most basic requirement—programs to make the machines function—had to be pirated. So the Bulgarians began copying Western programs, cracking any copy-protection schemes that stood in their way, and they became more and more skilled at hacking—in the classic sense of the word. They could program their way around any problem; they learned the ins and outs of the IBM and Apple operating systems; they became skilled computer technicians as they struggled to keep their unreliable and poorly manufactured computers functioning. In short, they were assimilating all the skills they would need to become first-class virus writers.

On November 10, 1988, Teodor Prevalsky, a 27-year-old engineer, sat down at a computer at the technical institute where he worked and started to write his first virus. He had managed to get a copy of a 1987 virus called Vienna, which had been published in a German book, and he used it as a model for his own bug. On November 12, Teodor proudly made an entry in his diary: "Version 0 lives."

Version 0 was, in all probability, the first homegrown Bulgarian virus. It did very little except replicate, leaving copies of itself on what are called COM files— simple program files of limited length. When the virus infected a file, it beeped.

JUST TWO DAYS AFTER WRITING VERSION 0, TEODOR HAD PREPARED VERSION 2. IT WAS MORE CLEVER THAN THE ORIGINAL IN that it could infect both common types of executable files: COM and EXE. The latter are the more sophisticated programs—like word-processing, for instance—and because they are structurally complex they are more difficult to infect. But Teodor's Version 2 employed a little trick that would convert short EXE files into COM files. When the operator called up, or loaded, an EXE file, the lurking virus saw the load command, jumped in ahead, and modified the structure of the EXE file so it resembled a COM file. The next time a restructured EXE file was loaded up, it could be successfully infected by the virus, just like an ordinary COM file.

Teodor was also experimenting with antiviral software at the time, and he developed a program that would hunt down and kill Versions 0 and 2. It was called Vacsina, the Bulgarian word for vaccine. However, by Version 5 Teodor had adapted his virus so that it was immune to his own killer program. He accomplished this by simply adding the character string "Vacsina" to the virus. When his antivirus program saw the string, it would leave the bug alone.

It was shortly thereafter that Version 5 escaped. Like most Bulgarians, Teodor had to share his computer with colleagues at the institute; with four people using one machine, with software copying rampant, and with the casual transfer of diskettes, it was only a matter of time before one of the bugs began to propagate out of his control. Within weeks Version 5 had spread throughout Bulgaria. In less than a year it had reached the West—the first Eastern virus to jump the iron curtain. When the virus was examined, researchers discovered the text string "Vacsina," which immediately gave a name to Version 5.

Meanwhile, Teodor continued experimenting. By December 15, 1988, he had advanced to Version 8. On this variant the payload—the innocuous beep—now sounded only when an infected computer was restarted from the keyboard (a "warm reboot"), allowing it to remain hidden for longer. In the best programming tradition, all his improvements were duly documented and given version numbers as they appeared.

Later in December a new Bulgarian virus was discovered. It carried a text string that said it had been authored by a Vladimir Botchev. The bug was almost certainly written in response to a magazine article stating that it would be "difficult" to write a virus that could infect all EXE files, including the longer ones. Vladimir had presumably seen that as a challenge. His virus appeared less than a month after the article was published. It employed a novel and technically elegant device that enabled it to attach itself to any EXE file, no matter what length. After it infected a file it played the tune "Yankee Doodle"—in celebration, perhaps.

This virus was generally not damaging—its payload was the tune—and because it was easy to detect, it never spread. But the new bug's payload was immediately copied by Teodor in his Version 18, which appeared on January 6, 1989. This one didn't beep; instead it played "Yankee Doodle," which Teodor had lifted, note for note, straight from Vladimir's program.

Five days later Teodor produced Version 21, which could remove the virus from infected files if a more recent version of this bug attacked the same system. Then, on February 6, 1989, Version 30 appeared. It incorporated a "detection and repair" capability, which would warn the virus if it had been modified or corrupted while replicating. Eerily, it could then fix the damage itself by changing the corrupted instructions back to their original form. It was a kind of artificial life, though the repair capability was limited (it could handle only changes of up to 16 bytes in length).

By the end of February Teodor was on to Version 39 and his virus was now full of tricks: it could infect EXE files of any size and could even evade antivirus software. As soon as it noted the presence of a detection program, it would detach itself from the infected file and hide elsewhere in the computer's memory.

With Version 42, which appeared in March, his virus took on a new role: virus fighter. The Ping-Pong boot-sector virus, which is believed to have been created at Turin University in Italy, had now reached Bulgaria. Ping-Pong (also called Bouncing Ball) was a joke virus: from time to time it simply sent a dot careening around the screen, like a ball in a squash court. Teodor's new virus could detect Ping-Pong and was able to modify it in such a way that, after a time, it destroyed itself, leaving behind its corpse. He persisted with the tune "Yankee Doodle" as his payload, but he varied the time and frequency it would play. One of his next variants was Version 44, which plays the tune every eight days at 5 P.M. This was the version destined to become the most widely traveled of all Teodor's viruses: once again, it escaped from his office machine, probably on a diskette, and spread through Bulgaria; on September 30, 1989, it was sighted in offices of the United Nations in Vienna; and from there, now known as Yankee Doodle, it traveled the world. It was this version that caused mayhem at the California publishing house in July 1991.

Teodor continued to develop his virus. The last variant was Version 50, by which time it had been given the additional power to detect and destroy the Cascade bug, which had just arrived in Bulgaria from Austria. Cascade was another joke virus: it caused the letters on a computer terminal to fall down and pile up in heaps at the bottom of the screen to an accompanying clicking noise. After the virus had finished its performance, a user could resume his work—though he would need to replace the letters and words that had fallen from his screen. It wasn't particularly damaging, though the operator's nerves could well be frayed.

Teodor also experimented with "stealth" viruses—silent, deadly, and almost undetectable bugs that evade antiviral software in much the same way that the Stealth plane evades radar detection. Stealth technology has been exploited by virus writers since 1986, but Teodor's was the first that could add itself to a program file without, apparently, increasing the length of the file. Of course it was only an illusion: the virus would simply deduct its own length from the infected file whenever it was being examined.

With his stealth bug Teodor had more or less reached the pinnacle: there was little he could do to improve the programming of his latest virus except, perhaps, to add a destructive payload. But, for Teodor, destruction of data or programs was never the point. He wrote viruses as an intellectual challenge. None of his viruses had ever been intentionally damaging, though he had become aware that they could cause collateral losses. He had also realized that a completely harmless virus was an impossibility. All viruses, by their mere presence on a computer, can accidentally overwrite data or cause a system to crash.

In 1989 Teodor decided to retire from virus writing. His own career until then had, curiously, mirrored that of his friend, Vesselin (Vesko) Bontchev. Teodor and Vesko had been close friends for many years. They were both engineering graduates from professional families, which made them part of the privileged class in Bulgaria at the time. The Bulgarian computer industry was in full swing by then, but the country had few uses for the new machines. In response, a magazine was started called *Komputar za vas* ("Computer for You"), to show readers how to do something constructive on their relatively worthless PCs. The magazine needed technical writers who could explain how the machines worked, and Vesko found that he could double his income of $45 a month by writing the articles. By Bulgarian standards his salary was already high; with the additional income from the magazine he was positively wealthy.

---

*Most computers in Bulgaria had been hit with viruses at least once, and many had been hit with multiple viruses at the same time.*

---

While Teodor wrote viruses, Vesko wrote about them; as Teodor became more proficient at writing bugs, Vesko became more accomplished at analyzing them. By 1989 Vesko had become Bulgaria's most important virus researcher and a major contributor to Western literature on the subject. He had been invited to submit papers and lecture at Western European computer security conferences.

Vesko's reputation was due, in large part, to having been in the right place at the right time. First, there were his friend Teodor's bugs. Teodor would often pass on the programming codes to Vesko for analysis; Vesko would then report on their capabilities. It was a convenient arrangement, and the resulting publicity would encourage other virus writers. Eventually, what became known as the Bulgarian virus factory started to pump out bug after bug, each more dangerous than the last, and Vesko was there to record it. By 1991 he was reporting two new locally grown viruses each week.

In a country with so many bugs flying around, it was inevitable that Bulgarian computers would become overrun. Most computers in the country had been hit at least once; many had been hit with multiple viruses at the same time. Because Vesko was the country's leading authority on the malicious programs, he was eventually given responsibility for coordinating Bulgaria's effort to fight them off. He was constantly on call. By day he worked in his office in the Bulgarian Academy of Sciences, where he was given the dour title of assistant research worker engineer. Weekends and nights he continued the fight from his own cramped room, on a borrowed Bulgarian clone of an IBM PC. He dealt with 10 to 20 phone calls each day from institutions or firms that had been attacked by viruses.

By then Bulgaria had spawned some of the most skilled and prolific virus writers in the world. Many programmers and students took a stab at writing viruses, with varying degrees of success. It became something of a fad among computer freaks in the late 1980s. There was, of course, no "factory" in the usual sense of the word—just a group of young men (they were all male), probably unknown to one another, who had learned the tricks of writing viruses through the techniques perfected while stealing Western software. Since 1988 the Bulgarian virus factory has produced around 200 new viruses; only a few have reached the industrialized West. The scale of the problem may not become apparent for several years.

In any event, in late 1990 and early 1991, Bulgaria itself, no longer Communist and not quite democratic, was going through an identity crisis. Public confidence in the government, in state institutions, and in the currency had evaporated, to be replaced by a deeply cynical, almost anarchic national ethos. Bulgaria had become a country of shabby, small-time dealers, of petty black marketers and crooked currency changers. The symbols of the immediate past, of the near half-century of communism, had been pulled down; little had been erected in their place. But the computers remained, and indeed offered themselves to the new generation of computer programmers as weapons to be turned against the state, to drive an electronic stake through the heart of the system. In this gray time of shortages and rationing, of cynicism and despair, writing viruses was a sort of protest—perhaps against the Communists, possibly against the transitional state, almost certainly against the lack of opportunity and hope.

The man who was to become known as the Dark Avenger began work on his first virus—Eddie—just weeks before Teodor sat down to write the first of his Vacsina–Yankee Doodle series. Teodor's virus was ready first, but the Dark Avenger's bug was much more malicious and infective. "It may be of interest to you to know that Eddie is the most widespread virus in Bulgaria," the Dark Avenger once boasted. "I also have information that Eddie is well known in the United States, West Germany, and Russia too."

The Dark Avenger likes to leave teasing references to his identity in his viruses. As in the Eddie virus, he sometimes "copyrights" his bugs and often gives Sofia as the source. The text string DIANA P. was assumed to be a reference to his girlfriend, except that Diana isn't a particularly Bulgarian name. It's now believed to be a reference to Diana, Princess of Wales.

The Dark Avenger also likes heavy-metal music: the other text string in his first virus, the mysterious EDDIE LIVES, apparently refers to the skeletal mascot Eddie used by the British heavy-metal group Iron Maiden in its stage act. Heavy-metal symbols and motifs run through many of the other viruses written by the Dark Avenger. His Number of the Beast virus (the name is a reference to an Iron Maiden song) contains the 3-byte signature 666, the mystical number believed to refer to the "beast," the Antichrist in the Book of Revelation.

The Dark Avenger has produced four versions of Eddie and six versions of Number of the Beast, as well as four variants of a virus called Phoenix and four of another one known as Anthrax (the name of an American heavy-metal group). In a way, the Dark Avenger has become so well known that any particularly destructive and clever Bulgarian virus will almost automatically be attributed to him. The alternative is too dire for the computer security industry to contemplate.

THE DARK AVENGER'S FAME WAS EVIDENT FROM THE RESPONSE TO HIS CALLS TO THE WORLD'S FIRST "VIRUS EXCHANGE" BULLETIN board, which was established in Sofia by 20-year-old Todor Todorov on November 1, 1990. The idea was eventually copied by others in Britain, Italy, Sweden, Germany, the United States, and Russia, but Todorov was the first. The board describes itself as "A PLACE FOR FREE EXCHANGE OF VIRUSES AND A PLACE WHERE EVERYTHING IS PERMITTED!"

Todorov built up a large collection of viruses after callers learned of his exchange procedures: "IF YOU WANT TO DOWNLOAD VIRUSES FROM THIS BULLETIN BOARD, JUST UPLOAD TO US AT LEAST 1 VIRUS WHICH WE DON'T ALREADY HAVE. THEN YOU WILL BE GIVEN ACCESS TO THE VIRUS AREA, WHERE YOU CAN FIND MANY LIVE VIRUSES, DOCUMENTED DISASSEMBLIES, VIRUS DESCRIPTIONS, AND ORIGINAL VIRUS SOURCE COPIES!"

The Dark Avenger made his first call on November 28, 1990, four weeks after the bulletin board was set up. "I'M GLAD TO SEE THAT THIS BOARD IS RUNNING," he wrote. "I'VE UPLOADED A COUPLE OF VIRUSES TO YOU. I HOPE YOU WILL GIVE ME ACCESS TO THE VIRUS AREA." To which Todorov replied, "THANK YOU FOR THE UPLOAD, YOUR SECURITY LEVEL HAS BEEN UPGRADED. . . . AND YOU HAVE ACCESS TO THE VIRUS AREA NOW."

When it was learned that the Dark Avenger frequented Todorov's bulletin board, other users began leaving messages for him. "HI, DARK AVENGER! WHERE HAVE YOU LEARNED PROGRAMMING? AND WHAT DOES 'EDDIE LIVES' MEAN? AND WHO IS 'DIANA P.'? IS SHE YOUR GIRLFRIEND OR WHAT?" The queries were from Yves P., a French virus writer. Free Raider posted his salute on December 9: "HI, BRILLIANT VIRUS WRITER." Another message said, "HI, I'M THE SYSOP [system operator] OF THE INNERSOFT BULLETIN BOARD. SHOULD I CONSIDER MY BOARD NOT POPULAR BECAUSE YOU DON'T LIKE TO CALL IT? PLEASE GIVE IT A CALL."

The messages from his fans reflected the Dark Avenger's new status: he had become a star. The Dark Avenger's viruses were known to be the most destructive and among the best-engineered ever seen. His fame, as he knew, had spread throughout Europe and to North America as well.

So it's not surprising that he wanted to be treated like the star he was and reacted badly to criticism. In March 1991 he sent the following message to Fidonet, the international bulletin board network: "HELLO, ALL ANTIVIRUS 'RESEARCHERS' WHO ARE READING THIS MESSAGE. I AM GLAD TO INFORM YOU THAT MY FRIENDS AND I ARE DEVELOPING A NEW VIRUS THAT WILL MUTATE IN 1 OF 4,000,000,000 DIFFERENT WAYS! IT WILL NOT CONTAIN ANY CONSTANT INFORMATION. NO VIRUS SCANNER CAN DETECT IT. THE VIRUS WILL HAVE MANY OTHER NEW FEATURES THAT WILL MAKE IT COMPLETELY UNDETECTABLE AND VERY DESTRUCTIVE!"

Fidonet may not have been the best outlet for his boasting: its users are mostly ethical computer enthusiasts. The Dark Avenger received a flood of replies from all over Europe. Most were critical; some were abusive. The Dark Avenger replied testily, "I RECEIVED NO FRIENDLY REPLIES TO MY MESSAGE. THAT'S WHY I WILL NOT REPLY TO ALL THESE MESSAGES, INSTEAD SAYING 'FUCK YOU.' THAT'S WHY I WILL NOT SAY ANY MORE ABOUT MY PLANS."

VESKO BONTCHEV, ALTHOUGH UNASSUMING, IS PROUD OF HIS REPUTATION AS THE COUNTRY'S FOREMOST virus fighter and of his contacts with other researchers in the West. His position is ensured by his oddly symbiotic relationship with the Dark Avenger, one that almost parallels his earlier relationship with Teodor. Vesko contributes to the Dark Avenger's fame by publicizing his activities abroad. In a curious way the two need each other.

Cynics who have noticed this have argued that if the Dark Avenger hadn't existed, it would have been in Vesko's interest to have invented him. Some have even theorized that the two are one and the same: that the quiet, intense virus researcher has an alter ego—the demonic heavy-metal fan, the admirer of Princess Diana, the virus writer called the Dark Avenger.

In an interview in a Bulgarian newspaper, Vesko was asked about the rumors. "Can you give me the name of Dark Avenger?" the reporter queried.

"No."

"Is it possibly you?"

"I have been asked similar questions both in the West and in the Soviet Union. But it is not true."

Despite the rumors, Vesko isn't the Dark Avenger. The two young men—the hunter and the outlaw—are locked in an unfriendly embrace. The relationship between the two is one of mutual distrust, which neither attempts to disguise. It is the classic relationship between a cop and his adversary: hatred, tinged with a measure of respect.

On several occasions, Vesko says, he has tried to smoke out the virus writer. Once Vesko announced that he had carefully analyzed two viruses attributed to the Dark Avenger: the Number of the Beast and Eddie. He said that in his view they could not possibly be the work of the same writer. One was clever, the work of a professional, the other sloppy, the work of an amateur. Furthermore, he said, he intended to present his evidence at a lecture that would be held in Sofia. He guessed that the Dark Avenger would appear, if only to hear what Vesko had to say about his programs.

The meeting was well attended, particularly for a cold Friday night in early December. Vesko presented his evidence. Number of the Beast, he said, was obviously written by an extremely skilled specialist whose style contrasted in every way with the poor quality of Eddie. He watched the audience during his presentation, Vesko says, looking for someone who might be the Dark Avenger; during the questions and discussion afterward he listened for anyone defending the programming of Eddie. He saw and heard nothing that gave him any clues.

But two days after the lecture he received a letter from the Dark Avenger. According to the letter, the virus writer had attended the meeting. Vesko published his comments in the magazine *Komputar za vas*. "The author of the Eddie virus is writing to you," the Dark Avenger began. "I have been reading your pieces of stupidity for quite a long time, but what I heard in your lecture was, to put it boldly, the tops." The virus writer went on to complain about Vesko's critique of his programming skills. Then he added: "I will tell you that my viruses really destroy information, but on the other hand, I don't turn other people's misfortunes into money. Since you [get paid to] write articles that mention my programs, do you not think I should get something?"

Virus writing is not a lucrative field. The Dark Avenger had once before alluded to getting paid for his skills, in a message to a local bulletin board operator, when he had suggested, none too hopefully, that "maybe someone can buy viruses." So far as is known, he has never sold any of his bugs.

In 1990 Vesko put together a psychological profile of the Dark Avenger, a compilation of all the known facts about him: his taste in music, his favorite groups, his supposed interest in the Princess of Wales, his need for money, and so on. From his letter Vesko gleaned he had been a student at Sofia University and, from sarcastic remarks he had made about Vesko's engineering degree, that he was either a mathematics or science student (there is a traditional rivalry between engineering and the other two faculties). He sent the profile to seven former students at the university, asking if they knew anyone who fit the criteria. All seven replied, Vesko says, and all seven mentioned the same name—that of a young man, then 23, a programmer in a small private software house in Sofia.

Vesko didn't turn him in. Even had he wanted to, there was little point: writing viruses is not illegal in Bulgaria.

The virus the Dark Avenger had promised in his message on Fidonet duly appeared in May 1991. He called it the Mutating Engine, and it may well be able to disguise itself in 4 billion different ways.

A virus like this one, which can continually change its appearance, is potentially the most difficult to detect. It contains no constant characteristic, such as a text string, that could be used by virus scanners to register its presence. All that can be detected of the Mutating Engine is a mass of encrypted code—a code that changes every time it infects a file. It may be the most dangerous virus ever produced. Worse, it isn't only a virus: it was distributed as a routine that other writers could build into their own bugs, giving them the same ability to evade detection. A number of these have now been discovered, all of them Mutating Engine clones, with names like Coffee Shop, Cryptlab, Fear, Groove, Little, Pogue. . . .

But the Dark Avenger now has competition from the East. Russians are developing whole new families of clever and malicious bugs, so many that they may soon replace Bulgaria as the leading virus-producing country.

As the sources of viruses multiply—from pirate boards, construction sets, or manic Thai, Russian, and Bulgarian computer freaks—incidents of infection will become much more common.

One of the more malicious Russian viruses is called LoveChild. When it infects a computer, the virus initiates a countdown that begins at 5,000. As long as the virus remains undetected, the counter ticks down with each successive use of the computer. Nothing happens until the counter reaches zero.

Then it wipes out the hard disk.

No one knows how many LoveChild viruses are in existence. Or how many counters are now silently approaching zero.

# Philosophical Frontiers

In recent years, a number of technologies have brought new hope for improving the length and quality of human life. In some instances, such as medical scanning and life support systems, the contributions of computing technology are direct and obvious. In other fields such as biotechnology, computers play indirect yet vital support roles. As dramatic as recent developments have been, we are likely to witness ever more spectacular achievements in our abilities to manipulate nature as computers become more powerful, and perhaps even achieve "artificial intelligence" (AI).

The current and potential benefits of these trends are significant. For example, new reproductive technologies such as in vitro fertilization (which may or may not be used in conjunction with surrogate parenting) offer hope to infertile couples desperate to have a child. DNA mapping, gene splicing, and cloning may lead to the elimination of genetically inherited disorders such as Huntington's disease and cystic fibrosis. Fetal tissue transplants may someday free sufferers from the devastation of diabetes, Alzheimer's, and Parkinson's disease. On the other hand, we also have new technologies that allow their users to inflict death and destruction on an unprecedented scale. Nuclear weapons, which depend heavily on computers, are an obvious example.

Paradoxically, *both* the potentially life-saving and life-taking technologies have spawned enormous controversies over whether or not, and under which conditions, their development should be considered morally and ethically acceptable. In previous issues of *Computers in Society*, several articles have highlighted dilemmas surrounding the life-sustaining potential of organ transplants and artificial life-support systems. In this issue, however, the context for introducing new philosophical dilemmas is a nuclear weapons laboratory. In "Coming of Age in a Weapons Lab," anthropologist Hugh Gusterson relates how physicists, engineers, and computer scientists who develop and test nuclear weapons at Lawrence Livermore National Laboratory in California reconcile their work with their ethical, political, and religious values. He also recounts challenges posed by the demise of the cold war and the reduction in the arms race.

The second article in this section examines whether researchers are on the verge of creating new life forms.

Mark Nichols explains that some scientists believe that "digital creatures," which exist only as computer programs, are the beginnings of artificial life forms and will lead to artificial intelligence (AI). In the next article, "Is Thinking Computable?" Peter Denning reviews opposing sides of the AI debate and concludes that, for now at least, "We can rest a little easier." The prospect of having "godlike power to create beings more advanced than ourselves" is a philosophical frontier we do not as yet have to confront.

The concluding article of this section and issue of *Computers in Society* moves from the topic of whether computers will think to the way that humans think. According to James Bailey, in "New Computers, New Thoughts," the approach to human thinking has always followed a logical, sequential process. With the advent of more powerful computers that use "parallel processing," we are now able to perform previously inconceivable tasks of vast complexity. These new powers, argues Bailey, will not only be immensely useful, but they will fundamentally reshape the way we think and what we think about.

### Looking Ahead: Challenge Questions

Are you a "consequentialist"—someone who believes that whether a course of action is ethically justifiable depends on whether or not it leads to a desired outcome (the ends justify the means)—or are you a "deontologist"—someone who believes that certain actions are intrinsically right or wrong regardless of their consequences?

Which do you think will pose the greatest philosophical and ethical implications—the ability to prolong or alter biological life and processes? the potential to inflict mass death and destruction? the prospect of creating artificial life and/or artificial intelligence?

Can you identify ethical or philosophical issues that would have been impossible for people unacquainted with cars, telephones, electricity, or space travel to think about? Is James Bailey right? Will advances in computing change the nature and content of our thoughts?

Should the people who develop powerful new technologies be held responsible for any negative consequences that might result from their use?

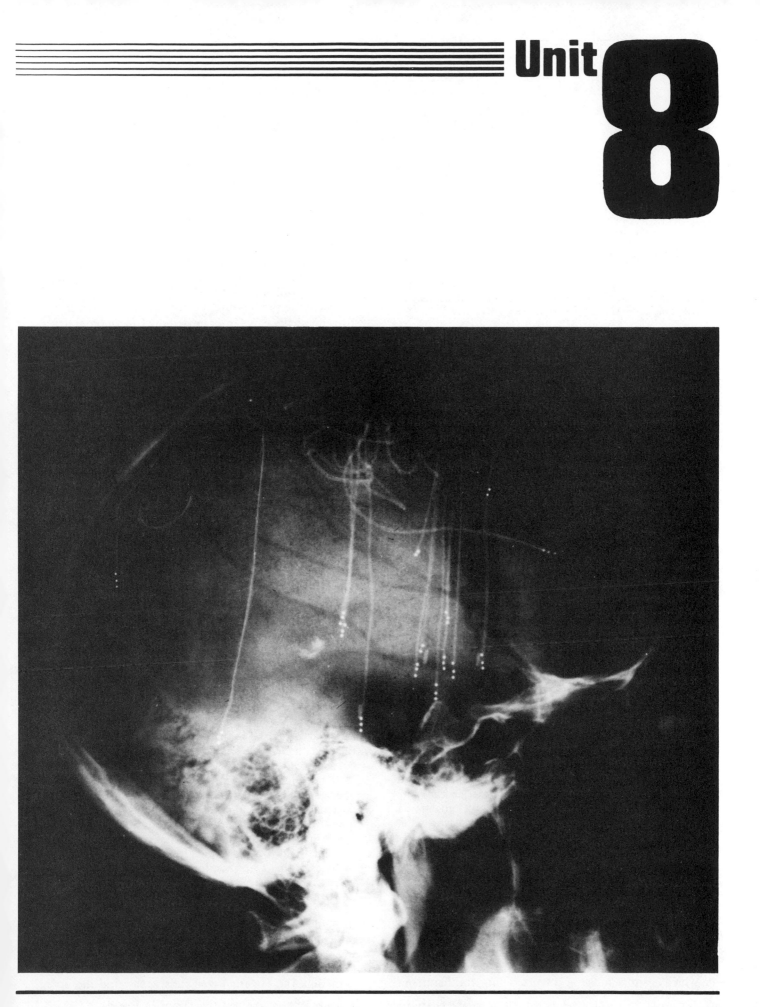

# COMING OF AGE IN A WEAPONS LAB

## Culture, Tradition and Change in the House of the Bomb

### Hugh Gusterson

HUGH GUSTERSON is a social anthropologist at the School of American Research in Santa Fe. He is at work on a book about his research at the Lawrence Livermore National Laboratory.

PETER, AS I SHALL CALL HIM, is in many ways a stereotypical resident of the San Francisco Bay area: he belongs to the Sierra Club; he protested the Vietnam War in the 1970s; and he currently supports a smorgasbord of liberal causes, from women's rights to gun control. He also does what a few thousand other local residents do, quietly, week in and week out: he helps develop nuclear warheads at the Lawrence Livermore National Laboratory.

Many people might find those two sets of pursuits incongruous. Yet Peter himself sees no contradiction. "I don't think of these weapons as things that will ever be used," he explains, sipping wine in the living room of his modest suburban home. His wife sits at the dining room table, helping the children with their homework. "When you're a physicist and you know how a nuclear weapon works and what all the parts are, it's no more strange than a vacuum cleaner," he adds. "You don't fear it at all. I understand that to people who don't work on them, nuclear weapons are an alien thing. I felt the same way before I went to the lab." He frowns. "I feel very bad that people are afraid. I feel bad for them."

Peter is one of sixty-four nuclear-weapons scientists I interviewed at the Livermore Laboratory between 1987 and 1990. I went there as an anthropologist interested in modern American society, intrigued in particular by the arms race and the cultural politics of science. I knew well enough how nuclear-weapons scientists were viewed by antinuclear activists. But I wanted to learn how nuclear scientists viewed themselves, especially at a time when their world was being turned upside down: first by the continual drumbeat of antinuclear protests, and later by the reforms of the Soviet president Mikhail Gorbachev. I was also seeking to work with a group of people who were, to my way of thinking, even more exotic and inaccessible than the people studied by my graduate adviser—a group of headhunters in the Philippine jungles.

In the latter respect, the Livermore scientists were no disappointment. I soon came to think of their world as a kind of high-tech, ritual secret society, one in which members wear badges and spend most of their working hours sealed off from the rest of the world by armed guards and barbed wire fences; in which trash cans have locks on them for the safe disposal of secret documents; in which visitors must be escorted into the bathroom ("Uncleared person coming in!" the escort shouts to those within); in which secretaries must lock up their typewriter ribbons during coffee breaks for fear that spies will steal the ribbons and reconstruct classified data. For two and a half years I interviewed the Livermore staff scientists, lived and ate with a few, attended their churches, participated on the fringes of their social life—and in the end I began to open a window on their secret world.

It is a world whose future has recently come into question. With the end of the cold war and the debut of a new world order, some politicians are talking of converting the laboratory for nonmilitary work or even closing it. For the first time, Livermore scientists, as well as their counterparts at both the Los Alamos and the Sandia national laboratories in New Mexico, may have to engineer a new future for themselves or face extinction.

UNTIL THE EARLY 1950s all nuclear weapons, including the bombs dropped on Hiroshima and Nagasaki, were designed and built at the Los Alamos National Laboratory. As the Korean War intensified, however, and as the cold war broadened, as McCarthyism stirred at home and scientists pressed to test the first hydrogen bomb, the federal government decided to establish a second weapons laboratory. And so it was that in 1952 the Livermore Laboratory, a ramshackle collection of huts and trailers in a small town known formerly for its horse ranches and vineyards, came into being.

The laboratory was established under the leadership of two physicists: Ernest O. Lawrence, a professor at the University of California at Berkeley; and Edward Teller, popularly known as the father of the H-bomb and widely rumored to have been the inspiration for Dr. Strangelove, the title character in Stanley Kubrick's 1964 film. At the outset Livermore was a small lab, staffed by unusually young scientists: its director, Herbert York, was thirty-one years old; Harold Brown, in charge of thermonuclear design, was twenty-four. The new lab saw itself as a place quite unlike Los Alamos, a haven from bureaucracy where creative young scientists could explore novel ideas without rigid management from above. The consequences of that freewheeling approach were unhappy at first: Livermore's first two hydrogen bomb tests were duds, or fizzles, as weapons scientists call them. After one fizzle the mathematician John von Neumann, alluding to the lab's main rival, remarked, "There will be dancing in the streets of Los Alamos tonight." (As one Livermore scientist told me, "the Soviets are the competition, but Los Alamos is the enemy.")

In time the Livermore scientists mastered the art of

atomic- and thermonuclear-weapons design and went on to design warheads for the Poseidon, Polaris, Minuteman II and Minuteman III missiles, among others. More recently, and more controversial, Livermore developed the neutron bomb and the warheads for the MX and the ground-launched cruise missiles. In the 1980s Livermore became a prime contractor of research into the controversial Strategic Defense Initiative, working to develop the X-ray laser, the free-electron laser and Brilliant Pebbles—a system of computer-guided projectiles that would be fired from orbiting satellites at incoming missiles.

The laboratory has grown from an institution with 540 employees and an annual budget of $3.4 million in late 1952 to one with 8,000 employees and a $1 billion budget today. Livermore scientists are engaged in many non-weapons projects, including the human genome project and the quest for a laser fusion reactor capable of producing energy by firing lasers at minute pellets of tritium and deuterium. Nevertheless, roughly two-thirds of the laboratory's budget is devoted to weapons research—a fraction that, in a post–cold war world, makes Livermore a prime target for politicians in search of a peace dividend.

I ARRIVED AT LIVERMORE harboring two stereotypes about nuclear-weapons scientists. First, I expected all of them to be political conservatives, perhaps even with a touch of Strangelove about them, whose daily work would be animated by an unquestioning patriotism and an antipathy toward communism. Second, I expected them to feel, somewhere deep down, guilty and conflicted about their potentially genocidal work. On both counts I could not have been more wrong. Roughly half the people I interviewed could be described as liberals, many of whom had actively opposed the Vietnam War or supported the civil rights movement. Approximately half the laboratory's elite group of warhead designers voted for Michael Dukakis, the Democratic candidate in the 1988 presidential election—a higher proportion than in the country as a whole.

I also arrived with the preconception, reinforced by critics of the lab, that scientists work there only because they are highly paid or because they are second-raters and cannot find jobs elsewhere. In either case the presumption is that, in effect, the employees of the lab have made a Faustian bargain, checking their consciences at the laboratory gates. But in fact most of the employees I interviewed had turned down job prospects elsewhere, and they earn substantially less after promotion at the lab than they would in the corporate sector. (A neophyte warhead designer at Livermore can earn about $65,000 a year, and a senior designer $90,000.) Most had chosen Livermore for three reasons: they enjoyed its casual, campuslike atmosphere; unlike university professors, they would not be required to teach or to write grant proposals; and unlike corporate scientists, they could pursue basic research unrestrained by concerns about profitability, and they could do so on state-of-the-art equipment.

Nor have most Livermore scientists tuned out the ethical issues, although the precise contours of their moral thinking may seem odd to opponents of the arms race. One scientist, for instance, noted that whereas he felt comfortable designing nuclear weapons, he could never reconcile himself to working as a lawyer defending murderers or drug dealers, because he might cause more harm than good if he did his job well. Others drew an ethical distinction between the people who design weapons and those who "figure out what to do with them." One scientist noted that he "could never be a button presser in a missile silo." Another agreed, asking: "Is an automobile manufacturer responsible for the people killed by drunk drivers?"

Yet another said that, although nuclear weapons appear morally problematic because of their great destructive force, he felt it was more ethical to work on them than to develop conventional weapons. The latter, he maintained, are designed to kill people, whereas the former are intended to prevent killing. In fact many Livermore employees argued that, in an anarchic world filled with nuclear weapons, it may be as morally problematic *not* to design nuclear weapons as it is *to* design them. "Your conscience should trouble you either way," said one staff scientist. "If you don't work on weapons, think of all the people you may be endangering by leaving them [the people] undefended. The moral questions aren't simple."

MORAL PHILOSOPHERS distinguish two primary approaches to the complex moral dilemmas raised by nuclear weapons: the deontological and the consequentialist. Adherents of the former position are guided by the so-called wrongful-intentions principle: one must not do evil even to bring about good; and one must not threaten a wrongful act, even if one never carries out the threat. Thus deontologists condemn the nuclear threat, even if its intended purpose is to prevent war. The U.S. Catholic bishops' pastoral letter on war and peace, which questioned the moral basis of nuclear deterrence, is the best example of deontological thinking.

Consequentialists, on the other hand, maintain that actions should be judged by their consequences rather than by the purity of the methods involved: the ends justify the means. Needless to say, the Livermore scientists I interviewed are consequentialists. In their view, the lab designs nuclear weapons not to kill people but to deter other countries from starting wars and thus to ensure "stability"—the closest word in the Livermore lexicon to *peace*. According to that logic, nuclear weapons are designed solely to threaten, not to be used in battle. Some of the interview subjects said they could not think of any circumstances, even a nuclear attack against the United States, in which they would approve the use of nuclear weapons.

The narrow terrain of nuclear ethics leaves little room for originality, so it should come as no surprise that most nuclear-weapons scientists offer similar rationales for their work. More intriguing, however, is how they arrive at their rationales. When I began interviewing Livermore employees, I was startled to hear one after another tell me how lucky I was to be interviewing him or her; unlike his or her colleagues, each one said, he or she had thoroughly thought through the ethical questions raised by weapons work. It soon became clear that many people at the lab were mulling over the implications of their work but were doing so in private. At the same time they were convinced that their colleagues had given the matter far less thought. "I sometimes have this sense that we're not supposed to discuss it," said one engineer.

Instead, in a process that might be thought of as collective privatization, the employees pick up cues for their ethical thinking from managerial pronouncements and other public discourse at the lab, but they largely work through the issues alone, in silent struggle. Antinuclear writers often assert that weapons scientists suffer from denial, that they ignore the consequences of their work; after all, how could they continue working if they stopped to think? But that view confuses a lonely, quiet way of thinking with an evasion of thinking altogether.

The loneliness of the scientist's confrontation with conscience is reinforced by the laboratory's rules of secrecy. Individuals cannot (at least in theory) discuss any of the classified details of a specific weapon or weapons project with any of their colleagues except the ones who have an official "need to know." Yet according to consequentialist logic, moral thinking requires that the consequences of introducing new kinds of weapons be carefully weighed. Suppose, for instance, that earth-penetrating warheads could be improved in such a way that it became possible to target enemy leaders in underground bunkers: Would that development make the world more or less stable? The issues are complex, and the answer is by no means clear. But by compartmentalizing and stanching the flow of technical information, the secrecy rules restrict the scope of an ethical debate that logically depends in part on informed judgments. Moreover, security regulations prevent weapons scientists from discussing their work, except in the vaguest terms, with family members—with whom, in any event, they spend little time, as they are not allowed to work on secret documents at home . The effect is to enlarge the social vacuum in which individual scientists confront the ethical implications of their work.

THE ONE INSTITUTION that might be expected to foment discussion about the lab's mission is the church, particularly since the national leaderships of the Catholic, Presbyterian, Methodist and most other mainline American congregations condemned the arms race in the 1980s. Churches are important institutions in Livermore, as they are in many American communities, and two-thirds of the people I interviewed identified themselves as Christians. I therefore followed the churches with some interest.

I found that although the various churches in Livermore had different ways of coping with the laboratory, nearly all gave succor to its work. In a few cases ministers took an active interest in the details of laboratory work and overtly endorsed the official view that nuclear weapons are necessary to maintain peace. Some evangelical ministers took a more fatalistic stance. Given the sinful nature of humankind, they argued, America had no alternative but to pursue deterrence—even though nuclear Armageddon may be inevitable. Said one evangelical physicist, sad but resolute in his point of view: "What scares me more than the weapons themselves is that my colleagues think they'll never be used. That's a form of denial. That's worshiping the human race."

More typically, however, the ministers reinforced the collective privatization of moral thinking largely by avoiding public discussion of the issue. Avoidance often entailed taking a stance different from that of the national church governing body or neighboring churches of the same denomination. The local Methodist church tried to play down the actions of a Methodist bishop from nearby

Oakland who had been arrested for civil disobedience at the lab gates; a few Catholic weapons scientists said they had been personally challenged by priests and parishioners in nearby towns, but not in Livermore. Only a few years after the Catholic bishops had issued their pastoral letter, I asked a local Catholic priest whether being in a parish with a nuclear-weapons lab presented a challenge to his ministry. No, he replied. "My main issues in Livermore are the same I'd have anywhere that I was a priest: primarily to try to help people spiritually, but also materially, and to provide psychological and marital counseling."

WITH THE EXCEPTION of the two evangelical scientists, the Livermore employees I interviewed were supremely confident that nuclear weapons would never be used. In fact not a single interviewee had ever had a nightmare about nuclear annihilation. How had they come to feel so safe, I wondered.

Several scholars who have asked that question in recent years have focused on the specialized, "technostrategic" language in which nuclear professionals discuss their work. The language does for nuclear war what Victorian English did for sex, so greatly blurring a lurid subject with euphemism and abstraction that it becomes difficult to connect the words with their possible real-life consequences. Thus bombs are no longer bombs but "devices" or "physics packages," and their explosions "events"; cities are "countervalue targets," and the deaths of thousands, even millions of civilians are disguised by the neutral term "collateral damage." Carol E. Cohn, a professor of social change at Swarthmore College, argued that this language creates an "astounding chasm between image and reality."

I would argue that the reduced anxiety also derives from the sense of mastery that Livermore scientists gain by conducting nuclear tests at the Nevada Test Site near Mercury, Nevada. To ensure that a warhead design is reliable, the intricate device is attached to diagnostic equipment, buried deep underground and then detonated. Such tests have tremendous technical value. From the anthropologist's point of view, however, they also share some of the characteristics of more traditional rituals. According to one school of thought in anthropology, such rituals are staged as a means of dealing with anxiety, especially anxiety about death, by simulating human knowledge and control over events that otherwise seem mysterious and uncontrollable. In this light, nuclear tests can be seen as providing an arena in which weapons designers can tame their fears of mass destruction. And, more telling, they can also be viewed as rites of passage whereby new scientists are initiated into a community, namely the community to which nuclear weapons are "no more strange than a vacuum cleaner."

The rite of passage is particularly important for the laboratory elite of about a hundred physicists who direct the design of weapons. It is mostly from this group that the laboratory's managers are chosen. New designers spend years studying the esoteric secrets of bomb-design physics, known only to employees with high-level clearances, before they are permitted to develop their own design ideas. Ninety percent of those ideas are rejected by colleagues in design-review meetings.

Even after an idea is accepted, another long and arduous process follows, in which designers test one another's skills in review meetings and then work in teams coordinating large numbers of physicists, engineers, computer scientists and technicians in building the device. The process demands endurance: it puts the designers in jeopardy of humiliation if the device does not perform as predicted. As the test proceeds and a new nuclear device is lowered into a test shaft, the designers begin to worry that it will not work as it should. Will the initiating burst of neutrons fire properly? Were the specifications for the radiation implosion mechanism calculated correctly? Whereas the average citizen worries that at some point a nuclear weapon will explode, the designers worry that on this occasion it won't. "You're kind of helpless," said one physicist. "You just take your hands away and hope everything works out all right."

That feeling of helplessness, mixed with a confidence that the weapons can be made to do our bidding, is central to the psychology of nuclear deterrence. Scientists who build conventional weapons experience the success and efficacy of their labor directly: an artillery shell explodes during combat or it does not. The success of nuclear weapons, however, is defined in terms of deterrence, a nontechnical phenomenon with no physical manifestation beyond the absence of catastrophe. Tests and simulations, then, play a critical role in the lives of nuclear-weapons developers by making the abstract real and the ineffable tangible. The very rhythm of the testing process is such that designers experience, again and again, the fear that a nuclear weapon cannot be controlled—only to learn, in most instances and within certain parameters, that it can.

THE CULTURE THAT Livermore employees have nurtured and thrived in for the past forty years is now endangered as the result of events outside the laboratory gates. The astonishingly rapid disintegration of the Soviet Union has deprived the laboratory of the adversary that largely legitimized its work. If, as the Russian president Boris Yeltsin says, the nuclear weapons of the former Soviet Union are no longer aimed at the U.S., Livermore's raison d'être is no longer self-evident. Meanwhile, an international ban on nuclear testing is more likely than ever to be instituted—bringing to an end an activity that, technically and symbolically, constitutes the core of the laboratory's culture.

The future of the lab is also endangered by changes closer to home. The city of Livermore is no longer what it was in 1952: an isolated town of 7,000 deferential citizens who either worked for the "Rad Lab" or tried to ignore the "propeller-heads," as workers at the lab were known among the local people. Today some 56,000 people live within the city limits, many of them young and well educated, and commute to their offices in Silicon Valley or San Francisco or work for the high-tech companies being drawn to Livermore by relatively inexpensive real estate. Livermore's weapons designers survived the protests at their gates in the early 1980s (in one, 1,200 people were arrested in a single day), only to find that many of their neighbors are now turning against them.

Many residents also have grown concerned about the health and environmental impact of the laboratory and the detrimental effect it may have on property values. After discovering groundwater contamination, the Environmental Protection Agency in 1987 declared the lab a Superfund site, and lab administrators subsequently an-

nounced their intention to build a waste incinerator. In 1989, 10,000 residents of the Livermore valley petitioned against the incinerator, plans for which were later canceled. That year the city's congressman, Pete Stark, urged his constituents to sue the laboratory "as soon and as often as possible" and suggested in public that the laboratory might want to move elsewhere.

Given the end of the cold war and the lab's shaky relations with the local community, some commentators have suggested that all nuclear-weapons research be consolidated at Los Alamos. If the federal government decides that only one weapons-design laboratory is needed, Los Alamos seems the better of the two options: three-quarters of the current U.S. nuclear stockpile was designed there, and the facility itself is more isolated, easing the handling of plutonium. Livermore, for all intents and purposes, is now a suburb of San Francisco.

REACTING TO THE RUMORS OF DOOM, some Livermore scientists argue that if the lab is to survive, it must aggressively seek funding for new fields of research. Some of the existing hardware and expertise at the lab can be applied directly to environmental and energy studies. The enormous supercomputer codes developed by physicists to model nuclear explosions and nuclear-winter scenarios, for instance, could be used to model global warming. The NOVA laser, employed in both military and fusion-energy research, could be devoted solely to the latter.

The transition would not take place smoothly, however. If the lab wants to pursue its new ambitions with taxpayer funds, it must renegotiate its budget with the White House, Congress and the many Washington agencies that will no doubt view the lab as an intruder in their turf wars. The lab is seeking partnerships with corporate sources of funding, but corporations that have experimented with such agreements complain of Livermore's culture of secrecy and its employees' socialized indifference to budgetary restraints. Moreover, some staff scientists complain that many of the new, proposed research missions are not as challenging as the old ones and would not make direct use of existing capabilities. To a skilled physicist, devising ways of cleaning up contaminated groundwater is simply not as compelling a task as designing weapons that replicate, for the fraction of an instant in which they burn, the internal processes of stars.

Many scientists and managers, then, still look upon weapons work as the core of the lab's mission. In so doing, however, they have reconceptualized the role of—and rationale for—weapons design in a post–cold war world. In previous years Livermore employees considered their work critical because it maintained the equilibrium between the ever more potent nuclear arsenals of the superpowers. Since those arsenals are now being reduced, some lab scientists envision other ways of contributing to global stability and safety.

FOR EXAMPLE, they suggest that instead of working to improve the effectiveness of nuclear weapons, the lab should redesign existing weapons to make them less likely to explode by accident and find safe and verifiable ways of dismantling U.S. and ex-Soviet nuclear weapons. (In 1990 the *Washington*

*Post* reported that the W-79 nuclear artillery shell and the W-69 short-range attack missile contained design flaws that could lead to accidental explosion in peacetime. Weapons experts also question the safety of the warhead for the Trident II submarine-based missile.) The shift in agendas betrays a certain irony: at the height of the cold war, Livermore steadfastly vouched for the safety of its products. Now that new weapons are no longer needed, the old ones have become a cause for concern.

Responding as well to growing environmental concerns, some employees propose designing a "green bomb": a nuclear weapon built from relatively nontoxic materials that, during production, would be less likely to cause the kind of contamination that disgraces nuclear-weapons facilities such as the Rocky Flats Plant in Colorado, the Hanford Nuclear Reservation in Washington State and the Savannah River Plant in South Carolina. Some workers also feel the lab should continue its SDI research—which accounts for 10 percent of its budget—to counter a perceived growing nuclear threat from third world nations. And the scientists who want to see the lab retain its weapons mission often argue that the current high quality of the U.S. nuclear stockpile is the result of competition. Give Los Alamos a monopoly franchise, they say, and quality will suffer.

At a period of flux in the international system, as some politicians search desperately for a peace dividend while others search equally hard for new reasons to maintain old military programs, only time will tell whether Livermore can retain its niche in the weapons culture. Meanwhile, many of its scientists are optimistic they can survive beyond the age of deterrence, and with good reason: the moral framework in which they pursue their profession may be delicate, but it is not inflexible. After all, humankind owes its success in large part to an unceasing ability to adapt to adversity and change. The trait is no less prominent in the nuclear-weapons culture than it is in any other.

# Compelling signs of artificial life

*Digital 'creatures' that clone themselves may really be alive*

Three years ago, Thomas Ray, a biologist at the University of Delaware, began testing a model of evolutionary principles that he had created on a computer. To set the system in motion, Ray fashioned a digital creature made up of a string of computer instructions and injected it into the model. Within a few hours, the solitary creature had begun to proliferate, spawning a race of clones that lived, died, evolved and gave rise to new groups of mutants that competed with each other in a struggle to survive. Ray was amazed. When he designed the system, called Tierra, "nobody knew what was going to happen," he remembers. "But it turned out that evolution worked just as well in a computer system as in the real world." And Ray maintains that systems like Tierra do more than just mimic living things, they *are* living things. "To me, anything that lives and replicates is alive," says Ray. "It doesn't have to be wet and squishy."

Ray is not alone in believing that some electronic creatures squirming through a digital world or darting across computer screens may share the spark of life with humans, animals and plants. During the past decade, the idea of creating artificial life has attracted a following among North American and European scientists. Working on computers, they have devised systems whose colorful displays show digital creations that resemble insects and plants flourishing in a silicon world. Even scientists who stop short of claiming that some computer inhabitants are really alive say that they sometimes seem eerily lifelike. Christopher Langton is director of the artificial life program at the Santa Fe Institute in Santa Fe, N.M. After setting up an artificial life system in 1981, recalls Langton, "I wondered if I had the right to turn it off. I had created a universe in which there existed something that resembles life. I began to wonder what rights the creator has."

So far, there is little agreement among scientists about what constitutes life, and whether ingenious squiggles on a computer screen meet any valid definition of it. But many researchers in the field share a burning ambition to help give birth to nonbiological creatures that will qualify as life forms. In the process, they expect to gain a greater understanding of the cosmic logic that underlies organic life. "Nobody yet has made life in a computer," says Steen Rasmussen, a Danish physicist who has worked at the Santa Fe Institute since 1988. "But we are getting closer. And I think that within the next 10 years, somebody will make something that we will have to call a living process."

The origins of computer-based artificial life systems can be partly traced to the work of John von Neumann, the brilliant Hungarian-born, American mathematician. During the 1950s, he devised a tool for investigating artificial life called a cellular automaton. Consisting of an array of squares on a vast checkerboard, the automaton behaves according to a set of rules governing each square; as well, each square is affected by the state of the squares bordering it. During the 1960s, mathematicians at England's Cambridge University began playing an elaborate board game, called Life, which worked on the basis of a cellular automaton. Once set in motion, with each square in a giant grid being "alive" or "dead" (a dead square would be empty) depending on the state of the squares adjacent to it, the grid appeared to take on a life of its own. Patterns and shapes mysteriously appeared in the grid. As journalist Steven Levy wrote in his 1992 book *Artificial Life,* "sometimes objects broke up only when other newborn cells tampered with the equilibrium; at other times they were temporary configurations, doomed to dispel into quiescence."

The behavior of cellular automatons fascinated scientists. Within a few years, theoreticians at American universities had begun playing Life on computers, creating dazzling images as thousands of cells on their screens, obeying a few simple rules, winked on and off, forming complex and unexpected patterns. Part of the fascination was the idea that computer-generated systems might mirror nature itself. In the new field of study known as chaos theory, which developed during the 1980s, scientists had discovered that structures, or patterns, could be discerned even in systems that appear to be completely disorganized. One of the basic questions that they wanted to answer, says Rasmussen, is "what is it in matter that enables it to have an incredible variety of forms, including life?"

During the past decade, a cadre of scientists have pursued the answer to that and other related questions. One of them was Langton who, after graduating with a science degree from the University of Arizona in Tucson, decided to see if he could create a self-reproducing artificial organism on his computer. He began by creating four-sided loops with a short tail extending from one side. The loops contained information that determined their behavior, instructing the tail to extend itself to create a new loop. The process worked, and the loops began to multiply, forming a colony of identical loops. The experiment convinced Langton that biological processes could be reproduced in machines.

Meanwhile, Stuart Kauffman, a leading biologist and artificial life theorist who is affiliated with the University of Pennsylvania medical school in Philadelphia, had developed a theory to explain how organic life may have developed on earth as the result of a set of underlying rules working in a complex, primordial "soup" of chemicals. Rasmussen, during the late 1980s, created a computer model that imitated primordial conditions with an artificial chemistry consisting of millions of computer instructions. As the computer ran through thousands of generations, digital "proto-organisms" died and new ones were created. Rasmussen concluded, among other things, that the evolution of lifelike forms depended on symbiotic, or co-operative, structures, which seemed to emerge spontaneously within the system. "I think this is a law of the universe," says Rasmussen. "and it makes possible the jump from nonliving to living."

In a dramatically different approach to artificial life, a Calgary scientist has developed a way of simulating plant growth on computer screens. In the system devised by Polish-born Przemyslaw Prusinkiewicz, strikingly lifelike computer graphics can show a lily-of-the-valley growing from a seed to maturity in less than a minute. To make his digital plants grow, Prusinkiewicz, 41, uses a few lines of computer instructions to represent the genetic code contained in a real plant's seed, then adds the digital equivalent of nutrients, sunlight and water. Since he began developing his system during the mid-1980s, Prusinkiewicz has created models for about 20 plants. He can even simulate a stand of pine trees, complete with millions of needles, on his computer screen. Prusinkiewicz's blending of science and art is already being used by biologists to test hypotheses about plant life. Prusinkiewicz does not claim that the plants he creates are alive, but that "they simulate processes that take place in real organisms."

At the Santa Fe Institute, Langton is currently trying to create in a computer the digital equivalent of the conditions needed to support cellular life. To do this, Langton will provide in digital form the molecules needed to produce water, enzymes, nutrients and the other essential ingredients needed to sustain life. Then he will try to introduce into the chemical "soup" an artificial cell and watch to see if it survives—and reproduces. Langton, who is also a research scientist at the U.S. National Laboratory at Los Alamos, N.M., predicts that it will be several years before he can achieve his goal.

Even if Langton succeeds, he is unlikely to persuade skeptics that a synthetic cell is a genuine form of life. Doyne Farmer, a Santa Fe-based expert on artificial life, concedes that creating such a cell would be "a significant breakthrough." But critics, he adds, might object that the cell does not really possess the attributes of life, because "Langton has to some extent rigged up his environment to produce the results he wants to see." In fact, some scientists maintain that the promise that artificial life studies once seemed to hold has already begun to fade. William Macready, a 30-year-old Ottawa physicist who is currently doing postgraduate studies on complex systems at the Santa Fe Institute, says that once he "found the idea of artificial life intriguing. But now I'm not so sure that people in the field are learning as much as they think—or whether the systems they build are anything more than computer simulations."

Artificial life scientists, including Langton and the University of Delaware's Ray, have different ways of looking at the issue. Life on earth, Langton argues, has developed along hierarchical lines, with single-celled organisms evolving into more complex creatures. Now, says Langton, after billions of years of evolution, the human race may be at the point of constructing "the basis for a new organization of life." Ray is convinced that the digital creatures he has created on a computer can evolve into more complex forms of life. "And for such creatures," he says, "intelligence is the next frontier. We are living proof that evolution is capable of creating intelligence out of virtually nothing." Like other scientists in their field, Langton and Ray contend that life may not exist only in organic form—that silicon worlds can also teem with forms of life that human beings are helping to create.

**MARK NICHOLS**

## The Science of Computing

# Is Thinking Computable?

## Peter J. Denning

*Peter Denning is Director of the Research Institute for Advanced Computer Science at the NASA Ames Research Center.*

The vision of thinking computers fascinates people and sells magazines and books. For decades the advocates of "strong AI" (artificial intelligence) have claimed that within one or two hundred years electronic machines will be able to do everything a human can do. They see our minds as "computers made of meat," subject to the laws of physics; as soon as we understand those laws and the physical structure of the brain, we will be able to construct computing machines that solve the "differential equations of mind" in real time and exhibit behavior exactly like ours. These machines will experience emotions, judge truth, appreciate beauty, understand, be self-conscious and intelligent, and have free wills. A few advocates go so far as to speculate that the machines will be better than we are in every way and will eventually succeed *Homo sapiens* on the evolutionary scale.

Some philosophers and scientists strongly disagree. They see computers as no different from machines of levers, wheels, moving balls, valves, or pneumatic pipes; although electronic machines can perform tasks of much greater complexity in a given time, there is nothing essentially different about them. These skeptics see no way that any such machine could come to "understand" what it does. Indeed, they argue that "understanding" and "thinking" are meaningless concepts for machines. Expert systems are unlikely to achieve competence beyond what a "mindless, procedural bureaucracy" is capable of. Even though computers now play chess at the grand-master level, almost no one says that they have insight or an understanding of chess; they are programmed simply to perform "brute-force searches" of possible future board configurations.

I have summarized these arguments in two previous columns *(1, 2)*, and I am returning to them now because of two new contributions to the ongoing discussion. The first is a debate in *Scientific American* [January 1990] between John Searle and Paul and Patricia Churchland. The other

is a new book by Roger Penrose. I will discuss these works and add some reflections of my own.

In the *Scientific American* debate *(3, 4)*, Searle, a philosopher from the University of California at Berkeley, argues that no computer program can function like a mind; the Churchlands, philosophers from the University of California at San Diego, argue that systems mimicking the brain's structure can do so. The editors arranged an exchange: each side challenges the other's arguments and refutations. Neither is swayed by the other's arguments.

Both sides begin with the test Alan Turing proposed in 1950, an imitation game in which an interrogator asks questions of a human being and a machine; if the interrogator is unable to distinguish between the two, the machine passes the test and is declared intelligent *(5)*. Turing replaced the question "Can a machine think?" with "Can the interrogator distinguish the two in an imitation game?" because he considered the former question so imprecise as to be meaningless. His own opinion was that by the year 2000 there would exist machines capable of fooling the interrogator for at least five minutes in 30% of the games played. Turing's test is taken as a criterion of machine intelligence by advocates of strong AI.

Searle reviews his own Chinese Room argument, in which a man who understands no Chinese translates between incoming messages in Chinese and outgoing messages in Chinese by performing pattern replacements following rules in a book. According to Chinese observers on the outside, the room passes the Turing test by conversing in Chinese, but the man in the room has absolutely no understanding of what is going on. Searle maintains that a computer is no different: any machine that might pass the Turing test cannot be said to be thinking. Human brains have the capacity, conferred by their specific biology, to attach meanings to symbols, a fact that differentiates them from computer programs. Simulation is not the same as duplication, and so Searle wonders why so many are prepared to accept a simulation of thinking as actual thought when they would not do the same for a computer simulation of digestion.

From *American Scientist*, March/April 1990, pp. 100-102. Reprinted by permission of *American Scientist*, journal of Sigma Xi, The Scientific Research Society.

## 8. PHILOSOPHICAL FRONTIERS

The Churchlands agree that the Turing test is not a sufficient condition for conscious intelligence. But they reject Searle's claim that an algorithm cannot be intelligent in principle. They argue that a brain is a finite, complicated web of neurons, each of which performs a definite function governed by the laws of physics. A set of mathematical equations relates all the signals appearing in the web; a sufficiently powerful computer would

---

*Searle wonders why so many are prepared to accept a simulation of thinking as actual thought when they would not do the same for a computer simulation of digestion*

---

be able to solve for (or simulate) what a given brain does in solving those equations. The Churchlands recognize that the required computational power is likely to be achieved only within the architecture of neural networks that mimic the structure of the brain. In such systems, intelligent behavior arises macroscopically, from the collective effects of simple neuron firings, and thus the individual neurons do not need to "understand" anything.

I found it fascinating that both sides presented coherent interpretations of strong AI—with conflicting conclusions. Each side is sure it is "right" and is impervious to the other's counterarguments. None of the theories of machine intelligence I am aware of addresses this all-too-human phenomenon.

It is also interesting that both sides, following the tradition begun by Turing, dismiss the question "What is thinking?" as meaningless. But this question remains at the heart of the debate. You will see shortly that it is central to Penrose's investigation.

What we think thinking is has been a moving target throughout history. For two hundred years under the ascendancy of Newtonian mechanics beginning in the early 1700s, everyone accepted the universe as a marvelous clockwork system governed by a few simple laws. In this tradition the epitomy of human thought was problem-solving through logical deduction, man's path to exploring God's universe. The quest for a complete understanding of thought led to attempts beginning in the 1800s to formulate a universal system of logic in which all statements could be mechanically checked for validity. But the hope for such a system was dashed in the 1930s by the incompleteness theorem of Gödel and the incomputability theorem of Turing. Still, the idea that thinking was somehow a mechanical process lived on in Turing and guided his formulation of testing for intelligence. The idea of a computer thinking didn't seem the slightest bit strange to him.

Today a different interpretation of thinking is challenging the old idea. Many of us believe that thinking is not logical deduction, but the creation of new ideas.

Logical deduction seems too mechanical. When we recall our moments of insight, we often say that our emotional state affected us and that we had a bodily sense of our creation before we could put it into words. We regard thinking as a phenomenon that occurs before articulation in language, and it seems that machines, which are programmed inside language, cannot generate actions outside language.

I have no doubt that fifty years from now there will be many machines performing tasks that today we associate with thinking—and people will still regard them as only machines. Interpretations of thinking will have shifted farther, preserving a clear distinction between human and machine.

I turn now to Penrose's book, *The Emperor's New Mind* (6). Penrose, a mathematician and physicist at Oxford University, mounts the most serious attack on strong AI that I have yet seen. This is not an easy book: Penrose leaves few stones unturned as he considers a broad range of speculations about mind, consciousness, and thinking. He takes his readers on an odyssey through a heady array of topics, including algorithms, Turing machines, Mandelbrot sets, formal systems, undecidability, incompleteness theorems, nonrecursive sets, Newtonian mechanics, space-time, phase spaces, relativity, quantum mechanics, entropy, cosmology, black holes, quantum gravity, brains, neurophysiology, animal consciousness, and more. In each topic he finds abundant evidence of human actions that are not algorithmic, concluding with the claim that a full understanding of mind awaits the development of quantum theories of physics as yet unknown to us.

Penrose agrees with Searle that the Turing test is an inadequate description of intelligence, but he challenges Searle's assumption that computers might pass the test. He asserts repeatedly that mental processes are inherently more powerful than computational processes. He points to the principle of universal computation—the idea that a general-purpose computer can simulate any other machine—as the basis for the widespread belief that algorithms must be the essence of thought. As a consequence, Penrose devotes considerable attention to the subject of noncomputable functions, such as the halting problem (is there a program which any given algorithm halts for a given input?), and he returns frequently to the idea that most of the questions about science that we consider interesting are not solvable by any general algorithm. Minds are constantly coming up with solutions to questions for which there is no general algorithm. How, he asks, could an algorithm have discovered theorems like Turing's and Gödel's that tell us what algorithms cannot do?

Penrose next takes on the strong-AI claim that we will one day have a sufficient understanding of the laws of physics and the structure of the brain to conduct an exact simulation by computer. What is physics? he asks. Is physics capable of complete understanding? What is an exact simulation? After exploring the failures of Newtonian physics that led to the formulation of relativity theory and then quantum mechanics, Penrose argues that the laws of physics at the quantum level may be determinate but not computable. Because some mental phenomena operate at scales where quantum effects may exert an influence, the functions representing the mind may not be computable, and thus an exact mechanical simulation may not be possible.

Although these suggestions are not provable given our current state of knowledge, Penrose has nonetheless offered a sharp metaphysical challenge to strong AI. The presupposition of a definite set of computable equations that determine a thinking being's next response begs the question because it implicitly assumes that all mental processes are algorithmic. If, as Penrose suggests, important physical processes of the brain are not computable, then computable equations would be only an approximation; they would leave out the quantum effects on which the conscious thought of the brain may depend.

Penrose does not, in my view, deal adequately with the shifting interpretations of consciousness and thinking. It is precisely the motion of these moving targets that must be dealt with. Penrose holds that consciousness has something to do with awareness of timeless Platonic realities: "When mathematicians communicate, [mathematical understanding] is made possible by each one having a *direct route to truth*, the consciousness of each being in a position to perceive mathematical truths directly" (p. 428).

I have found the biological interpretation of self and consciousness offered by Humberto Maturana and Francesco Varela (7) to be a good corrective to the narrow view expressed by Penrose. Maturana and Varela say that consciousness is associated with (but not uniquely determined by) the way we observe things. There are levels of consciousness, ranging from responding reflexively and following rules mindlessly to observing oneself as an observer. Each observer operates within a system of interpretation that includes biases, prejudices, presuppositions, culture, history, and values and that affects what can be seen or not seen, what is important or not important, and what is held as true or not true. As conscious beings, we must constantly reckon with different observers of the same phenomena. For example, Searle and the Churchlands are different observers of

---

*Although it intrigues us that we might have a godlike power to create beings more advanced than ourselves, we are also threatened by that possibility*

---

strong AI and have reached different conclusions from their observations of the same phenomena.

The invention of interpretations is a fundamentally human activity that is intimately involved with our understanding of truth. As scientists, we like to say that scientific laws and mathematical theorems already exist awaiting discovery. But if we carefully examine the processes of science, we find paradigms other than discovery. Roald Hoffmann says that the creation of new substances not found in nature is the dominant activity in disciplines such as chemistry and molecular biology

(8). Bruno Latour goes farther, observing that in practice a statement is accepted as true by a community if no one has been able to produce evidence or an argument that persuades others to dissent (9). Science is a process of constructing facts, and different scientific communities can construct different systems of interpretation of the same physical phenomena. Western and Eastern medicine, for example, are two scientifically valid systems of interpretation about disease and human disorders; each recommends different interventions for the same symptoms and sees phenomena that are invisible to the other, and their interpretations are not easily reconciled.

Considerations such as these about the variousness of truth make it difficult for me to accept Penrose's speculations about links between consciousness and Platonic truth. For me, the existence of multiple, incomplete interpretations actually supports Penrose's basic claims about mental as opposed to computational processes. Like a system of logic, an interpretation cannot include all phenomena. Our powers of conscious observation give us a capacity to step outside a particular interpretation and devise extensions or alternatives. Thus consciousness itself cannot be captured by any fixed description or interpretation. How then can consciousness be captured by an algorithm, which is by its very nature a fixed interpretation? This question applies also to algorithms that are apparently designed to shift their interpretations, because the rules for shifting constitute an interpretation themselves.

Although Penrose has left us with a great many questions that will occupy the philosophers among us for years, it is well to remember that we will continue to build practical systems that perform increasingly sophisticated tasks, such as recognition of speech and visual shapes, diagnosis, advising, symbolic mathematics, and robotics.

We humans see ourselves at the top of the current evolutionary scale. Although it intrigues us that we might have a godlike power to create beings more advanced than ourselves, we are also threatened by that possibility. Searle, the Churchlands, and Penrose have bolstered our confidence in the belief that we are more than mechanical devices. We can rest a little easier, always keeping a watchful eye on the literature in case someone comes up with a plausible argument that machines may, one day, think.

## *References*

1. P. J. Denning. 1986. Will machines ever think? *Am. Sci.* 74:344–46.
2. P. J. Denning. 1988. Blindness in the design of intelligent systems. *Am. Sci.* 76:118–20.
3. J. R. Searle. 1990. Is the brain's mind a computer program? *Sci. Am.* 262(1):26–31.
4. P. M. Churchland and P. S. Churchland. 1990. Could a machine think? *Sci. Am.* 262(1):32–37.
5. A. M. Turing. 1950. Computing machinery and intelligence. *Mind* 59:433–60. (Reprinted in D. R. Hofstadter and D. C. Dennett, *The Mind's I*, Basic Books, 1981.)
6. R. Penrose. 1989. *The Emperor's New Mind*. Oxford Univ. Press.
7. H. Maturana and F. Varela. 1987. *The Tree of Knowledge*. Shambhala.
8. R. Hoffmann. 1990. Creation and discovery. *Am. Sci.* 78:14–15.
9. B. Latour. 1987. *Science in Action*. Harvard Univ. Press.

# NEW COMPUTERS, NEW THOUGHTS

## James Bailey

*From "First We Reshape Our Computers, Then Our Computers Reshape Us: The Broader Intellectual Impact of Parallelism," by James Bailey, in the Winter issue of* Daedalus, *the journal of the American Academy of Arts and Sciences. The issue, entitled "A New Era in Computation," is dedicated to the subject of massively parallel computing, a new technology that allows a computer, or a number of computers, to work on various parts of a problem simultaneously. Bailey is the director of marketing at Thinking Machines Corporation, in Cambridge, Massachusetts.*

Today we marvel at the ingenuity of engineers who, in the 1930s and 1940s, created a new and seemingly unprecedented wonder: the computer. Amid the marveling, however, we often overlook a curious point: the fact that it took no time at all for these supposedly unprecedented wonders to be filled up with useful work. As soon as the first electronic computers were put together, established sets of problems were waiting to be fed into them. It was almost as if computers had existed and been used all along.

In fact, they had. Prior to 1940, though, all "computers" were people—the scribes, clerks, and attendants who for centuries had performed the calculations that scientific progress had demanded. Over the course of 2,500 years, these human computers had developed a method of expressing and formulating science that was sequential: calculations followed one another progressively. The first electronic computers of the 1940s were accepted so quickly because they copied the sequential architecture of their human counterparts. Their inventors left essentially unchanged the partnership between scientist and computer that scientists were accustomed to; the only difference was that the computers were now machines.

It is only today, for the first time in history, that we are genuinely *reshaping* our computers. We are making them parallel. Instead of being organized around what human brains are good at—sequential thinking—parallel computers are organized around what electronic circuits are good at. Parallel computers can operate on thousands of pieces of data at once and can keep track of extremely complex interactions among them all. They are adept at carrying out computations that no human computer would ever attempt. As this new form of computing gains wider acceptance, the stakes are wonderfully high. Parallel computers have the potential to transform modes of thinking that have gone unchallenged since the time of Newton, Descartes, and even Aristotle. As we finish reshaping our computers, they are already beginning to reshape us.

Looking back into the history of human computers is not easy, because the profession was such a lowly one. Its influence, however, was profound: the kind of science scientists chose to pursue was limited by the abilities of the human computers on which they had to rely. What fruitful avenues of scientific investigation were never pursued, for want of the appropriate computational resource? How did the scientist's computer shape him and his science?

Pierre Duhem, writing at the turn of the century, comments on the way that human memory affects the expression of science: "He [the physicist] will choose a certain formula because it is simpler than the others; the weakness of our minds constrains us to attach great importance to considerations of this sort." For human computers a memorable formula is, in fact, preferable to an efficient one: a computer that reckons slowly will still get the answer eventually, but a computer that forgets its formula, or program, is doomed. Aristotle, in his treatise *On Memory*, focuses on an aspect of memory architecture that goes even deeper. He observes that human memory is designed to read out data sequentially, not

From *Harper's,* May 1992, pp. 28-30, 32. Originally from *Daedalus,* Journal of the American Academy of Arts and Sciences, from the issue entitled, "A New Era in Computation," Winter 1992, Vol. 121, No. 1. Reprinted by permission.

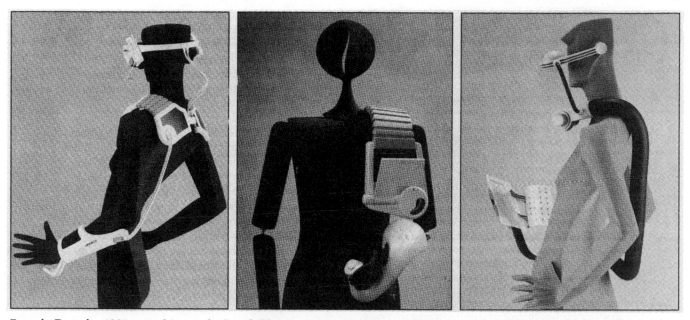

*From the December 1991 issue of* Across the Board: The Conference Board Magazine. *These wearable computer terminals, currently in development at the NEC Advanced PC Design Center in Tokyo, are designed to blend "the machine with the body" in order to maximize a user's freedom of movement. The Tender Loving Care Computer (at left) allows emergency medics to work on a patient without interruption. A hand-held "track ball," with special sensors and video camera, lets the medic check the patient's vital signs and sends information and pictures to the hospital; the information is also displayed in the medic's goggles. At the same time, the medic dictates data about the patient's condition into a microphone attached to the headpiece; this information is matched against a medical encyclopedia stored in a CD-ROM database in order to produce a diagnosis. The Wearable Data Terminal (middle) is used to keep track of inventory. Using an optical scanner worn on the wrist, a worker transmits bar-code information into a computer system, where it can be checked against data stored on CD-ROM. The Porto Office (at right) allows executives to input data using a keyboard, writing pad, or microphone. The system also includes a fax machine, a 35mm camera, and a speakerphone. NEC plans to begin marketing the computers in the late 1990s.*

randomly. "Whatever has some order, as things in mathematics do, is easily remembered," he writes. "Other things are remembered badly and with difficulty."

Aristotle's observation raises an unsettling question. Why exactly is it that mathematics "has some order"? How much of the reason for this is independent of the historical accident that mathematics was invented at a time when all the computers available to carry it out were sequential? In his *Discourse on Method* René Descartes elevates sequentialism—"conducting one's thoughts in order"—to be one of his four laws of correct thinking. Descartes felt that his own mental processes were more efficient when he put them into order, and so, naturally, he sought sequential methods to solve problems. But to then extrapolate from the workings of his own mind to the nature of the physical world, as Descartes did, may have been a mistake; he may have imposed the notion of sequentiality on a nonsequential world.

Because of the sequential architecture of human memory, the science that was pursued most vigorously in the age of human computers relied on sequential calculations. Celestial mechanics, ballistics, and navigation, all of which involve a single object following a single path, align strongly with Descartes's desire to "conduct one's thoughts in order." The computations involved are an ideal fit with the strengths and weaknesses of human computers. The formulas are short and easy to remember, and the number of active variables remains small throughout the computation. Generations of computers found both their training and their careers in these computations.

It was only in rare instances that scientists did not follow the sequentialist approach. In Galileo's *Two New Sciences*, for example, the reader is asked to "imagine" a series of objects moving out from one point at the same time, at different angles and rates of acceleration. Because Galileo's musing (which amounted to a very early theory of an expanding universe) depended on a great number of objects being changed at once, it would have required parallel computation to actually calculate. Galileo, stuck in the age of sequential computers, was forced to leave his ponderings unresolved. His foray into parallel science—and cosmology—was brief.

At one level the difference between sequential computation and parallel computation is mechanical. Any computation that can be carried out by a parallel computer can also be carried out by a sequential computer; parallel processors merely allow algorithms to be carried out faster, on larger sets of data. For this reason alone, they are likely to become predominant.

But the opportunities for exploiting parallel computation are already moving beyond mere

[Computer Program]

# THE DIGITAL COUCH

*From the program code for PC Therapist III, an interactive computer program written by Joseph Weintraub and sold by Thinking Software in Woodside, New York. The program, which is designed to simulate the responses of a psychotherapist, looks for certain words and phrases, such as those shown in brackets below, in remarks typed in by its "patient," the human operator. The program then chooses its reply from a list of relevant responses; it often repeats part of the patient's comments in its own response. This is PC Therapist's most basic level of conversation; at more complex levels, the program has a database of thousands of sentences to choose from. Last November PC Therapist III won the First Annual Loebner Prize for the computer program best able to mimic human interaction; during a series of typed conversations, PC Therapist III convinced five of the contest's ten judges that it was human.*

[I feel _____]
Tell me more about such feelings.
Do you often feel _____?
Do you enjoy feeling _____?

[I am _____]
Do you like being _____?
Did you come to me because you are _____?
How long have you been _____?
Do you believe it's normal to be _____?

[I want _____]
What would it mean if you got _____?
Why do you want _____?
What if you never got _____?
I sometimes also want _____.

[Are you _____]
Why are you interested in whether
   I am _____?
Would you prefer it if I were not _____?
Perhaps in your fantasies I am _____.

[Dream]
What does that dream suggest to you?
What persons appear in your dreams?
Are you disturbed by your dreams?

[Maybe]
Why the uncertain tone?
Can't you be more positive?
You aren't sure?

[Machine]
Do machines worry you?
Are you frightened by machines?
Are you talking about me in particular?
Do you think I am different from you?

mechanical improvements. Today at least three new threads of development are becoming visible. The first is the shift from presenting results as numbers to presenting results as pictures, a process known as "scientific visualization."

The shift to visual forms is closely tied to parallelism. Pictures communicate information in a parallel form: the viewer sees innumerable relations simultaneously, at a glance. Numbers and words—discursive communication—communicate information in a sequential form. Just as Galileo discovered scientific problems that could not be solved sequentially, so there are things one can "say" in pictures that simply cannot be said discursively. A modern computational fluid dynamicist, analyzing the flow of air over the wing of a supersonic airplane, studies a graphic computer display, not a series of equations; the complex set of relations between wing and air—the countless vortices within vortices—cannot be comprehended simply from a printout of numbers. When the relevant science lies in the *relations* among elements, as it did in Galileo's multiple moving objects, words fail, and so do individual numbers.

In Galileo's time artists communicated one set of truths in the parallel mode, while scientists communicated a different set of truths in the sequential mode. So when the skies spoke to the poetic imagination of Galileo, he had no computational place to go with his insights. Today's Galileos do, and that is becoming one of the most significant impacts of parallelism.

A second radically new form of parallel computation is growing up around the realization that numbers are not necessarily the best medium for representing complex processes. This method, which uses what are called lattice gas algorithms, is useful in charting processes that seem chaotic, like the movement of a fluid. Lattice gas algorithms use no numbers at all; instead, they allow millions of "simple-minded" objects to interact on a computational playing field, colliding and bouncing off one another. Depending on the rules of movement used, a distinct pattern of behavior emerges. Such an algorithm is a natural fit with a science like fluid dynamics, since a brook is, in fact, made up of myriad jostling water molecules. These algorithms are also well suited to what electronic circuits do best. Real numbers are quite ungainly from the point of view of an electronic circuit; blacks and whites or zeros and ones are much more simpatico with the way an electronic circuit operates.

The third line of development, known as genetic-algorithm computation, takes its inspiration from Darwin's theory of natural selection. Again, this method holds great promise for modeling the behavior of systems that seem to us chaotic and

[Computer-Network Postings]

# LOST
# IN NINTENDOLAND

*The messages below, regarding techniques for playing Nintendo video games, were posted last December on the video-games bulletin board of the Prodigy interactive computer service. The exchange appeared in the Winter issue of* Meanwhile . . . , *published in Philadelphia.*

Has anyone out there ever beat The Immortal? I'm at the very end (the dragon) and I can't get past him! Someone please help! I've been stuck here forever!

In "Chrysalis," where is the love necklace? Please respond in 24 hours, please.

I need help on "Bart vs. the Space Mutants." I can't figure out if you need to change the color of the trash cans. I also don't know if you need to change the color of the fountains. If you need to hide or color these, then how? I am on the first level.

Does anyone know where to find the red and blue switch palaces? Also, how do you pass the Chocolate Mountain 3 without going in a circle?

I found out how to get to the star road from the vanilla dome. You must have the cape. Go to the red dot before the pipe. Go to the first jumping board. Fly to the left. There should be a tube you can go into and finish the area.

On "Super Mario Bros. 3," in the third world, sixth part, there appears a green block. At times it appears whole, at times only part of it appears. What does it mean and what can I do with it? I've also seen it in the fourth part of the same world. It used to be a bush but changes once I complete a sequence of moves with a turtle at the beginning. Any ideas?

In "Mega Man II," how do you defeat the Blobs in Dr. Wiley's castle? I really need to know.

How do you get through the Ghost World? I have lost about five men and I can't seem to get through it!

Okay, exactly how many missiles does it take to destroy Mother Brain?

How do you get out of the Forest of Illusion? I need help from anyone.

that defy analysis by traditional numerical techniques. (The behavior of a nation's economy is a pertinent example.) Instead of a single all-knowing program, the computer is given myriad imperfect programs, called "agents." Initially, all agents have an equal voice in the way the overall computation proceeds. At each stage each agent's results are compared with what the answer should have been; the agents that were the most helpful in reaching the desired result are rewarded with a larger voice next time. They become more dominant while the more feckless agents wither away.

These three new ways of thinking about problem solving underscore the difference between the current revolution in computing and the transition that occurred in the 1940s. There was no anxiety then about the validity of the results that the first electronic computers produced, because the answers could be checked directly. The results from the electronic computer were compared with the results of the same calculation, using the same algorithm, made by a human computer. The results of lattice gas and genetic computations enjoy no such prior cultural acceptance, yet their potential to change the way we think about the world is all the greater for their unorthodoxy. Fifty years after the first electronic computers were built, their potential to reshape what we think about, and even how we think, may be taking hold at last.

It is not uncommon for the true impact of a new technology to remain veiled for a generation or two. Such was the case with the steam engine. Early steam engines were often relegated to a relatively minor downstream role by mill owners. Their job was simply to pump water back up into the millpond after it had passed over the water wheel. It was a role dictated not by what the engines were inherently good at but rather by a preexisting need—a seasonal bug in the way millstreams work. Only decades later did the culture recognize and reorganize itself around the unique capabilities of the engines themselves. Only then did the Industrial Revolution truly take hold.

The partnership between human scientist and human computer is even more ancient than the partnership between miller and millstream. It is reasonable to assume that there will be a lag between the time when we reshape our computers and the time when they begin to reshape us. Or maybe this assumption is not reasonable at all. Maybe it only *sounds* reasonable because we are all still trained to believe that orderly, sequential processes (first this happens, then that) are more likely to be true. Maybe it will turn out to be more accurate to have said, "As we were reshaping our computers, so simultaneously were they reshaping us." Maybe when things happen in this world, they actually happen in parallel.

# Glossary

*This glossary of computer terms is included to provide you with a convenient and ready reference as you encounter general computer terms that are unfamiliar or require a review. It is not intended to be comprehensive, but, taken together with the many definitions included in the articles, it should prove to be quite useful.*

**Alphanumeric.** Data that consists of letters of the alphabet, numerals, or other special characters such as punctuation marks.

**Applications software.** Software designed to accomplish a specific task such as accounting, financial modeling, or word processing.

**Archive.** Storage of infrequently used data on disks or diskettes.

**Artificial intelligence.** Hardware or software capable of performing functions that require learning or reasoning (e.g., a computer that plays chess).

**ASCII.** American Standard Code for Information Interchange. (The acronym is pronounced "as-key.") An industry standard referring to 128 codes generated by computers for text and control characters (for example, A = 65, Z = 90, a = 97). This code permits the computer equipment of different manufacturers to exchange alphanumeric data with one another.

**Authoring language.** A high-level language, usually created expressly for use by educators, that allows a user to program with minimal knowledge of computer languages. PILOT.

**Automatic Teller Machine (ATM).** A machine that provides 24-hour banking services.

**Auxiliary storage.** A storage device in addition to the core or main storage of the computer. (Includes magnetic tape, cassette tape, floppy disk, and hard disk.) Sometimes called external storage or secondary storage.

**Babbage, Charles.** Frequently considered the father of the modern computer; in the early 1800s he outlined the ideas that have become the basis for modern computational devices.

**Backup.** An extra copy of information stored on a disk. If the program or other data stored on the first disk is damaged, it is still available on the backup copy.

**Bar code.** A code that consists of numerous magnetic lines imprinted on a label that can be read with a scanning device. Often used in labeling retail products.

**BASIC.** Beginners All-purpose Symbolic Instruction Code. A high-level computer language, considered by many authorities to be the easiest language to learn, and used in one variation or another by almost all microcomputers.

**Batch processing.** An approach to computer processing where groups of like transactions are accumulated (batched) to be processed at the same time.

**Baud rate.** The speed of serial data transmission between computers or a computer and a peripheral in bits per second.

**Binary.** The base-two number system in which all alphanumeric characters are represented by various combinations of 0 and 1. Binary codes may be used to represent any alphanumeric character, such as the letter "A" (100 0001), the number 3 (000 0011), or characters representing certain computer operations such as a "line feed" (000 1010).

**Bit.** Binary digIT. The smallest unit of digital information. Eight bits constitute one byte.

**Bit-mapped.** Any binary representation in which a bit or set of bits corresponds to an object or condition.

**Board.** Abbreviation for printed circuit board. Can also refer to any of the peripheral devices or their connectors that plug into the slots inside a microcomputer.

**Boolean.** An expression that evaluates to the logical value of true or false (e.g., 1 + 1 = 2 or 3 < 2).

**Boot.** (Short for Bootstrap.) To start the computer; to load an operating system into the computer's main memory and commence its operation.

**Buffer.** A temporary memory that is capable of storing incoming data for later transmission. Often found on printers to allow the printer to accept information faster than it prints it.

**Bug.** An error in a program that causes the computer to malfunction. *See also* Debugging.

**Bus.** A collection of wires that transmit information in the form of electrical signals from one circuit to another.

**Byte.** The sequence of bits that represents any alphanumerical character or a number between 0 and 255. Each byte has 8 bits.

**CAI.** Computer-Assisted Instruction or Computer-Aided Instruction. An educational use of computers that usually entails using computer programs which drill, tutor, simulate, or teach problem-solving skills. *See also* CMI.

**Card.** Refers to a peripheral card that plugs into one of the internal slots in a microcomputer.

**CAT Scanner.** A diagnostic device used for producing a cross-sectional X ray of a person's internal organs; an acronym for computer axial tomography.

**Cathode-ray tube (CRT).** *See* Display screen.

**CBT.** 1. Computer-Based Testing. Refers to the use of computers to present, monitor, or correct examinations. 2. Computer-Based Training. *See also* CAI.

**CD ROM.** Compact Disk Read Only Memory. An auxiliary storage device that uses a rigid disk to store information capable of being read by a computer. Its major advantage is that it can store many times more bytes of information than floppy diskettes or a hard disk.

**CD-I.** Compact Disc-Interactive. A format available to personal computer users that allows access to picture databases and large text; a compact disc standard that includes music compact discs (CD audio), static data (CD ROM), and graphics.

**Central Processing Unit.** *See* CPU.

**Chip.** An integrated circuit used inside a microcomputer and on boards. They contain such electronic devices as transistors, capacitors, and circuits.

**CMI.** Computer-Managed Instruction. An educational use of computers that usually entails the use of computer programs to handle testing, grade-keeping, filing, and other classroom management tasks.

**COBOL.** COmmon Business Oriented Language. A high-level language, used mostly in business.

**Compatibility.** 1. Software compatibility refers to the ability to run the same software on a variety of computers. 2. Hardware compatibility refers to the ability to directly connect various peripherals to the computer.

**Compiler.** A program that translates a high-level computer language into machine language for later execution. This would be similar to a human translating an entire document from a foreign language into English for later reading by others.

**Computer.** Any device that can receive, store, and act upon a set of instructions in a predetermined sequence, and one that permits both the instructions and the data upon which the instructions act to be changed.

**Computer Bulletin Board Service (CBBS).** A computerized data base that users access to post and to retrieve messages.

**Computer literacy.** Term used to refer to a person's capacity to intelligently use computers. May also be used to refer to programs in schools designed to help students acquire this capacity.

**Computer program.** A series of commands, instructions, or statements put together in a way that permits a computer to perform a specific task or a series of tasks.

**Computer-Aided Design (CAD).** An engineer's use of the computer to design, draft, and analyze a prospective product using computer graphics on a video terminal.

**Computer-Aided Instruction.** *See* CAI.

**Computer-Aided Manufacturing (CAM).** An engineer's use of the computer to simulate the required steps of the manufacturing process.

**Computer-Assisted Instruction.** *See* CAI.

**Computer-Based Testing.** *See* CBT.

**Computer-Based Training.** *See* CBT.

**Configuration.** The components that make up a computer (referred to as hardware—a keyboard for text entry, a central processing unit, one or more disk drives, a printer, and a display screen).

**Control key.** A special function key found on most computer keyboards that allows the user to use the remaining keys for other specialized operations.

**Copy protected.** Refers to a disk that has been altered to prevent it from being copied.

**Courseware.** Instructional programs and related support materials needed to use computer software in the classroom.

**CPU.** Central Processing Unit. The "brain" of the computer consisting of a large integrated circuit that performs the computations within a computer. CPUs are often designated by a number, such as 6502, 8080, 68000, and so on.

**Crash.** A malfunction of a computer's software or hardware that prevents the computer from functioning.

**Crossfooting.** The ability of a computer to total numeric amounts that have been arranged in columns and rows, and then placing the answers at the end of each row or bottom of each column.

**CRT.** Cathode-Ray Tube. *See* Display screen.

**Cursor.** The prompting symbol usually displayed as a blinking white square or underline on the monitor that shows where the next character will appear.

**Data.** All information, including facts, numbers, letters, and symbols, that can be acted upon or produced by the computer.

**Data base.** A collection of related information, such as that found on a mailing list, which can be stored in a computer and retrieved in several ways.

**Data base management.** 1. Refers to a classification of software designed to act like an electronic filing cabinet, which allows the user to store, retrieve, and manipulate files. 2. The practice of using computers to assist in routine filing and information processing chores.

**Data processing.** Also known as electronic data processing (EDP), it is the mathematical or other logical manipulation of symbols or numbers, based on a stored program of instructions.

**Debugging.** The process of locating and eliminating defects in a program that causes the computer to malfunction or cease to operate.

**Default format statement.** Formatting instructions, built into a software program or the computer's memory, which will be followed unless different instructions are given by the operator. (A common default format is a 6.5-inch line, with 1.5-inch margins.)

**Desktop publishing.** The system that processes text and graphics and, with page layout software and a laser printer, produces high-quality pages that are suitable for printing or reproduction.

**Directory.** A list of files that are stored on a disk.

**Disk, Diskette.** A thin plastic wafer-like object enclosed in a plastic jacket with a metallic coating used to magnetically store information. The standard size on microcomputer is 5 $1/4$ inches in diameter, though many are beginning to use smaller $3^1/4$ inches or $3^1/2$ inches diameter diskettes that are stored in more rigid jackets.

**Disk drive.** A peripheral device capable of reading and writing information on a disk.

**Disk envelope.** A removable protective paper sleeve used when handling or storing a disk; must be removed before inserting in a disk drive.

**Disk jacket.** A nonremovable protective covering for a disk, usually black plastic or paper, within which the disk spins when being used by the disk drive.

**Disk Operating System.** *See* DOS.

**Display screen.** A peripheral that allows for the visual output of information for the computer on a CRT, monitor, or similar device.

**Documentation.** Instructional materials that describe the operations of an individual computer program or a piece of system hardware.

**DOS.** Disk Operating System. (The acronym is pronounced to rhyme with "boss.") Refers to the program that enables a computer to read and write on a disk.

**Dot-matrix.** A type of printing in which characters are formed by using a number of closely spaced dots.

**Downtime.** Any period of time when the computer is not available or is not working.

**Dumb terminal.** Refers to a terminal that can be used to input information into a computer and to print or display output, but which lacks the capacity to manipulate information transmitted to it from the host computer. *See also* Intelligent terminal.

**Dump.** Mass copying of memory or a storage device such as a disk to another storage device or a printer so it can be used as a backup or analyzed for errors.

**Duplexing.** The procedure that permits two computers to transmit data to each other simultaneously.

**DV-I.** Digital Video-Interactive. Optical storage media that delivers full-motion, full-screen video, three-dimensional motion graphics, and high-quality audio capabilities.

**Electronic Funds Transfer System (EFT).** A system that eliminates the exchange of cash or checks by automatically transferring funds from one account to another.

**Electronic mail (E-mail).** Sending and receiving information by computer.

**Electronic spreadsheet.** *See* Spreadsheet.

**Electronic worksheet.** *See* Spreadsheet.

**Elite.** Any typeface that allows the printing of 12 characters to an inch.

**ENIAC.** Electronic Numerical Integrator and Calculator. The first electronic digital computer produced in the United States.

**EPIE.** Educational Products Information Exchange. A nonprofit group associated with Consumer's Union, which, among other things, evaluates computer hardware and software.

**Error message.** A message displayed or printed to notify the user of an error or problem in the execution of a program.

**Expert systems.** Software packages designed to copy how expert humans in a certain field think through a problem to reach the correct solution.

**Exponential notation.** Refers to how a computer displays very large or very small numbers by means of the number times 10 raised to some power. For example, 3,000,000 could be printed as 3E + 6 (3 times 10 to the sixth power).

**Fan fold.** A type of paper that can continuously feed into a printer (usually via tractor feed).

**FAX.** (n.) Short for the word facsimile. A copy of a document transmitted electronically from one machine to another. (v.) To transmit a copy of a document electronically.

**Field.** Group of related characters treated as a unit (such as a name); also the location in a record or database where this group of characters is entered.

**First-Generation Computers.** Developed in the 1950s; used vacuum tubes; faster than earlier mechanical devices, but very slow compared to today's computer.

**Fixed disk.** *See* Hard disk.

**Floppy, Floppy disk.** *See* Disk.

**Format.** (n.) The physical form in which information appears. (v.) To specify parameters of a form or to write address codes on a blank disk in preparation for using it to store data or programs. *See also* Initialize.

**FORTRAN.** FORmula TRANslation. A high-level language used primarily for mathematical computations; though FORTRAN is used by some microcomputers, it is mainly used by mainframe computers.

**Function keys.** Computer keyboard keys that give special commands to the computer (for example, to format, to search text).

**GIGO.** Garbage In, Garbage Out. Serves as a reminder that a program is only as good as the information and instructions in the program.

**Global.** The performance of any function on an entire document without requiring individual commands for each use. For example, a global search-and-replace command will allow the computer to search for a particular word and replace it with a different word throughout the text.

**Graphics.** 1. Information presented in the form of pictures or images. 2. The display of pictures or images on a computer's display screen.

**Hard copy.** A paper copy of the computer's output.

**Hard disk.** A magnetically coated metal disk, usually permanently mounted within a disk drive; capable of storing 30 to 150 times more information than a floppy disk.

**Hardware.** Refers to the computer and all its peripheral devices. The physical pieces of the computer.

**HDTV.** High Definition TV. A television with quality resolution that is higher than current international standards.

**Head.** Refers to the component of a disk drive or tape system that magnetically reads or writes information to the storage medium.

**Hex or Hexadecimal.** A numbering system based on 16 (digits 0–9 and letters A–F) rather than on 10. Most computers operate using hex numbers. Each hexadecimal digit corresponds to a sequence of 4 binary digits or bits.

**High-level language.** An English-like computer language (BASIC, Pascal, FORTRAN, Logo, COBOL) designed to make it relatively convenient for a person to prepare a program for a computer, which in turn translates it into machine language for execution.

**Hypermedia.** The connecting of data, texts, video, graphics, and voice in an information system that allows a user to move easily from one element to another.

**Hypertext.** A technique that organizes and connects information in a nonsequential or nontraditional manner.

**IAV.** Interactive Video. The merger of two electronic media, computers and television, and two design areas, instructional and visual.

**IC.** Integrated Circuit. *See* Chip.

**ICAI.** Intelligent Computer-Assisted Instruction. A type of CAI on which the interaction between the computer and learner is subject to a complex algorithm that uses student responses to questions to determine subsequent interaction (level of problem difficulty, remedial work, etc.).

**Icon.** Refers to the use of a graphic symbol to represent something else. Its use is central to the use of advanced computers such as the Macintosh and Amiga.

**Indexing.** The ability of a computer to accumulate a list of words or phrases, with corresponding page numbers, in a document, and then to print out or display the list in alphabetical order.

**Initialize.** 1. To set an initial state or value in preparation for some computation. 2. To prepare a blank disk to receive information by dividing its surface into tracks and sectors. *See also* Format.

**Ink jet printer.** A dot-matrix printer in which the characters are formed by using a number of closely spaced dots that are sprayed onto a page in microscopic droplets of ink.

**Input.** Information entered into the computer.

**Integrated circuit.** *See* Chip.

**Intelligent terminal.** A terminal that is capable of doing more than just receiving or transmitting data due to its microprocessor. *See also* Dumb terminal.

**Interactive multimedia.** Back-and-forth dialogue between user and computer that allows the combining, editing, and orchestrating of sounds, graphics, moving pictures, and text.

**Interface.** (v.) To connect two pieces of computer hardware together. (n.) The means by which two things communicate. In particular, it refers to the electrical configuration that allows two or more devices to pass information. *See also* Interface card.

**Interface card.** A board used to connect a microcomputer to peripheral devices.

**I/O.** Input/Output. Refers usually to one of the slots or the game port in a microcomputer to which peripheral devices may be connected.

**Joy stick.** An input device, often used to control the movement of objects on the video display screen of a computer for games.

**Justification.** A method of printing in which additional space is inserted between words or characters to force each line to the same length.

**K.** Abbreviation for kilo, or 1000. In information processing, K stands for kilobyte (1024 bytes) and is often used to describe a computer's storage capacity.

**Keyboard.** The typewriter-like keys on a microcomputer. Each microcomputer will have basically the same keyboard as a typewriter, with major differences limited to special function keys such as ESCape, RESET, ConTRoL, TABulate, etc.

**Kilobyte.** *See* K .

**Language.** Characters and procedures used to write programs that the computer is designed to understand.

**Large-Scale Integration (LSI).** Refers to a generation of integrated circuits that allowed the equivalent of thousands of vacuum tube switches to be installed on a single chip.

**Light pen.** An input device, shaped much like a mechanical pencil, which, when touched to a display screen, can be used to select or execute certain computer functions.

**LISP (LISt Processing).** Programming language primarily used in artificial intelligence research.

**Local Area Networks (LAN).** The linking together of computers, word processors, and other electronic office equipment to form an interoffice network.

**Log on.** To execute the necessary commands to allow you to use a computer. May involve the use of a password. More common on mainframe systems.

**Logo.** A high-level language specifically designed so that it may be used by both small children and adults. It involves a "turtle"-shaped cursor for much of its operation.

**M.** *See* Megabyte.

**Machine language.** A fundamental, complex computer language used by the computer itself to perform its functions. This language is quite difficult for the average person to read or write.

**Macro.** Refers to the use of a simple command to execute a sequence of complex commands while using a computer program. The use of macros can save the user a considerable amount of time and reduce the chance of typing an incorrect key when executing a sequence of commands.

**Magnetic Ink Character Recognition (MICR) devices.** Computer hardware capable of reading characters imprinted with magnetic ink, such as on checks.

**Mainframe.** Refers to large computers used primarily in business, industry, government, and higher education that have the capacity to deal with many users simultaneously and to process large amounts of information quickly and in very sophisticated ways. *See also* Time share.

**Management Information System (MIS).** A systems approach that treats business departments as integrated parts of one total system rather than as separate entities.

**MB.** *See* Megabyte.

**Megabyte.** 1,048,576 bytes.

**Memory.** Chips in the computer that have the capacity to store information. *See also* PROM; RAM; ROM.

**Menu.** The list of programs available on a given disk to guide the operator through a function.

**Menu driven.** Refers to software in which the program prompts the user with a list of available options at any given time, thus eliminating the need to memorize commands.

**Merge.** A command to create one document by combining text that is stored in two different locations (e.g., a form letter can be merged with a mailing list to produce a batch of personalized letters).

**Microcomputer.** Refers to a generation of small, self-contained, relatively inexpensive computers based on the microprocessor (commonly consists of a display screen, a keyboard, a central processing unit, one or more disk drives, and a printer).

**Microprocessor.** The CPU. It holds all of the essential elements for manipulating data and performing arithmetic operations. A microprocessor is contained on a single silicon chip.

**Microsecond.** One millionth of a second.

**MIDI.** Musical Instrument Digital Interface. A protocol that allows for the interchange of musical information between musical instruments, synthesizer, and computers.

**Millisecond.** One thousandth of a second; abbreviated "ms."

**Minicomputer.** Refers to a class of computers larger than micros but smaller than mainframe computers, many of which support multiple keyboards and output devices simultaneously.

**Mnemonics.** A computer's system of commands, which are structured to assist the operator's memory. Abbreviations are used for the command functions they perform (e.g., C for center, U for underline).

**Modem.** MOdulator/DEModulator. A peripheral device that enables the computer to transmit and receive information over a telephone line.

**Monitor.** The display screen of a computer.

**Motherboard.** The main circuit board of a computer.

**Mouse.** A hand-operated device that is used to move the cursor around on the CRT screen.

**Nanosecond.** One billionth of a second; abbreviated "ns."

**National Crime Information Center (NCIC).** A computerized information center maintained by the FBI that serves agencies throughout the United States.

**Network.** A structure capable of linking two or more computers by wire, telephone lines, or radio links.

**Nibble.** 1. Half a byte. 2. Refers to copy programs that copy small portions of a disk at a time, often used to copy otherwise copy-protected programs.

**Nonvolatile memory.** Memory that retains data even after power has been shut off. ROM is nonvolatile; RAM is volatile.

**Numeric keypad.** An input device that allows the user to input numbers into a microcomputer with a calculator-like key arrangement.

**Off-line.** An operation performed by electronic equipment not tied into a centralized information processing system.

**On-line.** An operation performed by electronic equipment controlled by a remote central processing system.

**Operating system.** A group of programs that act as intermediary between the computer and the applications software; the operating system takes a program's commands and passes them down to the CPU in a language that the CPU understands; application programs must be written for a specific operating system such as DOS 3.3, Pro-DOS, MS-DOS, TRS-DOS, and others.

**Optical Character Reader (OCR).** Also called an optical scanner, it is a device that can read text and automatically enter it into a computer for editing or storage.

**Output.** Information sent out of the computer system to some external destination such as the display screen, disk drive, printer, or modem.

**Parallel.** A form of data transmission in which information is passed in streams of eight or more bits at a time in sequence. *See also* Serial.

**Pascal.** A high-level language, with a larger, more complex vocabulary than BASIC, used for complex applications in business, science, and education; named after the seventeenth-century French mathematician.

**Password.** A code word or group of characters required to access stored material. A protection against unauthorized persons accessing documents.

**PC.** Personal Computer. *See* Microcomputer.

**Peripheral.** Hardware attachments to a microcomputer, (e.g., printer, modem, monitor, disk drives, or interface card).

**Peripheral card.** A removable printed-circuit board that plugs into a microcomputer's expansion slot and expands or modifies the computer's capabilities by connecting a peripheral device or performing some subsidiary or peripheral function.

**Pica type.** Any typeface that allows the printing of 10 characters to an inch.

**PILOT.** Programmed Inquiry, Learning, or Teaching. A high-level language designed primarily for use by educators, which facilitates the wiring of computer-assisted instruction lessons that include color graphics, sound effects, lesson texts, and answer checking.

**Pitch.** A measurement that indicates the number of characters in an inch (e.g., pica yields 10 characters to an inch; elite yields 12 characters to an inch).

**Pixel.** PIXture ELement. Refers to the smallest point of light that can be displayed on a display screen.

**Plotter.** A printing mechanism capable of drawing lines rapidly and accurately for graphic representation.

**Port.** An input or output connection to the computer.

**Printout.** *See* Hard copy.

**Program.** A list of instructions that allows the computer to perform a function.

**PROM.** Programmable ROM. A ROM that is programmed after it has been made.

**Prompt.** A message given on the display screen to indicate the status of a function.

**Protocol.** A formal set of rules that governs the transmission of information from one piece of equipment to another.

**RAM.** Random Access Memory. The main working memory of any computer. In most microcomputers, anything stored in RAM will be lost when the power is shut off.

**Read Only Memory.** *See* ROM.

**Retrieve.** The transfer of a document from storage to memory.

**RF Modulator.** Radio Frequency Modulator. Refers to a device that converts video signals generated by the computer to signals that can be displayed on a television set.

**RISC.** Reduced Instruction Set Computer. A computer architecture requiring assemblers and compilers to generate a limited series of instructions to perform complex functions.

**Robotics.** The science of designing and building robots.

**ROM.** Read Only Memory. A memory device in which information is permanently stored as it is being made. Thus, it may be read but not changed.

**RS-232.** Industry standard for serial transmission devices.

**Run.** 1. To execute a program. 2. A command to load a program to main memory from a peripheral storage medium, such as a disk, and execute it.

**Save.** To store a program on a disk or somewhere other than a computer's memory.

**Scanning.** Examining text on a display screen for editing purposes.

**Screen.** A CRT or display screen.

**Search and replace.** Locating a character string in a document and replacing it with a different character string.

**Second-Generation Computers.** Used transistors; smaller, faster, and had larger storage capacity than the first-generation computers; first computers to use a high-level language.

**Serial.** A form of data transmission in which information is passed one bit at a time in sequence.

**Software.** The programs used by the computer. Often refers to the programs as stored on a disk.

**Sort.** To arrange fields, files, and records in a predetermined sequence.

**Speech synthesizer.** Refers to a peripheral output device that attempts to mimic human speech.

**Split screen.** A type of dual display that allows some computers to view two or more different video images on the screen at the same time. *See also* Windowing.

**Spreadsheet.** A program that provides worksheets with rows and columns for calculating and preparing reports.

**Stack.** A list used to keep track of the sequence of required program routines.

**Store.** Placing information in memory for later use.

**System.** An organized collection of hardware, software, and peripheral equipment that works together. *See also* Configuration.

**Telecommunication.** Transmission of information between two computers in different locations, usually over telephone lines.

**Terminal.** A piece of equipment used to communicate with a computer, such as a keyboard for input, or video monitor or printer for output.

**Third-Generation Computers.** Refers to the present generation of computers based on microchips. Compare to first generation (tubes) and second generation (transistors).

**Time share.** Refers to the practice of accessing a larger computer from a remote location and paying for services based on the amount of computer time used. *See* Mainframe.

**Tractor feed.** A mechanism used to propel paper through a printer by means of sprockets attached to the printer that engage holes along the paper's edges.

**TTD.** A TTY communications device used by the deaf.

**TTY.** A TeleTypewriter.

**Turning test.** A person asks questions and, on the basis of the answers, must determine if the respondent is another human being or a machine.

**Typeover.** Recording and storing information in a specific location to destroy whatever had been stored there previously.

**Universal Product Code (UPC).** A bar code that appears on virtually all consumer goods; can be read by a scanner or wand device used in point-of-sale systems.

**User friendly.** Refers to hardware or software that is relatively easy for a new operator to learn, and which has features to help eliminate operator error.

**User group.** An association of people who meet to exchange information about computers or computer applications.

**Very Large Scale Integration (VLSI).** *See* LSI.

**Voice Recognition System.** A system that allows the user to "train" the computer to understand his or her voice and vocabulary.

**Volatile.** Refers to memory that is erased whenever the power is removed, such as RAM.

**WAN.** Wide-Area Network. The movement of data between computers in various areas through high-speed links.

**Windowing.** The ability of a computer to split a display screen into two or more segments so that several different documents can be viewed and several different functions performed simultaneously.

**Word processing.** Refers to the use of computers as electronic typewriters capable of entering and retrieving text, storing it on disks, and performing a wide range of editing functions.

**Wraparound.** A computer's ability to automatically move words from one line to the next or from one page to the next as a result of margin adjustments, insertions, or deletions.

**Write protected.** A disk in which the write-enable notch is either missing or has had a write-protect tab placed over it to prevent information from being written to the disk.

**Write-enable notch.** A notch in a floppy disk that, if uncovered, allows a disk drive to write information to it, and which, if covered, prohibits such writing.

**Write-protect tab.** A small adhesive sticker used to write-protect a disk by covering the write-enable notch.

### Sources for the glossary include:

*Apple Computer Incorporated, Apple IIe Owner's Manual,* Cupertino, CA, 1982.

"Apple II New User's Guide"; B. Gibson, "Personal Computers in Business: An Introduction and Buyer's Guide," *MECC,* Apple Computer, Inc., 1982.

*Computer-Based Training Start Kit,* Department of Treasury, Internal Revenue Service, Document 6846 (5–83).

Craig W. Copley and Stephen J. Taffee, Minnesota Educational Computing Corporation, St. Paul, MN, 55126.

"Glossary of Computer Terms," *Printout,* April 1983.

"Glossary of Computer Terms," S. Richardson, *Noteworthy,* Winter 1982, pp. 27–29.

"Glossary of Computer Terms," William A. Sabine, *Gregg Reference Manual,* 1992, pp. 480–490.

*Softalk,* January 1983, January 1982.

Stephen J. Taffee, Department of Education, North Dakota State University.

"Using the Computer in the Classroom," *Today's Education,* April–May 1982.

"VisiCalc Glossary," *Apple Orchard,* July–August 1982.

A. C. Nielsen, 144
accommodation, Americans with Disabilities Act and reasonable, 75–77
AC/ES system, 75–76
active badges, 139
adaptive technology, for disabled persons, 71–78, 87–88
adults only computer games, 156, 157–158
Advanced Field Artillery Tactical Data System (AFATDS), 183–185
Advanced Micro Devices (AMD), 120
Advanced Research Projects Agency (ARPA): optoelectronics and, 31, 32; speech-recognition technology and, 39, 40
aeronautical charts, strict liability in text for, 192
aerospace, optoelectronics and, 33
*Aetna Casualty & Surety Co. vs. Jeppsen & Co.,* 194
Africa, information technologies in, 202–206
Ahlbom, Anders, 180
Air Travel Information System (ATIS), 8–9
airlines: computer reservation systems and, 211–212; speech-recognition technology and, 39
airplanes, optoelectronics and smart, 33
Alliance for Employee Growth and Development, Inc., 63
American Airlines Inc., 211, 212
American Federation of Government Employees (AFGE), 65
American Standard Inc., 26
Americans with Disabilities Act (ADA): adaptive technology and, 71; reasonable accommodation and, 75–78; telecommuting and, 70
*America's Choice: High Skills or Low Wages,* 59, 60
animation, use of computer, in Mitchell brothers murder trial, 43, 153–155
Aristotle, 232–233
armed forces: Advanced Field Artillery Tactical Data System and, 183–185; Advanced Research Project Agency and, 31, 32, 39, 40; training for, and computers, 10; war and human-factors and, 174–175
ARPANET, 80
artificial intelligence (AI), thinking by computers and, 229–231
artificial life: computer created, 227–228; virtual reality and, 46
atomic-force microscopes (AFMs), 36–37
authenticated badges, 139
automation, 25; fixed, 199
automaton, cellular, 227

badges, 139–140
barfogenic zone, 46–47
Barlow, John Perry, 14
Berman, Jerry, 17
Bontchev, Vesko, 217, 218–219
braille printers, 72, 75
brain, versus computers, and thinking, 229–231
Bulgaria, computer viruses and, 213–219

CAD-CAM, 25–26, 80
calculators, 190
callback routines, 111–112
campus culture, 149

Canadian Airlines International Ltd., 211, 212
cancer: cellular phones and, 178–180; testicular, 90–91
*Cardozo vs. True,* 191
CAT scanners, rising cost of health care and, 52, 53, 54, 55
Catalina Marketing, 22, 143
CD-ROMS, 29, 31
cellular automaton, 227
cellular phones: cancer and, 178–180; computer crimes and, 163
Chips (Clearing House Interbank Payments System), electronic money and, 48, 49, 50, 51
Chisum, Donald S., 117–118
Chrysler Corp., 25, 26–27
churches, role of, in life of nuclear-weapons scientists, 224
Churchland, Patricia Smith, thinking by computers and, 229, 230, 231
Churchland, Paul M., thinking by computers and, 229, 230, 231
Clearing House Interbank Payments System (Chips), electronic money and, 48, 49, 50, 51
cognitive-impaired persons, adaptive technology for, 74–75
Commission on the Skills of the American Workforce, 59, 60
communications, fusion of computers with, 6–11
compact disk (CD) players, 29, 30, 31
complexity problem, 172–177
computer abuses, 148–150
computer animation, use of, in Mitchell brothers murder trial, 43, 153–155
computer crime, 160–163; corporate viruses and, 164–169; electronic money and, 49–50; piracy and, 127–131
computer ethics, 148–150; computer games and, 156–159
computer games, 97; ethics and, 156–159
computer imaging, 151–152
computer reservation systems, airlines and, 211–212
Computer Software Protection Act, 118
computer transactions, electronic conflicts and, 110–113
computer viruses, 213–219; law and, 164–169
computers: disabled persons and, 84–89; do-it-yourself movement and, 80; ethics, 148–150; fusion of communications with, 6–11; as pleasure machines, 95–99; superduperitis and, 108–109
consequentialists, 223
contracts, electronic, 110–113
"Copyleft," 135, 137–138
copyrights, for software, 124–125
Corinthian Pharmaceuticals, 113
Crawford, Chris, 156, 157, 158, 159
criminal law, computer viruses and, 167–169
crytography, 111–112
Cyrix Corp. 116–117, 119–120

Dark Avenger, 214–215, 217–219
data superhighways, 14–20
"dataglove," 42
death games, 156–157

de-fragmenting, of work force, 61
democracy, electronic, 100–107
deontologicalists, 223
Descartes, René, 233
desktop publishing, do-it-yourself movement and, 80
*Diamond v. Diehr,* 122
disabled persons: adaptive technology and, 71–78; computer usage and, 84–89
discotheque, disabled persons and, 79–81
do-it-yourself movement, 79–81
DRAMs (dynamic random access memories), 118, 119
drugs, computer game ethics and, 158–159
dyslexia, 74, 75

economy, self-service, 79
Eddie virus, 214–215
education, 10; scientific literacy and, 93–94; use of computers in special, 84, 85, 89
E-forms, 8–9; voice, 9
Egypt, 207
electromagnetic radiation, cancer from cellular phones and, 178–180
electronic contracts, 110–113
"electronic cottage," 66, 67
electronic curbcuts, 88
Electronic Data Gathering, Analysis and Retrieval (EDGAR) system, 111
electronic data interchange (EDI), 8, 111
Electronic Data Systems, 21, 22
electronic democracy, in Santa Monica, California, 100–107
electronic forms, 8–9; voice, 9
Electronic Frontier Foundation (EFF), Kapor and, 14–20
electronic information, liability for defective, 190–195
electronic mail, 79–80, 98
electronic money, 48–51
electronic serial numbers (ESNs), 163
EMACS, 132, 136
encryption, 111–112
Engelberger, Joseph, 200
entertainment: computer networks and, 10; virtual reality and, 44
ergonomics, complexity problem and, 172–177
errors, computers and software, 181–182, 183, 186, 189
ethics, computers, 148–150
European Economic Community (EEC), software piracy and, 130
extortion, computer crimes and, 161
extremely low frequency (ELF) electromagnetic fields, cancer and, 178–179
eyegaze systems, 72, 75

factories, future of, 24–28
fastballs, virtual reality and, 42
Federal Reserve, electronic money and, 48, 49, 50
Feynman, Richard, 35
flexible manufacturing systems, 198
"flexible workplaces," 69
forensic animation, use of, in Mitchell brothers murder trial, 43, 153–155
Free Software Foundation (FSF), free-software movement and, 132–138

Galileo, 233, 234
Galileo Electro-Optics Corp., 37
Gates, Bill, 14
GCC, *see* GNU C Compiler
genetic-algorithm computation, 234–235
Germany, micro-mechanical devices in, 36, 37
GMFanuc, 199
GNU, 135–138
GNU C Compiler (GCC), 135–137, 138
Gordon, Gil, 65–66, 67, 68, 69, 70
*Gottschalk v. Benson,* 122

hackers, lawsuits concerning, and computer viruses, 164–169
*Hack-Tic,* 162
health care: information revolution and, 22; patient information sources and, 90–92; rising cost of, and medical technology, 52–55
hearing-impaired persons, adaptive technology for, 74
*Hessenthaler v. Farzin,* electronic contracts and, 113
high-definition television (HDTV), computer networks and, 10
high-performance organization, 59
hotlines, for patient information, 91–92
human-factors, complexity problem and, 172–177
Hwang, George, 116, 117

implied warranty, 194; information in books and, 191
industrial design, 22–23
information, 7–8; infrastructures, 10–11, 14–20; liability for defective electronic, 190–193
information security breaches, computer viruses and, 164–169
information technologies (ITs): in Africa, 202–206; in Middle East, 207–210
infrastructures, information, 10–11, 14–20
instructional systems design (ISD) approach, 62
insurance, information revolution and, 22
Integrated Device Technology Inc., 116
integrated services digital networks (ISDNs); data superhighways and, 15–16; telecommuting and, 67
Intel Corp., 116, 117, 119–120
Iran, 207–208
ISDNs, *see* integrated services digital networks

Japan: nanotechnology in, 37; robotics in, 198–201
Jordan, 208

Kapor, Mitch, 14–20
"keyboard solutions," 72–73
Kimble, 160, 162
King, Rodney, trial of, 151
Knowbot, 9

labor unions, telecommuting and, 65
Laderle Laboratories, 113
Lanier, Jaron, 45
lasers, 29; semiconductor, 30
"laudable crowding," 142
learning-disabled persons, adaptive technology for, 74–75
less developed countries (LDCs), information technologies in, 202–206, 207–210

liability: categories of, 192–193; defective electronic information and, 190–193
light-emitting diodes (LEDs), 30, 32
linear accelerators, software errors in, 186–187, 189
liquid-crystal displays (LCDs), 32
Lisp Machine, 134–135
literacy, scientific, 93–94
Livermore Laboratory, life of nuclear-weapons scientists at, 222–226
Lotus, 14
LoveChild, 219
low-wages option, 59, 60

*MacPlaymate,* 156, 158
Magnavox, Advanced Field Artillery Tactical Data System and, 184–185
mainstreaming, of disabled persons, 85
manufacturing, in future, 24–28
marketing: information revolution and, 22; research, 141–145
mathematics: do-it-yourself movement and, 80; methods of computation and, 232–235
Mauro, Charles, 172–173, 174–176
Maytag Corp., 27
McKesson, 21
medical technology: rising cost of health care, 52–55; software errors and, 186–187, 188, 189
microchips, 36
micro-mechanical devices, 36
microscopes, advances in, and nanotechnology, 36–37
Microsoft, 14
Middle East, information technologies in, 207–210
Mitchell, Jim, use of computer animation in murder trial of, 43, 153–155
miniaturization, 35–37
mobile identification numbers (MINs), 163
mobility-impaired people, adaptive technology for, 72–73
Motorola Inc., 24, 25
M.R.I. scanners, rising cost of health care and, 52, 53, 54, 55
Mutating Engine, 219

nanotechnology, 35–37
NASA: computer imaging and, 151; virtual reality and, 43–44
National Nanofabrication Facilities (NNF), 37
negligence, 192–193
New Global Economy, 58
nuclear-weapons scientists, life of, at Livermore Laboratory, 222–226

optoelectronics, 29–34

parallel computation, 232, 233–234, 235
*Parker v. Flook,* 122
passwords, electronic contracts and, 111–112
Patent Office, 122, 123–124, 125–126
patents: computer piracy and, 127–131; intellectual property litigation and, 116–120; software, 121–126
patients, information for, 90–92
Penrose, Roger, thinking by computers and, 229, 230–231
PET scanners, rising cost of health care and, 52, 53, 54, 55
pixels, smart, 34

*Polaroid v. Kodak,* 118
Prevalsky, Teodor, 215–217
"prior art," 123–124
product development, 23, 25–26; for disabled persons, 71–78, 87–88
Productivity Software, 121
"proto-organisms," 227–228
Public Electronic Network (PEN), electronic democracy and, 100–107
public-key cryptography, 112
publishing, computer networks and, 10
PWA Corp., 211, 212

radio frequency (RF) fields, cancer and, 178–179
reading machines, 72, 75
"real-time design," 26
reasonable accommodation, Americans with Disabilities Act and, 75–77
Refac International, 122
remedies, breached implied or express warranties, 193
reservation systems, airlines and computer, 211–212
retail: distribution, and information revolution, 21–22; market research and, 141–145
rhetoric, of disability, 84–87
robotic computers, 6
Roman, Mark, 90–91
Rottenberg, Marc, 18
Russia, computer viruses in, 219
Rust, Langbourne, 142
Rytex Co., 25

Saenz, Mike, 158
safety, avoiding software errors and, 188–189
Santa Monica, California, electronic democracy and, 100–107
scanning tunneling microscopes (STMs), 36, 37
scientific literacy, 93–94
screen-reader systems, 72, 75
Searle, John R., thinking by computers and, 229, 230, 231
Security and Exchange Commission, 110–111
Semiconductor Chip Protection Act, 118
semiconductor lasers, 30
sensor technology, optoelectronics and, 33
sensory computers, 6
sequential computation, 232–234, 235
signed writing, 111
smart pixels, 34
smart planes, 33
society, computers and, 181–185
soft skills training, 62
software: errors, 181–182, 183, 186, 189; free-, movement, 132–138; liability for defective, 190–193; patents and, 121–126; piracy of, 127–131
Software Publishers Association, software piracy and, 127–128
source cards, free-software movement and, 133–138
source code, trade secrecy in software and, 125
special education, use of computers and, 84, 85, 89
speech-recognition technology, 38–40
Square D, 22–23

Stallman, Richard M., free-software movement and, 132–138
Stanley Magic Doors, 26
stickykeys, 73
strict liability in tort, 193; in aeronautical charts, 194; in books, 191, 194
stunt hackers, 161–162
supercomputers, 6
support groups, for patients, 91–92
Sweden, research on effects of electromagnetic radiation in, 180
Syria, 208

telecenters, 69
Telecommunications Devices for the Deaf (TDDs), 74, 75
telecommuting, 64–70
"telepresence," 44
testicular cancer, 90–91
Texas Instruments (TI), 23, 118–119
Therac-25, software errors in, 186–187, 189
thinking, computers and, 229–231
3-D printing, 25–26

Todorov, Todor, 217–218
town meetings, electronic democracy and, 100–107
trade secrets, software and, 125
transistors, 36
*Transport Indemnity Co. v. Seib,* electronic contracts and, 112
*2600, the Hacker Quarterly,* 162

ULSI Systems Inc., 116–117
Underhill, Paco, 141, 142, 145
Uniform Commercial Code (UCC), 191, 192, 193
Unimation Inc., 199, 200
unions, telecommuting and, 65
United States: nanotechnology in, 37; robotics in, 198–201
Unix, 133–134, 135
user-centered design, 175–177
USAA, 22

VCRs, complexity problem and, 173
video display terminals (VDTs), cancer and, 178, 179, 180

virtual reality, 41–47
viruses, computer, 213–219; law and, 164–169
visually impaired people, adaptive technology for, 72
von Neumann, John, 222, 227
VPL Research Inc., 45

war human-factors, 174–175
warranty, 192; implied, in books, 191
"waterfall method," 175
*Winter vs. G. P. Putnam's Sons,* 191, 194
word-predictive software, 73, 75
work force: shortage in, 199; skilled, 58–63; training of, 58–63
*Workforce 2000,* 60
wristwatches, complexity problem and, 172

XyQuest, Inc., 121–122, 125
XyWrite III Plus, 121, 125

Yankee Doodle virus, 213–214

Zimbabwe, 202–203

## SELECTED REFERENCES
### (Of Works Cited in the Introduction and Overviews)

Bender, Mark. EFTS: Electronic Funds Transfer Systems. Port Washington, New York: Kennikat Press.

Evans, Christopher (1979). *The Micro Millenium*. New York: Washington Square Press.

Kocker, Bryan (1989). "President's Letter." *Communications of the ACM*, June: 660, 662.

Masuda, Yoneji (1981). *The Information Society as Post-Industrial Society*. Washington, D.C.: The World Future Society.

McWilliams, Peter A. (1984). *The Personal Computer Book*. Garden City, New York: Quantum Press.

Samarajiva, Rohan (1989). "Appropriate High-Tech: Scientific Communication Options for Small Third World Countries." *The Information Society* 6(1/2); 29–46.

# Credits/
# Acknowledgments

Cover design by Charles Vitelli

**Introduction**
Facing introduction—IBM Corporation.

**1. The Changing Economy**
Facing overview—Matsushita. 30—Illustration by Jared Schneidman. 32—Illustration by Builbert Gates. 33—Illustration by Rob Doyle/BW.

**2. Employment and the Workplace**
Facing overview—Wharton Econometric Assoicates, Inc., Philadelphia, PA, photo by Don Walker, Atco, NJ.

**3. Computers, People, and Social Interaction**
Facing overview—Apple Computers.

**4. Intellectual Property and Individual Privacy**
Facing overview—TRW.

**5. Computer Ethics and Crime**
Facing overview—IBM Corporation.

**6. Technological Risks**
Facing overview—United Nations photo by Andrea Brizzi.

**7. International Perspectives and Issues**
Facing overview—TRW.

**8. Philosophical Frontiers**
Facing overview—Medical World News.

# ANNUAL EDITIONS ARTICLE REVIEW FORM

■ NAME: _____ DATE: _____

■ TITLE AND NUMBER OF ARTICLE: _____

■ BRIEFLY STATE THE MAIN IDEA OF THIS ARTICLE: _____

_____

_____

_____

_____

■ LIST THREE IMPORTANT FACTS THAT THE AUTHOR USES TO SUPPORT THE MAIN IDEA:

_____

_____

_____

_____

_____

_____

■ WHAT INFORMATION OR IDEAS DISCUSSED IN THIS ARTICLE ARE ALSO DISCUSSED IN YOUR TEXTBOOK OR OTHER READING YOU HAVE DONE? LIST THE TEXTBOOK CHAPTERS AND PAGE NUMBERS:

_____

_____

_____

_____

_____

■ LIST ANY EXAMPLES OF BIAS OR FAULTY REASONING THAT YOU FOUND IN THE ARTICLE:

_____

_____

_____

_____

■ LIST ANY NEW TERMS/CONCEPTS THAT WERE DISCUSSED IN THE ARTICLE AND WRITE A SHORT DEFINITION:

_____

_____

_____

_____

_____

*Your instructor may require you to use this Annual Editions Article Review Form in any number of ways: for articles that are assigned, for extra credit, as a tool to assist in developing assigned papers, or simply for your own reference. Even if it is not required, we encourage you to photocopy and use this page; you'll find that reflecting on the articles will greatly enhance the information from your text.

# COMPUTER STUDIES: COMPUTERS IN SOCIETY
## Fifth Edition
### Article Rating Form

Here is an opportunity for you to have direct input into the next revision of this volume. We would like you to rate each of the 47 articles listed below, using the following scale:

1. **Excellent: should definitely be retained**
2. **Above average: should probably be retained**
3. **Below average: should probably be deleted**
4. **Poor: should definitely be deleted**

Your ratings will play a vital part in the next revision. So please mail this prepaid form to us just as soon as you complete it.
Thanks for your help!

Annual Editions revisions depend on two major opinion sources: one is our Advisory Board, listed in the front of this volume, which works with us in scanning the thousands of articles published in the public press each year; the other is you—the person actually using the book. Please help us and the users of the next edition by completing the prepaid article rating form on this page and returning it to us. Thank you.

| Rating | Article | Rating | Article |
|---|---|---|---|
| | 1. Communications, Computers, and Networks | | 27. Supermarket Spies |
| | 2. The New Democrat From Cyberspace | | 28. Dispatches From the Front Line: Computer Ethics War Stories |
| | 3. Who's Winning the Information Revolution? | | 29. Computer Imaging, A New Branch of Science That Can Turn Truth on Its Head |
| | 4. Tomorrow's Factory | | 30. Evidence Set in Motion |
| | 5. The Light Fantastic | | 31. World of Electronic Games: Computer Game Ethics |
| | 6. How Small Is It, Johnny? | | 32. "The Playground Bullies Are Learning How to Type" |
| | 7. At Last! Computers You Can Talk To | | 33. Legally Speaking: Can Hackers Be Sued for Damages Caused by Computer Viruses? and Viruses and Criminal Law |
| | 8. Virtual Reality | | |
| | 9. Fast Money | | |
| | 10. Medical Technology 'Arms Race' Adds Billions to the Nation's Bills | | 34. The Complexity Problem |
| | 11. The Skilling of America | | 35. Do Cellular Phones Cause Cancer? |
| | 12. Telecommuting: A Better Way to Work? | | 36. A System on Overload |
| | 13. Adaptive Technology for the Disabled | | 37. Programmed for Disaster |
| | 14. Do It Yourself | | 38. Liability for Defective Electronic Information |
| | 15. Challenging the Myth of Disability | | |
| | 16. The Powerful Patient | | 39. Why Japan Loves Robots and We Don't |
| | 17. The 20 Percent Solution | | 40. Sub-Saharan Africa: A Technological Desert |
| | 18. The Pleasure Machine | | |
| | 19. Electronic Democracy | | 41. Computing in the Middle East |
| | 20. Superduperitis | | 42. New Technology Propels Air Travel |
| | 21. Contracts Without Paper | | 43. The Bulgarian Connection |
| | 22. The Great Patent Plague | | 44. Coming of Age in a Weapons Lab |
| | 23. Why Patents Are Bad for Software | | 45. Compelling Signs of Artificial Life |
| | 24. Warning: Here Come the Software Police | | 46. Is Thinking Computable? |
| | 25. Programs to the People | | 47. New Computers, New Thoughts |
| | 26. Orwellian Dream Come True: A Badge That Pinpoints You | | |

*(Continued on next page)*

**ABOUT YOU**

Name_____ Date_____
Are you a teacher? ☐  Or student? ☐
Your School Name _____
Department _____
Address _____
City_____ State _____ Zip _____
School Telephone #_____

**YOUR COMMENTS ARE IMPORTANT TO US!**

Please fill in the following information:

For which course did you use this book? _____
Did you use a text with this Annual Edition?  ☐ yes  ☐ no
The title of the text? _____
What are your general reactions to the Annual Editions concept?

Have you read any particular articles recently that you think should be included in the next edition?

Are there any articles you feel should be replaced in the next edition? Why?

Are there other areas that you feel would utilize an Annual Edition?

May we contact you for editorial input?

May we quote you from above?

COMPUTER STUDIES: COMPUTERS IN SOCIETY, Fifth Edition

**BUSINESS REPLY MAIL**

First Class        Permit No. 84        Guilford, CT

*Postage will be paid by addressee*

**The Dushkin Publishing Group, Inc.**
**Sluice Dock**
DPG **Guilford, Connecticut 06437**

No Postage
Necessary
if Mailed
in the
United States